CATHOLIC RECORD SOCIETY
PUBLICATIONS

MONOGRAPH SERIES
VOLUME 7

Editor for Catholic Record Society

Peter Doyle

Editorial Committee for Catholic Record Society

T. A. Birrell
P. R. Harris
M. Hodgetts
V. A. McClelland

Vincent Alan McClelland

VICTORIAN CHURCHES AND CHURCHMEN

Essays Presented to Vincent Alan McClelland

Edited by
Sheridan Gilley

PUBLISHED FOR
THE CATHOLIC RECORD SOCIETY
BY
THE BOYDELL PRESS
2005

© The Catholic Record Society 2005
Registered Charity No. 313529

All rights reserved. Except as permitted under current legislation no part of this work may be photocopied, stored in a retrieval system, published, performed in public, adapted, broadcast, transmitted, recorded or reproduced in any form or by any means, without the prior permission of the copyright owner

First published 2005

ISBN 0 9028322 2 0

ISSN 1747–5287

A Catholic Record Society publication
Published by The Boydell Press
an imprint of Boydell & Brewer Ltd
PO Box 9, Woodbridge, Suffolk IP12 3DF, UK
and of Boydell & Brewer Inc.
668 Mt Hope Avenue, Rochester, NY 14620, USA
website: www.boydellandbrewer.com

A CiP catalogue record for this book is available
from the British Library

Information about the Catholic Record Society
and its publications may be obtained from the Hon. Secretary,
c/o 114 Mount St, London, W1X 6AH

This publication is printed on acid-free paper

Typeset by Pru Harrison, Hacheston, Suffolk
Printed in Great Britain by
Cromwell Press, Trowbridge, Wiltshire

CONTENTS

Introduction *Sheridan Gilley*		ix
Notes on Contributors		xv
1	Cardinal Manning and his Political Persona: The Education Act of 1870 *Jeffrey von Arx*	1
2	Henry Edward Manning, Priscilla Maurice, and the Pastoral Care of the Sick *Peter C. Erb*	12
3	The Cardinal and the Penitent: Cardinal Manning and Virginia Crawford *Robin Gard*	28
4	Henry O'Callaghan: Manning's Reluctant Episcopal Protégé *Leo Gooch*	58
5	'Education and correct conduct': Randal Lythgoe and the Work of the Society of Jesus in Early Victorian England and Wales *Maurice Whitehead*	75
6	The English Benedictines and the British Empire *Aidan Bellenger*	94
7	Varieties of Modern Scottish Catholic Conservatism *Bernard Aspinwall*	110
8	The Myth and Reality of Sr Barbara Ubryk, the Imprisoned Nun of Cracow: English Interpretations of a Victorian Religious Controversy *Rene Kollar*	139
9	Bernard Ward: Edmundian and historian *Stewart Foster*	163
10	Tradition and Conversion in English Literature *Joseph Pearce*	183

11	Newman's *Idea of a University*, 'the Circle of the Sciences', and the Constitution of the Church *Wulstan Peterburs*	200
12	Thomas Arnold: A Bicentenary Appraisal *David Newsome*	234
13	Tractarians and National Education, 1838–1843 *James Pereiro*	249
14	The Reverend Canon Henry Kingsmill Moore, DD, Ball. Coll. Oxon., FLS, and Church of Ireland Education, 1880–1927 *Susan M. Parkes*	279
15	'Scott's Folly': John Scott and the Development of the Wesleyan Educational System *John Smith*	292
16	Anglicanism 'represented' or 'misrepresented'? The Oxford Movement, Evangelicalism, and History: The controversial use of the Caroline Divines in the Victorian Church of England *Peter B. Nockles*	308

Selected Publications of Vincent Alan McClelland	371
Index	377

INTRODUCTION

SHERIDAN GILLEY

Vincent Alan McClelland, MA PhD FRHistS, Emeritus Professor in Educational Studies at the University of Hull, was born on the third day of the third month of 1933. He was educated at the Royal Grammar School at Clitheroe in Lancashire, and took the degrees of MA and PhD and a PGCE at Sheffield University and an MA at the University of Birmingham. Beginning as a teacher in Lancashire, he went on to become a Lecturer at the Mount Pleasant College of Education in Liverpool (1962–4) and at Liverpool University (1964–9). In 1969, he became Professor of Education at the National University of Ireland in Cork, where he was Head of Department for nine years. He became Professor of Educational Studies at Hull in 1978, where he was also Dean of the School of Education and/or Head of Department until 1998. He retired as an Emeritus in 1998. He was a Foundation Fellow of the Maryvale Institute near Birmingham, and remains its Dean of Graduate Research. His other public duties have included the chairmanship of The History of Education Society of the UK and of Committee B of UCET, and more recently, of the Audit of Special Educational Needs Provision in Gibraltar in 1997.

Academics usually choose to be scholars or administrators. The mere management to the highest standard of efficiency of a succession of Departments, and the amount of committee work required of a modern professor, together with Alan's own conscientious discharge of duties as a representative or chairman on other public bodies when he was in Lancashire, Ireland and Yorkshire, would have been enough to exhaust the energies of the ordinary academic. What is remarkable, however, is the steady and imperturbable manner in which he has achieved his stature in the world of scholarship, through both his own writings and his encouragement of others.

Alan's own opus includes two major monographs, seven edited books and more than a hundred articles, which have appeared in a steady stream throughout an otherwise busy career. He has been a major influence upon the world of Victorian Catholic historiography and the history of Catholic education since the appearance of his first major work, *Cardinal Manning: His Public Life and Influence*, more than four decades ago, in 1962. By showing the seriousness and significance of Manning's commitment to both social and religious reform, this did much to restore to Manning the reputation which had been injured by his first biographer, E.S. Purcell, and by the distillation afterwards of Purcell's poison into an elegant essay by Lytton Strachey. During the following forty years Alan's programme of study of Manning has been carried forward through numerous articles and in two collections, one of which he edited for the centenary of Manning's death in 1992 in *Recusant History*, and the other, *By Whose Authority? Newman, Manning and the* Magisterium (1996), the product of an international symposium that Alan expertly managed from the English side, which met over a number of years in the University of Freiburg-im-Breisgau. Alan's study of Manning most recently bore fruit in his essay on Manning and his patron and predecessor, Cardinal Wiseman, in *From without the Flaminian Gate: 150 Years of Roman Catholicism in England and Wales 1850–2000* (1999), which Alan edited with Michael Hodgetts. Manning also appears in Alan's second major monograph, *English Roman Catholics and Higher Education 1830–1903* (1974), which showed its author's mastery of the main sources for nineteenth-century Catholic historiography, and which remains the central and indispensable authority on its subject and a key monograph for anyone interested in the Victorian Catholic Church.

Alan's work for Roman Catholic historical scholarship has included his expert editing of *Recusant History* to the highest of academic standards since 1989, and his Chairmanship of the Council of the Catholic Record Society since 1990. He was the Founding Chairman, in 1968, of the North West Catholic History Society, of which today he is President, and he is the current Chairman of the Andrew C. Duncan Catholic History Trust. He was the first Anatole von Hügel Fellow at St Edmund's College, Cambridge.

Alan's achievement as an historian is closely bound up with and rooted in his concern with Catholic education, both past and present, and with his tremendous contribution to education in general and to the education of teachers in particular over more than four decades.[1] His first experience as a school-teacher was the foundation for his work in three universities, Liverpool, the National University of Ireland, and Hull – in Ireland and Hull as Professor of Education. His doctoral thesis on the early development of English Catholic higher education was undertaken at the University of Sheffield under the supervision of the late Professor Walter Harry Green Armytage (1915–98), a true polymath of distinction and the foremost historian of education in Britain at that time. Harry Armytage encouraged Alan to develop his educational and historical interests to the full, and for Alan, as for his mentor, everything has always interconnected: he has always seen research, educational theory, classroom practice and civic and private values as part of a single outlook and activity. Alan's response to others – colleagues, students

---

[1] I am grateful to Professor Maurice Whitehead for assistance with the remarks which follow.

and heads of schools – has had the same sort of completeness and integrity, the marks of the complete educationalist and professional who has thrown all his energies into his work, as much for others as for himself.

Through forty years of rapidly changing social, moral and educational values Alan has, therefore, been unwavering in his breadth of vision and resolve over what constitutes sound education and an effective teacher education. His research and writing continue to occupy an increasingly important intellectual space, currently populated by very few other academics in the British Isles, by demonstrating the necessary interconnectedness of the Catholic family and community in wholeness and integration to one another. In one of his most recent publications he argues cogently that Catholic schools ought to 'have the communion of saints at the very heart of their religious teaching and experience, their catechesis and their daily living' if they are to 'challenge a society that delimits and narrows its world in all sorts of ways but especially by its espousal of materialism, individualism and utilitarianism'.[2] This analysis points to the very heart of his philosophy of education and throws an important light on the range of his record of publication and research.

Alan's contribution to Catholic teacher education in the British Isles is unparalleled. A recent survey by the Centre for Research and Development in Catholic Education at the University of London Institute of Education has shown that a quarter of the doctoral and masters' dissertations on Catholic education in the British Isles during the past decade has come from the University of Hull – a testimony to Alan's commitment.[3] His most notable successes in this area have been through collaboration with and support for the Maryvale Institute in Birmingham where, as has been said, he is a Foundation Fellow and is currently Dean of Graduate Research, and for the Christian Leadership in Education Office (CLEO) operated by the Presentation Brothers in Cork. Over the past six years, more than one hundred Cork-based students from CLEO have graduated with masters' or doctoral degrees in Education from the University of Hull, many with distinction.

This collection only touches upon Alan's accomplishment as a leading light of the contemporary Catholic educational world, but it does attempt to cover his interests in both Catholic historiography and the history of education, as the numerous references to his writings in these pages bear testimony. Here pride of place must go to the papers which embody Alan's enduring concern with the life and work of Cardinal Manning. The first, by Jeffrey von Arx, unites Alan's fascination with both Manning and educational history in a crisp

---

[2] V.A. McClelland, 'Religious Instruction in Schools: A Theology of Catholic Education', in John Redford (ed.), *Hear, O Islands: Theology & Catechesis in the New Millennium* (Veritas: Dublin, 2002), p. 134.

[3] Mary Atherton and Gerald Grace, *Doctoral and Masters Theses and Dissertations on Catholic Education in the UK and Ireland* (University of London Institute of Education: London, 1999).

and elegant discussion of Manning's attitude to the 1870 Education Act, which Manning did not understand at first in its ultimate function of creating a secular education system in England. Peter Erb shows the influence upon Manning's conception of pastoral care of Priscilla Maurice, who was the sister of the liberal Anglican theologian F.D. Maurice and a writer on the spiritual guidance of the sick. In a model piece of editing by Robin Gard, Manning's tenderness and humour with his female penitents also appear in the diary of his penitent Mrs Crawford, the survivor of the spectacular divorce trial involving Sir Charles Dilke, and a Catholic convert, a writer and life-long social worker among the poor. Leo Gooch, the historian of Catholicism in north-eastern England, charts the trials and tribulations, climaxing in an almost immediate resignation, of Manning's protégé Henry O'Callaghan as Bishop of Hexham and Newcastle.

Two essays deal with Catholic religious. Manning's *bête noire* was the Society of Jesus, one of the major obstacles, in his eyes, to the conversion of England, but Maurice Whitehead's study of the vigorous Fr Randal Lythgoe, SJ, says much about the Jesuit achievement in the expansion of Roman Catholicism in England in the nineteenth century, in terms of institutional growth, the building of parishes and schools and the making of converts. The study of the English Benedictine contribution to the British Empire by Dom Aidan Bellenger belongs to this same period of Roman Catholic expansion, and to the Catholic attempt to combine a vigorous sense of Englishness with practical work and the ideal of the religious life.

Given Alan's interest in Scottish Catholic history, there is a particular appropriateness about Bernard Aspinwall's richly textured account of the conservative strand in Glaswegian twentieth-century Catholicism. The notes to the text demonstrate Dr Aspinwall's unsurpassed knowledge of the literature and sources for modern Scottish Catholic history. Dom Rene Kollar evaluates a body of ambiguous and contradictory evidence to show how the anti-Catholic and anti-conventual Protestant culture of the nineteenth century shaped the reception of news of the release of an allegedly ill-treated or mentally-ill nun from confinement in her nunnery in Cracow. He also shows the defensiveness of the Catholic response to this, and the difficulty in such a controverted matter of finding the truth.

Fr Stewart Foster has supplied this volume with a learned account of Bernard Ward, President of St Edmund's College and first Bishop of Brentwood, whose seven pioneering volumes on the history of the Catholic Church in England between 1781 and 1850 laid the foundations for sound English Catholic historical writing for this period. Without this work, and that of Ward's friend and fellow-Edmundian Edwin Burton on Richard Challoner, and of Bernard's brother, Wilfrid Ward, on Cardinals Wiseman and Newman, modern English Catholic historical scholarship could hardly exist, and Bernard Ward himself anticipated Alan in combining a large scholarly output with great practical achievement.

Joseph Pearce is now well known to a wide public for his writings on Catholic literary figures. His exploration here of the relationship between tradition and conversion to Catholicism, rooted in Romanticism and passing through such celebrated individuals as Newman and Gerard Manley Hopkins, reaches far into the twentieth century. It serves to honour Alan's interest in Catholic culture in its widest sense and in the gifted laymen of many talents in the Church.

Forming a link between the essays on historical and educational themes, Dom Wulstan Peterburs finds a key to the theological work of Manning's rival Cardinal, Newman, in the idea of the interdependence of competing and sometimes contradictory elements within the Church's life and thought, within the circle of the sciences in *The Idea of a University*, between laity and clergy in the essay 'On consulting the faithful', and among the priestly, prophetical and regal offices in the Preface to *The Via Media*. The balanced catholicity of this vision is one that Alan shares.

Most of the remaining essays illustrate Alan's interest in educational and ecclesiastical history beyond the borders of Roman Catholicism. In the Thomas Arnold Memorial Lecture for 1995 David Newsome, one of Alan's oldest friends and another great expert on Manning, gives a characteristically elegant interpretation of the significance of Thomas Arnold, the liberal Anglican historian and theologian and reforming headmaster of Rugby School. Alan's former research student James Pereiro, who has contributed so much to the study of Manning's theological development, charts the Tractarians' reaction to the beginnings of the secularising movement to free British education from religious control, and suggests that their work for the entrenchment and the expansion of the Anglican educational system, especially of the area under the influence of the National Society had, despite its unrealistic aim of preserving an Anglican monopoly, a lasting effect upon the preservation of the Churches' role in English education. Susan Parkes provides a narrative account of the educationalist Canon Henry Kingsmill Moore, showing the Church of Ireland's understanding of itself and of its educational aims and aspirations in an unecumenical age, while John Smith, in his study of John Scott, chairman of the Wesleyan Educational Committee for many years, furnishes the reader with a comprehensive view of the educational achievement of the Wesleyan Connexion.

These essays reflect the variety and disunity of Victorian Christianity. The last chapter in the volume is a classic study of the disunity of the Anglican tradition itself, in the warfare between Victorian Evangelicals, old High Churchmen and the new Tractarians over whether the Church of England was Protestant or Catholic or someway between these. Dr Nockles examines one aspect of this conflict, the Tractarian appeal to the Caroline Divines of the seventeenth-century Church of England, and the complexities and ironies which such an appeal entailed, given the theological ambiguities and ironies of Anglican churchmanship in both the seventeenth and nineteenth centuries.

Here again, Manning makes his appearance and his contribution. Despite the length of this chapter, the editor was unwilling to make it shorter by omitting any of the extensive evidence which the writer brings to his task in a powerful piece which is a definitive statement on its subject, and makes a suitably learned conclusion to this volume.

This collection is offered to Alan in love and humble admiration. May he live long to continue with his work, with Marie, increasing further the respect and gratitude which he has already won, and the affection to which this volume is a memorial.

CONTRIBUTORS

Professor Jeffrey von Arx, SJ, is President of Fairfield University, Connecticut, and the author of an extensive body of writing about Cardinal Manning. He is the author of *Progress and Pessimism: Religion, Politics, and History in Late Nineteenth-Century Britain* (1985), and has edited *Varieties of Ultramontanism* (1998).

Dr Bernard Aspinwall, Senior Research Fellow in History at the University of Glasgow, is the author of *Portable Utopia: Glasgow and the United States, 1820–1920* (1984); *The USA* (1986); *Reinido e America: Influencia Religiosa* (1992), and numerous articles on Scottish Catholic history.

Dom Aidan Bellenger, OSB, is Prior of Downside Abbey, Somerset. He is the author of *The French Exiled Clergy in the British Isles after 1789* (1986) and numerous articles in this area, and co-author of *Princes of the Church: A History of the English Cardinals* (2001).

Professor Peter Erb, of the Wilfrid Laurier University in Ottowa, Canada, is editing the Gladstone–Manning correspondence for the Oxford University Press. His recent works include *Newman on the Idea of a Catholic University* (1996).

Fr Stewart Foster is the Archivist of the Diocese of Brentwood, chairman of the Essex Recusant Society and author of *The History of the Diocese of Brentwood* (1994) and other historical works.

The late **Robin Gard** was Northumberland County Archivist (1965–87), editor of *Catholic Archives*, and editor of *Northern Catholic History*.

Dr Sheridan Gilley is a Reader Emeritus of the University of Durham. He is the author of *Newman and his Age* (1990: reprinted 2003) and numerous articles on modern religious history, and co-editor, with Dr Roger Swift, of three works on the Irish in nineteenth-century Britain (1985, 1989 and 1999), and with W.J. Sheils of *A History of Religion in Britain* (1994).

Dr Leo Gooch is Secretary of the Catholic Record Society, and is the author of *The Desperate Faction? The Jacobites of North-Eastern England 1688–1745* (1995), editor of *The Revival of English Catholicism: The Banister–Rutter Correspondence 1777–1807* (1995), co-author of *Down Your Aisles:*

The Diocese of Hexham and Newcastle, 1850–2000 (2000) and author of many articles on recusant history.

Dom Rene Kollar, OSB, is Professor of History at St Vincent College and St Vincent Seminary, Latrobe, Pennsylvania. He is the author of five books on nineteenth- and twentieth-century religious history.

The late **Dr David Newsome** was Fellow and Senior Tutor of Emmanuel College, Cambridge, and lecturer in ecclesiastical history in the university, and Headmaster of Christ's Hospital and Master of Wellington College. He was the author of *Godliness & Good Learning: Four Studies on a Victorian Ideal* (1961), *The Parting of Friends: A Study of the Wilberforces and Henry Manning* (1966), *The Convert Cardinals: Newman and Manning* (1993), and *The Victorian World Picture: Perceptions and Introspections in an Age of Change* (1997).

Dr Peter Nockles is librarian at the John Rylands University Library Manchester, and archivist for the Methodist Church. He is the author of *The Oxford Movement in Context: Anglican High Churchmanship 1760–1857* (1994) and of numerous articles, including a major contribution to the official history of the University of Oxford.

Susan M. Parkes was formerly Senior Lecturer in Education at Trinity College, Dublin, of which she is now an Emeritus Fellow. She is the author of *Kildare Place: the History of the Church of Ireland Training College, 1811–1969* (1984) and editor of *Education and National Identity: The Irish Diaspora* (1987) and of *A Danger to the Men? A History of Women in Trinity College, Dublin 1904–2004* (2004), to which she is also a contributor.

Joseph Pearce is the author of numerous books on Catholic literary figures, including Chesterton, Belloc and Roy Campbell, as well as Alexander Solzhenitsyn. His approach to his subject in this volume is writ large in *Literary Converts: Spiritual Inspiration in an Age of Unbelief* (1999). He is also co-editor of the *Saint Austin Review*.

Dr James Pereiro is the Chaplain of Grandpont House, Oxford, and the author of *Cardinal Manning: An Intellectual Biography* (1998).

Dom Wulstan Peterburs, OSB, is a monk of Ampleforth Abbey, Yorkshire. His publications include 'Newman and the Development of Doctrine' in V. Alan McClelland (ed.), *By Whose Authority? Newman, Manning and the Magisterium* (1996).

Dr John Smith is Senior Lecturer in Education at the University of Hull and author of *Methodism and Education 1849–1902: J.H. Rigg, Romanism, and Wesleyan Schools* (1998).

CONTRIBUTORS

Maurice Whitehead is Professor of History at the University of Wales in Swansea. He has written *The Academies of the Reverend Bartholomew Booth in Georgian England and Revolutionary America* (1996) and numerous articles on Catholic education in England, Wales and continental Europe in the eighteenth and nineteenth centuries.

1

CARDINAL MANNING AND HIS POLITICAL PERSONA: THE EDUCATION ACT OF 1870

JEFFREY VON ARX

GIVEN that the great majority of Roman Catholics in England by the time Henry Edward Manning became Archbishop of Westminster in 1865 were poor Irish, it is not surprising that elementary education was the public issue that first and most concerned him. And, of course, Manning's own concern with elementary education coincided with a public concern, following the Reform Act of 1867, that England was significantly behind France and Prussia in providing education for its populace.

A significant literature has grown up regarding Manning's involvement with the Education Bill of 1870. Beginning with his first biographer, Edmund Sheridan Purcell, it was thought that Manning, absent from England during most of 1870, and distracted by the role which he assigned himself at the Vatican Council, failed to protect the interests of the existing Catholic school system. He allowed the passage of a bill that established a rival rate-funded secular system that was a threat to the very existence of denominational education. The strongest statement of this position is that of Christopher Howard, who wrote in 1951 that Manning allowed the Education Bill to pass into law 'without his taking any step to protect the Catholic schools whose vital interests were so closely affected.'[1] V.A. McClelland, however, has demonstrated conclusively that Manning was indeed both concerned and active before, during and after the Vatican Council in the interests of Catholic education specifically and denominational education in general. This activity was carried on principally, although not exclusively, through his efforts to influence the Prime Minister, William Ewart Gladstone. In regular correspondence with Gladstone on the issue, even during his absence in Rome, Manning

---

[1] Edmund Sheridan Purcell, *Life of Cardinal Manning*, 2 vols (London, 1895–1896), vol. II, p. 494; C. Howard, 'Manning and Education,' in John Fitzsimons (ed.), *Manning: Anglican and Catholic* (London, 1951), p. 377.

believed he had in him a sympathetic ear.[2] The most detailed study of Manning's work for education has been undertaken by D.E. Selby, who certainly confirms and even amplifies McClelland's portrayal of the activist archbishop at the time of Forster's Bill.[3] Interpretation has, in a sense, come round full circle in the recent views of Dermot Quinn, who, while not questioning the depiction of an activist Manning, has certainly doubted the effectiveness of his interventions, especially with Gladstone. Quinn believes that Manning seriously over-estimated his influence on Gladstone; offered him often unwelcome and inappropriate advice; and did not appreciate how the Vatican Council and his own role there had undermined his credibility with Gladstone and his position in English politics more generally in the early 1870s.[4]

If there is a lack of consensus about how effective Manning was in his efforts for Catholic education in 1870 and afterwards, this may be because there is even less agreement in judging the motives and goals of his educational policy. This was the case from the very beginning. As early as 1868, with an earlier version of an education bill in prospect, Manning had written to the Catholic bishops suggesting a common approach with the Established Church to protect denominational education. This suggestion was not accepted.[5] When the bishops first met in Rome to discuss Forster's impending Bill, they effectively repudiated, in the name of the independence of Catholic schools, an understanding that Manning had reached with the government before leaving England, that Roman Catholic schools would accept government inspection of their secular instruction in return for aid from the rates.[6] When the Bill reached its final form, Manning was willing to accept what became, in effect, a 'dual system' of secular education assisted out of the local rates and denominational education supported by partial grants from the central government. He even went so far as to encourage Roman Catholics, including the clergy, to stand for the School Boards that would oversee the

---

[2] V.A. McClelland, *Cardinal Manning: His Public Life and Influence, 1865–92* (London, 1962), chapter III, 'The Act of 1870 and its Consequences,' pp. 61–86.

[3] D.E. Selby, 'Henry Edward Manning and the Education Bill of 1870,' *British Journal of Educational Studies*, vol. 18, no. 2 (June, 1970), pp. 197–212. See also his 'Cardinal Manning and Free Education,' in K. Dent (ed.), *Victorian Education, History of Education Society Occasional Publications*, No. 2 (1976), pp. 24–33; and *Towards a Common System of National Education: Cardinal Manning and Educational Reform, 1882–1892*, Educational Administration and History Monograph No. 6, Museum of the History of Education (Leeds, 1977), pp. 1–60.

[4] Dermot Quinn, 'Manning as Politician,' *Recusant History*, vol. 21, No. 2 (October, 1992), pp. 273–5. For Quinn's views on the ineffectiveness of Roman Catholic political action in the second half of the nineteenth century in general, see his *Patronage and Piety: The Politics of English Roman Catholicism, 1850–1900* (Stanford, 1993).

[5] Selby, 'HEM and the Education Bill of 1870,' pp. 200–1.

[6] Selby, 'HEM and the Education Bill of 1870,' pp. 202–3. The meeting took place in mid-February, 1870.

provision of elementary education in the localities. These Boards, which would run secular schools where they were necessary, were also responsible for judging the adequacy of denominational provision of education in their areas. Manning believed that it was important for Roman Catholics and other denominationalists to be on the Boards in order to protect the interests of the voluntary system. He was bitterly attacked by some among his co-religionists for conceding the principle of secular education and even cooperating with it.[7]

Disagreement and difference over what Manning wished to achieve by his involvement in the negotiations over the Education Act of 1870 have continued among historians. For those who believe that Manning, unfocussed and unprepared for the legislation, had no consistent policy to guide his actions, his subsequent campaign to revise the Act, culminating in the appointment of a Royal Commission in 1885, represented a belated recognition that Forster's Act had been a disaster for denominational education. For those who see Manning functioning – albeit none too effectively – within the context of interest politics, his support of the legislation represents expediency: 'The Act was a *pis aller*,' writes Dermot Quinn, 'and Manning realized it better than others.'[8] Even those like McClelland and Selby, who see policy in Manning's activities, disagree as to its motive. McClelland sees Manning as 'not averse to the entry of the State into the field of education' and maintains that he had 'always advocated' the dual system.[9] Selby disagrees, saying that 'Manning consistently opposed the State assuming an active role in the provision of elementary education . . . With the publication of Forster's Bill, however, he came to accept the inevitability of State entry, and realizing that financial considerations precluded any real alternative other than acceptance of the Dual System, endeavored to safeguard the Catholic schools against interference with their religious teaching and management.'[10]

Selby offers an interesting explanation of Manning's policy and tactics in 1869 and 1870 in regard to education. 'The key to an appreciation of both,' he writes, 'lies in his cognisance and dread of the emergence of secularism as a force in English life and society.' Manning, in Selby's view, saw the nineteenth century as a 'continuous struggle between Christianity and the revolutionary and secularist principles of 1789,' and was 'concerned, almost to the point of obsession, with the idea that some impending cataclysm was facing "Christian society"' – a cataclysm being prepared by 'the progressive alienation of society from the Church and the consequent de-Christianization of civil and political life.'[11] At the time of his early writing about the Temporal Power, an apocalyptic strain occurs in Manning's thinking: he believed that

---

[7] McClelland, pp. 70–2.
[8] Quinn, 'Manning as Politician,' p. 275.
[9] McClelland, pp. 62, 70.
[10] Selby, 'HEM and the Education Bill of 1870,' p. 198.
[11] *Ibid.*, p. 198.

civil and political life in the West was becoming 'desacralized' or, as he later came to call it, secularized.[12] But does the apocalyptic vision of contemporary events of Manning's early thinking also characterize his educational policy? Or do his actions in regard to education express the more dispassionate analysis of secularization that led him to seek an active, critical, but responsible engagement of the Church with the liberal state? In 1882, Manning was willing to acknowledge the compelling interest of the state in universal elementary education: 'Putting away all ecclesiastical questions,' he wrote in that year, 'it cannot be denied that the State is justified in providing for the education of its people. It has the right to protect itself from the dangers arising from ignorance and vice, which breed crime and turbulence.'[13] D.E. Selby is correct, however, in maintaining that in the years leading up to the passage of the 1870 Act, 'Manning consistently opposed the State assuming an active role in the provision of elementary education.'[14] If one consults the Pastoral Letter he wrote in June 1869 in anticipation of Forster's Bill, it is apparent that Manning was far from being an advocate of the direct entry of the state into the field of education. He believed that education was the responsibility in the first instance of parents, who, as Christians, had an obligation to see that their children were educated according to the truths of the Christian faith in schools where that faith was taught. In a country united in faith, such schools would be schools of both Church and state and supported by both. In a country divided in religion, denominations would found their own schools by voluntary effort. The state might choose to assist in the support of these schools, but it must do so in an even-handed way, and without interfering in their religious character or direction.[15] It is significant to note that Manning never advocated total state support of denominational education. As a duty incumbent on parents, education had to engage their voluntary participation in their organized denominations (or, indeed, in non-religious associations for those who required it). This voluntarism should be complete as far as the initiative to establish schools was concerned, and substantial as far as financial support was concerned, according to the ability of parents to pay.

It need hardly be stated that if Manning advocated the expansion with state aid of the Catholic school system, he necessarily favoured the same advantages for the schools of the Established Church and of the Nonconformist denominations. In fact, the 1869 Pastoral is unusual in being addressed not only to his own clergy and faithful, but also to non-Catholics whom he hoped

---

[12] Jeffrey von Arx, 'Manning's Ultramontanism and the Catholic Church in British Politics,' *Recusant History*, vol. 19 (May, 1988), pp. 332–47.
[13] Manning, 'Is the Education Act of 1870 a Just Law,' in *The Nineteenth Century*, vol. 12 (December, 1882), p. 959.
[14] Selby, 'HEM and the Education Bill of 1870,' p. 198.
[15] Henry Edward Manning, 'Pastoral Letter, Feast of the Sacred Heart' (1869), Westminster Archdiocesan Archives: St. Edmund's College Archives, Box 15, No. 10, pp. 271–5.

to win over to the cause of denominational education. He wrote to Cardinal Cullen in Dublin describing the Pastoral as a *'political* declaration. I have carefully avoided giving it a predominantly Catholic character. Christian education as the *genus* and denominational as the *species* will cover all we want. And if we are to rally the Anglicans and the Nonconformists, we must, I fear use a language intelligible to them, rather than our own.'[16] Manning had proposed making common cause with the other denominations as early as February 1868, when he circularized the Catholic bishops, recommending that Catholics send representatives to a public meeting organized by the Established Church to support denominational education. Although the bishops were reluctant to support this proposal, Manning requested that the (lay) Chairman and Secretary of the Catholic Poor School Committee, the principal funding body for Catholic elementary education, attend meetings of the Anglican National Education Union.[17] Interdenominational cooperation and the effort to forge a common religious front on education would dominate Manning's policy.

In 1869 Manning was prepared to admit that the state, too, had moral obligations in regard to education, which were a function of the moral character of the state. Not surprisingly, Manning's developing thought on the true nature of the liberal state accounted for the situation of religious division or pluralism. Here the state as educator had a moral responsibility to recognize the rights and duties of its members to educate their children according to the dictates of their consciences in religious schools of their own choosing. As far as the state's obligations were concerned, Manning maintained in 1869 that 'the State has neither the commission nor the power to educate . . . A civil power holding the balance of justice even in a firm neutrality among the religious sections of a divided people, [will] assist them to educate their children, partly by private and partly by public means, in schools proper to their respective religious convictions.'[18] Only a tyranny usurped the obligations of parents and religious educators. Manning thought this deification of the civil power the essential perversion of the liberal state. The preservation, therefore, not only of Christianity and public morality but also of civil liberty required the 'independent action of the Church interposing itself between the State and the people' in the matter of education.[19]

Manning recognized that there would be both a variety of denominational schools and gradations in the amount of religious teaching: 'Between a denominational school and a secular school there are gradations of religious teaching which would reconcile nearly all our divisions and yet preserve the

---

[16] Manning to Cullen, 15 August 1869, Cullen Papers, Archives of the Archdiocese of Dublin, quoted in Selby, 'HEM and the Education Bill of 1870,' p. 200.
[17] *Ibid.*, pp. 200–1.
[18] Manning, 'Pastoral Letter,' pp. 274–5.
[19] *Ibid.*, p. 277.

Christian character of the school.' Without conceding the point, Manning implies that the state might play a direct and just role in education where religious divisions were so great that only a school to all intents and purposes secular would meet the objections of all concerned. In such situations, something like the non-denominational Irish national schools might have to be established.[20] Such cases, in Manning's view, were bound to be few in number, but in the light of his subsequent and fairly rapid acceptance of the dual system, the exception is significant.

Manning did not at first believe that the state should have a direct role in the provision of education as long as voluntary associations could meet the need. But he was willing to concede the principle of the government's right to inspect religious schools to ensure the responsible and efficient use of increased public funds in respect to the non-religious aspect of the schools. Here Manning's model was the agreement the Church had reached with the government over reformatories and industrial schools, where Catholic children were sent to Catholic-run institutions open to state inspection at partial public expense. This was the substance of Manning's discussions with Lord de Grey in 1869 before his departure for the Vatican Council. The English Catholic bishops in Rome repudiated Manning's understanding with de Grey in February 1870 because it allowed for more extensive inspection by non-Catholic government inspectors than advocates of the complete independence of Catholic schools, like Bishop Bernard Ullathorne of Birmingham, were willing to accept.[21]

Manning's position in the pre-Bill period was, therefore, as follows. He recognized, at least by implication, the need for a much-expanded system of elementary education to fill the gaps where it was not available. He wished to see the need met and gaps filled by an expansion of the voluntary, denominational system that had already gone a long way toward providing universal elementary education in England. This expansion was to be effected by increased voluntary effort, augmented, stimulated, funded and audited by government. In the very few circumstances where voluntary efforts on the part of the denominations were not practicable or sufficient, he was willing to contemplate a very limited role for government in setting up what would, in effect, be secular schools.

In its initial conception, Forster's Bill was not that far from what Manning had envisioned. It accepted existing denominational schools, which currently provided instruction to about two-thirds of English school-children, as the basis of a national system. It offered the denominations the opportunity to meet existing deficiencies in the provision of elementary education over the

---

[20] *Ibid.*, p. 280. Although, clearly, Manning thought the national system inappropriate for Ireland, where the five-sixths of the population who were Catholic deserved schools of their own. Cf. p. 273.

[21] Selby, 'HEM and the Education Bill of 1870,' pp. 202–3.

period of a year with the benefit of assistance by grant from the central government. Where, after a year, deficiencies persisted, School Boards would be set up that could establish schools assisted from the local rates. In the original Bill, the Boards could choose the kind of religious instruction to be offered in the schools they established, subject to a conscience clause (i.e., parents who objected to the religious instruction offered in a Board School could withdraw their children for the period of those lessons). The School Boards could, if they chose, offer assistance from the local rates to voluntary schools.

The first version of Forster's Bill seemed to accept the notion of voluntary (denominational) effort as the backbone of a universal system of elementary education, with the possibility of board-run, possibly secular schools as a stop-gap where denominational efforts did not meet the need. As such, it was a disappointment to groups like Joseph Chamberlain's National Education League, which favoured a universal, secular system, and so they campaigned against it. Manning, writing to Gladstone from Rome on first seeing published reports of the Bill, expressed both hopes and fears as to the proposed legislation. He had reservations about the shortness of the time being offered denominations to remedy deficiencies, and about leaving the ability to assist denominational schools through the rates up to local School Boards.[22] Because Manning had had unfortunate experiences of the anti-Catholicism of local bodies like the Poor Law Guardians in his efforts to rescue Catholic children from workhouses, he feared the new Boards. When he received the full text of the Bill, Manning expressed guarded approval, but with some prescience sounded a warning that the ability of the new School Boards to set up schools assisted from the rates would result in competition that would eventually disadvantage voluntary schools. Less presciently, he indicated to Gladstone the willingness of Catholics to give up assistance to denominational education from the rates, contenting themselves with grants from the central government, in order not to be answerable to local Board administration. We shall see that Manning would later alter his opinion about local versus central administration of education – and *ipso facto*, his unwillingness to see denominational education assisted from the rates.[23]

Lobbying by those like Chamberlain, who believed the Bill gave too much away to denominational education, paradoxically met some of Manning's reservations about the bill.[24] Boards would no longer be in a position to assist from the rates (and thus, perhaps, to control) denominational schools, which were compensated by an increase in grants from the central government. Indeed, Boards were taken out of the business of providing denominational education entirely with a prohibition of any denominational teaching in

---

[22] Manning to Gladstone, 24 February 1870, Gladstone Papers, British Library. Quoted in McClelland, p. 65.
[23] Manning to Gladstone, 7 March 1870.
[24] Selby, 'HEM and the Education Bill of 1870,' p. 210.

rate-aided schools (the Bible could be read, but without "denominational" commentary). Although these provisions precluded local Boards from interfering with denominational education, it also meant that the Board Schools for which they were responsible would be almost entirely secular. This went some way further toward the creation of the dual, competitive system that Manning had wished to avoid. Additionally, the period of grace in which denominations were offered the opportunity to fill the gaps in the national system before Board Schools would be established was reduced from a year to six months.

Even so, Manning wrote to Gladstone in July of 1870 that 'The Education Bill is decidedly improved.'[25] For his part, he urged his fellow Roman Catholics to take advantage of the opportunities to establish new schools with government assistance in the six month grace period being offered. Making every effort to do so within his own diocese, he also urged, as we have seen, that Roman Catholics should stand for the new Boards. 'It seems to me,' he wrote to Bishop Ullathorne of Birmingham, 'that our best course is to cooperate to the utmost of our power, and thereby obtain a share in the treatment of questions which may affect us. If they should offer to include our clergy on any Boards, I think we ought to accept it.' When Ullathorne indicated that he and many other Roman Catholics found his policy incomprehensible, Manning tried to explain: 'The Boards may destroy our lesser schools by reporting them to be insufficient or inefficient . . . By opening negotiations with the Boards, as I have done with the Privy Council [in regard to grants for the building of schools during the grace period], I hope to save these. By standing aloof from the Boards, we should be exposed to the danger of their hostility.'[26]

It is difficult to evaluate Manning's support of the 1870 Act without the distorting influence of hindsight. As we have seen, the Bill, at least in the intent of its initial version, was substantially what Manning hoped it would be: an endorsement of voluntarism as the basis for a system of national education, with the incentive of government assistance to expand that system. At first, the prospect of competing rate-funded secular schools was a cloud no bigger than a man's hand: Board Schools, as religious or secular as Boards desired, would be established only where denominations had not succeeded in setting their own schools up. Some of these Board Schools might end up being secular, but there was no deliberate or systematic attempt to make them so. This was the Bill that first gained Manning's approval, although with reservations over the Board Schools – not, it is to be noted, in regard to secularism, but in regard to their advantage over voluntary schools in the matter of funding.

It is ironic that some of the amendments to the Bill that made a dual system

---

[25] Manning to Gladstone, 10 July 1870, quoted in McClelland, p. 70.
[26] Manning to Ullathorne, 17 September 1870, Ullathorne–Manning Correspondence, Manning Papers, Archives of the Archdiocese of Westminster; also McClelland, pp. 70–1.

of religious and secular schools inevitable were sought not only by the secularists of Chamberlain's National Education League, but also by Manning on behalf of denominational schools. Manning wanted the local Boards to have no direct control over denominational schools, which they might if they were in a position to grant or to withhold assistance from the rates. The secularists wanted the Boards out of religious education entirely, and the result was the Cowper-Temple clause, which forbade the use of 'religious catechism or religious formulary distinctive of any particular denomination' in Board Schools.[27] Denominational religion might be taught to students at Board Schools, but it would have to be outside normal school hours and on a non-compulsory basis. Instruction during school hours would be essentially secular, with the exception of non-denominational reading of the Bible.

This meant that between them, the secularists and representatives of denominationalism like Manning had succeeded in severing all connections between the Board Schools and religious education. If denominational education remained the centrepiece of a system of national education, the character of schools established by the Boards might not matter that much. But if Board Schools grew and multiplied, a full-blown dual system of voluntary schools, partially funded by government, and secular schools established by the state and supported from the rates, would result. If Manning had foreseen this possibility in 1870 he would not have given Forster's bill even the qualified endorsement he did. And by encouraging Roman Catholics to stand for the boards, he must have thought it still possible to use them to check the growth of secular education, which he was convinced the great majority of English people did not support. Manning's 1870 stance on the Bill only makes sense on the assumption that, even as amended, Forster's Bill was still basically an acceptance of voluntarism and denominationalism as the basis for a system of national education. Secularists like Chamberlain and the National Education League, understanding the Bill as a victory for the Church, looked for ways either to amend the Act or to use its provisions to erect the rival system of secular education that the Act and its supporters neither desired nor foresaw.

It is difficult to evaluate Manning's support of the Act because such an evaluation involves both his foresight and our hindsight. But it is not so difficult to come to a conclusion about the questions with which we began this chapter: what were Manning's motives, what were his goals in the field of national education? Did he have a policy, and can one understand his actions in regard to Forster's Bill in the light of consistent policy? Did that policy commit him, as McClelland seems to believe, to acceptance of the role of the state in education and a dual system of denominational and secular education from the beginning? Or do we understand Manning's policy and tactics in 1870 as Selby suggests, in light of an apocalyptic vision of 'social

---

[27] Act of 1870, quoted in McClelland, p. 73.

disintegration' that led him to try to save what he could of denominational education in the face of the unavoidable encroachment of the secular state?[28] Or, rather, is it not the case that Manning's policy in regard to education is best understood as part of the effort to seek accommodation and engagement – critical but constructive – of the churches with the liberal state?

A number of things stand out in Manning's response to the issue of national education in England that will help to answer these questions. The first is that from the very beginning of his involvement in the education question he tried to ally Roman Catholics with the Established Church (which had by far the largest stake in the survival of the voluntary system) and similarly committed Nonconformist denominations like the Methodists. This effort was concerted and persistent and, as we have seen, pursued over the opposition of his co-religionists. As has been said, Selby sees this policy as reflection of Manning's obsession with the 'continuous struggle between Christianity and the revolutionary and secularist principles of 1789,' in which it was necessary for Christians to present a common front.[29] Now it is true that Manning believed in a struggle between Christianity and secularism, and it is true that he believed civil and political life had been de-Christianized. But he was also convinced that de-Christianized civil and political life offered unique opportunities to the churches to combat secularism. Churches could sustain and even advance Christianity in society, and especially among the masses, precisely by active engagement in the political life of the liberal state. And because the liberal state was bound to observe neutrality among them, the churches were free to pursue these political goals as equals on an even playing field. They all had equal opportunity and obligation to take political stands, to form political alliances, and to act in concert when they shared common goals. Manning's efforts to form political alliances with the other churches in the interest of denominational education is surely best understood not as a rejection, but as an acceptance of the political forms and process of the liberal state.

Manning's participation in the controversies over the Bill shows his distinctive view of the role of the liberal state in a religiously pluralistic and secular civil society. He clearly admitted a role for the state in the matter of national education: the state had an interest in seeing that its populace was educated. But Manning did not believe that in a religiously divided society the state could undertake the responsibility of education directly, as it might in a religiously united society. The right and responsibility for educating children belonged in the first instance to parents, who had the duty of educating their children according to their convictions about religious truth. Where there was not unanimity about religious truth, this meant that the principal agencies in conducting education could only be those religious associations to which

---

[28] Selby, 'HEM and the Education Bill of 1870,' p. 198.
[29] *Ibid.*, p. 198.

parents belonged. The state might choose to assist these associations, but it could not assume the responsibility that belonged to them of establishing and conducting educational institutions, except in extraordinary circumstances.

There were two reasons for this. The first had to do with the necessarily secular character of the state in a religiously divided society. The state could not, except in extraordinary circumstances, undertake to establish or conduct educational institutions on its own in a religiously divided society because, in Manning's view, education could not be separated from religion. For the state to involve itself directly in education was to put itself in charge of an essentially religious enterprise, and in a religiously divided society this was one of the things a liberal, secular state must not do.

The second reason the state could not have a direct role in education in a religiously pluralistic society had to do with the very identity of the liberal state as a limited form of government. If the state was to be authentically liberal and secular (in Manning's terms, neutral and even-handed among religious groups in society), it must respect and even foster the legitimate autonomy of voluntary religious associations. The state could not usurp the responsibility of parents to educate their children or to delegate that responsibility, by default of religious unity, to the various voluntary religious associations. We shall see that in subsequent controversy over the workings of the 1870 Act, Manning's thinking on the importance of voluntarism and even of localism would develop much further (to include, for example, the right and responsibility of non-believing parents to establish non-religious schools to their liking!). Even in 1869–70, however, it is clear (for example, in the 1869 Pastoral on education) that Manning believed that state support for – but not control of – the intermediate role of the churches in education was critical to the essential character of the liberal state. The state's willingness to allow the 'independent action of the Church interposing itself between the State and the people' made the difference between limited as opposed to despotic exercise of the power of the state.

The state might play a direct role in the establishment of schools as we have seen, in the very few situations where the denominations would be unable to do so. These state-sponsored schools would be religious in some form according the desires of the local population. State-sponsored schools might be secular only when people in a locality were so divided by religion that an essentially secular school was all that could be agreed on. These exceptions, however, would prove the rule that the proper role for the secular, liberal state in education was to facilitate the work of the churches in providing religious education to the people.

2

HENRY EDWARD MANNING, PRISCILLA MAURICE, AND THE PASTORAL CARE OF THE SICK

PETER C. ERB

IT HAS now been a half-century since H. Francis Davis reflected on 'Manning the Spiritual Writer' in a collection celebrating the centennial of the Cardinal's conversion.[1] A decade later in a much changed theological setting and in a volume of quite different intentions, the Bishop of Salford, George Andrew Beck, took up the issue again, remarking on the general dearth of attention given to this aspect of Manning's career.[2] Although Bishop Beck, like Davis before him, was limited in his study primarily to printed sources, and although both studies were brief, they pointed to an important aspect of Manning's life and character, often under-emphasised by friends and overlooked by foes: both as an Anglican and as a Roman Catholic, as an Archdeacon and as an Archbishop, his pastoral objective played a central role in his decisions and reflected a striking warmth of character.[3]

---

[1] John Fitzsimmons (ed.), *Manning: Anglican and Catholic* (London, 1951), pp. 149–60.
[2] George Andrew Beck, 'Cardinal Manning,' in Charles Davis (ed.), *English Spiritual Writers* (London, 1961), pp. 161–71. Beck does note the brief comments on the issue in E.E. Reynolds, *Three Cardinals: Newman–Wiseman–Manning* (London, 1958), and the much earlier chapter on Manning as a writer and preacher in Arthur Wollaston Hutton, *Cardinal Manning* (London, 1892), pp. 215–37.
[3] For background on the negative appraisal of Manning, beginning with Edmund Sheridan Purcell, *Life of Cardinal Manning: Archbishop of Westminster*, 2 vols (London, 1895; 2nd ed., 1896), and particularly marked with Lytton Strachey, *Eminent Victorians: Cardinal Manning, Florence Nightingale, Dr. Arnold, General Gordon* (London, 1918), see Sheridan Gilley, 'New Light on an Old Scandal: Purcell's Life of Cardinal Manning,' in D.A. Bellenger (ed.), *Opening the Scrolls: Essays in Catholic History in Honour of Godfrey Anstruther* (Stratton on the Fosse, 1987), pp, 166–98, and note, as well, Maisie Ward, *The Wilfrid Wards and the Transition*, 2 vols (New York, 1934–37), vol. 1, pp. 205 ff. and 411 ff. For balanced and full studies of Manning see, above all, James Pereiro, *Cardinal Manning: An Intellectual Biography* (Oxford, 1998); David Newsome, *The Convert Cardinals: John Henry Newman*

Thus, Davis began with a depiction of a painting of Newman and Manning at Oscott and struggled with the juxtaposition between the two men established by contemporary public discourse, attempting to make certain that Manning was not thereby denigrated. Beck too was anxious over portraits of Manning as the austere Cardinal. As a result, he emphasised the human aspect of the man and quite usefully quoted at length Manning's 1865 directions to his Oblates on spiritual care, which call for a gentle, kind openness on the part of the director – a characteristic quite the opposite of those often ascribed to Manning during his own time and in the century thereafter.

1. Try to be gentle, calm, silent as possible.
2. Never contradict anybody.
3. If you are forced to differ say: 'I should hardly have thought so,' or 'I thought it was so and so,' or 'Can you be sure that is so?' Contradictions seldom convince and almost always irritate.
4. Never reprove anyone in the presence of others.
5. Find all the excuses you can for them, that they may be ashamed of excusing themselves.
6. Never refuse permission unless compelled, and then with gentleness, kindness and regret. Let them know that you are going against yourself.
7. Try to cheer and amuse everybody especially if they are ill, or in trouble or out of sorts, that they may return to you as the *refugium* and *requies peccatorum*.
8. Watch over your manner and tones of voice and look. Be very courteous, considerate and delicate in dealing with others, especially those you are a little impatient with.
9. Pray very much against prejudice and dislike of persons.
10. Look through the largest window in the house, not through the keyhole.
11. In giving obedience don't order but ask 'Be as good as to do so and so.' 'Would you do so and so,' and offer to do it sometimes yourself.
Here are ten commandments for you and one over.[4]

Manning's directions in this case are not surprising either in the personality or the interests they reflect. Spiritual direction and pastoral care had long been his preoccupation and his talents in these areas are amply documented,

---

and Henry Edward Manning (London, 1993); David Newsome, *The Parting of Friends: A Study of the Wilberforces and Henry Manning* (London, 1966); V. Alan McClelland, *Cardinal Manning: His Public Life and Influence 1865–92* (London, 1962), and note the earlier works by Shane Leslie, *Henry Edward Manning: His Life and Labours* (New York, 1921).

[4] Beck, pp. 165–66. On the institutional context of Manning's directives see V. Alan McClelland, '*O Felix Roma!* Henry Manning, Cutts Robinson and Sacerdotal Formation 1862–1872,' *Recusant History*, vol. 21 (1992), pp. 180–217 (quotation at p. 193) and his 'Changing Concepts of the Pastoral Office: Wiseman, Manning and the Oblates of St. Charles,' *Recusant History*, vol. 25 (2000), pp. 218–36. For a broader portrait of Manning's character as reflected in the directives both as an Anglican and a Roman Catholic note, above all, Professor McClelland's first, fifth and final chapters in his *Cardinal Manning*.

particularly over the years immediately before and following his conversion in 1851. In Rome in 1847, for example, he met Florence Nightingale (1820–1910),[5] a woman who became well aware of his pastoral skills and who sought him out five years later as she faced a religious and vocational crisis.[6] In the late 1840s as well, Manning met Mary Stanley (1813–1879), to whom he offered direction for many years as she struggled with theological choices and personal decisions from the early 1850s, through her contentions over nursing with Nightingale in the Crimea in 1854–1855 and her family's sensitivity to her decision to enter the Roman Catholic Church in 1856.[7] In the 1840s Manning was also directing, among many others, Marianne Caroline Byles (1822–1880), later the second Mrs Coventry Patmore;[8] Manning's sister-in-law, Mary Sargent Wilberforce (1811–1878), wife of Henry Wilberforce (1807–1873);[9] and Henry's brother, Robert Isaac Wilberforce (1802–1857).[10] In all these cases Manning's personal concern with and affection for those under his care is ever evident and is perhaps best related by another of his directees, Elizabeth Herbert (1822–1911), the wife of Sidney Herbert (1810–1861).[11] In a later autobiographical pamphlet Lady Herbert outlined her relationship with Manning, speaking of him as 'always loving and tender,'

---

[5] For details see Mary Keele (ed.), *Florence Nightingale in Rome: Letters Written by Florence Nightingale in Rome in the Winter of 1847–1848* (Philadelphia, 1981).

[6] For the correspondence of Manning with Nightingale see Peter C. and Elizabeth J. Erb, 'Florence Nightingale For and Against Rome: Her early Correspondence with Henry Edward Manning,' *Recusant History*, vol. 24 (1999), pp. 472–506.

[7] Mary Stanley was the second of five children to Catherine and Edward Stanley, the Bishop of Norwich, and was slightly older than her more famous brother, Arthur Penrhyn (1815–1881), with whom she remained in close contact to her death on 24 November 1879. Well known for philanthropic work throughout her life, she was active in the recruitment of nurses for the Crimea in 1854 and served in Westminster and Lancashire during the cotton famine of 1861. See Frederic Boase, *Modern English Biography*, 1st ed., 1892; reprint: 6 vols (London, 1965), vol. 3, p. 711, and Rowland E. Prothero and G. G. Bradley, *The Life and Correspondence of Arthur Penrhyn Stanley*, 2 vols (London, 1894). The full correspondence of Stanley and Manning is preserved in Bodleian MS Eng. lett. c. 660.

[8] The Manning–Byles correspondence, including some 110 letters written between 1840 and 1883, is preserved at Pitts Theology Library, Emory University, Atlanta, Ga.

[9] For the remaining correspondence between Manning and Mary Wilberforce see Ushaw College MSS OS/P1–42.

[10] Robert Isaac Wilberforce was Vicar of East Fairleigh, Kent, 1833–1840 and of Burton Agnes, Yorkshire, 1840–1856, serving as Archdeacon of the East Riding from 1841; he entered the Roman Catholic Church in 1854. Henry Wilberforce was Perpetual Curate of Bansgore, Hampshire, 1834, Vicar of Walmer 1841–1843, Vicar of East Farleigh, Kent, 1843–1850, and entered the Roman Catholic Church in September 1850, shortly after the reception of his wife, Mary.

[11] Sidney Herbert, 1st Baron Herbert of Lea, served as a Member of Parliament for South Wiltshire from 1832, was Secretary to the Admiralty, 1841–1845, Secretary at War, 1845–1846, 1852–1855, Secretary of State for the Colonies, 1855, and Secretary of State for War, 1859. Elizabeth married Sidney Herbert in 1846; she converted to Roman Catholicism in 1862.

(p. 5) 'shar[ing] in our anxiety as our joy,' (p. 6) and not placing any pressure on her to convert after he had done so.[12]

Manning as Maurice's Early 'Editorial' Consultant

In all of this, perhaps nowhere more fully than in his relationship with Priscilla Maurice, the sister of the noted Anglican theologian, Frederick Denison Maurice (1805–1872),[13] Manning's gifts as a pastoral counsellor[14] are made clear. Born in 1810 into a Unitarian family which eventually included seven

---

[12] Lady Herbert, *How I Came Home* (London, n.d.).

[13] John Frederick Denison Maurice was educated at Trinity College, Cambridge, left without a degree, refusing to subscribe to the Thirty-Nine Articles, but later entered Exeter College, Oxford. In 1840 he was appointed Professor of English Literature and History at King's College, London, formed the Christian Socialist movement with other like-minded writers, and in 1866 was appointed Professor of Moral Philosophy at Cambridge. For details see Frederick Maurice (ed.), *The Life of Frederick Denison Maurice: Chiefly Told in His Own Letters*, 2 vols (London, 1884; hereafter: Maurice); Leslie Stephen's biographical article in *The Dictionary of National Biography* (hereafter *DNB*, electronic edition) and Boase, vol. 2, p. 804.

[14] The term 'pastoral counsellor' is here used in its traditional sense of the pastor as spiritual guide, not in the later, more therapeutically-directed usage of the pastoral counselling movement, working as it does in a buffer created by modern methods of pain control and advanced medical technique, not thereby needing to face so consistently the close connection between sickness and death as experienced a century and a half earlier. In spite of the wide popularity of the pastoral counselling movement in the later twentieth century, however, surprisingly little study has been directed to pastoral care in the Victorian period (or to the early modern and modern periods generally), although there is a rich primary literature available. There, thus, remains a need for a closer analysis of Maurice's use of such classic Anglican and other popular manuals for visiting the sick such as Lancelot Andrewes (1555–1626), *A Manual of Direction for the Sick* . . . translated by Richard Drake (London, 1684; the volume was highly popular in the nineteenth century. See also *The Private Devotions of Lancelot Andrewes* . . . *Translated by* . . . *Peter Hall* . . . *To which is added The Manual for the Sick* [London, 1830] referred to by Manning to Priscilla Maurice, January 17, 1851, Bodleian MS Eng. lett. c. 659, ff. 211–14; note as well the later popular edition of the *Manual* by Henry P. Liddon [London, 1869]); Jeremy Taylor (1613–1667), *The Rule and Exercises of Holy Dying: in which are described the Means and Instruments of Preparing Ourselves and Others respectively for a Blessed Death*, which was already in its 28th edition in the early nineteenth century (London, 1812). Compare as well his *A Discourse of the Divine Institution, Necessity, Sacredness, and Separation of the Office Ministerial. With Rules and Advices to the Clergy*, published with his *Eniautos: A Course of Sermons for all the Sundays of the Year*. . . . [3rd ed., London, 1668] and *The Sick Man's Guide to Acts of Patience, Faith, Charity, and Repentance: Together with Two short Exercises, 1. Against unreasonable Fears in Sickness, 2. Against Despair extracted and abridged from Bishop Jeremy Taylor's Holy Dying*, by William Hale (London, 1838); Nathaniel Spinckes (1654–1727), *The Sick Man visited; and furnish'd with Instructions, Meditations, and Prayers, suitable to his Condition, for putting him in Mind of his Change, for supporting him under his Distemper, and for preparing him for, and carrying him through his last Conflict with Death* (2nd ed., London, 1717); Richard Batty (d. 1758), *The Clergyman's Companion in Visiting the Sick: Being a Collection of the following Particulars for that

sisters, their brother, and two orphaned nephews,[15] Priscilla Maurice was sent to school during her brother's first years at Cambridge[16] and returned to help at her home in 1828 when the family's financial fortunes declined. Like Manning, her brother recognised her fine mind and accordingly corresponded with her on theological matters throughout her life. In September 1821 her mother decided to leave Unitarianism for Trinitarian faith, and was followed thereafter by the older sisters. On 22 March 1831 Maurice's brother told her of his decision to be baptised as an Anglican,[17] and in 1834 when he came late to an ordination examination, she concluded that he required her care and joined him in a small cottage in his first curacy at Bubbenhall in Warwickshire.[18] She was already very ill in October 1836 and her sister Lucilla came to nurse her while she, in turn, continued to serve their brother.[19] Her illness (never clearly described in the correspondence) advanced throughout her life. By 12 February 1853 she had declined badly at her residence at Hastings,[20] and died there at Easter, 1854, following her mother's death a short time earlier.[21]

Purpose; viz. I. The Manner of Visiting the Sick; extracted chiefly from Bishop Taylor. II. The Order for Visitation of the Sick out of the Common-Prayer Book. III. The Communion of the Sick. IV. Some other Prayers and Forms, with a very great Variety of occasional Prayers for the Sick: Collected, for the most Part, from the devotional Writings of Some of the most eminent Divines of the Church of England. To which are annexed, the Offices of Publick and Private Baptism (8th ed., London, 1752); James Stonhouse (1716–1795), *Every Man's Assistant, and the Sick Man's Friend.* New edition, revised by . . . T. Stonhouse (London, 1825); Joseph Hordern, *Plain Directions for Reading to the Sick* (3rd ed., London, 1830); *A Manual of Instructions for the Time of Sickness* (Bristol, 1831); *Devotions for the Sick: Prayers and Thanksgivings, with Instructions for the Use of Sick Persons and their Friends during Sickness or upon Recovery* (Oxford, n.d.); and *The Priest's Companion in the Visitation of the Sick* [W. Dodsworth, compiler] (London, 1843), among others. Note, as well, the Roman Catholic manuals: John Gother (d. 1704) *Instructions and Devotions for the Afflicted and Sick,: with Some help for Prisoners, such especially as are to be tried for life* (London, 1756) and John Bede Polding, *Instructions and Devotions for the Afflicted and Sick* (London, 1834).

[15] Florence Higham, *Frederick Denison Maurice* (London, 1947), p. 13; Maurice, vol. 1, p. 8.
[16] Higham, p. 21; Maurice, vol. 1, pp. 57–9.
[17] Maurice, vol. 1, p. 123.
[18] Higham, p. 34; Maurice, vol. 1, pp. 153, 161. Maurice held the position until her brother's marriage on 7 October 1837, and then returned to help him at Guy's Hospital in 1844, the year before his wife's death (Higham, p. 53; Maurice, vol. 1, p. 405). The relationship was well known at the time and depicted in Elizabeth Gleghorn Gaskell's *Ruth* (1853) as that between the characters Thurstan Benson and his sister, Faith (Higham, p. 40). On their theological discussions see Maurice, vol. 1, p. 106 (February 1830); vol. 1, p. 107 (May 1830); vol. 1, pp. 118–19 (4 January and February 1831 on miracles), vol. 1, pp. 412–16 (May 1845), vol. 2, p. 63 (June 1851), vol. 2, pp. 124–5 (September, 1853); vol. 2, pp. 164–6 (May, June 1853).
[19] Higham, p. 41; Maurice, vol. 1, p.207.
[20] Maurice, vol. 2, p. 155.
[21] Her sister, Lucilla, was with her at the time and tells of Maurice slipping a hymnbook into her hands a few moments before her death. The book was open at Baxter's hymn: 'Christ leads us through no darker rooms/ than he went through before,/ And he who to Christ's kingdom comes,/ Must enter by that door.' (Higham, pp. 105–6).

Maurice was the sister-in-law of Manning's colleague, Julius Hare, Archdeacon of Lewes,[22] through whom Manning was regularly informed about her state, and through whose family, as well, Priscilla Maurice was acquainted with Mary Stanley, who shared with her an interest in the spiritual treatment of the sick.[23]

Manning seems to have met Maurice first in the early 1840s and continued in contact with her through to the close of 1853, from which period there are extant some 140 letters.[24] On 29 November 1881 he gathered his correspondence with her, introducing the collection with a general commentary on their relationship and a warning as to its tone: 'They might give the impression of too much human emotion & affection. But nothing could be further from the truth. The letters to Miss Stanley are not perhaps open to such a thought: but those to Miss Maurice might be.'[25] The affectionate tenor of the correspondence noted by Manning is most evident in the second section of the letters, those following the Gorham decision of the Privy Council in March of 1850[26]

---

[22] Julius Charles Hare (1795–1855) was educated at Trinity College, Cambridge, where he was elected a Fellow in 1818, and appointed to a lectureship in 1822. Well-versed in contemporary German theology, he served the parish of Hurstmonceaux, Sussex from 1832, and was appointed Archdeacon of Lewes, 1840. He married Esther Maurice, the sister of F.D. and Priscilla Maurice. For details see Augustus John Cuthbert Hare's biographical article in the *DNB* and N. Merril Distad, *Guessing at Truth: The Life of Julius Charles Hare (1795–1855)* (Shepherdstown, W. Va., 1979).

[23] Mary Stanley's aunt, Maria Leycester, younger sister of the wife of Edmund Stanley, Bishop of Norwich, and the sister-in-law of Julius Hare, lived at Hurstmonceaux after the death of her husband. She was there visited by Stanley and her brother, Arthur. See Arthur Penrhyn Stanley, *Memoir of Edward and Catherine Stanley* (London, 1879). On Mary Stanley's concern for the sick, note in particular the opening chapter of her anonymously published *Hospitals and Sisterhoods* (London, 1854; 2nd ed., 1855), which, in quite the opposite direction from that of Florence Nightingale, insists that the physical nursing of the sick is relatively well done, but that what is lacking is spiritual care by the nurses.

[24] Bodleian MS Eng. lett. c. 659; the collection comprises 340 folios and is arranged in chronological order. The Manning side of the correspondence alone is extant.

[25] Bodleian MS Eng. lett. c. 659, ff. 1–2; The statement is on Archbishop's House, Westminster, S.W. letterhead and is signed 'H.E. Card[inal] Archb[isho]p.' Manning here neglects to note the far more intimate tone of his correspondence with his sister-in-law, Mary Sargent Wilberforce, the person with whom, at least in his letters, he reflects the closest personal relationship.

[26] George Cornelius Gorham (1787–1857) was installed by Bishop Henry Phillpotts into the parish of St Just, Penwith, Cornwall in 1846, but was soon in controversy with his bishop over a fund appeal for Church building through the evangelical Church Extension Society and an advertisement in the *Ecclesiastical Gazette* for a curate 'free from Tractarian Error.' When Gorham was offered the parish of Bampford Speke in August 1847, Phillpotts insisted on an extensive examination. On 11 March Phillpotts declared that Gorham's baptismal doctrine was defective and he refused to induct him. Gorham issued a published complaint and in June 1848 opened a case in the Court of Arches in his own defense. The decision was against Gorham and the latter appealed to the Judicial Committee of the Privy Council. The case was heard from 11–18 December 1849. The decision in favour of Gorham was announced 8 March 1850. For details Henry Parry Liddon, *Life of Edward Bouverie Pusey*, edited by J.O.

and the completion of Maurice's major work, *Sickness, its Trials and Blessings* (London: Francis and John Rivington, 1850) at about the same time.[27] The present paper, however, is concerned with the first part of the correspondence during which both Manning and Maurice developed their particular views of sickness and pastoral approaches to the sick person.

It was concern over Maurice's illness which may have first drawn her to Manning for counsel,[28] but in March 1843 (the first date for which we have concrete information regarding their contact) she was also seeking editorial and theological advice, sending him notice of notes she had written on 'The Order for the Visitation of the Sick' and 'The Communion of the Sick' in *The Book of Common Prayer*. As one who suffered directly she felt that her advice to clergy visiting the sick was of special value. Manning agreed, as he wrote her on 8 April 1843:

> That which gives to your notes their especial value is that they are the things which the Comforter 'hath taken' & shewn unto you in times of suffering. This gives them a reality which nothing else could confer on them. And it is this that makes me delay in attempting anything myself. Unless one's mind is brought by illness, or watching a sick bed, or by affliction, or by a very vivid reawakening of old perceptions, to the point of sight from which alone trial is legible it seems almost irreverent and hardhearted to write upon it.[29]

With Maurice, as with others, Manning's epistolary style was shaped by his own view of the pastoral office – all of the functions of which he argued were directed by 'sympathy & guidance . . . blessings obtained for us by the incarnation of our Saviour under, & in whom his Pastors stand.' Manning's words in this case were initiated by his response to Maurice's question concerning the place of confession, but he is clear that 'sympathy and guidance' are applicable to *all* pastoral offices, and that those blessings, as 'obtained by the Incarnation' even when practised by such an individual and private act as one pastor writing to one parishioner, are blessings within community. Maurice had spoken to him of the 'loneliness of heart' experienced in her illness, an isolation he is finding increasingly 'hard to bear.' 'Whether it is harder to bear in

---

Johnston and Robert J. Wilson, 4 vols (London, 1893–1897), vol. 3, pp. 201–71 and J.C.S. Nias, *Gorham and the Bishop of Exeter* (London, 1951).

[27] The preface by F.C. Massingberd was dated St. Leonard's-on-Sea, 20 March 1850. The volume went through five editions by 1857. For later editions, see 1868, 1869, 1877, 1880, 1884, 1885, and an American edition, New York, 1857.

[28] See Bodleian MS Eng. lett. c. 659, ff. 1–2: 'She was in incurable illness & bedridden before I first saw her. I do not remember, I may be wrong after many years, that I ever saw her except in extreme illness, and very rarely. She lived chiefly at Hastings. I was very seldom there in all the years I knew her. And our meetings altogether were exceedingly few. But our intimacy was by letter. She was like her brother & had a very *able* and *subtle* mind, more the mind of a man than of a woman.'

[29] Bodleian MS Eng. lett. c. 659, ff. 3–4.

weakness & passiveness' such as she experiences or in 'the activity of life & mind' Manning does not know. What he does insist on, however, is that 'nothing can fill the solitude of heart but He who stands at the door and knocks [Rev. 3:20],' that is, that all 'religious fellowship is an expression and so a part of His presence.' Both sympathy and guidance are communal functions, the first as much as the second. The two are inseparable, the manifestation of sympathy as important as the expression of guidance. Thus in the letter in which he raises the issue, Manning is strikingly open as to his own feelings, reiterating to Maurice at the beginning of his letter what he had earlier told her at a private meeting: 'I know what the relief is of being able to utter what we have pent up but always growing in depth and emotion: & I hope you will write freely: trusting that nothing you write can be read by me without sympathy.' And he returns again to the issue at the close, offering the reader insights into his own deeply affectionate nature and his practice of reservation in regard to it, a practice that might appear to some as iron emotional control:

> I have as I am aware given you no help in the question how you are learning more of the great and severe lesson of living without the gifts and happiness of this life. Indeed I feel to know too little of it myself. I suppose one thing is to cease from efforts to persuade ourselves into any state differing from our actual feeling: and to bear that feeling, be it loneliness or sadness as God's will for a time: to suppress the sensitiveness which desires to taste of the gladness of life: & to wait for peace, with our eyes shut; we know not when nor how. If it tarry wait for it. It will come & not tarry.
>
> Do not distress yourself about selfishness. It is not so because you yield no consent to it. To have such feelings only reminds you that the world is fallen & you along with it
>
> I will only add that I hope you will not fear to write openly even of weaknesses. I know that time & delicate sympathy is too high a gift for me to promise, but I trust I may revise more of that great grace from Him in whom clear it is.[30]

Such words were auspicious for a friendship, but relations between the two over the next several years were not without struggles. Manning warned her in his 8 April letter of his own reservations concerning his role as an editor of her works: His 'employments are so many and so distracting that they make me feel unfit to approach the great mysteries of suffering: for we ought to draw near with feet unshod, the ground where on we stand being holy [Exodus 3:5],' he wrote, adding: 'This much at least I will say that it will be a most grateful by-work to which I may turn when I think I can set down any thing of instruction or consolation for the elects sake – and I am thankful to you for suggesting it to me.'[31] In fact, so caught up was he with other matters that he was still having difficulty finding time to work through Maurice's manuscript

---

[30] Manning to Maurice, 31 August 1844, Bodleian MS Eng. lett. c. 659, ff. 19–22.
[31] Bodleian MS Eng. lett. c. 659, ff. 3–6.

with care on 22 December 1843, promising to do so in the coming winter,[32] although by 30 June of the following year, having finally met her at Reading a few weeks previously, he was required to repeat the promise.[33] On 12 October 1844, Manning having returned from a trip to Normandy, Maurice's manuscript was before him once more and this time he immediately reviewed it. The manuscript was not in good order. Maurice had assembled the notes of others, there was at least one metaphor 'a little strained and prominent in style,' the 'tone & texture' as a result were not integrated, and there was need for some expansion. Nevertheless, Manning was willing 'to proceed at once' to the publisher on Maurice's behalf, if she so wished.[34]

What her response was is not clear. By 22 February 1845, however, one has the sense, Maurice's patience was strained, the more so when she was offered as excuse a fleeting comment on 'two or three months . . . unusually full of work, and lately, of a most anxious kind . . . In addition to all ordinary duties . . . three books reprinting which require . . . constant attention.'[35] Fortunately her health was improved slightly, and she took action. On 6 March 1845 Manning at last returned the manuscript with a self-indulgent apology for his delay, expressing his willingness to have the piece passed on to Francis Charles Massingberd:[36] 'I am really glad that the notes will be edited by one who is himself a partaker in sickness, from which God has hitherto so graciously spared me.'[37]

There remained some troubles with the publisher (with which Manning may have helped)[38] but by mid-year Maurice's *Hints on the Service for the Visitation of the Sick* (London: Francis and John Rivington, 1845) appeared anonymously with a preface by Massingberd dated at Torquay, 15 April 1845, announcing that it was 'drawn up by one who has been long tried by sickness and has experienced the deep consolation and support which the Visitation Service of the Church is calculated to afford . . . published at the suggestion of some clergymen, having been written originally only for private use,' (p. iii) and that '[a]t the request of the writer, [Massingberd] willingly certif[ied his] belief as a Presbyter of the Church, that what has been written is according to Sacred doctrine, and is calculated to lead other sufferers to a better understanding and fuller appreciation of this beautiful and Holy Service.' Manning

---

[32] *Ibid.*, ff. 7–8.
[33] *Ibid.*, ff. 11–12.
[34] *Ibid.*, ff. 23–8.
[35] *Ibid.*, ff. 29–30.
[36] Francis Charles Massingberd (1800–1872) was educated at Rugby and Magdalen College, Oxford. He served as rector of South Ormsby, Lincolnshire from 1825, was appointed a prebend at Lincoln Cathedral in 1847 and chancellor in 1862. A High Churchman he was an active proponent and supporter of Convocation throughout his life. For details see the biographical article by Edmund Venables in the *DNB*.
[37] Bodleian MS Eng. lett. c. 659, ff. 31–2.
[38] See Manning to Maurice, 27 July 1845, Bodleian MS Eng. lett. c. 659, ff. 37–8.

had suggested that the *Hints* be printed in parallel columns, the 'Order of Visitation' on the one side and Maurice's notes on the other, but in its final form, Maurice's notes appeared after the 'Order.' Nor did Maurice immediately return for other publishing advice to Manning. Less than a year later *Sacred Poems for Mourners* with an Introduction by the Rev. R. C. Trench[39] (London, 1846) was published. The volume contained almost 400 pages of poetry, selected, according to the introduction, by 'one who was alone,' [Priscilla Maurice] (p. vi) from writers such as Crashaw, Southwell, Herbert, Herrick, Jonson, Taylor, Milton, Baxter, Southey, and Longfellow, and grouped under the general headings of 'the Office for the Burial of the Dead': Psalm 39, Psalm 90, 1 Corinthians 15:20 ff., Sentences and Prayers, and the first and second collects.

'Sickness, its Trials and Blessings'

There is no reference to *Sacred Poems* in Manning's letters, but in spite of this and the tension over the publication of *Hints*, the correspondence between the two not only continued thereafter, but intensified. For the next several years a symbiotic relationship developed between them, Manning's illness, on the one hand, modifying certain less agreeable aspects of his approach and Maurice focusing, on the other, on the nature of her isolation as a result of her illness and the implications of this for understanding her 'vocation.'

Manning's own illness struck him seriously in December of 1846 and his doctor ordered him for a curative rest to the Continent in the summer. He was initially too weak to travel, although in the fall of the year he did have the strength to go to Italy. As a result of his illness his relationship with Maurice was to a degree reversed. On 19 February 1847 he wrote thanking her for her advice and adding candidly – perhaps with a touch of irony regarding his earlier 'wisdom':

> You know how often I have told you my difficulty about entering into the meaning of sickness. I feel able to do so better just now. As you ask about me I will tell you, & get rid of myself. I have been ailing for nearly two months & it has now settled on my throat – not the chest, thank God. I am sufficiently unwell to understand many things I have talked about very wisely. I can truly say and I

---

[39] Richard Chenevix Trench (1807–1886) was educated at Trinity College, Cambridge, where he met F.D. Maurice and Julius Hare. Curate at Hadleigh under Hugh James Rose, 1833, and associated with High Church views, he was appointed to the perpetual curacy of Curdridge, Hampshire, 1835, and served as curate to Samuel Wilberforce, 1841. From 1846–1858 he was Professor of Divinity at King's College, London, was appointed Dean of Westminster, 1856, and Archbishop of Dublin, 1863–1884, leading the Irish Church through the turmoil of Disestablishment in 1870. For details see Ronald Bayne's biographical article in the *DNB* and Boase, vol. 3, p. 1013.

thank God; & as I do; and, though it may perhaps be that I do not really think I have much the matter with me, yet I feel it a blessed thing not to pray to be otherwise than I am, but just to lie on the waterflood, knowing who sitteth above it.[40]

Four months later, and little improved, Manning responded to Maurice's counsel once again.[41] In this, as in the former, letter Manning turned at the close to a direct discussion of Maurice's own increased difficulties with her health, but by 12 October he gained a new sense of the depths to which disease can reduce one:

> Every day convinces me how deeply wanting I am in love, trust, gratitude: or in short, in faith, hope, & love. Nothing I feel more destitute of than the final confiding love of God, the full fraternal trustful love of our Lord & Saviour. I have found it to be my special want and the want of it as you say sets all things wrong. We grow morbid & gloomy in our sense of sin, & unloving, unfilial in our heart towards God.
>
> From my remembrance of our conversation I am sure I gave you more than a full reason to see this. I trust it is not really so unbalanced, however honour by distinct desires & prayers as our partial treatment of the subject w[oul]d make appear.[42]

It was in this context that Maurice went to Manning for advice with her next, largest, and most popular project, *Sickness, its Trials and Blessings*. On 26 October 1848 he promised to look at the manuscript. Quotations from it which she had taken from his sermons, he is willing for her to 'count all your own. The lines are not in print, but are freely yours.' Sensitivity over possible plagiarism was a minor problem for Maurice at the time, however; shortly after Manning's note to her, she was opposed on part of her text by persons she trusted, and turned to him again. His response on 14 November 1848 is carefully measured, acknowledging her pain, endeavoring to depersonalise the

---

[40] Bodleian MS Eng. lett. c. 659, ff. 58–60.
[41] Manning to Maurice, 14 June 1847. Bodleian MS Eng. lett. c. 659, ff. 61–62: 'I cannot thank you enough for what you wrote. It comes home with much directness to my own personal feelings. You remember I once told you I c[oul]d not write anything about sickness "having never learnt". And now I fail to know so little that I dare not say more than to tell you that while I was ill I tried to put some sermons together on subjects relating to preparations for death. They are far short of even what I intended: but such as they are I hope soon to send them to you. I w[oul]d ask you not to say what I have written: as I wish nothing less than to connect them with myself. They will not be published till the end of the year but I shall hope to send you the sheets, for your own use &, if so be, any the least comfort.' On the sermons referred to here see Henry E. Manning, *Sermons* (London, 1847): Sermon XII: 'The Cross The Measure of Love,' pp. 217–39; Sermon XVII: 'Preparation for Death A State of Life,' pp. 311–30; Sermon XVIII: 'The Death of Christ our Only Stay,' pp. 331–51; Sermon XIX: 'The Fearfulness of Death,' pp. 352–69; Sermon XX: 'The Blessedness of Death,' pp. 370–87; Sermon XXII: 'The Great Betrothal,' pp. 411–30, to three of which (XII, XVII, XXII) he directs Maurice on 12 October 1847, Bodleian MS Eng. lett. c. 659, ff. 65–8.
[42] Bodleian MS Eng. lett. c. 659, ff. 65–8.

issue, and, above all, encouraging her to continue, assuring her of the value of her project and of her person and work as she completes it:

> For my own part I am glad you have written it: for it must contain a record of things made known to you by suffering. The thought of such reasons are, if any, from God and we are not intended to slight or squander but to fix & to lay them up, for our own good, & for the good of others. I have a very deep belief that this is the duty of those when God tries: that what we take may be given to others ... To him you say that you wrote as the God of Truth dictated. I understand you to mean much what I have said. I could conceive your friends misliking the expression & misunderstanding it to mean more than you intended. I should revise it as the work of your own mind under the teaching of sickness, and with the help which God gives to all in trials each for his hour & his day.
>
> What your brother says is wholly my own mind about all writings. I have only patience for the books which are written on spiritual trials by those who have never tasted this reality.[43]

By 9 March 1849 the manuscript was in his hands and he reviewed it carefully, knowing as he did so that Massingberd was again seeing the whole through the press.[44] The final printed version did not appear for another full year, Maurice's illness and her own reworking of the piece playing a major role in delaying final publication. Certainly the project led her to a close self-scrutiny and in June 1849 she presented Manning with an autobiographical piece in which she 'analysed the evils & dangers of [her] life.' It may be that she intended to integrate parts of it into her new work, but whatever the case, her self-reflections at the time were directly the result of 'vocational' concerns which had been with her from the beginning of their correspondence as she struggled to understand the meaning of her sickness, her sense of isolation in it, and the possible parallels between her situation 'alone' and that of those in a sisterhood.[45]

On 2 October, having read her June autobiographical paper, Manning outlined what he understood to be the psychological effects on her development in a family 'disinterested ... out of unity and ... out of Faith.'

---

[43] *Ibid.*, ff. 81–2.
[44] *bid.*, ff. 92–5.
[45] As early as the opening months of 1848 she was in consultation with Elizabeth Lockhart, possibly on matters related to the foundation of sisterhoods. See Manning to Maurice, from Rome on the Monday after Easter, 1848, Bodleian MS Eng. lett. c. 659, ff. 71–72. Elizabeth Lockhart (1812–1870) was the daughter of Alexander Lockhart (d. 1831) and after her father's death lived with his second wife, Martha (Jacob) Lockhart (1798?–1872), at Hastings and Chichester. Manning is said to have forbidden either mother or daughter to speak with Elizabeth's step-brother, William (1819–1892), following his conversion to Rome in August 1843 (*DNB*, Boase, vol. 2, p. 469). Elizabeth was the first superior of the Anglican Sisters of St. Mary the Virgin at Wantage from 1848 and was received into the Roman Catholic Church in 1850, her mother four years earlier on 9 July 1846.

I seem to see how you suffered from the absence of Truth & Love: truth to steady your mind: Love to soften it.

You had seeking, craving, questioning, doubting and a blank, instead of seeing, grasping, believing, knowing & a reality. So much for the intellectual part which might be expanded into a volume.

As for the moral

Isolation, selfconsciousness, irritation, exhaustion, excitement and helplessness took the place of peace, order calm discipline contentment, self-denial and a submitted will.

The cause of this seems to me to be the absence of the Object of Faith, & the Discipline of the Soul which God has ordained in His church.

The absence of this objective reality & system leaves us in a state of practical *atheism*. Self then becomes our centre & law, our Altar & God, belief, opinion, affections all begin & move round self. We love others as they please us, love us, minister to us, make us happy. Even in doing them good it is as being their Maker Redeemer & Sanctifier.[46]

Six weeks later, on 14 November 1849,[47] he wrote her again, as he did once more on 21 November[48] in each case taking up the topic of her 'aloneness' and the best structure for the formation of a sisterhood. For Manning, Maurice's difficulties stemmed from her formation in the ultra-Low Unitarian tradition and the Low Church traditions to which her mother and sisters converted when she was yet a child. What she requires, he insists, is 'objective' religion. Although he will not deny the need for the subjective element in the religious life,[49] he understands her situation well enough, he believes, to sense that a person limited by an illness such as she has, will inevitably fall prey to self-centredness if she is not 'guided' and 'empathetic' to the incarnated realities of truth and love, particularly as they are manifest in the communal nature of the faith.[50] For a person like Maurice, as she understands herself in sickness and

---

[46] Bodleian MS Eng. lett. c. 659, ff. 108–9.

[47] *Ibid.*, ff. 110–13.

[48] *Ibid.*, ff. 114–20.

[49] This he knew from personal experience as he told her a year later. See Manning to Maurice, 30 August 1850, Bodleian MS Eng. lett. c. 659, ff. 110–13: 'What I always felt was that the low Ch[urch] had no *objective Truths* the High Church little *subjective religion*. All my opinions being of what w[oul]d be thought the latter school, I therefore turned all my *preaching* on the former or *subjective* matter, as your brother truly remarks.' Note as well Manning's letter to Maurice of 20 October 1846 in which he presses her on the need for a sisterhood as a means for avoiding 'Rome,' on the one hand, and offering a permanent objective calling, on the other. Such a calling, he proposes can be taken up even in a semi-permanent manner, if, for example, a full commitment would result in a 'breach with her Family. And then I think nothing but a decided choice for life formed in faith of God's vocation, would make it right to take such a step.' Bodleian MS Eng. lett. c. 659, f. 53.

[50] On Maurice's difficulty with the 'objective' in worship, note Manning's comments to her early in the correspondence on the nature of the Holy Spirit, 3 July 1844, Bodleian MS Eng. lett. c. 659, ff. 13–16.

'alone' (a descriptor applied to her by Trench earlier), the communal function that is most suitable is that of a sisterhood, the only 'objective' alternative to marriage. The self must either be contained by and redeemed in community or it will force the community to circle round it. Although attracted to the option Manning placed before her, she did not follow it finally, the opening lines of her *Sickness, its Trials and Blessings* hinting at what she had learned from Manning of sympathy, but reiterating and universalising her sense of the importance of the solitary aspect of her 'vocation':

> Each one knows that he must *die* alone. How few realise that, for the most part, it is God's appointment that each one should *live* alone, and suffer alone! Each one must 'bear his own burden [Gal. 6:5],' feel his own incommunicable grief . . . Solitude and a sense of isolation are not peculiar to sickness. They who walk abroad in the busy world have their own 'loneliness of heart' . . . This deep weary sense of isolation is a call to the sick to sympathize with, and better to understand the trials of those in health. There is in every heart more or less a craving for sympathy; a restless craving for those who have not learned where to turn for true sympathy, and that 'One only and one is enough' to satisfy all their yearnings. (p. 3)

How Manning initially reacted to such words we do not know. The 'One' to whom she was turning was the same as the 'Maker, Redeemer & Sanctifier' to whom Manning had directed her, but the tone of her opening paragraph in *Sickness* offers no hint that she understood his emphasis on objective religion. Her modifier 'only' and her added statement that 'one is enough' suggests that she had not shifted as far as Manning would have liked, and explain in large part his conclusion in the introductory epistle to his 1881 collection of the correspondence: 'She was advancing towards much Catholic truth but was by all her family influences & antecedents' hindered in finally reaching the goal. He had earlier replied to her regarding the use of his sermons in the introduction that there was no need for her to indicate any particular words as quotations – they were as much hers as his, he noted.[51] After all, those offering pastoral sympathy and guidance were together in the body of Christ. But, whether she understood this in the same way as he did or not, Manning continued to offer her aid, reviewing the proofs of *Sickness* on 6 and 14 May 1850[52] and reporting to her on 18 June that Henry Wilberforce had come on a copy of the volume and had commented positively on it, not realising it was Maurice's.[53]

There is no mention of Manning reviewing Maurice's two later collections, both printed anonymously. *Prayers for the Sick and Dying By the Author of 'Sickness, its Trials and Blessings'* (London, 1853) and *Help and Comfort for*

---

[51] Manning to Maurice, 20 April 1850, Bodleian MS Eng. lett. c. 659, ff. 138–9.
[52] Bodleian MS Eng. lett. c. 659, ff. 143–4, 147–8.
[53] *Ibid.*, ff. 149–50.

the Sick Poor By the Author of 'Sickness, its Trials and Blessings' (London, 1853).[54] But this does not indicate any break in their relationship. Certainly Manning had learned much from her over the years as the correspondence indicates, reflecting his growing movement away from the more sermonic tones of Newman's early sermon on affliction, to which Manning had pointed Maurice in his first letter to her,[55] his voice growing ever more assured and more direct (as she advised clerical visitors to be) in respect both to her illness[56] and to personal matters: Manning's increasingly strained relationships with the Low Church orientation of Hare,[57] Manning's own shifts in religious direction,[58] Maurice's brother's negative views of the High Church patterns,[59] and Manning's more open acknowledgment of the importance for him of her expressions of consolation.[60]

Manning had gained the core of these personal virtues earlier, but his skill in their practice appears to have peaked after 1848, following his serious illness and his direct work with her on the principles of her pastoral care of the sick. In his earlier writing he expressed close sympathy with the poor and the suffering among his parishioners, but those pastoral admonitions bear the marks of a reserved homiletic voice compared with his comments in the last five years of his correspondence with her. The same argument might be made for his later writing in which his function as a pastor or his treatment of the topic are raised – the institutional and theological emphasis in *The Pastoral Office* (Printed for Private Use Only, 1883) for example, or in his highly popular *The Eternal Priesthood* (London, 1883) – but underlying such works one can note that human and intimate tone reflected in the correspondence with Maurice and for which he felt the need to write the 1881 monitum to his collection. Thus in *The Eternal Priesthood*, the mark of what he had learned in the Maurice and other relationships over the years immediately before and after his conversion is less personally, but accurately expressed: when speaking of the joys of the pastor, what comes first to Manning's mind is

> ... the [threefold] relation of pastor and flock ... mutual knowledge, mutual love, mutual charity. The mutual knowledge is to know the number, the name,

---

[54] A third edition was published in 1859 and a 'New Edition' in 1869.
[55] John Henry Newman, *Parochial Sermons for the Winter Quarter, Being the weeks between Advent Sunday and Lent*, vol. V (London and Oxford, 1840), Sermon XXI: 'Affliction, a School of Comfort.'
[56] 10 April 1850, Bodleian MS Eng. lett. c. 659, ff. 136–7.
[57] 29 January 1849, Bodleian MS Eng. lett. c. 659, ff. 86–9; 20 April 1850, *ibid.*, ff. 138–9; 21 November 1850, *ibid.*, ff. 191–2.
[58] 21 March 1850, Bodleian MS Eng. lett. c. 659, ff. 128–31; 5 and 20 August 1850, *ibid.*, ff. 155–9; 25 October 1850, *ibid.*, ff. 178–82.
[59] 14 May 1850, Bodleian MS Eng. lett. c. 659, ff. 143–4; cf. ff. 145–6); 5 April 1850, *ibid.*, ff. 155–7; 30 August 1850, *ibid.*, ff. 160–2; 29 February 1851, *ibid.*, ff. 226–7; undated letters from 1853, *ibid.*, ff. 324–7; 28 December 1853, *ibid.*, ff. 337–40.
[60] 26 September 1850, Bodleian MS Eng. lett. c. 659, ff. 165–6.

and the needs of his flock one by one, and to be known by them as their father, friend, and guide: the mutual charity is that he loves them for our Lord's sake, for their own sake, as heirs of eternal life, and as his spiritual children in Jesus Christ; and the mutual service is that he bestows upon them his care, labour, time, strength , health, and if need be, life itself; and that they render to him the service of filial charity, generosity, and obedience. When pastor and flock are so united, then the words of S. John are fulfilled: 'I have no greater grace than this, to hear that my children walk in truth.' (p. 225)

With such pastoral empathy and guidance, then, are united truth and love, the flock's response in gratitude before the open kindness, as Manning described the pastoral virtues to his Oblates when he left them to serve as Archbishop in 1865.

3

THE CARDINAL AND THE PENITENT: CARDINAL MANNING AND VIRGINIA CRAWFORD

ROBIN GARD

ON THE evening of 10 March 1888 a young lady reporter, Miss Eustace, nervously rang the bell of the archiepiscopal residence in Westminster, the plain, barrack-like dwelling, formerly an army officers' club, in Carlisle Place. She had come by prior appointment made by her editor, W.T. Stead,[1] the campaigning journalist of the *Pall Mall Gazette*, to seek Cardinal Manning's views on the death of the German Emperor, William I. She had already attended the afternoon service in the Chapel Royal in Whitehall, at which the royal family had been present, and had filed her copy, 'In Praise of Inequality of Brotherhood', largely a résumé of the sermon by the Bishop of Peterborough, and was both tired and doubtful of her reception. She had good cause to be nervous since she must have realised that His Eminence, whose reputation for being well informed on most topics of the day was common knowledge, would immediately identify her. Thus, climbing the bare staircase and passing through the sparsely furnished, curtain-less rooms of the gloomy mansion to meet the piercing eyes of the gaunt prelate must have severely tested her resolution.

What occurred at that interview is not known: the Chapel Royal service was featured in the *Pall Mall Gazette* on 12 March, but the Cardinal's views were not reported. It is probable that Stead, in his note arranging the meeting, would have told Manning who Miss Eustace was and, indeed, may have contrived the interview so that the two should meet. It cannot be doubted that Manning would have recognised Miss Eustace as Mrs Virginia Crawford, whose confession of adultery with the Cabinet Minister, Sir Charles Dilke, a close

---

[1] William Thomas Stead (1849–1912), editor of the *Pall Mall Gazette*, 1883–89, founded the *Review of Reviews*, 1890. Died in the Titanic disaster.

friend of the Cardinal, which led to two sensational divorce hearings in 1886, had made her the most notorious woman in Britain at the time.

It is unlikely that Manning would have met Mrs Crawford beforehand, but he would have known about her background and about her role in the case from Dilke, who, shortly after the divorce proceedings were begun in July 1885, is said to have told the Cardinal 'everything'. During the meeting, Manning would have been sure to have questioned Mrs Crawford about her life, doubtless touching on the divorce case, and is reputed to have told her that 'she had been badly brought up'. Mrs Crawford, however, was a woman of spirit, gifted with a sharp mind, and despite, or perhaps because of, their differences of age, sex, temperament, attitudes and experiences, the austere Cardinal and the young erstwhile delinquent lady found a friendship which lightened his last weary years and inspired the friendless, social outcast to lead a reformed life. As was his wont, Manning gave his visitor a book, which he signed and dated, and in which Mrs Crawford wrote later, 'This was the first book given to me by Cardinal Manning'.

The next day, Mrs Crawford discussed with Stead various commissions on which she was engaged. In a letter dated 12 March, Stead urged her 'to keep a copious diary of your visits and impressions of people like Cardinal Manning, Canon Liddon, the Salvation Army and the like'. If Mrs Crawford followed this advice straightaway, no such diary survives, but a journal of interviews does exist from 6 June 1890 to 16 February 1892, with three later entries dated 1893, 1896 and 1899.[2] In this Mrs Crawford records thirty-three visits to Cardinal Manning between 27 March 1890 and 31 December 1891, just two weeks before his death. The entries of these visits are here reproduced in full and offer unaffected testimony of Manning's private opinions on a wide range of spiritual, religious, moral, ecclesiastical, literary and other matters.

Very little is known of any visits which Mrs Crawford almost certainly made to the Cardinal between her first interview on 10 March 1888 and the first visit recorded in the journal on 27 March 1890. Evidently, Manning wrote her many letters, which Shane Leslie, who went to see her in 1911 on an introduction from Wilfrid Meynell, had been anxious to read, but he 'gathered that they were too sacred and would accompany her to the grave', and there are no Manning letters among her surviving papers. However, Leslie later obtained a copy of the journal from her relatives and published the Manning entries, first selectively in *The Quarterly Review* in 1951 and then fully in *The Dublin Review* in 1967.[3]

It is likely that the Dilkes became aware of Mrs Crawford's contacts with Manning since Sir Charles wrote to him, sending notes of new material

---

[2] Dilke–Crawford–Roskill Collection, Churchill College, Cambridge, REND.12/7.
[3] Shane Leslie, 'Cardinal Manning in Mrs Crawford's Journals', *The Quarterly Review*, No. 587 (January, 1951), pp. 68–83; 'Virginia Crawford, Sir Charles Dilke, and Cardinal Manning', *The Dublin Review*, vol. 241, no. 513 (Autumn, 1967), pp. 177–205.

collected by the committee investigating the case on his behalf. In his reply on 26 February 1889, Manning wrote: 'I could hardly have believed that so many oversights and omissions, and all against you, could have happened as in these two trials. Nor how so many contradictions should have been possible. God grant that some light may spring up to clear you; and lift off from you the great suffering that is upon you'.[4] This guarded letter may have been composed in knowledge derived from Mrs Crawford, but reassured Dilke that his own relationship with the Cardinal had not changed.

The journal contains only one indirect reference to the divorce case, in the note of the visit made to the Cardinal at his request by Mrs Crawford's sister Maye, when he thanked her for befriending Virginia, as Mrs Crawford will henceforth be called. The recorded visits were made on a Thursday, Friday or Saturday, but there is no indication of the time of day or how they were arranged. However, Virginia recalled in 1942 that she used to visit the Cardinal every Friday and was always admitted without delay, which suggests that she had an open invitation and that there were probably more visits than are recorded.[5] Virginia was by no means Manning's only private visitor, and from other accounts one gets the impression of an endless stream of persons climbing the stairs to the private sanctum. Only once did Manning keep her waiting, apologising afterwards that she surely would not mind if she knew his previous visitor was Mr Gladstone, with whom he was now reconciled.[6]

This is not the place to review the Dilke case in any detail as it has been exhaustively examined in many publications, even though several mysterious aspects remain to be convincingly explained.[7] Apart from Dilke and Virginia, Manning probably knew the intimate history better than anyone. He had been a close friend of Sir Charles Dilke from 1874, and of Lady Dilke from 1886; he was a warm friend of J.E.C. Bodley, Dilke's secretary, and the person he wished for his own biographer; he was in frequent touch with W.T. Stead, who was hostile to Dilke and hounded him throughout his life, and, above all, he was the spiritual mentor and friend of Virginia. Manning counselled silence on all parties and was even able to restrain Stead. Stead claimed in 1891 that the Cardinal was on his side in the controversy about the case he was conducting in his paper, whereupon Manning wrote to a correspondent: 'Neither directly nor indirectly have I expressed either judgment or sympathy in what Mr Stead

---

[4] Roy Jenkins, *Dilke, A Victorian Tragedy* (London, 1996), p. 368.
[5] Francis Bywater, 'Virginia Crawford', unpublished MSS, p. 225.
[6] *Ibid.*, p. 226.
[7] Jenkins, *Dilke, passim*; David Nicholls, *The Lost Prime Minister, A Life of Sir Charles Dilke* (London, 1995), *passim*; Betty Askwith, *Lady Dilke, A Biography* (London, 1969), *passim*; Vivian Green, *Love in a Cool Climate, The Letters of Mark Pattison and Meta Bradley 1879–1884* (Oxford, 1985), pp. 237–46; R. Rhodes James, *Rosebery* (London, 1963), pp. 181–9; Francis Bywater, 'Cardinal Manning and the Dilke Divorce Case', *The Chesterton Review, Cardinal Manning Special Issue*, vol. 18, no. 4 (November 1992), pp. 539–53; Bywater, 'The Dilke Divorce Case' and 'Virginia Crawford', unpublished MSS, *passim*.

has done. The relation of confidence in which I have stood to both persons involved has absolutely closed my lips.'[8]

Much of what has been published has been unsympathetic to Virginia Crawford and her family, and Virginia herself deserves a full biography. However, it is necessary here only to sketch her life before her meeting with the Cardinal, and then, after the journal entries, it will be fitting to trace her subsequent career.

Virginia Mary Crawford was born on 20 November 1862, the fourth of six daughters and of ten children of Thomas Eustace Smith (1831–1903) of Gosforth House, Northumberland, a Newcastle shipping magnate, Liberal MP for Tynemouth (1868–1885), and Martha Mary Dalrymple (1835–1919). Smith left the management of his shipping interests to his second son, Eustace, and he and his wife, a leading London hostess, travelled widely and were patrons of the Pre-Raphaelite and other artists. Their London home, 52 Princes Gate, was a popular meeting place for painters such as Watts, Rossetti, Leighton and Whistler, poets and men of letters such as Browning and Meredith, politicians like G.O. Trevelyan, Joseph Chamberlain, L. Courtney and Dilke, and philosophers like Herbert Spencer, many attracted by the beauty and the intelligence of Mrs Smith, known as Eustacia, as by the repute of other guests. Only Oscar Wilde seems to have resisted her charms, and her chagrin at finding him entertaining the guests of another hostess, having declined her invitation, is recorded.[9] Neither Smith nor his wife were religious, although he built a handsome church on his Gosforth estate for his tenants and people in the neighbouring colliery villages, a church ornamented with William Morris and Company stained glass designed by Burne-Jones, Ford Madox Brown, Rossetti and Morris himself. Virginia and her sisters were educated by a Calvinist governess, Mlle Friedel, at home and at Lausanne, where Virginia – a precocious child dubbed by her sisters 'V.S. (Very Scientific)' – at a very young age acquired a European outlook, a life-long devotion to literature and the arts, and a fluency in languages.

Mrs Smith was a strong-willed mother and ensured that her six daughters 'came out' in turn at 17 years and were sensibly married, only two marrying husbands of their own choice. Maye, the eldest, married Ashton Wentworth Dilke (1850–1883), the younger brother of Sir Charles Dilke, in a love match. Ashton Dilke was a European traveller, a writer on Russian politics and literature, proprietor of the *Weekly Dispatch*, and MP for Newcastle from 1880 to 1883. Helen, the second daughter, who features in the divorce case, married Robert Richens Harrison, younger brother of Frederic Harrison, the positivist writer, and twenty years her senior. When Olive, the third sister, was married, Virginia became her mother's next companion to be found a husband. She

---

[8] Jenkins, p. 368; Bywater, 'Cardinal Manning and the Dilke Divorce Case', pp. 548–9.
[9] Bywater, 'Virginia Crawford', pp. 38–9.

refused two men, one being the young Baden Powell. Virginia told her father that if she was made to marry one of them 'I know I should throw a book at his head', to which her indignant father said, 'Very well, my dear, there is nothing more to be said'.[10] It was only after her mother locked her up in her room on short rations that she agreed to marry Donald Crawford (1837–1919), Fellow of Lincoln College, Oxford, a Scottish Advocate, later MP (1885–1892) for N.E. Lanark, who was twenty-five years her senior. When Mrs Smith told the painter, later Lord Leighton, about the match, he was indignant: 'Do you mean to say you are marrying off that child. I call it shameful'.[11] All the daughters had generous marriage settlements, so that her marriage on 27 July 1881 afforded Virginia, still only 18 years of age, a welcome degree of financial and personal independence. Glimpses of the Crawfords' married life appear in the correspondence of Mark Pattison (1814–1884), Rector of Lincoln College, and his young admirer, Meta Bradley.[12] Meta noted in December 1881 that Virginia looked on marriage 'very much as a matter of course, a business to be got over at 18', and in 1882, 'she's very young and has never felt anything very much. It amuses me to hear such a child babble in her fresh way. I can't imagine what they have in common.' Mark Pattison agreed: 'she and her husband have nothing in common, and from her eagerness to contradict him, one might infer that there existed at present a secret antipathy, but this she will no doubt get over when she finds her interests are identified with her husband's and how necessary it is for a pair to make common cause against the world.'[13]

There were no children of the marriage, though Virginia wanted a child and late in life remarked that if she had had children 'nothing that happened would have happened'. While in London, Virginia led a full social life with her sisters, Maye and Helen, while she had her first experience of practical social work for the poor, assisting Canon Barnett in his East End Mission. This contrast between the frivolous and serious aspects of Virginia's character was shrewdly observed by Meta Bradley in April 1884: 'she is a curious mixture of worldliness by education and straightforwardness by nature. She flirts by night and is most energetic at the East End by day.'[14] Physically, Virginia at this time was rather on the plump side, not pretty, but had 'milk maid looks', which made her attractive to men.

At some time after her marriage Virginia met a Captain Henry Forster, with whom she formed an attachment which soon became gossip, leading to letters sent anonymously to Crawford, warning him of his wife's behaviour. Two of these actually referred to Dilke, a third mentioning Virginia being seen at a

[10] Family notes, REND.13/1.
[11] Family notes, REND.13/1.
[12] Green, *passim.*
[13] *Ibid.*, pp. 127–8.
[14] *Ibid.*, p. 183.

hotel with Forster. Crawford had both watched, but it was only on the receipt of a fourth letter that he confronted Virginia on 17 July 1885 with his suspicions, only to be told that her lover had been Sir Charles Dilke (1843–1911), then President of the Local Government Board. Dilke had long been a close friend of the Smith family, and after his brother Ashton's marriage to Maye Smith in 1876 was related, and even permitted to be called 'Charlie' by her younger sisters. Within the closed world of London society, Dilke had a 'reputation', and the family relationship was complicated by liaisons between Mrs Smith and Dilke in 1868 and again in 1874–5. Eustace Smith was clearly a tolerant husband, as their marriage continued until his death in 1903.

Crawford sued for divorce, naming Dilke, who tried unsuccessfully to induce Virginia to withdraw her allegations. Dilke's immediate political career was ruined and Gladstone omitted him from the new government formed at the beginning of February 1886. The case, Crawford v. Crawford and Dilke, was heard on 12 February 1886, when Crawford obtained a decree *nisi* solely on his recital of Virginia's confession to him. This was unsworn and therefore in law could not be considered as evidence of Dilke's guilt, and the case against him was dismissed. The judgment thus implied, paradoxically, that Virginia had committed adultery with Dilke but that he had not done so with her, a conclusion worthy of the Savoy operas of Gilbert and Sullivan entertaining London at the time. Dilke had the opportunity to appear and to deny on oath the alleged adultery but his counsel advised him not to do so, lest he be examined about possible 'indiscretions' in his earlier life. This created the public suspicion that Dilke, despite being legally cleared of the charge, had something to hide.

Dilke was determined to restore his name but, the case against him having been dismissed, he could not begin proceedings himself, and these had to be instituted through the intervention of the Queen's Proctor, to whom Dilke applied to have Crawford's decree rescinded on the grounds that it had been pronounced 'contrary to the justice of the case'. Accordingly, a new hearing took place from 16 to 23 July 1886, the six-day trial exposing all the sordid details of the evidence to public gaze.

Virginia thus had the opportunity of adjusting her answers where necessary. She was forced to admit adultery with Forster, but Dilke, likewise, had to confess the same with Mrs Smith. Virginia almost certainly fabricated some details of allegations, but was the more convincing, as well as the more attractive, witness. Her life style had clearly been wayward, but she was self-assured in court and gave her evidence succinctly and without hesitation, whereas Dilke was diffuse. His otherwise strong case was undermined by several circumstances, including the contrary evidence of a certain Mrs Rogerson, a friend expected to deny that Virginia had once told her of her adultery, but who, instead, confirmed the damaging conversation; the failure to produce a crucial witness, Fanny Stock, who could have contradicted Virginia's most sensational charge; and the testimony on Virginia's behalf of her sister Maye against her brother-in-law. The jury took only a few minutes to uphold Crawford's decree.

The motives which induced Virginia to accuse Dilke are still debated. If not guilty of all Virginia's charges, Dilke, in his intimacy with the Smith family, may yet have behaved improperly towards her before her marriage (he was barred from visiting the family after 1880), which if true and disclosed would have also damaged his reputation. Virginia was patently anxious to shield Forster, of whom she seemed genuinely fond, although there was no prospect of their marrying as he was already engaged. Dilke was probably right in suspecting a female conspiracy, one involving Mrs Rogerson, to whom he may once have proposed and who wished to marry him. Her changed evidence in the second hearing suggests that she played a key role in the case.[15] Shane Leslie and others fastened on Mrs Smith as the master-mind, but there is no evidence that she had any influence over Virginia, and the Smiths had much to lose and, indeed, were obliged to withdraw from London society, sold their lavish house, 52 Princes Gate with all its treasures, and went to live in Algiers.[16] Both Rosebery and Chamberlain, Dilke's colleagues and putative rivals, knew Virginia socially but the idea of a political conspiracy is to be dismissed, although Bodley, Dilke's secretary, had misgivings about Chamberlain, and Dilke about Rosebery. A perverted desire on Virginia's part for notoriety may even have been a factor in her conduct,[17] but it is hard to believe that she concocted the whole story and sustained it in detail through the most rigorous examination. Whatever her reasons, Virginia never wavered in her allegations nor was faulted in court. The popular verdict was that even if Dilke were innocent of the offences alleged, he was probably guilty of others with which he was not charged. Despite continued protestations of innocence, Dilke had no further legal course of action, but his friends formed a committee which found new evidence against Virginia and her sister Helen, and other material, which, had it been available in 1886, might have affected the verdicts. Dilke retired temporarily from politics but, supported by Lady Dilke (Emilia Francis, widow of Mark Pattison), of whom he had long been a close friend (they were married on 3 October 1885) he re-entered Parliament and sat as MP for the Forest of Dean until his death in 1911.

After her separation from Crawford in 1885, Virginia travelled in Europe, lived for a while in Italy, and when in London stayed with her sister Maye, a widow since 1883. Maye was 'advanced' in her views, a strong advocate of

---

[15] For Mrs Rogerson, later Mrs George Stevens, see Ted Morgan, *Somerset Maugham* (London, 1980), pp. 102–3; Marie Belloc Lowndes, *The Merry Wives of Westminster* (London, 1946), pp. 190–2; H. Montgomery Hyde, *Henry James at Home* (London, 1969), pp. 44–5; R. Calder, *Willie, The Life of Somerset Maugham* (London, 1989), pp. 81–3.

[16] 52 Princes Gate and much of its contents were sold privately to Alexander Henderson, created Lord Faringdon in 1915. Several of the family's paintings have been traced.

[17] V.M. Crawford, *Ideals of Charity* (Edinburgh & London, 1908), pp. 90–1.

women's suffrage, and had succeeded her husband as proprietor of the *Weekly Dispatch*. During 1886 Virginia toured Germany and visited Russia, making notes of political and social topics, and during 1888 she worked as a district nurse in Soho.[18] Maye introduced her to W.T. Stead, the editor of the *Pall Mall Gazette*, for whom she began working as a reporter, posing as Miss Eustace, in March 1888. Stead, a Nonconformist, advised Maye that Virginia needed a religion and introduced her to Canon Henry Parry Liddon, with whom she corresponded on religious beliefs between March 1888 and February 1889.[19] Liddon gave Virginia a copy of *The Confessions of St Augustine*, which she duly annotated. On Stead's behalf she wrote features for the *Pall Mall Gazette* – such as on the work of the Salvation Army in the East End, and interviewed people in the news, including General Boulanger – records of which appear in her journal. Her journalistic career with the paper ended, however, when its proprietor discovered her identity.

Virginia recorded no meetings with Manning during her spiritual journey in 1888, but as she claimed to have been one of his converts he presumably counselled her, and he arranged for her instruction by Fr Robert Butler, one of his fellow Oblates of St Charles Borromeo, and she was received into the Catholic Church on 4 February 1889. The same day she went to see Stead and that evening wrote to thank him for his sympathy 'after the amused derision of some of my friends. Whether I am right or wrong, it is to me the most solemn event in my life, and I can conceive of nothing so dreadful than that I should grow faithless to the promises I have made today.' She then retired for some days to the Franciscan nuns at Mill Hill, to whom Manning had introduced her, and to whom she became devoted. Whatever she may have confessed privately, no public retraction of the charges against Dilke, if false, was required, and she kept the silence advised by Manning on all parties. Stead was even dissuaded from announcing her conversion. 'The right and only prudent course', Manning wrote to him, 'is complete silence and retirement. For this reason you will take no public notice of what you have heard from her. She will write to you as before; and it is good for her to have wide popular and social subjects before her. She has been very calm, and has done nothing without conviction.'[20]

Manning introduced Virginia to the editor and literary figure Wilfrid Meynell, whose friendship enabled her to appear in public again, one occasion being a visit to the Royal Academy, prompting Manning to observe drily, 'I suppose they will expect to see a Magdalen skulking among the saints'. Manning encouraged her to resume social work and she spent much time in

---

[18] 'Life in the London Slum', *Temple Bar*, February 1891, REND.12/5.

[19] Henry Parry Liddon (1829–90), Canon of St Paul's, a noted spiritual counsellor and said to preach 'even better than Manning'. There are eight letters from Liddon to Virginia, REND.12/3.

[20] Bywater, 'Cardinal Manning and the Dilke Divorce Case', p. 548.

literary research, her first publication under her own name being a translation from Russian of *The Scarlet Letter* of G.S. Tourgenief, in *Time*, August 1890. Her journal witnesses how Manning sought to strengthen her faith by spiritual reading, regular habits of prayer and observance of religious duties. Thus, as one of mutual affection and free of obvious inhibitions when Virginia first records her meetings with Manning, their relationship was already established, although, of course, it is only Virginia's story.[21]

> *March 27th* [1890] *Thursday*) We were talking about Gladstone's first article in *Good Words* on the Authority of the Bible in which more or less he takes the orthodox Catholic rather than the orthodox Protestant view. The Cardinal was saying what a wonderful man he is, and then added 'What I admire in him most is the facility with which he takes up his pen and writes on a subject quite outside his own lines. When I do such a thing, I quake in my shoes'. 'But I comfort myself', he went on, 'with the thought that young men of his age can do these rash things; but when he is eighteen months older he won't be able to do more than I can'.
>
> *April 3rd* (*Holy Thursday*) Speaking of Huxley – for whom he entertains a special antipathy – the Cardinal said 'I consider him quite contemptible as a politician – he ought to be a radical and he clings to the upper ten. Tyndall is just as bad – they are both guilty of what seems to me odious toadyism'. Apropos of the *Religio Medici* of Sir Thomas Browne – for which the Cardinal expressed considerable partiality – being on the Index, he told me a fascinating story. An old French ecclesiastic, a Consultor of the Index Congregation, remarked to Bishop Ullathorne that there were a great many wicked books in England. The Bishop sorrowfully agreed. 'For instance', said the Frenchman solemnly, 'there is *Uncle Tom's Cabin*, a very wicked book!' 'The fact is', said the Cardinal, 'they know nothing about English literature in Rome'. I wondered how long it is since he read Sir Thomas Browne, for he quoted several passages and particularly praised the essay on urn burial.
>
> The Cardinal approves the new Code (1890) – spoke of the School Board as 'the survival of the unfittest'.
>
> *April 19th* (*Saturday*) The Cardinal said he never read the *Tablet* – it had no views and no politics to speak of. 'I always say it is the most unprincipled paper I know'. I asked if it really expressed the opinions of the Bishop of Salford,[22] to whom it belongs. 'I'm afraid it does', said the Cardinal, with a shake of his head and added that the Bishop knew nothing about politics – he had never given his

---

[21] Virginia's journal is here printed from the contributor's personal transcript of the original in the Dilke–Crawford–Roskill Collection (REND.12/7) and includes Virginia's own contemporary, or later, corrections and some errors. It shows minor differences from the copy published by Shane Leslie in *The Dublin Review* in 1967, which was printed from a typescript copy borrowed from the family, the whereabouts of which is at present unknown. The dates are as recorded by Virginia, but the day of the week has been added in parenthesis.

[22] Herbert Vaughan (1832–1903), second Bishop of Salford (1872–92), succeeding Cardinal Manning as Archbishop of Westminster (1892–1903).

mind to the subject. I said it was rather a sad outlook for the future in that case, to which the Cardinal only smiled. He very much regretted the non-existence of a Liberal Catholic organ and recommended the *Catholic Times* [*Weekly Register* inserted in pencil and *Catholic Times* underlined too] as the least objectionable.

Referring to extracts about Dr Döllinger and himself in this month's *Review of Reviews*, he said it was quite true that the second time he met Döllinger he was reserved, as by that time he had already written a great many things against the Church, and many people foresaw the probability of his leaving it. As to the anecdote about himself and *Cardinal* [erased] Archbishop Darboy of Paris and the Cardinal's hats, he said of course it was sheer invention. What did happen was that the Archbishop had written some letter about the religious orders in France which very much displeased the Pope, and the Cardinal, then on his way to Rome (in 1867), was asked to stop in Paris and see the Archbishop and represent the matter to him in its true light, which he did.[23]

May 9th (*Friday*) We discussed Deceas'd Wife's Sister Bill today and I tried to discover that the Cardinal had any better reason for his opposition than most people. But he could only produce the time-honoured arguments: that wives wouldn't like it, that they couldn't have their sisters *in law* [crossed out] to stop in the house, that it would give a blow to the family life which is the foundation of England's greatness, etc. All of which the dear old man firmly believes. However he doesn't expect me to believe him for at least he said 'Ah well, we needn't discuss it any more. I don't expect to convince you and I don't suppose you entertain any hopes of convincing me!'

May 16th (*Friday*) The Cardinal is in the midst of O'Brien's novel *When we were Boys*,[24] and warmly recommended it to me. He said he was much struck by it – it shewed wonderful versatility and imagination and of course he is delighted with *the* [inserted in pencil above] intense Catholicity of tone.

May 23rd (*Friday*) Speaking of his approaching Jubilee the Cardinal said he had presents from seven among the different bodies of Dock Labourers, one union sending him £25 and said how touched he was by their gratitude.[25] I told him the story of the docker who at a meeting held to discuss the question of a testimonial said: 'I noticed His Eminence wore a very shabby coat. I don't know whether he would take it amiss if we gave him a new one', and he was quite delighted and laughed heartily. I asked the Cardinal what he was going to do with the testimonial money, when he got it, and he said he should first pay his debts and then make his will and divide it up between five or six objects which he is particularly anxious to help on.

June 6th (*Friday*) The Cardinal talked today about the wonderful influence that

---

[23] 'Dr Döllinger's Reminiscences of Cardinal Manning. An Incredible Story', *Review of Reviews*, April 1890.
[24] William O'Brien, *When we were Boys* (London, 1890).
[25] Cardinal Manning had been instrumental in settling the four-week-long London Dock Strike of 1889. The bodies of Dock Labourers mentioned here were doubtless members of the Strike Committee, at a meeting of which Manning had effected the successful compromise.

priests had over people, as priests, quite apart from their personal qualifications. 'Priests are sometimes very disagreeable people, in fact they very often are', he said, with a smile. 'But', he added, 'it was almost impossible to get parishioners to complain of their priest – even in occasional cases of Irish priests given to drink, which he has wanted to investigate, it has been almost impossible to get any evidence, as the people feel it is a sort of insult to the Church to say anything against a priest.' The Cardinal then gave me a little book he has had printed for private circulation only, and which he usually only gives to his friends. It is extracts from the Meditations of a wonderful Poor Clare Abbess, on the duties and sacred functions of the priesthood – the Cardinal regards them quite as inspirations and having read the book in French, had it translated into English specially. He told me not to lend it to anyone.

June 12th (*Thursday*) This morning at 12 o'clock the Cardinal was presented with his Jubilee Personal Testimonial, got up by Monsignor Gilbert, the Vicar General, and the Duke of Norfolk. The big drawing-room was crowded to suffocation with clergy and laity and a sprinkling of ladies, and punctually at 12 o'clock the Cardinal entered on the arm of the Duke of Norfolk and took his post in front of his episcopal cross and below the smiling and canopied portrait of His Holiness. The Cardinal looked quite beautiful and impressive in his new cassock with a red cloak over his shoulders and he smiled a great deal to everybody, and seemed altogether very brisk and happy. He took off his biretta and looked at his best in his red skull-cap as he stood facing the crowded room. 'My Lord Duke' presided over the function: he struck me as quite devoid of 'side' but also of brilliancy, intelligent, practical and commonplace. But he spoke well and read the address well announcing the £7,500. Then the Bishop of Clifton, portentously dull, spoke for the bishops, and the V.G. enthusiastically eulogistic for the diocese, and Sir Francis Sandford, with graceful references to the Cardinal's educational efforts, for the outsiders, and Lord Ripon a few well-chosen words in his pleasant voice for everyone. And then we all cheered hard and the Cardinal responded in capital voice and with his usual felicity. He had looked quite shy and uncomfortable during the prolonged eulogisms of the various speakers, but had his revenge on the Duke of Norfolk, who was soon blushing hard while His Eminence patted him on the back for the way he had spent his money and reminded him of having seen him *as a school-boy* [added in ink above, by VMC?] in cassock and cotta swinging the incense in the old Oratory Church. Then the Cardinal told us what he was going to do with the money – a scholarship for a priest to be called the Jubilee Burse, repairs to his Church of St Gregory at Rome, according to custom, a bed at the London Hospital for his friends the dockers, the debts of two schools and a mission, legacies to five old servants and the residue to St Edmund's College, all of which was received with much applause. In fact we were all growing quite enthusiastic and the Cardinal received a tremendous ovation at the end. Then the Duke asked for his blessing which we all knelt to receive and then there was a perfect rush to kiss his hand, a feat which Marie Belloc and I only performed after a lot of scrimmage, and the dear Cardinal was born [*sic*] off to his own room.[26] I think he was touched and

[26] Marie Belloc Lowndes (1868–1947). Manning introduced her to W.T. Stead, who engaged

pleased with it all, and on both sides there was the feeling that perhaps he might never again address such a gathering of his people, which gave some of us lumps in our throats, and anyhow it was an interesting historical occasion which it will be a pleasure to look back upon.

June 13th (Friday) The Cardinal did not seem any the worse for his fatigues of yesterday and was evidently pleased with his reception, although he remarked that prolonged public eulogism was rather a trial. Speaking of the Duke of Norfolk he said it was really remarkable what a steady useful life he had lead [*sic*], with all the temptations of great wealth ever since he came of age. He had given thousands of pounds for churches and schools, and his goodness, and utter absence of 'side' is all the more striking as he is not an able man in any way, and so has not an opportunity of distinguishing himself in public life.[27]

July 5th (Saturday) I asked the Cardinal what was the use of saying one's prayers when one did so perfectly mechanically and feeling utterly indifferent on the subject. He said 'If you ask me what the immediate good to yourself is, I can't tell you, though it certainly does you good in the long run; but that is not actually the question. The question is, is it right? Don't trouble yourself about the reason of a thing or the good of anything but if you know it is right that ought to be a sufficient reason'. Then he quoted the verse of a psalm, (only I don't know which) which as far as I can remember was 'keep innocency; do that which is right, and it will bring a man peace in the end'.[28] That is one reason why the Cardinal is so helpful; he never gives you the minor reasons for doing a thing like most people who tell you the Bible *tells* [crossed out] says so, or the Church says so. That always makes me contradictious. He just says, in his solemn way 'My dear child, it is right', and you have to feel that is conclusive even if you don't want to. He objects himself very much, I know, to the expression 'abstract morality' – but I always think that the abstract morality point of view helps one more than any other.

July 11th (Friday) The Cardinal has been quite absorbed in reading Marie Bashkirtseff – how on earth he finds time I can't think – and confided his impressions in me.[29] He said he thought it one of the most fascinating and tragic *souls* [crossed out] books he had ever read and that it contained a great moral lesson for anyone who thought, but as nine persons out of ten never thought, it was feared her readers would for the most part fail to see it. He said he thought it quite

---

her to report on the Paris Exhibition of 1889. Marie Belloc Lowndes, *Where Love and Friendship Dwelt* (London, 1943), p. 145; Susan Lowndes (ed.), *Diaries and Letters of Marie Belloc Lowndes, 1911–1946* (London, 1971), pp. 69, 114–16.

[27] Henry Fitzalan-Howard, 15th Duke of Norfolk (1847–1917), lay leader of the English Catholics, a staunch Conservative but with a genuine concern for the poor, a builder and benefactor of churches (notably St Philip's, Arundel, and St John's, Norwich), with a deep interest in all Church matters.

[28] Possibly Psalm 37, verse 27 (*Jerusalem Bible*).

[29] Matilde Blind, *The Journal of Marie Bashkirtseff*, 2 vols (London, 1890). A well-born Russian lady who recorded her intimate thoughts, mostly while a student of painting in Paris, 1873–84. She died on 31 October 1884.

unfair to dismiss her as a detestable and selfish young woman, for he said he thought we were most of us just as bad only we hadn't got the frankness to write it down, or the wonderful vividness of mind which allowed Marie to seize and describe her most fleeting sensations. But of course he admits that her egotism was intense *but* [erased] and when I remarked that it was extraordinary she had never fallen in love he said she was too selfish, and too absorbed in herself to be able to do so. Referring to her deafness, the Cardinal said he could sympathize with her feelings for he knew from personal experience what it meant. Apropos of which he treated me to a little bit of autobiography. He said nearly 30 years ago, when he had been working very hard, on awaking one Sunday morning he heard a sort of grinding noise. At first he thought it was some workmen close by but then remembering it was Sunday he knew it could not be: but he was so convinced it came from outside that he openned [*sic*] his window and looked out so as to discover the cause. At length, it dawned across him that the noise was in his own head, and he has had it ever since from that day to this, and it was the beginning of his deafness which of course is very painful. It runs in his family, as he told me once, some months ago, that his father and brother were also deaf. His eyesight however is wonderful, even now he never puts on glasses except to read small print, and then only pince-nez and not spectacles.

July 18th (*Friday*) The Cardinal has been speechifying to St Anselm Society[30] on the fascinations of Marie Bashkirtseff, and Mrs Jackson who was present told me that everyone was much amused as it had really nothing to do with the subject in hand, but the dear old man is so full of the book that he can't help talking about it.

August 15th (*Friday*) The Cardinal feels the death of Cardinal Newman very much. Coming so closely after the death of Fr Anderdon SJ, his nephew,[31] it gives him a great feeling of solitude in his old age. He remarked that he had had two warnings within 10 days of one another of the nearness of death, and that he had realized anew how soon his turn must come. 'There is hardly any of the old set left', he said, 'and it is very sad to be one of the last to be called'. I am thankful to say he is not going to the funeral in Birmingham, only to the Requiem Mass on Wednesday at the Oratory.

The Cardinal had a visit from my sister Mrs Dilke a day or two ago, and they seem to have been mutually charmed with one another. He persisted in expecting her to be a sort of grim forbidding female, and was quite relieved at finding her youthful and charming and declared she hadn't frightened him a bit. They discussed all sorts of things, and he thanked her for having been so good to me, and evidently was quite charming to her. She wrote to me, too, how much she had enjoyed her visit which was made at his request. Nothing is more attractive in the Cardinal than his intense love for children. Every time I see him he asks

---

[30] St Anselm Society was founded before 1870 'for the dissemination of the best literature' and ceased to exist just before the Great War.
[31] William Henry Anderdon (1816–90), nephew of Manning, convert (1850), ordained (1853), secretary to Manning (1863), popular preacher and giver of retreats, prolific writer of books, pamphlets and articles, died 29 July 1890.

about my Children's Country work[32] and how the children enjoy Harrow. So I showed him some of the letters that the Ogle Street children wrote to me from Weybridge, and he was delighted with them, entering so keenly into their little children's pleasures.

Sept 2nd (Tuesday) The Cardinal is very interested in the Liverpool Trades Union Congress which is sitting just now. He characterized the *Times* leader this morning, with great energy, as 'simply infamous': it preaches the old political economic doctrines of the supremacy of capital and the sacred right of the employer to engage labour at the lowest price, etc. 'It is simply the apotheosis of self-worship', said the Cardinal.[33] He considered it premature to decide on the 8 hours Bill, until workmen have part of the day for self-culture and until women are not dragged away from their home duties by the necessity of earning.

Sept 26th (Friday) The Cardinal has been ill for the last three weeks with a bad chill, and I saw him today for the first time. He was looking very old and shaky, although he is on the mend, and the attack has evidently tried his strength a great deal. But he was full of interest in things as ever – expressed great indignation over the brutality of the Tipperary Police yesterday at the opening of the trial of Dillon and O'Brien,[34] and asked me to lend him the *Rassegna Nazionale* with an article against the Temporal Power by a Jesuit father, which had excited his interest. He recommended me to read the *Oeuvres Spirituelles* of Fénélon,[35] and said he thought they stood quite alone: also to study the New Testament with the help of Quesnel's Commentary.[36] I'm afraid I said the New Testament didn't interest me particularly – he said that was because I didn't understand it enough. Hence the Commentary.

Oct 17th (Friday) The Cardinal has made me a lovely present of Fénélon and Quesnel's Commentary. I was delighted as I had not yet invested in them. I have

---

[32] Crawford, *Ideals*, pp. 70–8.
[33] *The Times* leader of 2 September 1890 noted, *inter alia*, the distinction between the older unions which had recognised 'the hard facts' of capital and labour and had discovered that the 'laws of human action in the gross' could not be set aside, and the newer unions which aimed 'at the complete control of industrial undertakings, or, in other words, at the wholesale appropriation of the property of the employers'.
[34] John Dillon (1851–1927), MP, and William O'Brien (1852–1928), newspaper editor, Irish nationalists who advocated agrarian reform, were among twelve defendants prosecuted before the Tipperary magistrates under the Criminal Law and Procedure (Ireland) Act, 1887, for inciting the tenants of a Tipperary landlord to withhold their rents. A large crowd of supporters, including John Morley MP, was prevented from entering the court house and in the scuffle which ensued the police charged the crowd with batons, inflicting many injuries. *The Times* fully reported the daily proceedings throughout the trial.
[35] François de Salignac de la Mothe-Fénélon (1651–1715), bishop and spiritual writer. Virginia refers to works under two titles, *Oeuvres Spirituelles* and *Lettres Spirituelles*, but presumably the same collection.
[36] Pasquier Quesnel (1634–1719), spiritual writer. His *Réflexions morales sur le Nouveau Testament*, possibly the Commentary referred to here, was condemned for its Jansenist errors by Clement XI in the Bull *Unigenitus* (1713), which precipitated a half century of controversy in France.

begun Fénélon's *Lettres Spirituelles* at once, and am quite fascinated by them. The Cardinal is immensely good about giving books – he has given me lots. He told me two rather nice stories about Monseigneur de Mérode, chamberlain to Pius IX and brother-in-law to Montalembert, whom he used to know in Rome.[37] He said he liked him immensely, he was so full of energy, with a great sense of humour. He told the Cardinal himself that one day travelling in France at *table d'hôte* on a Friday opposite a rather blustering Frenchman, who declared that as for him he eat [*sic*] meat every day of the week, he didn't care what day it might be. 'Mon cher ami', answered Mérode in bland tones, 'mais c'est un fait bien singulier que vous me racontez là, car savez-vous que dans ma jeunesse mon père possédait un chien qui faisait précisément la même chose?'

When de Mérode had to resign his office of Minister of War to the Pope, he was furious, his great friend Monsgnr. Bastide called to condole with him expecting to find him very depressed but found him instead in such a rage that he remarked 'Mais, mon ami, je suis venu croyant vous trouver dans le Jardin des Olives, au lieu de cela je vous trouve dans le Jardin des Plantes!'[38] The Cardinal told both stories in French which he speaks admirably with only a slight British accent – I always enjoy hearing him tell an anecdote. He always does so with such a keen appreciation of their humour.

Oct 24th (*Friday*) I have promised His Eminence never to read another French novel – it is rather sad, but I daresay he is right, and even if he isn't I don't mind doing it to please him. French literature is like a red rag to a bull to the Cardinal and many is the discussion we have had on the subject. Boccaccio too is *fruit défendu*, and of course Huxley and Darwin and Herbert Spencer and all the scientific atheists one used to read with so much zeal, so I feel on dreadfully short commons in the literary line and occasionally positively don't know what to read. Fortunately, he has no views on Russian literature so on that side I can read what I like.

Nov 7th (*Friday*) The Cardinal told me rather a nice little story apropos of the house in Bayswater where the Oblates of St Charles live. To the left of the entrance are the reception rooms for visitors: beyond is a door which no woman is allowed to pass and which is kept locked. One day the Cardinal let himself in with his latchkey, when to his amazement on entering, he saw a tall lady coming down the stairs towards him. He put on his sternest manner and asked 'Where do you come from?' 'From America'. 'Leave the house this minute or you shall be excommunicated'. So she left smiling. 'Wasn't she rather overwhelmed?' I asked. 'Oh dear no, not in the least', said the Cardinal, who had evidently been intensely amused by the incident.

Speaking of Catholic prospects, he said prophetically 'I have no fear for the Catholic Church in the future. If only she will free herself from dynastic influences'. He is immensely touched and gratified by the gorgeous testimonial

---

[37] Frédéric Ghislain de Mérode (1820–74), archbishop, minister of war, almoner, chamberlain, Belgian friend of Pius IX, also responsible for modernising streets in Rome.

[38] The Paris Zoo.

presented to him last week by the Jewish Community headed by the Chief Rabbi, and which he shewed me today.[39]

Dec 6th (*Saturday*) The Cardinal is unable to be present at the Guildhall meeting on behalf of the Jews on the 10th, but he has written a letter to be read out.[40] He feels immensely strongly on the subject and regrets very much that Catholics should always side against them. He said 'Whereas Christ prayed for them in the last hour of His Life on earth, I feel we ought to treat them with all the justice of the old law, and all the charity of the new', and a great deal more to the same effect, and at the end he said with a laugh 'Now, if my Catholic subjects like to break their teeth against that file they are welcome'.

Dec 12th (*Friday*) Speaking of the death of Dean Church,[41] the Cardinal said he used to know him very well, and of late years they often met at the Athenaeum. In 1845, he said, he had to preach a University sermon on Nov. 5th: he took the line that the temporal power of the Papacy, as exemplified in the Armada, the Gunpowder Plot, etc., must be kept quite separate from the spiritual power. In fact, he said, there were very few things in the sermon which he would not say now, if he had to preach it over again. Dean Church, however, wrote him an extreme *clever* [inserted] letter (which he still retains) strongly remonstrating against his line of argument, on the grounds that the temporal power of the Papacy was the strongest civilising influence throughout the Middle Ages.[42]

Speaking of the old Oxford days, the Cardinal referred to Dr Moberly,[43] the late bishop of Salisbury: he was one of his most intimate friends, was a tutor and fellow of Balliol during the Cardinal's last year at Oxford, but promptly dropped him when the Cardinal came into the Church. However, 'I am glad to say', said the Cardinal, 'that we exchanged friendly letters before he died'.

Feb 8th [1891] (*Sunday*) The Cardinal is at present brewing a great scheme of Catholic evangelistic work something on Salvation Army lines. He will establish two or three *priests* [inserted] in some house in the middle of the slums, and they will have a hall and preach Christianity to the heathen, with all the

---

[39] Manning expressed public sympathy for the Jews, and in 1890 moved a resolution at a meeting at the Mansion House protesting against Russian massacres of Jews. The testimonial referred to was probably that presented to him on his Jubilee, signed by Lord Mayor Isaacs, Chief Rabbi Adler and Lord Rothschild, in recognition of Manning's defence of the Jews.

[40] Manning's letter for the Guildhall meeting on 10 December 1890, held to condemn further Russian persecution of Jews, was written to Sir John Simon on 8 December, and included the words quoted by Virginia. See Shane Leslie, *Henry Edward Manning, His Life and Labours* (London, 1921), pp. 485–6; also *The Times*, 10, 11 December 1890.

[41] Richard William Church (1815–90), fellow of Oriel College (1838–52), friend of Newman, leading member of the High Church party, Dean of St Paul's (1871–90), died 9 December 1890.

[42] Dean Church's letter to Manning, dated 12 July 1844, commenting on Manning's sermon on 5 November 1843 (not 1845 as noted here) is printed in full in Edmund Sheridan Purcell, *Life of Cardinal Manning*, 2 vols (London, 1896), vol. I, pp. 696–9.

[43] George Moberly (1803–85), fellow of Balliol College (1826), headmaster of Winchester College (1835–66), Bishop of Salisbury (1869).

distinctively Catholic doctrine dropped out. They are to be helped by the Little Sisters of the Poor, the St Vincent de Paul Sisters and other Sisters of Charity; also a body of lay workers, male and female, if they are to be found. The rest seems rather vague, so far, and nothing is to be done until after Easter; but in the meanwhile H.E. is tremendously keen about it. I wanted him to work it through the tertiaries under the Franciscan Fathers at Upton, but he was very scornful about that, and declared the tertiaries wouldn't be worth 2d! He has asked me to be a Slum Sister, but I don't quite know how much it implies. Of course I promised. It is extraordinary at his age the Cardinal making all these vast plans, but he said to me cheerfully only the other day 'Thank God! I have still life before me!', quite ignoring his 82 years. And his feeling like that is the best sign of his health. Of course he admits that money is one of the first difficulties, but how he expects to collect his audiences without a brass band & drum I really don't know.

April 16th (Thursday) It is weeks since I put down anything the Cardinal has said, but often it is only personal. But, after all, that need not prevent me and it will all be precious after he has gone. Today he was rather annoyed about a paragraph that had appeared in the *Pall Mall Gazette* announcing the formation of a sort of Catholic Toynbee Hall. He had no previous news of it and remarked 'some young idiots no doubt', in a severe tone. He is very severe on R.C.s going to Oxford. I suggested that it was no use expecting the young men of the aristocracy staying at Catholic colleges till they were 21, but he declared he did not see why they shouldn't, that now when they were just beginning to learn something, they waste their time at Oxford and remain ignorant and useless all their lives! It is evidently a sore point with him.

I asked the Cardinal today to let me join the Confraternity of Expiation[44] and he willingly agreed, but Fr Kenelm Vaughan was out, so it had to be deferred.

May 14th (Thursday) I asked the Cardinal whether he had taken the drive that all the papers had been predicting for him. He said No and didn't mean to, and that he was so happy and comfortable indoors that he felt no inclination to move. He intends being present at High Mass on Whitsunday if possible, but will not preach. 'The fact is I'm not up to it any longer', he added, 'in two months time I shall have reached my 84th year and I think at that age, people are justified in taking care of themselves'. He was very cheerful over it all, but it was sad to hear him, for it made me realize with a pang that with all his keenness of intellect, his strength must be slowly ebbing away. He told me he had received the Papal Encyclical on the Social Question the night before.[45] Both it and the résumé have still to be translated into English. The Cardinal only received it from Rome late last night, and had only had time to glance through it, but he seemed very satisfied with it, and said the whole problem was approached in the broadest spirit. It

---

[44] The Confraternity of Divine Expiation was established at 28 Beaufort Street, Chelsea in 1887 by Frs John Stephen Vaughan (1853–1925) and Kenelm David Vaughan (1840–1909), younger brothers of Cardinal Vaughan, and continued until 1898. Kenelm Vaughan wrote an appreciation of Manning's spiritual life in 'The Cardinal's Inner Life', *The Tablet*, 1892, pp. 128–9.

[45] The Papal Encyclical *Rerum Novarum*, 1891.

was 50 pages in length. The Pope does not make use of the expression Catholic Socialism and does not formally condemn it, but the Cardinal told me he knew from private sources that the Holy Father objects to the expression and that he quite agrees with him.

May 14th [bis] (Thursday) I have just got back from ten days in Paris and the Cardinal, I am afraid, regards me as somewhat contaminated by the inevitable wickedness of the place. He didn't want me to go at all, and from his point of view no doubt he was right, for Paris always makes me feel dreadfully frivolous, however he was very nice about it and let me have my own way. And, yesterday, when he asked me what I had been doing, he tried to be stern, but couldn't help being amused by my lively description. I sometimes think the Cardinal's greatest grace is his sense of humour. I told him about Mrs Chapman beginning her speech three times with 'Moi, je suis libre penseur!' and he was immensely amused and said she was a triple goose.[46]

He told me that the evening before he had received the Papal encyclical from Rome on Socialism, that it was very long, over 50 pages, so he had only had time to glance through it, but on the whole he seemed very pleased with it, and said it dealt with whole question in a very broad spirit. A short résumé is to be published in English, as well as the Encyclical. I asked the Cardinal where I could get it and he promised to send me a copy, this morning an advance proof arrived by post. I thought it so good of him – one of the many little things in which he shews his immense thoughtfulness. (I have accidentally written two accounts of this interview, but they complete one another).

May 29th *(Friday)* We talked today about Women's Rights, in which the Cardinal goes much further than many of its opponents. He quite approves of women voting and sitting on Boards of Guardians, etc., and even on County Councils, which I thought a great concession, but when it comes to parliamentary franchise, then he is quite obdurate. I told him I thought it was merely a remnant of prejudice on his part. He declared the Catholic Church was the only power which had known how to make use of its women, and that when Catholic women wanted to work they became nuns, and all their efforts were disciplined and directed, which was more to the purpose than in Protestant countries. I suggested the only objection was that the residuum of the world was so very worldly, and that mothers brought up their daughters either for the world or the cloister, and that if the former they were allowed to be as worldly as they liked. The Cardinal said 'Yes, that is a misconception of duty, bordering on heresy, which I am sorry to say is very common', and went on to say that 'a great many women, and some of the best women too, are quite unfitted by nature for either marriage or for the cloister'. He professes himself very pleased with the Papal Encyclical on the labour question, and said we were all to model our Socialism

---

[46] Virginia had been to Paris for W.T. Stead to interview a Peter Lavrov (1823–1900), Russian historian, social activist and internationally renowned radical, to whom she had an introduction from Prince Peter Kropotkin (1842–1921), Russian anarchist theoretician. The meeting at which Mrs Chapman spoke may have been of the Union des Institutions Feminines Chrétiennes. REND.12/7, 3 pages.

upon it. He is gratified and rather amused at Stead's anxiety to publish it and said 'Really, Mr Stead has got the Pope on the brain'. He said a great many Catholics, while accepting the Pope doctrinally, quite failed to grasp the vast dogmatic position he holds and can hold in social questions; whilst Stead, on the contrary, is immensely impressed with his social importance, but of course rejects his position as infallible entirely.

June 20th (Saturday) I asked the Cardinal if he wasn't very pleased at the Government defeat in the House of Commons over Sydney Buxton's amendment raising the age of half-timers from ten years in factories to eleven.[47] He said 'Yes, indeed, it is the best victory for education we have had for a long time', and his whole face beamed with pleasure. He added that he opened the paper the moment he came to breakfast to see the result of the division, and when he saw the figures 'I was so pleased I positively couldn't eat my breakfast!'

June 26th (Friday) The Cardinal has given me the *Life of Christ* by the Abbé Fouard, of which he has a very high opinion. He prefers it to the Père Didon, as it is less rhetorical and he is always great at severity of style for devotional works; he says it fills up the gaps in the Gospel history better than any book he knows. So I am to read some every day.[48]

The Cardinal has been pitching into me for not going to Mass every day. He quite took it for granted that of course I did, and declared I ought to do ¼ of an hour meditation on every *day* [erased] *morning as well* [inserted above]. I'm afraid that implies an amount of virtue for which I am quite unequal. However, I had to confess to a great deal of extra slackness lately, as I'm always in a hurry in the morning to get off to the B[ritish] Museum. But H.E. declined to accept Mme de Krudener as a valid excuse, so I suppose I must try and reform.[49]

July 3rd (Friday) The Cardinal is absolutely opposed to the Government Education Bill and dislikes the principle of Free Education altogether, although of course the 10/- a head grant is very advantageous to the R.C. schools, where half the children are educated free. The Cardinal calls the profit blood money. I think he regards the principle has [sic] transferring the duty of education entirely from the parent to the State and thus weakening parental authority. He talked a long

---

[47] Sydney Charles Buxton (1853–1934), Liberal politician, MP for Peterborough (1883–5), Poplar (1886–1914), member Dock Strike Conciliation Board (1889), member Royal Commission on Education (1886–9), instrumental in raising the half-time age limit for children in factories from 10 to 11 years (1891), Under Secretary for Colonies (1892–5), Postmaster-General (1905–10), President of Board of Trade (1910–14), Governor General of South Africa (1914–20), created Earl Buxton (1920).

[48] Henri Constan Fouard (1837–1903), French Biblical scholar and spiritual writer. His *La Vie de Notre-Seigneur Jésus Christ* was published in 1880. Henri Didon (1840–1900), French Dominican preacher and spiritual writer. His *Life of Christ* was published in 1890 and translated into English in 1891.

[49] Clarence Ford (pseudonym adopted by Virginia Crawford), *The Life and Letters of Madame Krudener* (London, 1893). Barbe Julie de Krudener, née Wietinghoff (1764–1824), friend of Tsar Alexander I, prophetess of the downfall of Napoleon, and inspirer of the Holy Alliance, a 'repentant Magdalen who preached forgiveness throughout the length and breadth of Europe'.

time today about living in the presence of God, and said he would like to give me a rule of life: Prayer 24 hours a day. He said it was better to say quite short prayers scattered through the day than long ones morning and evening, so as to accustom ourselves never to be long without remembering that we are in the presence. As a practical application of which he told me to say the Angelus 3 times a day. It reminded me of Hope-Scott, who confided in a friend that he had just time to say the mid-day Angelus as he ran up the stairs from the House of Commons Committee rooms to the House of Lords at twelve o'clock: I have often wondered how many lawyers would say as much.[50]

Oct 23rd (*Friday*) It is months since I have entered anything about the Cardinal. Just now he seems particularly bright and keen intellectually. He is very interested in our magazine project, and expressed a hope that his flock would be enterprising enough to take it up. I said I thought it was only converts who were enterprising and he said 'Yes, but it would never do to say so'. He then went on to point out that the ablest of the Jesuits, Oratorians, Passionists, etc. and many of his Parish priests were all converts. I think he feels very much the sort of hidden antagonism to all his views which exists among the Catholic upper ten thousand; he knows quite well that they only just tolerate him because they must, and because they hope for better things when he is gone. He is dreadfully annoyed just now with the Bishop of Salford who dined with the Licensed Victuallers Association and patted them on the back.[51] Putting aside the moral question, I do think it was horribly wanting in tact and respect to the Cardinal's known views. Having incautiously introduced the topic, the Cardinal put on his very grimmest and most withering expression and said 'I am exceedingly annoyed' – after which I hastened to change the conversation.

Decr 4th (*Friday*) It is an open secret that the Cardinal has not much sympathy with the Jesuits; the other day he spoke to me of Farm Street as 'the worst gossip-shop in London'.

Dec 12th (*Saturday*) We were talking over St Charles Borromeo and the Cardinal was expressing unbounded admiration for him. I said I thought he was very like St Charles himself. The Cardinal smiled and said 'No, St Charles was meek', as he got up to go to speak to someone. I think the dear old man is quite aware how imperious and obstinate he can be at times.

The Cardinal is very great on the purity of the English language and is often amiably lecturing on the subject. He amused me very much by giving me a solemn injunction never to say 'Thanks awfully' or 'Don't you know' again. However, he admits that talking slang is venial compared with writing slang; he himself believes in a very concise simple style, and is always impressing on me

---

[50] James Robert Hope-Scott (1812–73), friend of Newman, convert (1851), benefactor of several Scottish missions and convents, founded churches at Galashiels, Kelso and Selkirk, married (second) Victoria, daughter of the 14th Duke of Norfolk.

[51] Herbert Vaughan, then Bishop of Salford, had spoken at this dinner advocating, in the interests of Temperance, the consumption of lighter beers. See J.G. Snead-Cox, *The Life of Cardinal Vaughan*, 2 vols (London, 1911), vol. 1, p. 475.

the duty of never using a superfluous word. He himself is extremely concise in all his writing, especially his letters.

Xmas Eve (*Thursday*) The Cardinal was inveighing today as usual against modern society. He says it is quite as corrupt and luxury-loving and selfish as the old French noblesse and it will all go smash of a sudden. 'I shall not see it', he said prophetically, 'but you will'. The immediate cause of the outburst was that the Cardinal was denouncing the theatre (on which he admits his views are extreme) and private theatricals, and I said I thought they were innocent compared with the dancing in short skirts which was becoming the fashion for girls in private houses. The dear Cardinal of course had never heard of such a thing and nearly stood on his head with horror.

He is much exercised in his mind just now over the English workhouses and the Poor-Law. He says he can remember as vicar of some parish [marginal note *Lavington?*] helping to carry out the old poor-law in 1832–3–4, and so he has watched the operation of the new Poor Law since its passing in 1835 – which is more than most people have done.[52] He maintains that the present Poor Law is the outcome of the combined selfishness of capitalists, ratepayers and political economists. He said he had sent for Mr Charles Booth,[53] to talk the matter over with him and stir him up about it. 'If I were younger, I would do it myself', he said, 'but as it is I have to content myself with saying the few words that are possible'. 'It makes me quite impatient', he said later, 'when people talk as though becoming a Catholic meant merely accepting the decrees of the Council of Trent. That is only a small part of it. Becoming a Catholic means becoming again as a little child and having a new heart'.

New Year's Eve [1891/2] (*Friday*) This was really my last visit to the Cardinal, but so little did I expect it that I never even wrote down the conversation at the time. But now that my dearest friend and father has gone to his rest I must put down what little I can remember. I have never known him more kind and tender than he was that day. We talked of the old and the new year. I said New Year's day was depressing for it made one feel how little one had done in the old. 'Ah, my child', he said, 'no doubt we all feel that of ourselves, but I can only say that I do not feel it about you at all. And my New Year's wish for you *may* [erased] *shall* [inserted over] be that you may do as well in the next year as you have done in the last two'. Of course I said I hoped to do heaps better. But he said 'No, I shall be quite content if you do as well'. He went on to say that the perseverance I had shewn convinced him that I was capable of anything, 'by which of course I mean', he added, 'any course of duty which the will of God may seem to point out to you'. 'As for me', he continued, 'I can't expect to see any more New Years, my life may be measured by months and weeks, perhaps even days, and I

---

[52] Manning had been curate of Woollavington cum Graffham (West Sussex) in 1832, its rector in 1833. He was Rural Dean in 1837 and Archdeacon of Chichester in 1840. See David Newsome, *The Parting of Friends* (London, 1966).

[53] Charles Booth (1840–1916), shipowner and writer on social questions, author of *Life and Labour of the People of London* (1891–1903). See T.S. Simey and M.B. Simey, *Charles Booth, Social Scientist* (Oxford, 1960).

should not like to die feeling that you had no one to turn to, and were left without an adviser'. He then said he thought I could not do better than always go to Fr David, Provincial of the Franciscans,[54] for advice, that he had complete confidence in him and was sure he would always direct me wisely. That besides there was Fr Butler whom I could always rely upon in any trouble. I said I had the greatest confidence in Fr David and should prefer him to any one else, so he said 'Very well, my child, then that is settled'. In reality, I had been longing for him to settle the question for months, but had not liked to broach it, so it was really wonderful that he should speak of it himself, as though he had a premonition of approaching death. At confession I said that I did not deserve a quarter of all the kind things he has said to me and that he could not know how indifferent and bored I often feel over my prayers and spiritual duties. But he said again that fervour did not mean what one might happen to feel at the moment; it meant perseveringly doing your duty day by day whether you wanted to or not. 'And that I feel satisfied you do, my child', he said. Though the Cardinal had been talking about the shortness of life before him and so on, he was not in the least depressed or feeble in health; on the contrary, he seemed to me particularly bright and vigorous. I asked him, jokingly, to dispense me from Friday abstinence on New Year's day, as I was dining with the R[ussell] Cookes,[55] on the ground that the Pope had dispensed the French nation, and he answered laughingly, 'Wait till I am Leo XIV and perhaps I will think about it. In the meanwhile, it is good for you to eat fish'. I said I always liked fish until I was a Catholic and ever since I've hated it. On which he answered in his dry tone but with a twinkle of humour in his eyes 'How like you!' and we both had a good laugh. I could never resist leading up to his somewhat scathing retorts – they were so characteristic of him and he never expected one to feel squashed by them. *(Janr 19th 1892)* [added in parentheses]

After Manning's death, Virginia spent the next few years travelling, researching, writing and publishing studies on a variety of subjects, before long under her full married name, her reformed life, evident sincerity, and social work earning her such public respect that the name of Mrs Crawford ceased to be associated with the bygone scandal. Through Manning's contacts Virginia met may of the pioneers of Catholic Social Action in Europe who had prepared the way for *Rerum Novarum* (1891), and whose work she was to describe in 1933 in *Catholic Social Action, 1891–1931*. She also met

---

54 Fr David Fleming (1851–1915), OFM, born Killarney, professed in Belgium (1870), ordained at Ghent (1875), Definitor of Belgium Province (1884), first Superior at Forest Gate, London (1887), first Provincial of restored English Province (1891–3), Vicar General of Order (1901–3), assisted Commission on Anglican Orders (1894), as Definitor General helped to draft the Bull *Felicitate Quadam* (4 October 1897) uniting branches of the Friars Observant, Consultor to Holy Office (1896), Secretary to the Biblical Commission (1903), again Provincial of English Province (1905–8), died at Forest Gate 11 November 1915. (From a biographical note by the late Fr Justin McCloughlin, by courtesy of the Archivist, Franciscan Study Centre, Canterbury.)
55 Maye, Virginia's eldest sister and widow of Ashton Dilke, married secondly William Russell Cooke, 19 September 1891.

churchmen and employers who were putting into practice in their institutions the Church's newly expounded social teaching (visits recorded in notes among her papers) and she translated Leon Harmel's *Catéchisme du Patron* under the title *A Key to Labour Problems* in 1893. In 1889 she had reported in her journal a visit to the Catholic District School for Boys at Mill Hill, and in 1892 she visited Fr Nugent's Industrial School for Boys in Liverpool,[56] at the same time going to see the Good Shepherd Convent, Notre Dame Training College and Industrial School for Girls.

One of the most touching entries in her journal is the record Virginia wrote in May 1893 of her visit to Lavington.

> I was at Midhurst the other day, staying with the Sisters of Mercy and Mrs Mylne and I drove over to Graffham and Lavington to see the Cardinal's early home. Lavington now belongs to Reginald Wilberforce, son of the Bishop of Oxford; it is an ugly house but a lovely place. The little Gothic church nestles in the trees behind the house; it is a simple little country church, with an oak rood-screen. The Cardinal restored both it and Graffham church, which is more picturesque but rather dark. They are only ¼ of a mile apart and are served by one parson. The main door of the Lavington church opens straight out on to the lawn of Lavington House; on the other side is the little church yard, and here against the wall, is the tomb of Mrs Manning, unmarked by any stone, but in line with the Wilberforce and Sargent tombs. It is awful to think how he must have suffered when she was laid there. Then we went on to the parsonage, a few minutes walk down the lane, a low white house covered with roses, with long French windows opening on to smooth lawns, with fine trees round and a lovely view. A very ideal home, simple yet beautiful, in an exquisite English setting, just outside the Lavington grounds. Inside, everything just as it was in his day, with solid deep-seated chairs and sofas and old cabinets and family portraits; the drawing room with bow-windows, his study long and narrow, overlooking the garden, and a print of Richmond's early portrait. No wonder he loved it all his life. No wonder it was an awful wrench to leave it. It was all so sad and pathetic, and so strange to be in the rooms where the ascetic Cardinal lived with his beautiful wife and adored her passionately. It made one understand better his intense love of nature and of English rural life, and also the infinite depths of tenderness in his character. The celibacy of half a century did not mould his character as much as those three years of ideal home life and married happiness. And then the years of loss and renunciation and rigid self-suppression and hard work for others. One realised it all so vividly as one stood there. I felt I never understood him so

---

[56] James Nugent (1822–1905), the 'apostle' of Liverpool, social reformer, educator, and temperance advocate. Trained at Ushaw and Rome (1838–46), ordained (1846), introduced Notre Dame Sisters to Liverpool (1851), opened Catholic Institute (1853), chaplain to Walton Prison (1863–85), established Refuge for Boys (1865), founded *Northern Press* (1867), which became the *Catholic Times* (1872), organised the temperance League of the Cross (1872), set up a Refuge for Fallen Women and Night Shelter for Women (1891) and a House of Providence for Unmarried Mothers (1897). A statue was erected in his honour in Liverpool in 1906. REND.12/7, 5 pages.

clearly or loved him so much. I picked some roses in his garden and some leaves from an old climbing rose which I knew must have been there in his day. It was a visit I shall never forget. I am so thankful I went. The house is let now!

Virginia continued to write for Stead and indeed corresponded with him until his death in the *Titanic* in 1912, though she gave him no assistance in his continued campaign to discredit Dilke. She spent much time also in the British Museum researching the lives of Madame de Krudener and the Princess Amelia Gallitzin – both of whom experienced spiritual conversion and were influential European figures – editing the journals of the former in 1893 and a biographical article on the latter in 1895, both under the pseudonym of Clarence Ford.[57] This research took her to Paris where she always felt at home.

In early 1896, Virginia paid a two-months visit to Rome and Umbria, keeping a prosaic record[58] of the places she visited and the company of many English expatriates, for whom she did not greatly care. On 23 February she attended a papal Mass and at a short audience which followed found Leo XIII 'not nearly as alarming as Cardinal Manning'. In the brief exchange allowed she spoke to the Pope in French saying she was 'a convert of Manning's, at which he seemed very pleased and turned to Mgr Del Val[59] with an exclamation of pleasure. I explained I had a Catholic sister and two nephews, and asked for his blessing for the Mill Hill nuns and he said so impressively, as a definite message, "Donnez vous-même ma bénédiction à toutes les religieuses franciscaines dont vous me parlez". Then I kissed his foot in its glorious red and gold slipper and it was all over'.

Virginia then went on to Assisi in March and found it 'the most beautiful, soul-satisfying place I have ever been in'. The Franciscan Father Superior said Mass for her intentions at the tomb of St Francis, where she received 'one of the most perfect communions I have ever enjoyed. I don't run easily to pious emotions but it was wonderfully moving to know oneself so close to the remains of the great saint. And his spirit seemed specially to penetrate the whole place, and made me realize somehow as I had never realized before how vain and worldly I am and how utterly unworthy to call myself a child of St Francis'. It is probable that she had long been a Franciscan tertiary. Next she went to Perugia, and discusses the respective merits of painters whose works she examined in the Palazzo Comunale, notably those of Perugino, Pinturicchio, Piero della Francesca, and Fra Angelico, doubtless making notes

---

[57] Clarence Ford, *Krudener*; 'An Eighteenth Century Conversion', *The Month*, January 1895, a biography of Princess Amelia Gallitzin (1748–1806), whose life was redeemed by conversion to the Catholic faith.

[58] REND.12/7.

[59] Rafael Merry del Val (1865–1930), born in London, studied at Ushaw College (1883–5) and in Rome (1885–91) and employed in the Vatican, Secretary to the Papal Commission on Anglican Orders (1896), Secretary to the College of Cardinals (1903), Cardinal (1903), Pontifical Secretary of State (1903–14), Secretary of the Holy Office (1914–30).

on Franciscan art, on which she published monographs on *Fra Angelico* (1900) and *Raphael* (1904), and published articles and gave lectures.

Virginia's travels in Europe and her interest in literature brought her into touch, and correspondence, with many contemporary authors, including Maeterlinck, Daudet, Huysmans, Sienkiewicz and D'Annunzio, whose works she reviewed, collecting her articles into *Studies in Foreign Literature* in 1899.

As in her court evidence, Virginia's writing is direct and avoids digression. She goes straight to the point and pursues her argument succinctly to its conclusion. She was unusually observant, had a good memory, could marshal her facts, and express her views lucidly. In 1897 Stead recommended her to George Moore (1852–1933), who was looking for a Catholic to advise him on convent life for his coming book, *Evelyn Innes* (1898), and this proved the beginning of a lifelong friendship. Although Virginia did enter a convent briefly in 1903 to try her vocation,[60] at this time her qualifications as an expert on the life of an enclosed nun seem dubious, but Stead knew her as a thorough researcher. The collaboration was successful and Virginia helped Moore from time to time, notably on twelfth-century costume and architecture for his *Heloise and Abelard* (1921), and once confessed to a friend 'I dressed Heloise and built the house she lived in!' Virginia liked Moore, but their friendship was neither one of love nor discipleship and she was not uncritical of his work, but Moore knew he could rely on her. Shane Leslie stated that Virginia wrote all the letters in French on which Moore acquired his epistolary fame among French writers, and that they were even published as Moore's.[61] Virginia was one of the very few select friends present at Moore's obsequies at Lough Carra in 1933. Her last letters to Moore were published.[62]

That Virginia had once assisted Canon Barnett in his East End mission may have initially warmed Manning to her, and she in turn must have been inspired by his concern for the poor and, as the journal witnesses, she agreed to undertake work he recommended. They were sympathetic too in political philosophy, and while Manning had limited political opportunities, Virginia was free to engage in direct social action. Her first step was to stand and be elected as a Poor Law Guardian for Marylebone, and she was re-elected until the end of the Poor Law in 1930. This was by no means a nominal commitment but entailed several meetings a week, regular visits to the workhouse and infirmary, and dealing with hundreds of applications for outdoor relief every week. She soon came to know intimately the living conditions and problems of the poor in London and, recognising the weaknesses of the Poor Law in practice,

---

[60] St Mary's Abbey, the Franciscan convent at Mill Hill, London.
[61] Shane Leslie, 'Virginia Crawford, Sir Charles Dilke, and Cardinal Manning', *The Dublin Review*, No. 513, Autumn 1967, p. 204.
[62] V.M. Crawford, 'George Moore: letters of his last years', *The London Mercury*, No. 206 (December, 1936), pp. 133–9.

she strongly advocated its reform, writing and lecturing as effectively as she could. She found that the system tended to create a permanent class of paupers, able-bodied as well as the helpless, trying to relieve indiscriminately the needs of unmarried mothers, deserted wives, orphans and abandoned children. As early as 1908 she was recommending the transfer of infirmaries to the metropolitan boards, pauper schools to the education authorities, and the workhouses themselves to the municipal councils. In the Marylebone workhouse she was especially concerned for its Catholic inmates, Cardinal Bourne, always a great support, complimenting her for ensuring that the Catholics could make their Easter duties.

At the turn of the century Virginia, still only in her late thirties, seemed to be always travelling. In 1897 and again in 1900 she visited Belgium to see at first hand the schemes and institutions founded by churchmen and employers of social conscience to improve educational opportunities and working conditions, thus putting into practice the principles of *Rerum Novarum*. These she quickly publicised in articles. In 1900 she paid another visit to Rome and met both Cardinal Rampolla and Mgr Merry del Val. The following year she was in Vienna reporting on basic solutions being employed to relieve the homeless, and later in the year she went to Milan and other Italian cities on a like errand, taking time off to study more Italian painting. Hardly any topic in which she became interested and knowledgeable was not made the subject of an article, one even describing the work of the Franciscan sisters in Uganda, presumably from letters received at Mill Hill. In 1902 she went to Canada to see how the children sent by the Catholic Emigration Society were settled, and crossed the continent reporting on convent schools and institutions.

At home, Virginia was engaged not merely in 'hands-on' work, from which she never shied, but was always alert to promote new initiatives to remedy practical problems. She decried 'the time-honoured distribution of soup and flannel petticoats', or alms, as a remedy for poverty, preferring to offer the poor the means of raising themselves from their conditions. Much of her experience she described in *Ideals of Charity* (1908), in which she emphasised the importance of training for social work and identified where this could be obtained. In the book she covered a whole range of practical work, such as district visiting, the problem of girl mothers, children's country holidays, work in the Kent hop fields, problems of the Poor Law, retreats, work the poor could usefully do at home, and reforms to deal with rural poverty. Some of the problems discussed in this short book still await solutions today – Virginia had little confidence in legislation. In its day the book was well regarded as a valuable training manual for voluntary social workers. Few students of the divorce case have noticed a curious statement which Virginia makes in the chapter on girl mothers, when, deprecating any attempt to encourage the girl to talk about her experience, she writes: 'Woman's vanity often takes strange forms, and an unbalanced emotional nature will crave for notice and notoriety on almost any terms. Hence an indiscreet sympathiser runs the risk of encouraging the recital of imaginary and distorted versions of the actual facts. My own experience is that very few women can be trusted to give a truthful account of how they fell into trouble'.[63] However, lest this should have specific relevance to the case, Virginia remarked, late in life, to her niece: 'I have never been any good at lying. That was one of my troubles'.

Virginia was one of the founders in 1909 of the Catholic Social Guild 'to promote the study of social questions on Catholic lines and to facilitate intercourse between social students and workers'. From 1912 until 1919 she was its London-based secretary, working from home at first and from 1914 from a small office in Victoria Street, where, assisted only by a lady clerk, she coped with correspondence, study schemes, publications, book boxes, and other administrative work, surrounded by stacks of literature, and interrupted by visits, purchases of Guild literature, packing books for the post, and other mundane tasks. However, at this time she wrote her best known pamphlet, *The Church and the Worker*, one of the Guild's best sellers at 50,000 copies. Within a mere fifty pages and nine chapters, she outlined the Industrial Revolution, the Manchester School of Political Economy, and the rise of the Trade Unions, describing the Catholic attitude to these and the part played by Catholics before and after *Rerum Novarum*, completing the study with the Catholic teaching on the Living Wage and the Family. This and *Ideals of Charity* were among the Guild's earliest essential reading. Virginia also drew up the Guild's six points which the hierarchy in 1912 approved as a plan for social reform: the Living Wage, Housing, Mutual Help, Poor Law Reform, Child Hygiene, and Fuller Education. However, when the Guild moved its offices to Oxford after the War, leading to the foundation of the Catholic Workers College in 1921, Virginia resigned her post.[64]

Never one to waste the idle hour, Virginia, now in her late fifties, soon took on another heavy commitment. She stood and was elected as the first woman Labour Councillor on the Marylebone Borough Council, and was re-elected until 1930, during which time she served on the Housing, Public Health, Baths, and Library committees, and represented the Council on London-wide committees, and this when she was still a Poor Law Guardian. This was possibly the busiest time of her life. She had come a long way from the irresponsible *femme fatale* of the divorce case, and even the novice convert and social worker of her thirties, and was now regarded as wholly trustworthy. Thus, when Maurice Moore, brother of George Moore, for whom she was researching for his *Heloise and Abelard* at the time, asked for a reliable witness to see the situation in strife-torn Dublin in 1920, Virginia went at some risk to her safety and duly recorded her experiences.[65]

---

[63] Crawford, *Ideals*, pp. 90–1.
[64] J.M. Cleary, *Catholic Social Action in Britain, 1909–1959* (Oxford, 1960), *passim*.
[65] REND.12/8.

Virginia was a strong advocate of women's rights and shared her sister Maye's campaigning for women's suffrage. She was a committee member of the Catholic Women's Suffrage Society, later St Joan's Alliance, from 1919 to 1929, and chairman in 1925 and 1926 – in which year she organised a national meeting in London demanding equal franchise, attended by Dame Millicent Fawcett – and she represented St Joan's Alliance at the Berlin Congress of the International Women's Suffrage Alliance in 1929.[66] Even so, she did not neglect one of her domestic concerns, the plight of the girl, or unmarried, mother. The prevailing, indeed presumed best, solution was for the baby to be taken from its mother and fostered or adopted, enabling the mother to resume her previous life. Virginia had, however, long argued that the mother and child should be kept together and the mother trained to earn a sufficient living to keep and bring up her child. This was the objective of St Joseph's home in London, of which Virginia was the co-founder and chairman in the 1920s. Its President was Bishop Brown of Southwark,[67] ever a stalwart support to Virginia, and its secretary was Dorothy Butt, daughter of Sir Charles Butt, the judge in the first divorce case, with whom she formed a lasting friendship.

After the First World War and into the 1920s, at an age when many people contemplate leisurely retirement, and when still heavily involved in her Poor Law work and local municipal politics in Marylebone, and in her various charitable activities, Virginia became engaged once more in international affairs. Because of her early contacts with the pioneers of Christian democracy and her wide knowledge of Catholic social movements in Europe (which she reviewed in *Catholic Social Doctrine, 1891–1931* in 1933) she was able to contribute to the meetings of the Christian Democratic Union, which brought together leaders of the Christian Democratic parties in different countries. She was among the first to see the dangers of fascism, beginning with the rise of Mussolini and the eclipse of Don Luigi Sturzo's Popular Party in 1922. She assisted the Italian Refugees Relief Committee in 1927, and from 1929 to 1932 edited *Italy Today*, which published pamphlets issued by the Friends of Italian Freedom, her campaigning earning her *persona non grata* status from Mussolini in 1934.

The Spanish Civil War presented a dilemma for left-wing Catholics and Virginia devoted her energies to promoting the peace plans drafted by the British, French and Spanish Committees for Civil and Religious Peace in Spain. She served on the British Committee, which contained such eminent

---

[66] Obituary notice in *The Catholic Citizen*, 15 November 1948. The archives of St Joan's International Alliance are held in the Fawcett Library, London Guildhall University, Old Castle Street, London, E1 7NT. For a description of these see *Catholic Archives*, No. 21, 2001, pp. 65–9.

[67] William F. Brown (1862–1952), Bishop of Pella and Auxiliary Bishop of Southwark (1924). Leader for the hierarchy in national policies affecting Catholic schools. Published *Through Windows of Memory* (London, 1946).

figures as Viscount Cecil, Dr C.P. Gooch, Dr Gilbert Murray, Harold Nicholson and Don Luigi Sturzo, with Virginia's protégé, Barbara Barclay-Carter, as secretary. Spain, however, was only part of a wider international crisis, and in 1936 Virginia and like-minded liberal friends formed the People and Freedom Group, which sought to apply Christian principles in national and international life. The Group's news-sheet, *People and Freedom*, continued until after the Second World War. In this work, Virginia found encouragement from Cardinal Hinsley, while in Archbishop William Temple she recognised a prelate in the mould of Cardinal Manning.

In 1944, following an illness, Virginia, now in her eighty-second year and suffering acutely from the deafness which had begun in 1905, retired from the People and Freedom Group, and moved from the Camden home she had bought in 1934, to live for a while in Winchcombe. Her mind, however, was still clear and she wielded her pen as effectively as ever. For more than sixty years she had turned out a constant stream of articles, essays, pamphlets on art, literature, social problems, Poor Law reform, women's rights, indeed on almost every topic on which she had worked or studied, and she had published at least a dozen books. Yet she now embarked on a biography close to her heart. This was the life of Frederic Ozanam (1813–1853) whose academic study of Franciscan art and poetry, his practical action in relieving the poor in Paris, where he founded the Society of Saint Vincent de Paul in 1833, and above all his commitment to Christian democracy, foreshadowed her own work. She lived to see the book published by the Catholic Social Guild in 1947.[68]

During Virginia's last meeting with Manning, two weeks before his death, he had told her what her mission in life would be: 'Any course of duty which the will of God may seem to point out to you'. After her conversion and Manning's death, Virginia led an exemplary single life, fully occupied to the end with useful work, sustained by her Catholic faith. Despite her deafness, she kept much of her boyish vitality which had endeared her to Manning and to her many lifelong friends. The Franciscan spirit never left her but in her late years she became friendly with the Prioress of Princethorpe and made a habit of saying the Benedictine office. She never forgot the debt she owed for her regeneration, first to Canon Barnett, who had introduced her to practical social work, then to W.T. Stead, for encouraging her literary talent and directing her towards religion, to Canon Liddon for his spiritual guidance, but, above all, to Cardinal Manning, her 'dearest friend and father' who had befriended the penitent Magdalen in her time of great humiliation, and whose teaching she tried to follow faithfully throughout her life.

Virginia outlived all her brothers and sisters and all those involved in the

---

[68] V.M. Crawford, *Frederic Ozanam, Catholic and Democrat* (Oxford, 1947). Ozanam had visited London and recorded vivid impressions of London's poor.

Dilke case, and died in London, aged 85 years, on 19 October 1948. In her will, after family legacies, she left bequests to the Catholic Workers College, the Josephine Butler Memorial House in Liverpool, to the Franciscan Mission in Uganda, the Abbot of Prinknash and the Assumption Convent at Ramsgate. She kept few personal papers but those that survive, including her published articles and books, are preserved at Churchill College, Cambridge.[69]

---

[69] The Dilke–Crawford–Roskill Collection, ref. REND., Churchill College, Cambridge.

4

HENRY O'CALLAGHAN: MANNING'S RELUCTANT EPISCOPAL PROTÉGÉ

LEO GOOCH

IN THE only Pastoral Letter Henry O'Callaghan addressed to the diocese of Hexham and Newcastle (given from Monte Porzio, the *casa di villegiatura* of the Venerable English College, Rome, on 17 February 1888) he remarked that when he had been nominated to the see he had felt it his 'duty to make earnest endeavour to escape from the responsibilities of the Episcopate'. It is, of course, quite usual for bishops-elect to make comments of that sort, but in this case it was genuinely meant and he made great efforts to have his nomination rescinded. The faithful in the north became aware of his reluctance to become their fourth bishop but they had little idea of the unusual events which had led to his appointment in the first place, nor did they suspect the true cause of his stay among them of barely two months, or of his resignation the following year.

The credentials of the first three bishops of Hexham and Newcastle (Hexham from 1850 to 1861) had certain similarities and provide the context for the events to be narrated. William Hogarth, the first, was born at Dodding Green in Westmorland and, in 1809, was one of the first to be ordained priest at Ushaw College which had opened the previous year. He stayed on as a professor for some years but in 1824 he took over the mission at Darlington and would remain there for the rest of his life. He was highly energetic with a marked capacity for business; somewhat bluff in manner, wisely he steered clear of ecclesiastical politics and concentrated on diocesan development. He died in 1866 aged eighty and was succeeded by James Chadwick, fifty-three years old, who came of Lancastrian Jacobite stock though he was Irish-born. He, too, was ordained at Ushaw College and stayed on as a professor. In 1850 he joined a small group of secular priests to form the Diocesan Missionary Establishment at St Ninian's, Wooler, from which they conducted parochial missions and conventual retreats throughout northern England. St Ninian's was destroyed by fire in 1857 and Chadwick rejoined the staff at Ushaw

College; he later served four years as chaplain to Charles, Lord Stourton (XIX) at Allerton Park in Yorkshire, and was elected a Canon of Beverley. He returned to Ushaw in 1863 and was consecrated bishop there in October 1866. Mgr George Talbot remarked that Chadwick had been 'the only man whom the Holy See could choose out of the three names sent by the Chapter',[1] but that was not quite the full story. Talbot was a papal chamberlain to and a close friend of Pope Pius IX; having the ear of the pontiff he therefore had great influence with the Congregation of Propaganda. He was also an intimate of Archbishop Manning, whose personal representative in the Vatican he effectively was, and they colluded to ensure that Manning's policy on all matters to do with the English church was accepted. When Bishop Hogarth died Talbot confided to Manning that there was 'so narrow a spirit in the North of England'[2] (that is, of cisalpinism) that a new sort of bishop was required, but the Chapter of Hexham and Newcastle could not be relied upon to make the right choice. The Chapter's *terna* listed Canons Ralph Platt, James Chadwick and William Knight in that order. Manning forwarded the names to Propaganda but he also wrote to Talbot prompting the decision he wanted:

> The first and third are impossible, the second is good. He is a man of interior spirit, love of souls, a true missionary and ecclesiastical in every way. In all questions he is on the higher side. I should be very glad to see him bishop. This, I may add, is the judgement also of [Robert Cornthwaite] the Bishop of Beverley.[3]

Presently, Talbot was able to inform Manning that Chadwick had indeed been appointed. Manning expressed his satisfaction and added that if Mgr Charles Eyre, the Vicar General, were to be made Archbishop of Sydney, the new bishop's entry into the diocese would be eased. As it happened, there was a suitable vacancy closer at hand which Talbot could use to fulfil Manning's wish – the Vicariate of the Western District of Scotland, and Eyre was nominated to it as Archbishop of Anazarba *in partibus infidelium*.[4]

In 1877 Chadwick became the eighth President of Ushaw College but he resigned the following year because the combined presidential and episcopal round was so demanding. He died at Newcastle in May 1882 aged sixty-nine and was buried at Ushaw. It was confidently expected that Edward Consitt would succeed Chadwick since his name headed the *terna,* but Manning did not approve of him, presumably for reasons similar to those which had previously disqualified Platt and Knight or because Consitt was hostile to Manning's Oblates of St Charles. In 1861 they had corresponded on the matter, with Manning telling Consitt that his 'conviction of the absolute

---

[1] HNDA, List 17: Thompson Papers No. 16, G. Talbot to Wm. Thompson, 14 October 1866.
[2] E.S. Purcell, *Life of Cardinal Manning Archbishop of Westminster*, 2 vols (London, 1896), vol. II, p. 269.
[3] *Loc. cit.*
[4] *Ibid.*, p. 270. Eyre was consecrated in Rome on 31 January 1869.

necessity of giving to the Secular Clergy in England, both in the Colleges and on the Mission, a rule of life and a common spirit [had] grown to a point hardly to be exceeded.'[5] Consitt doubtless took exception to that slight on his brethren and may have said so when they met subsequently; at any rate, he was passed over in favour of John William Bewick.

Bewick was born in 1824 at Minsteracres in Northumberland, where his father was steward to the Silvertop family. Like his predecessors he, too, was an Ushawman, and was said to have been both a brilliant scholar and an accomplished athlete and was generally well-liked. He was ordained in 1850 and served all his priestly life on Tyneside; he became diocesan treasurer and in 1868 he was appointed Vicar General (after Eyre). Subject to a consideration of £70 a year, Fr J.S. Rogerson, one-time chaplain at Minsteracres but then living in retirement in Paris, gave Canon Bewick a house on the north bank of the river at Tynemouth formerly known as 'Villa Tyne' but which Rogerson had renamed 'The Martyr's Peace'. Bewick subsequently bought three adjacent properties to consolidate the mission in the town and at his elevation in 1882 he decided to remain there and make 'The Martyr's Peace' the episcopal residence. Bishop Bewick's health declined rapidly (he was diabetic) and he died on 29 October 1886, aged sixty-three, having held the see for only four years; ten days previously he had presided at the eighth Diocesan Synod in which 141 priests had participated. Thus the family origins, the education, and the missionary lives of the first three bishops of the diocese (like most of the Vicars Apostolic of the Northern District before them) lay firmly in northern England, and the diocesan clergy could be forgiven for thinking that a tradition had been well-established and that one of their own would be appointed fourth bishop, even if he was not their first choice.

On 24 November 1886 the Cathedral Chapter met under the presidency of Robert Cornthwaite, (now Bishop of Leeds) to draw up the *terna* of nominees to succeed Bishop Bewick. The names were given in alphabetical order but, since that corresponded with the Chapter's preferred order, they were bracketed with the capital letters A, B and C to ensure that the order of preference was clearly understood:

[A] Edward Consitt
[B] Gabriel Coulston
[C] Thomas William Wilkinson[6]

Moreover, whereas the minutes of Chapter meetings were normally signed by the Provost, on this occasion they were signed by the Secretary because the

---

[5] HNDA, Misc. LP/13: Manning to Consitt, 8 August 1861. *The Tablet*, 30 July 1887, p. 183, surmised that Consitt's 'advanced years' had told against him; An Old Alumnus, *Records and Recollections of St Cuthbert's College, Ushaw* . . . (Preston, 1889), p. 258. Consitt preached the panegyric at Chadwick's funeral.

[6] HNDA, [St Mary's Cathedral] Chapter Records 13/27.

meeting concluded with the earnest request that Bishop Cornthwaite 'represent to the Cardinal and the bishops the strong expression of the wish of the Chapter, speaking for themselves, for the body of the Clergy, and also for the Laity, that one individual specially named by the speaker, should be appointed our future bishop'.[7] Obviously, he referred to the Provost, Edward Consitt, who had been elected Vicar Capitular early in November. Furthermore, five days after the Chapter meeting some eighty of the regular and secular clergy met at Bishop Bewick's 'month's mind' and resolved all but unanimously to send a Memorial to the Pope stating that they would welcome Consitt as their new bishop.[8]

The youngest nominee in the *terna* was Coulston, a fifty-seven-year-old Lancastrian who had spent his entire working life at Ushaw as professor in turn of Classics, Philosophy and Dogmatic Theology. Wilkinson was sixty-one; he was an old Harrovian and a Durham graduate who had become a Catholic under Newman's influence. His priestly life had been spent ministering to the Irish migrants in west Durham where he created four substantial parishes: Wolsingham, Crook, Tow Law and Willington. He was elected to the Chapter in 1865 but he retired five years later exhausted from overwork. He became a gentleman-farmer near Wolsingham and gained something of a name as a breeder of Durham shorthorn cattle. Consitt was the oldest at sixty-seven. His father had been born near Middlesbrough and, as a retired naval officer (who had served under Nelson in the battles of Cape St Vincent and the Nile), had emigrated to Canada where Edward was born. After his mother's death five years later his father brought him back to Europe and settled at Bruges. Consitt was educated first in the Benedictine College at Douai and then at Ushaw, where he was ordained priest in 1843. His priestly career included a period with Chadwick at the Diocesan Missionary Centre at Wooler, short placements at Haggerston Castle, Gateshead and Durham and latterly twenty-five years as Professor of Moral Theology at Ushaw. He was elected a member of the Chapter in 1863, was appointed Canon Theologian and then Provost.[9]

The strong expressions of support for Consitt were genuine, of course, but they were also intended to forestall the Archbishop of Westminster's intervention, for the northern clergy did not want their wishes brushed aside yet again. Manning, however, had resolved upon the promotion of Henry O'Callaghan, Rector of the Venerable English College, Rome, and a fellow Oblate of St Charles Borromeo.[10] Some reasons may reasonably be conjectured for his

---

[7] HNDA, Chapter Records: Minute Book (1854–1890), 24 November 1886.
[8] T.C. Hayward, 'College Rectors VIII: Henry O'Callaghan (1867–1888)', *The Venerabile*, vol. XVI, no. 4 (May 1954), p. 227.
[9] J.M. Tweedy, *Popish Elvet* I (Durham, 1981), p. 147.
[10] Oblates were secular priests living a community life but who were committed to serve in any capacity required by their ordinary, i.e., 'Oratorians with a diocesan remit'. H.E. Manning established the Congregation on 1 June 1857 and was its first Superior; it was accepted into

choice: Manning may have thought that after twenty years at the Venerabile it was time O'Callaghan was replaced and this episcopal vacancy provided the opportunity; it may have been that the cardinal thought the northern clergy needed a strong hand, for O'Callaghan was widely known to have one; or, most probably, Manning, almost eighty years old, calculated that this could be the last opportunity he would have to raise another Oblate to the English hierarchy. There had been fourteen episcopal vacancies in the English and Welsh hierarchy between Manning's appointment to Westminster in 1865 and Bishop Bewick's death in 1886. The first was for Hexham and Newcastle in 1866, and we have seen that Manning ensured Chadwick's elevation. Two more arose in 1872: as diocesan in Salford and auxiliary in Westminster. Manning was not so insensitive to appoint an Oblate his auxiliary, but the Oblate Henry Vaughan was appointed to Salford (he would found the Mill Hill Missionaries and succeed Manning as third Archbishop of Westminster). Four others were to auxiliary posts (Menevia, 1873, Birmingham, 1879, Shrewsbury, 1879, Southwark 1885) but the diocesan bishops rather than Manning would have had the final word about those appointments. Vacancies for diocesans which arose in Liverpool (1872), Nottingham (1874) and Northampton (1880) came too early (in the interests of the Venerabile) to move O'Callaghan. Bishops were required for two new dioceses (Middlesbrough, 1879, Portsmouth, 1882) but the appointment of an Oblate to either would not have been politic. Vacancies arose in 1882 in Southwark and in Hexham and Newcastle. Vaughan's suggestion that an Oblate (O'Callaghan, in fact) take over the second London diocese was rightly ignored and a Redemptorist was appointed; in the north, having vetoed Consitt, Manning could hardly object to Bewick as well, particularly as he had been Chadwick's vicar general. That left Hexham and Newcastle in 1886 as the first practical opportunity for O'Callaghan to be moved and Manning intended to seize it.[11]

Henry O'Callaghan was born of Irish parentage in London in 1827. He became a student at St Edmund's, Ware, at the age of sixteen; he was ordained in 1851 and became Prefect of Discipline at the college. Herbert Vaughan was appointed Vice President in 1855; he was preparing to become an Oblate and he recruited three members of staff to join him, one of whom was

---

Westminster by Cardinal Wiseman. The most recent historical treatment of the Oblates is in two articles by V.A. McClelland: *'O Felix Roma!* Henry Manning, Cutts Robinson and Sacerdotal Formation, 1862–1872', *Recusant History*, vol. 21, no. 2 (October, 1992), pp. 180–217; 'Changing Concepts of the Pastoral Office: Wiseman, Manning and the Oblates of St. Charles', *Recusant History*, vol. 25, no. 2 (October, 2000), pp. 218–36.

[11] It may be noted that there was no reason why Oblate-bishops should not continue to be members of their Congregation; in 1865, on his elevation to Westminster, Manning told the Oblates' Chapter meeting that he would be *'semel oblatus, semper oblatus'*, and he would always try to keep the Rule as far as possible' (McClelland, 1992, p. 185). Vaughan attended meetings of the Congregation while at Salford but not after his translation to Westminster, though he continued to be a member and its unofficial 'protector' [*Ex inf.* V.A. McClelland].

O'Callaghan. The ceremony of their oblation took place in July 1859 but their presence in the seminary was soon deemed to be threatening, largely because Manning, their Superior, was distrusted by most of the ecclesiastical establishment of Westminster and Southwark and he was suspected of wanting to take over the college. In an attempt to keep the peace, and on advice from Rome, the Oblates were withdrawn in 1861 and O'Callaghan joined Manning at St Mary of the Angels, the London church of the Oblates which had been opened by Cardinal Wiseman four years before. In March 1865 Manning (who would be named as Archbishop of Westminster a month later) sent O'Callaghan to Rome to establish and become the first rector of a House of Studies for the Oblates at S. Nicola. O'Callaghan proved to be an ideal superior; he enforced a strict regimen and was appropriately reserved and punctilious, yet he knew when and how to relax with his charges and it is clear that he created a well-managed, hard-working and happy community. His own academic endeavours lay in biblical studies and he was proficient in Hebrew, Syriac and Chaldean.[12]

O'Callaghan's evident success indicated to many that he was destined for higher dignities and his first preferment was not long in coming. At Manning's instigation, without the agreement of the hierarchy and after merely two years in Rome, he was appointed Rector of the English College in place of Frederick Neve, who had been Rector for only four years. The circumstances which prompted this change have been well documented and need not be rehearsed here save to say that poor discipline under Neve was the reason given for his removal. (Neve was a convert parson whose laxity was attributed by Mgr Talbot, Pro-Protector of the Venerabile, to his education at Eton and Oxford.)[13] In any event, having failed to secure St Edmund's, Manning now had the English College under Oblate control and hence, of course, his own. In addition to the cardinal, the Oblate Herbert Vaughan (now Bishop of Salford) and Bishop Chadwick, O'Callaghan's appointment was supported by Bishop Cornthwaite, a former rector, who remarked that O'Callaghan is 'the best man I know either here or in Rome' for the post. Talbot said that O'Callaghan had been nominated because he was a young, active and efficient superior, well used to college life, and was highly esteemed by the Pope and the Roman authorities.[14] Notwithstanding these recommendations, however, O'Callaghan's appointment was opposed by others in the hierarchy, largely because he was an Oblate, because he was not an alumnus, and/or because they were not consulted – the *fait accompli* being as reprehensible as the *coup d'état*.

O'Callaghan took over at the Venerabile in October 1867. He introduced a

---

[12] Hayward and McClelland, *passim*.

[13] T. Duggan, 'College Rectors VII: Frederick Neve (1863–7), *The Venerabile*, vol. V, no. 4 (1932), p. 346. E.S. Purcell, *Life of Cardinal Manning*, vol. II, pp. 365–77 reprints the correspondence between Manning and Mgr George Talbot; Duggan gives Neve's version.

[14] Hayward, p. 219. Talbot to Manning, 1 October 1867, copy at HNDA, Misc. LP 1/22.

stricter *horarium*, stopped theatricals, dissolved the debating society and curtailed the students' social life. But he was not entirely without a sense of proportion: he refused to allow Manning to address the college on temperance,[15] he provided hot wine on festive occasions, and he was kindly to students in difficulty or need. In fact, he conducted himself very much as he had in the Oblates' House of Studies. Furthermore he demonstrated considerable self-assurance during an unusually difficult period. The fall of Rome to Victor Emmanuel in 1870 and the loss of the Pope's temporal power led to the confiscation of church property with the consequent loss of rental income and an increase in taxation, which placed the college in considerable financial difficulty. The expropriation of the college buildings was only prevented by transferring their ownership to the Duke of Norfolk.[16] On a happier note, O'Callaghan was made a Doctor of Divinity and a Domestic Prelate by the Pope. He hosted the English bishops during the First Vatican Council 1869–70, then for the golden jubilee of Pius IX in 1877, and again in 1881 for the promulgation of the Bull *Romanos Pontifices* which settled relations between the regulars and the hierarchy in Britain. O'Callaghan was joint postulator of the cause of sixty-three of the English Martyrs, of whom the best known were John Fisher and Thomas More, which came to fruition on 29 December 1886 when fifty-four of them were beatified (the others were beatified on 13 May 1895). Finally, over the twenty years of his rectorship O'Callaghan supervised the building of the college's new church, dedicated to St Thomas of Canterbury. No one doubted that he was *episcopabile*. Bishop Vaughan, writing to Edward, Cardinal Howard in 1881, said that he was 'in favour of O'Callaghan for Southwark . . . [he] is a disciplinarian and that is what is somewhat needed in Southwark . . . He would get on well with H.E. a thing to be considered in a nomination to Southwark'. The following year Manning lauded O'Callaghan to Cardinal Howard and remarked that, like many rectors of the English College before him, he deserved a bishopric.[17] Such, then, were the antecedents of Manning's nominee as fourth bishop of Hexham and Newcastle.

The first indication of Manning's intervention came at the end of March 1887 when he passed Consitt a letter from the Prefect of Propaganda rejecting the Chapter's *terna,* 'having taken into consideration the reasons given by Your Eminence and others of your colleagues'.[18] Naturally, speculation about the bishops' preferred candidate was rife and when it became known that it was O'Callaghan the diocese was said to have gone into 'a state of crisis'.[19] An

---

[15] *Ibid.*, pp. 222–4.
[16] M.E. Williams, *The Venerable English College Rome* (privately published, London, 1979), pp. 133–7.
[17] *Ibid.*, p. 138.
[18] HNDA, Chapter Records 13/28. Translation from the Italian kindly made by Fr S. Foster.
[19] Hayward, p. 227.

attempt was made to have the fifty-year-old Northumbrian Arthur Riddell, Bishop of Northampton, translated but he declined.[20] On 14 April the Chapter met 'in special and secret session', again under the presidency of Bishop Cornthwaite, to comply with the 'command of His Holiness [Leo XIII] to send up a new *terna* in place of that sent by the Chapter in December 1886'.[21] The Chapter's archives do not contain a copy of the second *terna* but it is safe to say that the principal nomination at least was unchanged. It was 'a matter of notoriety', *The Tablet* would later remark, that Consitt's name had been twice submitted to the Holy See; the *Newcastle Daily Chronicle* had it that: 'More than twice a mitre was within his reach'.[22] But Divine Providence took a hand to break the looming impasse: Consitt died on 21 July. William Brown remarked that his death 'ended a much-feared, but influential, regime in the Diocese'; as Consitt's erstwhile curate, however, he was not perhaps an entirely objective observer.[23] At any rate, the way was now clear for O'Callaghan; two days after Consitt's funeral the English bishops met to select their *terna* and there can be little doubt that his was the first name in it.

The Chapter reconciled themselves to O'Callaghan's nomination after Consitt's death but it is uncertain when O'Callaghan himself first knew of it, though he did not seem to have been altogether taken unawares early in August to receive a kindly letter with helpful information about the diocese from Canon Wilkinson – now Vicar Capitular in succession to Consitt. O'Callaghan replied on 23 August saying that he was 'praying continually that the probability to which you allude may not become a fact' but, in any event, he said, the decision would not be made for at least two months.[24] His reluctance to accept the nomination was soon common knowledge; on 19 September the *Newcastle Daily Chronicle* reported that he preferred to remain in Rome 'but it is more than probable that his *nolo episcopari* will be gently put aside by his Holiness Pope Leo XIII, with whom the suave and cultured President [*sic*] of the English College is a *persona grata*'. Indeed it was, for he had been named to St Cuthbert's see by the Pope the previous day. Since the information was not confidential, the bishop-elect immediately sent a telegram to Wilkinson which he followed up with a letter observing: 'I have not yet received any formal communication from Cardinal Simoni and therefore the last word on the matter has yet to be said by the Holy Father when I have my Audience. I will let you know immediately I find that his decision is irrevocable.'[25] He received the formal Brief of appointment on 1 October.

A few days later he thanked Wilkinson for the advice offered in the 'work

---

[20] *NDC*, 15 April 1887.
[21] HNDA, Chapter Minutes.
[22] *The Tablet*, 30 July 1887, p. 183; *NDC*, 22 July and 20 September 1887.
[23] Tweedy, p. 147.
[24] HNDA, List 78, O'Callaghan to Wilkinson, 23 August 1887.
[25] *Ibid.*, same to same, 21 September 1887.

so utterly beyond my capacity as that of governing the important diocese of Hexham and Newcastle' which he still hoped to evade. But the audience with the Pope a few days later did not go O'Callaghan's way:

> After making the last objection which I considered it my duty to lay before him, I begged him to dispose of me as he thought fit. The question was about my health and the consequences likely to ensue from such a great change of climate. I gave him the pros and cons and he then told me to make no further objection.[26]

The Pope, however, knowing that the new church at the Venerabile was due to be opened in December and that the English bishops would be visiting Rome to celebrate the papal priestly jubilee in January, allowed O'Callaghan until February before having to leave for England. O'Callaghan was delighted about this, being disinclined to follow the recommendation of Manning and Propaganda that he be consecrated as soon as possible so as to spend Advent and Christmas in his diocese, for he was due to have another audience of the Pope on 8 December, at which he intended again to seek a release. Meanwhile he received the congratulations of the Chapter through Wilkinson, for which he was appropriately grateful, though he still could not suppress his 'fear and confusion' or overcome his 'great dread of responsibility and . . . deep sense of demerit'.[27]

O'Callaghan's consecration was arranged for 18 December. The principal celebrant was to be Edward, Cardinal Howard. He had served in the Life Guards as a young man and had carried the Standard at the funeral of the Duke of Wellington in 1852. He had been ordained in 1855 and had lived in some state in Rome since receiving the red hat in 1877.[28] He was now fifty-seven years old, Canon of S. Lorenzo in Damaso, Bishop of Frascati, Archpriest of the Vatican Basilica, a member of the Congregation of Propaganda Fide and, more pertinently, Protector of the English College. With his great height, burly physique and handsome, ruddy features, the 'gran cardinale Inglese' brought an imposing presence and full-throated voice as well as a rigorous military precision to the ceremonies in St Peter's. Howard may have put the fear of the Almighty into the Italian sacristans but he was evidently unable to stiffen O'Callaghan's backbone, for the latter's agitation increased as the date of his consecration approached and his 'nerves were wrought up to such a pitch by 6 December as seriously to indispose him'. He told Wilkinson a month later that this was the point at which he 'broke down so lamentably'.[29] Both the papal audience and his consecration were deferred indefinitely and he was

---

[26] *Ibid.*, same to same, 7 October 1887.
[27] HNDA, Chapter Records 12/26 and 12/27, Wilkinson to O'Callaghan, 15 October 1887; replies, 27 and 29 October.
[28] M. Bence-Jones, *The Catholic Families* (London, 1992), p. 224, says Howard lived in the Villa Negroni; Hayward, p. 226, says the Palazzo della Pigna.
[29] Burton, p. 150; HNDA, List 78, O'Callaghan to Wilkinson, 10 January 1888.

despatched to Sorrento to recover. It was taken for granted in English circles that he would be passed over and another candidate appointed in his place but no such recommendation was made by Propaganda.[30]

Most of the English bishops (but not Manning, who was infirm) went to Rome for the Pope's sacerdotal jubilee (31 December 1887) and were given audience two days before, the anniversary of the Beatification of the English Martyrs. The pontiff hoped that O'Callaghan's consecration would take place before long and he felt sure that the new bishop would be an ornament to the diocese. He also welcomed the arrival in Rome of Canons Robert Franklin (Cathedral Administrator in Newcastle) and George Waterton (Missionary Rector at Carlisle) together with ten priests who had gone out 'to conquer the scruples of the bishop-elect and to promise him a hearty welcome to his diocese'.[31] O'Callaghan received them coldly and his continuing recalcitrance gave rise to renewed speculation about his replacement; the front-runners were Monsignor Patrick Fenton, ex-President of St Edmund's, Monsignor Edward Goldie of Leeds, and Canon Waterton.[32]

The English hierarchical and lay delegation to the Papal Jubilee celebrations had their main audience on 10 January 1888. O'Callaghan went in taking the diocesan contribution of £592 to the Jubilee Fund, intending to use its presentation as the pretext to importune the Holy Father yet again. The correspondent of *The Tablet* reported that he approached the throne after the bishops and addressed the pontiff 'at some length and very earnestly, but what he said was not heard'. O'Callaghan told Wilkinson that he had urged on His Holiness that 'it would be for the good of the Diocese' if he were to be allowed to resign. But, after enquiring about his health, the Pope gave instructions to William J. Clifford, Bishop of Clifton, who was standing at his right hand, 'to arrange for a speedy termination of the matter', by which he meant that there was to be no further delay in the consecration.[33] Clifford had already strongly pressed O'Callaghan to accept the appointment. George Burton, a student at the Venerabile for Hexham and Newcastle, went in with the bishops but was dismissed after kissing the Pope's hand and having been given his jubilee medal. He hung around outside waiting for the bishops to emerge and he noted in his diary that his Rector had made

> a final effort with Leo to get out of the Hexham business, but the Pope stood firm. Mgr Fenton brought out the news to the loggia: Canon Waterton seemed

---

[30] *NDC*, 12 December 1887, p. 8. The paper was kept well informed by Burton, its 'Special Correspondent' (cf. Burton pp. 154/6). The 1888 edition of *Northern Catholic Calendar* anticipated the consecration but the date was corrected in 1889.
[31] *NDC*, 30 December 1887.
[32] *NDC*, 7 January 1888.
[33] *The Tablet*, 21 January 1888, p. 98; HNDA, List 78, O'Callaghan to Wilkinson, 10 January 1888.

piqued, ran down 'O'Callaghan' and misbehaved generally; [the Revd. Patrick] Matthews of Gateshead gave him two years; Franklin two months.³⁴

The patience of the canons, bishops and pontiff was exhausted.

The following morning Bishop Clifford went into O'Callaghan's room and 'expressed his determination to remain there until the day was fixed for the latter's consecration', and 18 January was decided upon. Cardinal Ricci remarked to Burton that he hoped there would be no 'bust-up' this time.³⁵ Reluctantly, then, and under obedience, O'Callaghan was consecrated on the nominated day by Mgr. Parocchi, the Cardinal Vicar (Howard was indisposed), assisted by the Bishops of Clifton and Portsmouth (John Vertue). It was the first ceremony to be held in the English College's new church and was attended by all the English ecclesiastics and layfolk in Rome for the Jubilee, chief among them the Duke of Norfolk. The Venerabile gave a dinner that evening for the bishop and the clergy of Hexham and Newcastle; Burton observed that Waterton was phlegmatic and smoked cigars but Matthews was 'on the spot [and] Franklin quiet'.³⁶

O'Callaghan drew little strength from his consecration or from the private audience he had the same evening; indeed, the imminence of his new responsibilities made him worse: 'I am not likely to get rid of the insomnia now that the cares of the Episcopate intrude'.³⁷ On 17 February, however, having been dined out of college and having sent his Lenten Pastoral Letter ahead, he took leave of the Pope and set out for England 'much cut up'. Burton wished him well: 'Poor old Rector! He's been kind and considerate towards me despite an involuntary stiffness of manner, and I wish him life and health and happiness:– and may I find him blooming in 1890'.³⁸

O'Callaghan got to London by the end of the month and after resting for a week at Archbishop's House took the train to Newcastle, arriving on 8 March, Thursday in the third week of Lent, almost a year and a half after the death of his predecessor. He went on to Tynemouth where the weather was cold, wet and windy – the onset of a week-long easterly gale. He was enthroned on 13 March (oddly, the impending patronal feast of the diocese, 20 March, seems not to have been considered, or perhaps it was but the possibility of further procrastination was judged to be too risky). When the preacher, Fr William Humphrey, SJ, lightheartedly pointed out that the new bishop had turned his 'back upon the glad Roman sunshine to face these leaden skies', and had left the Venerabile where he had 'loved to live and where [he had] hoped to die', tears were seen to stream down O'Callaghan's face.³⁹ The grand celebratory

---

34 Burton, p. 154.
35 *Ibid.*
36 *Ibid.*, p. 155.
37 HNDA, List 78, O'Callaghan to Wilkinson, 16 February 1888.
38 Burton, p. 157.
39 *NDC*, 14 March 1888; Hayward, p. 228.

lunch at the County Hotel did little to revive the bishop's spirits, nor did the weather, which made it 'about as wintry as any day could be'. The next day was worse: 'The gale continue[d] to rage with unabated violence, the sea breaking with deafening force on the coast and shipping being absolutely at a standstill'. From his window in Bishop's House O'Callaghan could see ships standing off the harbour-mouth unable to get into the Tyne and take refuge.[40] He had no intention of staying long at 'The Martyr's Peace'.

Provost Wilkinson was immediately made Vicar General and continued to help O'Callaghan get to grips with his new responsibilities, supporting him in confirming over five hundred people within the first ten days, and then in the Holy Week ceremonies at Ushaw. At the beginning of April three senior canons organised a whip-round for the bishop among the clergy to make up 'a purse of gold' as 'a substantial mark of our affectionate welcome to him'. The great sacrifice in surrendering the many ties which had bound him to Rome 'to undertake a laborious episcopate . . . must have been accompanied by [a] personal outlay which cannot have been inconsiderable'.[41] The subscription list remained open until 4 May but, with or without the purse, O'Callaghan fled the north a day or two after the Feast of the Ascension, 10 May, and Wilkinson was again left alone to administer the diocese. On 14 May O'Callaghan wrote to him from Archbishop's House in Westminster:

> I find my position quite unendurable and must go to Rome to settle matters. The Cardinal has opposed my return to Tynemouth as he wishes me to remain under the doctor's hands. But the doctor can do very little for me and things have now come to such a pass that it matters very little what becomes of me. I am grieved for you and the poor Diocese.[42]

Events moved swiftly. A week later Wilkinson got a letter from the cardinal's secretary telling him that O'Callaghan had arrived in Rome; letters were enclosed from Propaganda and Manning informing Wilkinson of his appointment as O'Callaghan's auxiliary as Bishop of Cisamus *in partibus infidelium* (Crete). Manning wrote: 'The decision has been made with full and mature deliberation: and you may take it as coming directly from the Vicar of our Lord laying you under obedience'.[43] Wilkinson wrote to a friend, 'God help me. I have sought nothing, I wanted nothing. I have neither learning, knowledge or virtue, so they must take what they can get. I am put under obedience to accept, so here goes. I will do my best, no-one could do more than that.'[44]

Early in June Manning told Wilkinson that since the Pope had forbidden O'Callaghan to return to the diocese until his health was restored he would

---

[40] *NDC*, 9–14 March 1888 weather reports. There were several accounts of ships grounding.
[41] *The Tablet*, 7 April 1888, p. 585.
[42] HNDA, List 78, O'Callaghan to Wilkinson, 14 May 1888.
[43] *Ibid.*, Manning to Wilkinson, 4 June 1888.
[44] HNDA, List 17, Thompson Papers no. 22, 22 May 1888.

keep him in London. But O'Callaghan wrote to Wilkinson from Bruges (on his way back to England) hoping that they would still be friends despite the trouble he had caused, and saying that now he was so much better he would like to consecrate Wilkinson.[45] That was the last thing Wilkinson expected or wanted, for he had already engaged Bishop Clifford. (Manning had headed off an invitation from Wilkinson asking him to do it by saying he was 'too old to travel'.)[46] That apart, O'Callaghan's intention of returning to the north at all so appalled Wilkinson that he wrote the following impassioned letter to Manning, which serves to show that it was not just physical ill-health, or the weather, that O'Callaghan was suffering from:

> I would ask you that my Briefs might be allowed to lie dormant and so die out. I so greatly fear friction hereafter, and at least the appearance of two authorities in the Diocese. I tremble at the thought of anything of the kind and yet I know now so well, nobody can know better, the mind, the sentiments, the whole tone and way of thinking and acting of our good Bishop that I feel that in a very few weeks he and I must necessarily drift asunder. If he is utterly changed in nature and character from what he was when at Tynemouth, then undoubtedly he is, or may be at any rate, perfectly able to rule his Diocese alone and without my help and I should only be in the way; but if he is in any kind or degree the same, then our working together is simply an impossibility . . .
>
> The very thought of what I went through at Tynemouth fills me still with terror and nothing would induce me to subject myself again to such an ordeal. He is a younger, a stronger, and in every respect a better man than I. If he is capable of the work he should do it, but I cannot possibly with any fruit act as an Auxiliary to him . . .[47]

From the first O'Callaghan had counted on Wilkinson as an experienced missionary to advise and support him and Wilkinson had responded willingly. But that was at a distance; when they came face to face the partnership broke down. Wilkinson was an able and businesslike administrator but O'Callaghan found it difficult to make, and then keep to, even the simplest of decisions. Priests obtaining rulings from him would often find them cancelled by the next post. The Vicar General had also to deal with his bishop's scruples; it seems that when O'Callaghan was in Rome prolonged wrestling with his conscience often made him late for, or even miss, his Mass.[48] Wilkinson, who was known to be testy, would not put up with that for long. Whether there was a scene it is impossible to know but Wilkinson was adamant that their parting be final.

Manning tried to pacify Wilkinson by pointing out that O'Callaghan only wished to go north to collect his things but at the same time make

---

[45] HNDA, List 78, O'Callaghan to Wilkinson, Bruges, 8 June 1888.
[46] *Ibid.*, Manning to Wilkinson, 4 June 1888.
[47] *Ibid.*, Wilkinson to Manning, 7 July 1888.
[48] Hayward, p. 228, n. 36.

some public act that everybody might see that he is not finally declined in a hopeless state. He expressed the wish to be your consecrator as such an act. This is very reasonable and his absence would give an exaggerated impression of his state. He is much better and perfectly master of himself . . .

He said that he had warned O'Callaghan that unless he returned to Archbishop's House immediately after the ceremony,

> and unless he is restored to health both of body and mind I am bound to ask the Holy See to accept his resignation. You will see therefore that there is no danger of dualism in the diocese . . . In truth my belief is that he may never sufficiently recover or that if he should recover he could not long bear the strain. You are therefore safe from all such trials as you fear. Accept him as consecrator and avoid disturbing the marked return of health and peace of mind.

Manning would get Bishop Clifford to ensure that his instructions were enforced.[49] The latter assured Wilkinson that if O'Callaghan were to recover then Wilkinson would be free to retire. He expected O'Callaghan to resign but 'the Holy See prudently requires that a little time should elapse before such a step is resorted to'.[50] In a concluding exchange, Wilkinson accepted Manning's advice but made quite sure that the cardinal was in no doubt about the conditions on which he would accept consecration and added:

> I am 40 years a Priest this year. I have lived in the greatest peace and happiness during the whole of that period in the midst of missions founded by myself, keeping quite clear of the gossip, the bickerings and the miseries I so often saw around me. It would be to me simply appalling now at 63 to be dragged into anything like ecclesiastical misunderstandings and cross purposes with the Bishop of the Diocese. The clergy are thoroughly with me.[51]

Manning reassured him: 'What you fear will never be!'[52] In the event, O'Callaghan was unable to consecrate Wilkinson; it was done instead by Bishops Clifford and Riddell and Archbishop Charles Eyre at Ushaw on 25 July 1888; Bishop John Cuthbert Hedley OSB preached. (Wilkinson was made a Freeman of Newcastle in October.)

---

[49] HNDA, List 78, Manning to Wilkinson, 9 July 1888.
[50] *Ibid.*, Clifford to Wilkinson, Bristol, 22 July 1888.
[51] *Ibid.*, Wilkinson to Manning, 11 and 13 July 1888. Wilkinson had always been diffident about accepting preferment. In 1865, two years after being elected to the Chapter and appointed Canon Theologian, he told Canon Bewick that he had accepted the honours only 'under obedience to the Bishop on the election of the Chapter. They are not exactly in my way; my ambition was to labour away in the parish [Wolsingham] I was first appointed to at my ordination and not in any way to mix myself with affairs external to that parish. As my superiors have willed otherwise I am content that it sh[oul]d be so and if I can be of any use whatsoever in promoting the cause for which alone I live I shall be for ever thankful.' (HNDA, Various, 18 December 1865).
[52] HNDA, List 78, Manning to Wilkinson, 11 July 1888.

A little over a year later the cardinal's secretary informed the Chapter of Hexham and Newcastle that Propaganda had accepted O'Callaghan's resignation on 27 September 1889 and that the Chapter's *terna* to fill the vacancy was required.[53] The Chapter met under the presidency of Bishop Clifford and their nominations, again in alphabetical order but with no indication of preference, were: Canon John Carroll of Shrewsbury diocese;[54] Canon James Rooney, Wilkinson's Vicar General;[55] and Bishop Wilkinson. Rome was not long in coming to a decision: Bishop Wilkinson was translated to Hexham and Newcastle in December 1889. He received his Briefs on 6 January and was enthroned on 18 February 1890.

The nomination of O'Callaghan, then, was not an example of Manning's customary good judgement. The climate of northern England, the state of O'Callaghan's health and the diocesan clergy's initial hostility were major disincentives to giving up the congenialities of Rome, but there was another factor which Manning should certainly have considered even though he had not seen O'Callaghan for four years (the cardinal's final visit to Rome had taken place in 1883) and the two do not appear to have corresponded on the matter. From the outset O'Callaghan had let his unsuitability on temperamental grounds be generally known. He had been an academic all his working life with a brief interval from 1861 to 1865. For the twenty-five years preceding his episcopal nomination he had enjoyed the prestigious title of Rector but the responsibilities which went with it were not exactly demanding: in the first case he had charge of six students and in the second sixteen. And they were (more or less) compliant young men destined for the priesthood, well within the supervisory capacities of one who had started out as Prefect of Discipline at St Edmund's. The Pope had once said that the Oblate students were so good that they did 'not require much to keep them in order'.[56] Now aged sixty, O'Callaghan was being asked to govern an enormous diocese with which he had no connection and of which he knew nothing, comprising the four counties of Northumberland, Durham, Cumberland and Westmorland, with an estimated Catholic population of 128,000, 137 priests in 95 missions, 77 church schools and 25 religious communities.[57] He knew he was unequal to

---

[53] HNDA, Chapter Records 13/32/1, W.A. Johnson to Rooney, 11 October 1889.
[54] The *terna* is at *ibid.*, 13/30, 15 October 1889. Carroll, aged 51, became coadjutor in his home diocese in 1893 and succeeded Bishop Edmund Knight in 1895. He died in 1897.
[55] Aged 40. He would outlive Bishop Wilkinson and his two auxiliaries, Bishops Preston and Collins, and act as Apostolic Administrator of the diocese during the latter's incapacity 1922–4. Rooney died in 1931 aged 82.
[56] Purcell, vol. II p. 368; Hayward, p. 225 and n. 20: 'Between 1875 and 1887 the Venerabile contained an average of no more than sixteen students in any given year'. There were 105 students between 1867 and 1887.
[57] J. Lenders, 'Statistics of the Diocese . . . [1890]' *NCC* (1932), between pp. 80–81. Both O'Callaghan and Wilkinson put the diocesan Catholic population at 180,000 to 200,000 – a total that was not reached until 1920.

the task and only accepted it under strict obedience; then, having taken the measure of his new duties at firsthand, not the least of which was the two- to three-year backlog of diocesan business, he recoiled at the prospect and had the good sense to vacate his chair. (The nearest comparable case is that of Robert Cornthwaite, his predecessor but three at the Venerabile, who became bishop of his native diocese of Beverley in 1861 when he was forty-three.) It is a lesson of perennial importance that not all clerics have episcopal attributes just because they have risen to minor prominence or are favoured by high-ranking patrons.

Within a year of his translation Wilkinson was also appointed twelfth President of Ushaw College, and he would lead both the diocese and the college (where he took up residence) into the twentieth century. He inherited a vigorously growing diocese which needed stability rather than reform, which was just as well, for as a north-country Tory he was disinclined to radical change. He rapidly cleared the arrears of episcopal work and soon became known as a highly efficient administrator and financial manager who would brook no secretarial prevarication or, indeed, liturgical sloppiness. He carried out his public duties energetically but they took their toll. He offered to retire in January 1894 but he was told that his resignation would be 'a great injury to the diocese itself, and a distinct loss to the whole English Episcopate' and that it would be better to apply for an auxiliary.[58] But, as we have seen, he had always been averse to 'dualism', as he termed it, in the diocese and he held back for several years before he would agree. Even then he never quite withdrew his guiding hand from either of his auxiliaries (Richard Preston – a *Venerabilino* – from 1900 and Richard Collins from 1905) who found themselves subject to his strong personality until the last.[59] Wilkinson was made an Assistant Prelate at the Pontifical Throne by Pope Pius X in November 1905. The twenty years of his combined episcopate and presidency culminated with the centenary of Ushaw College in July 1908 and the diamond jubilee of his priesthood in December. He died four months later in April 1909, aged eighty-four, and was buried at Ushaw. He left his entire fortune of over £50,000 for the education of priests for County Durham.[60]

O'Callaghan was made titular Archbishop of Nicosia *in partibus infidelium*

---

[58] Ushaw College Manuscripts, OS/H 29, Wilkinson to Cardinal Vaughan, n.d. [early 1894]; OS/H 30 Propaganda and Cardinal Vaughan to Wilkinson, 27 February 1894.

[59] Six months after his appointment Preston remarked that 'being a bishop even in the mitigated auxiliary form is, I assure you, very terrible', but he was probably referring to the rôle in general rather than Wilkinson's manner. (A. Watts, 'Bishop Preston' [obituary], *Ushaw Magazine*, vol. 15 (1905), p. 7.)

[60] H. Burton, 'Thomas William Wilkinson, Late Bishop of Hexham and Newcastle, Twelfth President', *Ushaw Magazine*, no. 56 (July 1909), *passim*. Wilkinson wrote to Canon Stark towards the end of his life saying: 'I am feeling very feeble and worn out. The weather has been terribly against an old man in his 84th year. Still I may possibl[y] wear on until the centenary but I shall be glad for very little at it', HNDA, Chapter Records 14/17 n.d.

and went back to live in Italy; he did not attend Manning's funeral in January 1892. Wrenched from his accustomed habitat and respected position, he was 'quite broken' and without a job or a home; his successor at the Venerabile would not have him in permanent residence.[61] Wilkinson volunteered to pay him £150 a year from his private income rather than allow O'Callaghan to become a burden on the diocese but, when he was reminded about it, he acceded to the requirement of Canon Law that such payments had to be made from the ordinary's *mensa*, or household account. Accordingly, a quarterly remittance was made through the London and Westminster Bank from the date of O'Callaghan's resignation to the week after his death.[62] O'Callaghan spent his time in Florence and Rome making guest archiepiscopal appearances at ordinations and so on until the end of the century, when he suffered a sudden stroke which paralysed him and he was placed in the care of the Little Company of Mary (the Blue Nuns) in Florence. He attended Mass in a wheelchair but his scrupulosity became so bad (he asked for Confession every day) that he had to be put under strict ecclesiastical obedience. He died in October 1904, aged seventy-seven, and was buried in the cemetery of San Miniato. His passing was marked by a short obituary in *The Edmundian* and a brief notice in *The Tablet* but the memoir promised for *Northern Catholic Calendar*, his own diocesan annual, never appeared.[63]

Abbreviations and Acknowledgements

Burton	George Burton's Roman Diary: Liber 824, Archives of *Venerabile Collegio Inglese* (bound ms., pagination added). I am grateful to Delia Gallagher and Nicholas Schofield for photocopies.
HNDA	Hexham and Newcastle Diocesan Archives. I am obliged to the archivist, Robin Gard, for his ready assistance. I am also grateful to Canon Robert Spence for permission to cite the Cathedral Chapter Records.
NDC	Newcastle Daily Chronicle

[61] HNDA, List 78, Clifford to Wilkinson, 22 July 1888; Hayward, p. 229, n. 33.
[62] HNDA, List 78, Manning to Wilkinson, 8 July 1890; reply, 9 July 1890; HNDA, Diocesan Ledgers, 'Bishop's Mensa Account' 1890–1904, *passim*. Hayward, p. 229, mistakenly says the diocese paid him £240 a year. Perhaps the difference was paid by the Venerabile.
[63] *The Edmundian* (1904), pp. 120–1; *The Tablet*, 15 October 1904, p. 611; *Northern Catholic Calendar* (1904), p. 109.

5

'EDUCATION AND CORRECT CONDUCT': RANDAL LYTHGOE AND THE WORK OF THE SOCIETY OF JESUS IN EARLY VICTORIAN ENGLAND AND WALES

MAURICE WHITEHEAD

The exclusive, narrow, military, aristocratic character of the Society [of Jesus] shown in the time of James I with the arch-priest figment and the continual thwarting of the English clergy down to good Father Lythgoe, whom I just remember, seems to me to be a mysterious permission of God for the chastisement of England.[1]

HENRY EDWARD MANNING's well-known antipathy towards certain aspects of the activities of the Society of Jesus, reflected in one of his autobiographical notes, quoted above, clearly did not extend to the life and work of 'good Father Lythgoe'. In January 1851, only three months before the future cardinal's reception into the Roman Catholic Church at the Jesuit church at Farm Street, London, Fr Randal Lythgoe, SJ (1793–1855), had left London for East Anglia, to take up what was to prove to be his last post. The magnificent new church at Farm Street was one of the many, enduring expressions of the achievements of Lythgoe's recently completed six-year period of office as provincial superior of the English Jesuits, from 1841 to 1847. Though his life's work was almost at an end by 1851, Lythgoe had laid the very foundations on which the restored English Jesuit Province was to grow over the next century. The purpose of the present paper is to explore the ways in which Lythgoe's background and education influenced his work, particularly as a provincial superior.

---

[1] Manning's statement is quoted in Shane Leslie, *Henry Edward Manning: His Life and Labours* (London, 1954), p. 297.

Background and Education, 1793–1827

Randal Lythgoe, the son of Thomas and Elizabeth Lythgoe, was born on 28 November 1793 at Eccleston, near St Helens, in Lancashire, and was brought up at Southworth Hall in the parish of Winwick, three miles north of Warrington.[2] A prosperous farming family, apparently of Scottish origin, the Lythgoes had been established in south-west Lancashire since the Tudor period, principally in the adjoining parishes of Wigan, Leigh and Winwick. Though their surname was spelled and pronounced in a variety of different ways in the locality, this particular branch of the family employed the pronunciation 'Lígo'.[3]

The corner of Lancashire in which Southworth Hall lay had been noted since Elizabethan times for its unwavering recusancy, and the domestic milieu into which Randal Lythgoe was born was one heavily influenced over generations by both the missionary and the educational work of the Society of Jesus. A half-timbered manor house first built in the medieval period, Southworth Hall had been rebuilt in the seventeenth century. As early as 1420, the private chapel within the Hall had been granted a licence by the bishop of Lichfield and, after the Reformation, it had remained in Catholic hands, being served by Jesuit missionaries throughout much of the penal period. By the eighteenth century the property was in the hands of the Gerard family of Ashton-in-Makerfield, several members of which were Jesuits. When, in 1797, Southworth Hall and some twenty acres of farmland were bequeathed by one of the

---

[2] ABSI, *Province Register*, 12/2/6, f. 32. Despite considerable research, the marriage of Thomas and Elizabeth Lythgoe has not yet been located in either Catholic or Anglican sources. Circumstantial evidence strongly suggests that Elizabeth Lythgoe was the daughter of Robert Rockliff (died 1782) and his wife, Elizabeth Howard. Rockliff was the land agent for Lord Molyneux's estates at Croxteth, near Liverpool. His grandson, Robert Rockliff (1797–1874), was the founder of the Liverpool printing and publishing house of the same name, which still exists. See Adrian R.L. Bush, *A History of the Rockliff Family of Liverpool* (Liverpool, 1984), pp. 1–8, 65.

[3] Oral tradition suggests that the Lythgoe family migrated from Scotland to Lancashire after the battle of Culloden in 1745. However, surviving documentary evidence suggests a much earlier date – more probably some time after the battle of Flodden in 1513. The family name is recorded in parish registers and testamentary records for south-west Lancashire from Tudor times onwards and is variously spelled Ligo, Lithgo, Lithgoe, Lithgow, Lygo, Lygoe or Lythgoe. A Randle Lythgoe was born at Wigan, circa 1560; and one Randall Lygo was born at Abram, near Wigan, circa 1608 (see International Genealogical Index, registers of Wigan parish, Lancashire). A ceramic jug, still extant, presented to Fr Randal Lythgoe's father, Thomas, in 1831, and bearing the inscription 'Thomas Ligo', attests to the particular pronunciation of the family surname employed by the Southworth Hall branch of the Lythgoe family. I am indebted to Mr Bernard Lightbound, a descendant of Thomas Lythgoe, for this information.

Gerard family to the president of Stonyhurst College, the tenancy of the property passed to Thomas and Elizabeth Lythgoe.[4]

The Southworth branch of the Lythgoe family was closely allied through kinship over several generations with the neighbouring recusant families of Arrowsmith, Brownbill, Holme, Howard, Polding and Rockliff, all of whom had extensive Jesuit connections and, in the case of the Poldings, both Jesuit and Benedictine connections. These included, over a time span of two centuries, the martyr St Edmund Arrowsmith, SJ (1585–1628), also born in the parish of Winwick; the saintly and mystic Fr John Howard [*vere* Holme], SJ (1718–1783), first president of the English Academy at Liège, from the suppression of the Society of Jesus in 1773 until his death; Fr Thomas Brownbill, SJ (1788–1844), superior of the Jesuit novitiate at Hodder, near Stonyhurst from 1827 to 1842; his two brothers, Fr Francis Brownbill, SJ (1793–1875) and Fr James Brownbill, SJ (1798–1880), the latter of whom, as superior at Farm Street, London, from 1841 to 1854, received Henry Edward Manning into the Church; Fr John Polding, SJ (1807–1858), rector of Mount St Mary's College, Spinkhill, Derbyshire, from 1843 to 1844; and John Bede Polding, OSB (1794–1877), first archbishop of Sydney, Australia.

Where the young Lythgoe received his earliest education is not known, but, in January 1808, at the age of fifteen, he became a boarder at Stonyhurst College in his native Lancashire.[5] He was destined to remain in the vicinity of Stonyhurst for the next fifteen years, first as a lay pupil at Stonyhurst College and subsequently as a Jesuit novice at nearby Hodder, on the Stonyhurst estate. His experience in both locations was to play an important part in the shaping both of his outlook and of his future life.

In 1808, Stonyhurst College was in a state of transition and looking towards the future. Forced to escape the impending atrocities of the second French invasion of the principality of Liège in the summer of 1794, the suppressed English Jesuits had migrated to England. Soon thereafter, they had settled at Stonyhurst, thanks to the munificence of Thomas Weld of Lulworth, Dorset, who ultimately presented part of his Stonyhurst estate to the English Province of the Society of Jesus.[6] Educational continuity between Liège and Stonyhurst had been assured by the last president of the academy and the first president of the college, Fr Marmaduke Stone (1748–1834), who had held office since his appointment to the position in Liège in 1790. On his nomination in 1803 as the first provincial superior of the newly restored English Jesuit province, Stone had continued to reside at Stonyhurst, combining his new duties with those of

---

[4] Thomas E. Gibson, *Lydiate Hall and its Associations* (Edinburgh and London, 1876), p. 210; Joseph Gillow, *Catholic Registers of Southworth Hall, Lancs., 1795–1827*, Catholic Record Society, vol. 13 (1913), p. 327.

[5] ABSI, *Province Register*, 12/2/6, f. 32.

[6] Maurice Whitehead, ' "In the Sincerest Intentions of Studying": The Educational Legacy of Thomas Weld (1750–1810), Founder of Stonyhurst College', *Recusant History*, vol. 26 (May, 2002), pp. 169–93.

the presidency of the recently transplanted college.[7] This combination of work soon proved too onerous. It led in 1808 to the appointment of the Maryland Jesuit, Fr Nicholas Sewall (1745–1834), as president of the college, allowing Stone to concentrate on his work as provincial superior and the new rector to concentrate on educational developments in conjunction with the prefect of studies. Innovation was soon evident on three main fronts: improvement of the fabric; lighting of the buildings; and development of the curriculum.

First, Sewall and the procurator of Stonyhurst, Fr Charles Wright (1752–1827), lost no time with the business of extending and remodelling the ancient buildings of Stonyhurst Hall, better to equip them as a modern place of education. Part of the older structure, extremely solidly built, was demolished dramatically with the use of gunpowder, no doubt delighting and making a lasting impression on the pupils. The replacement building, however, was erected without any regard to architectural beauty or harmony, a matter that was to make an equally lasting impression on the young Randal Lythgoe.[8]

Second, the enterprising Fathers Sewall and Wright decided in 1811 to adopt the as yet untried experiment of using gas for lighting purposes. Commissioning Samuel Clegg to install a gasworks in the grounds of the college, they introduced gas lighting on a grand scale throughout the entire college building. Stonyhurst had the distinction of becoming the first public building in the British Isles to be so lit, on 18 February 1811, while Lythgoe was a pupil there.[9]

Third, in the hurried flight from Liège in 1794, a fine collection of scientific and mathematical instruments used in the teaching of the secondary level course of studies at the English Academy had had to be abandoned. Wishing to continue and build on the distinguished and innovative scientific educational work of the Liège Academy, the Jesuits launched an appeal in 1808 for the construction of a new scientific library and a new chemical laboratory to complement a mathematical apparatus room that had recently been completed.[10] In achieving their scientific goals, the Jesuits of Stonyhurst were

---

[7] The restoration of the English Jesuit Province in 1803, ahead of the universal restoration of the Society of Jesus in 1814, was made possible through the affiliation of the English Jesuits to the Jesuits in White Russia. The latter had survived the universal suppression in 1773, thanks to the refusal of Catherine the Great to promulgate the papal brief of suppression in her dominions. See G. Holt, 'The English Province: The Ex-Jesuits and the Restoration', *Archivum Historicum Societatis Iesu*, vol. 42 (1973), pp. 288–311.

[8] J. Gerard, *Stonyhurst College: Its Life Beyond the Seas, 1592–1794 and on English Soil, 1794–1894* (Belfast, 1894), p. 128.

[9] Gerard, p. 125; and T.E. Muir, *Stonyhurst College, 1593–1993* (London, 1992), p. 78. The experiment was so successful that it led, through the influence of Fr Joseph Postlethwaite of Stonyhurst and Fr Joseph Dunn of Preston, to the creation of a gas company in Preston, which was the first provincial town in Britain to introduce gas street lighting.

[10] SA, F/1/2/7, C.IV.6 and C.IV.7; G. Holt, 'The March of Science', *Stonyhurst Magazine*, October 1958, pp. 211–13.

far advanced: it was not until 1857 that a comparable school – Rugby – possessed a science laboratory. All this innovative activity left its mark on the young Randal Lythgoe and, together with subsequent experiences elsewhere, would help to influence his outlook later in life.

Lythgoe entered the Jesuit novitiate at Hodder in September 1812, began his study of logic two years later, and, in 1816, embarked on a course of natural philosophy. From 1817 until 1823, he was engaged as a scholastic, teaching at Stonyhurst, taking a class up through the full course of studies from Elements to the class of Poetry.[11] By the summer of 1823, he was ready to embark on his theological studies and his superiors judged that he would best flourish if he were sent for this purpose to Rome.

Setting out from Stonyhurst on 7 August 1823, Lythgoe accompanied two young Stonyhurst students, Walter and Robert Clifford, at the request of their father, Lord Clifford, as far as Paris. There he showed them the Louvre and Versailles and, from Lady Clifford and Lady Constable in Paris, he gained letters of introduction to the papal nuncio there, Monsignor Macchi. From Paris, Lythgoe made his way to Turin and Rome on a very deliberate and carefully planned route that took him via the small town of Jougne, on the road between Besançon and Lausanne. There his former novice master, rector and provincial superior, Fr Charles Plowden (1743–1821), had been buried two years before, following his sudden death *en route* home to Stonyhurst from attending in Rome the election of a new Jesuit General.[12] As subsequent events were to prove, Lythgoe's pilgrimage to Plowden's grave, on his path to Rome, was a hugely symbolic gesture. He was almost certainly the first English Jesuit to visit the grave after Plowden's death. As well as being a mark of respect for a remarkable Jesuit priest who had lived through the darkest days of the suppression of the Society of Jesus, it was also a silent pledge to take forward Plowden's pioneering work in restoring the English Jesuit Province.

Arriving in Rome on 26 October 1823, shortly before his thirtieth birthday, to study at the *Collegio Romano*, Lythgoe was keen to use his time to the full – and not solely on his studies. As one of the first English Jesuits to study in Rome after the restoration of the Society of Jesus, he saw himself as a representative, however unofficial, of English Jesuit affairs. Accordingly, he lost no time in paying a visit to the new Jesuit General, Fr Aloysius Fortis, to discuss English Province matters with him. He was also quick to obtain a place at the foot of the stairs of the Vatican as the Pope entered his carriage; and the crowds thronging around the Pope in the courtyard of the papal palace overwhelmed him.[13]

---

[11] ABSI, *Province Register*, 12/2/6, f. 32; Gerard, p. 300.
[12] ABSI, *Foreign Correspondence, 1776–1859*, ff. 203–5, Randal Lythgoe to Nicholas Sewall, 15 October 1823.
[13] *Ibid.*, ff. 207–9, Lythgoe to Sewall, November 1823.

Lythgoe was soon writing back to his provincial, Fr Nicholas Sewall, informing him that 'Fr General says that we must pray for success and pray hard – but then ought we not to imitate the champions of old who wielded the sword whilst they prayed to the Lord?'[14] In England and Wales, there was continuing friction between the Jesuits and the Vicars Apostolic. Suspicion of the Jesuits had increased around the time of, and after, the universal restoration of the Society of Jesus by the Pope in 1814. However, local restorations depended on the approval of national hierarchies, and a majority of the English and Welsh Vicars Apostolic successfully held out until 1829 against such a restoration in England and Wales. Undeterred by this level of opposition, Lythgoe reported excitedly in 1823 that Cardinal della Somaglia had 'absolutely promised Fr General that an order shall be sent to the Vicars Apostolic [in England and Wales] to treat us as they treat the other religious orders'.[15] The Jesuit General clearly found Lythgoe an interesting and helpful young man. As the latter was to admit privately to Fr Nicholas Sewall, '[he] is very affable and kind to me, and this affability and kindness on his part has emboldened me to say many things, particularly with regard to the Missions, which I trust have corrected some erroneous ideas that were previously entertained upon that subject'.[16] Lythgoe's easy access to, and frank discussions with, the Jesuit General were soon to win him enemies: within a matter of months he was reporting to Sewall that an unknown fellow Jesuit had lodged a complaint against him, accusing him of overstepping himself in his dealings with the General.[17]

Some of Lythgoe's early hopes were ambitious, if not unachievable. Within a few months of arriving in Rome, he was looking forward to the restoration of the English College in Rome to the custody of the English Jesuits, a hope that never materialised. He also strongly urged Fr Joseph Tristram (1766–1843), the rector of Stonyhurst, to invite Monsignor Macchi, the papal nuncio in Paris, who was soon to be made cardinal, to Stonyhurst. Macchi was about to leave Rome on a visit to England, and Lythgoe warned that 'if we do not get round the nuncio, others will, and instead of being our friend, he will be our foe'.[18]

Notwithstanding his status as a student, Lythgoe was soon also playing another minor diplomatic role in Rome. Hearing that the Marquess of Hastings was staying close to the Vatican, Lythgoe enquired indirectly and discreetly whether or not a visit to him from the Jesuit General would be acceptable. The Marquess was greatly flattered and Lythgoe arranged the visit, reporting back to Fr Sewall that the General had thanked the Marquess for his friendship to

[14] *Ibid.*, f. 209.
[15] *Ibid.*, f. 214, Lythgoe to Sewall, 27 December 1823.
[16] *Ibid.*, f. 222, Lythgoe to Sewall, 7 April 1824.
[17] *Ibid.*, f. 226, Lythgoe to Sewall, n.d. [mid-July 1824].
[18] *Ibid.*, f. 219, Lythgoe to Tristram, 7 February 1824.

Catholics in England and Wales – and to Stonyhurst in particular. He had also assured the Marquess that the object of the Society of Jesus 'is to make all its members men of letters and friends of their country'.[19]

If Randal Lythgoe were to contribute personally to the future work of the English Jesuits, he needed to survive the consumption that was then raging in Rome and that was taking the lives of so many of his fellow students. As he wrote to Fr Thomas Glover (1781–1849) at Stonyhurst, 'I recommend myself to your good prayers and those of all my friends at Stonyhurst that I may live ... *to do good* and not to leave my body ... in one of the niches here, to be eaten away by scorpions'.[20] Potentially fatal maladies apart, Lythgoe was impressed with the 'comparative ease' in which the Italian Jesuits lived, having everything provided for them, including 'an abundant table' and, for those of literary tastes, 'a copious library and leisure for improvement and study'. Furthermore, he noted that 'each one in his respective sphere enjoys a degree of consideration among men in the world which education and correct conduct are always sure to inspire'. Lythgoe believed that young Jesuits could not expect to meet with these advantages in England, where 'scanty conveniences and the want of little attentions' were the norm.[21]

Besides the advantages of Rome, there were also many disadvantages to be encountered there, both physical and intellectual. Lythgoe reported from Rome to one of his English Jesuit confrères that 'the want of cleanliness and the confinement are very troublesome. The confinement and discipline of Juniors or even Novices in England is *Liberty* when compared with what we have here'; and he complained that, as a student in Rome, he was being 'subjected to the treatment of a boy'.[22] Furthermore, as he reported to Fr Sewall, 'the Theology here is not such as is well adapted to England. All the books that would be of most service to us are upon the *Index*, and of these we cannot read a single line.'[23] In many ways, his being in Rome was a complete frustration. Though he had managed to visit the Vatican Library once, he found that the antiquities of Rome were 'as inaccessible to us as were the mysteries of the Bona Dea to the Ancients. Indeed ... a man must be exceedingly *industrious* to see anything of consequence. I have had the reputation of being sufficiently industrious, but I have not as yet been able to see a single picture gallery or museum in Rome, not even that of the Vatican'.[24]

The shortcomings of the theological education then available in Rome were matters that Lythgoe clearly broached openly in his private meetings with the Jesuit General. By mid-July 1824, he was able to report to Fr Sewall that the

---

[19] *Ibid.*, f. 214, Lythgoe to Sewall, 27 December 1823.
[20] *Ibid.*, f. 218, Lythgoe to Glover, 14 January 1824.
[21] *Ibid.*, f. 256, Lythgoe to Sewall, 19 February 1826.
[22] *Ibid.*, f. 225, Lythgoe to Fr John or Fr James Laurenson, 11 April 1824.
[23] *Ibid.*, f. 222, Lythgoe to Sewall, 7 April 1824.
[24] *Ibid.*

General had told him that he believed that the discipline of the scholasticate in Rome was not suited to someone of his age and standing in the Society of Jesus and that he would be better studying elsewhere.[25] Indeed, the General's closest advisers believed that a house of higher studies should be established in England as soon as could conveniently be arranged.[26] Lythgoe was not afraid to voice his own opinion on this matter to his provincial superior. He informed Sewall that he thought that such an establishment would be best situated in the Midland District of England, where Bishop Milner was more favourably disposed to the Jesuits than many of his episcopal brethren.[27] However, he foresaw that 'our enemies might attempt to have an enquiry instituted in Propaganda into the grounds on which we possess our several missions, and though they would probably fail in their object, still such an investigation might be very unpleasant'.[28]

Randal Lythgoe's continuing education and preparation as a Jesuit was a matter of urgent discussion between Fr Nicholas Sewall and the Jesuit General, and it was finally decided that, from the autumn of 1824, he would continue his theological studies in Paris. Lythgoe's initial reactions to life in France were hardly positive and, by Christmas 1825, he was uncharacteristically gloomy and even homesick and lonely. Writing on Christmas Day, 1825, from Paris, to Fr Charles Wright at Stonyhurst, the naturally gregarious Lythgoe recorded his private sentiments graphically:

> Alas! How different is Christmas in every other country from what it is in England. There, the simple carol, the blazing sea-coal fire, the smoking goose, the good mince-pie, the cordial pledge all conspire to excite and keep alive kindly mirth and fellowship. In Rome you were indeed reminded of the approach of Christmas by the shepherds in their uncouth guise descending from the mountains into the eternal city and there, pipe in hand, tuning the glories of the new-born king. But alas here in France all is one, same, unvaried, cheerless scene; here there is no token of approaching Christmas; here all seasons are alike; the most horrid blasphemies constantly rend your ears, and the most shameless vice stares you in the face at every turn. So much for Christmas time.[29]

He was soon back in his usual good spirits, which were uplifted by Leo XII's encyclical, *Caritate Christi,* published in Rome on Christmas Day, 1825. The year 1825 had been celebrated in Rome as a Jubilee or Holy Year and, as events would turn out, it was to prove the only Jubilee of the nineteenth

---

[25] *Ibid.*, f. 226, Lythgoe to Sewall, n.d. [mid-July 1824].
[26] *Ibid.*, f. 228, Lythgoe to Sewall, n.d. [October 1824].
[27] Many of the Vicars Apostolic other than Milner would ordain Jesuits, but only 'for the mission' and not as religious 'sub titulo pauperitatis'.
[28] ABSI, *Foreign Correspondence, 1776–1859*, f. 229.
[29] *Ibid.*, f. 249, Lythgoe to Fr Charles Wright, 25 December 1825.

century, the potential Holy Years of 1850 and 1875, like that of 1800, passing by uncelebrated owing to major political upheavals in Europe. Leo XII, anxious to extend the 'treasures of the Church to all the regions of the world', decreed that the year 1826 should be marked as a year of Jubilee generally throughout the Church.[30]

As Randal Lythgoe reported to Fr Sewall, the opening ceremony in France of the extended Jubilee took place at Notre-Dame Cathedral in Paris with a splendour and an effect that had not been expected. The ensuing series of spectacular Lenten sermons preached at Saint-Sulpice particularly inspired him, not least because of the regular presence there of the newly restored king, Charles X, the dauphin, the dauphiness, and the duchesse de Berry. Lythgoe was awe-struck by the powerful preaching, to congregations of up to ten thousand people, of the Irish-born French Jesuit, Père Nicolas Tuite de MacCarthy (1769–1833)[31] who, he reported, 'scourges his auditory . . . but with a dignity and good breeding which precludes almost the possibility of offence'.[32] Equally inspiring as preachers of the 1826 Lenten sermons were his young French contemporaries as Jesuits, Père Claude Guyon (1795–1845)[33] and Père Xavier Lacroix de Ravignan (1795–1858),[34] the latter of whom was to preach at Henry Edward Manning's first Mass at Farm Street, London, twenty-five years later.[35]

By the late summer of 1826, Lythgoe was waiting to be sent imminently to Turin or Fribourg for ordination, but he was eventually ordained a priest in France, at Pignarol, on 1 October 1826.[36] Three weeks later, he was sent to complete his theology studies at the newly opened Jesuit *Séminaire de l'Arc* at Dole, in the Jura. Here he found himself happily 'further removed from the

---

[30] *Caritate Christi*, §1, 25 December 1825.
[31] MacCarthy was born in Dublin on 19 May 1769 and moved to Toulouse at the age of four years. Ordained at Chambéry in 1814, he began a clerical career that placed him in the first rank of modern preachers. He declined nomination as bishop of Montauban in 1817 and entered the Society of Jesus the following year. MacCarthy died in Annecy on 3 May 1833. See C. Sommervogel, *Bibliothèque de la Compagnie de Jésus*, vol. 5 (Paris, 1894), pp. 238–239.
[32] ABSI, *Foreign Correspondence, 1776–1859*, f. 256, Lythgoe to Sewall, 19 February 1826.
[33] Claude Guyon was born at Régny (Loire) on 18 July 1795 and joined the *Missionnaires de Lyon*. When Napoleon prohibited the preaching of missions, Guyon exercised an ordinary ministry until 1816, when he entered the *Société des Missionnaires de France*. He entered the Society of Jesus in November 1821 and was thereafter a missioner until his death, while preaching, in 1845. See Sommervogel, vol. 3 (Paris, 1892), pp. 1976–1977.
[34] Ravignan, born at Bayonne on 1 December 1795, abandoned a promising legal career to enter the Society of Jesus in November 1822. He was one of the greatest preachers of his day and died in Paris on 26 February 1858. See Sommervogel, vol. 6 (Brussels, 1895), p. 1499.
[35] ABSI, *Foreign Correspondence, 1776–1859*, f. 256, Lythgoe to Sewall, 19 February 1826.
[36] ARSI, *Anglia 1002*, VI, 8, Lythgoe to Fr Thomas Glover, 6 August 1826; ABSI, *Province Register*, 12/2/6, f. 32.

horrible blasphemies and curses of the gentlemanly rabble of Paris'[37] and found himself instead in the gentlemanly company of a small, select band of seventeen young Jesuits completing their studies. These included the formidable preacher, Père Ravignan, who had so inspired him a few months before; Alexis Canoz, a future missionary vicar apostolic, administrator of the diocese of Bombay and later bishop of Trichinopoly, India; and Christian de Châteaubriand (1791–1843), nephew of the celebrated writer.[38] Though Lythgoe was to remain only five months at Dole, returning to Stonyhurst in February 1827, the august company of his fellow students in France was to provide him both with intellectual stimulation of a high order and enduring, powerful international contacts within the Society of Jesus.[39]

Missionary and Educational Activity, 1827–1847

Randal Lythgoe's first appointment after ordination was as a missioner in Preston, Lancashire, where he was to remain until 1832. During this time he was identified at the Jesuit curia in Rome as a 'high flyer' destined for a significant future role in the work of the English Province.[40] His intellectual powers, combined with his large frame – he was more than six feet tall – and his very considerable physical bulk, marked him out as force to be reckoned with. Perhaps it was his forceful personality that set him at odds with Lord Arundell, who refused to accept his appointment as a missioner on his estates at Wardour in Wiltshire in 1832. Certainly, during his brief posting to the Jesuit mission in Lincoln in 1832, he made a large impact in every sense of the term, with one lay correspondent, Mrs Young of Market Rasen, reporting that Lythgoe walked about 'as if he would convert all the city . . . and he weighs 20 stone'.[41]

On his appointment as vice-rector of the Jesuit community in London in 1833, Lythgoe became increasingly conscious of the growing challenges ahead of him. He was also fully aware of the extent to which the English Province was in a state of transition. The leadership of those who had been Jesuits before the suppression in 1773 was now gradually passing to those of a younger generation who had been members only of the restored Society of Jesus. As his former novice master and provincial superior, the eighty-eight-year-old Marylander Fr Nicholas Sewall, lay dying early in 1834, Lythgoe

---

[37] ARSI, *Anglia 1002*, VI, 8, Lythgoe to Glover, 6 August 1826.
[38] A. Rosette, *La Compagnie de Jésus à Dole après son Rétablissement* (Paris, 1945), p. 48.
[39] ABSI, *Province Register*, 12/2/6, f. 32.
[40] ARSI, *Assistentia Angliae, Prov. Angl. I, 1830–1850*, f. 13, English Assistant to Fr Charles Brooke, 14 June 1831.
[41] ABSI, *Foreign Correspondence, 1776–1859*, f. 315, Fr Edward Scott to Fr Thomas Glover, 11 July 1832.

enquired of Fr Thomas Glover in Rome, 'Is [Father Sewall] not the Dean of the Society? If I am not deceived, he, Fr Stone and Fr Angier are the only surviving members of the Old Society.'[42] Within three years, Fathers Marmaduke Stone and Thomas Angier were both dead and the future of the English Province now lay firmly with members of the restored Society of Jesus, among whom Lythgoe was now a prominent figure.

From his continental European education, during which he had witnessed at first hand the assaults that had been inflicted upon Christianity in the wake of the French Revolution, Randal Lythgoe fully appreciated the need for Catholic education in the widest sense. If the work of the Catholic Church in England and Wales in general, and that of the English Jesuit Province in particular, were to flourish in the future, robust and fearless intellectual leadership would be needed as part of the overall mission. On his appointment to London in 1833, Lythgoe's duties had included responsibility for the small Jesuit day school which had operated in the capital since 1824 and which was then located at Marylebone Park House.[43] Despite many efforts, the number of pupils never exceeded thirty and, with great reluctance, Lythgoe, operating on the instructions of his provincial superior, Fr Richard Norris (1792–1846), was obliged to close the school. It was a bitter blow to one so committed to education.

In December 1838, Lythgoe received Frederick Lucas (1812–1855) into the Church in London and maintained a friendship with him thereafter. When Lucas determined early in 1840 to launch *The Tablet* as a Catholic weekly newspaper, Lythgoe quietly gave his fullest support behind the scenes – and there is even some evidence that the idea of the creation of *The Tablet* was Lythgoe's own.[44] Lythgoe was also committed to the pursuit of historical scholarship relating to the Catholic Church in England and Wales. Just as Lucas was preparing to launch *The Tablet*, Lythgoe was instrumental in acting as an intermediary between the Jesuit provincial superior, Fr John Bird (1783–1853), and the Catholic historian and secular priest, Mark Tierney (1795–1862), who was anxious to re-edit Charles Dodd's monumental *Church History of England* (Liège, 1734–1739).[45]

---

[42] *Ibid.*, f. 319, Lythgoe to Glover, 4 February 1834.
[43] The school at Marylebone Park House was situated on the site now occupied by the Royal Academy of Music.
[44] J. Gillow, *A Literary and Biographical History, or Bibliographical Dictionary of the English Catholics, from the Breach with Rome, 1534, to the Present Time*, 5 vols (London, 1885–1902), vol. 5, p. 338; B.Ward, *The Sequel to Catholic Emancipation 1830–1850*, 2 vols (London, 1915), vol. 2, p. 31; Michael Walsh, *The Tablet 1840–1990. A Commemorative History* (London, 1990), pp. 3–4. Lythgoe's support for *The Tablet* was on-going. When, in 1842, Lucas ran into a legal dispute with his printers and was forced to continue his journal temporarily under the title *The True Tablet* in order to avoid a law suit in Chancery, Lythgoe made an important speech in Preston on 1 November 1842 in favour of Lucas's position. See *The True Tablet*, 5 November 1842.
[45] The volumes were actually published in Wolverhampton. See John Vidmar, 'The Jesuits and

Lythgoe gave Tierney the fullest encouragement in his plans, writing to him warmly:

> You may rest assured that Fr Bird, as well as every member of the Society, is most anxious that you should have every means of information that can be put within your reach, respecting the facts touched upon in Dodd's History and we all of us sincerely hope that the results of your labours may be to secure for you the character of a high minded and honest Historian. It is surely true that all little, petty jealousies should give way to our combined and hearty effort to advance the great cause in which we are all equally interested. The time will come when we shall all wish that we had so laboured.[46]

When the first volumes of Tierney's historical study, based heavily on manuscript sources from Stonyhurst loaned to him by the English Jesuits, appeared in the early 1840s, their hostile anti-Jesuit tone caused consternation in Jesuit circles. Volume IV, dealing with the reign of James I, was deemed to go beyond the bounds of an agreement, made between Tierney and the Jesuits, stipulating that he would not publish anything 'of which the Society should have reason to complain'.[47] It is unclear precisely why Tierney's publishing project was so abruptly abandoned after 1843. Both the Jesuits and the Vicars Apostolic found the re-examination of ancient quarrels between the secular clergy and the Society of Jesus in England and Wales unhelpful and embarrassing, particularly at a time in the early 1840s when contemporary secular-Jesuit relations were highly sensitive. There is some evidence that both parties exerted pressure for the project to be abandoned.[48]

The 'little, petty jealousies' between the secular clergy and the Jesuits formed part of Lythgoe's inheritance on his appointment as Provincial Superior of the English Jesuits on 14 September 1841, a position that he was to hold until 31 December 1847. All the grievances on both sides were well known in Rome and Lythgoe's challenge was now to steer a *via media* through these difficulties.[49] Lythgoe met the challenge by throwing himself with enormous energy into ambitious plans for missionary activity and educational development unparalleled in the English Jesuit Province before or since.

Lythgoe's tireless round of visitations of Jesuit parishes in the English Province did much to foster the widespread revival of the spiritual life of the laity whom the Jesuits were serving. In 1846, in Richmond, North Yorkshire,

---

Mark Tierney (1795–1862)', *Archivum Historicum Societatis Iesu*, vol. 64 (1995), pp. 217–36.

[46] ABSI, Z/1/6, Lythgoe to Mark Tierney, 23 March 1840.
[47] ABSI, SB/1, Lythgoe to Tierney, 18 January 1842, quoted in J. Vidmar, p. 228.
[48] For a fuller analysis of Lythgoe's supposed role in the Tierney affair, see Vidmar.
[49] For a full list of all the problems facing Lythgoe in 1841, see ASR, *Amministrazione camerale del Patrimonio Ex-Gesuitica*, Segnatura 201/6, *Inghilterra*, undated document of c. 1840. A nuncio probably drew up this detailed document, written in Italian, as a memorandum to Propaganda. It carries a brief, later annotation by the Jesuit General, Fr Pieter Beckx.

for example, 102 people were converted to the Catholic faith and 110 were brought back to the practice of their religion. At Stourton, in rural Wiltshire, also in 1846, 48 adults were converted and 70 brought back. In the same year at Wakefield, 29 people were converted and there was standing room only at all the services in the church there, while at Pontefract, 200 children were being educated under the auspices of the Jesuits.[50] These few examples reveal, in microcosm, what was already happening across the length and breadth of the English Province.

This spiritual and educational revival was accompanied by an extensive and far-reaching building programme initiated by Lythgoe immediately before, and vigorously pursued during his period as provincial superior. An analysis of his work in these fields awaits and merits detailed research and, within the bounds of the present essay, no more than the briefest of sketches can be attempted. Lythgoe's initiatives included:

- the construction of a church and presbytery at Tunbridge Wells in 1837;
- the opening of St Francis Xavier's College, Liverpool, in October 1842 as the first day-school to flourish in the restored English Province;[51]
- the opening of Mount St Mary's College, Spinkhill, Derbyshire, in 1842 as a boarding school 'on terms sufficiently economical to meet the wishes of parents having large families or limited incomes';[52]
- the demolition at Stonyhurst in 1843–44 of the utilitarian buildings of Fr Charles Wright, and construction of a new western wing including the Bay Library;
- the construction in 1843 of a new wing and an elegant church at Mount St Mary's;
- the construction of a new Infirmary at Stonyhurst in 1844;
- the laying in 1844 of the foundation stone of the church at Farm Street, London, opened in 1849;
- the opening in 1845 of a college in Malta, at the invitation of the British government;
- the construction of St Francis Xavier's Church, Liverpool, 1845–48, opened in 1848;[53]
- the laying in 1847 of the foundation stone of St Beuno's College, Tremeirchion, North Wales, opened in 1848 as the theologate of the English Jesuit Province;[54]

[50] ARSI, *Anglia 1601, Litterae Annuae 1846–1853*, f. 218.
[51] For a detailed analysis of this, see Maurice Whitehead, 'The Contribution of the Society of Jesus to Secondary Education in Liverpool: The History of the Development of St Francis Xavier's College, *c*. 1840–1902', PhD thesis, University of Hull, 1984; and Maurice Whitehead, 'The English Jesuits and Episcopal Authority: The Liverpool Test Case, 1840–1843', *Recusant History*, vol. 18 (October, 1986), pp. 197–219.
[52] ABSI, MQ/9, *Prospectus* for Mount St Mary's College, undated [c. 1843].
[53] See Nicholas Ryan, *St Francis Xavier's Church Centenary, 1848–1948* (Liverpool, 1948).
[54] On a visitation to the Jesuit mission at Holywell in the mid-1840s, Randal Lythgoe went to

- the construction of new churches at Clitheroe and Yarmouth in 1847;
- the construction of the Talbot Schools at St Walburge's, Preston, in 1847.[55]

In many other places, as Lythgoe was to report to his superiors in Rome, churches were being extended or decorated and poor schools were opened in the late 1840s at Accrington, Clitheroe, Market Rasen, Mount St Mary's, Prescot, Preston, St Beuno's, St Helens and Tunbridge Wells.[56] In Bristol, in 1847, Lythgoe received back from Bishop Ullathorne the old Jesuit mission at Trenchard Street, which had been in secular hands for many years.[57]

In these undertakings, Lythgoe would not consider anything other than the best. The buildings of Fr Charles Wright at Stonyhurst had long offended the eye of Lythgoe who had witnessed their construction during his years as a young student there. If makeshift arrangements had been acceptable at Stonyhurst in the immediate aftermath of the flight from Liège, Lythgoe made it absolutely clear that they were not acceptable in the fully restored English Province of the Society of Jesus. In every instance of construction, whether of churches or colleges, prominent architects were used, such as J.J. Scoles at Liverpool and at Farm Street and Joseph Hansom at Mount St Mary's and St Beuno's, and the best materials were used. Nor was any building undertaken without a large vision. At Liverpool, the building of the magnificent, large church of St Francis Xavier in a sparsely inhabited neighbourhood on the edge of the town raised eyebrows in certain quarters in 1848. Yet Lythgoe anticipated the unprecedented growth of Liverpool in the following thirty years: by 1880, the Liverpool church was serving a population of 10,000 Catholics – the largest parish in the English Jesuit Province.

To serve such an expanded province, Lythgoe needed both additional manpower and money. His dynamism and boundless energy certainly attracted young men to join the Society of Jesus and, in the ten years between 1840 and 1850, the English Province grew numerically from 140 to 180 members.[58] As provincial superior, Lythgoe was constantly on the move, making contacts and building alliances, especially among the large network of lay friends of the Society of Jesus in England and Wales on whom he was dependent for financial assistance.

---

inspect an outlying farm, called Bryngwyn, to which was attached a field, called from time immemorial St Beuno's Field. It had belonged to the Holywell mission for nearly two centuries. Lythgoe was taken by the beauty of the location and declared that he would build there his theologate. See *LLNN*, vol. 20 (1889–1890), pp. 159–160.

[55] *LLNN*, vol. 33 (January, 1915), p. 4.
[56] ARSI, *Anglia 1601, Litterae Annuae 1846–1853*, f. 211.
[57] ABSI, *Province Register*, 12/2/6, f. 32.
[58] ARSI, *Catalogus Provinciae Angliae Societatis Jesu Ineunte Anno MDCCCXLI* (Rome, 1841); and manuscript *Catalogus Provinciae Angliae Societatis Jesu Ineunte Anno MDCCCL*, in the search room at ARSI.

What drove Lythgoe to conduct himself so dynamically? In all his enterprising activity, Lythgoe kept in close and regular contact with the Jesuit General in Rome, the Dutchman Fr Jan Philip Roothaan (1785–1853), who has often been called the 'second founder' of the Jesuits. Elected General in 1829 at the young age of forty-three, Roothaan had a clear vision of the directions in which the Jesuits should develop worldwide, notwithstanding the momentous political events that were taking place in Europe in the 1830s and 1840s. With his international educational background, Lythgoe shared many of the ideals and aspirations of a General superior who, like himself, had received his education and formation as a Jesuit far away from his homeland, in Russia, Switzerland and Italy.[59]

Lythgoe's long letters to Roothaan – thirty-two in number during his period as provincial – attest to the affinity that existed between these two men of action. Many of the letters were written 'on the road' as Lythgoe diligently travelled about attending to the work of the province: fourteen were written from London, seven from Stonyhurst, three from Holywell, and the remainder from Bristol, Dover, Dublin, Ghent, Liverpool, Lulworth, Spinkhill and Wakefield.[60]

Final Years, 1848–1855

After the completion of his term of office as provincial at the beginning of 1848, Lythgoe went to North Wales for eleven months to supervise the arrangements for the completion of the buildings and the opening in that year of the new theologate of the English Province at St Beuno's. This project, involving the transfer of theology students from Stonyhurst to St Beuno's, and the transportation of ten tons of theology books from the library at Stonyhurst, was one close to Lythgoe's heart: twenty-four years had passed since the Jesuit General had suggested to the English provincial, through the young Randal Lythgoe in Rome, that a separate theologate was needed.[61]

All of Lythgoe's reported activity in the English Province over the previous seven years attracted the Jesuit General, Fr Roothaan, to come and see at first hand what was happening, not least at St Beuno's. As revolution swept through Italy in 1848, Roothaan left Rome and established his headquarters

---

[59] For a full account of Roothaan's life and work, see C.J. Ligthart, *The Return of the Jesuits: The Life of Jan Philip Roothaan*, translated from the Dutch by Jan J. Slijkerman (London, 1978).

[60] ARSI, *Anglia 1003*, III, 1–39. The series of letters from Randal Lythgoe to Fr General Roothaan runs from 25 January 1842 until 19 December 1847 and includes seven letters from Jesuits other than Lythgoe, including Fr John Bird (1), Fr James Brownbill (3), Fr John Costa (1) and Fr William Rowe (1).

[61] Gerard, p. 143.

temporarily, until 1850, in Marseilles. During this period he visited almost all the Jesuit houses in France, and, in 1849, a large number in the Netherlands, Belgium, Ireland and Britain. Arriving in England on 6 October 1849, he began a tour of the English Province, beginning in Preston and proceeding to Stonyhurst, Wigan, Liverpool and St Beuno's, where he planted a 'General's Tree', symbolic of the new spiritual and educational life that was taking root in England and Wales. After visiting Ireland, he returned to Liverpool, where on 29 October he held a major meeting of all Jesuits from the neighbouring missions in the very heartland of the English Province. He was anxious to know about and to appreciate the exacting nature of their work more closely. Fr Roothaan's satisfaction with what he found in England and Wales was, in large measure, a reflection and an endorsement of the exceptional labours as provincial of Fr Randal Lythgoe in the period 1841–1847, and his visit gave the English Jesuits new heart to pursue their work further.[62]

No sooner had the theologians settled in their new Welsh environment than Lythgoe was asked to go to Malta to inspect the development there of the college that he had founded four years earlier. After a perilous Mediterranean voyage, Lythgoe arrived safely in Malta, where he was warmly received by the Governor.[63] By the end of the 1840s, six priests, six scholastics and six brothers from the English Jesuit Province were working at the college in Malta.[64]

When Lythgoe arrived back in London in the late summer of 1849, there was uncertainty as to how best to re-channel his energies now that he was no longer provincial superior. After a few months of hesitation, during which time Lythgoe served as a missioner in London, the new provincial, Fr William Cobb (1804–1877) and his consultors, 'after mature deliberation', agreed unanimously to propose to him 'to try Yarmouth'.[65] He was accordingly

---

[62] For an account of Roothaan's visit to England and Wales, see Ligthart, pp. 319–29 and ABSJ, *Epist. Gen. 1750–1853*, ff. 362–4.

[63] Embarking at Marseilles on a three-day voyage to Malta, Lythgoe's ship hit a violent storm that kept the vessel at sea for eight days. After four days provisions began to run out and the ship had to take shelter in a cove off Sardinia. It then ran aground near the island of San Pietro, on the southern side of Sardinia, and all attempts to refloat the ship failed. Undaunted, Lythgoe turned his prayers to Our Lady, Star of the Sea, and threw a miraculous medal that he had in his possession into the sea. Next morning, without any efforts from the crew, the ship floated free and proceeded safely to Malta, where the Governor received Lythgoe cordially. This episode is recounted by Lythgoe in a letter, in his own hand, written in French, and dated 22 January 1849, to the Abbé Le Francour at the *Missions de France* in Marseilles. See ARSI, *Anglia 1009*, 1, 18.

[64] ARSI, *Anglia 1601, Litterae Annuae 1846–1853*, f. 221 and *LLNN*, vol. 32 (October, 1913), pp. 234 *et seq.*

[65] ABSI, *Provincial Consultations, 1832–1882*, entry for 28 January 1851. I am indebted to the Very Reverend David Smolira, SJ, the present provincial superior of the British Province of the Society of Jesus, for allowing me to consult this volume which forms part of the archives of the Jesuit curia in London.

appointed rector of the territorial College of the Holy Apostles, which covered all the Jesuit missions in Lincolnshire and East Anglia, including Market Rasen, Lincoln and Boston as well as Norwich and Bury St Edmunds – and Great Yarmouth, which formed his base.

Lythgoe's national and international experience and expertise was not neglected. When the Jesuit General, Fr Roothaan, in January 1853 gave orders for the twenty-second General Congregation of the Society of Jesus to be convened in Rome the following June, Lythgoe was invited to attend. He was joined by Fr John Etheridge (1811–1882), the new English Jesuit provincial, and Fr William Cobb, who had stepped down as provincial after only two years in post, in representing the English Jesuit Province.[66] The death of Fr Roothaan in May 1853, before the General Congregation began, meant that Randal Lythgoe became an elector of Fr Pieter Beckx as the new General. For one who had given so much new direction to the English Province and who was now near the end of his own life, this unexpected visit to Rome, to provide continuity to the Society of Jesus worldwide, was a fitting *finale*. After the election, suffering from the excessive heat of Rome, Lythgoe was obliged to absent himself from the General Congregation and return to England.

Though weakened by his visit to Rome, there was still life and some of the old spark left in Randal Lythgoe – and he was still ready to contribute to the further development of the English Province in any way that he could. Lythgoe's activity as provincial in expanding the work of the English Jesuits had highlighted the narrowness of the training and formation of scholastics who were destined to spend at least part, and, in some cases most of their lives as Jesuits teaching either at Stonyhurst, Liverpool or Mount St Mary's. Fr Thomas Tracy Clarke (1802–1862), novice master at Hodder, determined to move the novitiate to a more distant locality, just as Lythgoe had done in moving the theologate from Stonyhurst to St Beuno's. Like Lythgoe, he judged it unwise and inappropriate for Stonyhurst boys entering the Society of Jesus to test their vocation in the vicinity of their old school, as he himself had had to do. In 1854, with the approval of the new General in Rome, a start was made in the search for a suitable property. A large building close to St Francis Xavier's Church in Liverpool was viewed by Brother Henry Foley, SJ, in 1854, but was not purchased.[67]

Eventually, a young solicitor, acting on behalf of Fr Clarke, saw a property called Beaumont Lodge at Old Windsor. Learning that the property was

---

[66] J.W. Padberg, M.D. O'Keefe and J.L. McCarthy, *For Matters of Greater Moment: The First Thirty Jesuit General Congregations* (St Louis, 1994), p. 731; ABSI, *Province Register*, 12/2/6, f. 32.

[67] *History of St Stanislaus' College, Beaumont. A Record of Fifty Years. 1861–1911* (Old Windsor, 1911), p. 13. The building inspected by Brother Henry Foley was probably Rupert House, Everton, purchased in March 1854 by Mother Emily Bowles, SHCJ, for her new training college.

suitable, Fr Clarke proceeded from Stonyhurst to Windsor, dressed as a farmer, and, by prior arrangement, was joined there by Randal Lythgoe in similar attire. Lythgoe is alleged to have enquired politely of the vendor if the acquisition of the property would entitle him to a pew in the local parish church.[68] These ploys were resorted to in order to avoid the slightest suspicion, so soon after the anti-Catholic agitation of the early 1850s, that a Jesuit novitiate might soon be set up beneath the very walls of Windsor Castle.

The acquisition of Beaumont Lodge, formerly the home of Warren Hastings, in August 1854, in one sense completed Lythgoe's educational work, which was to be carried on by others after his death. The novitiate was to move again, in 1861, to Bessborough Lodge, Roehampton, where it was to remain for a century, being renamed Manresa House; but the property vacated at Old Windsor was immediately transformed into Beaumont College, another boarding school of the English Province, further extending Lythgoe's pioneering educational work.

Conclusion

The death of Fr Randal Lythgoe at Great Yarmouth on 25 January 1855 brought to an end an important chapter in the development of the English Jesuit Province.[69] Lythgoe's significance lay in the manner in which he lifted the English Jesuits out of a narrow rut. Through force of circumstances in the aftermath of the suppression of the Society of Jesus, and through the extraordinary survival of the English ex-Jesuits of Liège before and after their flight to Stonyhurst in 1794, horizons had grown very limited. Lythgoe had been able to view the universal restoration of the Society of Jesus in 1814, and the delay until 1829 of the recognition of the English Jesuits by the Vicars Apostolic, through the wider perspective of a continental European education. This had provided him with the vision to take his brethren forward, according to the ideals that he shared so closely with Fr Jan Philip Roothaan. For Lythgoe, the restoration of the English Jesuit Province was not simply about achieving permission to exist, but about promoting Ignatian ideals to the full, both in the fields of missionary activity and of education. The 'education and correct conduct' which, from an early age, he believed should be the hallmark of the English Jesuits, was promoted throughout his lifetime, particularly as provincial. This won him respect, even from Henry Edward Manning, and Lythgoe's Jesuit brethren continued to pursue his ideals and ambitious plans long after his death.

---

[68] *History of . . . Beaumont*, p. 13; *LLNN*, vol. 33 (1915–16), p. 374.
[69] A copy of the will of Randal Lythgoe of Great Yarmouth, clerk, dated 18 October 1852, and for which probate was granted on 25 May 1855, can be found in ABSI 27/6/5.

Through circumstances beyond his control, Lythgoe, despite his lifelong commitment to the promotion of education, had failed in 1836 to revive the flagging fortunes of the Jesuits' fledgling school in London. Manning, for his part, throughout his years as archbishop of Westminster, vehemently opposed any suggestion that the Jesuits should re-open a school in the capital. Yet on 18 January 1892, almost thirty-seven years after Lythgoe's death, as Manning's obsequies were taking place in central London, the English Jesuits were quietly continuing to build upon Lythgoe's work. In Wimbledon, just a few miles away in the diocese of Southwark, with the full support of Bishop John Butt, Fr James Nicholson, SJ, was busy welcoming the first students at the Jesuits' new London day-school, Wimbledon College, opened that very day.[70] The irony of the timing of that particular initiative was one that would have appealed to Fr Randal Lythgoe.

Acknowledgements

Research for this papper was made possible thanks to a major grant from the Spencer Foundation in Chicago. For archival assistance in the preparation of this chapter, I am indebted to Fr Thomas M. McCoog, SJ, and Brother James Hodkinson, SJ, in London; the late Fr Frederick Turner, SJ, at Stonyhurst; Frs Joseph De Cock, SJ, and José Antonio Yoldi, SJ, in Rome; and to staff at the *Archivio di Stato* in Rome. I wish to thank Fathers Kevin Fox, SJ and Geoffrey Holt, SJ, and my colleague Professor Gareth Elwyn Jones, for their helpful comments on a draft version of this chapter.

Abbreviations

ABSI	Archivum Britannicum Societatis Iesu, 114 Mount Street, London
ARSI	Archivum Romanum Societatis Iesu, Borgo Santo Spirito, Rome
ASR	Archivio di Stato di Roma, Corso del Rinascimento, Rome
LLNN	*Letters and Notices* – the private journal of the British Province of the Society of Jesus, 1862–
SA	Stonyhurst Archives, Stonyhurst College, Lancashire.

---

[70] A. Poole, *A History of Wimbledon College* (London, 1992), p. 15. Fr James Nicholson had himself been educated at the college founded in Liverpool by Randal Lythgoe fifty years earlier. In 1894, Nicholson founded a second Jesuit day-school in London, St Ignatius's College, Stamford Hill.

6

THE ENGLISH BENEDICTINES AND THE BRITISH EMPIRE

DOM AIDAN BELLENGER, OSB

THE taking of Jerusalem by the British Army in December 1917 was one of the most resonant moments in imperial history. As Armageddon was being played out, the Holy City itself came under British rule. The British Minister to the Holy See reported back to the Foreign Office in London:

> The news of the taking of Jerusalem at the end of 1917 was received with expressions of considerable satisfaction at the Vatican; a solemn *Te Deum* was sung in the Church of Santa Croce in Gerusalemme. To indignant criticism from the other side that this was little in accord with the Papal policy of political neutrality, reply was made in that in such a matter as the recovery of the Holy Places from the domination of the infidel the Holy See could not fail to take sides.[1]

On the Feast of the Assumption, 15 August 1918, as a result of the British occupation a great Catholic pilgrimage was organised for British soldiers in Jerusalem. It was a day of extraordinary events in which Imperial pride and Catholic piety walked hand in hand, as much 'Land of Hope and Glory' as 'Faith of Our Fathers'. The celebration, supervised by the Catholic chaplains and the military authorities, included a sermon by the Benedictine, Dom Bede Camm (1864–1942), well known as a writer on the English martyrs and their shrines, whose *Pilgrim Paths in Latin Lands* includes a detailed recollection of the day:

> It was always one of the dreams of my life (as it is, I suppose, of most men) to see Jerusalem. But I never expected to see it as I did Jerusalem delivered, delivered from the age-long tyranny of the Turk, with the Union Jack flying over her towers, streets thronged with British soldiers, the 'Vision of Peace' begirt indeed

---

[1] T.E. Hachey (ed.), *Anglo-Vatican Relations 1914–1936: Confidential Annual Reports of the British Ministers to the Holy See* (Boston, 1972), p. 20.

by the tramp and panoply of war, and yet the visible promise of the peace that was about to dawn upon a distracted and blood-stained world. I saw sights at Jerusalem that had never been seen since the days of the Crusaders, saw the victors prostrating themselves, as their forefathers had done centuries ago, before the Tomb of Christ, long processions of Catholic soldiers making the Stations of the Cross along the Via Dolorosa, British Tommies on guard at the doors of the Holy Sepulchre, and in the very cave where Christ was born for us at Bethlehem.

I heard that vaults of the old Crusading church of St Anne echo to the familiar strains of English hymns, the well known bugle calls of our Army ring out from the Mount of Olives, mingling with the hoots of the lorries which in almost ceaseless stream carried supplies and ammunition to our troops in the Jordan Valley, or on the Nablus front . . . it was at such a time as this that the British military authorities in Palestine permitted, nay, deliberately encouraged, a great pilgrimage of Catholic soldiers to Jerusalem for the Feast of Our Lady's Assumption.[2]

The First World War probably marked the high point of British (and specifically English) Catholic national patriotism, and in this movement the Benedictines played a significant role. In the nineteenth century, the Benedictines became a part of the imperial fabric and contributed to the propagation of an English-style Catholicism to the empire's furthest parts. It was, in some ways, a surprising process. Seventeenth- and eighteenth-century monks had been hostile to the Hanoverian establishment, favouring the Stuart counter-court and excluded by law from participation in English political society.[3] Incipient anti-Catholicism remained a feature of English life and monks were perceived as figures of fear as much of affection, but somehow the Benedictines managed to remain patriotic Englishmen; Westminster Abbey had, after all, once been home to a black monk community. Yet the return to Englishness did not come all at once. Like the British Empire itself the English Benedictines reinvented themselves in the reign of Victoria. The English Benedictines in the nineteenth and twentieth centuries refocused their spheres of influence and their allegiances. Before the French Revolution their headquarters had been in continental Europe (and mainly in France), with their English centres being chiefly small one-man missions. By the end of the nineteenth century they were well settled on English soil, with established schools and populous parishes and confident enough to celebrate their nationalism. They had become part of Victorian England and its Empire:

> Those who heard the hearty cheers that welcomed her from all sides on Jubilee Day will be able to realise how grateful her subjects are for the many benefits they have received during her long and glorious reign. In Victoria's reign the

---

[2] B. Camm, *Pilgrim Paths in Latin Lands* (London, 1923), p. 254.
[3] See D. Lunn, *The English Benedictines 1540–1688* (London, 1980), and G. Scott, *Gothic Rage Undone: English Monks in the Age of Enlightenment* (Bath, 1992).

growth of the Colonies in numbers and importance had been enormous . . . During the reign there has been a great and general improvement in Art and Literature. Education has been brought to the door of the poorest and strenuous efforts are being made to make life happier and brighter for them. There is indeed no one in Her Majesty's mighty Empire – upon which the sun never sets – who, honestly thinking over those sixty years of reign, does not feel his heart glow with thankful admiration.[4]

The rapprochement between the Benedictines and the Empire was partly the consequence of the relatively warm reception given to the monks on their return to England following the forced closure and repatriation of their monasteries. The monks themselves helped to ease the transition. Many of the Benedictines who came to prominence in the great years of empire came from the merchant class who were to be among the chief beneficiaries of empire. Many, too, were Lancastrians associated with Liverpool and its sea port, the second port of empire. The monks were to take part in the heroic mission to the victims of plague in the city which was to make several of them 'martyrs' of charity.[5] Benedictine monks of the early nineteenth century were far from precious or faint-hearted; their gritty, mission-based monasticism responded clearly to the needs of the time and attuned the English Benedictines perfectly to the imperial ideal; adventure and enterprise entered the monastic vocabulary and the empire beckoned; the *peregrinatio* to the open seas had been more a Celtic than an English monastic characteristic, but for the Victorian Benedictine the world did not seem big enough.

In the period from the revival of the English Benedictines in the early seventeenth century until the French Revolution the missionary activity of the monks had been confined to England and Wales. There were some significant connections with Maryland in the American colonies, but they were personal rather than institutional. John Bede Tatham, alias Gray, was born in Yorkshire about 1640 and entered the monastery of St Gregory's, Douai, where he made his profession in 1657. He abandoned the community, married and emigrated (in 1685) to the New World where he pursued a successful career in trade and built a palatial house (since demolished) at Burlington, West New Jersey. He was a justice and a councillor and may even have been considered as governor of New Jersey in 1690. On his death, in 1700, his property included a library of some five hundred books (with many Benedictine items), religious relics and a collection of mathematical instruments.[6] Richard Paul Chandler, a native of Maryland (a colony which had close associations with the English Jesuits), was educated at St Gregory's, Douai, where he made his monastic profession in 1705 and was ordained in 1710. He died young at Douai in 1712; he was

---

[4] *The Raven* (Downside School Magazine), 22 October 1897, p. 85.
[5] See A. Hood, 'Fever in Liverpool', *E.B.C. History Symposium*, vol. 11 (1992), pp. 2–21.
[6] See H.H. Bisbee, 'John Tatham, Alias Gray', *The Pennsylvanian Magazine of History and Biography* (1959), pp. 253–64.

probably the first American Benedictine monk;[7] at least three women from Maryland entered English Benedictine convents.[8] The crucial personal connection between the English Benedictines and the first British Empire (albeit after American Independence) was provided by Bishop Charles Walmesley (1722–97), Vicar Apostolic of the Western District, who, on 15 August 1790 consecrated John Carroll (1735–1815) at Lulworth Castle Chapel in Dorset as the first bishop of Baltimore and as the father of the North American Catholic hierarchy. Walmesley's role in the making of the American church is commemorated in his handsome twentieth-century tomb at Downside Abbey, which was paid for by the American bishops.[9]

A closer, institutional link became possible in the 1790s, when the monks made homeless by the French Revolution were offered a substantial property in the United States by Carroll, who regarded the monks, 'the Apostles of England, Germany and many other countries', as the potential apostles of America.[10] This was not to be, but the estate on offer, near Pittsburgh in Pennsylvania, was settled in 1846 by German Benedictine monks from Metten, to become St Vincent's Abbey, Latrobe, one of America's greatest monasteries.[11] The three American monasteries of the English Benedictines now existing (2005) at Portsmouth, Rhode Island, Washington and St Louis were much more recent foundations: Portsmouth, 1919; Washington, 1924; St Louis, 1955 – as was the mission in Peru.[12]

In the heroic nineteenth century period it was the southern hemisphere which was to be the principal arena of overseas English Benedictine missionary activity. Mauritius was to be the first area of opportunity, and it proved to be the most sustained Benedictine missionary territory; English monk-bishops presided over the Mauritian church for almost a century (1819–1916).[13] Mauritius, or the Ile de France as it was then called, had been a

---

[7] H.N. Birt, *Obit Book of the English Benedictines from 1600 to 1912* (Edinburgh, 1913), p. 73.

[8] D.A. Bellenger, 'Early North American Connections of the English Benedictine Congregation', *E.B.C. History Symposium*, vol. 11 (1992), p. 24.

[9] *Ibid.*; 'An Anglo-American memorial: Bishop Walmesley's Tomb at Downside', *South Western Catholic History*, vol. 8 (1990), pp. 40–46.

[10] John Carroll to Michael Benedict Pembridge, 19 September 1794, Downside Abbey Archives, Birt Papers B66.

[11] P. Guilday, *The Life and Times of John Carroll* (New York, 1922), pp. 369–71.

[12] See R. Wilson, 'The Worth Mission to the Apurimac Valley, Peru 1969–1975', and J. Hodkinson, 'Belmont in Peru', *E.B.C. History Symposium*, vol. 11 (1992), pp. 63–77 and pp. 78–81 respectively.

[13] The Jesuit, Leo Meurin, was Bishop of Port Louis between 1887 and 1895. All other bishops in those years were English monks. A useful survey of the Benedictine contribution to the Mauritian Church is provided by A. Nagapan, *L'Eglise à Maurice 1810–1841* (Port Louis, 1984), which is well documented and illustrated. English summaries of part of this work are found in A. Nagapan, 'A Century of English Benedictine Apostolate in Mauritius 1819–1916', *E.B.C. History Symposium*, vol. 16 (1998), pp. 91–131. See also J. Mamet, *Le Diocèse de Port Louis* (Port Louis, 1974).

French colony from 1715 to 1810, and its population (which included many slaves) was predominantly Catholic. On 3 December 1810 the island capitulated to the British and reverted to its original Dutch name, Mauritius; it remained under British control until 1968. The British authorities were concerned that French-born priests should not be allowed to serve in Mauritius and, prepared to tolerate the Catholic religion as that of the majority of the population in this distant colony, looked for English-speaking priests. As David Cannadine has argued in his *Ornamentalism* (Harmondsworth, 2001), the Empire always tried to make colonies seem like home, and took abroad their preoccupations with class and status.

British imperial policy was helped by church developments. The creation of a vicariate apostolic for much of the Southern Hemisphere by the Holy See led in 1818 to the appointment of the Benedictine Edward Bede Slater (1774–1832) as Vicar Apostolic of Mauritius and to his consecration as bishop of Ruspa. Born in Liverpool, a student at Lamspring, and later a monk of St Laurence's (not yet at Ampleforth), his elevation seems more related to his physical presence at Rome in 1817–18 rather than to any innate missionary skills. He died at sea on his way home from the colony. His successor was William Placid Morris (1794–1872), a Londoner and a Downside monk, who was working as a priest in London when called to Mauritius. He was consecrated Bishop of Troy, an exotic *in partibus* titular, on 5 February 1832. Like Slater he was not a success, and had severe problems in his administration especially concerning financial management. Both Slater and Morris were appointed with little or no consultation with the English Benedictine President. In common with the other providers of clergy for the Catholic Church in England at the time, the Benedictines had a manpower shortage which appeared to many as a sign of terminal decline.

The Holy See under Pope Pius VII (1800–23) and Gregory XVI (1831–46), despite the onslaught of rationalism and the devastation inflicted on the Church by the French Revolution, was experiencing a great revival of interest in missions. Gregory XVI was a monk himself and undertook a reorganisation of *Propaganda Fide* to make its work more effective. Gregory XVI was a man of action and had a very high view of the papal office, prefiguring many of the ideas of his more famous successor, Pius IX (1846–78). He was hostile to the Portuguese practice of *padroado* (crown control of the church) and his appointment of vicars apostolic (directly answerable to Rome), including that of Mauritius, was in part an attempt to reassert papal power; Gregory XVI created more than seventy new dioceses and vicariates and appointed 195 missionary bishops. 'More and more extra-European churches owed their organisation and leadership to the papacy rather than to a colonial power.'[14] The first English Benedictines were personal appointments by the pope, not part of a well thought out Benedictine missionary campaign.

[14] E. Duffy, *Saints and Sinners: A History of the Popes* (London, 1997), p. 221.

As far as Mauritius was concerned the crucial episcopate was that of William Bernard Collier (1803–90), a native of Yorkshire and a monk of St Edmund's, Douai, working in Rome as Benedictine procurator from 1833–40. All the later Benedictine bishops of Mauritius were monks of Douai, the only one of the English communities which remained on French soil and presumably giving its monks at least some French. Collier was in Mauritius from 1841–63, first as vicar apostolic (and bishop of Milevis) and from 1847 as Bishop of Port Louis. He retired to England in 1863 and ended his life in Coventry. He was responsible not only for organising his diocese but also for a programme of evangelisation. This latter process included the encouragement of new missionaries to Mauritius, especially the recently founded Holy Ghost Congregation. He trawled France, Ireland and the United States as well as England for potential candidates; he did not consider fostering native vocations, perhaps sharing 'the general feeling of the superiority of western men, and believing that the future of the Church would be safer if it was kept in their own hands'.[15] Inculturation, so strong a feature of the Jesuit missions of the Counter Reformation, had given way to triumphant Eurocentricism. Collier regarded the work of religious sisters (native as well as European) as essential for the growth of the Church. He organised, with the aid of Jacques Laval (1803–64), now a *beatus*, and a team of Holy Ghost Fathers, the evangelisation of emancipated black slaves; some 66,000 people were said to have been baptised. Catholic clergy were paid from the public treasury but were regarded, in a British colony where 'Establishment' was taken for granted as, in effect, second-class citizens. Collier was succeeded by successive pairs of Benedictine bishops, first, Michael Adrian Hankinson (1863–70) and William Benedict Scarisbrick (1871–87) and, later, Peter Augustine O'Neill (1896–1909) and James Romanus Bilsborrow (1910–16).

Hankinson, born in Warrington, Lancashire, in 1817, was a monk of Broadway, Worcestershire (the short-lived successor to Lamspring) before joining Douai, where he was prior from 1854–63. He died in 1870. Scarisbrick, from Liverpool, had served on many home missions and retired from Port Louis in 1888 to become titular Archbishop of Cyzicus. He died at Malvern, a great imperial retirement place, and is buried at St Wulstan's, Little Malvern, not far from Sir Edward Elgar. Hankinson and Scarisbrick consolidated Collier's work in education and the creation of parishes, but Scarisbrick came into conflict with the first Catholic governor of Mauritius, Sir John Pope-Hennessy (1834–91), who had already served as governor of Barbados, Hong Kong and the Gold Coast; in the last place his reforms led to an annual 'Pope-Hennessy's Day'. Pope-Hennessy was a sympathetic supporter of persecuted groups and took the side of the Mauritian creoles against the English ascendancy. Pope-Hennessy, who coined the phrase 'Mauritius for

---

[15] S. Neill, *Christian Missions* (London, 1964), p. 404.

the Mauritians' (echoing Polding's 1868 Australian statement) was seen by Scarisbrick as insufficiently patriotic; perhaps he was too Irish for the stolid English Scarisbrick, whose racial views would provide grist for Edward Said's mill in his study of *Orientalism* (Harmondsworth, 1979), which has been so influential in its opening up of the study of empire. Mauritius was in turmoil and an enquiry into Pope-Hennessy's governorship, ordered by the British Government and recounted in his entry in *The Dictionary of National Biography*, although it exonerated him of maladministration, considered him guilty of 'want of temper and judgement', 'of vexatious and unjustifiable interference' with magistrates and of an unbecoming partisanship. Pope-Hennessy dedicated his later years to Irish politics. Scarisbrick, as stubborn as Pope-Hennessy in his own way, brought the Benedictine episcopate to a temporary halt, and Archbishop Meurin's perceived success led many to petition for either a Holy Ghost or a Jesuit prelate as his successor rather than a monk.

O'Neill was a return to Benedictine control, perhaps because the Benedictines were seen by the British Colonial Office as 'safer' in patriotic terms than members of a more international order. O'Neill was another Liverpudlian, and after studies at Douai and Belmont (the English Benedictines' house of studies in Herefordshire), where he became professor of philosophy and held various offices until 1888, he was elected President General of the English Benedictine Congregation from 1888 to 1896. O'Neill's episcopate, like many of his predecessors', was beset with controversy and debt, although he loved his adopted land; two years after his resignation as bishop he returned to Mauritius in retirement and died there in 1911. O'Neill himself, fully aware of the emerging monastic priorities of his religious congregation (as a monk he was often seen as a leader of the 'mission' party) suggested a bishop chosen from a missionary congregation, but the last of the Benedictine bishops, Romanus Bilsborrow (1862–1931) was duly appointed. He was later transferred to Wales where he was to become first Archbishop of Cardiff in 1916. Bilsborrow retired to Mauritius, where he died. In Wales, the difficulty of combining episcopal authority, monastic life and Benedictine missionary activity was played out as actively as in Australia, particularly in the long episcopate of Bishop Thomas Joseph Brown (1798–1880), a Downside near-contemporary of Polding and Ullathorne.[16] One leading English monk of the time, Paul Wilfrid Raynal (1830–1904), was born at Port Louis and was prior of Belmont from 1873–1901, responsible for the formation of the junior monks.

More significant perhaps than the work in Mauritius was the Australian mission. This began as an extension of the endeavour in Mauritius, but soon took on a life of its own. Australia, with its population made up largely at first

---

[16] See A. Hood, 'Bishop Thomas Joseph Brown O.S.B. (1798–1880) and the Dispute between the Hierarchy and the English Benedictines', *Recusant History*, vol. 25 (2000), pp. 304–24.

of convicts, was not at first sight the most attractive place to work as a priest, but it provided opportunities for heroism and adventure not lost on the monks. John Augustine Birdsall (1775–1837), President-General from 1826 to 1837, was the great encourager of the Australian mission and had the vision to see it as the start of a great empire-wide expansion of Catholicism, using the imperial trade routes to bring the Catholic faith to the four corners of the world, with 'our island' as 'a sort of Head Quarters from which the Church would be able to exercise its authority and dispense its blessings to all around us'.[17] The high hopes of the enterprise are captured by William Bernard Ullathorne (1806–89), in his ebullient autobiography.[18] He was sent in 1832, still only twenty-six, as Vicar General of Bishop Morris in Australia, in whose history he was to play a crucial role in giving telling evidence to the Molesworth Commission (1837) which was central in the abolition of transportation.[19] The key figure in the Australian mission was, however, not Ullathorne but Bede Polding.

John Bede Polding (1794–1877) was born in Liverpool and was a cousin of Bishop Slater and of Dom Paulinus Heptonstall (1798–1869), who acted as English agent for Polding in his Australian years. Polding, for many years a key figure in the Downside community (serving as novice master from 1819 to 1834), was a great enthusiast for the overseas missions and, having refused an appointment as Vicar Apostolic of Madras, he was in 1834 made Vicar Apostolic of New Holland and consecrated Bishop of Hiero-Caesarea. In 1842 he became the first Archbishop of Sydney and as such the first Catholic metropolitan in the Empire. His organisation of a new church and hierarchy was taken as a model for the restored English hierarchy in 1850. He was a great missionary whose personality formed a new church. He identified himself strongly with his new country. In 1868 he used the phrase 'Australia for the Australians' as a peacemaker at a time of much sectarian bitterness. In a Lenten pastoral letter in 1856 he had written 'Before all else we are Catholics; and next, by a name swallowing up all distinctions of origin, we are Australians'. He ordained the first Australian-born priest and saw the need for Australian bishops long before the first was consecrated in 1898.[20]

---

[17] J.A. Birdsall to N. Wiseman, 15 August 1829, Archives of the Venerable English College, Rome, Ben VIII, 1.

[18] The most recent edition of Ullathorne's autobiography, edited by L. Madigan under the title *The Devil is a Jackass*, was published at Bath in 1995.

[19] For an overview of Ullathorne see D.A. Bellenger, ' "The Normal State of the Church": William Bernard Ullathorne, First Bishop of Birmingham', *Recusant History*, vol. 25 (2000), pp. 325–34.

[20] Polding has attracted much attention from scholars. He is the central figure in H.N. Birt, *Benedictine Pioneers in Australia*, 2 vols (London, 1911), and the subject of F. O'Donoghue's biography, *The Bishop of Botany Bay* (London, 1982). A three-volume collection of his letters, a great resource for the early history of Australia, has been published by the Good Samaritan Sisters (a religious congregation he founded), *Letters of John Bede Polding OSB*

Polding dreamed of an abiding Benedictine mission in Australia but this was not to be, despite two of his fellow monks, Charles Henry Davis (1815–54) and Roger Bede Vaughan (1834–83) coming in turn as his coadjutors. Davis died young and Vaughan, who became coadjutor archbishop in 1873, only survived six years as metropolitan, although these were crucial years in the growth of the church. The Australian church passed into Irish hands and the English Benedictines themselves began to emphasise their monastic rather than missionary inheritance. Polding's ideal of an abbey-diocese, the most complete expression of the Benedictine commitment to pioneer overseas missions, evaporated, and Vaughan, who lacked Polding's charisma but had greater administrative gifts, brought the dream to an end. St Mary's Cathedral, still the dominant ecclesiastical building on the Sydney skyline, its Gothic lines in contrast to much of the modern city, is an exuberant expression of Polding's dream, completed as late as 1928. The most lasting memorial to Polding is the Australian Catholic Church itself, but the community of Benedictine nuns founded in 1849 still flourishes at Jamberoo, seventy miles south of Sydney, and the parallel missionary work of the Spanish Benedictine Bishop Rudesindo Salvado (1814–1900) continues at New Norcia in the north of the continent.[21]

The perceived conflict between the life of the missionary and the monk, encouraged by the Holy See's patronage of revived monasticism, came to dominate the debates of the English Benedictine Congregation in the years leading up to the promulgation of new, more monastic constitutions in 1899, but among the first generation of reformed Benedictine monks of the Subiacan congregation there appeared to be no such contradiction. The monastery at Ramsgate in Kent, inaugurated in 1865, owed its inspiration to the Italian Abbot Pietro Francesco Casaretto (1810–78), the Subiacan reformer, who was both an admirer of the work of Polding and in 1846 the founder of a Benedictine missionary college in Genoa. This college hoped to provide English-speaking priests for the Australian mission. Ramsgate, a monastery always dedicated to 'the primitive observance' of the Benedictine Rule had, too, a

---

(Sydney, 1994, 1996 and 1998), which throws light on both his continuing contacts with the English Benedictines and the gathering opposition to Benedictine episcopacy. *The Eye of Faith* (Kilmore, 1978), gathers his pastoral letters. A two-volume collection of *Documents and Resource Material Relating to the Episcopacy of Archbishop John Bede Polding OSB*, entitled *Adjutor Deus*, containing more than six hundred pages of text, and edited by Srs M.X. Compton, P.D. McKinley and D. Dyson of the Good Samaritan Sisters (Sydney, 2000), provides a comprehensive guide to Polding's remarkable period of office.

[21] The Spanish character of the mission settled by Salvado comes out in R. Rios, *Las Missiones Australianas de las Benedictinos Espanoles* (Barbastro, 1930). A personal memoir, more ordered than Ullathorne's, is provided by R. Salvado, *Memorie Storiche dell' Australia particolarmente della Missione Benedittina di Nuova Norcia* (Rome, 1851). A. Linage, *Rosendo Salvado or The Odyssey of a Galician in Australia* (Galicia, 1999) provides a good introduction.

missionary dimension which went far beyond its hinterland in the Isle of Thanet. In 1877, for example, of the twenty-five priests in the community four were working in the vicariate apostolic of Eastern Bengal, two were in Australia and two in Ireland. It was in New Zealand, and particularly in the diocese of Auckland, however, that Ramsgate made its special mark. Dom Edmund Luck (1840–96), a Ramsgate monk, became Bishop of Auckland, and like Polding's mission to the aborigines in Australia, was remembered as apostle of the Maoris. Like Polding, too, he saw his dream of an abbey-diocese disappearing, and in 1888 the General Chapter of the Subiaco Congregation refused to sanction the continuance of Auckland as a Benedictine mission. This reflected the tensions within Casaretto's reform. Casaretto was Abbot-President of the Cassinese Congregation from 1852 to 1858, but his supporters, increasingly dedicated to the primitive observance, became separated from the Cassinese and formed the distinct Subiaco Congregation in 1872.[22]

Monastic formation, with its period of probation (the novitiate), its structured day and its hierarchical organisation with a lifetime dedication to an ideal was, in its inspiration, an attempt to flee the world and to create a perfect society in miniature. Yet, with its elevated sense of duty, purpose and service, monasticism could be an effective paradigm for an infant missionary church and, slightly adapted, the model for an educational system which could train neophytes for a secular destiny. A threefold apostolate stemming from the Benedictine ideal, personal sanctification through community life under a rule and an abbot, mission to the waste places, and education beyond the cloister, were all to play a crucial part in the Victorian Benedictine experience.

The reform of the monastic order in the last quarter of the nineteenth century, a reform with more the character of a rediscovery of lost ideals, led to many questions about the future of missionary work, especially foreign missionaries, but it encouraged the growth of the lay schools attached to the English Benedictine monasteries, which were to make their own special contribution to the Benedictine imperial theme by becoming part of the public school provision which acted as a nursery for the colonies and for the armed forces. Ampleforth and Downside both had schools attached to their monasteries from their re-foundation in England. Douai, in France, had its Benedictine school re-founded in the 1820s. The three schools, especially the two English ones, changed out of all recognition in the period leading up to the First World War. The utilitarian converted 'manor houses' acquired in the early 1800s were supplemented by new buildings. What had been small domestic and ecclesiastical seminaries became schools of national importance. The great school block opened in 1861 at Ampleforth was on the model

---

[22] D. Parry, *Monastic Century: St Augustine's Abbey, Ramsgate, 1865–1965* (Tenbury Wells, 1965).

and scale of a major English public school. It was perhaps ironic that many of these schools had based their buildings on medieval monastic antecedents. The even more ambitious plans for the rebuilding of Downside to the designs of Leonard Stokes (only partly completed) reflected a growing self-confidence in the new-found freedom of living in England. The schools (or colleges as they were invariably described in the Victorian period) were moving away from their continental roots and acquiring an English identity which preserved their Catholicism as their chief defining characteristic. Integration was more characteristic than segregation and this was reflected both in the life and culture of the schools and in their curriculum.

Bishop Cuthbert Hedley (1837–1915) argued in 1877 that the Benedictine schools offered a very good education for the upper classes. The traditional 'old' English Catholics were hesitating about their educational needs as they moved away from ecclesiastical colleges, and Hedley agreed that the monks would fill the gap. The Benedictines hoped 'to initiate, develop and polish all the faculties – physical, intellectual, moral and religious and to give a boy's whole nature its completeness and perfection, so that he may be what he ought to be and do what he should as, to form him as a man, and to prepare him to do his duty in life to those about him, to his country, to himself, and so, by perfecting his present life, to prepare him for the life to come . . .' (The chant of the monks) 'resounding at all hours with the Divine praise, and slow and solemn vesper', and 'the festivals of dim and far-off saints who lived simple lives and ruled men in their day' were 'fitted to attract young hearts'.[23]

Dom Cuthbert Almond, in his history of Ampleforth (1903), commented on the 'family likeness' of the Catholic schools with continental origins: places like Ampleforth and Downside and also the Jesuit college at Stonyhurst and, on their resettlement in England, the secular colleges at Old Hall in Hertfordshire and Ushaw in County Durham. Their customs and structures owed more to continental models than to the English equivalents. Even games were characteristically unusual. Thus a form of hand-ball existed in all the colleges and led to the construction of great walls. Catholic cricket as played in the schools was singular, an old-fashioned 'swiping' cricket with no overs and unlimited sides.[24] Over the second half of the nineteenth century, the old identity was swept away. Inter-school games competitions ironed out singularities of rules. Public examination and the gradual assimilation into the English university system began with colleges becoming centres of external study for degrees of the University of London and culminated, in the late 1890s, with the foundation

---

[23] *Bishop Hedley's Address on School-Work, Delivered at Ampleforth College on the reopening of Studies*, 28 August 1877, Ampleforth Abbey Archives, quoted by V.A. McClelland, 'School or Cloister? An English educational Dilemma 1794–1880', *E.B.C. History Symposium*, vol. 15 (1997), pp. 1–30 and pp. 19–20. Hedley was Bishop of Newport and Menevia from 1881 until his death.

[24] L. Almond, *History of Ampleforth College* (London, 1903), p. 350.

of Benedictine houses of study at both Oxford and Cambridge. In 1895 Catholic students were allowed at Oxford and Cambridge by the Catholic authorities on condition that there would be Catholic lectures. Bishop Hedley became the first chairman of the Oxford and Cambridge Education Board.[25] The first of the convert clergymen began to enter the Congregation around 1900 and brought with them, too, their own brand of Englishness. An exaggerated Englishness (including a model parliament) was fostered by Mgr Lord Petre (1847–93), an educational reformer who was deeply influential in the Downside of the 1870s. Petre considered the Benedictines as more English than the Jesuits and argued against the 'unbending discipline, excessive surveillance, (and) the denial of all leisure' characteristic of the Society of Jesus, arguing that such attributes gave rise to 'contracted mental power or a coarseness of character fitted for the reclamation of land in Australia or New Zealand [rather] than for competition with the cultivations, refinement, knowledge and mental grasp, the *scholarship* of which our Protestant fellow-subjects offer so many bright examples'. He made a contrast between the life of 'individuality and freedom characteristic of an English Protestant Public School with the 'over-strict and prison-like discipline' of certain Catholic colleges.[26]

Such arguments led to the integration of the Benedictine colleges in the wider educational world. Dom Leander Ramsay (1863–1929), head master of Downside from 1902, consciously remodelled his school on the English ideal inspired, it is said, chiefly by Wellington College. At Ampleforth, more successfully than any of the other Catholic schools, a house system on the English Public School model replaced a line (or year group) structure on the Jesuit scheme. The head masters of Downside and Ampleforth were invited to join the Headmasters' Conference in 1913 and 1917 respectively; the head master of Douai (back in England from 1903) in 1920.[27]

Herbert Vaughan (1832–1903), the future Cardinal Archbishop of Westminster and founder of the Mill Hill Missionaries, England's largest Catholic foreign missions society, spent a year at Downside (1850–1) as a parlour boarder. His brother Roger (Bede) later joined the community and became Archbishop of Sydney, but Herbert Vaughan himself was warned off. Thinking of becoming a monk, Dom Placid Hall (1819–90) cautioned him, 'Young man, you will want more elbow room than you would find here.'[28] The generation after Polding had different, more school-centred priorities.

---

[25] See H. Wansbrough and A. Marett-Crosby, *Benedictines of Oxford* (London, 1990), and *E.B.C. History Symposium*, vol. 15 (1997) dedicated to Benedictine educational history.

[26] W.J. Petre, *Remarks on the Present Condition of Catholic Liberal Education* (London, 1877), and *The Problem of Catholic Liberal Education* (London, 1877), quoted by V.A. McClelland, 'School or Cloister?', pp. 18–19.

[27] For the English Benedictines in the twentieth century see D. Rees, 'The Monastic Mission in the Twentieth Century', in D. Rees (ed.), *Monks of England* (London, 1997), pp. 235–50.

[28] R. O'Neil, *Cardinal Herbert Vaughan* (London, 1995), p. 46.

The change of mentality was reflected significantly in the transformation of the musical and choral tradition at Downside under the influence of Richard Terry (1865–1933), Downside's music master in the 1890s. Downside's choral musical repertoire, from its settlement in 1814, had consisted of the great continental masterpieces performed alongside contemporary Catholic composers. Terry, who had been a choral scholar at King's College, Cambridge, introduced the works of the English Tudor polyphonic school of forgotten masters like Byrd and Tallis not only into the Downside choral orbit but also into the wider world of music. He became the first Master of Music at Westminster Cathedral, was knighted, and began a tradition which was to create a uniquely national Catholic 'sound'.[29] Edward Elgar, the most imperial of composers, was born a Catholic and for some time attended the Catholic Church served by the English Benedictines of Little Malvern in Worcestershire and was a frequent visitor to Stanbrook Abbey.[30]

Patriotism, complicated by Irish nationalism and the Catholicism of many of Britain's rivals (and sworn enemies), was becoming an accepted public stance for the Catholic community.[31] Among the Benedictines this was also seen in the formation of cadet corps in the schools and work as chaplains to the forces.[32] In 1837 Polding, as missioner to the people of the village of Stratton-on-the-Fosse, had arranged a coronation procession of his village schoolchildren, one of the earliest post-Reformation Catholic parades.[33] A number of monks had served in the Boer War, but it was in the First World War that their profile became very high indeed; there were some fifty Benedictine chaplains as compared to nearly eighty Jesuits. The chaplains brought their Benedictine spirituality to the soldier on the front.

> The work of a chaplain is extraordinarily fascinating and you really feel that you are doing the good God's work here among these poor fellows who today are in robust health, and tomorrow are twisted and contorted in agonies or just asleep in death . . . One just rushes here and rushes there, trying to get at them whenever one can find them. Tommy is always ready to make his confession and appreciates work done for him. Even those with no religion stand by in solemn silence awed by the gravity of the priest's work.[34]

Dom Stephen Rawlinson (1865–1953), became the senior chaplain on the

---

[29] See D.A. Bellenger, 'Sir Richard Terry and Downside', *The Raven*, vol. 276 (1995), pp. 53–6.

[30] See P.M. Young, *Elgar, Newman and the Dream of Gerontius in the tradition of English Catholicism* (Aldershot, 1995).

[31] As reflected in the attitudes of the twentieth century English Cardinals, see, D.A. Bellenger and S. Fletcher, *Princes of the Church: The English Cardinals* (Stroud, 2001), Chapter Six.

[32] For Catholic Chaplains in the Forces, see T. Johnstone and J. Hagarty, *The Cross on the Sword* (London, 1996).

[33] J.A. Harding, *The Diocese of Clifton 1850–2000* (Bristol, 1999), p. 179.

[34] Quoted by J. Hagarty, 'Benedictine Military Chaplains during the First World War', *E.B.C. History Symposium*, vol. 16 (1998), pp. 134–51, at p. 138.

Western Front with eight hundred chaplains under his care. In October 1917 Field Marshal Haig, following a dinner party at which both Rawlinson and Cardinal Bourne were present, reflected that (without much knowledge of Catholic religious orders) 'the cardinal is neither eminent in appearance or in conversation. On the other hand Rawlinson is a most agreeable fellow and seems to have all the qualities of an efficient Jesuit father.'[35] The first chaplain of any faith in all the British services to die in World War I was Dom Basil Gwydir (born 1867) of Douai Abbey, who went down with the hospital ship *Rohilla* in October 1914. Another naval chaplain, Dom Odo Blundell of Fort Augustus, who had served as a naval officiating chaplain since 1905, and was to serve throughout the War, was the first Catholic priest to celebrate Mass on a Royal Naval Ship on a home station since the days of King James II.[36] The Benedictines, despite many military allusions in the *Rule of Benedict*, are more associated with peace than the Jesuits (whose college, Stonyhurst, became celebrated as the school which produced seven VCs),[37] and it was perhaps appropriate that it was an old Downside boy, Sir Percy Fitzpatrick (1862–1931), who first had the idea of the two minutes silence, peace as a memorial to conflict.[38] The nave of the abbey church at Downside was completed as a memorial to the War dead. Opened on 25 July 1925, in the presence of the Cardinals Gasquet and Bourne, the nave was intended to stand as 'a lasting memorial of the Old Boys who had fought for their country, and also as an external reminder of the Christian ideals for which so many of them had died'.[39] In a sermon the Bishop of Clifton, George Ambrose Burton (1852–1931), reminded the congregation that in 1914 England

> Called on her youth and manhood to stand up for right as against might, for the old culture as against the new *kultur* of triumphant atheism, her appeal at once fired the imagination of Catholics, and nowhere, perhaps, found a more willing response than in the hearts of those of our body whose ideals and character had been moulded on Benedictine lines.[40]

Dom Bede Camm, who served as a First World War chaplain, a convert from Anglicanism, was a crucial figure in the creation of an imperial English Catholicism. He popularised the cause of the martyrs of the Reformation period and developed the theme of 'Country House' Catholicism begun

---

[35] *Ibid.*, p. 137.
[36] *Ibid.*, p. 145.
[37] See T.E. Muir, *Stonyhurst College 1593–1993* (London, 1992), and also F. Irwin, *Stonyhurst War Record* (privately printed, 1927). A similar volume, L. Graham, *Downside and the War*, had appeared in 1925.
[38] Sir Percy Fitzpatrick, a South African, and the Two-Minutes' Silence are discussed in his *DNB* entry (*DNB, 1931–40*, Oxford, 1949), p. 282.
[39] 'The Opening of the War memorial', *Downside Review*, vol. 43 (1925), p. 173.
[40] *Ibid.*, p. 178.

perhaps by Robert Hugh Benson and brought to perfection in Evelyn Waugh's *Brideshead Revisited*. In his *Forgotten Shrines*, a lavish illustrated volume, he traced the relics and places of the martyrs' lives and works.[41] Historical research had always formed part of the work of the English Benedictine Congregation but it found in Francis Aidan Gasquet (1846–1929) a writer of great industry if not accuracy, who in the years around 1900 contributed greatly to the revival of an English Catholic historiography. Created a cardinal in 1914, as Vatican librarian and as cardinal *in curia* during the First World War, he acted as an outspoken opponent of the Germans and as an unashamed Englishman. The bombastic, if dignified, Gasquet summed up, perhaps, in his person the English patriot as Benedictine.[42]

The First World War did not bring to an end the partnership of the Benedictines with the British Empire, but it marked a watershed for the monks, as for so many others in European society. By 1918 the reforms of the new monastic constitutions of 1899 had made their mark and the Benedictine communities were settling (at different paces) into a more monastic rhythm of life. Disillusionment with the imperial ideal was perhaps, in a few cases, beginning to set in. One such case was Dom Francis Sweetman (1872–1953) a chaplain in the Boer War, who attempted to establish a Benedictine monastery in Ireland, at Gorey, County Wexford, ended up as a supporter of Irish independence and was suspected of being an IRA sympathiser.[43] In the nineteenth century, Benedictine-educated Irishmen had been characteristically loyalist.[44]

Benedictine life was always marked by individuality, but as the twentieth century progressed old certainties evaporated. The public schools became as much a service industry as nurseries for empire with an international and multi-cultural clientele as well as a traditionally-run one. The monasteries discovered *angst* as well as triumphalism. Some influential critics like Dom David Knowles (1896–1974), the greatest of the historians of English monasticism, sensed an inherent contradiction between running a public school and true monastic observance,[45] a problem already perceived (from another viewpoint) by those Catholic parents in the nineteenth century who were worried by the stifling impact of clerical education on their children.[46] Yet the patriotic

---

[41] D.A. Bellenger, 'Dom Bede Camm (1864–1942), Monastic Martyrologist', *Studies in Church History*, vol. 30 (1993), pp. 371–81.

[42] D.A. Bellenger, 'Cardinal Gasquet (1846–1929) An English Roman', *Recusant History*, vol. 24 (1999), pp. 552–60.

[43] D.A. Bellenger, 'An Irish Benedictine Adventure: Dom Francis Sweetman (1872–1953) and Mount St Benedict, Gorey', *Studies in Church History*, vol. 25 (1989), pp. 401–15.

[44] See, for example, Richard More O'Ferrall, Rowland Blennerhasset, George Lambert, Charles Owen, O'Conor Don, listed among *Distinguished Alumni* in *The Downside Review*, vol. 33 (1914), pp. 212–20. This also includes Richard O'Gorman, involved in the Smith O'Brien rebellion of 1848.

[45] See A. Morey, *David Knowles* (London, 1979), especially pp. 61–79.

[46] See McClelland, 'School or Cloister?', note 23.

tradition continued through the twentieth century and this characteristic aspect of Benedictine life was found as strongly in the second English Benedictine cardinal of the century, Basil Hume (1923–99), a monk as staunchly English (and both were half French) as the first, Gasquet, and the first Roman Catholic cleric to be given the Order of Merit.

7

VARIETIES OF MODERN SCOTTISH CATHOLIC CONSERVATISM

BERNARD ASPINWALL

Identity *is* equality: it is equality at first sight, an equality that takes no lengthy reasoning or painstaking investigation to discover. Therefore all political or social forms . . . inspired by the idea of equality will almost inevitably point to the concept of identity and foster the herd instinct, with the subsequent suspicion, if not hatred, for those who dare to be different or who claim superiority.[1]

ERIK VON KUEHNELT-LEDDIHN's view was shared by a small, if neglected, Catholic group in Cold War Scotland. In particular three diverse men deserve a place in Scottish Catholic historiography. Colm Brogan, acerbic journalist, his academic brother, Sir Denis, and ex-Communist Hamish Fraser broke from ethnic, class or ideological herds, through the popular press, history or experience of Communism.[2] To them social engineering brought hell rather than heaven on earth. As professionals emerging from a minority, they endorsed meritocracy.[3]

In the Second World War and the generation following, James E. Handley celebrated Catholic advance in education and affluence: solidarity, self-denial and education had transformed a poor community. Tom Gallagher later, more concerned with 'Irishness' and the Left, largely ignored Conservatives.[4] His work appeared as ecumenism, industrial decline and social change were pushing the Church towards social outreach and New Labour to abandon the

---

[1] *Leftism Revisited: From Sade and Marx to Hitler and Pol Pot* (Washington, DC, 1990, originally published 1953), p. 5. He contributed to *The National Review* from the first issue. To him Atheism and Agnosticism were the established religions of the USA, *The Tablet*, 31 March 1962.

[2] Colm Brogan was a life-long Catholic. Denis abandoned Catholicism in the 1930s and kept a keen interest in developments, returning shortly before his death. Fraser was a convert in 1948.

[3] See Wolfram Kaiser, 'Co-operation of European Catholic Politicians in Exile in Britain and the United States during the Second World War', *Journal of Contemporary History*, vol. 35 (2000), pp. 439–65.

[4] Tom Gallagher, *Glasgow: The Uneasy Peace. Religious Tension in Modern Scotland, 1819–1914* (Manchester, 1987).

Old Left. Some scholars still associate Catholics with 'ghetto' instincts: deference to their clergy, support for Irish nationalism – or later the Labour party – in defence of their narrow interests.[5] Even Scottish Communists like Mick McGahey and others followed their failed religious faith to a logical conclusion with another herd. To left wing interpreters, Catholics were finally following their providential class role.[6] But as Sir Denis Brogan saw, the irrational, mystical, naive faith of the Left, like the 'invincible ignorance' of heretics, was impenetrable.[7]

With inclusive 'Scottishness' today, professionals desert old loyalties. David McCrone and others have shown that Catholics share similar social and political attitudes with their fellow citizens.[8] Education and upward mobility in a changing economy have understandably made Callum G. Brown question religious identity as a useful concept.[9] Identity, however, is a complex religious, social and political package. Faith creates a real community and so Catholic socialisation makes the individual 'want to do what he has to do', and the more institutionalised conduct becomes, the more controlled it becomes.[10] Even today, more Scots are in churches than at soccer grounds each week: more are in Stirling chapels than at the local Albion ground any week.

In that respect the Brogan family embody transformation and continuity within Scottish Catholicism. In particular Colm Brogan's successful career as a Conservative political apologist reinforced a belief that socialism is the philosophy of failures. His challenge to the myth of Glasgow and 'the wild political creed of its swarming half-Irish proletariat', suggests that McCrone's transformation may have earlier roots.[11] Tories dropped Orangeism and, as Brogan forecast, Catholics voted for them.[12]

---

[5] Raymond Boyle and Peter Lynch (eds), *Out of the Ghetto? The Catholic Community in Modern Scotland* (Edinburgh, 1998).

[6] See E. von Kuehnelt-Leddihn, *Leftism Revisited* and *Liberty of Equality: The Challenge of Our Time* (London, 1952). I differ from Tom Gallagher 's emphasis on mixed marriages, *Glasgow*, p. 53. We might as well draw conclusions from the illegitimacy of Keir Hardie, R.B. Glasier, Ramsay MacDonald and Bevin.

[7] *Is Innocence Enough?* (London, 1941), p. 149. J.E. Handley, *The Irish in Scotland, 1798–1845* (Cork, 1943); *The Navvy in Scotland* (Cork, 1970). Also Noel Ignatiev, *How The Irish Became White* (London, 1995), especially pp. 52, 70, 93. Also Tom Gallagher, *Glasgow*, and his *Edinburgh Divided: John Cormack and No Popery in the 1930s* (Edinburgh, 1987).

[8] His essay with Michael Rosie, 'Left and Liberal: Catholics in Modern Scotland', in *Out of the Ghetto?*, pp. 67–94. On the USA, James T. Fisher, *The Catholic Counterculture in America, 1933–1962* (Chapel Hill, 1989).

[9] In his review of *Out of the Ghetto . . .*, *Scottish Historical Review*, vol. 79 (2000), pp. 277–9.

[10] C. Lasch, *Haven in a Heartless World: The Family*, quoted in Sarah Lyons Watt, *Order Against Chaos: Business Culture and Labor Ideology in America, 1880–1915* (Westport, Connecticut, 1991), p. 21.

[11] A. Dewar Gibb, *Scotland in Eclipse* (London, 1930), p. 148. The short-lived *Scottish Catholic Monthly*, 1893–6, suggested more sophisticated diverse tastes.

[12] *Glasgow Observer*, hereafter cited as *GO*, 28 September 1962. Also 7 September, 21 December 1962, quoted in Tom Gallagher, *Glasgow*, pp. 274–5.

Born in 1902, Colm Brogan and his three brothers were educated at St Aloysius's, Glasgow. Born to a Donegal family of merchant tailors, their father, Denis (1856–1934) spent two years in California before settling in Rutherglen.[13] The head of an immensely successful branch of the United Irish League, his business flourished in Glasgow. A founder of the Glasgow Gaelic League, and along with Professor Phillimore, the Glasgow Catenians (1913) and the Catholic Institute, he promoted lay intellectual improvement.[14] From his mother, Margaret Toner, Colm inherited a Jacobite highland tradition and claimed descent from a founder of Celtic Football Club. He was raised in a pro-Boer, Liberal and Irish Nationalist atmosphere.[15]

Brogan developed his literary bent at St Aloysius' College, Glasgow where he sub-edited the first issue of the school *Magazine* (1919) on the occasion of the school's fiftieth anniversary.[16] He described the visit of an old boy of humble origins, Dr William P. Larkin, an American lawyer, manager of *Collier's Weekly* and now on the board of the Knights of Columbus: Larkin's secretary, Mr. Glen, was another alumnus.[17] The Knights were then the most vociferous anti-socialist and anti-Communist of American organisations.[18]

Conservative aristocratic influence and clerical leadership in working-class areas had declined in Scotland from the 1880s.[19] By 1914 the future lay with Jesuit pupils as they entered professions and contracted mixed marriages with their Protestant counterparts. The old order was fragmenting.[20] The head-

---

[13] His interest continued with *Century* and *Munsey's Magazine. Spectator*, 21 March 1970 and D. Brogan Sr, obituary, *GO*, 27 January 1934.

[14] 'The Last of the Great Whigs', *Spectator*, 14 February 1970, pp. 208–9. His father presided at lectures by the pacifist and Stanford University president, David Starr Jordan, *The Days of Man*, 2 vols (New York, 1922), vol. 2, pp. 539–49; Sir Bertram Windle, Bernard Vaughan, SJ and others. *GO*, 29 November, 6 December 1913. The League branch members included John Wheatley. Peter Lane, *The Catenian Association, 1908–1983* (London, 1982), pp. 46–7.

[15] H.G. Nicholas, Obituary in *Proceedings of the British Academy* (1976), pp. 399– 410. Sir Denis said an imperialist uncle suggested he should be christened Paul Kruger! *The English People*, p. 19, footnote 1; 'The Good Queen and the Highlands', *Spectator*, 3 March 1970, with Barra, Eriskay and Deeside. Miss Thompson, his teacher with two nephews who were priests, hailed from Banff.

[16] The magazine carried an advertisement for the family firm, 193 George Street.

[17] C. Brogan, 'A Distinguished Visitor from America', *St Aloysius's College Magazine*, 1919, p. 13. A pupil under the Revs Chandlery and Bacon, leaving in 1891, he directed the two hundred Knights' centres in wartime France. *Ibid.*, December 1919, p. 19.

[18] Richard Gid Powers, *Not Without Honour: The History of American Anti-communism* (New Haven, 1998 edition), pp. 54–5. Also Christopher J. Kauffman, *Faith and Fraternalism: The History of the Knights of Columbus* (New York, 1982). After receiving his KSG from the Pope, Larkin returned to the school again in May 1919. *St Aloysius's College Magazine*, December 1919, p. 19.

[19] See Jose Harris, *Private Lives, Public Spirit: A Social History of Britain, 1870–1914* (Oxford, 1993), p. 157 and M.L. Bush, *The English Aristocracy: A Comparative Synthesis* (Manchester, 1984), and Mark Bence-Jones, *The Catholic Families* (London, 1992).

[20] See my study of Galloway diocese in R. McCluskey (ed.) (Ayr, 1997), and June G. Alexander,

master, convert English don the Rev Eric Hanson, SJ, built on the work of convert evangelical missionary the Rev Edward Bacon, SJ (1839–1922).[21] Pupils, he said in 1905, were not to blame Jewish, Masonic or Protestant prejudice for *their* failure. He demanded the highest standards, and pupils like the Brogans whose families were moving into the new suburbs proved it. 'Lace curtain' respectability suggested a new element in Scottish Catholicism.

During Hanson's leadership prospects for an integrating, intellectual base developed. His College excelled. By 1921 pupils had secured the highest examination results in the Glasgow area; their 82 per cent success rate was far and away the best.[22] In 1905 around six Catholics attended the University of Glasgow; by 1920 more than four hundred entered, mostly from the College.[23] Boys like the Brogans won scholarships to Glasgow University and graduated as lawyers, doctors, academics and teachers. Several alumni also won the coveted Snell Scholarships to Balliol.[24] Jesuits made parents of able children more 'British' by encouraging them to transform the existing social order from within.[25] A small, significant professional base grew with different ideas of 'progress' from their socialist coreligionists.[26] Their British patriotism, boosted by the Rev Bernard Vaughan, SJ, showed: eighty former pupils died in the First World War and the adjoining Jesuit parish lost three hundred.[27]

The Immigrant Church and Community: Pittsburgh's Slovak Catholics and Lutherans, 1880–1915 (Pittsburgh, 1987), p. 30.

[21] Report of Bacon's jubilee and 45 years of service, *Glasgow Herald*, 16 February 1918, 18 September 1920. He introduced drama, temperance, the cult of Scottish Jesuit martyr, the Rev John Ogilvie, and organised the Archbishop MacHale Branch of the Gaelic League and Heart of Erin Branch of the Irish National Federation. On Hanson, 'Catholics and Education', *Glasgow Herald*, 27 February 1904 and 5 February 1927, quoting him: 'The greatest of all Tories are the clergy. You might educate the children and the parents but never attempt to educate the clergy. He had made the mistake of his life when he attempted it.' *St Andrew*, 4 January 1906. The Jesuits 'presented everything as having an immediate significance' and fostered 'competition and argument'. 'Reminiscences of the Early Days', *The College Magazine*, June 1973, p. 35.

[22] The Rev W. Crofton, Provincial to the General, 10 April 1911, Rome, Jesuit Archives Rome 20.11.18 and Report, 1920–21, Jesuit Archives, London.

[23] *GO*, 2 January 1926.

[24] B.F. Costelloe, later an MP, was reputedly the first. He had visited the USA, *The Tablet*, 9 August 1884. Archibald McAlpine, 1911, J.F. Scanlan, 1913, Vincent Lyon seem to have been the next three scholars. The school had six bursary winners in 1909. Patrick McGlynn won the Clarke scholarship and later the Ferguson. College Mss Diary, St Aloysius's, Glasgow, December 1914. *Glasgow Herald*, 30 December 1910, 26 December 1914; *St Aloysius's College Magazine*, December 1920, pp. 10–13. But *GO*, 2 March 1956 claims Leo Esdaile was the first. Few entered the closed worlds of banking or insurance.

[25] See A. Lynn Martin, *The Jesuit Mind: The Mentality of an Elite in Early Modern France* (Ithaca, 1988), pp. 206–7, 232. In 1979 Gerry Malone was the first pupil to become a Tory MP.

[26] See details in my 'The British Identity within Scottish Catholicism, 1830–1914', R. Pope (ed.), *Religion and National Identity*, pp. 268–306.

[27] *Dowanhill Education College Magazine*, January 1914, July 1915, January 1917; *The Tablet*,

A.J. Cronin, the novelist of bitter Catholic experience, was a former pupil.[28] As the war ended Belloc, Chesterton, Gill and other luminaries were regular visitors to Glasgow. Dr W.P. Larkin visited a second time as Chief Director of the American Knights of Columbus.[29] Then amid the 'Red Clydeside' crisis of 1919, Gordon Highlanders were billeted on the College. Italian Jesuits ministered to immigrants, a Glasgow Jesuit founded the Apostleship of the Sea in 1920 and the Rev Charles Dominic Plater and the Rev Leo O'Hea promoted the Social Gospel on their visits and in special courses.[30] In 1921 the American Jesuit pioneer of the social apostolate, the Rev J.L. Garesche, closed the parish mission.[31] Socially, the Knights of St Columba, the cinema chains of English Catholics, Kemp and Green, and Celtic Football Club, flourished within the established order, displacing the recreational role of the Ancient Order of Hibernians.[32]

That conservative influence was reinforced by the Rev Dominic Plater, SJ, who developed a social ideal of retreats to unite Catholics, expand the lay apostolate and uplift the toiling masses.[33] Glasgow Catholic Socialists were

---

1914–16 *passim* for samples; Mss Diary St Aloysius's, 14 November 1918, and *GO*, 18 September 1920.

[28] *Shannon's Way* (London, 1931), and *Hatter's Castle* (London, 1948).

[29] Mss St Aloysius College Diary, June 1919 and Colm Brogan in *College Magazine*, June 1919, p. 13.

[30] The Revs Ambruzzi, a student at Cambridge, Rota and Mosca, 2 April 1914, 23 July, 17, 8, 18 September, – n.d., October, 16 December 1918. 26 June 1920 notes '47 boys and three Italians' making their First Holy Communion. By contrast *UFC Assembly Proceedings*, 1912, p. 359, rejected 'the sons of sunny Italy' for 'flouting our dearest traditions.' Its reports of 1893, 1903 and 1906 lamented proliferating ice cream and chip shops. Mss Sodality Library Catalogue, St Aloysius's College. The school offered three prizes in Catholic social study. *Catholic Times*, 3 October 1913, 30 April 1915; C.C. Martindale, *The Rev Charles Dominic Plater* (London, 1920); *College Magazine: Social Study Course* and Library listing, St Aloysius' College; *Dowanhill Education College Magazine*, July, 1919, on their visits, 20 January, 4 April 1919, p. 32; Joan Keating, 'The Making of the Catholic Labour Activist: Catholic Social Guild and the Catholic Workers' College, 1909–39', *Labour History Review*, vol. 59 (1994), pp. 44–56. The Rev William Barry preceded them. See his *Memories and Impressions* (London, 1924), and his CTS address on Scotland and education, *The Tablet*, 12 July 1890; CYMS conference, *ibid.*, 9 August 1890, and *Notre Dame Magazine*, July 1916, pp. 19–22, Plater; February 1919, p. 32, O'Hara; *Catholic Social Yearbook* (1928); C. Plater, 'The Clergy and Social Action in Ireland', *Catholic World*, vol. 98 (1913–14), pp. 43–53. See C.C. Martindale, *Plater*, pp. 117 and 139.

[31] Mss Diary, St Aloysius's, 22 March 1921. See J.M. Cleary, *Catholic Social Action in Britain, 1909–1959* (Oxford, 1961), pp. 10–120 and Georgiana P. McEntee, *The Social Catholic Movement in Great Britain* (New York, 1927).

[32] T. Gallagher, *Glasgow*, p. 109 claims devotionalism diverted popular attention from nationalism or socialism. Cinemas served a similar purpose.

[33] See C.D. Plater, 'A Great Social Work', *The Month*, vol. 102 (1903), pp. 4, 66–73; his 'A Work, *ibid.*, vol. 114 (1909), pp. 449–60; 'The Teaching of Civics in Catholic Schools', *ibid.*, vol. 115 (1910), pp. 598–605; 'Social Study in Seminaries', *ibid.*, vol. 116 (1910), pp. 364–73 and pp. 596–606; 'The C.S.G. Summer School', *ibid.*, vol. 136 (1920), pp. 97–103. The Rev H. Lucas often wrote in *The Month* in favour of social improvement free from state control.

ignorant of history, European Catholic social action or how 'Sacraments do compensate for bare feet.' Marxism described situations but failed to understand people. His retreat movement ran counter to an idealised Middle Ages, Irish nationalism or Christian Socialism. More significantly women were invisible.[34] The Scottish Right was a *male* phenomenon.

Catholics, as C.S. Devas claimed, saw socialism and strikes as threats to the family, the essence of social stability.[35] Self-improvement and self-help were far better in providing the faithful with a Scottish, or more accurately, British, identity.[36] Many Glasgow parishes ran savings banks until the First World War. Even in the 1880s, Glasgow Catholics raised almost £1,200 for starving Ireland and a St Mary's, Glasgow, parishioner left £10,000 to charities.[37] Emigration was preferable to illusory socialism as Catholic imperialism dismissed Irish nationalism.[38] To Catholicism, flourishing in a voluntary system, the 'Protestant' state remained a threatening force. A change from landlord to bureaucrat was hardly an improvement. Catholic Modernists were scathing of socialism. Belief in oneself and God brought amelioration and only the inadequate, *The Tablet* frequently implied, failed.[39] Conservatism was in place.

Popular Protestantism thought otherwise. A Scottish Catholic peer observed in the Spanish Civil War that 'the Armada and *Westward Ho!*' still

---

[34] Reported but hardly discussed. *GO*, 6 January 1952, on leakage, 12 November 1954, 4 May 1956 on many troubled Catholic marriages in Liverpool. The Grail only entered Scotland in 1956. See *SCD*, 1956, *GO*, 11 January 1957. CWL and UCM had begun in 1913. Winifred Hayes, 'Woman's Place in the Future World Order', *Catholic World*, vol. 157 (1943), pp. 482–7, shows a rare awareness.

[35] C.S. Devas, *Plain Words on Socialism, A Lecture delivered at Oddfellows Hall, Edinburgh, 20 February 1906* (Edinburgh, 1908). Also *The Tablet*, 1 January 1887. He reinforced the social assumptions of Catholic revivalism and aristocratic patronage. Also *The Tablet*, 17 April 1880 and 2 April, 27 August 1881. Anthony Clare, *On Men: Masculinity in Crisis* (London, 2000), is an excellent contemporary discussion. Mrs. Gertrude Parsons' magazine, *The Literary Workman*, 22 April 1865, reports the Rev Gregory Holden's successful intervention with a Catholic union strike leader made the anti-Catholic Lord Lonsdale give £100 and free stone for Cleator Moor Catholic church.

[36] An example is Sir John Lavery. See his *The Life of a Painter* (Boston, 1940), and Kenneth McConkey, *Sir John Lavery* (Edinburgh, 1993). He also rejected socialism, p. 30.

[37] *The Tablet*, 17 March 1883, 6 June 1885 (Will of Mrs Peter McLoughlin); 12 September 1885, B.F.C. Costelloe.

[38] Cf. B.F.C. Costelloe, 'The Boyhood of England and the Farms of Canada', *The Tablet*, 3, 24 January 1885.

[39] C.S. Devas in *The Tablet*, 1 January 1887. G. Tyrrell, 'Socialism and Catholicism', *The Month*, vol. 87 (1896), pp. 280–88. Darrell Joddock (ed.), *Catholicism Contending With Modernity* (Cambridge, 2000). See letter of Joseph Monteith, *The Tablet*, 2 April 1887. Also Anon, 'Socialism and Liberty', *The Month*, vol. 55 (1885), pp. 141–3 and J. Rickaby, 'Three Socialist Fallacies', *ibid.*, vol. 91 (1898), pp. 151–65. He predicted their leaders would be 'men of blood and action, of explosives and anarchy.' Elite Catholics like Monteith, T.C. Anstey, Acton, Montalembert, Balmes and others favoured decentralisation.

dictated popular perceptions of Catholicism.[40] The Catholic and Protestant bourgeoisie alike detested working-class bigotry around the Catholic Celtic and the Protestant Rangers, but working-class paranoia made the headlines, so Catholic Tory converts, the Rev David Hunter Blair, abbot of Fort Augustus, the Marquess of Bute or the Lothian families were invisible.[41] In 1918 reputedly the only Conservative defeated in Scotland was a distinguished Catholic soldier.[42] A descendant of the influential nineteenth century Tory convert, Robert Monteith stood as the first Catholic Conservative candidate at Motherwell in 1950.[43] Even that forlorn task was indicative of a changing body.

Colm Brogan, then, came to maturity at a very creative period. John Wheatley's Catholic Socialist Society, extensively covered in the *Catholic Observer* and the socialist *Forward*, were challenging from 1906. Class, ethnicity and religious values clashed in 'How the Duke of Norfolk Plundered the Catholic Church.'[44] In response the Rev Reginald Middleton, SJ, a conservative social reformer, a product of Beaumont, Downside, Ampleforth, Yorkshire acres and a Berkeley Square home, had begun a Catholic Social Reform organisation 'to combat anti-religious socialism'.[45] To inculcate social Catholic ideas over two years he gave over fifty lectures. In 1916 Middleton

---

[40] Lord Rankeillour quoted in Tom Buchanan, *Britain and the Spanish Civil War* (Cambridge, 1997), p. 9.

[41] Colm Brogan, 'Redskins and Conks', *Spectator*, 7 October 1955, and D.W. Brogan, footnote 69. Or the more pertinent commentary by Joseph Bradley, *Ethnic and Religious Identity in Modern Scotland: Culture, Politics and Football* (Aldershot, 1995); Martin Clarke, *Scotsman*, 5 November 2000, *The Tablet*, 9 July 1887, 19 October 1889. The Laird of Alva, J.A.J. Johnstone, President of the Catholic Caledonian Association, *The Tablet*, 12 April 1890. Sir W.J. Hope Johnstone, Dumfriesshire, a convert with one daughter a nun, *The Tablet*, 25 July 1891. D.W. Brogan noted Arthur Griffith, founder of Sinn Fein, denounced a renowned English preacher as 'a Catholic in Christian clothing' while the Scottish-born Archbishop Davidson of Canterbury, not Cardinal Bourne, protested effectively against Black and Tan atrocities: *The English People: Impressions and Observation* (London, 1943), p. 128, footnote 1. In England, Norfolk and de Lisle were Unionists.

[42] *Parliamentary Elections, 1918–50*, however, shows two Tory defeats in Fife and Perthshire. The Anti-Partition League significantly made a last electoral stand in 1950.

[43] See *Glasgow Free Press*, 12 January 1861, for Monteith's Lanark New Year speech. See among my essays on Monteith, *Downside Review*, vol. 97 (1979), pp. 46–68 and *Innes Review*, vol. 31 (1980), pp. 57–70. Archbishop William Smith in Edinburgh, bitterly opposed the Irish, *The Tablet*, 18 August, 1 September 1888.

[44] *Forward*, 24 October 1908. Also *Forward*, 2 February, 9, 16, 23 March, 24 August, 7 September, 5 October 1907; 21 November 1908; the Rev M. Power, SJ, 19 December 1908. Also Sheridan Gilley, 'Catholics and Socialists in Glasgow, 1906–12', in Ken Lunn (ed.), *Hosts, Immigrants and Minorities* (Folkestone, 1980), pp. 160–200.

[45] The Rev R.R. Middleton, SJ, to General, 26 December 1912, and the same, 10 July 1911, JAP 20–11–24, Jesuit Archives, Rome, hereafter cited as JAP. But Professor John S. Phillimore and the Rev Meyer had established the Glasgow Catholic Social Reform Association with public lectures and regular classes of forty. London, Farm St, Jesuit Archives, the Rev W.J. Crofton to Provincial, 6 June 1910. From 1903, Plater wrote of spiritual *and* social benefits in *The Month, American Catholic Review* and elsewhere.

inaugurated retreats at Craighead to foster harmonious class encounters in pleasant spiritual surroundings.[46] His friend, the Swiss-born Rev Joseph Egger, SJ, supported the Cowcaddens Social Reform Association and with Bro. Shields, SJ, founded the Apostleship of the Sea.[47] Middleton's Glasgow Catholic Institute, inspired by Professor J.S. Phillimore, had 530 members and six social study libraries and had numerous luminaries address its meetings.[48] Jesuits were already lamenting leakage and declining Mass attendance especially among the poor.[49] Middleton was concerned that Labour, *the* party of the future, 'should be leavened by Catholic principles.' The future lay with the toiling laity. Although *The Month* supported that initiative some, like Stuart Coats, the ultra conservative convert of the Scottish textile family, were outraged: to them the reliable Jesuits had lost their way.[50]

In the inter-war period Catholics were seen as fecund Hottentots, 'unScottish' and inferior: 'The finest manure makes no impression on concrete.' Hardly surprisingly, Catholic mistrust of mass democracy peaked during the Spanish Civil War.[51] In that climate Colm Brogan's pugnacity came into its own. In his west of Scotland accent he had, as William Buckley observed, 'the most searing tongue.'[52] To the end of his days, 'an ongoing alembic', he never stopped writing.[53] He was a leading light in the University Boxing Club, the *University Magazine* and later the *Catholic Students Magazine*, before starting to write for the *Glasgow Herald* from 1930. In the

---

[46] *GO*, 17 February 1956. On the eve of the First World War, a scheme for a retreat centre was accepted. London, Farm St, Jesuit Archives, the Rev J. Ritchie, Glasgow to the Rev R. Middleton, SJ, 7 February 1914. Parishes and organisations began to go on residential retreats. By 1922 they included most parishes in the central belt. London, Farm St, Jesuit Archives, Craighead, List of retreats 1922. In spite of the 1920 coal strike, their popularity slowly improved. By 1925 severe depression failed to dent the growth. Around 1200 that year undertook such exercises. Three even decided upon a religious vocation. The centre continued to thrive until the 1960s. Then after a downturn numbers recovered. By 1971 some 2,229, including an increase of 500 lay folk, attended retreats at Craighead. *Ibid.*, Craighead Report, 15 December 1971.

[47] The Rev W. Crofton, SJ, to the Provincial, 6 June 1910 Archives, SJ, London. Egger obituary, *Letters and Notices,* vol. 182 (January, 1911), pp. 60–70; *ibid.*, vol. 290 (October, 1938), pp. 140–1, *Glasgow Herald*, 1908 and 1910 reports Cowcaddens meetings several times. P.F. Anson, *Harbour Head* (London, 1944), pp. 102–4.

[48] The Rev W. Crofton, SJ, to Provincial, 10 July 1911, 17 March 1914, 16 March 1915. JAP 20–11–24. See S.N. Miller, 'J.S. Phillimore: A Memoir', *Wiseman Review*, vol. 234 (1960–1), pp. 316–34 and vol. 235 (1961–2), pp. 23–47.

[49] The Rev W. MacMahon, SJ, 2 January, 7 October 1914, 20 ii 38, 46; 6 April 1915, 20 ii 46.

[50] S. Coats, letter to the Rev Provincial, 18 August 1913, JAP, 20–6–4.

[51] Andrew Dewar Gibb, *Scotland in Eclipse*, p. 61. See Tom Gallagher, *John Cormack . . .* and Colin Holmes, 'Alexander Ratcliffe, militant Protestant and antisemite', in Tony Kustner and K. Lunn (eds), *Traditions of Tolerance* (Manchester, 1989), pp. 196–217.

[52] Obituary, *National Review*, vol. 29 (4 March 1977), pp. 254–5. Buckley and he corresponded over many years. Buckley Mss, Yale University, New Haven, Connecticut, USA.

[53] *Ibid.*

Spanish Civil War, like the majority of British Catholics, he backed General Franco and scorned the gullible British left.

His stance was a culmination of improved education, innovative converts, English religious orders and American influence. The Jesuit St Aloysius's College, Glasgow (1859), had transformed Catholic life by fostering Jesuit vocations and over a hundred Scottish secular priests, who were more acculturated, a little more conservative and undoubtedly more British.[54] Jesuit education opened up new careers for laymen to escape the tenements where three-quarters of the population lived in one or two rooms, where, in 1874, two-thirds of children dying under five had no medical attention whatsoever and where, in 1907, the S.V.P. helped one in seventeen Catholics.[55]

The Catholic Student Magazine was indicative of a growing Catholic university presence. Until his untimely death in 1926 the convert Professor John S. Phillimore embodied the Catholic new self-confidence.[56] G.K. Chesterton's unsuccessful rectorial campaign was followed in 1932 by the election of Scottish Nationalist and Catholic convert, Compton Mackenzie. The new Catholic university chaplaincy under convert and former History lecturer the Rev W. Eric Brown (1893–1957) began the magazine in October 1932.[57]

In the first issue Colm Brogan wrote scathingly that socialist progress meant 'The Deadly Virtues yield the same conclusions as the Vices', a view the Spanish Civil War strengthened.[58] Moral outrage demanded effective action. 'We are struggling towards the Promised Land but the Philistines are making for it in forced marches.' From Spain, he described the struggle as a crusade of 'the hordes of Attila', whose savagery demanded, as in Kenya and Rhodesia later, uncompromising resistance: it was 'ideological Mau Mau'.[59]

---

[54] See my paper on 'Jesuits and Scottish Catholic Identity', in Robert Pope (ed.), *Religious Identity: Wales and Scotland, c.1700–2000* (Cardiff, 2001), pp. 268–306.

[55] M.F.S., The Labour Question', *American Catholic Quarterly*, vol. 17 (1892), pp. 21–46, p. 742. The Rev J. Elder Cumming, 'Neglect of Infants in Large Towns', *Transactions of the National Association for the Promotion of Social Science* (Glasgow, 1874), pp. 723–9, 727; *Forward*, 5 October 1907.

[56] *Glasgow Herald*, 23, 27 December 1921. Obituary in *Glasgow Herald*, 2 January 1926. His comments at St Aloysius's prize day were published as 'The Prospects of the Catholic Church in Scotland', *Dublin Review*, vol. 171 (1922), pp. 183–98.

[57] It included an early essay by the young John Durkan, 'The Return of Mani', *Catholic Student*, March 1935, p. 22. Also 'An Opinion on Modern Poetry' *ibid.*, November 1934, pp. 14–15. John Bayne, the University Distributist Club founder, later the first Catholic sheriff in Lanarkshire, was another regular contributor. Brown's obituary, *GO*, 6 December 1957. Colm Brogan saw him off from Southampton to South Africa, *GO*, 12 September 1947.

[58] 'The Work, Wealth and Happiness of Mankind', *Catholic Student*, October 1932, pp. 16–9. Also Literature and Contemporary Thought', *ibid.*, March 1933, pp. 4–6; 'The Contemporary Novel', *ibid.*, November 1934, pp. 9–11 and 'Noblesse Oblige', pp. 16–17; 'The Gradgrind Letters', *ibid.*, March 1935, pp. 12–13; 'G.K. Chesterton', *ibid.*, September 1936, pp. 5–6 and 'The Human Touch', *ibid.*, pp. 15–16; *ibid.*, November 1934, p. 11.

[59] 'A Glance Around Spain', *ibid.*, March, 1939, pp. 4–5; 'Journey's End in Spain', *Glasgow Herald*, 29 April 1967. He stressed Left wing racism against Franco's Moorish troops.

Justice and religious freedom were doomed under Communism. His fellow contributors, however, were rather more guarded in their support for Franco.[60]

The Jesuit meritocrat demanded realism and practical success: escapism was irresponsible. Brogan found Belloc and Chesterton impractical romantics, Bruce Marshall merely entertaining, Graham Greene barely Catholic. The faithful living in Scotland were *Scottish* and needed native hard headedness. Like Sir Denis, he rejected Irish fantasies, utopian visions and government by the ignorant. Convert intellectuals might enliven faith but the mass of philistine Catholics drifted into suburbia or socialism: 'We can't for ever live on injections.' He was hardly 'an ignis fatuus of the Irish bogs by way of Glasgow and now in London.'[61]

Colm's three brothers were William, a noted university athlete and classics teacher, Diarmid, an English and Classics teacher, and the renowned Sir Denis W. Brogan, authority on the United States of America and France, *Spectator* columnist and almost infallible on radio's 'Round Britain Quiz' and 'Transatlantic Quiz'.[62] In contrast to Colm, Denis made a judicious case for Conservatism. He was akin to his near contemporary at St Aloysius's, A.J. Cronin, 'a Catholic who strayed occasionally into the less dark corridors of scepticism but who still at heart clung to his belief.' His liberal views would seem to have followed the classic statement of L.T. Hobson:

> The heart of liberalism is the understanding that Progress is not a matter of mechanical contrivance, but one of the liberation of living spiritual energy. Good mechanism is that which provides the channels wherein such energy can flow unimpeded, unobstructed by its own exuberance of output, vivifying the social structure, expanding and ennobling the life of the mind.[63]

Contrary to popular notions of Scottish Catholicism, Denis first attended an Old Firm game in 1968, his sixty-fifth year! His identity was formed through Queens Park and boxing. Middle-class Irish Catholics had little interest in Fenianism or militancy.[64] The United States more than ethnicity formed him.[65]

---

60 E.g. Frank Macmillan, 'The Press and Spain', *Catholic Student*, September 1936, pp. 10–13; 'The Genesis of the Struggle in Spain', *ibid.*, May 1937, pp. 4–7; 'Further Fascist Ramp!', *ibid.*, February 1938, pp. 14–15; 'Mounier', *ibid.*, March 1939, pp. 24–6.

61 *GO*, 24 January, 5 December 1947; 25 November 1949 at Paisley CTS rally; 17 November 1961; 9 March, 11 May 1962. *The Catholic Student*, February 1938, pp. 8–9; *GO*, 15 February 1963.

62 Obituary, *Times*, 7 January 1974. *Spectator*, 12 January 1974 is disappointing. He was also a director of Hamish Hamilton, the publishers. His father talked much about California. *The English People*, p. 239, footnote 1. His early reading came from Rutherglen Public Library and Maclehose's Circulating Library, Glasgow. He voted for Lord Russell in the 1919 Glasgow rectorial election but subsequently regarded him as 'credulous'. *Spectator*, 7 March, 20 June 1970. Massive numbers of his annotated books, donated to Glasgow University Library, testify to his breadth.

63 A.J. Cronin, *Shannon's Way* (London, 1975), p. 46. L.T. Hobson, *Liberalism* (London, 1911).

64 Ken Fones-Wolf, *Trades Union Gospel*, pp. 66, 7–13, 99, 106, 125.

65 D.W. Brogan, 'The Old Firm is a Great Spectacle', *Glasgow Herald*, 31 August 1968. Bob

When, in April 1922, he returned to his old school to talk on the American Civil War, 'All present were astounded at Mr. Brogan's extensive knowledge.'[66]

At Glasgow University, like Colm, he switched from medicine to arts, and went on to Balliol, Harvard, Paris and Rome.[67] Although educated in a cosmopolitan world, he reputedly never stayed a night in London before his appointment to University College.[68] After his marriage in Nice cathedral, he subsequently became Professor at Cambridge and Fellow of Peterhouse on the eve of the Second World War.[69] An adviser to the British political warfare executive, he became increasingly critical of leftist 'rationalised violence and ideological short cuts.'[70] Moral outrage, however admirable, required adequate means to have effect. To lead men by candlelight was harder than demanding the moon.[71] In the real world, the pure had first to survive.[72] He rejected the simple notion 'Europe is the Faith and the Faith is Europe.' Equally, nationalism sustained irrational self-righteousness.[73] Unlike the far Right or Left, he had few illusions.[74]

History Brogan saw as commanding and organising reality. A preoccupation with infallible ideology was a preposterous rejection of historical reality: 'The Millerites, waiting in their Pentecostal robes for the Second Coming, at least noticed that something had gone wrong with the true schedule; they spared our world wild explanations of miscalculations no more absurd than those of the party in which so much good Left capital has been sunk.'[75]

Their distorted ideology failed: 'the decadent bourgeoisie of 1919 were more formidable than the emergent proletariat.'[76] Slaves to 'blind faith', their

---

Crampsey too was reared on Queen's Park F.C. D.W. Brogan, 'Matière d'Amerique', *Spectator*, 2 March 1956.

[66] *St Aloysius's College Magazine*, June, 1922, p. 26.

[67] D.W. Brogan, 'Unnoticed Changes in America', *Harper's Magazine*, vol. 214 (1957), pp. 27–34.

[68] *The English People*, p. 8.

[69] *St Aloysius's College Magazine*, June 1932, p. 4.

[70] See his *Proudhon* (London, 1934), p. 94; obituary, *British Academy*, p. 408. He readily admitted errors. 'A stand on the Marne in 1940', *ibid.*, p. 207, footnote 1. He was also wrong on Indian independence. Dalton's father, Dean of Windsor, had employed Donegal Glasgow novelist Patrick Macgill.

[71] *The English People*, p. 9. Quoted *ibid.*, p. 204. Asked his religious persuasion at a 1950s Chicago party, he replied 'Agnostic' to which the questioner said 'I did not know you were as old as that.' *Harper's*, vol. 214 (1957), p. 31. D.W. Brogan, 'The Balance Sheet of Vichy', *Spectator*, 23 September 1955, and review of L.J. Halle, *Nature of Power*, *ibid.*, 27 May 1955; 'Socialites and Social Life (Negro style)', *ibid.*, 28 January 1955; 'T.V.A.'s Majority', *ibid.*, 8 July 1955.

[72] *Ibid.*, p. 222.

[73] *Ibid.*, p. 77, quoting Gavan Duffy. Also quoting Fanny Parnell's poem, *ibid.*, pp. 223–4. Colm is identical in *GO*, 10 May 1963.

[74] *Worlds*, p. 225. His wartime apology for the allies was directed to an American audience.

[75] *Is Innocence Enough?*, p. 149.

[76] *Worlds in Conflict*, p. 94. See also his *Is Innocence Enough?*, p. 154.

dreams were 'thin food'.[77] Equally 'The Illusion of American Omnipotence' was flawed.[78] Men did not live by abstractions.[79] A humane order meant an inclusive national culture where all were given equal respect.[80] Liberty empowered creative individuals, so whatever ideologues imagined, society would never be blandly conformist.[81]

Brogan followed Catholic tradition in discriminating between fads and eternal truths.[82] Although later an agnostic, he addressed the Catholic Social Guild in Oxford (1928) and remained an informed observer of Catholicism.[83] He rejected Chesterbelloc and the puritanical Irish Diaspora: Irish moral superiority was as suffocating as imperialism.[84] Reviewing James E. Handley, *The Irish in Scotland* (1943), he drew interesting conclusions.[85] Moral outrage was self-defeating. Constantly playing upon the 1923 Church of Scotland General Assembly anti-Irish outburst merely prevented Catholics moving on. It was a theme he developed again later in *Harper's Magazine*, May 1950.[86] His incisive analysis of American Catholicism saw Thomas Merton and Jesuit civil rights campaigners as more significant than the anti-intellectual immigrant masses.[87] History, a liberating, dynamic experience, recognised facts of the past and did not serve a party, creed or class.

His observations were a catalyst for a major debate about Catholic intellectual failings.[88] The Catholic Right was equally distressed by that failure:

---

[77] *Ibid.*, pp. 154–5. See the North Ayrshire debate between G.J. Monaghan, Catholic Workers' Guild and H. Millar, Saltcoats Communist Party re forced labour in USSR, *Ardrossan and Saltcoats Herald*, 27 January, 3 February 1950. Clashes continued: 3, 31 July, 15 September 1953; 7, 21 January, 4 February 1955. Cf. H. Belloc, *An Essay on the Nature of Contemporary England* (London, 1937), p. viii. They agreed on little else especially Belloc's anti-Semitism, pp. 66–70. Brogan's annotated copy is in Glasgow University Library. *The English People* is something of a riposte. Also H. Belloc, *The Servile State* (London, 1909).

[78] *Harper's*, vol. 205 (1952), pp. 21–8.

[79] *The Study of Politics* (Cambridge, 1946), p. 5. Also Edmund Burke, p. 6.

[80] *Worlds in Conflict*, p. 56.

[81] *The Study of Politics*, p. 7.

[82] *Ibid.*, p. 55, p. 113, p. 118 and p. 48.

[83] D.W. Brogan. 'Home, Sweet Home', *Spectator*, 7 February 1970, p. 176.

[84] *The English People,* p. 126, footnote 2, and probably L'Action Française of Maurras. *Ibid.*, p. 132 and p. 198, footnote 1. In American student days he still thought the Incarnation 'very important', *ibid.*, p. 240, footnote 2. He had met Sir Michael O'Dwyer, later murdered in India, 'A First Without A Star', *Spectator*, 20 June 1970.

[85] *Glasgow Herald*, 13 January 1944. Besides his major scholarly works he contributed a vast array of essays and reviews to numerous papers and magazines. He contributed to 'The Kennedy Dynasty, An Appraisal', *Esquire*, vol. 72 (November, 1969), p. 1623; in October, p. 48; vol. 73 (January, 1970), p. 32; 'English Sickness', vol. 224, *Harper's* (June, 1967), pp. 57–62; 'Vietnam', *Atlantic Monthly*, vol. 220 (July, 1967), pp. 48–55, and numerous others. Admired by Alistair Cooke, he also wrote for *The Manchester Guardian*.

[86] 'The Catholic Church in America', *Harper's*, vol. 207 (May, 1950).

[87] *Harper's*, vol. 214 (1957), p. 34.

[88] J.T. Ellis, *American Catholics*. Also Walter Ong, *Frontiers in American Catholicism* (New York, 1957); Daniel and Sidney Callahan, 'Do Catholic Colleges Develop Intellectuals?',

'Today we wish only to become Men in Gray Flannel Suits. The literal dream of the Full Life has conquered the content and thus destroyed its old reforming zeal.' As the debate reached Scotland, more varied Catholic attitudes were developing in the trans-Atlantic world.

Catholic Conservatives trumpeted their patriotism during the Cold War. It provided a simple answer in a more complex post-war order. Anti-Communism, affluence and religiosity hid a fragmenting Catholic body. Affluent Scottish Catholics went on pilgrimage to Rome and Lourdes as Marian devotions obscured the 'new' educated Catholic women.[89] Never before had so many Scots celebrated Christmas: a cultural revolution was underway. By the 1950s, Catholics were a seventh of the population, but their herd-like cohesion hid a limited intellectual base. Catholics had already come a long way.[90] More then four hundred Catholic students were at Glasgow University and seminaries boomed as some 200,000 visited the Glasgow Vocations Exhibition. Jesuits from Oxford galvanised Catholic trade unionists into action against Communism. The Association of Catholic Trade Unionists met at St Aloysius's, as did the Catholic Transport Guild.[91] The Jesuit Charles Pridgeon and Paul Crane lectured throughout Scotland while occasionally the Rev Tom Corbishley, SJ, added his weight.[92] The outsider, through merit rather than esoteric ideology, would transform society .

In 1953 the seventy-fifth anniversary of the restored hierarchy celebrated a success.[93] Massive expansion, however, masked increasing mixed marriages and falling Mass attendance.[94] Unity had become an end in itself, evading

---

Commonweal, December 1957, pp. 180–5; T.F. O 'Dea, *American Catholic Dilemma: An Inquiry into the Intellectual Life* (New York, 1958).

[89] E.g. *GO*, 23 July 1954. Two thousand left on three special trains for Lourdes. In 1958 Bishop Scanlan was noted opening two churches in eight days and weekly pictures abounded of new schools, churches and expansion.

[90] *GO*, 10 October 1950; 11 December 1955. G. Highet, 'The Churches', in *The Scottish Economy*, A.K. Cairncross (ed.), (Cambridge, 1954) pp. 297–308. At Galashiels, twent-one White Fathers were ordained, *GO*, 24 May 1957.

[91] *Ibid.*, 27 January, 30 May 1950; 20 June 1952.

[92] *Ibid.*, 27 January, 24 March, 1 September, 11 November 1950; 11 May, 8 June 1951; 31 October 1952 headlined 'Catholics Dont Know Their Own Social Policy'; 9 April 1954; 27 March, 30 November 1953; 14 June 1957, Crane at Catholic Workers Guild and Catholic Transport Guild meetings; the Rev Cecil Keane, SJ, urged workers 'to take up cudgels against Communists', 8 October 1954; 3 December 1954. Corbishley came to rebut Paul Blanshard's Gifford lectures, *ibid.*, 7 March 1952.

[93] *GO*, 15 February 1952 and 17 February 1956 with supplement. 110 churches were dedicated to Our Lady. See *GO*, 19, 29 December 1952 on changed Christmas observances.

[94] *Ibid.*, 25 July 1947 reports seven thousand at Carfin to pray for the conversion of Scotland; also 30 January, 17 July 1953, the first Galloway diocesan pilgrimage to Lourdes. Throughout the 1950s it reported numerous new churches, schools and growth. *Ibid.*, 6 January 1952, Bishop Douglas on marriages; *ibid.*, 9 April 1954, two million weekly miss Mass; Lord Wheatley, Catholic and youngest judge, *GO*, 5 February, 12 November 1954; Bishop Scanlan on 'The Evils of Mixed Marriages', *ibid.*, 6 January 1952.

issues and confirming clerical dominance over a laity already showing signs of diversity. Irish partition, allegedly an issue used by Communists, disappeared from the *Glasgow Catholic Observer* between 1949 and 1962.[95] Silence soon enveloped Catholic support for the Scottish Covenant in the 1950s.[96] Initiatives like the Notre Dame Child Guidance Clinic revealed problems of affluence more than of poverty.[97] Anti-Communism hid cracks as the faithful fumbled towards a new identity in a larger political world.

In Scotland upwardly mobile Catholics, as Colm Brogan stressed, had only limited sympathy with a traditional Conservative and *Unionist* party, but more with the transatlantic Radical Right. A strong American current underpinned their outlook: the Brogan connection; the Distributist movement; Fraser's network; the Lanarkshire-born Catholic scourge of Communists, Philip Murray of the American CIO; the American origins of the Jesuit activist Paul Crane; visits by the exiled Ukrainian Bishop Buczko, Bishop Fulton J. Sheen, Russell Kirk and numerous Scottish, particularly Lanarkshire emigrants on return trips. Or even Lou Costello and his Paisley-born wife who visited Scotland.[98] Like their American coreligionists, Catholics 'betrayed' by a White Anglo-Saxon Protestant (WASP) establishment asserted their uncompromising anti-Communism.

A form of Catholic 'revenge politics' against thirties liberals, it echoed their 'out' group experience at the hands of militant Protestantism: public purification at home demonstrated their inability to strike a blow against Communist oppressors abroad. Eastern European émigrés shared that hostility and founded The League for European Freedom (1945).[99] Cheated by Communists at home and rejected by xenophobic Scottish trade unionists,

---

[95] *Ibid.*, 10, 17, 24 January 1947; 27 January 1947; 27 February, 30 July 1948; 3 June 1949; 17 November 1950; 5, 12 January 1962.

[96] *Ibid.*, 20 January 1950, John Bayne. Also J.H. Fichter, 'A Comparative View of Agrarianism', *Catholic World*, vol. 143 (1936), pp. 654–9.

[97] See *Annual Reports*, 1926 to date, SND Clinic, Athole Gardens, Glasgow W12.

[98] B. Aspinwall, 'Broadfield Revisited: Some Scottish Catholic Responses to Wealth', *Studies in Church History*, vol. 24 (1987), pp. 393–406. Grandson of the American consul in Manchester, son of an American-born British barrister, Crane had spent four years there, *GO*, 16 February, 16 March, 11 May 1951; Blantyre-born Murray expelled Communists, *ibid.*, 13 April 1951; Sheen had spoken at Possilpark and Dunfermline pre-war; Buczko was in the USA when Russia invaded, *ibid.*, 6 January 1951; *GO* carried regularly reports on emigrant gatherings in USA as 3 March 1950; George H. Nash, *The Conservative Intellectual Movement in America since 1945* (New York, 1976), p. 72; *GO*, 7 July 1950 on Costello's wife from St Catherine's, Paisley.

[99] *GO*, 15 December 1950; 27 November 1953. John F. Stewart chair. It published numerous pamphlets, 1946–54. J.J. Campbell made a good will visit to Formosa, *GO*, 7 April 1961. *Glasgow Herald*, 3 January 1941 on the Catholic Union. Sponsored by MI6, S.L.E.F. was supported by Douglas Woodruff and Tom Burns of the *The Tablet*. The Scottish branch included the anti-Catholic Andrew Dewar Gibb and many right wing, nationalist émigrés. Stephen Dorril, *MI6* (London, 2000), pp. 25–49.

they were mobilised by Archbishop Gordon Gray and lawyer J.J. Campbell of the Scottish-Polish Society, by reports of oppressed Lithuanians or visits of Bishop Buczko to the Ukrainians.[100] In his pastoral letter of Advent 1947, the Bishop of Galloway described Archbishop Stepinac as 'a living protest against the fiendish hatred of all things Catholic, a hatred which atheistic Communists so loudly proclaim'. The Scottish hierarchy followed with a stern warning on Communism in 1949. Archbishop Campbell of Glasgow took the lead, often gathering two thousand at anti-Communist rallies.[101] Cardinal Griffin, a patron of Fr Peyton's Rosary Crusade, invited Glasgow Labour and Anti-Partition campaigner ex-Baillie Alex McGregor to a huge London rally and came to hear three thousand faithful in Glasgow addressed by Colm Brogan.[102] The combative Bishop John Carmel Heenan also assisted.[103] The *Catholic Observer* ran weekly articles by Douglas Hyde, former editor of *The Daily Worker,* as Catholic study groups and miners fought Communist influences. Through the Catholic Social Guild, Fraser generated opposition to Communist penetration of trades unions and organised visits from Jesuits like Paul Crane and others.[104]

In that climate a conservative Catholic outlook grew as anti-Communism allowed differing agendas to flourish. Demonstrations against Communism had a double significance. They exercised an influence on local MPs and

---

[100] *GO*, 9 May, 19 September 1947; 9 January, 13 February, 13 May, 11 June 1948; 17 June, 9, 30 September, 28 October, 4 November 1949; 7 April 1950; 2 October, 30 November, 11 December 1953; 11 June, 3 September, 12 November, 10 December 1954; 13 January, 17 February, 2 March, 13, 27 April, 7 December 1956; 28 August 1958. See 14, 23 December 1956 on Hungarian refugees at Largs and three thousand at Prestwick en route to the USA. 'Michael Collier' (J.J. Campbell?) wrote many articles in *GO* on the Poles and the naive miners' leader, Abe Moffat, e.g. 4 February, 12 August, 2 September 1949. The former Ukrainian prime minister, Yaroslav Stetzko visited, *GO*, 26 August 1949. On Lithuanians, 11 August 1949. Xenophobia was a labour tradition from Keir Hardie onwards. E.g. *Forward*, 16 November 1907 on Polish miners and 27 June 1908, Glasgow Green Labour demonstration against the Chinese.

[101] *Ibid.*, 23 February 1947; 16 January 1949; 21 November 1952; 20 November 1953. He attended a Ukrainian rally, *ibid.*, 11 June 1954. A rally was held in Ayr, *ibid.*, 9 February 1947; Greenock, *ibid.*, 30 May 1947.

[102] *Ibid.*, 13, 27 June 1947; 21 January, 4 February 1949, 11 July 1952.

[103] *GO*, 25 November 1955. His views on Spain, *GO*, 31 October 1952. He published many articles in *GO*, and possibly many others by 'A staff correspondent' on Spain and Communism were by him.

[104] E.g. *GO*, 23 March 1956, for a Saltcoats meeting with the Revs Paul Crane and J. Christie, SJ; Douglas Hyde was unable to come. See Hamish Fraser correspondence, 1955–6, in the Scottish Catholic Archives, Edinburgh, CSG, DG 19/9. The Rev J. Christie had ready quotes for the press. E.g. *GO*, 28 August 1953 on Kinsey. On infiltration John McIlroy, 'Reds at Work: Communist Factory Organisation in the Cold War, 1947–1956', *Labour History Review*, vol. 65 (2000), pp. 181–201 and in new industries, Bill Knox and Alan McKinley, 'Working for the Yankee Dollar: American Inward Investment and Scottish Labour, 1945–70', *Historical Studies in Industrial Relations*, vol. 7 (1999), pp. 1–26.

developed Catholic self-confidence. Less defensively, they moderated the hard Labour left. There were demands for a ban on Communist teachers and a ban on Communist use of council halls. Organising exile communities of Poles and Ukrainians, debating with Harry McShane or denouncing the treatment of Cardinal Wyszcinski, Catholics believed a great day was coming.[105] Standing firm abroad would yield fruit at home.

Back-to-the-Land enthusiasts in the 1930s had opted out, but post-war Catholics sought to transform 'immoral' industrial society.[106] Douglas Hyde and Fraser provided propaganda in the *Glasgow Observer*, lectured to Glasgow University Catholics and helped to defeat the last remaining Communist MP, Willie Gallacher.[107] Through the Catholic Truth Society, Catholic Men's Guild, Catholic Social Guild and the Association of Catholic Trade Unionists (A.C.T.U.), the laity mobilised.[108] Attacked by the Catholic Right, Sir John Dollan, former Labour Lord Provost of Glasgow, condemned Communist abuses. Scottish Catholic trade unionists similarly defended themselves against agitators.[109] They wanted social democracy, not Red fascism. Improved standards of living, with the first televised Mass and high profile conversions, increased the Catholic stake in the social order.[110] Over the next decade, although distanced from Brogan and Fraser, they made common cause against Communism.

Weakness in the face of Communism was naive.[111] Although linked with the American Radical Right, Fraser and others drew on a ragbag of ideas. In trying to reinvent the ideal of a 'Catholic' state they drew on the Abbé Barruel (the ideological scourge of the French Revolution) and the contemporary French Catholic Right, and expelled missionaries to China. Even the footballer Harry Haddock reported his dreadful experiences in Hungary.[112]

---

[105] E.g. *GO*, 11 June, 3 September, 12 November, 10, 17 December 1951; 1 February 1952 (Quille); 2, 30 October, 20 November, 4 December 1953; 1 October 1954. Colm Brogan wanted Communists banned from the Civil Service and BBC broadcasts, *ibid.*, 4 March 1948; 21 January, 4 February 1949.

[106] See my 'Broadfield Revisited . . .', pp. 393–406.

[107] Douglas Hyde wrote a weekly column in *GO* throughout the 1950s and Fraser organised rallies. *Ibid.*, 13 January, 10 February, 3 March 1950, 3 December 1954, 2 March 1956. H.W. Henderson, another former Communist, prolific pamphleteer, assisted. *Ibid.*, e.g. 2 March 1956. See 25 March 1949 for his debate with Harry McShane.

[108] *Ibid.*, 27 January, 24 February 1950; 3, 10 February 1956.

[109] *Ibid.*, 4 July 1947; 9, 30 January, 20 February, 30 December 1949.

[110] *Ibid.*, 8 January 1953, first televised Mass; 6 April 1956, the conversion of Alec Guiness.

[111] Frank Macmillan, 'Christians of the Left', *The Tablet*, 10 March 1956. Labour councillor Alexander McGregor, lawyer, Hon. Secretary of Catholic Truth Society, chairman of the Catholic Evidence Guild, prominent Friend of Nationalist Spain, Anti-Partionist, continued his anti-Communist campaigns after World War II. *GO*, 13 January 1950. Colm Brogan, *GO*, 27 February, 7 May 1948. Also Gallagher, *Glasgow* . . ., pp. 208–9; Tom Buchanan, *Britain and the Spanish Civil War*, especially the bibliography and his *The Spanish Civil War and the British Labour Movement* (Cambridge, 1991), pp. 167–95.

[112] Abbé Barruel, *Memoirs Illustrating the History of Jacobinism*, 4 vols (London 1797–8). F.

By the 1960s, however, public opinion had mellowed: unquestioned unity and Catholic social and religious structures were less secure. Conservatives rejected Vatican II: Protestantism, Communism and change in the Church were their enemies. More populist than their elite Catholic predecessors, the 'new' conservatives resisted innovation. Their faith made change unnecessary. Like the young Maritain, they argued social stability rested in the faith; Protestantism had failed the test. With few exceptions, they were hostile to socialists, Liberals and Protestants alike. With less wit, they followed the reassuring Scottish convert novelist, Bruce Marshall (1899–1987), in *Father Malachy's Miracle* (1931) or *All Glorious Within* (1944) and his disenchantment in his *Marx the First* (1975).[113] Colm Brogan similarly despatched Protestant assaults with his acerbic pen.[114] But their stance brought them into conflict with less strident Catholic apologists.[115]

Conservatives a generation older than post-war graduates, perhaps jealous of their coreligionists' opportunities, were sceptical about the quality and desirability of educational expansion.[116] Their emergence coincided with Catholic intellectual angst over public credibility, achievement and loyalty. Catholics were moving out from their defensive bulwarks.[117] Catholic suburbia welcomed reassuring simplicity in complexity as they 'arrived' on the social scene.[118]

A less populist, more restrained Conservatism emerged. Successful Glasgow businessman Jack MacGavigan, an Oxford graduate, patron of the arts and chair of the Newman Association, was indicative. Rejecting Catholic paranoia, he engaged with the conservative social order: 'Catholic Art' was as alien as 'Catholic Mathematics'.[119] In 1953 Scottish Nationalists allegedly

---

Macmillan in *GO*, 26 January, 12 February, 9 March, 18 June 1951. Some believed Scotland's conversion imminent and demanded a daily Catholic newspaper, *GO*, 4 April 1947. At the Paisley rally, *GO*, 9 November, 7 December 1951; 3 December 1954; 2 March 1956. The Rev John P. Conway (1914–80) and the Revs J. van Cuillie and Haddock on return from an international match.

[113] Bruce Marshall (1899–1987). Born Edinburgh, educated Glenalmond, St Andrews and Edinburgh Universities, lost a leg in World War I, lived much of his life in France. *Annual Obituary*, 1987.

[114] Review of Paul Blanshard, *The Irish and Catholic Power* (London, 1955), *The Tablet*, 7 May 1955. He was equally sharp in 'Mauriac is a Bore', *GO*, 2 December 1955.

[115] *Ibid.*, and 17, 24, 31 March, 7, 28 April, 5, 12 May, 28 July 1956 over French 'Progressive' Catholics and then latterly in 1957–9 with Catholic trade unionists over their reactions.

[116] E.g. Christopher Hollis, review of Russell Kirk's works, *The Tablet*, 30 March 1957, and Colm Brogan, 'Lucky George', *Spectator*, 6 July 1956, *GO*, 15 July 1958. F. Macmillan and H. Fraser, *ibid.*, 18 May 1958; 5, 12 May 1961.

[117] John Tracy Ellis, 'American Catholics and the Intellectual Life', *The Tablet*, 17, 24, November, 1 December 1956. These extracts from his book (Chicago, 1956), provoked considerable British discussion.

[118] C. Brogan, 'The Grievance of the Middle Class', *GO*, 25 May 1956.

[119] *GO*, 26 January 1951. In between Michael de la Bedoyere promoted his conservative views

bombed his shop displaying 'ER' decorations.[120] The Newman Association and the later Scottish Catholic Renewal Movement in the sixties and seventies encouraged a more independent minded laity. Subsequently Gerry Malone, MP, former Jesuit pupil and Glasgow lawyer, and aristocratic Michael Ancram, MP, Conservative party chairman, proved the diversity of Catholicism. Conspiracy theorists failed, but they opened a path to Conservatism.

As old industrial and educational barriers collapsed, older Conservative Catholics challenged the new agenda and leadership. Instinct made the self-made sophisticated Catholic scorn the carnival of naive political correctness and neo-Marxist materialism.[121] He came from a hard school, not a welfare system. To reject McCarthyism was not to ignore 'the clear and present danger' of Communism.[122] Unlike gullible White Anglo-Saxon Protestant liberals, they would be ever ready. With American links, their posture coincided with the first formal statements of American Conservative philosophy.[123]

Colm Brogan and Fraser savaged the Left; like 'Fitba daftness [it] reflects the sterility of Scottish life'.[124] Contributing to the *Spectator* and national newspapers, Brogan was an abrasive critic of modern education in his respected *The Educational Revolution* (London, 1954) and *The Nature of Education* (London, 1962).[125] Seen by Evelyn Waugh as 'a better Brogan', he became a close associate of Lord Beaverbrook.[126] His Conservatism was idiosyncratic: opposed to the Common Market he endorsed market forces: 'You want the Goods? Capitalism has them.' Brogan was a free marketeer in education, business and unions.[127]

---

in the paper. See his 'My Window on Fleet Street', *Catholic World*, vol. 172 (1950), pp. 39–43.

[120] *GO*, 23 March 1953.

[121] See Tom Gallagher, *Glasgow*, p. 274, quoting Lord Wheatley and Brother Clare (James E. Handley). Also D.W. Brogan, 'The Course of Empire', *Spectator*, 26 December 1953.

[122] D.W. Brogan, 'McCarthy', *Spectator*, 12 February 1954; 'Truman in the Saddle', *ibid.*, 13 April 1954.

[123] Russell Kirk, *American Conservatism* (New York, 1954), *Beyond the Dreams of Avarice* (Chicago, 1957), *Prospects for Conservatives* (Chicago, 1957). Also Clinton Rossiter, *Conservatism in America* (New York, 1959). The American *Catholic World* was vehemently anti-Communist from 1938–9 through World War II and beyond. E. Kuehnelt-Leddihn 'Do Jews Tend Toward Communism?', *ibid.*, vol. 164 (1946–7), pp. 107–13.

[124] *GO*, 3 June 1962. 'Fitba' vernacular Scottish expression for football.

[125] Obituary, *St Aloysius's Magazine*, June 1977, p. 49. *GO*, 21 June 1963, on Strathclyde University, 9 August 1963, but especially 'A Meal Ticket for Life That's Teaching (for some!)', *ibid.*, 28 June 1963.

[126] 'Lord Beaverbrook', *ibid.*, 25 August 1964, pp. 722–4. He claimed Beaverbrook, whom he met frequently, might have become a Catholic but for his Presbyterian minister father. *The Letters of Evelyn Waugh*, p. 234, letter of 26 August 1946. Brogan returned the compliment, *GO*, 6 March 1953.

[127] E.g. his articles in *GO*, 5 December 1947; 25 November 1949; 17 June, 3 August, 14 September, 26 October 1962.

An early recruit to Cold War rhetoric, he was appalled by the intelligentsia's uncritical view of Communism. But American and British spy scandals, the collapse of Eastern Europe and China to Communism reinforced the stampede from the far left to saner shores. The titles of their publications revealed all: *The God that Failed, I Believed, I Confess, School of Darkness, Fatal Star*.[128] He was contemptuous of the 'nihilism' that 'masquerades as liberalism', colonial nationalists and the corrupt incompetence of independent African states.[129] His unique journalistic assault on the idols of the Left, and, according to the *Glasgow Herald*, 'a superb intolerance with which he maintained it reduced some to speechlessness' and so achieved his objective.[130]

Even in the post-war period he bitterly opposed democratic socialism. In a 1948 echo of Robert Monteith he even suggested that some Labour Members of Parliament were Russian agents.[131] His disdain for the nanny state was clear in his best seller, *Our New Masters* (London, 1947, reprinted 1948). *They Were Always Wrong*, he trumpeted in a 1949 Conservative Central Office pamphlet.[132] Free access to higher education, and lower standards and welfare gave 'The Right to Sponge on Everyone'.[133] Butskellism and the 1964 British election, 'The Great Bore', lacked principles.[134] Parodying Lord Acton, he observed 'it is precarious power, plus Harold Wilson, that corrupts absolutely'.[135] His contempt for Wilson was brutal.[136]

His scathing style, more suited to Glasgow University debates, made his point. The Communist treatment of Cardinal Mindzenty and Archbishop Stepinac was scandalous. The Communist MP William Gallacher's *Catholics and Communism* (London, 1945) and his *The Case For Communism* (1949), were tissues of falsehoods.[137] Brogan's *The Case Against Gallacher* (1949), a Catholic Truth Society pamphlet, savaged this dupe of murderous Leninism.[138]

---

[128] R.H. Crossman (ed.), (London, 1952); I. Kravchenko (New York , 1949); Douglas Hyde (London, 1952); Bella V. Dodd (New York, 1954), and Hamish Fraser, (Glasgow, 1954). For a concise statement, see Owen Chadwick, *The Christian Church in the Cold War* (London, 1993 edition).

[129] 'The Comfort of Cold Friday', *National Review*, 29 December 1964, p. 1153 and *GO*, 17 November 1961.

[130] *Glasgow Herald*, 30 March 1977. He was hardly politically correct. *Times*, 29 January 1977. Also 12 March 1977.

[131] *Glasgow Herald*, 9, 16 March 1948.

[132] (London, 1949). The tract is a long denunciation of nationalisation, pacifism and Russia.

[133] *National Review*, 30 August 1958, pp. 557–8; 'England's Upper Class Proletariat', *ibid.*, 15 June 1957, pp. 571–2.

[134] 'The Great Bore', *ibid.*, 17 November 1964, pp. 1015–16; 'Ten Days That Shook the Exchequer', *ibid.*, 26 January 1965, pp. 57–8; 'The Crooked Road of Harold Wilson', *ibid.*, 16 November 1965, pp. 1026–7; 'Fast Shuffle at 10 Downing Street', *ibid.*, 3 October 1967.

[135] 'The Crooked Road of Harold Wilson', *ibid.*, 16 November 1965, p. 1027.

[136] 'Wilson Agonistes', *ibid.*, 24 August 1971, p. 930.

[137] *Ibid.*, p. 5.

[138] *Ibid.*, pp. 7, 11, 19. See *GO*, 24 April 1963 for his continued fierce assaults.

In 1956, at a Glasgow meeting, he opposed the visit of Krushchev and Bulganin: 'Can You Negotiate With Liars?' Compromise was impossible.

He began to operate on the larger American stage. The first formal expression of an American conservative philosophy by Russell Kirk and others prepared the way.[139] Brogan and Frank Macmillan, whose contributions to *Dublin Review, The Tablet* and *Glasgow Observer* were usually committed pieces, resisted any drift to the left. Brogan scorned protesters at Faslane and Archbishop Thomas Roberts's pacifism.[140] In *The Tablet*, Macmillan portrayed 'Progressive' theologians as leftist stooges.[141] But Brogan's world and his health were in decline. The sixties were to him disastrous. Swinging London and Angry Young Men confirmed cultural decline.[142] Even his beloved *Spectator* lost its principles.[143] After the various scandals his 'homeless' Conservatives welcomed the advent of Lord Home.[144]

W.F. Buckley, Jr had begun the lively right wing American journal, *National Review*, in 1955. Two years later he provided what would be a platform for Brogan's increasingly acerbic views on Britain over a period of twenty years.[145] On occasion Brogan was joined by his brother Denis, Sir Arnold Lunn, and the novelist John Braine.[146] They retreated in horror from 'The Effluent Society boys.'[147] Their link coincided with the unravelling of American Catholic homogeneity: minds across the sea had more in common

---

[139] *The Conservative Mind* (London, 1954 edition), and Eric Kuehnelt-Leddihn, *Liberty or Equality*. See also his novel, *The Gates of Hell* (London, 1933), and his *Leftism from De Sade and Marx* . . .

[140] *GO*, 10 September, 6 , 20 October 1961; F. Macmillan, 20 January, 5, 19 May 1961; Hamish Fraser, 29 June 1962.

[141] See *The Tablet*, 10, 17, 24, 31 March, 28 April, 5, 12, 26 May, 5, 26 June 1956. Macmillan reviewed French literature in the *Dublin Review*, 1951–2, 1958; French analysis to the *The Tablet* and to *GO*, 14 , 28 April, 26 May, 5, 12 June, 7 July, 11, 18 August 1950; 18 June 1951; 18 July, 5, 19 September, 31 October 1952; 24 January, 18 March, 13 May, 19, 26 September 1953; 26 November 1954.

[142] 'This Happy Breed', *National Review*, 16 January 1960, pp. 40–1; 'No Language But A Cry', *ibid.*, 25 February 1961, pp. 111–13; 'The State of the Nation', *ibid.*, 17 May 1966, pp. 467–8; 'Gin Fizz', *ibid.*, 26 July 1966, pp. 722–3, p. 729.

[143] Under Ian Gilmour. See 'Low Life Above Stairs', *ibid.*, 25 February 1964, pp. 153–5.

[144] 'Britain's Scandalous Spy Case', *ibid.*, 12 March 1963, pp. 95–6 and p. 210; 'The Profumo Affair', *ibid.*, 2 July 1963, pp. 528–34, p. 543; 'At Home with Sir Alec', *ibid.*, 31 December 1963. *GO*, 26 July 1963.

[145] Many other contributors were former prominent American leftists like James Burnham, Max Eastman, Ralph de Toledano and Communists including Freda Utley, and Eugene Lyons. Another F.D. Wilhemsen, with Jane Bret, wrote *The War in Man: Media and Machines* (Athens, Georgia, 1970), and *Christianity and Political Philosophy* (Athens, Georgia, 1978).

[146] D.W. Brogan, *National Review*, 18 March 1972, p. 25; Sir Arnold Lunn, 'On Selective Indignation', *ibid.*, 18 July 1960, p. 172; 'The New Olympics', *ibid.*, 10 September 1960, p. 149, and 'The Flight from Pity', *ibid.,* 16 January 1960, p. 43, and John Braine, *ibid.*, 16 February 1973, p. 205.

[147] C. Brogan, 'No Language but a Cry', *ibid.*, 25 February 1961, p. 113.

than hands across the local aisles. Buckley's father, a wealthy oilman, had witnessed the Mexican Revolutionary persecution of the Church. His son had similar doubts about visionary politics. A man of great charm and wit, Buckley was renowned for his books, *God and Man at Yale* (1951), *Up From Liberalism* (1959), and his unrepentant defence of McCarthyism.[148] A lecturer on the American celebrity circuit, a novelist, candidate for mayor of New York, he was an urbane television personality.[149] He loathed murderous communism. If mercy was 'bourgeois sentimentalism' . . . 'It is theologically wrong, historically naive and strategically suicidal to assume that the forces of communism, like those of the devil, are routed by personal or even corporate acts of justice and love.' His determined intellectual anti-Communism survived McCarthy.

Brogan's hostility to the welfare state had free rein. It destroyed self-esteem, self-discipline, social order and efficiency: work-shy British, immigrants on welfare and vandalism were symptoms of that collapse.[150] He revelled in flaying Labour government failings.[151] The hypocritical cant of the upwardly mobile Scottish beneficiaries of welfarism was fuelled by 'working class bigotries because they still carry the working class badge'. Their sterile lives were still bound by class consciousness, ethnicity and sport. America, he warned, was following British 'indiscriminate handouts'.[152] Believing that

---

[148] W. Buckley and L. Brent Bozell, *McCarthy and His Enemies* (Chicago, 1954); W. Buckley, *Modern American Conservative Thought* (New York, 1988) and his *The Committee and Its Critics: A Calm Review of the House Committee on UnAmerican Activities* (New York, 1962). He attracted admirers, Nick Clark, *Alistair Cooke* (London, 1999), pp. 495, 504. Also Donald C. Crosby, *God, Church and Flag: Senator Joseph McCarthy and the Catholic Church, 1950–1957* (Chapel Hill, 1978). Dr John C. Docherty, Old Aloysian and Glasgow graduate, qualified as a doctor in Canada, then worked with oil companies. He aided the Mexican rebels but after being captured but escaped to USA. *St Aloysius's Magazine* (June, 1930), pp. 13–14.

[149] William F. Casey, later Director CIA, Charlton Heston and Tom Sellek were close supporters. See John B. Judis, *William F. Buckley* (New York, 1988); Richard Gid Powers, *Not Without Honour: The History of American Anti-communism* (New Haven, 1998 ed.), pp. 51–2, 282–407; W.F. Buckley, *The Unmaking of A Mayor* (New York, 1966). Graham Greene had scant regard for him or his monthly. Donald Greene, 'Graham Greene and Evelyn Waugh: Catholic Novelists', pp. 5–37 in Jeffrey Myers (ed.), *Graham Greene: A Revaluation in New Essays* (London, 1990). I met Buckley in Indiana, 1962 after he gave a superb, if wildly controversial, lecture. He was proud of his time at Beaumont, the English Jesuit public school. Kuehnelt-Leddihn taught there in 1930s.

[150] 'Mayhem at Notting Hill', *National Review*, 27 September 1958, pp. 203–4, 210; 'Alabama Here We Come', *ibid.*, 9 March 1965, pp. 195–6, and 'British Make Work Takes a Blow', *ibid.*, 28 March 1959, pp. 615–16; 'Notting Hill and the Murders to Come', *ibid.*, 4 July 1959, pp. 173–5.

[151] 'Beavan Czar of Britain's Proletariat', *ibid.*, 21 December 1957, pp. 565–6, and 'The Deserted Tillage', *ibid.*, 4 November 1961, pp. 297–8; The State of the Party', *ibid.*, 2 April 1976, and 'Exit Harold, Enter Jim', *ibid.*, 9 July 1976, pp. 226, 346–9; 'I'm Alright Jack', *ibid.*, 4 February 1977, pp. 151–2.

[152] 'A View of the Goldwater Administration From Abroad', *ibid.*, 14 July 1964, pp. 595–7.

'*No help should be given except to the helpless*', he backed Goldwater for president in 1964.¹⁵³ *The Catholic Herald* replied that 90 per cent of National Health Service patients fell into that category: 'It is doubtless owing to the lamentable paupering of the working class, people are objecting to dropping dead on quite so grandiose a scale.'

Like many of his generation Brogan, shocked by the end of Empire, retreated to a little Britisher position. Coloured immigration to Britain was proof of social decay. 'Many of the immigrants bring the primitive conditions of their native life . . . Whole streets sink rapidly into squalor.' In the *Glasgow Observer* he claimed that Pakistani Muslims brought disease, deception and social division.¹⁵⁴ Although of immigrant descent himself, he loathed more recent arrivals.¹⁵⁵ Like the late nineteenth-century Californian Irish, he believed that Asian immigrants threatened health, stability and Christian tradition.¹⁵⁶

In short he lamented the passing of an order within which he had succeeded. His once denigrated Church, about to bask in success, found herself in chaos. His social, political and religious concerns merged. In rapid social change Brogan understandably looked favourably upon Senator Joe McCarthy, his resistance to Communism, change and liberalism.¹⁵⁷ Political correctness he found repellent: with Chesterton, he warned that one who ceases to believe in God, far from believing in nothing, believes in everything. Original Sin overshadowed utopian humbug.

Vatican II was unacceptable. Like Kuehnelt-Leddihn of *The National Review,* he was appalled by 'the braying of the Trojan asses from the theological demi-monde' in the post Vatican II Church.¹⁵⁸ Another contributor, sociologist and former Communist Will Herberg, wrote the Church needed 'a more adequate, more intelligent and discriminating *Syllabus of Errors* for our Time'. His conservative mentor, Buckley, questioned the later Papal social encyclical with his notorious 'Mater Si, Magister Non'. That shared outlook reflected Brogan's rise from modest background to mixing with the great and good.

---

[153] *Ibid.* In his outlook he mirrored 55 per cent of the Irish Catholics in New York who voted for Goldwater. Ronald H. Baylor and Timothy J. Meagher (eds), *The New York Irish* (Baltimore, 1996), p. 427.
[154] *National Review*, 9 March 1965, pp. 195–6; *GO*, 2 February 1962.
[155] 'Churchill, A Profile in Greatness', *National Review*, 9 February 1965, pp. 99–100, p. 121. He claimed Churchill's name never appeared in a D.C. Thomson publication during the Second World War. He was always referred to as 'the Prime Minister'.
[156] *Ibid.*, See his claim *GO*, 18 August 1952, more Irish immigrants deported under Immigration Act.
[157] 'London Letter', *ibid.*, 26 March 1960, p. 202 and p. 215.
[158] The expression comes from Dietrich von Hildebrand, *Trojan Horse in the City of God* (Chicago, 1967). E. von Kuenelt-Leddihn, *Leftism Revisited* . . ., p. 332. I had lengthy exchanges with Brogan in *GO*, 1973–5.

To the end, the ailing Colm Brogan maintained his faith in an unchanging Church and in the unquestioned superiority of talent and of independence of mind. Considered too vitriolic by the Scottish Catholic press, he found an intellectual home across the Atlantic.[159] Although seriously ill, he retained his humour, comparing Job with his own painful lot as a 'peevish hypochondriac'.[160] Even in his dying days he sent a scathing article to *The National Review* which attacked British social and education policies.[161] He died in St Margaret's Hospice, Clydebank, in January 1977.

In contrast to Brogan, Hamish Fraser was schooled in hard experience. Like his American counterparts he brought a ginger element to the cause.[162] His progress was chequered. After dropping out of Edinburgh University as a Young Communist, he became the only British member of the International Brigade in SIM, the Spanish branch of the KGB, during the Civil War. On his return he was a Communist trade unionist on Clydeside during the Second World War. Received into the Church in 1948, he came into contact with the idiosyncratic Rev John McQuillan, former seminary professor, founder of the ill-fated Catholic Land Colony at Biggar. With his conversion his outlook radically changed: 'One Yalta is too much for One Generation.'[163] Now Labour were 'mere fellow travellers of Soviet totalitarianism'.

His campaign against Gallacher convinced Fraser that the 'hard' Left would destroy the 'soft' Labour party. By 1951 he was in demand as a speaker at anti-Communist rallies and conferences around the west of Scotland.[164] In November 1951 Fraser debated with Saltcoats socialist Bob Lambie and sparked a lengthy corrspondence in *The Glasgow Observer*. In December he addressed several meetings, including a thousand in Paisley and a thousand in Greenock the same evening.[165] Fraser, with the secretary of the Friends of Spain and the poet Roy Campbell, his former Nationalist enemy, urged Spain be brought into the western alliance.[166] Campbell, a convert South African,

---

[159] Gallagher, *Glasgow*, pp. 215–16, p. 256, p. 283, citing Michael Bedoyere and *The Daily Express*.

[160] *National Review*, vol. 29 (4 March 1977), pp. 254–5.

[161] 'I'm Not Alright Jack', *ibid.*, 4 February 1977, pp. 151–2. See his *House of Horror* (London, n.d.) on socialism.

[162] Nash, *The Conservative Intellectual . . .*, p. 129.

[163] *GO*, 9 February 1951. His obituary *Times*, 29 October 1986. He was received by a conservative American Jesuit at St Aloysius's. His autobiography *Fatal Star* (Glasgow, 1954) was unenthusiastically reviewed in *The Tablet*, 22 January 1955. Thomas McGettagan, Glasgow, complained, *ibid.*, 5 February 1955. Also see Fraser on China, *ibid.*, 12 February 1955. He supported the Soviet-Nazi pact in his *The Intelligent Socialist's Guide to the Second World War* (Glasgow, circa 1941?).

[164] E.g. Coodham, *GO*, 1 September 1950, 2, 9 November 1951; article 'We Have Been Warned', *ibid.*, 10 November 1950.

[165] Also Wellshot, *GO*, 2, 9, 23, 30 November, 7 December 1951.

[166] *Ibid.*, 9 December 1949, 5 October 1951. He wrote *The Truth about Spain* (CSG, Oxford, 1949), and *Spain and the West* (Glasgow, 1951).

later dedicated part of his 'The Flowering Rifle' to him.[167] Militant anti-Communism was Fraser's life.

Renewed Marian devotion fed into this concern. The papal definition of the dogma of the Assumption (1950), the Rosary Crusade and an interest in Our Lady of Fatima rallied the apprehensive faithful. Popular prayer, processions and pilgrimage grew markedly. Like Lourdes, the movement renewed faith, care and compassion in the face of the atheist challenge and channelled women's apirations into 'safe' areas.[168] The intensification of public devotion peaked in the 1954 Marian year. Thousands attended Marian rallies at Celtic Park, Glasgow and throughout Scotland: 40,000 attended a Marian rosary rally in Coatbridge and 8,000 at Bishopbriggs. Some 3,500 attended a Blue Army rally at Howwood.[169] Before a rally of 100,000 in Fatima itself, Bishop Fulton Sheen confirmed two Glasgow Jewish converts.[170] Millennarianism flourished as 'all the hallmarks of a final clash' were at hand.[171]

Fraser was deeply involved with the Blue Army of Fatima. Three weeks after the inaugural Glasgow meeting, it denounced Stalin as 'Satan's field marshal' and 'Kremlin's Satanic fury'. The following year, the founder, the Rev Harold Colgan, New Jersey, and his newspaper editor, J.M.H. Haffert, arrived, declaring 'Russia will be converted'. In 1950 Passionists at Fatima House, Coodham hosted a Catholic Workers' Guild conference at which the Rev Mgr John McQuillan attributed social evils to the Reformation; the Rev Tom Corbishley, SJ, to the lack of moral law; J.J. Campbell, of the Scottish-Polish Society, to a denial of private ownership; and Fraser to the Labour government.[172] In October 1951 Fraser recounted 'The Road from Communism' in the Edinburgh Jesuit magazine, *The Mercat Cross*, and three years later in his spiritual autobiography, *The Fatal Star* (Glasgow, 1954). Passionists

---

[167] Roy Campbell, *Collected Works*, 4 vols (Craighall, South Africa, 1985–8), vol. 1, *Poetry*, p. 564 and p. 672, note 1. Fraser is not identified in the footnote. Campbell's homophobia and anti-Semitism were greatly modified from the 1939 edition. Descended from a Scottish grandfather, Campbell like his friend Colm Brogan contributed to *National Review*. 14 December 1955, 15, 29 February, 25 April, 27 June, 1, 22 December 1956, 11 May 1957. See his autobiography, *Light on A Dark Horse* (London, 1951), and Peter Alexander, *Roy Campbell* (Oxford, 1982).

[168] Cf. Ruth Harris, *Lourdes: Body and Spirit in a Secular Age* (London, 1999), pp. 357–66. Hundreds of emigrants to the USA returned for the summer Dunfermline pilgrimage, 1948–58.

[169] *GO*, 10 October 1951; 5 June, 17 July, 16 October, 30 November, 11 December 1953; 4 June, 10, 17 September 1954. Also Coodham CWL lecture on 'The Maternity of Our Blessed Lady'. *Ibid.*, 8 October 1954. Ten thousand attended St Margaret's rally, Dunfermline, *ibid.*, 31 June 1957.

[170] *Ibid.*, 10, 26 October 1951. He spoke in Dunfermline and Possilpark in the 1930s, *ibid.*, 1 June 1951.

[171] *Ibid.*, 7 December 1951. See Jay P. Dolan, *Catholic Revivalism, The American Experience, 1830–1900* (Notre Dame, 1978).

[172] *Ibid.*, 1 September 1950.

enthusiastically backed Fraser as the next few years often saw five thousand at Marian rallies, monthly services and occasional torch-light processions. Passionists enthused a Garnethill rally, even claiming that 'if we had Communist zeal' Scotland would be converted in three years.[173] Scots were seeking to contain domestic changes and international threats.

At a Blue Army rally in Saltcoats the Rev Paul Crane, SJ, and the Rev Andreas Johannes Fuchs, president of the Blue Army from Germany, came to speak on 'The Way Ahead' and 'The Social Apostolate and Fatima'. Fraser and Fuchs had addressed the founding meeting of the European Blue Army of Fatima in Paris on 8 December 1952.[174] Fraser circulated its official publication, *L'Homme Nouveau*, as Marian devotion identified Communism as the root of all evil.[175]

The following year Fraser spoke on 'The Social Message of Fatima' at a Coodham conference which included the Rev Charles Pridgeon, SJ, Principal of the Catholic Workers' College, Oxford and John Lynch of the CTS and Newman Society.[176] Only Our Lady of Fatima would end Communism. Fraser, an indefatigable newspaper correspondent, publicist and dynamic organiser, gave up his Kilbirnie teaching post to become Director of the Laetare Centre, Linlithgow. Working closely with Bishop McGee to promote the Galloway Catholic Workers' Guild, he encouraged the Rev Paul Crane, SJ, and vigorously backed the Marian rosary crusade for the conversion of Russia. Like the liturgist the Rev Clifford Howell, SJ, influenced by his American experiences, he sought to create 'a Mystical Body awareness' to regenerate the social order through the Mass.[177] He brought the expelled Belgian missionary the Rev J. van Coillie to his British campaign against religious persecution in China.[178] He even sent the Pope a telegram. In 1956, after his campaign against Bulganin and Krushchev, he, the Rev James M. Lillis (1902–79),

---

[173] *Ibid.*, 1 June, 2 November 1951; 13, June, 3 October 1952; 11 December 1953; 7 May 1954.

[174] H. Fraser to Bishop J. McGee, 16, 23 April, 19 September, 14, 24 November 1955; the Rev G. Fuchs to H. Fraser, 20 April 1955, DG 19/9, Scottish Catholic Archives, Edinburgh.

[175] *GO*, 18 January 1857; 9, 16 January, 17 July, 6 November 1958. See Thomas A. Kselman and Steven Avella, 'Marian Piety and the Cold War in the United States', *Catholic Historical Review*, vol. 72 (1986), pp. 312–19; Kauffman, *Faith and Fraternalism*, p. 385; James T. Fisher, *The Catholic Counterculture in America, 1933–1962* (Chapel Hill, 1989), pp. 157–66. Following in a tradition, Fraser linked contraception and Marxism, *GO*, 28 May 1952. See the Rev Joseph Husslein, 'The Invasion of Race Suicide and Socialism', *American Ecclesiastical Review*, vol. 45 (1911), pp. 276–90.

[176] *GO*, 30 November 1953. A Spanish priest, the Rev Gonzalez, was an observer. Article in *ibid.*, 12 July 1957.

[177] *Ibid.*, 26 September 1953; *Clergy Review*, vol. 34 (1950), pp. 245–57 and vol. 35 (1951), pp. 311–23. On this idea see Fisher, *Catholic Counterculture*, pp. 163–5. On the background, Paul Marx, *Virgil Michel and the Liturgical Movement* (Collegeville, Minnesota, 1957), and the Papal encyclical, *The Mystical Body* (1943).

[178] *GO*, 3, 17, 24 December 1954; 3 September 1955. Bishop McGee pastoral on industry, *ibid.*, 9 December 1955.

chaplain to the Blue Army in Scotland, and Vincent Donnelly, Glasgow publisher of its organ, *Immaculata*, joined half a million pilgrims in Fatima.[179]

Anti-Communism degenerated into resistance to virtually any change. By 1958, papal warnings about atomic warfare showed a changing mood. Fraser's claims about decolonisation or that seventy Labour MPs were fellow-travellers had a sceptical reception. He and the Rev Paul Crane demanded the liberation of 'the people' from depressing housing schemes, state schools or mediocre universities, the victims of inadequate government planning.[180] They were speaking to the true believers, as mainstream Catholics were more relaxed about Communism.[181]

Critical voices were raised against Macmillan, Crane and others.[182] The calling of the Second Vatican Council further stunned conservatives. But Fraser insisted that Communists never change. In welcoming *Mater et Magister*, he emphasised its hostility, like *The Syllabus of Errors*, to 'modernity' and to Communism. His ecumenism envisioned united opposition to the Left.[183] Unlike Brogan he favoured aid to underdeveloped nations and encouraged Scottish devolution to contain socialist centralisation.[184]

Even amid Vatican II, Fraser's associate veteran campaigner, the headmaster Frank Macmillan, translated Marcel Clement, *The Communist Challenge to God. A Christian Textbook on Communism* (Glasgow, 1961), which he used in his 'How Real is the Devil to You?' Macmillan worried over Algerian independence; for him Christian imperialism was alive and well.[185] Together they would oppose the Scottish Catholic Renewal Movement (1968), the visits of the Rev Hans Küng and the Rev Daniel Berrigan, SJ. But their tide was ebbing.

After Vatican II Fraser continued his campaign through his magazine *Approaches* (1965), writing for *Christian Order* and lecturing in Britain and India.[186] He corresponded with Buckley but did not write for *The National*

---

[179] *Ibid.*, 12, 19 October 1956. The Goldsteins, Glasgow Jewish converts, brought two hundred pilgrims from America. A rally of over three hundred of the Legion of Mary was held at Howwood, *ibid.*, 14 September 1956.

[180] *Ibid.*, 24 April, 8 May 1958; F. Macmillan, *ibid.*, 15 May 1958, H. Fraser article, *ibid.*, 13 June 1952, *ibid.*, 3 August 1957. Also his letter against Nationalisation, *ibid.*, 30 August 1958. Fraser and Macmillan questioned Algerian independence from French barbarism, *ibid.*, 9 October 1958; *The Tablet*, 9 June 1962.

[181] *GO*, 26 June 1958, F. Macmillan, 'No Love for McGovern.'

[182] *Ibid.*, 30 August, 13 November 1957. J.J. Campbell campaigned against televised smut, *ibid.*, 7 April 1961, 9 August 1963. He served on the Public Morality Committee from 1943.

[183] *Ibid.*, 11, 25 January, 22 February, 8, 26 March, 26 April, 3 May, 28 June. *Ardrossan and Saltcoats Herald*, 21 January, 4 February 1955; *GO*, 20 April 1956 on 'Fatima and Atheistic Communism'; *Scotsman*, 9 December 1985; *Approaches*, 1969–85. But Saltcoats officials welcomed the Soviet guests, *GO*, 2 November 1956.

[184] *Ibid.*, 24 May, 14 June, 12 July, 9, 23 August, 6, 29 September 1963.

[185] *GO*, 5, 19 May 1961. Fraser agreed, *GO*, 18 August 1961.

[186] *Christian Order*, February 1960, pp. 67–71; August 1961, pp. 451–6; November 1961, pp.

Review. He supported Una Voce, Archbishop Lefebvre and the Latin Mass Society. In America, the right wing Catholic weekly, *The Wanderer,* sponsored his lecture tour.[187] With Colm Brogan, Fraser held many views in common. He felt betrayed by the Catholic intelligentsia who were socially engineering an unrecognisable faith. In *Approaches* and *The Christian Democrat,* he reiterated his anti-Communism and unease with Vatican II. His aim was 'to promote lay initiative in the temporal order independent of the hierarchy yet in a spirit of uncompromising fidelity to the social doctrines of the Teaching Church'. It was a conservative variation on the role of the laity.[188] His scorn for 'modernity' was clear.

He had more sympathy with Paul Johnson, Evelyn Waugh or the former American liberal Michael Novak.[189] At a popular level he reflected the confusion of an older generation. His targets were 'subversive' innovators: Teilhard de Chardin, John Courtney Murray, Cardinal Suenens, Hans Küng and new style catechetics. He was supported by the Canadian Catholic *Register* and associated with the appropriately named magazine, *The Remnant*. His *Approaches* even reprinted the Jesuit Rev E. Cahill's *Freemasonry, Its Character and Purpose* (1944) and ultra-conservative essays and backed Archbishop Lefebvre against 'Occupied Rome'.[190] In short *aggiornamento* was repellent. His zeal remained undimmed until his death in October 1986.

Changing newspaper headlines from 'Diabolic Force Inspires the Communist Drive' to 'Dont Always Blame the Communists', reflected that shift. Self-confident Catholics were less concerned as they had other possessions than Irish cultural identity, were less influenced by older apologists and reached different convictions.[191] As the Brogans followed careers down south, their influence diminished. After 1960, the metropolitan Colm and the Cold War warrior Fraser were adrift from mainstream Scottish Catholicism.

70–103; December 1977, pp. 733–43; Colm Brogan contributed articles in January 1962, pp. 12–16; April 1962, pp. 294–8; October 1962, pp. 592–600. *GO*, 6 March 1953, Brogan on Waugh, Macmillan on De Gaulle, *Christian Order*, April, 1960, pp. 196–205.

[187] *Approaches*, Easter 1970, pp. 14–30; March 1972, pp. 46–50; September 1975, pp. 3–9; November 1976, pp. 1–9; the Ascension, 1981, pp. 80–88; the Holy Innocents, 1985, pp. 32–44; the Immaculate Conception, 1986 posthumous last issue of the magazine which reputedly had a circulation of three thousand worldwide. Buckley Mss.

[188] See J. Coulson (ed.), J. H. Newman, *On Consulting the Faithful* (London, 1969). Montalembert famously observed when Bishops have a girls' mentality, the laity should be like Crusaders' sons.

[189] See Novak's *The Catholic Ethic and the Spirit of Capitalism* (New York, 1993).

[190] *Approaches*, March, 1972, pp. 46–50; September, 1975, pp. 3–9; November, 1976, pp. 1–9; March, 1976; the Ascension, 1981, pp. 80–8; the Immaculate Conception, 1986, posthumous last issue. W.F. Buckley, 'Catholics and Abortion', *National Review*, vol. 15, December, 1970, pp. 1366–7, shared his misgivings. A local councillor, Fraser opposed more municipal housing, *Glasgow Herald*, 22 May, 16 June, 9 August 1971.

[191] Headlines in *GO*, 5 December 1947 and 5 May 1961.

Ironically the cosmopolitan outsider, Denis, impressed by Vatican II, began his return to the faith. They had each played a pioneering lay role in breaking the Catholic mould.

Colm Brogan and Fraser diverged in the early sixties. They developed different strategies to deal with *the* enemy, Communism. From London, Brogan believed that education and market forces would eliminate poverty and incompetence. Only a return to truly Conservative values would regenerate Scotland and the faith.[192] Scotland had prospered under Adam Smith and Brogan had succeeded in that competitive world. From his provincial position, Fraser saw *Mater et Magister* as a model anti-Communist plan.[193] Scotland should have greater power over her economic affairs, universities, and concern for the Third World.[194] A supporter of Opus Dei, concerned for Catholic education and massive out migration, Fraser reflected his more vulnerable position as a provincial schoolmaster.

These attitudes paralleled declining traditional industries.[195] They found themselves at odds with Vatican II, post-war affluence and the rising generation. Faithful were becoming property owners, independent of state power but succumbing to other challenges. They represented the clash of two views of faith: 'liberated 'and 'captive'. The first saw Catholicism as freeing the human spirit for fulfilment and the other saw only narrow sectarian boundaries. They were victims of earlier Catholic experience. Their clergy, preoccupied with building programmes, were unable to meet the demands on their limited resources and imaginations. Under Protestant pressure, Catholic leadership failed to develop an imaginative *Scottish* response to the pastoral and intellectual crisis. However, under Thatcher and Reagan, Brogan's views were back in favour. Laissez-faire might seem a long way from the Irish nationalist background, but it stood for independence from the dominant state.

These three Conservatives were indicative of a Catholic stereotype. They stood firm against the excesses of secularism and Communism and produced a *masculine* consensus. Their hopes of a Christian state faded as a new multi-faith Scotland took shape. As their monocultural 'Christian' world faded, a more diverse Catholic identity developed, as women began to challenge traditional male hegemony. Sir Denis Brogan's Conservatism was more sympathetic with that view. All had to be recognised.

Ultra-Conservative male Catholics no longer dominate Scottish Catholicism. They are merely a section of Catholic opinion. The Catholic body has been transformed out all recognition. Even its official leadership in Scotland,

---

[192] Brogan, *ibid.*, 3, 17 June, 3 August, 14 September, 7, 21 December 1962; 4 January, 5 February, 15 March, 12 April, 30 August 1963.
[193] *Ibid.*, 3, 17 November, 8, 26 December 1961.
[194] Fraser, *ibid.*, 7 April, 13 November, 15 December 1961; 2, 9 February, 2, 9, 16 March, 13, 27 April, 7, 21 September, 5 October, 30 November 1962.
[195] *Ibid.*, 3 February 1957, on the closure of Albion Works, Kilmarnock.

more open to question, was often less in tune with clergy and faithful. The Communist empire was crumbling. Routine, ethnicity, male working-class solidarity and female subservience were slowly disappearing. 'Faith of Our Father' had run its course.[196] 'Liberation' was in progress.

---

[196] Andrew O'Hagan, *Faith of Our Father* (London, 1999), or younger Catholic women like the Saltcoats writer, Maggie Graham, *Sitting Among the Eskimos* (London, 2000).

8

THE MYTH AND REALITY OF SR BARBARA UBRYK, THE IMPRISONED NUN OF CRACOW: ENGLISH INTERPRETATIONS OF A VICTORIAN RELIGIOUS CONTROVERSY

DOM RENE KOLLAR, OSB

A RECENT American television programme began with scenes of a building where someone had painted Botticelli's *The Birth of Venus*. The unknown artist sarcastically painted the following phrase, 'All History Is Myth,' coming from her mouth. This statement might seem true, especially when one studies the rancour and hostile emotions which frequently coloured religious controversies in nineteenth century England, where fantasy, falsehood, and hyperbole frequently replaced reality. Stories about nuns and convents were no exception and often supplied the material for a number of hateful legends. In William Makepeace Thackeray's *The Irish Sketch Book*, for example, the narrator visited an Ursuline convent at Blackrock, near Cork, and admitted 'this is a great privilege for a heretic.'[1] He encountered a nun, and acknowledged that he had never been in the presence of one before this meeting. The reader quickly learns, however, that the narrator harboured some anti-Catholic prejudices. After some caustic comments about Roman Catholicism, the narrator wondered out loud, 'has she any of her sisterhood immured in *oubliettes* down below . . . is her poor little weak delicate body scarred all over with scourgings, iron collars, hair-shirts?'[2]

In some circles of Victorian England a number of educated people also held this impression of nuns and conventual life. Many reasons gave rise to this hostile and critical view of convents. In addition to a general anti-Catholic prejudice which saw all practices associated with that religion as either

---

[1] W.M. Thackeray, 'The Irish Sketch Book' in *The Complete Works of William Makepeace Thackeray* (New York, 1903), p. 328.
[2] *Ibid.*, p. 331.

immoral or idolatrous, a stereotype of the inhuman existence which nuns allegedly endured might have developed out of specific happenings or events which people had either exaggerated or misinterpreted. A Benedictine monk in London understood this possibility. Writing in 1899, this cleric described an event at a local convent. A nun, obviously suffering from mental problems, threatened to harm herself and to set fire to the buildings. The other sisters, consequently, kept a close watch on her, but she managed to escape. The nun 'got out of the window, and halfdressed [sic] as she was making for the garden, through the hedge across a field and into one of the new roads close by.'[3] A kindly man eventually rescued the fleeing nun and took her home, where his wife cared for her until authorities from the convent arrived. The monk understood the possibilities for trouble, which, however, did not materialize: 'we are likely to have the "escaped nun" cry for a time.'

By the 1860s the figure of the poor, imprisoned nun, languishing in a dank convent cell on the orders of a diabolical mother superior or churchman, had become a symbol of the baseness of Roman Catholicism. *The Monk*, written by the nineteen-year-old Matthew Lewis in 1794, had already told the sad and horrific story of Agnes, a young Spanish girl who suffered imprisonment within the vaults of the convent. In 1836 the fabricated story of Maria Monk shocked and titillated readers on both sides of the Atlantic with tales of a Montreal convent where seduction, murder, infanticide, and, of course, imprisonment, formed part of the daily routine of the nuns. The quantity of literature and publications that attacked conventual life and emphasized its abuses was phenomenal, and those Victorians who read the memoirs of Henrietta Caracciolo and Sister Lucy became well acquainted with themes of imprisonment and loss of personal freedom.[4] From north of the border, *The Bulwark*, a publication of the Scottish Reformation Society, reported several escapes from convents,[5] and *Priests and Their Victims; or, Scenes in a Convent*, published in 1852, illustrated another theme which would play an important role in the case of Sr Barbara, namely, the immoral actions of those priests associated with convents.[6]

Criticisms of sisterhoods were not confined to print. Beginning in 1851 with a bill introduced by Henry Charles Lacy, several attempts, especially

---

[3] G. Dolan to H.E. Ford, 10 October 1899, Dolan Papers, Ealing Abbey Archives, London.

[4] H. Caracciolo, *Memoirs of Henrietta Caracciolo* (London, 1865); and *The Marvellous Escape of 'Sister Lucy,' and Her Awful Disclosures Respecting New Hall Convent, Boreham, Essex* (London, 1865).

[5] See, for example, *The Bulwark*, August 1852, 2 February 1857, 1 April 1859, 1 May 1865 and 1 June 1866.

[6] *Priests and Their Victims; or Scenes in a Convent! In Which the Reader Is Shown the Cause of a Nun's Entry into a Convent, the Manner of Her Education, the Cunning of the Priesthood, Their Midnight Orgies, the Mode of Getting Rid of the Offspring, with a Correct Copy of the Secret Instructions of the Jesuits; and an Account of Their Brutal Treatment of an Italian Lady, Compiled from M. S. "Confessions of a Nun," etc. etc. by Signor —* (London, 1852).

those associated with Charles Newdigate Newdegate, were made to require parliamentary or government inspection of sisterhoods. Naturally, those who argued for inspection made references to the alleged imprisonment or the incarceration of nuns, and the supporters of state supervision tried to educate the British public to the evils of convent life by means of lectures and pamphlets.[7] In 1869 an event occurred in Cracow, then part of the Habsburg Empire, which concerned a Carmelite nun, Barbara Ubryk, who had been imprisoned within the walls of her convent. The incident quickly caught the attention of individuals in England who had already watched with interest the developments of the Hull convent case[8] and who saw this foreign incident as another example of the cruelty practised by Roman Catholic sisterhoods.

The news of Sr Barbara's incarceration first reached England in July 1869, when *The Times* reported some disturbances that occurred on 21 July when a mob broke a door and several windows at the convent of Carmelite nuns in Cracow. According to the paper, 'The cause of the demonstration was that a nun had been in close confinement in the Convent for 20 Years, and was only liberated . . . by the interference of a judicial Commission.'[9] The rabble returned to the convent four days later and attempted to break into the convent where the nun had been held captive. Driven back, the mob continued to cause havoc within the city and threatened other Catholic establishments. The paper noted that a number of arrests had been made and that government officials had already initiated an investigation into the case of Sr Barbara. Several days later *The Times* again devoted more space to these religious riots in Poland, and the British public soon became acquainted with the life and trials of Barbara Ubryk.

The 31 July edition of *The Times* printed a hostile article dealing with the imprisoned nun. It contained reports from two Austrian correspondents who sketched the background and the events surrounding her discovery. This story most certainly repulsed and shocked British readers. One correspondent stated that 'an anonymous letter stating that a nun had been immured in a neighbouring cloister since 1848, and begging that justice might be done to her'[10]

---

[7] See W.L. Arnstein, *Protestant versus Catholic in Mid-Victorian England. Mr. Newdegate and the Nuns* (Columbia, Missouri, 1982) for Newdegate's campaign to legislate for government inspection of England's convents. Several groups opposed to Anglo-Catholicism and what they believed was the growing influence of Roman Catholicism in the British Isles supported Newdegate's programme with an outpouring of pamphlets, for example, *A Plea for the Inspection or Suppression of Convents* (London, 1870).

[8] For accounts of the 'Great Convent Case,' see, W.L. Arnstein, *Protestant versus Catholic* and M. McClelland, 'The First Hull Mercy Nuns: A Nineteenth Century Case Study,' *Recusant History*, vol. 22 (October, 1994), pp. 199–221.

[9] *The Times* (London), 26 July 1869.

[10] *Ibid.*, 31 July 1869. A second article in the same edition, written by another correspondent, followed the outline of the first report, and also quoted at length from a Vienna newspaper which described the horrific conditions in which Sr Barbara was found.

had led to the discovery of Sr Barbara. The article pointed out that Sr Barbara had been born in 1817 and entered the Carmelite convent in 1841. After informing the Bishop of Cracow, Antonio Galecki, of a possible abuse at the convent, a representative of the city's magistracy, along with a delegate of the bishop, went to the convent, where they met with some resistance from a sister, who refused to receive them. The investigators, however, made their way to the cell of the nun 'with its strongly fastened double door,' and the sights and sounds which the rescue party encountered nauseated them.

According to the prejudiced language of *The Times*, on 'entering the cell, a spectacle met them scarcely to be described, and yet it ought to be told, for it shows what fearful wrongs may be perpetrated if individuals are handed over to the tender mercy of Concordats, and to arbitrary, irresponsible rule.'[11] The tiny room, it noted, measured seven feet by six feet, its window was walled up allowing only a sliver of light, and no furniture could be found. The appearance of Sr Barbara sickened the investigators.

> In a corner, lying on rotten, stinking straw, lay the poor crouching creature, '*halb Mensch, halb Thier*, half human, half a brute, half savage, half mad, utterly naked,' her body filthy, for she had not been washed for years. Her lean bones hanging loose, her cheeks sunken, her hair dishevelled and dirty – a fearful being, whom even Dante, with his amazing imaginative force could not have portrayed. This poor skeleton of a woman at the sight of her visitors shook herself up, and folding her hands and bitterly weeping said, 'I am hungry, have pity on me, give me food (*Fleisch*) and I will be obedient.'[12]

Immediately after this discovery, Bishop Galecki arrived at the convent and reprimanded both the mother superior and the confessor 'with the utmost severity.' The latter claimed that the ecclesiastical authorities had known about 'the immuring of the nun,' but the bishop denied this accusation. When asked why she had been imprisoned, Sr Barbara answered that she had broken her vow of chastity, but she immediately told the bishop that 'These nuns also are not pure; they are no angels.' Before he left, Bishop Galecki suspended both the mother superior and the priest from their duties at the convent. Sr Barbara's mental and physical health quickly became a concern. According to

---

[11] In 1855 a concordat was signed between the Holy See and Austria. 'Among other concessions to Rome were the freedom of communication between the bishops and the Vatican, the control of the elementary schools, the education of the clergy by the Jesuits, the surrender by the state of all share in the administration of ecclesiastical property, and the increase of clerical authority in questions connected with marriage.' K.S. Latourette, *A History of Christianity*, vol. 2 (New York, 1975), pp. 1108–9. In spite of an edict of toleration (1861) which eased restrictions on those who were not Catholic, elements within the empire resented concessions given to the Roman Catholic Church and agitated for the abrogation of the concordat. In 1870, however, the concordat with the papacy was suspended in response to the dogma of papal infallibility promulgated by Pope Pius IX in that year.

[12] *The Times*, 31 July 1869.

the opinion of the medical authorities who examined her on the day following her release, 'she is rather "*verwilder*"... wild and savage.' They did not diagnose her as 'deranged,' and held out hope for her recovery. As to her testimony – especially the breaking of her vows – *The Times* pointed out, 'it still remains to be seen whether this be not a delusion of the brain.' Sr Barbara was then immediately taken to a nearby asylum for the insane. The correspondent ended his report by hoping that justice would be carried out, but he also expressed concern that the local ecclesiastical authorities might try to obstruct any investigation, especially in respect to the testimony of the other nuns.

The Times printed another article concerning Sr Barbara on 2 August. This report, written by the paper's correspondent in Vienna, also described the hostile mood of the Cracow crowd after Sr Barbara's liberation from her confinement and the violence directed against the convent and a nearby Jesuit residence. The civil authorities cautioned the crowd against any more unlawful actions and urged the people to wait for the outcome of an investigation. A petition, however, had already been circulated demanding the removal of the Jesuits from the city. The correspondent also introduced some intrigue and mystery into the Sr Barbara incident. Citing a Cracow 2 August 1869 newspaper, he revealed that 'the proprietor of an intelligence office'[13] admitted writing the anonymous letter which had first led the civil and religious authorities to the Carmelite convent. Moreover, the Carmelite confessor to the convent, whom the paper incorrectly identified as Fr Lavkowick, had left the city before the discovery of Sr Barbara, and 'in a state of intoxication discovered [that is, revealed] the mystery to the parish priest, who in his turn told it to his cousin, the above-mentioned proprietor of the intelligence office.' (In the different versions of the Sr Barbara story, the confessor to the Carmelite convent would be known by different names.) But stranger and more suspicious things also allegedly happened.

The first was the sudden death of the confessor. This Carmelite priest died unexpectedly on 25 July, and according to the judgment of the Vienna correspondent, 'the chief witness is removed just at the most inopportune moment.' *The Times* also quoted a special edition of a Cracow newspaper, which added another element to the riddle. Early one morning in April 1848, a patrol of the National Guard had noticed a carriage before the gate of the convent. Two members of the guard peered into the carriage and saw two men, 'one of whom held on his knees a woman in a nun's dress, and having a nightcap on her head.' During some questioning, the woman fled and ran into the convent's courtyard and apparently yelled, 'I am lost.' No one knew what became of her. The guard arrested the men, but the members of the patrol became convinced that the incident was nothing more than a 'love adventure,' and released them. The Cracow paper now believed that some connection existed between this

---

[13] *Ibid.*, 2 August 1869.

1848 incident and the recent discovery of the imprisoned nun at the same convent, and it began a search to identify the members of the National Guard on duty that night.

By August 1869, therefore, all the elements for a gothic suspense story were in place to excite or to repulse the British public. The ambience of a foreign city, tales of the torture and imprisonment of a Roman Catholic nun at the hands of her community, tales of insanity and broken religious vows, mysterious letters, the sudden and suspicious death of one of the main participants in the drama, an array of shadowy characters, and the strange incident of that early morning in April 1848. Moreover, *The Times* continued to contribute to the controversy by attacking sisterhoods in general; this soon became an important ingredient in the unfolding mythology of Sr Barbara. Writing in the 31 July edition, the correspondent quickly vented his indignation and disgust at a religion which could allow so cruel an imprisonment to occur in a convent. 'Any one who, in tale or drama, should have represented such an event as happening in a civilized city in this age of humanity would have been accused of imagining impossible horrors to discredit a creed against which he had a fanatical antipathy.'[14] The article drew attention to the suspicions of some English concerning the morality 'engendered by the so-called religious life,' and described the Sr Barbara incident as a 'perversion of human instincts.' Nuns and convents did not naturally produce 'scenes of crime,' it argued, and a programme of state inspection would protect innocent young women against such crimes and misdeeds happening in England as had come to light in Cracow.

But was Sr Barbara mad? Was her incarceration necessary to protect herself and the other sisters? *The Times* reported that Sr Barbara claimed that she had been placed in solitary confinement because she had broken her vow of chastity, but her 'coarsest language' on her release and the lack of any evidence concerning sexual misconduct suggested that she had gone insane. Because of the nun's mental condition, some apologists might excuse the misguided but understandable actions of the nuns. The only other explanation, which could be taken from the pages of works inspired by Matthew Lewis, was unthinkable to the Victorian mind. According to *The Times*,

> To assume that the nuns shut up an erring Sister in a den and kept her there for twenty-one years in darkness, cold, and nakedness till she fell a victim to madness which they at first falsely imputed to her would be not unnatural if we could admit that the practices charged against the religious bodies of Western Europe three or four centuries since still linger among the Catholics of Poland.

But even the more charitable explanation of the imprisonment of a mad nun for twenty-one years could not be defended. Even a violently insane person

---

[14] *Ibid.*, 31 July 1869.

deserved better treatment. The article then recounted the events surrounding the discovery and release of Sr Barbara, and asked about the authorship of the letter which revealed her plight. Who wrote the anonymous letter which led to her freedom: a nun, a vindictive or hateful servant at the convent, or the intelligence officer? More importantly, however, who should bear the responsibility for the imprisonment and persecution of Sr Barbara?

The Roman Catholic officials must be held accountable. Taking into account all the circumstances of the case and all the possible explanations behind her long confinement, the London paper refused to accept any excuses for Sr Barbara's mistreatment. 'The ignorance of the Church authorities,' *The Times* declared, 'is the most extraordinary part of the business.' The newspaper dismissed the contention, which it had printed earlier, that influential churchmen in the city had known of Sr Barbara's situation for at least a decade. The surprised reaction of the bishop and his indignation suggested that he had no previous knowledge of the happenings at the convent. But ecclesiastical ignorance would not remove culpability: 'It is evident that, even if it was known that a Sister of unsound mind remained in the convent, there was no suspicion in any one's mind that she was being treated with such atrocious cruelty.' Moreover, nothing could excuse the actions of the other nuns. 'To shut up a woman, still young, in a dungeon a few feet wide, to leave her there year after year without clothing or fire, wallowing in filth, and, with her wailings . . . in their ears, to go daily through the long routine of religious service, has in it something diabolical!' The newspaper characterized the nuns as having 'seared consciences' and possessing 'perverted minds.' And what about the convent's confessor? Did he attempt to tell the nuns that the imprisonment of a member of their community constituted a crime which threatened her mental and physical health? Or did the nuns refuse to listen to their confessor's pleadings? Other accounts of Sr Barbara's sufferings, however, would later argue that this cleric was responsible for her incarceration.

With a sense of indignation and a helping of pious wrath against the nuns and Roman Catholicism in general, the rhetoric of *The Times* supplied the reading public with the circumstances surrounding the case of Sr Barbara. The article also predicted the possible consequences of the case. In the first place, it would inflame the passion of anti-Catholicism. According to the paper, 'The incident will tend to confirm the repulsion with which Protestants regard these institutions [convents].' Second, the privileged position of religious communities, particularly within the Austrian Empire, would be questioned and even altered. The advance of liberal ideas throughout Europe would eventually challenge and then destroy the domination of the Roman Catholic Church over the lives and minds of citizens. And last, the revelations of the Cracow convent would increase the demand for state inspection of all convents. 'If religious orders are to be maintained,' *The Times* demanded, 'their dwellings must be open to public inspection, and their customs and bylaws accommodated to those of the State.'

By August 1869, therefore, men and women in Great Britain who had read *The Times* had become acquainted with the saga and rescue of Sr Barbara. The 7 August edition of the paper reported that the inquiry into the nunnery case continued to hear evidence, Sr Barbara was making a good recovery in an asylum and no longer acted as a savage, the confessor to the convent had in fact died from natural causes, and the animosity against the Carmelite nuns for their supposed lack of compassion had subsided.[15] Regardless of its rhetoric, which clearly displayed its prejudice, the paper accurately supplied its readers with the facts of the case, but also raised many questions and introduced several mysterious incidents and persons into Sr Barbara's story. Like a playwright or director who writes a number of final scenes for a play or movie, reports of the events at the Polish Carmelite convent produced different interpretations of the incident. Religious prejudices and personal motives played a large part in the different versions, and the conflicting results shed some light on the human element in historical interpretation and the strength of religious passions in fashioning an historical narrative. This helped to create the myth of Sr Barbara Ubryk.

An anti-Catholic element quickly made use of Sr Barbara. *The Rock*, that inveterate opponent of the High Church party and practices associated with Roman Catholicism such as sisterhoods, printed a short piece dealing with Sr Barbara in its 6 August 1869 edition. The article paraphrased the reports from the Vienna press found in *The Times*. It did not, however, address the Cracow case *per se*, but rather used the example of Sr Barbara to attack all sisterhoods, both Roman Catholic and especially those in the Anglican Church. *The Rock* described the reports from Poland as 'a touching story of mingled suffering and horror . . .'[16] Instead of emphasizing the alleged cruelty and barbarism which Sr Barbara had to endure, this paper took up another of the positions of those who loathed and feared the conventual life: the harsh existence which a nun vowed to live constituted an unhealthy, unusual, and unscriptural life. 'It is not without cause,' the paper pointed out, 'that the Popish priests draw the veil, and keep it drawn very close, over the scenes enacted within convent walls.' If the facade disappeared, one would catch a glimpse of 'that strange and unnatural life – to which women devote themselves in the supposed interest of religion . . .'

As more and more information about the misdeeds occurring behind the convent walls became public knowledge, *The Rock* argued, people would no longer regard sisterhoods as 'nurseries of heaven,' or 'estimate their inmates as anything rather than angels.'

> Can we commit the greatest outrage on the social aptitudes of womanhood, and do the grossest wrong to her tenderest and most characteristic sympathies, as a

---

[15] *Ibid.*, 7 August 1869.
[16] *The Rock* (London), 6 August 1869.

woman, and then expect to find her as perfect as when her nature was left to its proper perfection and to its natural development? Can we take away the heart of woman and expect to find its emotions still beating in her bosom, still overflowing with the milk of human kindness?

Women committed acts of folly when they fled from the world and entered convents. Marriage and the family were the proper state for Victorian women; God had preordained this state of life as the ideal. According to this article, the Roman Church had sinned against the divine plan by its promotion and approval of sisterhoods. Moreover, the conventual life encouraged abnormal and inhuman activities, for example, 'by withholding a sister's sympathy, and intercourse, and affections from those who need it most, even to their own sister . . .' The events at the Carmelite convent in Cracow did not surprise *The Rock*. 'It is this hard and heartless want of sympathy to their own suffering sisters that is the crowning folly of convent life, and which will we trust,' the newspaper predicted, 'prove to be its ruin, if only allowed to develop its unnatural tendencies and tortures . . .' Naturally, the defenders of sisterhoods did not remain silent.

The Sr Barbara case also found its way into the columns of the English Roman Catholic press. In the summer of 1869 *The Tablet*, a London weekly, reported on the incident. The length of the articles and the emphasis of the reports differed greatly from those of *The Times*. On 14 August the paper commented on the campaign, currently being waged in England, that advocated government inspection of convents, and thanked 'the liberal papers generally for their consistent refusal to be startled by wild tales from Cracow . . . into the smallest of small tyrannies.'[17] In the same edition, a short article noted that the case of Sr Barbara had become the topic of numerous Protestant sermons which urged the state to inspect convents, and after sarcastically asking if 'lunatics have never been and never are illtreated [*sic*] in Protestant England,' it went on to describe the shocking case of an elderly man in Leicestershire. On 21 August, *The Tablet* tried to dispel wild talk of convent cruelty and consequently described the preliminary results of the investigation in Cracow. This Catholic paper pointed out that Sr Barbara had suffered from mental illness, and then praised the charity offered by the sisters. The account differed greatly from the reports and interpretations of *The Times*. 'There is no doubt,' the paper stated, 'that poor Barbara Ubryk has long been afflicted with the most distressing kind of madness; there is no doubt that she has been treated by the Carmelite Sisters with the most devoted and self-denying care and attention; there is no doubt that she was constantly well fed, and that her body health is excellent.'[18] The precautions taken by the Carmelites to restrain

---

[17] *The Tablet* (London), 14 August 1869.
[18] *Ibid.*, 21 August 1869.

Sr Barbara, moreover, 'were nothing more than the simple measures required for the sake, as well of her own safety as of natural decency.'

According to *The Tablet*, a sacristan, who had worked at the convent for thirty years, knew of Sr Barbara's madness and had walled up the lower part of the window in the room where she was confined in order to protect her. This person, contradicting other accounts, testified that her confinement was no secret. A doctor had paid her frequent visits, the former superior general of the Carmelites, Fr Natalis Hanzet, had ordered that she should be kept in the convent, and on several occasions several of the sisters had unsuccessfully applied to diocesan officials to have her removed to an asylum because of her 'fearful language.' Ecclesiastical officials had known of Sr Barbara's existence and her confinement: the diocese refused the request because 'the duty of the nuns was to take care of a mad sister, and not to sent her to a lunatic asylum.' *The Tablet* also told its readers that the mother superior and her assistants were still in prison, 'although the minute researches made in all the convent papers and in every part of the building, have not produced the slightest scrap of evidence in support of the slanderous charges of cruelty.' The article concluded by noting that the uproar and shock among the people of Cracow had subsided, and warned that other individuals would use this case as an example in their crusade to suppress religious orders and convents.[19] Roman Catholic opinion believed that the results of the public inquiry would eventually clear the Carmelites of any barbarous actions. Initial reports from Cracow seemed to justify this view.

The Tablet also printed a communication from Austria concerning the preliminary proceedings against the mother superior and other nuns accused of cruelty against Sr Barbara. These nuns were 'declared guilty of the *objective*, but not *subjective*, offence of overtly violating the right of personal freedom, and are adjudged to stand a special trial accordingly.'[20] They had already appealed this decision. The report, however, emphasized the changed public attitude toward the actions of the Carmelite nuns and also supplied new information about Sr Barbara. Before arriving in Cracow, it reported, Barbara Ubryk had formerly been a nun at a convent in Warsaw where 'she showed symptoms of insanity, and a change of scene was recommended.' The Carmelites received her, but the superior did not know about her history of mental health problems. If Sr Barbara's past had been known, the Cracow

---

[19] The same edition of *The Tablet* also reported that the Home Minister had recently withdrawn the annual state allowance to the Carmelite convent in Cracow because of the Sr Barbara incident. After appealing unsuccessfully to the Austrian Chancellor, the papal nuncio went directly to Emperor Francis Joseph. The emperor refused to interfere in the case officially, but promised to give the convent the annual allowance from his personal funds. The paper took this story as a sign that the furore over Sr Barbara was decreasing. 'Whether literally correct or not, this story is believed in Vienna, and is, in itself, a fresh sign that the original calumny is dying away.'

[20] *The Tablet*, 21 August 1869.

nuns would probably not have welcomed her. For seven years, the article continued, Sr Barbara exhibited no symptoms of insanity, and even wrote to her friends in Warsaw and described her contentment and happiness. Conditions at the convent then changed.

> In a short time her madness seized her more violently than ever, [and] it took the shape of 'Erotomania.' She seemed possessed of the devil of impurity, and believed herself to be the Holy Trinity. She tore off her clothes, destroyed her bed, her furniture, littered the floor with the straw of her mattress. Her clothes were renewed, her bed, her furniture restored, her cell cleaned out, continually. It was of no use. She wrecked everything again immediately. She showed herself at her window naked, and shouted the most horrible obscenities and blasphemies outside.

To stop this scandal, the convent officials walled up part of Sr Barbara's window, but she continued to receive the same food as the other sisters.

According to this Roman Catholic report, her condition remained unchanged after she had been released and removed to an asylum, where the authorities had to secure her with a strait jacket. Were the Carmelite sisters culpable for their treatment of Sr Barbara? Were they guilty of the cruel and inhumane treatment of another person, or were their actions only imprudent? The Catholic explanation stressed the naiveté of the convent's method of treatment. The sisters, for example, did not physically restrain her, as *The Times* had contended. In fact some noted the imprudence of the sisters for not sending Sr Barbara to an institution for proper treatment. Those who tried to view the case objectively drew attention to the cloistered state of the sisters' life and the horrible nature of Sr Barbara's illness. Moreover, they pointed out, several people, including her relatives, knew the seriousness of her mental condition and the manner of her confinement in the convent. This article, originating from Austria, offered an explanation for the curiosity and interest shown in the case of Sr Barbara: 'That the Cracow affair is another case among so many of gross and malignant slander and exaggeration, seems now taken for granted in the Catholic world here, while some non-Catholic journals of a more orderly sort are moderating their tone.' The report ended by noting that the Bishop of Cracow had recently withdrawn his 'harsh expression against the nuns.' Another writer in *The Tablet* pointed out that a doctor had visited Sr Barbara, who 'was suffering from a peculiar and most painful form of madness,' and had found no fault with the treatment she received from the nuns. Moreover, the paper concluded, 'Negligence and ignorance of the proper treatment may be urged against the nuns, but neither cruelty nor immorality.' Nonetheless, people in England, eager to blacken the reputation of Roman Catholicism and those suspicious of life behind convent walls, soon began to exploit Sr Barbara's trials to their own ends. At times, writers took great liberties with the facts of the case and diverged greatly from the reports in *The Times* and *The Tablet*.

In 1869, the year that the news of Sr Barbara became public, a small pamphlet, *The Horrors of Roman Catholic Convents and the Sufferings of Sister Barbara*, appeared in England.[21] The cover presented the reader with a shocking picture depicting the discovery of a sickly, emaciated woman in tattered clothes, chained in a dungeon. Her expression revealed a mixture of suffering and fear; her clerical rescuers displayed shock. The caption beneath this illustration captured the message of the publication: 'With an awful Description of her horrible condition when she was first discovered in her dismal, loathsome Den, and the fiendish treatment inflicted upon her by inhuman Priests, Lady Superioress and Nuns, who styled themselves "Spiritual Wives," and the "Brides of Heaven"!' The introduction by the editor called attention to the alleged wickedness of the Roman Catholic Church and the crimes this religion had perpetrated in the British Isles throughout history. The writer singled out wicked priests, the abominations of auricular confession, and the evils of convent life, and then called upon the readers to defend 'the Unalloyed Gospel of the Holy Scriptures' and the 'Unity of England's National Church, and the Purity of Her Christian Teaching.' For those who doubted the evil of the Roman Church, the case of Sr Barbara would open their eyes.

This version of her story began with a number of anti-papal diatribes that warned the English nation against the wicked designs of the Catholic Church, especially the increasing popularity of sisterhoods within Anglicanism. According to the pamphlet, these Anglo-Catholic convents 'have steadily gone on undermining Protestantism within and without the walls of our places of worship, and enticing our daughters into the numerous convents they [Roman Catholics] have everywhere established.' This posed a real threat to England's 'Civil and religious liberty.' The corrupting character of Roman priests and nuns seriously jeopardized 'those precious rights, liberties and principles for which the fathers of the Reformation suffered and died.' Sisterhoods promoted unnatural practices, and the sufferings of poor Sr Barbara visibly demonstrated the insidious and cruel nature of Catholicism. The outline of this story did not differ from the facts reported by *The Times* and *The Tablet*, and in many instances the report was based on the information already contained in the former newspaper, but its interpretation strayed from objective reporting.

In this anti-Catholic account of the rescue, Sr Barbara's cell was located 'close to a dung-hole.' The graphic description of the nun also differed somewhat from other portrayals : 'In a dark, infected hole adjoining the sewer, sat, or rather, cowered, on a heap of straw, an entirely naked, totally neglected,

[21] *The Horrors of Roman Catholic Convents, Exposed in a True Heartrending Account of the Shocking Imprisonment and Sufferings of Sister Barbara, a Polish Carmelite Nun, Who was Walled Up Alive for Twenty-One Years in the Cold Dark Cell of an Infected Underground Dungeon!* (London, 1869).

half insane woman, who, at the unaccustomed view of light, the outer world, and human beings, folded her hands and pitifully implored: "I am hungry" . . .' In addition to the disgusting description of the accommodation of Sr Barbara, the diatribe described the convent and the nuns as, 'This den, the inhumane sisters, who call themselves women, spiritual wives, the brides of heaven . . .' Closely following the language of *The Times*, the report described the astonished reaction of the Bishop of Cracow, recounted Sr Barbara's account that she was imprisoned because she had broken her vow of chastity, and quoted the mother superior, who stated that Sr Barbara had been kept in close confinement since 1848 'by order of the physician, because of her unsound mind.'

Other disturbing and shocking additions also found their way into this narration. The investigators discovered torture devices, and told the readers that these instruments had 'been used for torturing other poor nuns immured in the same convent and subjected to the iniquitous doings of their wicked father-confessors, as nuns formerly were . . .' Another example of editorial licence to discredit Catholicism and convents can be found in the alleged discoveries made by the government commission when it investigated the convent grounds.

> In passing through the refectory they discovered a secret chamber containing a whole collection of mediaeval instruments of torture. Amongst these are two huge crosses, weighing 80lb each, which guilty nuns had to wear on their backs as a punishment, two heavy stones of marble to be placed on the chest, and a number of 'crowns of thorns' with long and sharp iron nails. There were also several girdles, also fitted with nails pointing in wards [*sic*], which it is said were worn next to the skin by penitents, and a sort of knout for flogging the refractory.

These devices, unique to this rendition of the story but found frequently in numerous other anti-Catholic tracts, formed part of that sacred arsenal which all nuns supposedly used to punish or to mortify the flesh.

The pamphlet also examined the role of the confessor, following other published reports in describing the part played by the convent's confessor, Fr Lewkowicz, in the discovery of Sr Barbara and the eventual arrest of the mother superior after her discovery. But in this version the circumstances surrounding the death of the priest took on a new and diabolical character. (A different spelling of the priest's name appeared in the account printed by *The Times*.) According to both *The Times* and *The Tablet*, the confessor died suddenly, and the latter told its readers that the cause was natural. This publication, however, added a sinister element. 'The body of the former confessor, Father Lewkowicz, has been exhumed,' it claimed, 'and the news from Cracow is that traces of poison have been discovered in the body.' Additional tests would either confirm or disprove the report, but 'it seems certainly strange that the chief witness should have died just at the moment when the discovery [of Sr Barbara] became public.' The pamphlet also claimed that the superior of the nuns, a Carmelite priest, had visited the convent before her release, saw Sr Barbara 'in her horrible state, but had made no complaint.' *The Horrors of Roman Catholic Convents*, however, did acknowledge that Sr Barbara had a history of mental illness, but still described the manner in which the other nuns cared for her as an imprisonment.

The story of Sr Barbara only formed a part of this anti-Catholic polemic. The other pages contained allegations of cruel and inhumane treatment associated with Roman Catholicism and even mocked some of its doctrines and liturgical practices. The main theme running throughout, however, pertained to the question of freedom. English Protestantism had traditionally championed personal liberty, while Catholicism, on the other hand, sought to make vassals and slaves of its followers. Popery and Catholic institutions, such as convents, would destroy the freedom and independence of Protestant Britain. Like Sr Barbara, British citizens would become imprisoned and enslaved by Roman Catholicism. In concluding the discussion of Sr Barbara, the author stated: 'Leaving these sickening details to make their own impression, we will fill up the last part of our pamphlet with proofs, from the best sources (some Catholic) of the unchristian and soul-destroying character of Popery.' Sr Barbara, thus, had become a warning to those people who would welcome or embrace Roman Catholicism. State supervision would provide a safeguard against loss of liberty and freedom in convents. In 1870, for example, John Kensit, an anti-Roman Catholic writer and speaker and future secretary of the Protestant Truth Society, published *English Convents, What Are They?*[22] Kensit argued his case for parliamentary inspection of convents, and he used two short newspaper references to Sr Barbara as examples of convent abuse.

Anti-Catholic writers or those seeking state inspection of convents did not use the case of Sr Barbara and the circumstances surrounding her confinement and release again until the end of the nineteenth century. During the 1890s anti-convent writings still criticized sisterhoods. Alleged reports of the imprisonment of nuns in England and Europe, charges of mismanagement of orphanages operated by nuns, numerous pamphlets and novels which stereotyped the wickedness of sisterhoods, and the old campaign to force open convent doors to government inspection kept the question of convents before the public.[23]

---

[22] J. Kensit, *English Convents, What Are They? or, Is There Any Necessity for Conventual Inspection* (London, 1870). Kensit published another work in the 1890s, *The Inquisition and Confessional of the Present Century* (London, 1893?), which made explicit references to imprisoned nuns and their confinement in vaults located within convents. He drew special attention to a case of imprisoned nuns which occurred in Paris in 1871. To shock his readers, Kensit supplied a drawing of the three wooden cages in which were imprisoned three nuns.

[23] Examples of anti-convent propaganda during this decade are numerous. Three publications illustrate this type of literature. During the 1890s the Church Association published *The Fashionable Torture Instruments of the Ritualists; or, the Gospel of 'Expiation'* (London, 1890?). This short pamphlet printed drawings of torture devices or instruments allegedly used by nuns to impose self-discipline on their bodies. 'Convents as Prisons and Lunatic Asylums' appeared in *The Monthly Letter of the Protestant Alliance* (October, 1891), pp. 1–24. The

For example, a footnote in H. Rider Haggard's 1893 novel, *Montezuma's Daughter*,[24] claimed that the author had seen in a Mexican museum the remains of a nun who had been 'walled up.' The Jesuit writer Fr Herbert Thurston successfully attacked this allegation both in the press and in a pamphlet published by the Catholic Truth Society, and eventually forced the author to retract his misleading statement. And Sr Barbara was not entirely forgotten. At the end of the century the Rev W. Lancelot Holland, a vocal opponent and critic of sisterhoods, lectured on numerous cases of imprisoned nuns and wrote articles in Protestant papers attacking convents. He drew attention to the case of Sr Barbara, who had died in 1891, as an example of convent cruelty, and thus began the last great debate over the facts of the 'imprisoned nun of Cracow.'

Responding to some of Holland's remarks, the Rev Sydney Smith, SJ, wrote a pamphlet, *Calumnies against Convents*, which the Catholic Truth Society published in 1894.[25] This apologetic work critiqued some of the recent slanders addressed against convents in England such as 'the escape and the recapture of a nun from Colwich,' charges of cruelty made against a convent at Norwood, and hostile reports of the activities at an orphanage operated by nuns at Carlisle Place, London. Finally the author addressed the case of Sr Barbara. Smith began his discussion of the Cracow convent incident by quoting at length a report of the rescue of Sr Barbara that had appeared in a publication of the Protestant Association, and which closely paralleled the language contained in *The Horrors of Roman Catholic Convents*. Smith pointed out that 'This ghastly story was repeated by the journals of nearly every country at the time, and was received on every side with a chorus of indignation.'[26] Writers and publications hostile to Roman Catholicism gleefully blamed the institutions and beliefs of that religion for the alleged inhumane treatment of Sr Barbara. This Jesuit writer believed that another culprit had wickedly encouraged anti-Catholic feelings.

The opponents of Roman Catholicism throughout Europe feared a papal plot to convert the world, and the Catholics became convinced that in self-defence these forces had started a conspiracy against the threatened onslaught from Rome. According to Fr Smith:

---

work described numerous examples of the alleged imprisonment of nuns in England and on the Continent. A short mention of Sr Barbara was included. H. Grattan Guinness, Secretary of the Protestant Alliance, produced a book of poetry, *The City of the Seven Hills. An Illustrated Poem* (London, 1891). One poem, 'Rome's Convents,' ridiculed sisterhoods. The author also included a series of notes to back up his arguments and a series of pictures of victims allegedly 'walled up' by the Inquisition in Mexico.

[24] H. Rider Haggard, *Montezuma's Daughter* (London, 1893). The author later retracted his statement about immured nuns in Mexico after a lengthy debate with Fr Herbert Thurston, SJ, which appeared in the English press.

[25] Sydney Smith, *Calumnies against Convents* (London, 1894).

[26] *Ibid.*, p. 18.

Those, however, who understood the methods by which the Masonic Governments on the Continent were in the habit of arousing a popular feeling in favour of the measures that they were projecting against the Church, asked themselves what sort of Ministry were at the head of affairs in Austria, and what projects they had in contemplation.

This sinister Masonic threat, Smith believed, had unduly exaggerated and distorted the case of Sr Barbara. The Austrian ministry, according to this conspiracy theory, had used the public indignation and outrage against the Cracow convent to further its policy, which was 'bent on the suppression of the religious orders and the confiscation of their goods.' In fact, Fr Smith argued, a government official 'in a feigned female hand' had written the mysterious and anonymous letter which had exposed the existence of Sr Barbara. Moreover, the civil authorities had failed to act with dispatch when a mob attacked the convent in Cracow. The Masonic influence in the government, Smith told his readers, had followed a pre-arranged plan and moved quickly to 'withhold the annual pension on which the convent depended for its subsistence, and even suppress the convent altogether.'[27] Other Polish municipalities followed the lead of Cracow, and all this had transpired before the outcome of the trial and inquest. 'Why this indecent haste,' Smith reasoned, 'save because all had been arranged beforehand, and they were anxious to use the opportunity before it was destroyed by the detection of the fraud?'

Fr Smith noted that the major English newspapers, in particular *The Times*, had quickly lost interest in the Sr Barbara case. The curious reader in England did not know the results of the trial of the nuns accused of cruelty against Sr Barbara, and consequently he set out to inform them. The English Jesuit made no apologies for relying on the reports printed in *The Tablet*.[28] Smith repeated the 21 August 1869 story of that Roman Catholic paper, which stated that the two nuns were found guilty of an objective offence of violating the right of Sr Barbara to personal freedom and were ordered 'to stand a special trial accordingly.'[29] In other words, he pointed out, 'it was judged that they had *unwittingly* been guilty of a legal offence in locking the door on a mad woman without having first gone through the legal formalities.'[30] Fr Smith also revealed the outcome and verdict of 'the special' trial, information the anti-Catholic sources had failed to include in their histories of Sr Barbara. Quoting from the edition of 12 February 1870 of the *Civiltà Cattolica*, the Jesuit-operated publication located in Rome, Smith proudly announced:

> Hence Giska ['the Masonic' Minister for Home Affairs] and his fellow-conspirators had to put up with the passing of a verdict in good form to the effect

---

[27] *Ibid.*, p. 19.
[28] Fr Smith also made use of the reports contained the Catholic newspaper, *Civiltà Cattolica*.
[29] *The Tablet*, 21 August 1869.
[30] Smith, *Calumnies*, p. 20.

that Barbara Ubryk had in no way been shewn to have undergone any cruelty to which her madness could be imputed, and that throughout its course she had been treated as well as possible according to the method consistent with her deplorable state, and had received every attention which the most tender Christian charity could inspire.

No previous written accounts of the alleged Cracow cruelties had mentioned this verdict. Smith ended his short pamphlet by noting that the citizens of Cracow had started a subscription to replace those funds which the government had succeeded in sequestering. These arguments, however, did not convince the Rev W. Lancelot Holland.

Holland reacted immediately to the challenge thrown down by Fr Smith, and wrote a response which attempted to expose the evils and inhumanity of convent life. Its title, *Walled Up Nuns and Nuns Walled In*, captured the purpose of the author.[31] The introduction drew the reader's attention to the increasing power and nefarious influence of the papacy, and pointed out that the Roman Church had 'advanced in all the refinements of cruelty, practising every method or torture that human ingenuity and satanic influence could devise upon those who ventured to dissent from her principles, or attempted in any way to spread the light of truth.'[32] This type of punishment also applied to recalcitrant or erring nuns. The British public, Holland argued, must be informed of the true nature of the convent. Defenceless, young, and sentimental women in Britain needed protection from the inherent evils of sisterhoods. According to his reasoning, 'if the public would only grasp the real foulness so often underlying the whited sepulchres called Convents, there would not be many of these places left in Great Britain within a month after the discovery.' After illustrating the evils of conventual life from other examples of alleged abuses, the author discussed the case of Sr Barbara.

Holland began by telling his audience that he had earlier written a pamphlet concerning the Cracow incident,[33] and this had caused Fr Sidney Smith to reply with *Calumnies against Convents*, a defence of sisterhoods and a vindication of the treatment of Sr Barbara. In respect of the Cracow incident, the author attacked Smith's work and accused him of manufacturing 'palpable misrepresentations.'[34] Holland sneered at Smith's version of the story and questioned the veracity of the Jesuit: 'for unless the facts are well grasped, it would be impossible to withstand the varnished lies and subtle arguments of the trained sophists who are put forward by the Church of Rome to discredit

---

[31] W. Lancelot Holland, *Walled Up Nuns and Nuns Walled In* (London, 1895).
[32] *Ibid.*, p. 11.
[33] W. Lancelot Holland, *Somebody's Child: or Sister Barbara, the Carmelite Nun*. The pamphlet was out of print by 1895. This earlier work by Holland cannot be found, but probably contained the same material as *Walled Up Nuns and Nuns Walled In*.
[34] Holland, *Walled Up Nuns*, p. 163.

the truth.'³⁵ Holland's story of the rescue, however, introduced several new elements, and the narration now began to read like a gothic fiction. A new character and saviour, Sr Mary, appeared. This nun had discovered that Sr Barbara was confined to a 'dungeon,' and taking pity on her, Sr Mary had stolen the key from the mother superior and smuggled food into Sr Barbara. According to this rendition, Sr Mary found Sr Barbara sane, heard her story, and consequently vowed to rescue her. Moreover, Holland added another new twist, and claimed that Sr Mary had written the letter which eventually resulted in the release of Sr Barbara by the authorities!

Holland's narration of the rescue of Sr Barbara paralleled other accounts, but it appears that he exaggerated his description of the poor creature: 'her body entirely nude, bristling with long jagged hair, filth and vermin; her limbs shrunk and bent like withered sticks, her head and hair squalid and diseased; her thin, hollow cheeks nearly touching each other, and the great wild eyes flashing and glaring out from their deep sockets.'³⁶ An extremely disturbing drawing in this book depicted the scared and skeletal figure of a naked person cowering in the corner of a dark cell. As in the other accounts, the Roman Catholic bishop expressed horror at the discovery. Before leaving the convent, Sr Barbara explained that she had been imprisoned because she had broken her vows. In this version of the story, Holland identified the confessor as Fr Calenski, another new name for the priest, and he did not suggest poison to account for the confessor's sudden death. Rather, the priest committed suicide, and left a note which stated: 'I have resolved to kill myself: farewell to all on earth.'³⁷

After some criticism of Fr Smith and his interpretation of the case, Holland outlined his own interpretation of the results of the commission set up by the Austrian government to investigate the happening at the Cracow convent. He admitted that he had gleaned the information from the Vienna papers. The bishop, who sat on the commission, accepted the explanation of Sr Mary's authorship of the letter, but this story conflicted with Fr Smith's allegation that a government official had written it. Sr Mary testified next and stated that Sr Barbara had never exhibited any symptoms of mental illness when she first entered the convent. She also insinuated that Sr Barbara was 'imprisoned' because she resisted the advances of the confessor, and moreover the mother superior played a significant part in this conspiracy. The question of Sr Barbara's sanity remained a crucial issue. Sr Mary gave evidence which suggested that Sr Barbara had previously suffered from mental problems, but immediately before her release, the imprisoned nun 'returned sensible, rational replies, though she exhibited an excessive amount of nervousness.³⁸ Holland then revealed the decision of the commission, which clashed with Fr Smith's account:

---

[35] *Ibid.*, p. 165.
[36] *Ibid.*, p. 169.
[37] *Ibid.*, p. 171.
[38] *Ibid.*, p. 175.

> That the said Barbara Ubryk has been for 21 years unlawfully imprisoned in a loathsome, underground dungeon of the Carmelite Convent, and most cruelly and barbarously oppressed and maltreated by Mother Josepha, the Abbess thereof, and Father Calenski, the Confessor thereof. We also find that the said Barbara Ubryk was not of unsound mind, and therefore that it was unnecessary to deprive her of her liberty.

The commission noted that the convent's confessor had already committed suicide, but recommended, again conflicting with Smith's report, that the mother superior should be punished for her misdeeds.

Holland's book next introduced several new pieces of evidence. For the first time, interested people could actually read the testimony of Sr Barbara, who now appeared to be perfectly lucid and cured of any mental infirmities. The nun related that she had entered the Carmelite convent at Cracow, at the age of sixteen, after a failed romance. Holland presented additional testimony which stated that Sr Barbara had first joined another convent, and then transferred to Cracow after a bout of mental illness. She described her first years at Cracow in idyllic terms; both the mother superior, Sr Josepha, and the confessor treated her very well. However, the priest soon began to become more and more interested in her. One night he visited Sr Barbara's room to console her about some penances she had received from the mother superior. According to Sr Barbara, this did not 'excite her suspicions until he put his arm around her and kissed her full on the lips.'[39] She admitted that the actions of this cleric, who had also left some gifts of food, bewildered her. Sr Barbara's account of what happened next introduced the new twist of a sexual element into the already complex story.

Apparently the confessor had laced the cakes and fruit with drugs with the intention of sexually assaulting her, since she immediately fell into a deep slumber after enjoying the gifts. When Sr Barbara awoke, she discovered Fr Calenski, the confessor, lurking in her room. She then related the following scene:

> Evidently perceiving by his actions his wicked designs, she sprang away from him, struck him in the face, and screamed out, 'Go away from my cell, Father Calenski! Why do you behave so wickedly?' He struck her a heavy blow with his hand, and in a low hissing tone said, 'Silence; if you utter another scream I will kill you!'[40]

The frightened nun screamed, and the mother superior arrived. After consulting with the confessor, the mother superior left Sr Barbara's room, telling her, 'Girl, your silly lips have sealed your doom!' After a week's confinement in her convent room, Sr Barbara was eventually taken to a

---

[39] *Ibid.*, p. 178.
[40] *Ibid.*, p. 179.

dungeon in the basement of the convent, where the mother superior told her she would remain until her death. The confessor continued to visit her, but finally exclaimed, 'I am tired of you now, why don't you die or go really crazy?'[41] Sr Barbara admitted becoming insane and she also remembered the cold, the hunger, and the physical torture she had endured as a prisoner, especially at the hands of the priest. After threatening to murder her, the confessor began to attack her physically. According to her testimony, Fr Calenski, 'raising his cane and giving me several heavy blows with it, and causing me such agony that I became nearly crazy . . . [I] could not help screaming out . . .'[42] She suffered for days with a 'numbness in my neck and back' and the pain began to affect her mental state. But the abuse did not stop. 'On several occasions after this Father Calenski and Mother Josepha beat me, and I became so filled with despair . . .' Sr Barbara's story ended with a visit from Sr Mary and her eventual rescue.

If Holland's accusations were true, then cruel and inhumane punishments, similar to those allegedly used by the Inquisitors, had taken place in a Cracow convent. Moreover, nuns throughout England and Europe probably encountered similar punishments on a regular basis. The Roman Catholic newspapers and writers who had sought to explain the Sr Barbara episode as an example of naive nuns attempting to deal with an insane member of their convent had obviously lied. Consequently, the Rev Sydney Smith, SJ, whose earlier work on anti-convent literature had already irked the Rev W. Lancelot Holland, responded with another pamphlet published by the Catholic Truth Society. In this booklet, Smith branded Holland as a bigot and identified him as an important member of the Protestant Alliance, a violent anti-Catholic organization. Smith then returned to his central thesis: strong Masonic influences in the Austrian government had caused the furore and violence in Cracow against Roman Catholicism and its convents. He restated the contentions of his previous article, which contradicted all the main arguments of Holland, and reminded his readers that the accused Carmelite nuns, including the mother superior, had been acquitted. He referred the interested person back to the article in *Civiltà Cattolica* which vindicated the conduct of these nuns.[43] Fr Smith also repeated the evidence printed by *The Tablet*. He then addressed the charges brought by Holland's book dealing with Sr Barbara.

Smith totally dismissed Holland's evidence. According to his pamphlet, 'Mr. Holland's new authorities are not only false, but, it is to be feared, fraudulent.'[44] Fr Smith questioned the veracity of Holland's interpretation of the

---

[41] *Ibid.*, p. 180.

[42] *Ibid.*, p. 182.

[43] The article in the 12 February 1870 edition of *Civiltà Cattolica* reported a verdict which stated that no evidence proved that Barbara Ubryk had suffered any cruelty at the hands of the Carmelite nuns and that the nuns had treated Sr Barbara's madness in an appropriate and Christian manner.

[44] Sydney Smith, *The True Story of Barbara Ubryk* (London, 1897), p. 8.

commission's report, the evidence given, and the testimony of Sr Barbara. In fact, the Jesuit pointed out, Holland's chapter on Sr Barbara relied almost exclusively on an American pamphlet which dealt with the Cracow convent and Sr Barbara.[45] It did not utilize documentation from Poland. This booklet, Smith argued, represented 'nothing better than a romance absolutely unsupported by any reference whatever. Yet it is from it, not from any authentic document, in spite of his express declaration to the contrary, that his quotations within inverted commas are extracted.'[46] Smith set out to destroy the credibility of this factitious and spurious American pamphlet. As his ammunition, he identified and cited the medical and legal records associated with the case.

The most impressive of Holland's sources remained the testimony of Sr Barbara herself. Smith, however, named and then quoted four sources which attested that in her poor mental state she could not have given a coherent statement about her life and imprisonment in the convent. 'All concur in testifying to facts which prove that Barbara Ubryk could not possibly have made the alleged deposition either on 16 August 1869, or on any other date previous or subsequent.'[47] Smith urged cynics and unbelievers to visit the hospital in Cracow where Sr Barbara resided until her death in 1891. There they could enquire about her mental state after she was freed from the convent. Fr Smith also pointed out errors of fact in Holland's account of her life prior to becoming a nun and of her mental state before arriving at Cracow. For example, Sr Barbara had previously suffered from a history of mental health problems. Fr Smith dismissed the accusation of the alleged attempt at seduction and cruelty at the hands of the confessor, whom Holland had apparently falsely identified as Fr Calenski. He pointed out that 'no person of that name had at any time whatever to do with her case . . .'[48] Consequently, Fr Smith came to the following conclusion:

> In view of all this evidence it is excessive to say that Mr. Holland and his nameless American friend (who for aught we know may be himself under another guise) must share between them the responsibility of having attempted to pass off as genuine a palpably spurious document containing the grossest charges against others, and this with the express object of exciting prejudice and persecution against the peaceful priests, nuns, and other Catholics of English-speaking countries.

Smith next attacked the decision of the commissioners that Holland had

---

[45] See *The Convent Horror. Story of Barbara Ubryk. Twenty-One Years in the Dungeon, Eight Feet Long, Six Feet Wide. From Official Records* (Toledo, Ohio, 1896?). This booklet was also published in England.
[46] Smith, *Barbara Ubryk*, p. 9.
[47] *Ibid.*, p. 11.
[48] *Ibid.*, p. 12.

presented, and the Jesuit argued that this so-called evidence contained several errors or untrue statements, 'a plain proof that it is spurious.'[49] The signatures to Holland's questionable document which condemned the Carmelite nuns, Fr Smith contended, were 'made-up names.' He noted that only one commission had been established in Cracow, and the name of a judge (Gebhardt) which could be found in numerous other documents as a member failed to appear on Holland's list. As he had previously stated, Holland incorrectly identified the confessor as Calenski, and Fr Smith named the convent's confessor as Fr Piatkewicz. Smith also contradicted other false stories about this priest by pointing out that the confessor had died a natural death at the age of 75 in 1881. Moreover, Sr Barbara's place of confinement was not 'an underground dungeon,' but a room situated on the first floor of the convent at the end of a hall occupied by other nuns. Smith backed up these contentions with numerous references to documentary sources, reports in the press, and witnesses.

Fr Smith enumerated other errors in Holland's account, delighting in destroying the testimony of the heroine of his story, Sr Mary. The Jesuit laughed at her ignorance concerning the correct name of the confessor and the location of Sr Barbara's room, and he found it hard to believe that nuns living on the same corridor would be ignorant of her existence. At least, he reasoned, her cries and shrieks would have alerted others to her presence. The name of the mother superior of the convent came into question: Holland called her Sr Josepha; but Smith's sources identified this nun as Sr Maria Wenzyk. Smith then looked at the legal proceedings against the Carmelite superior and her accomplice, and he repeated the findings contained in his earlier work, *Calumnies against Convents*: sufficient evidence did not exist to prosecute the nuns; they had illegally locked Sr Barbara's door against her will, but had not acted in a cruel or criminal manner; and the charges against the two nuns had been dismissed. Moreover, Fr Smith again supplied the proper documentation to back up these statements. He also quickly dismissed Holland's other contentions: Sr Barbara was not sane; there was no attempt to conceal her mental condition or the method of dealing with her problems from ecclesiastical superiors; and the physical condition of her room was not as harsh and severe as some described. Fr Smith directed the interested reader to a list of sources to corroborate his statements, and he ended his pamphlet by surprisingly agreeing with his adversary, Holland, on one point: 'some fresh legislation in reference to convents is imperatively needed.'[50] He did not advocate parliamentary measures which would subject convents to inspection by the government, but rather 'a remodelling of the law of libel as shall enable the innocent and peaceful inhabitants of English convents to protect themselves against slanderers cowardly enough to attack them under the guise of charges against other convents in distant lands' such as Poland.[51]

[49] *Ibid.*, p. 13.
[50] *Ibid.*, p. 23.
[51] *Ibid.*, p. 24.

With the publication of Fr Sydney Smith's blistering and well-reasoned attack against Holland and the other critics of sisterhoods whom he mentioned, the literature devoted to mocking convents and describing alleged abuses within the cloister decreased markedly.[52] Anti-convent publications continued to decline as the new century opened in England, and along with other popular stories the figure of Sr Barbara also began to fade from memory.[53] To the end of the nineteenth century, individuals who interpreted Sr Barbara's life in a manner to fit their purposes – anti-Roman Catholic writers or defenders of Catholic sisterhoods who tried to justify the actions of the Cracow Carmelites – had distorted the real personality and the life of this woman, who died in 1891. Discrepancies can be seen in the numerous narrations. One interpretation of the case pointed the finger at the influence of the Masons, attempting to discredit Roman Catholicism, and another argued that cruel and heartless convents routinely tortured recalcitrant members, and consequently they should be suppressed or brought under government supervision. Moreover, disagreements about Sr Barbara's background, reasons for entering the convent, state of mental health before and after her release, and the reasons for her confinement appeared in the stories about her. Confusion surrounding the name of the confessor and the mode of his death, the author of the letter that prompted officials to visit the convent, and the correct name and the role of the mother superior also added to the mystery. Differing

---

[52] The anti-convent literature did not, however, disappear altogether. See, for example, Walter Walsh's critique of Anglo-Catholicism, which stated some harsh things about Anglican sisterhoods. W. Walsh, *The Secret History of the Oxford Movement* (London, 1899). In 1899 an anonymous author wrote *The Martyrdom of an Empress* (New York, 1899) which attempted to canonize the Austrian Empress Elizabeth, who had been assassinated in 1898. This biography took some liberties with the life of Sr Barbara, such as her background prior to entering the convent, the important role played by her brother in starting the investigation concerning her well-being, and the significant part played by the Empress Elizabeth, who asked the ecclesiastical authorities in Cracow to intervene. In addition to the graphic descriptions of the incarcerated nun, the account stated that the nuns had imprisoned Sr Barbara because she had kept up a correspondence with a former admirer and planned to elope with him. The story of the Cracow convent is included in this biography not necessarily to castigate the Roman Catholic Church, but to emphasize the charity of the murdered empress, who frequently sent flowers to Sr Barbara while she was in an asylum.

[53] The case of Sr Barbara did make another brief appearance. Early in the century S.J. Abbott, Secretary of the Convent Enquiry Society, published *The Empress and the Carmelite Nun. Twenty-One Years in a Convent Dungeon* (London, 1902?). This short pamphlet took its name from the recently-published biography of the Empress Elizabeth. It also contained excerpts from various newspapers that had carried the story of Sr Barbara during the previous century. Abbott used the case to argue for the necessity of government inspection of convents. Fr Herbert Thurston, SJ, published two pamphlets which attacked the stories that had developed out of H. Rider Haggard's *Montezuma's Daughter*. Thurston made no mention of Sr Barbara. See *The Myth of the Walled-Up Nun* (London, 1902) and *A Tale of Mexican Horrors* (London, 1904).

descriptions of Sr Barbara's sufferings and the condition of the room where she was discovered also appeared in print.

Some common elements, however, surfaced in all the accounts of her life. Sr Barbara Ubryk, by common agreement, was placed under confinement in a Carmelite convent in Cracow until she was set free in 1869. Cracow did experience some anti-Catholic violence because of rumours about her wretched physical and mental state, and numerous newspapers, some with an obvious prejudice, took delight in reporting the story. An inquiry did take place that eventually exonerated the convent's superior. The confessor to the convent appeared in all the accounts, and Sr Barbara did die in an asylum in 1891. Beside these accepted facts, the story of Sr Barbara had merged with fiction and legend by the end of the century. One became acquainted with the myth of Sr Barbara, and not the person.

Is history, as the figure of Venus painted on the wall announced to all onlookers, merely a collection of myths? The story or legend of Sr Barbara Ubryk clearly demonstrates the power of history. People can easily manipulate or misuse facts to fit pre-conceived stereotypes or agendas. In matters dealing with religion, people in nineteenth-century England often engaged in polemics or crusades against religious rivals, as the case of Sr Barbara clearly demonstrates. Most fierce and vitriolic was the suspicion and hatred directed against Roman Catholics in that country.[54] In the minds of some anti-Catholics, moreover, convents represented cruel and inhumane places of mental and physical torture. If one accepts and acknowledges the tendency in Victorian England to attack theological and doctrinal opponents in newspapers, pamphlets, and books, even to the point of creating falsehoods, one may arrive at a better understanding of the dynamics of religious hatred and bigotry. If, on the other hand, people accept uncritically stories which fit a stereotype, such as the wickedness of convent life, then the verdict of Venus about the mythic nature of history has some validity.

---

[54] For example, see D.G. Paz, *Popular Anti-Catholicism in Mid-Victorian England* (Stanford, California, 1992); Frank Wallis, *Popular Anti-Catholicism in Mid-Victorian Britain* (Lewiston, New York, 1993); and John Wolffe, *The Protestant Crusade in Great Britain* (Oxford, 1991).

9

BERNARD WARD: EDMUNDIAN AND HISTORIAN

STEWART FOSTER

I

IN HIS biographical memoir of Monsignor Bernard Ward, which formed the basis of an obituary notice in *The Edmundian,* Canon Edwin Burton referred to the death of the former President of St Edmund's College, Ware, and first Bishop of Brentwood as the disappearance into the past of 'one of the most prominent figures in the history of St Edmund's':

> Bishop Ward's name is likely to be remembered by the English Catholics of the future for his work as a historian and perhaps for his educational activities. At St Edmund's he must always be held in remembrance and honour as one of the greatest benefactors the College has ever known, and one whose work has already become an integral part of its tradition. Whatever place he may keep in the memory of posterity as a whole, his position in the future records of Old Hall is assured.[1]

In the late Victorian period Bernard Ward was in the vanguard of progress in Catholic education and epitomised the growing self-confidence of an English Catholic community increasingly concerned to record the history of its still recent struggle for Emancipation. Bernard Nicholas Ward was the third son and seventh of the eight children of William George ('Ideal') Ward and his wife Frances Mary Wingfield. A prominent convert to Catholicism from the Oxford Movement, W.G. Ward was professor of theology at St Edmund's College. His third son was born on 4 February 1857 at Old Hall House, the family home which Pugin had built for Ward in the college grounds in 1847. Cardinal Wiseman was a close friend of the family, hence Bernard Ward's

---

[1] St Edmund's College Archives (hereafter SEC) 14/17/18: n.d. [1920], E. Burton, typescript biographical memoir of Bishop Bernard Ward.

middle name, and Wiseman often visited the Wards at Old Hall. Bernard Ward was to spend more than forty of his sixty-two years at St Edmund's: from 1858 to 1861 the family returned to their estates on the Isle of Wight, but the remainder of Bernard's childhood and his entire schooling was passed at the college, and of the thirty-seven years of his priesthood all but eight were lived out at St Edmund's.[2] He was profoundly influenced by the place, and recalled with affection how, as a small child, he attended services in the college chapel, where the 'Ward staircase' led to a tribune for the family by the rood screen.

Bernard Ward was a lay student at St Edmund's College from 1868 to 1875, and soon exhibited great ability in the classroom, especially in mathematics and science. He was also the first boy in the school to wear the Eton suit. For the first three years of his schooling Ward's family continued to live at Old Hall House, but in 1871 his father left St Edmund's for good, two years after Archbishop Manning had transferred its theological students to his new seminary at Hammersmith. Bernard Ward received his First Communion in the college chapel on Maundy Thursday 1869, and in October of the same year was confirmed in the parish church, taking John, Philip and Edmund as his confirmation names.[3] The choice of the college's patron is an early indication of Ward's devotion to St Edmund. Indeed, he made his first visit to the saint's shrine at Pontigny in 1874 as a member of a pilgrimage party from St Edmund's led by the President, Monsignor Patterson.[4] This was to be the first of Bernard Ward's many visits to Pontigny.

At the end of his schooling at St Edmund's, Ward returned to the Isle of Wight, where he spent time on the family estates at Weston Manor and Northwood Park. At this point in his life he had no definite intention to study for the priesthood, and in the autumn of 1875 he left for a tour of Canada and the United States before returning to London to begin training as a land agent and surveyor. For six months in 1877–8, broken only by a visit to Italy and Rome at the end of 1877, he resided at Woburn Park near Weybridge, where the Rev William Petre, heir to the twelfth Lord Petre, had recently opened a school for the education of Catholic gentlemen. Ward was much influenced by Petre's somewhat novel method of pedagogy, which included a degree of self-government by the pupils and a regime more akin to a country house rather than a traditional boarding school.[5] Nevertheless, Ward was still destined for a

---

[2] For a description of the Ward household see W. Ward, *William George Ward and the Catholic Revival* (London,1893), pp. 66 ff., 211 ff.

[3] Cf. SEC 2/19/16: Bernard Ward to his mother, 11 October 1869.

[4] In 1873 he had taken part in a similar pilgrimage to Paray-le-Monial.

[5] For a summary of Petre's career and educational ideas see V.A. McClelland, 'The Liberal Training of England's Catholic Youth: William Joseph Petre (1847–93) and Educational Reform', *Victorian Studies*, vol. 15, no. 3 (1972), pp. 257–77; S. Foster, 'The Thirteenth Lord Petre', *Essex Journal*, vol. 19, no. 3 (1984), pp. 69–71; S. Foster, 'Monsignor Lord William Joseph Petre (1847–93): A Pillar of Downside', *Recusant History*, vol. 22, no. 1 (May 1994), pp. 88–101.

career as an estate bailiff, and duly entered employment in the City, where in moments of recreation he developed a taste for the opera and theatre. In 1878 he took up the post of land agent to the Catholic Jerningham family at Costessey near Norwich. The following Easter saw him in Rome, and then to Lourdes for the first of many pilgrimages to that shrine. Ward was still uncertain of his future when, on 8 October 1879, while praying in the chapel at Weston Manor, he made the decision to try his vocation to the priesthood.

In January 1880 Bernard Ward was sent to Oscott College as a candidate for the Diocese of Southwark, of which the Isle of Wight was then a part. He completed his studies in three years, during which time he assisted with the teaching of mathematics at the school. When the Diocese of Southwark was divided in 1882 and a new see established at Portsmouth, there was the question as to which diocese Ward should belong to. Cardinal Manning, having recognised his great promise, arranged for him to transfer to Westminster, and it was for the archdiocese that he was ordained deacon at Oscott on Holy Saturday 1882. In the following August he left Oscott and returned to St Edmund's College as Prefect of Discipline under Monsignor Fenton. Ward was ordained to the priesthood by Manning at Archbishop's House, Carlisle Place, on 8 October 1882, three months after the death of his father and three years to the day after his initial decision, made in the chapel at Weston Manor. The following day he celebrated his first Mass in the chapel at St Edmund's College.

As Prefect of Discipline until the end of 1885, Bernard Ward soon gained a reputation for being strict but fair. A tall figure, and then without the corpulence of later years, he directed his energies towards the growth of the college, which at that time was struggling to maintain its position as a lay school after the removal of the theological students. Ward was conscious of the need to strengthen the links with past pupils, and as Secretary of the Edmundian Association (1883–93) built up its membership and instituted an annual dinner in London. Early in 1886 Cardinal Manning sent Ward to establish a new mission at Willesden in north London. Here his first chapel was a room in the house where he lodged. Embracing a frugal lifestyle, he managed to restrict his living expenses to one pound per week and thereby to purchase land for a permanent church and school. Indeed, despite being a man of private means by virtue of his late father's settlement, there would always be a simplicity and frugality about Bernard Ward's personal life – spartan furnishings, a plain diet, and no tobacco or alcohol – not only as a young priest but also as President of St Edmund's and Bishop of Brentwood.

In October 1888 Ward returned to Oscott to teach Natural Sciences. He also attended scientific lectures in Birmingham in addition to performing his duties in the classroom. For the past fifteen years the situation at Oscott had been broadly similar to that at St Edmund's in that the clerical students – or at least a majority of them – had been moved to the new, purpose-built St Bernard's Seminary at Olton, Warwickshire, which Bishop Ullathorne had opened in

1873.[6] Although it now housed mostly lay boys, Olton was unable to accommodate all the clerical students, and Oscott had continued to receive seminarians, including Ward himself as a student for the priesthood between 1880 and 1882. However, in 1889 Ullathorne's successor, Bishop Ilsley, decided to gather all the seminarians under one roof and returned the clerical students to Oscott. The lay school therefore came to an end. Ilsley appointed himself Rector of Oscott in 1890, and among the small group of specially chosen professors for the new seminary was Bernard Ward. Ward's appointment, however, did not last long, because after a few months Cardinal Manning recalled him to work at St Edmund's.

If the first eight years of Bernard Ward's priesthood were marked by movement from place to place, his appointment as Vice-President and Prefect of Studies at St Edmund's in 1890, and thereafter President, was to allow him a quarter of a century in which to transform his *alma mater* into one of the leading Catholic educational establishments of the period. Immediately he set about the work of attracting more parents to send their sons to the College, a task made all the more important when Herbert Vaughan succeeded Manning as Archbishop of Westminster in 1892, closed the seminary at Hammersmith, and transferred his students to the new Central Seminary at Oscott under Ilsley. With such a move the future of St Edmund's as anything but a lay school was in doubt and Ward, having realised as much, was quite determined to do everything possible to secure its position. Even as Vice-President he began to exert an unusual personal authority, an authority which grew with the years. Monsignor John Vance, who had studied at St Edmund's and served as Professor of Philosophy (1912–17) while Ward was President, described him thus:

> tall, broad, bulkily heavy, of enormous girth, [he] walked heavily, in spite of a certain nimbleness, as his feet fell at a wide angle . . . Ward laughed loud, the old-fashioned, full-blooded squire laugh, bending his body jerkily forward as if to grasp or slap his knee; after this happy abandon there came a simmering 'hee, hee' . . . Ward's voice again was typical. It showed a strong and vibrant personality of intense sensitiveness. Through it there rang, as in an undertone, the challenging question, 'Am I the chief, or am I not?' and equally clearly there ran the emphatic affirmative answer.[7]

The same writer described Bernard Ward's face: 'A lofty brow, a fine head, features, if not of great refinement, at least of marked distinction, recalled William George Ward . . . [His] look was one of personal decidedness. Even his diffidences were those of a personal autocrat. He laughed, thought,

---

[6] See M. McInally, 'St Bernard's Seminary, Olton', in J.F. Champ (ed.), *Oscott College 1838–1988: A volume of commemorative essays* (Oscott, 1988), pp. 107–26.

[7] J.G. Vance, ' "Men of Little Showing" (6): The very Rev. Canon Burton', *The Clergy Review*, vol. 2, no. 5 (May 1931), p. 410.

doubted and moved decidedly'.[8] These qualities were to be crucial to the progress of St Edmund's in the last decade of the nineteenth century and the first decade-and-a-half of the twentieth.

Cardinal Vaughan appointed Bernard Ward Pro-President of St Edmund's College, in succession to Monsignor Crook, towards the end of 1892. He took up his duties as President in January 1893 and held office for twenty-three years, until July 1916. For the first three years he was ably assisted by Edmond Nolan as Vice-President.[9] He continued to serve as Prefect of Studies until 1904,[10] and during his term as President received a number of ecclesiastical honours: he was created a Domestic Prelate by Pope Leo XIII in 1895; was appointed a canon of the Westminster Chapter in 1903; and was elected a member of the Old Brotherhood of the Secular Clergy in 1909.

Throughout his years as President it was Ward's devotion to St Edmund's which enabled him to embark upon a steady programme of improvement and expansion which ensured the college was 'kept on the map' amidst Cardinal Vaughan's preoccupation with the Central Seminary scheme at Oscott. When Ward took charge of St Edmund's College numbers in the school were low, and Vaughan, having at one time considered it as a venue for the Central Seminary instead of Oscott, had even contemplated its closure altogether. It was for this reason that Ward's initial appointment was as *Pro*-President only. Moreover, and as will be seen in due course, Ward had the good fortune to take up his appointment at the time of the centenary of the establishment of St Edmund's College at Old Hall Green, following the dispersal of the English College at Douai in 1793. The timing proved decisive. As President, Monsignor Ward laboured to enhance the position of St Edmund's both materially and academically. Known to generations of students as 'Bunny', he was respected as a brilliant and energetic champion of the Edmundian cause. His obituary notice in *The Brentwood Diocesan Magazine* refers to the impression made by Ward on his pupils:

> the simplicity, obvious sincerity and absence of self-consciousness which were the outcome of his deep and strong faith, subtly influenced many among whom he lived, while his regularity of life and self-sacrifice were patent to all. It was by such means that he communicated to his boys something of his own high ideal of the priesthood.[11]

---

[8] *Ibid.*, p. 411.

[9] Nolan was the same age as Ward and had also been ordained in 1882. In 1896 he was appointed chaplain to the Catholic undergraduates at Cambridge, of which university he was a graduate. He was subsequently President of Prior Park College (1902–4) and Master of St Edmund's House, Cambridge (1904–9).

[10] When Archbishop Bourne returned the theological students to St Edmund's in 1904 Ward lectured in Moral Theology at the seminary.

[11] 'The Life and Work of Bishop Ward', *The Brentwood Diocesan Magazine*, no. 2 (February 1920), p. 44.

That same influence was in turn strengthened by a devotion to St Edmund, both personal and collegiate. Ernest Oldmeadow describes such devotion thus in his biography of Cardinal Bourne who succeeded Vaughan at Westminster in 1903:

> The 'love and veneration of St Edmund characteristic of the college' ... had in it something very much more than the old school tie. To many boys at Old Hall, St Edmund was not merely a long-dead thirteenth-century Archbishop of Canterbury. He was a living patron; even a friend and a companion.[12]

It was not without good reason that Ward considered the crowning glory of his presidency the opening in 1905 of the new Shrine Chapel of St Edmund as a resting-place for the College's relic of its patron. Moreover, the embellishment of the main Pugin chapel at St Edmund's was another of Ward's achievements: from his own resources he gave a set of windows to the Lady Chapel, presented a fine Gothic monstrance, and restored the liturgical use of Gothic rather than Roman vestments.

The opening of the Shrine Chapel took place one year after Archbishop Bourne's decision to transfer his church students to St Edmund's. The seminarians returned in the autumn of 1904 and new accommodation for them (the Divines' Wing) was opened in May 1905.[13] But Bourne also supported Ward's efforts to develop the education of lay pupils in a style more closely aligned to the traditions of the public schools. To this end Ward visited both Haileybury and Felsted, and from the latter in particular gained many fresh ideas. Indeed, he had already done much to enhance the College and its facilities. Among his many achievements he installed new heating and lighting systems in 1894–5, supervised the construction of the North Wing in 1895–6,[14] and in the same year defrayed the cost (£2,200) of a new swimming pool. He rebuilt the College library in 1897, presented his own share of the Ward Library to St Edmund's, and built the Exhibition Room in 1902. In his later years as President a second floor was added to the Prefect's Wing and renamed the 'Ward Wing'.[15]

Bernard Ward also developed the role of team sports among the students at St Edmund's. Although, according to his niece Maisie Ward,[16] in later life he took little exercise himself, in younger days he had been a good skater and an enthusiastic cricketer. Cricket was his favourite game: the grandson of William Ward, the famous cricketer and proprietor of Lord's, Bernard Ward

---

[12] E. Oldmeadow, *Francis Cardinal Bourne*, 2 vols (London, 1940), vol. 1, p. 73.
[13] This wing was destroyed by fire in 1907 and rebuilt in 1908. See D.J.S. Kay, *The Buildings of St Edmund's College* (Old Hall Green, 2000), pp. 69–78.
[14] *Ibid.*, pp. 55–68.
[15] *Ibid.*, p. 79.
[16] M. Ward, *The Wilfrid Wards and the Transition II: Insurrection versus Resurrection* (London, 1937), p. 115.

became a member of the MCC in 1874. He had been good enough to play for the club, and thereafter greatly treasured his MCC cap. Ward appreciated the value of sport for both lay boys and seminarians. In the summer two afternoons each week were set aside for cricket.[17] He built a pavilion in 1894, which he enlarged in 1906, and serialised the history of cricket at the college in *The Edmundian*.

Ward's other great hobby was his passion for steam trains and railways. He was an expert on *Bradshaw*, and his correspondence (and even his *Ad Clerum* letters as Bishop of Brentwood) contained detailed references to railway timetables. Guests arriving at St Edmund's were greeted by an enquiry as to their intended time of departure so that Ward might advise them of the most convenient train for their homeward journey.

Although the chief focus of Bernard Ward's work in education was directed towards his own college, his influence extended much further afield. He played a prominent part in national Catholic and local educational affairs. In 1896 he was appointed to what developed into the Standing Committee of Catholic Colleges.[18] Two years later he was elected secretary to the Conference of Catholic Headmasters, which he represented on the Catholic Education Council, and in addition he sat on the Hertfordshire County Council Education Committee for more than twenty years. Ward was also closely involved with the Universities' Catholic Education Board and plans for the provision of a Catholic chaplain at the University of Cambridge, following the lifting of the prohibition against Catholics attending Oxford and Cambridge in 1895. He offered to supply a chaplain, and early in 1896 Edmond Nolan, his Vice-President, was appointed.[19] At the same time negotiations were being conducted for the affiliation of St Edmund's College to Cambridge University and the opening of its own house of studies for the secular clergy. St Edmund's House was opened in 1896. Its chief benefactor ('the Founder') was the Duke of Norfolk, but Bernard Ward was one of its seven 'subscribers' and an *ex-officio* member of its Council.[20] Ward's generosity towards the new foundation continued, culminating in 1917 with his donation of the altar of St Edmund, which as Bishop of Brentwood he consecrated.

---

[17] For Bernard Ward's cricketing career see C.J. Gray, *The Willow and the Cloth: A Compendium of Cricketing Clergymen from the 18th Century* (Eureka via Lismore, 1999), pp. 281–2.
[18] See V.A. McClelland, *English Roman Catholics and Higher Education 1830–1903* (Oxford, 1973), p. 82.
[19] *Ibid.*, pp. 390 ff.; see note 9 above.
[20] *Ibid.*, pp. 409 ff.

II

It was during Bernard Ward's presidency of St Edmund's that he put his powerful intellect to work in chronicling the history of English Catholicism from the death of Bishop Challoner (1781) to the Restoration of the Hierarchy (1850). Although earlier in his career Ward had both studied and taught mathematics and science, it was to historical study that he now applied himself with great enthusiasm. In the light of the impending Modernist crisis in the Church and the dangers attached to more speculative disciplines, he ensured he was on safe ground. Indeed, Archbishop Edward Myers, another of Ward's pupils and then a professor at St Edmund's (1903-18) and subsequently President (1918–32), wrote of him: 'He understood the beaten tracks of ethics, politics, history, but not the "mistyness" of speculative flights. In all this he was vigorously English.'[21] Myers believed Ward to have considered the Church Fathers 'safe', and likewise Scripture, as long as it was read with devotion and without criticism, but he profoundly disliked any metaphysical treatment of theology.[22] Yet with some secular subjects he was less familiar:

> of English literature, even of the greatest names – except Dickens, Scott and Thackeray – Ward knew literally nothing. From the time he became a priest, for ascetical motives, he spurned all novels, all poetry and all plays . . . Ward, as a layman, had cared greatly for the theatre and the drama, but thought preoccupation with such interests, in a priest, a sign of frivolity . . . [he] had almost a platonic mistrust of music unless it was either ecclesiastical . . . or blaringly patriotic.[23]

But as an historian of English Catholicism Bernard Ward had few if any rivals in his generation. Ward's scholarship was imbued with a deep love of England's Catholic past, and of the Edmundian tradition in particular, together with a strong personal devotion to the English martyrs. He engaged in serious historical research from the beginning of his appointment as Vice-President of St Edmund's in 1890. He sifted through the rich archival collection at the college, mindful of the impending centenary of the foundation of St Edmund's at Old Hall Green, and was determined to write a fuller history than that produced by Doyle in 1869 to mark the centenary of the opening of the Old Hall Green Academy. As noted above, the timing of Ward's venture was fortunate given that his appointment as President in 1893 coincided with Cardinal Vaughan's preoccupation with the Central Seminary scheme and the

---

[21] Archbishop Edward Myers writing in *The Clergy Review*, vol. 2, no. 1 (February 1931), pp. 25–35.
[22] *Ibid.*
[23] Vance, p. 413.

very clear message that St Edmund's would have to close if it could not remain financially viable.

Ward's history of St Edmund's College was his first major publication. It appeared in the spring of 1893, a few weeks ahead of the centenary celebrations. While conducting his research he had begun to arrange the college archives, although Ward recognised that the task of producing a definitive history had been hampered by his inability to gain access to many of the deeds of the college property. It was only after the book had been published that Ward discovered among the Westminster Diocesan Archives evidence that the Standon Lordship School had been established in 1749 and not in 1753 as previously supposed.[24] Research for the book also engaged Ward in a wide correspondence, including for example a series of letters regarding details of Edmundians who fought in the Crimea.[25]

The publication of Ward's *History* set the tone for the centenary triduum of 23 to 25 July. Five of the six immediate past Presidents of the College joined a distinguished gathering of fellow prelates, Edmundians, guests, staff and students in what became nothing less than a triumphant celebration of the place of St Edmund's in English Catholicism and galvanised the whole place for Ward's subsequent programme of expansion. Moreover, the event did much to heal past quarrels and tensions, making the future of St Edmund's secure. And in the same way the appearance in 1893 of *The Edmundian*, a house journal founded at the initiative of Ward and under the editorship of Nolan, helped to reinforce the *esprit de corps* of St Edmund's, both past and present.

Proceedings on the first day of the centenary (Sunday 23 July) included a lecture on the history of St Edmund's College by the President 'illustrated by limelight views', and a special Centenary Catalogue was published.[26] In addition to various liturgical celebrations, which included a solemn procession with the relic of St Edmund, the three days of festivities witnessed a 'Past v Present' cricket match, an excursion to sites associated with the history of St Edmund's, including the old college, Hermitage, The Ship Inn, and Standon Lordship. There was a meeting of the Edmundian Association and a sumptuous dinner at which Cardinal Vaughan presided. Finally, in true Wardian style, a special train departed Standon station at 6.30 p.m. on 25 July to return the guests to London. Ward's commentary for the lantern-slide history of the college, a masterly synopsis of Edmundian history also published by the Catholic Truth Society in 1893, concluded with the following statement, which may be regarded as a summary of his aspirations:

---

[24] See E. Burton, *The Life and Times of Bishop Challoner 1691–1781*, 2 vols (London, 1909), vol. 1, p. 291, note 2.
[25] SEC 2/24.
[26] SEC 3/26/15.

> Let us join with the President in the hope he expressed that during the second century of its existence, while St Edmund's keeps in things material abreast of the age, it may at the same time continue to bring up priests and laymen devoted to their duty, with a spirit worthy of the traditions of the past.[27]

Ward's scholarly contribution to the history of St Edmund's College did not end with the 1893 monograph. During the summer months of 1899 he began research for his *Life of St Edmund of Canterbury* by visiting all the places associated with his subject's life. The book eventually appeared in 1903. The same year also saw the publication of the *History of St Edmund's College Chapel*, which Ward co-authored in six weeks with his then Vice-President and fellow historian Edwin Burton. Finally, in 1909 Ward published his *Menology of St Edmund's College*, a work requested and financed by his eldest brother Edmund Granville Ward, who had inherited the major part of the family fortune on the death of their father in 1882. Bernard Ward's Preface and Historical Introduction to the *Menology* provided yet another summary of the foundation of the English College at Douai and the history of St Edmund's. In the Preface Ward gave a succinct account of the very purpose of such a book:

> that it may be of service to the students, who will be able to peruse at their leisure the accounts which they have heard read; and that they may keep the book by them to recall the same lessons in after years. And there may be others, whether Edmundians or not, who live outside the College walls, and who will be glad to possess the records of so many great and holy men whose names are held in veneration at St Edmund's College, and may well be the subjects of special honour among the secular clergy of the South of England.[28]

III

The first decade-and-a-half of the new century found Monsignor Ward engaged in intense historical research of a broader kind, the result of which was a proliferation of books and articles, each breaking important new ground, and crowned by the publication between 1909 and 1915 of his celebrated trilogy surveying the background to, achievement and aftermath of Catholic Emancipation. A great deal of Ward's research was done at St Edmund's and in libraries and archives in England, but equally it was his visits, holidays and pilgrimages abroad, many of which were made for purposes of convalescence, which allowed him to make a systematic search for records pertaining to English Catholicism. Early in 1904 he visited Paris, where he investigated the archives of St Sulpice, and thereafter stayed at Milan and Athens before

---

[27] SEC 2/26/14.
[28] B. Ward, *Menology of St Edmund's College* (London, 1909), p. xii.

making for the Holy Land. His return journey was via Rome. Four years later he journeyed to Cologne, Paris, Valladolid (where he consulted the archives of the English College) and Switzerland, while in 1910 he made archival visits to Rome and Dublin. He returned to Rome in 1913, to Switzerland and Italy in 1914, and one year later turned his attention to the archives of the English College at Lisbon while on an official visitation on behalf of the Hierarchy.[29] Ward was also one of the founding members of the Catholic Record Society in 1904.

The first of the 'non-Edmundian' books was *Catholic London A Century Ago*, which appeared in 1905 and traced the history and development of Catholicism and its chief characters and sites in the capital at the turn of the nineteenth century. At the same time (1905) Ward made a MS transcript of Bishop Douglass's Diary,[30] the original of which had been temporarily misplaced by Canon Johnson, a member of the diocesan curia, when moving into the new Archbishop's House in Ambrosden Avenue, Westminster, in 1903. Bernard Ward had a great devotion to Bishop Douglass, and in the course of his work entered into a prolonged correspondence on both Douglass and Douai with Father Raymund Stanfield, whom Archbishop Bourne had appointed Diocesan Archivist. It was a great consolation to Ward that as President of St Edmund's he was able to arrange for the reinterment beneath the college chapel of the bodies of Douglass and others among the Vicars Apostolic.

Ward's scholarship continued unabated. He took on the joint editorship (with Father Herbert Thurston, SJ), of 'The Westminster Library' on behalf of the publishers Messrs. Longmans Green, who at that time were putting out a great many books on Catholic subjects and by Catholic authors. 'The Westminster Library' comprised a series of manuals for clergy and students on theological, pastoral and related topics, and among its contributors were Bishop Cuthbert Hedley, Dom John Chapman, Monsignor Benson and Father Adrian Fortescue. Moreover, such writers, together with Bernard Ward himself, were engaged as contributors to *The Catholic Encyclopedia*, a remarkable work in fifteen volumes edited in America and published from New York and London between 1907 and 1912. The articles penned by Ward are in themselves works of original scholarship and reflect his keen desire for the pursuit of historical knowledge and truth, yet are flavoured by an older Catholic outlook, a love of the traditions of Penal Times.[31] Among other

---

[29] See M.E. Williams, 'Lisbon College: The Penultimate Chapter', *Recusant History*, vol. 25, no. 1 (May 2000), pp. 90–2.

[30] SEC 6/9.

[31] An original 'Promoter' of *The Catholic Encyclopedia* (he purchased an entire set before publication), Ward was responsible for a total of thirty-one articles. His contributions appeared in all but one of the volumes. In Volume 1 (1907): Book of Advertisements, Aelnoth, William Allen; Volume 2 (1907): Peter Augustine Baines, Charles Berington, Joseph Berington,

contributors from England were Abbot Cuthbert Butler, Bishop Casartelli, Dom Bede Camm, and Fathers Thurston, Fortescue and John Hungerford Pollen, SJ. It has been noted already that Ward produced his history of the chapel at St Edmund's College jointly with his Vice-President, Edwin Burton. No account of Bernard Ward as Edmundian and historian would be complete without recognition of the scholarly co-operation and close personal friendship between Ward and Burton. Thirteen years his junior, Edwin Burton had been a lay pupil at the college during Ward's early years on the staff. He had also attended Ushaw College. Like Ward, he had not entered the seminary immediately upon finishing school. Burton studied for the law and was admitted a solicitor in 1893. It was then that he applied for the priesthood and was sent by Cardinal Vaughan to the Central Seminary at Oscott in 1894. He was ordained four years later and was appointed to the staff at St Edmund's, where he assumed the office of Vice-President in 1902. Burton's own historical interests focused on the period immediately before that favoured by Ward, and it was with Ward's encouragement that he set about producing his two-volume biography of Bishop Challoner, published by Longmans in 1909 and dedicated to Ward. It had been Bernard Ward who accompanied Burton to the parish church at Milton, Berkshire, in January 1907 to examine Challoner's burial place,[32] and throughout the years of his research for the book it was Ward to whom he turned for advice. Ward had often communicated to Burton material on Challoner discovered in the course of his own scholarly labours, as evidenced by the dozens of extant letters from Ward to Burton in the archives of St Edmund's College.[33] It was a somewhat fitting recognition of this co-operation, therefore, that both Ward and Burton were elected Fellows of the Royal Historical Society in 1907.[34]

It is the more remarkable that Ward (and indeed Burton) conducted such intensive research while performing so many other duties. Maisie Ward admired her uncle's devotion to scholarship amidst the cares of a busy life in

---

William Bishop; Volume 3 (1908): Alban Butler, Charles Butler, Cisalpine Club; Volume 4 (1908): Corporation Act of 1661; Volume 5 (1909): Douai, Douay Bible, Erastus & Erastianism, The Establishment (there was no entry for Bishop Douglass and another contributor was responsible for the article on St Edmund Rich); Volume 6 (1909): Thomas Flanagan; Volume 7 (1910): Thomas Griffiths; Volume 9 (1910): John Martiall, Gregory Martin; Volume 10 (1911): John Milner; Volume 11 (1911): Frederick Oakeley, Old Chapter, George Oliver, Henry Nutcombe Oxenham; Volume 12 (1911): Francis Plowden, William Poynter; Volume 13 (1912): College of St Omer; Volume 14 (1912): James Talbot, Ethelred Taunton; Volume 15 (1912): William Bernard Ullathorne.

[32] See Burton, vol. 2, p. 301.

[33] SEC 14/15A.

[34] Burton dedicated his two-volume biography of Challoner to Ward and also contributed articles to *The Catholic Encyclopedia*. At least one book has subsequently been dedicated to both Ward and Burton (and all Edmundians), viz. D. Newton, *Catholic London* (London, 1950) which acknowledges (p. 216) the debt owed to them by all Catholics for their research into the history of the capital.

education: 'With the Ward capacity for work . . . he added to his college administration the collection of records of English Catholicism which became five large volumes.'[35] In the course of preparing his major work, the trilogy covering the period between 1781 and 1850, Ward

> read in the library of every house or college he visited and never went away without some spoils for the book. He was a fine historian, for he never took anything at its face value . . . His large volumes were balanced and documented to a point that set them at once in the first rank of original work . . . Bernard Ward, like Lingard, held that fairness was not a matter of faith but of facts.[36]

It was for this reason that Ward was not afraid to return to the old controversies which formed so much a part of the story of English Catholicism in the period with which he was concerned: for example, he described the episcopate of Bishop Baines as 'one tortured history of quarrels and disputes';[37] and in the wake of Pugin's campaign for all things gothic, he considered the gulf between 'Roman' and 'English' Catholics to have widened until they were 'deeply and even bitterly opposed to one another on questions of far deeper moment than that of mere taste in ecclesiastical ornament'.[38] In one passage in particular Ward allowed his own celebrated wit somewhat unfairly to enter his description of Pugin's extreme enthusiasm:

> He called out for Gothic shops and Gothic railway arches, as being the only lasting and suitable kind, and he drew a Gothic railway station to contrast with the then new arch-entrance to Euston. In his own house, all the furniture was Gothic, and he even designed Gothic moulds for the cook to use in making his puddings and jellies. He was not insensible to the humour of his actions, and on one occasion he wrote to a friend that his wife was about to present him with a Gothic baby.[39]

Although very conscious of the need to preserve a sense of balance in his judgements, Ward never fought shy of offering critical appraisal when he believed it justified. This was true even in the case of such a revered figure as Cardinal Wiseman on the question of Lingard and the cardinalate, and the consequent dispute with Canon Tierney.[40] Indeed, one recent biographer of Wiseman has noted how indebted historians are to both Bernard Ward and his brother Wilfrid for their 'unsurpassed' and 'remarkably unbiased' books, even though it must be admitted that they were not entirely unaffected by their

---

[35] M.Ward, p. 115. In fact Bernard Ward's celebrated trilogy eventually ran to seven volumes.
[36] *Ibid.*, p. 116.
[37] B.Ward, *The Sequel to Catholic Emancipation*, 2 vols (London, 1915), vol. 1, p. 12.
[38] *Ibid.*, p. 82.
[39] *Ibid.*, pp. 94–5.
[40] See B.Ward, *The Eve of Catholic Emancipation*, 3 vols (Longmans: London, 1912), vol. 3, pp. 350–4.

father's influence.[41] Nevertheless, Bernard Ward's own prejudices, if that is not too strong a word, may occasionally be detected: for example, his disapproval and even dislike of Milner is never hidden – although such disapprobation did not prevent him from acquiring the bishop's walking stick as a personal souvenir.[42]

Ward's celebrated trilogy appeared in seven volumes between 1909 and 1915, published by Longmans in a style uniform with Burton's *Challoner*, and was at once marked by and acclaimed for its use of original documents. Indeed, chronologically, Ward continued where Burton had finished, viz. in 1781. Having received particular encouragement from Bishop George Ambrose Burton of Clifton to research the history of the later Vicars Apostolic, Ward rescued the period running from the death of Challoner to the Restoration of the Hierarchy from relative historical obscurity.

The Dawn of the Catholic Revival (2 volumes, 1909) was written within two years, and considered the period from 1781 to 1803. Completed despite Ward's prolific workload as President of St Edmund's, the book was very well received, although its author's modesty was such that he regretted his inability to devote as much time to the project as he felt was required.[43] Archbishop Bourne expressed his approval and encouraged Ward to continue his labours, and the first two volumes of *The Eve of Catholic Emancipation* appeared in the closing weeks of 1911, followed by a third in 1912. In *The Eve* Ward took the story to the threshold of the Act of Emancipation in 1829 – a piece of legislation which, incidentally, Ward considered to have been less significant in granting Catholics religious liberties than the 1791 Act. In support of this judgement he pointed to the rapid development of Catholicism in the period from 1791 to 1829, as compared to a more moderate growth in the immediate aftermath of Emancipation itself.[44]

His dedication and skill as an historian notwithstanding, one should never lose sight of the encouragement and assistance given to Bernard Ward by prelates, scholars and archivists in the preparation of his volumes. Bishop Burton and Archbishop Bourne have been mentioned, but there were others. For example, the records of the Archdiocese of Dublin were among the archival collections consulted by Ward while working on *The Eve*, and he

---

[41] R.J. Schiefen, *Nicholas Wiseman and the Transformation of English Catholicism* (Shepherdstown, 1984), p. viii. Wilfrid Ward's principal works include *William George Ward and the Oxford Movement* (London, 1889), *William George Ward and the Catholic Revival* (London, 1893), *The Life and Times of Cardinal Wiseman*, 2 vols (London, 1898), *Ten Personal Studies* (London, 1908), and *The Life of John Henry, Cardinal Newman*, 2 vols (London, 1912). Wilfrid assumed the editorship of *The Dublin Review* in 1906, to which journal Bernard contributed a number of historical articles and reviews.

[42] Cf. SEC 14/15A/8: Ward to Burton, 17 January 1897.

[43] Cf. Preface to Ward, *The Eve*, vol. 1, p. vii.

[44] See Ward, *The Eve*, vol. 1, pp. viii–ix; *Sequel*, vol. 2, p. 72.

acknowledged the interest in his work expressed by Archbishop Walsh and his generosity in placing the diocesan archives at his disposal.

He was also most grateful for the help offered by the archivist, Father Michael Curran, who was then in the process of re-arranging the collection. Curran read the chapters dealing with Ireland, and Ward was able to re-write his treatment of the Veto question of 1807–8 in the light of the new material brought to his attention by the archivist. In the same volume Ward also acknowledged the assistance of Father Pollen with material relating to the English Jesuits, and the help given by Albert Purdie, a student at St Edmund's College, in researching the history of the loss of the Douai funds following the French Revolution. Edwin Burton read the proofs. The final part of the trilogy, *The Sequel to Catholic Emancipation*, covered the period from 1829 to 1850 and appeared in two volumes in 1915.

One feature of the trilogy which is especially worthy of mention is the fact that Ward exhibited a particular sensitivity to the contribution of Ireland to the development of Catholicism in England. It was Denis Gwynn, writing at the time of the centenary of the Restoration of the Hierarchy, who noted this awareness of the role of the Irish poor in the establishment of Catholic parish life in nineteenth-century England: 'Their achievements in this respect were remarkably recognised by Bishop Bernard Ward, who had no recollection of the earlier phase (of Irish immigration) and whose instinctive sympathies were naturally repugnant to the Irish Catholics in England.'[45]

Ward paid tribute to the debt owed by English Catholics to their Irish co-religionists, 'without whose assistance in the time of struggle the modern development of Catholicity in this country would never have been possible';[46] and he, very much a son of his Tractarian father, considered the post-1846 phase of Irish immigration as having had a greater influence on English Catholicism than the Oxford Movement in terms of the expansion of missions and schools. *The Eve* was dedicated to the Catholics of Ireland.

Nevertheless, the research was not without its difficulties. In his preface to *The Eve* Ward made the following acknowledgements:

> The Archbishop of Westminster once more kindly offered the use of all the papers in his Archives, as did the Bishop of Clifton, and the other Bishops and heads of Colleges who had helped the former work (i.e. the *Dawn*) in this manner, repeated their kindness in the present instance. In addition to these, the Rector of the English College at Rome, Bishop Giles – who at the time of writing is believed to be the oldest living 'Edmundian' – threw open to me the most valuable collection of papers there, which include the greater part of the correspondence of the Agent of the English Bishops during the period under review; and

---

[45] D. Gwynn, 'The Irish Immigration', in G.A. Beck (ed.), *The English Catholics 1850–1950* (London, 1950), p. 269.
[46] Ward, *The Eve*, vol. 3, p. 285.

by the kindness of Cardinal Gotti, I was enabled to take advantage of my visit to Rome to spend several days in the *Archivium* of Propaganda, which contains documents which were practically essential to the work in hand.[47]

But Ward's private correspondence, especially his letters to Burton, tells a slightly different story. Ward invariably reported his scholarly findings to Burton. For the most part he met with co-operation. Thus, for example, in 1906 he informed Burton that there was a good deal of correspondence from Bishop Poynter among the archives of the Bishop of Clifton,[48] and two years later, while working on material for *The Eve*, he remarked of his labours at the English College, Valladolid, 'My visit here will substantially improve my chapter on the English Colleges abroad.'[49] Likewise in spring 1910 his visit to the English College in Rome was successful: the place was practically empty but the Rector, Bishop Giles, had left him two volumes of archives 'which will I think occupy me several days'.[50] A few months later he reported to Burton from Dublin: 'There are an enormous number of papers to look through, but not so very many to copy . . . about 200 Milner letters . . . Archives arranged in bundles & usually inaccurately labelled: this lends the fascination of surprise.'[51] And in 1915, while acting as Apostolic Visitor to the English College in Lisbon, Ward took advantage of the opportunity to work on the archives: 'I have been very hard at work here, 9 a.m. till 9 p.m., but am on the whole satisfied with what I have done.'[52]

But when it came to gaining access to various archives in Rome while working on the *Sequel*, Ward met with several obstacles. Essentially this was because the Holy See was unwilling to admit scholars to more recent nineteenth-century material. Ward, who was somewhat restricted by a lack of fluency in Italian, was allowed to consult some papers at Propaganda, but did not enjoy free access. On a visit to Rome in 1913 he found that Cardinal Gotti would not read Cardinal Bourne's letter of introduction requesting permission for Ward to consult the Vatican Archives. Ward was told that the collection must remain secret and that he was to make a list of the documents he wished to study. A typist would then copy the archival material if Cardinal Gotti considered it appropriate. 'Of course this is practically useless to me',[53] Ward informed Burton, and regretted that he was unable to assist his friend with material for his own period of research. He met with more success at the English College: 'The Rector has rummaged in his room and unearthed a large bundle of archives, some very important', which necessitated Ward staying on

---

[47] Ward, *The Eve*, vol. 1, pp. vii–viii.
[48] SEC 14/15A/28: Ward to Burton, 6 January 1906.
[49] SEC 14/15A/35: Ward to Burton, 31 January 1908.
[50] SEC 14/15A/43: Ward to Burton, 2 April 1910.
[51] SEC 14/15A/51: Ward to Burton, 23 August 1910.
[52] SEC 14/15A/56: Ward to Burton, 14 July 1915. Cf. note 29 above.
[53] SEC 14/15A/53: Ward to Burton, 21 April 1913.

for a few days in order to copy them; but when he enquired about the Archive of Propaganda he was simply told that there was a Russian priest somewhere in Rome who was reputed to possess a complete list of the contents, having spent fifty years working there. Ward was exasperated by such cloak-and-dagger treatment, and somewhat sarcastically told Burton, 'if the priest is susceptible of bribes, we might get lists for your period'.[54] Ward returned home disappointed.

IV

Much of Bernard Ward's research and writing took place during prolonged absences from St Edmund's College during the later years of his presidency, a period which he came to count as the most difficult of his life. Early in 1908, Ward had been considered for the vacant see of Northampton, where Bishop Riddell had died in the previous September. Ward's name appeared on the *terna* sent to Rome and a premature announcement was made of his appointment. In the event it was Canon Frederick Keating, the Administrator of Birmingham Cathedral and a former colleague of Ward at Oscott, who was named. Ward, although fearful of leaving St Edmund's, was much changed in character by his failure to secure Northampton. His humiliation turned to depression, and his heart was no longer in the presidency as it had once been. He turned more and more to his historical and literary work. Moreover, his relationship with the staff at St Edmund's began to deteriorate, and towards the end of 1915 a movement arose to have him replaced as President. Dogged by ill-health and tiredness, Ward virtually withdrew from all public duties. For much of 1916 he was absent from the college, taking spells of convalescence at Brighton, Bournemouth and other resorts. His own troubles had been worsened by the circumstances of the First World War – a general antipathy to war itself, the threat of bombing and the deaths of a number of Edmundians killed in battle[55] – and by the deaths of his brothers within a few months of each other. Edmund Granville Ward, the eldest of the sons, died in 1915. He was heir to his father and a man of considerable wealth, and the terms of his will led to something of a family rift when it emerged that Wilfrid Ward had been excluded, while Bernard received a handsome endowment.[56] Wilfrid died from cancer in April 1916 – a death no doubt hastened by the strained family relations – and Bernard's grief was intensified.

The illness of Edwin Burton, Ward's Vice President and friend, also disturbed him. Ward trusted Burton, but was also very dependent upon his

---

[54] SEC 14/15A/54: Ward to Burton, 25 April 1913.
[55] See SEC 14/17/161: Ward, sermon for fallen Edmundians, July 1916.
[56] See D. Greene, *The Living of Maisie Ward* (Notre Dame, 1997), pp. 46–7.

support: he wrote of Burton's appointment to St Edmund's, 'his coming has made the whole difference to my life and work here'. But there was a price to pay, since Bernard Ward was something of an autocrat, as Monsignor Vance later remarked:

> Ward demanded of those who worked under him – and everyone within his radius of authority perforce worked under him – a personal devotion to himself ... Ward, too, who, by instinct of nature, desired both praise and recognition – in receiving it he was often delightfully boyish – gave neither readily to others.[57]

There was also a certain vulnerability, as Ward 'longed for human sympathy, for understanding and for an affection that might endure in spite of his abrupt sallies, his curious jokes, his uneven temper, and his strange suspicions'.[58] Burton was his chief support and confidant, but Ward's isolation and loneliness persisted, and a number of the staff were of the opinion that he had been at St Edmund's for too long and that a change of presidency was required.

The movement to replace Ward was led by Edward Myers, the Professor of Dogmatic Theology and Patrology, an Edmundian ordained in 1902 and thus known to Ward since boyhood.[59] Myers was dissatisfied with Ward's presidency and sought to gain the support of his colleagues. Cardinal Bourne was very aware of Ward's poor health and the discontent among many at St Edmund's, and thus came to favour his resignation. Bernard Ward, having realised that his resignation was required, wrote a farewell letter to his staff on 19 July 1916,[60] by which date he had not appeared publicly in the college for some time. His departure was acrimonious. On 21 July Ward wrote to Burton about what he deemed to be a plot against him,[61] and later accused the Vice-President of keeping him in the dark about the affairs of the college.[62] Bernard Ward left St Edmund's on 29 July, having deposited in the archives the diaries he had kept of college life since 1890. He took up a new appointment as Rector of Holy Trinity, Brook Green, Hammersmith, and in due course was replaced as President of St Edmund's by Burton. In October 1916 Ward wrote to his successor to inform him that he would not be attending the college celebrations for St Edmund's Day, the first patronal feast he had missed in thirty-seven years.[63]

Bernard Ward's incumbency at Brook Green lasted only a few months. Although he had failed to secure appointment as Bishop of Northampton in

---

[57] Vance, pp. 414–15.
[58] *Ibid.*, p. 418.
[59] See SEC 14/15B/41: Ward to Burton, 16 January 1917.
[60] SEC 14/15B/8: Ward to the staff of St Edmund's College, 19 July 1916.
[61] SEC 14/15B/9: Ward to Burton, 21 July 1916.
[62] SEC 14/15B/20: Ward to Burton, 27 September 1916.
[63] SEC 14/15B/27: Ward to Burton, 26 October 1916.

1908, and despite an intimation from Cardinal Bourne in 1915 (in the midst of the dispute between Westminster and Southwark over the division of dioceses) that he had Ward in mind for the vacancy in Nottingham, it was not long before a successful nomination to the episcopate occurred. In March 1917 Monsignor Ward was appointed Apostolic Administrator of Essex, and four months later was translated to become the first Bishop of Brentwood.

An account of Ward's brief (1917–20) episcopate is to be found elsewhere,[64] but as Bishop of Brentwood, and with the borders of his diocese only a few miles from his beloved St Edmund's, his relations with the College continued to be strained. In January 1917, shortly before his appointment to Essex, Ward wrote to Burton about Bourne's insistence that he (Ward) should not interfere in affairs at St Edmund's.[65] Ward resented Bourne's attitude and the relationship between the two men deteriorated after Ward's episcopal appointment. When Essex was separated from the Archdiocese of Westminster and the Diocese of Brentwood established, a quota of clercial students at St Edmund's transferred to the new jurisdiction. This presented problems for Ward on a personal level in that, as Bishop of Brentwood, he was obliged to resume contact with the College. He visited his seminarians in May 1917, and again in June and July. In addition to his mistrust of Bourne, a further factor was introduced into Ward's relations with St Edmund's. Towards the end of 1917 Bishop Ward expressed his disapproval of the custom of seminarians serving in the military cadet force at the College, a practice endorsed by Cardinal Bourne.[66] As President, and while under Bourne's authority, Ward had accepted this practice, but as a bishop with jurisdiction over his own students he was not prepared to do so. The issue came to a head with the cessation of hostilities in November 1918. Ward refused to allow his church students to serve as cadets once the First World War had ended. The case was referred to Rome and Bishop Ward withdrew his students from St Edmund's in May 1919.[67] No student for the Diocese of Brentwood was to study at the college for another thirty years.

There was, however, a gradual reconciliation between Bernard Ward and Edwin Burton, and the bulk of Edmundians continued to hold their former President in great esteem. Money from an Edmundian testimonial was used by Ward to purchase his own crozier and episcopalia,[68] and an address was

---

[64] See S. Foster, *A History of the Diocese of Brentwood 1917–1992* (Brentwood, 1994), pp. 17, 18–46; S. Foster, 'A Bishop for Essex: Bernard Ward and the Diocese of Brentwood', *Recusant History*, vol. 21, no. 4 (October 1993), pp. 556–71.

[65] SEC 14/15B/39: Ward to Burton, 13 January 1917.

[66] See SEC 14/15B/97: Ward to Burton, 29 December 1917.

[67] See SEC 14/16B.

[68] At his consecration Ward used Bishop Weathers' mitre and the crozier of Bishop Stapleton, the first President of St Edmund's College. When Ward was appointed to Brentwood, Burton drafted a set of notes on the history of the clergy and missions in Essex (Brentwood Diocesan Archives: A2).

presented by the Edmundian Association on the occasion of Ward's episcopal appointment. Whatever the merits of the various disputes which had clouded Ward's final days at St Edmund's, and whatever might have occurred had Ward lived longer than his sixty-two years, his contribution to the College was of the first order and he remains one of the outstanding historians of English Catholicism. When his forty-eight-year association with St Edmund's came to an end in 1916, Bernard Ward himself described the parting as almost akin to 'leaving this world'. It was most fitting, therefore, that when Bishop Ward died in January 1920 his panegyric was preached by Edwin Burton and his body laid to rest at St Edmund's, in the spot he himself had chosen and in the tomb he had made ready for himself beside the altar of the patron saint.

10

TRADITION AND CONVERSION IN ENGLISH LITERATURE

JOSEPH PEARCE

ANYONE wishing to understand the relationship between tradition and conversion is confronted at the very outset with an inescapable paradox. Tradition, of its very nature, requires the tacit acceptance by those in the present of the ideas, beliefs and customs of the past. Tradition seems to require conformity. Conversion, on the other hand, requires the conscious rejection of the ideas, beliefs and customs that have been tacitly accepted in the past in order to embrace the creed to which one is converting in the present. Conversion seems to require nonconformity. Yet, in spite of this apparent contradiction, tradition and conversion are far from mutually exclusive. On the contrary, and as we shall see, they are ultimately in harmony.

A paradox, as G.K. Chesterton never tired of reminding us, is not simply a contradiction but, on the contrary, is only an apparent contradiction signifying a deeper unity. At its deepest, every conversion is not merely a rejection of a tradition to which one had previously subscribed but is, at the same time, the acceptance of another tradition which seems to make more sense than the one rejected. Conversion is, therefore, the acceptance of a tradition perceived as authentic in contradistinction to one perceived as false.

This is not simply a question of semantics. Since the Reformation, the received tradition of the majority of people in non-Catholic countries has been at loggerheads with the authentic tradition of the Church. In consequence, every conversion to Catholicism is a conscious rejection of the traditions of the non-Catholic majority in favour of the traditions of a minority. It is the rejection of prevailing fashion in the name of providential faith. As such, and contrary to the assumptions of many 'progressive' thinkers, authentic tradition's relationship with the modern world is both radical and revolutionary. It is radical in the sense that it counters the accretions of post-Reformation tradition in order to remain in communion with the roots of Christendom, i.e. the Apostolic Tradition of the Church. It is revolutionary in the sense that it seeks the repentance of post-Reformation society and its return to the Faith of its fathers. All revolution, properly and radically understood, requires a *return* – by definition. It is this understanding of the word that Chesterton must have had in mind when he wrote that evolution is what happens when everyone is asleep, whereas revolution is what happens when everyone is awake. Many so-called 'revolutions' in the past have been, in reality, either iconoclastic revolts against the *status quo* or else violent reformations of it. Neither is revolutionary in the true sense of the word. True revolution requires a return to basic truths, a return to authentic tradition. This revolution, in individuals and societies alike, is normally called conversion. Thus, authentic tradition and conversion are seen to be in sublime harmony.

Writing of the Victorians, Chesterton spoke of 'the abrupt abyss of the things they do not know'.[1] This 'abrupt abyss' was the result of chronological snobbery, the assumption, at least implicitly, that the age in which the Victorians lived was more advanced and 'enlightened' than any preceding era in history. With unquestioning faith in the concept of inexorable 'progress' the Victorians equated the wisdom of the ages with the superstition of the past. Thus mediaevalism was mere barbarism, scholastic philosophy was dismissed as being little more than an obsession with counting angels on the point of a needle, and the holy sacrifice of the Mass was mere 'hocus-pocus'.

The poetic counter-stance to this cold rationalism and its supercilious religious scepticism emerged several decades before the dawn of the Victorian era with the publication in 1798 of *Lyrical Ballads*, co-edited by William Wordsworth and Samuel Taylor Coleridge. In this ground-breaking volume, which served as the *de facto* manifesto of the Romantic Movement in England, the poets asserted their faith in the integrity of the human soul and derided the spiritual sterility of the sceptical philosophers. Coleridge and Wordsworth both embraced Christianity, and Coleridge, in particular, became an outspoken champion of religious orthodoxy.

In 'The Rime of the Ancient Mariner' there were early glimpses of Coleridge's later orthodoxy in the Marian invocation at the beginning of Part V:

> Oh sleep! it is a gentle thing,
> Beloved from pole to pole!
> To Mary Queen the praise be given!
> She sent the gentle sleep from Heaven,
> That slid into my soul.

In this, as in his beautiful translation of 'The Virgin's Cradle Hymn', a short Latin verse which he had discovered in a Catholic village in Germany, Coleridge was seeking a purer vision of Christianity untainted and untarnished by the embryonic scepticism of the more puritanical of the metaphysical poets

---

[1] G.K. Chesterton, *The Victorian Age in Literature* (London, 1912), p. 157.

of the seventeenth century. His defence of orthodoxy in both poetry and prose was an earnest endeavour to bridge the 'abrupt abyss' of the age in which he was living. In the course of his life's pilgrimage, his journey in faith, he had scaled the schism of sects and the chasm of secularism to rediscover the wonders of Christendom.

> I walk with awe, and sing my stately songs,
> Loving the God that made me!

Coleridge may have been the first of the 'moderns' to cast aside the 'progressive' traditions of the post-Enlightenment in order to rediscover the authentic traditions of the Church, but he was by no means the last. In many respects he blazed a trail that many others would follow.

The year before Coleridge died, the Oxford Movement was born. Those at the forefront of this traditionalist revolution in the Anglican Church – Keble, Pusey, Newman and others – were inheritors of Coleridge's orthodox mantle and shared his desire for a purer Catholic vision of Christianity beyond the fogs of puritanism. Nowhere was the plaintive cry of the Oxford Movement heard so starkly as in the opening lines of a hymn by John Mason Neale:

> Oh, give us back the days of old! oh! give me back an hour!
> To make us feel that Holy Church o'er death hath might and power.

A similar vision was the inspiration for a young architect, Augustus Pugin, who converted to Roman Catholicism, probably in 1834, and set about promoting the hugely influential Gothic Revival. The combined effect of the Oxford Movement and the Gothic revival changed the metaphysical atmosphere considerably. As Victoria ascended the throne in 1837, the mediaevalist winds of change were sweeping across England.

The prophet of neo-mediaevalism in the mid-nineteenth century was John Ruskin, whose influence on his contemporaries was gargantuan in its scope and impact. His art criticism developed into a spiritual history of Europe, epitomised by his famous essay 'On the Nature of the Gothic', and his love for the Italian Renaissance was infectious, introducing whole new generations to the art of the Church. For Ruskin aestheticism and morality were inseparable. Thus, he argued, the beauty of early Renaissance art flowed freely from its creative source in the moral foundations of mediaeval Christendom. Consequently, the aesthetic inevitably suffered when the humanism of the late Renaissance weakened the link with this Christian source. The more the Renaissance bloomed, he believed, the more it decayed.

Ruskin was an early champion of the Pre-Raphaelites, a 'brotherhood' of artists who shared his aesthetic vision. Seeking a purer perspective untainted by the decay of the late Renaissance, the Pre-Raphaelites chose Catholic religious themes and scenes of mythic mediaeval chivalry, painted in vivid colour and detail. Their opposition to the fashionable conventions of Victorian modernism, both in art and morals, was itself a dissatisfaction with the drabness of the Victorian spirit and a quest for the purity and adventure of a healthier age. Dante Gabriel Rossetti, perhaps the greatest of the Pre-Raphaelites, chose Marian themes such as *The Girlhood of Mary Virgin* and *The Annunciation*, or Dantean allegories such as *Beata Beatrix*, to convey a Catholic vision to a sceptical world. He also wrote fine religious verse, overflowing with mediaeval spirituality, akin to Coleridge's earlier poetic quest for pre-Reformation purity. Yet Rossetti, unlike his sister, was not an orthodox believer. Nor was Ruskin, who spent several months in a monastic cell in Assisi, basking in the Franciscan spirit, before declaring that he had no need to convert since he was already more Catholic than the Church.

Ruskin's vision, and that of the Pre-Raphaelites, was, at best, a baptism of desire into the Catholic spirit; at worst their vision lacked any ultimate reality. It would take a remarkable man to unite the vision with the reality.

John Henry Newman's conversion to Catholicism in 1845 sent shockwaves through the Anglican establishment. Already well known as a leading protagonist of the Oxford Movement, Newman's reception into the Church was a courageously decisive act by a catalytically incisive mind. His act of conversion united the Catholic vision with the Catholic reality, the artistic word with the flesh of the Divine Artist, and the creative mind with the Body of the Church. In Newman, the convert and the authentic tradition became one.

Newman endeavoured to explain the process of conversion in his first novel, *Loss and Gain*, a fictionalised semi-autobiographical account of a young man's quest for faith amid the scepticism and uncertainties of early Victorian Oxford. It remains one of the classic Victorian novels. The novelist Mrs Humphry Ward believed that it was one of the works to which 'the future student of the nineteenth century will have to look for what is deepest, most intimate, and most real in its personal experience'.[2] Newman also addressed the issue of conversion in his historical novel, *Callista*, and, most memorably, in his brilliant autobiography, *Apologia pro Vita Sua*. In his *Sermons addressed to Mixed Congregations*, published in 1849, Newman conveys with pyrotechnic profundity that the modern world faces a stark choice between authentic tradition and the abyss of nihilism:

> ... Turn away from the Catholic Church, and to whom will you go? it is your only chance of peace and assurance in this turbulent, changing world. There is nothing between it and scepticism, when men exert their reason freely. Private creeds, fancy religions, may be showy and imposing to the many in their day; national religions may lie huge and lifeless, and cumber the ground for centuries, and distract the intention or confuse the judgment of the learned; but on the long run it will be found that either the Catholic Religion is verily and indeed the

---

[2] Quoted by Alan G. Hill in his introduction to John Henry Newman, *Loss and Gain* (Oxford, 1986 edn).

coming in of the unseen world into this, or that there is nothing positive, nothing dogmatic, nothing real in any one of our notions as to whence we come and whither we are going. Unlearn Catholicism, and you become Protestant, Unitarian, Deist, Pantheist, Sceptic, in a dreadful, but infallible succession . . .[3]

Newman's message to his contemporaries, and to future generations, is clear: relearn Catholicism, i.e. convert, or perish. Perhaps the inextricable link between tradition and conversion has never been put so forcefully, either before or since.

Reading these lines it is easy to concur with the critic George Levine's judgement that Newman is 'perhaps the most artful and brilliant prose writer of the nineteenth century'. Such a judgement should not, however, detract from Newman's achievement as a poet. His most ambitious poem, and arguably his finest, is *The Dream of Gerontius*, which presents the vision of a soul at the moment of death, and its conveyance by its guardian angel to the cleansing grace of purgatory. Although it is steeped in Catholic doctrine, itself something of a novelty in Victorian verse, Newman's poem has been compared with *Paradise Lost*. 'It reminds us at times of Milton,' suggests the critic A.S.P. Woodhouse, 'and it strikingly anticipates T.S. Eliot in its presentation of Christ as the surgeon who probes the wound in order to heal.'[4] There is, however, none of Milton's deformed, darker spirit in Newman's poem. Instead it resonates with the hopeful spirit of Dante's *Purgatorio* and the glory of his *Paradiso*, which it resembles in faith, if not in form. *The Dream of Gerontius* is not a lament over a paradise lost but the promise of a paradise to be gained.

Newman returns to the purgatorial theme in 'The Golden Prison' in which purgatory is described as 'the holy house of toil, The frontier penance-place'. As in all else that he wrote, it seems that Newman is more intent on instructing his readers than on entertaining them. Poems such as 'The Sign of the Cross' and his hymn 'For the Dead' are deliberately designed to elucidate those aspects of Catholicism that aroused the ire and suspicion of his non-Catholic or anti-Catholic contemporaries.

Paradoxically perhaps, Newman is at his most charming when he is at his least Victorian. In 'The Pilgrim Queen', subtitled 'A Song', he throws off the formalities of Victorian verse to unleash his muse on the simplicity of mediaeval rhythm and rhyme.

> I looked on that Lady,
>   and out from her eyes
> Came the deep glowing blue

---

[3] John Henry Newman, *Discourses to Mixed Congregations*, pp. 283–4; quoted in William Samuel Lilly (ed.), *A Newman Anthology* (London, 1949), pp. 274–5.
[4] A.S.P. Woodhouse, *The Poet and His Faith: Religion and Poetry in England from Spenser to Eliot and Auden* (Chicago and London, 1965), p. 238.

>   of Italy's skies;
> And she raised up her head
>   and she smiled, as a Queen
> On the day of her crowning,
>   so bland and serene.
> 'A moment,' she said,
>   'and the dead shall revive;
> The Giants are failing,
>   the Saints are alive;
> I am coming to rescue
>   my home and my reign,
> And Peter and Philip
>   are close in my train.'

Newman's choice of this particular and uncharacteristic verse-form to convey the story of England's rejection of the Mother of God is intriguing. The jauntiness and joyful rhythm is reminiscent of pre-Reformation religious verse. It evokes England's Catholic past, the mythic Merrie England that still had the power to move Newman's contemporaries to feelings of nostalgia for a lost pastoral paradise in which people were united by a sure and simple faith. The jollity of the pre-Chaucerian metre serves as a counterpoint to the Pilgrim Queen's sorrowful lament that England had betrayed and deserted her to erect 'a palace of ice':

>   '... And me they bid wander
>   in weeds and alone,
>   In this green merry land
>   which once was my own.'

The betrayal, the desolation, the melancholy, are all reminiscent of the anonymous verse, 'The Ballad of Walsingham', which laments the destruction of England's Marian shrine, once the most prestigious in Christendom, under Henry VIII. Yet unlike the sorrowful and plaintive passion of the 'Ballad', Newman's 'Pilgrim Queen' transcends and transforms the sorrow with the promise of future glory. Beyond the passion is the resurrection. The Queen will rescue her people and, aided by the company of heaven, she will be restored to her rightful throne.

The balance, the symmetry, of 'The Pilgrim Queen' is the balance and symmetry of the Rosary. England's destiny, past, present and future, is reflected in the Rosary's mysteries. From Joy, through Sorrow, to Glory. As such, England emerges as a sub-plot in a far greater Mystery Play. The lost paradise of Merrie England is the lost Eden of humanity's primeval past. The paradise has been lost through betrayal and all that remains is the deep sense of exile at the broken heart of humanity. The broken-hearted can only look with hope for the promised glory – the conversion of humanity, and of England, through the restoration of the King and Queen to their rightful place. In tapping into authentic tradition, and calling for conversion, Newman had tapped into a well-spring of faith and hope.

Apart from his own prodigious literary achievement Newman was also the effective instigator of the Catholic literary revival. His example, his genius, his energy, and the impact of his life and work, provided the creative spark that ignited and inspired a new generation of Catholic literary converts. One in particular was to become arguably the greatest of all the Victorian poets. Gerard Manley Hopkins was received into the Catholic Church by Newman himself in 1866 and became, in literary terms, a sleeping giant. Although he remained utterly unknown, as a poet, during his own lifetime, he would emerge, thirty years after his death, as one of the most popular and influential poets of the twentieth century.

It is often said that Hopkins was ahead of his time and perhaps there are few people to whom such a judgement could be applied more truly. Yet Hopkins was more than merely ahead of his time. He was outside his time; beyond his time. His verse is ultra-temporal. It is essentially free, philosophically and culturally, of the fads and fashions of the Victorian age in which he lived. It is, however, equally free of the fads and fashions of the literary *avant garde* which 'discovered' and championed it during the period between the two world wars. Certainly there is no logic in the oft-repeated claim of many modern and 'post-modern' critics that Hopkins should be considered a twentieth-century poet. Regardless of his undoubted influence on the poetry of the twentieth century, the publication of his poems so long after his death was essentially no more than an accident of birth.

The ultra-temporal nature of Hopkins's poetry is rooted in scholastic philosophy. His Jesuit training had grounded him in the teaching of St Thomas Aquinas and Duns Scotus and this had inspired his notion of *inscape*, the central concept at the heart of his poetry, which was itself a reflection of the teaching of Duns Scotus that everything in creation has a unique spiritual identity, its *haecceitas* or 'thisness'. Distilling, through mediaeval philosophy, the purer spirit of faith and reason that had existed before the adulteration of the Enlightenment, Hopkins had served up Catholic theology to an unsuspecting modernity which, accustomed to lighter fare, became intoxicated by its heady effects. In effect, therefore, and with more than a modicum of irony, Hopkins's much-vaunted status as an honorary 'modern' springs from his adherence to the authentic tradition of the Church, a powerful reminder that orthodoxy is always dynamic.

Regardless of how they may be perceived by posterity, Hopkins and Newman saw themselves, first and foremost, as ordained ministers of the Church. They were priests first, and poets second. As obedient souls who sought to do God's will in their daily lives, they could be called converts of the light. There was, however, a parallel movement of rebellious souls who were intent on experiencing all aspects of life, both the licit and the illicit, and who, often shunning the light, walked in the shadows or stumbled in the darkness.

These were the Decadents, adherents of a movement originating in France, but which would spread infectiously across the Channel under the beguiling influence of Oscar Wilde.

In considering the relationship between the Decadents and the Church one is confronted with another paradox. At first glance the precociously *risqué* image of Wilde would appear to sit uncomfortably beside the primness and propriety of Newman. Appearances, however, can be deceptive. At the deepest level, saintly souls like Newman and Hopkins have more in common with 'sinners' such as Wilde and Beardsley than with the archetypal, stoically self-righteous and sceptic-souled Victorians. 'I have dreams of a visit to Newman,' Wilde confessed to a friend in 1877, 'of the holy sacrament in a new Church, and of a quiet and peace afterwards in my soul.'[5] Two years earlier he had scribbled in his Commonplace Book the words of the father of French Decadence, Baudelaire: 'O Lord! Give me the strength and the courage to contemplate my heart without disgust!'

In later years Wilde fell under the influence of Baudelaire's disciple, J.K. Huysmans, whose luridly licentious novel, *A Rebours*, had scandalised French society following its publication in 1884. In this novel, Huysmans had paid tribute to Baudelaire.

> ... writers had hitherto confined themselves to exploring the surface of the soul, or such underground passages as were easily accessible and well-lit . . . Baudelaire had gone further; he had descended to the bottom of the inexhaustible mine, had picked his way along abandoned or unexplored galleries, and had finally reached those districts of the soul where the monstrous vegetations of the sick mind flourish. There, near the breeding ground of intellectual aberrations and diseases of the mind – the mystical tetanus, the burning fever of lust, the typhoids and yellow fevers of crime – he had found, hatching in the dismal forcing-house of *ennui*, the frightening middle-age of thoughts and emotions. He had laid bare the morbid psychology of the mind . . .[6]

Huysmans, like Baudelaire, had chosen to look sin straight in the eye, probing its allure and its ugliness, whereas respectable, 'rational' society preferred to sweep it under the carpet or glance at it furtively or voyeuristically through a keyhole. Sin, for the prudishly prurient Victorians, was to be obscene but not heard. For the Decadents, however, the honesty of a sin confessed, even in the absence of contrition, was preferable to the hypocrisy of a sin concealed. For one as tormented by self-loathing as Wilde this candid vision of decadence was alluring. Temperamentally tempted to despair he saw Baudelaire and Huysmans as kindred spirits. They were seeking enlightenment from their own inner darkness. He was trying to do the same.

Far from vanquishing the religious question from their lives, the Decadents

---

[5] Rupert Hart-Davis (ed.), *The Letters of Oscar Wilde* (London, 1962), p. 31.
[6] Robert Baldick, *The Life of J.K. Huysmans* (Oxford, 1955), pp. 85–6.

discovered that plunging themselves into the depths of sin brought them into closer contact with religion, even if the contact only took the form of conflict. Sin and despair were, after all, religious concepts. They were not physical but metaphysical realities. Furthermore, and crucially, despair was distinct from desolation. The former is the absence or the denial of hope, the latter the longing or the hunger for it. A desolate soul does not seek suicide, it seeks consolation. Ultimately, the hunger for hope engenders a hunger for faith. Thus, in the final chapter of *A Rebours*, the novel's principle character, des Esseintes, discovers that his lustful appetites have not satisfied his inner hunger. In his hour of anguish he realises that 'the arguments of pessimism were powerless to console him, and the only possible cure for his misery was the impossible belief in a future life'. At the very last, utterly desolate, des Esseintes breaks into a faltering prayer to the 'impossible' God.

> Ah! but my courage fails me, and my heart is sick within me! – Lord, take pity on the Christian who doubts, on the sceptic who would fain believe, on the galley-slave of life who puts out to sea alone, in the darkness of night, beneath a firmament no longer illumined by the beacon-fires of the ancient hope![7]

In this agonising *cri de coeur* we hear the embryonic convert pining for the authentic tradition, the 'ancient hope', that is only dimly discerned. Leon Bloy, in a poignant review of *A Rebours* written within weeks of the novel's publication, wrote that Huysmans' supreme achievement was to demonstrate that man's pleasures were finite, his needs infinite. The choice that Huysmans had placed before his readers was 'whether to guzzle like the beasts of the field or to look upon the face of God'. A similar conclusion was drawn in another review by the ageing Romantic writer Jules Barbey d'Aurevilly, who highlighted the suggestive parallel between *A Rebours* and Baudelaire's *Les Fleurs du mal*.

> Baudelaire, the satanic Baudelaire, who died a Christian, must surely be one of M. Huysmans' favourite authors, for one can feel his presence, like a glowing fire, behind the finest pages M. Huysmans has written. Well, one day, I defied Baudelaire to begin *Les Fleurs du mal* again, or to go any further in his blasphemies. I might well offer the same challenge to the author of *A Rebours*. 'After *Les Fleurs du mal*,' I told Baudelaire, 'it only remains for you to choose between the muzzle of a pistol and the foot of the Cross.' Baudelaire chose the foot of the Cross. But will the author of *A Rebours* make the same choice?[8]

Twelve years after these words were published, Huysmans recalled Barbey's review: 'Strange! But that man was the only one who saw things clearly in my case . . . He wrote an article which contained these last prophetic

---

[7] *Ibid.*, p. 86.
[8] *Ibid.*, p. 91.

words: "There only remains for you to commit suicide or become a Catholic." '[9] By this time Huysmans had indeed become a Catholic and he would spend the last years of his life in a monastery. Wilde, whose novel *The Picture of Dorian Gray* was hugely influenced by *A Rebours* and contains the same desolate *cri de coeur*, responded approvingly when he learned that Huysmans had entered a monastery, declaring his own desire to do the same. In the event, he would be received into the Church on his death-bed. Other leading English Decadents were also received into the Catholic Church, most notably Aubrey Beardsley, Lionel Johnson, Ernest Dowson and John Gray, the last of whom, allegedly the original inspiration for Wilde's Dorian Gray, became a priest.

Ultimately, the Decadents were far more in revolt against the humanistic 'rationalism' of the post-Enlightenment than they were ever in revolt against the traditions of the Church. They sprang from the same Romantic tradition as Coleridge and Wordsworth, seeking the soul and its secrets in a world which had seemingly lost its soul through a lack of belief in its very existence. Whereas Coleridge and Wordsworth had become sceptical about scepticism, the Decadents had become cynical towards scepticism. Furthermore, when their cynicism led them to sin it brought them into contact with authentic tradition, specifically the Church's teaching on the Seven Deadly Sins, reflected most sublimely in art by the divinely-inspired infernal and purgatorial visions of Dante. The Decadents were groping uncertainly and sometimes blindly in search of the same Dantean vision. Their own visions may have been pale reflections of Dante's masterpiece, but they were visions of sublime reality nonetheless. The Decadents discovered the reality of sin and, having kissed it, recoiled from its embrace. Having experienced the dire consequences of the real absence of God, they hungered for His Real Presence.

Apart from the striking similarity between the Decadent and the Dantean, there is also an obvious affinity of inspiration and intent between Decadent works such as *A Rebours* and *The Picture of Dorian Gray* and the Faustian parables of Marlowe and Goethe. Perhaps the most striking example of a Decadent re-working of the legend of Dr Faustus was 'Finis Coronat Opus', a short story by Francis Thompson. The hero, or more correctly the anti-hero, of Thompson's tale is Florentian, a character cast in the same mould as Dr Faustus or Dorian Gray who also makes a pact with the devil in order to achieve his heart's desire. Whereas Dorian Gray had desired physical beauty and eternal youth, Florentian desires poetic genius and supremacy in the arts. In return for this, the devil demands the blood-sacrifice of Florentian's wife. Florentian removes the crucifix from the altar, treads the prostrate cross underfoot and places a bust of Virgil in its place. He then murders his wife on the altar of Art. His wish is granted but, as with Dorian Gray, it brings nothing but

---

[9] Barbara Beaumont (ed.), *The Road from Decadence, From Brothel to Cloister: Selected Letters of J.K. Huysmans* (London, 1989), p. 66.

misery and despair. At the very last, as the unbarred gate of hell looms menacingly, he is granted a glimpse of lost innocence: 'I met a child today; a child with great candour of eyes. They who talk of children's instincts are at fault: she knew not that hell was in my soul, she knew only that softness was in my gaze. She had been gathering wild flowers, and offered them to me. To me, to me!'[10]

In many respects, the figure of Francis Thompson stands symbolically as a unifying force between the Decadent converts of the 1890s and the decidedly non-decadent converts of the Edwardian and Georgian era, such as Chesterton, Benson, Baring, Noyes and Knox. Throughout the 1880s Thompson had led a life of penury, squalor and opium addiction in post-Dickensian London. Homeless, hungry and befriended by prostitutes, his experiences inspired his most famous poem, 'The Hound of Heaven', written in 1889. Although Thompson was a cradle Catholic, the poem, with its potent and poignant depiction of a reluctant soul's final acceptance of God's relentless and fathomless love, remains a classic of conversion literature. Yet if Thompson had been hounded by heaven in much the same way as many of his Decadent contemporaries, he was also inspired by a profound love for God's creation, most memorably evoked in his verse, 'To a Snowflake', with its echoes of Hopkins's Franciscan *inscape* and its prefiguring of Chesterton's philosophy of gratitude.

With the emergence of G.K. Chesterton, who entered the literary fray at the dawning of the new century, the Catholic literary revival entered its second dynamic phase. Indeed, it would be no exaggeration to say that Chesterton's role in popularising Catholicism in the twentieth century was as crucial as Newman's had been in the previous century. It would also be fair to say that Chesterton's mind was akin to Newman's in its ability to communicate timeless truth with seemingly effortless clarity. He hammered the 'heretics' in his book of that title and pitted their heresies against infallible 'orthodoxy'. Then, in 1909, he became embroiled in the controversy raging in the Church between the Traditionalists and the Modernists. In prose as profound as Newman's he argued the case for Tradition, labelling it the philosophy of the Tree.

> I mean that a tree goes on growing, and therefore goes on changing; but always in the fringes surrounding something unchangeable. The innermost rings of the tree are still the same as when it was a sapling; they have ceased to be seen, but they have not ceased to be central. When the tree grows a branch at the top, it does not break away from the roots at the bottom; on the contrary, it needs to hold more strongly to its roots the higher it rises with its branches. That is the true image of the vigorous and healthy progress of a man, a city, or a whole species.

---

[10] Wilfred Meynell (ed.), *The Works of Francis Thompson*, 3 vols (London, 1913), vol. 3, p. 133.

The Modernists, by contrast, did not subscribe to such a concept of Tradition, believing instead in 'something that changes completely and entirely in every part, at every minute, like a cloud . . . Now, if this merely cloudy and boneless development be adopted as a philosophy, then there can be no place for the past and no possibility of a complete culture. Anything may be here today and gone tomorrow; even tomorrow.'[11]

Elsewhere Chesterton would describe Tradition as the proxy of the dead and the enfranchisement of the unborn, and he also seems to have seen it as a weapon wielded by the Church Militant in its centuries-long war against heresy. The latter vision was never brought more vibrantly to life, quite literally, than in a memorable essay on Gothic architecture.

> The truth about Gothic is, first, that it is alive, and second, that it is on the march. It is the Church Militant; it is the only fighting architecture. All its spires are spears at rest; and all its stones are stones asleep in a catapult . . . I could hear the arches clash like swords as they crossed each other. The mighty and numberless columns seemed to go swinging by like the huge feet of imperial elephants. The graven foliage wreathed and blew like banners going into battle; the silence was deafening with all the mingling noises of a military march; the great bell shook down, as the organ shook up its thunder. The thirsty-throated gargoyles shouted like trumpets from all the roofs and pinnacles as they passed; and from the lectern in the core of the cathedral the eagle of the awful evangelist clashed his wings of brass.[12]

Chesterton's militant approach to the authentic tradition of the Church found expression in many aspects of his work. It was a central theme in his novel *The Ball and the Cross*, and surfaced in some of his finest verse, particularly in 'Lepanto' and 'The Secret People', in which the influence of his friend Hilaire Belloc is obvious. The combined influence of Belloc and Chesterton on the intellectual life of Edwardian and Georgian England won many converts to Catholicism, as did the best-selling novels of the convert R.H. Benson, whose historical romances brought Catholic Tradition vividly to life, most memorably in *Come Rack! Come Rope!* with its pot-boiling portrayal of the persecution of the Church in Elizabethan England.

If Belloc, Benson and Chesterton represented the voice of dynamic orthodoxy in the early years of the century, a new and radically different voice would be its principal exponent in the years between the two world wars. T.S. Eliot was hailed by the *avant garde* as the authentic voice of post-war pessimism and scepticism, particularly after the publication of *The Waste Land* in 1922. By contrast, many of the poetic old guard viewed him suspiciously as a dangerous threat to tradition, an iconoclastic aberration who was thumbing his nose at convention. In the confusion of the fray that followed the poem's

---

[11] *Church Socialist Quarterly* (January, 1909).
[12] *Daily News*, 13 May 1911.

publication, many on both sides of the critical divide had obviously missed the poet's point. Lack of understanding led inevitably to misunderstanding, so that battle lines were drawn according to erroneous preconceptions. The 'moderns' hailed it as a masterpiece of modern thought which had laid waste traditional values and traditional form. The 'ancients' attacked it as an affront to civilised standards. Both sides had made the grave and fundamental error of mistaking Eliot's pessimism towards the Waste Land of modern life for a cynicism towards tradition. In fact, Eliot's philosophical foundation and aesthetic sympathies were rooted in classical and mediaeval tradition, whereas he despised modern secular liberalism. It was, therefore, a perverse irony that he was being vilified by the upholders of tradition and championed by the doyens of secularism. Indeed, it would be fair to say that possibly no poem in the English language has been as admired, as abhorred and as misunderstood as T.S. Eliot's *The Waste Land*.

It would be many years before a true perspective would begin to appear of the poem, the issues it raised and the reaction it caused. More than forty years later, Eliot's obituary in *The Times* displayed a detached view of *The Waste Land* which had been sadly lacking in the midst of the fray following its publication.

> Its presentation of disillusionment and the disintegration of values, catching the mood of the time, made it the poetic gospel of the post-war intelligentsia; at the time, however, few either of its detractors or its admirers saw through the surface innovations and the language of despair to the deep respect for tradition and the keen moral sense which underlay them.[13]

Perhaps the hidden key to understanding *The Waste Land*, overlooked by almost everyone at the time and still ignored by many of the poem's postmodernist admirers today, is to be found in Eliot's devotion to Dante. Scarcely two years before *The Waste Land* was published, Eliot had written:

> You cannot... understand the *Inferno* without the *Purgatorio* and the *Paradiso*. 'Dante,' says Landor's Petrarch, 'is the great master of the disgusting.' ... But a disgust like Dante's is no hypertrophy of a single reaction: it is completed and explained only by the last canto of the *Paradiso* ... The contemplation of the horrid or sordid or disgusting by an artist, is the necessary and negative aspect of the impulse toward the pursuit of beauty.[14]

Eliot perceived that Dante had been grossly misunderstood by the undue emphasis placed upon the 'negative' *Inferno* at the expense of the other two 'positive' books of the *Divine Comedy* and there was something almost divinely comic in the fact that Eliot himself was to suffer the same fate after

---

[13] *The Times*, 5 January 1965.
[14] T.S. Eliot, *The Sacred Wood* (London, 1960), pp. 168–9.

the publication of *The Waste Land*. As post-Reformation puritanism had stressed the punishment of Hell in Dante and had ignored the 'papist' parts about the cleansing grace of Purgatory and the Church Triumphant in Paradise, so post-war cynicism had stressed the negative aspects of Eliot's Waste Land and had ignored the cathartic conclusion that pointed to a 'resurrection'. Typical of this myopic modernist miasma was the judgement of the literary critic, I.A. Richards, that Eliot in *The Waste Land* had effected 'a complete severance between poetry and *all* beliefs'.[15] This generally accepted assumption was blown asunder in June 1927 by Eliot's conversion to Anglo-Catholicism, news of which was greeted with incredulity. How could the arch-iconoclast have become an iconographer? It was all too much for Virginia Woolf, who declared to a friend that Eliot 'may be called dead to us all from this day forward'.[16]

Similar horror and incredulity greeted the news, three years later, that Evelyn Waugh had been received into the Catholic Church. By the end of the 1920s he was seen as the ultra-modern novelist in much the same way that Eliot had been perceived as the ultra-modern poet. As such, his conversion was treated with astonishment by the literary world. On the morning after his reception there was bemused bewilderment in the *Daily Express* that an author known for his 'almost passionate adherence to the ultra-modern' could have joined the Catholic Church. Two leaders in the *Express* had already discussed the significance of Waugh's conversion before his own article, 'Converted to Rome: Why It has Happened to Me', was published on 20 October 1930. Waugh's conversion, like that of Newman, Chesterton and Eliot, was rooted in tradition. The 'essential issue' facing European civilisation, he wrote, was 'between Christianity and Chaos':

> Today we can see it on all sides as the active negation of all that western culture has stood for. Civilization – and by this I do not mean talking cinemas and tinned food, nor even surgery and hygienic houses, but the whole moral and artistic organization of Europe – has not in itself the power of survival. It came into being through Christianity, and without it has no significance or power to command allegiance. The loss of faith in Christianity and the consequential lack of confidence in moral and social standards have become embodied in the ideal of a materialistic, mechanized state . . . It is no longer possible . . . to accept the benefits of civilization and at the same time deny the supernatural basis upon which it rests.

Waugh's contemptuous dismissal of 'talking cinemas and tinned food' as having any significance to civilisation was indicative of a deep mistrust of scientism and technolatry, i.e. the worship and idolisation of technological 'progress'. This anti-scientism was shared by Edith Sitwell and would

---

[15] Quoted in Peter Ackroyd, *T.S. Eliot* (London, 1984), p. 161.
[16] Quoted in Walter Hooper, *C.S. Lewis: A Companion and Guide* (London, 1996), p. 25.

contribute to her own conversion. She was horrified by the use of destructive technology during the Second World War and in her famous poem 'Still Falls the Rain' had likened the bombing of London during the Blitz to humanity's continual nailing of Christ to the Cross. Similar imagery was used five years later to convey her horror of the dropping of the atomic bomb on Hiroshima. 'The Shadow of Cain', the first of Sitwell's 'three poems of the Atomic Age' was, she explained, about 'the fission of the world into warring particles, destroying and self-destructive. It is about the gradual migration of mankind . . . into the desert of the Cold, towards the final disaster, the first symbol of which fell on Hiroshima.'[17] The poem's imagery was as chilling as its subject. 'The first two pages,' Sitwell explained, 'were partly a physical description of the highest degree of cold, partly a spiritual description of this.'[18] In 'Still Falls the Rain' she had employed the imagery of a relentless downpour to depict the misery of the Blitz. Now, in 'The Shadow of Cain', she was expressing the frosty fears of a whole generation as the world emerged from world war to cold war. *Après le deluge . . . the Cold.*

The horrors of Hiroshima also shocked Siegfried Sassoon, writer of some of the most disturbing poems of the previous war, to new heights of creativity. In 1945 he wrote 'Litany of the Lost', a verse which lamented the 'slavedom of mankind to the machine' and the 'terror of atomic doom foreseen'. Humanity was 'chained to the wheel of progress uncontrolled' and in spite of its 'marvellous monkey innovations' was 'unregenerate still in head and heart'. The poem is transformed into a prayer by the haunting refrain at the end of each verse: *Deliver us from ourselves.*

The alienation so evident in the post-war poetry of Sitwell and Sassoon, both of whom were received into the Church in the mid 1950s, illustrates a deep disillusionment with the modern world and its cult of 'progress'. In common with the many converts who had preceded them they were longing for depth in a world of shallows, permanence in a world of change, and certainty in a world of doubt.

Unfortunately, the Church's ability to win converts through the power of tradition seems to have been undermined in recent decades by the efforts of a new generation of Modernists hell-bent, seemingly, on tampering with Catholicism's timeless beauties and mysteries. The danger was perceived by Evelyn Waugh, who wrote in 1964 that 'throughout her entire life the Church has been at active war with enemies from without and traitors from within'.[19] To his great distress Waugh began to feel that the 'traitors' within the Church were working to deliver the faithful into the hands of the 'enemies' without. The Church Militant was being betrayed to a modern world seemingly

---

[17] Edith Sitwell, *Taken Care Of: An Autobiography* (London, 1965), p. 153.
[18] Victoria Glendinning, *Edith Sitwell: A Unicorn Among Lions* (London, 1981), p. 260.
[19] *Catholic Herald*, 7 August 1964.

triumphant. Alarmed at developments, Waugh devoted a great deal of his time during the last few years of his life to opposing the modernist tendency in the Church.

In a postscript to his biography of Waugh, Christopher Sykes endeavoured to put his friend's obstinate opposition into context. 'His dislike of the reform-movement,' Sykes wrote,

> was not merely an expression of his conservatism, nor of aesthetic preferences. It was based on deeper things. He believed that in its long history the Church had developed a liturgy which enabled an ordinary, sensual man (as opposed to a saint who is outside generalisation) to approach God and be aware of sanctity and the divine. To abolish all this for the sake of up-to-dateness seemed to him not only silly but dangerous . . . he could not bear the thought of modernized liturgy. 'Untune that string' he felt, and loss of faith would follow . . . Whether his fears were justified or not only 'the unerring sentence of time' can show.[20]

Perhaps the unerring sentence has not yet been passed, but it was certainly the case that Waugh was not by any means the only person who held these views. On 6 July 1971 *The Times* published the text of an Appeal to the Vatican to preserve the Latin Mass which was signed by a host of well-known Catholics, as well as many non-Catholic dignitaries and celebrities, including Harold Acton, Vladimir Ashkenazy, Lennox Berkeley, Maurice Bowra, Agatha Christie, Kenneth Clark, Nevill Coghill, Cyril Connolly, Colin Davis, Robert Graves, Graham Greene, Joseph Grimond, Harman Grisewood, Rupert Hart-Davis, Barbara Hepworth, Auberon Herbert, David Jones, Osbert Lancaster, F.R. Leavis, Cecil Day Lewis, Compton Mackenzie, Yehudi Menuhin, Nancy Mitford, Raymond Mortimer, Malcolm Muggeridge, Iris Murdoch, John Murray, Sean O'Faolain, William Plomer, Kathleen Raine, William Rees-Mogg, Ralph Richardson, Joan Sutherland, Bernard Wall, Patrick Wall and E.I. Watkin.

A moderate but nonetheless critical view was offered by Robert Speaight, actor, writer and Catholic convert, in his autobiography, published in 1970. Although he had sympathised with the reforms of the Council he complained that much had happened 'far beyond the intention of the Conciliar fathers':

> The psychology of adherence to Catholicism has subtly changed; authority is flouted; basic doctrines are questioned . . . The vernacular Liturgy, popular and pedestrian, intelligible and depressing, has robbed us of much that was numinous in public worship; there is less emphasis on prayer and penitence; and the personal relationship between God and man . . . is neglected in favour of a diffused social concern.[21]

---

[20] Christopher Sykes, *Evelyn Waugh: A Biography* (London, 1975), pp. 449–50.
[21] Robert Speaight, *The Property Basket: Recollections of a Divided Life* (London, 1970), pp. 398–9.

Ultimately Speaight's frustration with the modernists was linked to their evident contempt for tradition: 'What exasperates me in the attitude of many progressives is not their desire to go forward or even to change direction, but their indifference to tradition which is the *terra firma* from which they themselves proceed.'[22]

Alec Guinness was another thespian convert who found his initial enthusiasm for reform tempered by subsequent abuses of the Council's teaching. 'Much water has flown under Tiber's bridges, carrying away splendour and mystery from Rome, since the pontificate of Pius XII,' he wrote in *Blessings in Disguise*, his autobiography. Yet he remained confident about the future, rooted in the belief that the essential traditions of Catholicism 'remain firmly entrenched':

> The Church has proved she is not moribund. 'All shall be well,' I feel, 'and all manner of things shall be well,' so long as the God who is worshipped is the God of all ages, past and to come, and not the Idol of Modernity, so venerated by some of our bishops, priests and mini-skirted nuns.[23]

Guinness quoted one of Chesterton's 'most penetrating statements' as a prelude to his discourse on the reform of the Church. 'The Church,' wrote Chesterton, 'is the one thing that saves a man from the degrading servitude of being a child of his own time.' Perhaps he may also have added that tradition, as guarded and guided by dynamic orthodoxy, is the one thing that saves the Church itself from being a child of its own time. Certainly Chesterton had something similar in mind when he employed the imagery of the Church as a heavenly chariot 'thundering through the ages, the dull heresies sprawling and prostrate, the wild truth reeling but erect'.[24] It was this vision of a militant and dynamic tradition combating error down the ages that had inspired the host of converts from Newman to Chesterton; and from Waugh to Sitwell and Sassoon. If the flow of high-profile literary converts has been more noticeable by its absence than by its presence in the past quarter of a century perhaps it has something to do with the loss of that vision of tradition amidst the fogs of fashion. No matter. Fogs pass and the clarity of day reasserts itself.

Tradition remains. It not only remains, it also retains its power to win converts; for, as Chesterton also said, what is needed is not a Church that can move with the world but a Church that can move the world.

---

[22] *Ibid.*, p. 401.
[23] Alec Guinness, *Blessings in Disguise* (London, 1985), p. 45.
[24] G.K. Chesterton, *Orthodoxy* (London, 1908), p. 169.

11

NEWMAN'S *IDEA OF A UNIVERSITY*, 'THE CIRCLE OF THE SCIENCES', AND THE CONSTITUTION OF THE CHURCH

DOM WULSTAN PETERBURS, OSB

He who came for ever, came as a Spirit, and, so coming, did for His own that which the visible flesh and blood of the Son of man, from its very nature could not do, viz., He came into the souls of all who believe, and taking possession of them, He, being One, knit them all together into one. Christ, by coming in the flesh, provided an external or apparent unity, such as had been under the Law. He formed His Apostles into a visible society; but when He came again in the Person of His Spirit, He made them all in a real sense one, not in name only. For they were no longer arranged merely in the form of unity, as the limbs of the dead may be, but they were parts and organs of one unseen power; they really depended upon, and were offshoots of that which was One; their separate persons were taken into a mysterious union with things unseen, were grafted upon and assimilated to the spiritual body of Christ, which is One, even by the Holy Ghost, in whom Christ has come again to us. Thus Christ came, not to make us one, but to die for us: the Spirit came to make us one in Him who had died and was alive, that is, to form the Church.[1]

JOHN HENRY NEWMAN was received into the Catholic Church, at his retreat in Littlemore, just outside Oxford, on 9 October 1845 by the Passionist missionary Fr Dominic Barberi. His reception implied a rejection, at least in part, of the ecclesiology he had held as an Anglican, and the embracing of Roman Catholic ecclesial structures. Whilst intellectually convinced of the truth of the Roman Catholic claims by 1843, he had waited a further two years before asking to be received, delaying the moment until he felt himself as ready as possible for such a step.[2] Along with many of his

---

[1] J.H. Newman, *Parochial and Plain Sermons*, 8 vols (London, 1880–2), vol. iv, pp. 169–70.
[2] Cf. M. Peterburs, 'Newman and the Development of Doctrine' in V.A. McClelland (ed.), *By Whose Authority? Newman, Manning and the Magisterium* (Bath, 1996), pp. 49–78; esp. pp. 67–71.

fellow converts from Anglicanism in the 1840s and 1850s, Newman imagined that the Church of Rome would be ready to put him to work in her service, and indeed she was, but he found that actually living within her visible confines took much getting used to, and much to understand. The purpose of this essay is to elaborate that search.

As an Anglican, Newman had held that the Church should be one and be governed by the successors of the apostles, the bishops, whose position, in the first of the *Tracts for the Times*, he sought to underscore.[3] He further believed that the bishops could require the obedience of their subjects, but he also held that the Church was at her best when clergy and laity worked in a collaborative partnership. He discovered as editor of the *Rambler* that this was not the attitude of the English Catholic bishops, having already been similarly disappointed in Ireland, whilst establishing the Catholic University in Dublin. Newman agreed with the Catholic bishops that the Church was given unity and structure through the episcopal ministry, and despite misgivings about the opportuneness of its being defined by the First Vatican Council, believed in the pope's infallibility, but he argued that the Church was only given proper shape and form when the *ecclesia docens* was permitted to work alongside and with the *ecclesia discens*. It is argued here, that the relationship Newman envisaged among the different subjects in the 'Circle of the Sciences' in his *Idea of a University* is analogous to the relationship among the Prophetical, Priestly and Regal Offices of the Church described in the preface to the *Via Media*, with theology, the regulator of both systems, maintaining a delicate balance.

After his reception into the Catholic Church, Newman remained in Littlemore until February 1846, from where he moved to Old Oscott. He stayed there with several other converts, who had been with him in Littlemore, until September, when, accompanied by his devoted Ambrose St John, he set out for Rome, where both were to train for the priesthood. Upon his return to England, he established the English Oratory. The first house was in Birmingham, and a second was soon to be founded in London, although in 1853 it became independent.[4]

The *Idea of a University*

In November 1851, Newman was appointed Rector of the new Catholic University in Dublin, a post which he held until his resignation on 12 November 1858. He thus held office for seven years, although the university

---

[3] *Tracts for the Times*, 5 vols (London, 1834–40), vol. I.
[4] For the events of this period see I.T. Ker, *John Henry Newman: A Biography* (Oxford, 1988), pp. 316–75.

did not commence its work until November 1854, and so in practice his tenure of office was just four years.[5] The events of this period are well known, as are the reasons for his departure from office, and so need not be repeated here.[6] What are important, however, are the views which he put forward in a series of lectures delivered in 1852, *Discourses on the Scope and Nature of University Education.* These were later published, along with some *Lectures and Essays on University Subjects* (1859), written whilst he was Rector of the university, as *The Idea of a University*.[7] This volume was first published in 1873.

The preface to the *Idea* begins with the statement that a university exists for teaching 'universal knowledge'.[8] This does not mean that knowledge for its own sake is a good enough reason for a university to exist; its real purpose is to produce intelligent members of society, capable of thinking and reasoning for themselves.[9]

The first Discourse is introductory and it is here that Newman sets out his

---

[5] H. Tristram (ed.), *John Henry Newman's Autobiographical Writings* (London, 1956), pp. 283–4.

[6] Cf. F. McGrath, *Newman's University: Idea and Reality* (London, 1951); L. McRedmond, *Thrown Among Strangers: John Henry Newman in Ireland* (Dublin, 1990); and S.W. Gilley, *Newman and his* Age (London, 1990), pp. 275–97.

[7] The very title *Idea of a University* is in itself an indication of Newman's approach, since the term 'idea in his theology stands not for a mere concept, but for a principle with a life of its own and a power to develop into as yet non-existent forms and institutions: the very germ of a dynamic community, that ability . . . to embody high ideas in great institutions'. J. Coulson, 'Newman's idea of an Educated Laity – the Two Versions' in J. Coulson (ed.), *Theology and the University; An Ecumenical Investigation* (London, 1964), p. 53. Coulson's thesis in this and a subsequent article, 'Newman's Idea of an Open University and its consequences today' in J.D. Bastable (ed.), *Newman and Gladstone: Centennial Essays* (Dublin, 1978), pp. 221–37, is that in later years Newman changed his mind about the usefulness of a Catholic university as such, preferring an 'open' university in which Catholics would participate while retaining their own identity. This view is contested by I.T. Ker, 'Did Newman Believe in the idea of a Catholic University?', *Downside Review*, vol. 93 (1975), pp. 39–42, and also in his critical edition of *The Idea of a University* (Oxford, 1976), pp. 585–6. See also K. Flanagan, 'The Godless and the Burlesque: Newman and the other Irish Universities' in Bastable, pp. 239–78 for a comparison of Newman's views on the Catholic University with the other Irish universities, and in the same volume, pp. 279–86, and P.J. Corish, 'Newman and Maynooth' for a survey of his connections with the seminary. The possible application today of Newman's *Idea of a University* is discussed by J.M. Roberts, 'The *Idea of a University* revisited' in I.T. Ker & A.G. Hill (eds), *Newman after a Hundred* Years (Oxford, 1990), pp. 193–222; R. Jenkins, 'Newman and the *Idea of a University*' in D. Brown (ed.), *Newman: A Man for our Time* (London, 1990), pp. 141–58; and J. Pelikan, *The Idea of the University: a Reexamination* (New Haven & London, 1992), who refers to Newman's book as 'the most important treatise on the idea of the university ever written in any language', p. 9. Newman had already developed the themes of the place of religion in education in the *Tamworth Reading Room*, published in J.H. Newman, *Discussions and Arguments on Various Subjects* (London, 1878), pp. 254–305. Cf. C.S. Dessain, *John Henry Newman* (London, 1966), p. 102.

[8] J.H. Newman, *The Idea of a University*: edited and with an Introduction by I.T. Ker (Oxford, 1976), p. 5.

[9] *Ibid.*, p. 10.

qualifications for discussing university education, i.e. his time at Oxford, during which he learnt about liberal education.[10] In Discourse II Newman considers 'Theology a Branch of Knowledge'. In this lecture he argues that if one believes Christianity to be true, then it must be included in the curriculum of a university that claims to teach 'universal knowledge'. If theology is left out, then 'you will soon break up into fragments the whole circle of secular knowledge'.[11]

This argument is based on the belief expressed in Discourse III, 'Bearing of Theology on other Branches of Knowledge', in which Newman states that 'all knowledge forms one whole, because its subject matter is one.'[12] This he goes on to explain:

> As they all belong to one and the same circle of objects, they are one and all connected together; as they are but aspects of things, they are severally incomplete in their relation to the things themselves, though complete in their own idea and for their own respective purposes; on both accounts they at once need and subserve each other. And further, the bearings of one science on another . . . belongs . . . to a sort of science distinct from all of them, which is my own conception of what is meant by Philosophy, in the truest sense of the word, and of a philosophical mind.[13]

Newman is not, however, describing some sort of 'superscience':

> In default of a recognized term, I have called the perfection or virtue of the intellect by the name of philosophy, philosophical knowledge, enlargement of mind, or illumination.[14]

The relationship of the sciences, one to another, is further described in Discourse IV, 'Bearing of other Branches of Knowledge on Theology':

> I observe, then, that if you drop any science out of the circle of knowledge, you cannot keep its place vacant for it; that science is forgotten; the other sciences close up, or, in other words, they exceed their proper bounds, and intrude where they have no right.[15]

The danger then is that one particular branch of knowledge will put itself at the centre of the circle, and make the others subservient to it. For example,

---

[10] Newman had the double problem in overcoming opposition in being both an Englishman and a convert. Gilley, *Newman*, p. 278.
[11] Newman, *Idea*, p. 38.
[12] *Ibid.*, p. 57.
[13] *Ibid.*
[14] *Ibid.*, p. 114. This seems to have been misunderstood by Culler, who speaks of a 'science distinct from and yet in some sense embodying the materials of them all . . . a discipline . . . [with] a rather mysterious character'. A.D. Culler, *The Imperial Intellect: A Study of Newman's Educational Ideal* (New Haven, 1955), p. 182.
[15] Newman, *Idea*, pp. 73–4.

political economy may try to influence ethics, although it has no jurisdiction in that field.[16]

In the fifth Discourse, 'Knowledge its own End', Newman acknowledges that university students would not, in practice, be able to study all of the sciences,[17] but only a few of them. Narrow specialization in one area, however, should be avoided, and the student would benefit from living in a community in which the whole circle of sciences is taught. As Ker remarks: 'Clearly Newman would have regarded certain fundamental subjects – including theology – as absolutely indispensable, but it is ludicrous to suppose that he wanted a university to include every conceivable branch of knowledge known to man. In fact, in the last of the Discourses he makes the necessary modification when he states that "all branches of knowledge are, at least implicitly, the subject-matter of its teaching." [*Idea*, p. 183]. In other words, a university must be in principle hospitable and in practice not hostile to any kind of knowledge.'[18] The result of this will be the 'philosophical habit' of Discourse III, and it is in that sense that knowledge is its own end.

Newman was not, however, in favour of an education which would provide the student with merely a cursory knowledge of several different sciences. Rather, each separate science which is to be studied must be studied in detail:

> This is commonly and excellently done by making him begin with Grammar; nor can too great accuracy, or minuteness and subtlety of teaching be used towards him, as his faculties expand, with this simple purpose. Hence it is that critical scholarship is so important a discipline for him when he is leaving school for the University.[19]

That university education is for the 'enlargement of mind'[20] is made clear in Discourse VI, 'Knowledge viewed in relation to Learning':

> The enlargement consists not merely in the passive reception into the mind of a number of ideas hitherto unknown to it, but in the mind's energetic and

---

[16] 'Given that wealth is to be sought, this and that is the method of gaining it. This is the extent to which a Political Economist has a right to go; he has no right to determine that wealth is at any rate to be sought, or that it is the way to be virtuous and the price of happiness.' *Ibid.*, p. 84.

[17] In his use of the term 'science', Newman appears to be drawing on Aristotle for whom 'any body of knowledge may be called a science if it can be rationally organized in terms of principles which are either self-evident or are drawn from some higher sense whose own principles are self-evident.' A. Nichols, *The Shape of Catholic Theology: An Introduction to Its Sources, Principles, and History* (Edinburgh, 1991), p. 300. Such terminology appears to have been quite common in the nineteenth century: cf. H.E. Manning, *The Temporal Mission of the Holy Ghost or Reason and Revelation* (London, 1909), pp. 113–15.

[18] I.T. Ker, *The Achievement of John Henry Newman* (Notre Dame, 1990), p. 23.

[19] Newman, *Idea*, p. 12. The necessity of knowledge in detail, but avoiding narrow specialization, for the formation of a philosophical habit of mind is well described by Ker, *Achievement*, pp. 5–10.

[20] Newman, *Idea*, p. 114.

simultaneous action upon and towards and among those new ideas, which are making in upon it.[21]

That which is to be aspired to is the

> true enlargement of mind which is the power of viewing many things at once as a whole, of referring them severally to their true place in the universal system, of understanding their respective values, and of determining their mutual dependence. Thus is that form of Universal Knowledge, of which I have on a former occasion spoken, set up in the individual intellect, and constitutes its perfection.[22]

In the seventh Discourse, 'Knowledge viewed in relation to Professional Skill', Newman argues that the liberal education described above is 'useful' for two reasons. Firstly, because it is its own end, and 'has its use in itself',[23] and secondly, because it 'tends to good, or is the instrument of good'.[24] He concedes that it is not always the case that 'good' and 'useful' are identical, but he maintains that 'the good is always useful',[25] remembering that without education, professional and scientific studies will not advance.[26]

Critics, however, have argued that at this point Newman has contradicted himself over the question of whether a practical end must be assigned to a university course. Thus Culler argues: 'The whole burden of the fifth discourse was that . . . liberal knowledge is its own end, and now, under the guise of carrying this argument a step further, Newman has actually reversed it. Where before he had rejected utility as a criterion for evaluating knowledge, he now accepts that criterion and merely claims that liberal knowledge is useful too.'[27] To this Vargish adds: 'The confusion is real and the fault is certainly Newman's.'[28] But this is not Newman's argument. His point is that a practical end does exist, if one must be assigned. As he said in the fifth discourse, having first argued that 'knowledge is capable of being its own end', 'Further advantages accrue to us and redound to others by its possession, over and above what it is in itself.'[29] Yet, if 'a liberal education be good, it must necessarily be useful too.'[30]

Discourse VIII concerns 'Knowledge viewed in relation to Religion'. Here Newman contends that the 'pursuit of knowledge'[31] is of great benefit to the

---

[21] *Ibid.*, p. 120.
[22] *Ibid.*, pp. 122–3.
[23] *Ibid.*, p. 142.
[24] *Ibid.*, p. 143.
[25] *Ibid.*, pp. 143–4.
[26] *Ibid.*, p. 145.
[27] Culler, p. 222.
[28] T. Vargish, *Newman: The Contemplation of Mind* (Oxford, 1970), p. 132.
[29] Newman, *Idea*, p. 97.
[30] *Ibid.*, p. 144.
[31] *Ibid.*, p. 169.

study of religion, but he warns against forgetting about God, and arriving at a position where 'sin is not an offence against God, but against human nature'.[32] In other words, 'Newman suspect[s] liberal education for its sceptical, critical temperament.'[33]

Doubts about liberal knowledge are also voiced in the final Discourse, 'Duties of the Church towards Knowledge'. Here Newman considers the relationship between the Church and a Catholic university that teaches Catholic theology (which, of course, it must). It is pointed out that, unless the Church exercises some influence, the tendency of liberal knowledge is 'to impress us with a mere philosophical theory of life and conduct, in the place of Revelation.'[34] Thus, it should not be allowed to become the rival of the Church . . . in those theological matters which to the Church are exclusively committed.'[35]

To summarise, then, a university exists to teach 'universal knowledge'. Accordingly, all sciences, including theology, must be taught. The purpose of this is 'enlargement of the mind'. Warning shots, however, are fired across the bows of liberal knowledge, when it is argued that it must not be allowed to replace God. To this end, the Church must have some say in the running of a Catholic university.[36] As far as Newman's ecclesiology is concerned, the most important things to note at this juncture are the 'circle of sciences' and the role of hierarchical authority.

A critic of Newman has argued that in his description of the relationship of the sciences to one another, he employs two different images to describe the structure of knowledge, that of the 'circle of the sciences' and that of the 'hierarchy of the sciences', and that he makes no attempt to reconcile the two. The former, which is of classical origin, implies that theology occupies one segment of a circle, which is presided over by the science of sciences, but the latter, which is of medieval origin, implies that she is the queen of the sciences and herself has the ruling of all the rest.[37]

But, as Ker[38] has shown, this is to misunderstand Newman's argument. First, he never once mentions a 'hierarchy of the sciences'; second, he does not suppose that the sciences in the circle are equal with one another. He makes it quite clear, in fact, that some branches of knowledge, e.g. theology, 'impinge upon (not rule over) a great number of other branches of knowledge'.[39] The

---

[32] *Ibid.*, p. 165.
[33] K. Nichols, 'Education as Liberation', in D.A. Lane (ed.), *Religious Education and the Future: Essays in honour of Patrick Wallace* (Dublin, 1986), p. 138.
[34] Newman, *Idea*, p. 185.
[35] *Ibid.*, p. 184.
[36] Cf. Newman's now famous portrait of a gentleman. The point of the portrait is that liberal education can provide much, but not all that is required in a Catholic university. *Idea*, pp. 179–80.
[37] Culler, p. 258.
[38] Newman, *Idea*, pp. lxi–lxii.
[39] *Ibid.*, p. lxi.

image of the circle does not imply equality, but interdependence. It is, therefore, perfectly possible for one science to be the chief of the sciences, not in any hierarchical sense, but as a *primus inter pares*.[40] As will be seen later, the type of relationship envisaged here among the different sciences is the same as that envisaged among the three offices of Christ, exercised by the Church, as described in the preface to the *Via Media*. There, the Prophetical, Priestly and Regal Offices are seen to exist in creative tension with one another, but it is also contended that theology, the instrument of the Prophetical Office, is the regulating principle.

With regard to the role of hierarchical authority, it must be remembered that in the university Newman was trying to integrate clergy and laity. Such integration was not common, and clergy and educated laity often held radically different ecclesiologies. In order to achieve this integration, Newman felt that he needed to 'reconcile three factors – the autonomy required by the intellect to develop according to its proper nature, free from arbitrary and external constraints; the rights and function of theology within the economy of a university; and the extent to which the Church has the right to exercise a pastoral authority within the university'.[41] In this he was trying to achieve an equilibrium among competing claims. This, of course, reflects his view expressed in the image of the circle of sciences, that all are necessary and interdependent, but not necessarily equal.

The implications of this for Newman's ecclesiology are clear. The Church is not to be governed autocratically by the pope and the bishops. They are the prime governors of the Church, but their authority does not extend to all spheres. Coulson has summarised the matter well: 'Ecclesiastical authority can rightfully require an obedience to what is essential for the ordering of the Church as a polity or institution, but it cannot supersede conscience.'[42]

Thus, Newman can argue that the Catholic Church has some jurisdiction over a Catholic university, since that university is itself limited and defined by its concept of what constitutes knowledge and truth. There is to be, however, sufficient academic freedom to allow serious research to be conducted, without constant and unwarranted interference from the hierarchy. This relationship parallels the relationship described in the Discourses between liberal knowledge and the Church. Liberal knowledge can be of great benefit to

---

[40] *Ibid.*, p. lxii.
[41] J. Coulson, *Newman and the Common Tradition: A Study in the Language of Church and Society* (Oxford, 1970), p. 87.
[42] *Ibid.*, p. 100. The relationship between the Catholic university and ecclesiastical authorities is considered by Pope John Paul II in his 1990 Apostolic Constitution *Ex Corde Ecclesiae*, and P.C. Erb, *Newman and the Idea of a Catholic University* (Atlanta, 1997), whilst noting Newman's continuing importance for Catholic higher education, draws a number of parallels between the writings. See also J. Ratzinger, *The Nature and Mission of Theology: Approaches to Understanding its Role in the Light of Present Controversy* (San Francisco, 1995).

theology, helping it to make significant advances. This, of course, benefits the Church considerably. Left to its own devices, however, liberal knowledge is quite capable of dispensing with God, and substituting secular philosophy. Such study must therefore be kept in check by the Church. Similarly, academic and intellectual freedom in the liberal arts will benefit the intellectual standing of the university, which will, in turn, benefit the study of theology in the university, which then benefits the Church. The Church, however, must exercise such pastoral authority as is necessary to ensure that this is the case, and that the liberal arts do not take over and extend themselves into areas in which the Church is the arbiter. So, the broad boundaries of the university are to be set by the Church authorities, but these must not be too narrowly defined, and should allow ample academic and intellectual freedom. If the limits are too narrow, scholarship in general will decline, and the rights and functions of theology within the university will be severely impaired. The end result of this is that the Church as a whole will then suffer. This principle gives rise to Newman's views about the place of an educated laity in the Church.

Following his resignation as Rector of the Catholic University, Newman began working on a philosophical treatise in defence of Christianity. He labelled the notes 'Opus Magnum', but his work on this was delayed, first by a request from the bishops that he should become involved in a new translation of the Bible,[43] and second, by his involvement in what has become known as 'The *Rambler* Controversy'.

The *Rambler* Controversy[44]

The *Rambler* had been established in January 1848, by John Moore Capes. Capes was a convert, who had been received into the Catholic Church on 27 July 1845 by the future Cardinal Wiseman, who was at that time President of Oscott College. Since he was married, Capes was unable to seek ordination, but he managed to find a post as professor of mathematics at Prior Park College, near Bath. It was while he was there, in 1846, that he decided to found a periodical in which he and other converts 'should write for the present condition of the English mind, entering into all subjects of literary, philosophic and moral interest, treating them as a person who believes Catholicism to be the

---

[43] This project was abandoned by the bishops 'at the first difficulty.' Dessain, p. 111.
[44] The history of the affair is recorded by J. Altholz, *The Liberal Catholic Movement in England: The "Rambler" and its Contributors, 1848–1864* (London, 1962). Cf. also M. Sharkey, 'Newman on the Laity', *Gregorianum*, vol. 68, no. 1–2 (1987), pp. 339–46; and J.H. Newman, *On Consulting the Faithful in Matters of Doctrine*: edited and with an Introduction by J. Coulson (London, 1986), pp. 1–49.

only true religion'.[45] Bishop Ullathorne approved greatly of this idea, and the project went ahead, once Newman had been consulted and various difficulties had been ironed out. During the period 1848–54 the weekly sold reasonably well, developing into a monthly magazine in September 1848. The *Rambler* was smiled upon by the ecclesiastical authorities for the greater part of this period, and was actually favoured by Wiseman. From 1854, however, when Richard Simpson, a graduate of Oriel and convert to Catholicism, became heavily involved in the production of the magazine, the bishops began to frown upon it as it became associated with Liberal Catholicism.[46]

In fact, the now well-known controversy over the inspection of Catholic schools led to a meeting on 12 February 1859 in London at which Wiseman, Errington, Grant and Ullathorne decided that the editorship of the *Rambler* needed to be taken out of Simpson's hands. It was agreed that Ullathorne was to persuade Newman to take over the *Rambler*. This Newman did, after protracted negotiations between Simpson and the hierarchy in which he was the middleman.

Newman had been caught in a difficult situation. He was reluctant to take on the editorship of the *Rambler*, but believed that the ideals that lay behind it were worthy and proper, and deserved to be continued. In his advertisement for the first edition of the *Rambler* under his editorship, therefore, he did not mention the change of editor, nor did he change the name of the periodical, as his fellow Oxford convert and editor of the *Dublin Review*, W.G. Ward, had suggested, or merge it with the *Atlantis* as Simpson requested.[47] Instead he re-asserted, in more moderate form, the liberal ideals which underlay the work of Simpson and Acton, although he intended to change what had in so many ways displeased him.[48]

[45] Capes to Newman, 15 July 1846, cited in Altholz, p. 8.

[46] In 1858 Capes, who had suffered from ill health for many years, resigned and Simpson was joined as co-editor by John Acton. 'Acton was unique among his contemporaries . . . An Englishman by nationality, an aristocrat by inheritance, and a Catholic in religion, he had been made by circumstances of family and education into a thorough cosmopolitan, a competent scholar, and an accepted member of Protestant social and political circles.' Altholz, p. 45. Bishop Goss of Liverpool was the only English Catholic Bishop not to criticise the *Rambler* in a pastoral letter. P. Doyle, 'Bishop Goss of Liverpool (1856–1872) and the Importance of being English' in S. Mews (ed.), *Religion and National Identity. Studies in Church History*, vol. 18 (Oxford, 1982), p. 437.

[47] Cf. W. Ward, *The Life of John Henry Cardinal Newman*, 2 vols (London, 1912), vol. I, pp. 490–1; and Altholz, p. 94.

[48] Cf. Ward, vol. I, p. 492. Note also a letter that Newman wrote to Acton in December 1858: 'Let it go back to its own literary line. Let it be instructive, clever and amusing. Let it cultivate a general temper of good humour and courtesy. Let it praise as many persons as it can, and gain friends in neutral quarters, and become the organ of others by the interest it has made them take in its proceeding. Then it will be able to plant a good blow at a fitting time with great effect.' Cited by Coulson in Newman, *Consulting*, p. 6. For more detail on W.G. Ward see the two volumes by his son, Wilfrid Ward: *W.G. Ward and the Oxford Movement* (London, 1889) and *W.G. Ward and the Catholic Revival* (London, 1893).

Despite his intention, Newman immediately angered the bishops in his first number of the *Rambler* (May 1959). This he did by referring to the education question raised by Scott Naysmith Stokes, the Catholic school inspector, earlier in the year. The passage in which Newman caused offence was contained in his editorial note:

> Acknowledging, then, most fully the prerogatives of the episcopate, we do unfeignedly believe, both from the reasonableness of the matter, and especially from the providence, gentleness, and considerateness which belongs to them personally, that their Lordships really desire to know the opinion of the laity on subjects in which the laity are especially concerned. If even in the preparation of a dogmatic definition the faithful are consulted, as lately as the instance of the Immaculate Conception, it is at least as natural to anticipate such an act of kind feeling and sympathy in great practical questions, out of the condescension which belongs to those who are *forma facti gregis ex animo* . . . Surely it was no disrespect towards them to desire that they should have the laity rallying round them on the great question of education with the imposing zeal which has lately been exemplified in Ireland, in the great meeting which was held in Cork . . . Let them pardon, then, the incidental hastiness of manner or want of ceremony of the rude Jack-tars of their vessel, as far as it occurred, in consideration of the zeal and energy with which they haul-to the ropes and man the yards.[49]

The obvious purpose of the editorial was to placate the bishops, although some may feel that it was also intended as a swipe at them. In any event it unleashed their wrath, and Newman was drawn into conflict with John Gillow, professor of dogmatic theology at Ushaw College (the leading seminary in England),[50] over the use of the word 'consult'. Gillow understood Newman to mean by 'consult', to ask someone's opinion, and he was adamant that Pius IX and the bishops had not consulted the laity in that sense during the preliminary work to the promulgation of the dogma of the Immaculate Conception. Newman countered that his use of the word 'consult' was to be understood passively, i.e. in the way in which one might consult a barometer, and even quoted, in his defence, the Jesuit Perrone, whose work on the Immaculate Conception had been an important element in the promulgation of the dogma.[51] Although this pacified Gillow temporarily, he was to return to the attack following the July number of the *Rambler*.

It may be felt, however, that Newman's response to Gillow was rather disingenuous, and that Gillow is to be forgiven for being puzzled by Newman's use of the word 'consult'. Such a view is perhaps borne out by Newman's piece in the next number of the *Rambler*, which seems to be in

---

[49] Newman, *Consulting*, pp. 13–14.
[50] Gillow was later to approve of both Newman's *Apologia* and his *Letter to Pusey*. Ker, *John Henry Newman*, pp. 561, 588.
[51] Gilley, *Newman*, p. 303.

favour of an active role for the laity, and by his account of his meeting with Ullathorne on 22 May, a meeting at which the two disagreed as to the role of the laity. Newman argued that an educated laity had a very important role to play in the life of the Church, but his bishop would not allow the weight of his argument. Of the meeting Newman wrote:

> He saw one side, I another – He said something like, 'Who are the Laity? I answered that the Church would look foolish without them – not those words.[52]

It was at this meeting that Ullathorne advised Newman to resign as editor of the *Rambler* after the July edition, which he did.

Sharkey argues that confusion arose because Newman used the word 'consult' in two different ways. He summarises the matter thus: 'With regard to the education issue, he had wanted the bishops to enter into dialogue with knowledgeable laity about the provision of elementary schools. In matters of doctrine, though, the laity are to be questioned/consulted about what they believe.'[53]

It would appear, however, that this is a slight refinement of Newman's view. Certainly he used the word consult in two different senses, but only once he had been challenged by Gillow. In the May editorial, Newman believed 'that their Lordships really desire to know the opinion of the laity on subjects in which the laity are especially concerned' given that 'even in the preparation of a dogmatic definition the faithful are consulted'. Newman's point is that since the lay people are to be consulted about doctrine, their opinions should be consulted on less important matters also. He makes no distinction in the editorial between two different methods of consulting.

Furthermore, Sharkey seems to concede this to be the case when he offers 'questioned' as an alternative to 'consulted', since this necessarily involves more in the way of lay activity than Gillow's view, which expected lay opinion to be consulted in a purely passive way. He demanded a *fides implicita*, which is what is required if the laity is to be consulted in a purely passive sense. Newman would not, however, have allowed that a dogmatic definition may be disputed, and as his relations with Simpson and Acton show, he felt that the public questioning of authority put the questioner in a false position.[54]

But Newman's conception of the role of the laity is not purely passive, and as such it does not suggest a purely passive method of consulting the *sensus fidelium*. As will be shown, Newman acknowledged the legitimacy of the

---

[52] *The Letters and Diaries of John Henry Newman*, vols xi–xxxi, eds C.S. Dessain, E.E. Kelly & T. Gornal (London, 1961–71; Oxford, 1973–7); vols i–vi, eds I.T. Ker, T. Gornal & G. Tracey (Oxford, 1978–84); vol. vii, ed. G. Tracey (Oxford, 1995), vol. xix, p. 141.
[53] Sharkey, p. 343.
[54] Cf. Altholz, pp. 83–97.

divide between the *ecclesia docens* and the *ecclesia discens*, but he seems to have envisaged an organic partnership between the two, not a division between a purely passive laity (if only in matters of doctrine) and an active clergy. Such a divide is not the logical outcome of his policies in administering the Catholic University, nor is it the result of his views on the *Present Position of Catholics in England*:

> I want a laity, not arrogant, not rash in speech, not disputatious, but men who know their religion, who enter into it, who know just where they stand, who know what they hold, and what they do not, who know their creed so well that they can give an account of it, who know so much of history that they can defend it. I want an intelligent, well-instructed laity ... *You ought to be able to bring out what you feel and what you mean, as well as to feel and mean it.*[55] [My italics]

In his editorial to the May number and his discussions with Ullathorne following it, one can see Newman's view of the role of the laity in the infallibility of the Church. This was also in evidence during his time in Dublin, during which he felt it absolutely vital that there be an educated, intelligent laity, who would be 'a substantive power in the University'.[56] This view was fully expounded in the July issue in the essay, 'On Consulting the Faithful in Matters of Doctrine'. As Lease has commented: 'Here in all its pregnant fullness, is Newman's thought on the participation of the laity as guaranteed by the role played in the teaching function of the Church by the whole Church in its character as witnessing to its faith. It does not deny the active character assigned to the *ecclesia docens*; on the contrary it brings out in great clarity the cooperation essential for the full development of each in its respective role. It is the whole Church Newman is talking about, not one split into separate camps. The teaching office "ascertains" the fact of the whole Church's witness; on the basis of this witness, in which it itself is a co-witness; it determines the validity of the witness and its extent.'[57]

'On Consulting the Faithful' is split into three sections. In the first section[58] Newman defends his use of the word 'consult', re-stating the line of argument in his earlier correspondence with Gillow, that by 'consult' he meant 'ascertain as a matter of fact' what the views of the laity were, rather than ask the laity for a judgement. One might add that such consultation may be interpreted as being akin to looking in a mirror to see one's own reflection, and surely not what Newman was arguing for in his May editorial.

In the second section,[59] Newman argues that lay people have the right to be

---

[55] J.H. Newman, *Lectures on the Present Position of Catholics in England* (London, 1893), pp. 390–1.
[56] Newman, *Autobiographical Writings*, p. 327.
[57] G. Lease, *Witness to the Faith* (Pittsburgh, 1971), p. 89.
[58] Newman, *Consulting*, pp. 54–62.
[59] *Ibid.*, pp. 62–73.

'consulted', because the consensus of the faithful is an *indicum* or *instrumentum* of the judgement of the Church, which is infallible.[60] The term that Newman used for this was *phronema*. It was a sort of instinct or, perhaps better, a power of judgement

> deep in the bosom of the mystical body of Christ; as a direction of the Holy Ghost; as an answer to prayer; and as a jealousy of error, which it at once feels as a scandal.[61]

In the third section[62] of the essay, in order to prove the fidelity of the laity, Newman turns to the history of the Early Church, and to the Arian controversy:

> I shall set down some authorities for the two points successively, which I have to enforce, viz. that the Nicene dogma was maintained during the greater part of the fourth century,
> 1. not by the unswerving firmness of the Holy See, Councils, or Bishops, but
> 2. by the *consensus fidelium*
> I. On the other hand, then, I say, that there was a temporary suspense of the functions of the *Ecclesia docens*. The body of Bishops failed in their confession of the faith. They spoke variously, one against another; there was nothing, after Nicaea, of firm, unvarying, consistent testimony, for nearly sixty years. There were untrustworthy Councils, unfaithful Bishops; there was weakness, fear of consequences, misguidance, delusion, hallucination, endless, hopeless, extending itself into nearly every corner of the Catholic Church. The comparatively few who remained faithful were discredited and driven into exile; the rest were either deceivers or were deceived.
> II. Now we come secondly to the proofs of the fidelity of the laity, and the effectiveness of that fidelity, during that domination of the imperial heresy to which the foregoing passages have related.[63]

In the essay the first passage is followed by ten pages of evidence showing the apostasy of the bishops, and the second is followed by sixteen pages showing the fidelity of the laity. Newman conceded that, happily, the state of affairs, which he described as existing in the fourth century, did not exist in the nineteenth, but he was convinced that:

---

[60] *Ibid.*, p. 22.
[61] *Ibid.*, p. 23. It can be seen as the counterpart of the Illative Sense (or *phronesis*) of which Newman was to speak in the *Grammar of Assent*, in his description of that power in the individual to make real assents, going beyond merely notional assents, in matters of faith and conscience. Cf. J.H. Newman, *An Essay in Aid of a Grammar of Assent*: edited and with an Introduction by I.T. Ker (Oxford, 1985), pp. 222–47.
[62] Newman, *Consulting*, pp. 73–106.
[63] *Ibid.*, pp. 77 & 86. As W.P. Frost, 'On Celebrating Newman's Faith in the Laity', *Horizons*, vol. 6 (1979), has pointed out, the fact that the Catholic faith could withstand the corrosion of heresies was an important factor in Newman's conversion to Catholicism, p. 259.

> the *ecclesia docens* is more happy when she has such enthusiastic partisans about her as are here represented, than when she cuts off the faithful from the study of her divine doctrines and the sympathy of her divine contemplations, and requires from them a *fides implicita* in her word, which in the educated classes will terminate in indifference, and in the poor in superstition.[64]

As Gilley comments, 'The concluding sentence was a brutal hit at the actual state of the Church in Latin countries for combining aristocratic indifference with popular superstition.'[65]

For Newman, then, lay people have an important role to play in Church life, and are not mere reflections of the bishop's opinions. He wanted an educated laity, whose opinion would be taken into account in matters of doctrine. If the faith of the laity did not bear witness to a particular doctrine, then that doctrine could not be infallibly defined as dogma. Equally, in those 'mixed' questions, such as education, in which lay people were highly involved, the bishops should take their views into account, and not reserve these topics to themselves. For if the Church is to function properly, there must be an 'organic unity' between the two.[66] Should there be a 'temporary suspense', however, in the function of either party, the Church will still survive and its faith remain intact through the function of the other. So, although Newman allowed the validity of the divide between the *ecclesia docens* and the *ecclesia discens*, the above does not suggest the purely passive role for the laity he described to Gillow. Rather, he seems to favour some sort of organic partnership, perhaps at times, one of creative tension.

This essay, which one might almost think was designed to anger the bishops,[67] was an attempt to blunt the clerical tendencies of the hierarchy, which argued that lay people were there merely as mirrors of the bishops' opinions, and needless to say there was an immediate reaction against it. On 28 August 1859 Gillow wrote to Newman denying that there could be a suspense in the functions of the *ecclesia docens* and asserting that a *fides implicita* is what the Church rightly demands.[68] Newman responded to this that 'suspense' did not mean failure:

> I think it has a meaning far lighter even than 'suspension'. The 'body of bishops' was the 'actual mass at the time spoken of' – no more.[69]

---

[64] Newman, *Consulting*, p. 106.
[65] Gilley, *Newman,* p. 305.
[66] In *Consulting* Newman summarises Perrone: '*Conspiratio*; the two, the Church teaching and the Church taught, are put together, as one twofold testimony, illustrating each other, and never to be divided.' See p. 71.
[67] Coulson argues that the article was not aimed at the bishops, Newman, *Consulting*, p. 36. This view, however, is perhaps a little generous.
[68] Cf. *ibid.*, p. 31.
[69] Newman to Gillow, 2 September 1859, cited in *ibid.*, p. 32.

With regard to the *fides implicita*, Newman repeated his warning of inculcating an attitude which would result in the indifference and superstition he had mentioned in the essay.

Wiseman, Ullathorne and Manning also found the essay unfortunate.[70] Then in October, Bishop Brown decided to refer the matter to Rome. He said that he had been in contact with Wiseman, Ullathorne, Manning and Gillow, who said he had written to Newman, but not found his reply to be satisfactory. (Gillow had written a further letter to which Newman thought it pointless to respond, since Gillow had not grasped his method of argument, which, it might be added, appears to have been, at times, somewhat imprecise.) In his letter to Rome, Brown translated the offending terms into Latin to give 'greater theological accuracy'. 'Body of bishops' was translated as 'corpus Episcoporum' and 'general councils' as 'Concilia Oecumenica'. In their Latin sense Newman's treatment of these terms could indeed have been regarded as heretical.

Given that the English hierarchy shared the clerical views and autocratic tendencies of the Roman authorities, and taking into account the manner in which the issue was reported to *Propaganda*, it is not surprising that Newman came under suspicion of heresy. This cloud remained over him until 1867, when he sent Fr Ambrose St John and Fr Henry Bittleston to Rome to discuss the various misunderstandings which had arisen, despite Newman's willingness to submit to questions from *Propaganda*, and Wiseman's promise of help. The length of the dispute can be attributed to Wiseman's negligence, no doubt made worse by the onset of diabetes, and his preoccupation with the quarrel with Errington.[71] In addition, Manning did nothing to help Newman although he knew he was in trouble with *Propaganda*. It is unlikely that Manning deliberately withheld Newman's offer of explanation, but he certainly found it convenient not to rush immediately to Newman's aid.[72]

In summary, then, the '*Rambler* Affair' illustrates very clearly Newman's view of the role of the laity in the Church. He wanted an educated, intelligent, theologically aware laity, whose opinions would be taken into account by the bishops. The hierarchy is to exercise an authority that will keep the Church together as an institution, but within her fold, there must be room for legitimate private judgement and freedom of correctly understood conscience. Without such freedom, and proper interaction between the *ecclesia docens* and the *ecclesia discens*, the Church cannot hope to fulfil her missions as

---

[70] Gilley, *Newman*, p. 303.
[71] George Errington had been appointed Coadjutor Archbishop of Westminster to Wiseman with right of succession to the see, but Wiseman was highly sensitive to any criticisms from Errington and the old Catholic families of England he represented, partly due to his own favouring of (the Neo-Ultramontane) converts from Anglicanism, and eventually succeeded in having Errington's right of succession revoked. Cf. Gilley, *Newman*, p. 300.
[72] *Ibid.*, p. 307.

effectively as she could, were there to be effective co-operation between clergy and laity.[73] This is not just the case in matters of doctrine, in which the *sensus fidelium* is a true guide as to the faith of the Church, but in all areas, especially those in which lay people may have particular expertise, such as education. An obvious corollary of this stance is that the comment of Monsignor George Talbot, a Papal Chamberlain and fierce opponent of Newman's, should be rejected: 'What is the province of the laity? To hunt, to shoot, to entertain. These matters they understand, but to meddle with ecclesiastical matters they have no right at all.'[74] No wonder he regarded Newman as 'the most dangerous man in England'.[75]

The clash that occurred over the *Rambler* demonstrates the chasm that existed over the nature of the Church, between the bishops on one hand and the educated laity on the other; especially the converts from Anglicanism, who expected that the bishops would be only too keen to make the most of their talents. The bishops' conception of the Church was narrowly clerical. They ruled over a family which was to be protected from the outside world, and were not interested in how meaningful decisions could be made if there was no consultation with the laity, but with how they could resist encroachments onto 'their territory'. In March 1859 this was made absolutely clear in a letter from Bishop Ullathorne to Richard Simpson, in which he stated that the bishops regarded it as, 'absolutely unnecessary that the Catholic community should be informed of the grounds of our proceedings'.[76] Simpson's response came in an unpublished letter for Montalembert's *Le Correspondant*, in April 1859, and from which a preferred ecclesiology can be easily inferred:

> The English Hierarchy has been victorious; not over its enemies but over its friends; no new converts have been made, no enthusiasm excited, no burst of charity or zeal called forth by their artillery and their blows. They have triumphed over their own army, and have excited not the enthusiasm of Christian conquest, but the passions of civil war . . . this jealousy of the laity is a natural result of the strictness of the administrative organization which is now considered to constitute the strength of the clergy . . . The compactness of the clerical union makes it a caste, it has a separate professional education and separate habits of mind . . . The laity are to be kept in ignorance of all religious questions except those in the catechism, in order to misuse their obedience to a body of directors professionally educated to manage their religion for them. Religion is turned into administration, the clergy into theological police, and the body of

---

[73] Newman's preference for that system of authority in the Church can be seen from his decision to become an Oratorian, as well as his attitude to discipline in the university. In both the Oratory and the university, authority was to be exercised by personal influence, rather than by autocratic rule. Cf. Coulson, *Common Tradition*, pp. 95–101 and J.P. Marmion, 'Newman and Education', *Downside Review*, vol. 97 (1979), pp. 10–29.

[74] Coulson, *Common Tradition*, p. 125.

[75] *Ibid.*

[76] *Ibid.*, p. 111.

thinking laymen into a mass of suspects, supposed to be brooding on nothing but revolution, and only kept together by motives of fear, and by the external pressure of a clerical organization.'[77]

In other words, Simpson is calling for a Church in which the clergy and laity co-operate, rather than a society in which the hierarchy plays the role of Orwell's 'Big Brother'. The bishops are certainly the prime governors of the Church, but the laity must be consulted, and must be given sufficient trust and freedom to work for the good of the Church. This is the case both in matters of doctrine and in those areas in which lay people may have specialised knowledge and ability. This is a desire with which Newman, of course, sympathised, although he was not so outspoken in his public comments. In fact, he was deeply disillusioned with the attitude of the bishops, as is shown from his account of his meeting with Bishop Ullathorne, which led to his resigning the editorship of the *Rambler*. His fears about the then current situation in the Church were expressed in a letter to Henry Wilberforce:

> I fear deeply that our Bishops do not understand England and the English. Either the Catholic laity will kick, or, what I rather fear, they will more and more fall below Protestants in intellectual training and have no influence on the public mind.[78]

Here we see a reflection of Newman's thought about the Catholic University; without proper intellectual freedom the Church as a whole will suffer. If the laity are to be treated as 'children' and theological simpletons, rather than as responsible adult partners, then theology, and the life of the Church as a whole, will be severely distorted. This is with what Newman dealt in 'On Consulting the Faithful'.[79] Furthermore, given that it is the whole Church which is infallible, her teaching capacity would be severely undermined if a vital part of her were to be ignored. The implications for ecclesiology are clear. The laity should be encouraged, and should be allowed, to take part in the life of the Church to the full, since the *ecclesia docens* operates at its best at such times. The relevance of this to Newman's ecclesiology in the preface to the *Via Media* is that without the laity, theology would be impaired, and if that is the case it would not be able to perform its function properly as the regulating principle of the Church. This is what Newman saw happening in the Catholic Church of the nineteenth century, and both he and Simpson were concerned that it would result in Catholic opinion being of low intellectual quality and being held in contempt by Protestants. Newman's thought as this juncture is assessed well by Coulson: 'If the Church has a duty to consult the faithful, then it has a duty to manifest itself fully as a *conspiratio* of priests and laity, as distinct from the existing practice of acquiescing in a laity which was

[77] *Ibid.*, pp. 111–12.
[78] *Ibid.*, p. 113.
[79] *Ibid.*, p. 114.

either superstitious or indifferent, and capable of merely notional assent in matters of faith.'[80]

But the Church in Newman's thought was more than just a political grouping; it was also mystical. As such, he did not merely set the individual conscience against tyranny in the Church,[81] since he recognised that the former is only infallible when in accord with the *sensus fidelium*. It is the community that is important: *securus judicat orbis terrarum*. The whole Church is a living witness to the truth, and therefore, a living, dynamic reality, communicating God's presence on earth. Given this mystical conception of the Church, which is wide enough to embrace both the clergy and the laity, giving both the independence needed to ensure the spiritual and intellectual dynamism necessary to preach the Gospel and win converts, it is clear that a non-political regulator is necessary. This is theology.[82] Once again the image of the circle is relevant. The segments are the clergy, the laity and theology. All three are interdependent, but their overall relationship is to be governed by theology, the *primus inter pares*. This view of the interdependent, creative relationship among authority, the rights of the individual and the rights of scholarship was to find expression in the preface to the *Via Media of the Anglican Church*.

The Preface to the *Via Media*

The two-volume *Via Media of the Anglican Church* was published in 1877. The first volume is the third edition of the *Lectures on the Prophetical Office of the Church viewed relatively to Romanism and Popular Protestantism*,[83] but now with additional notes in which the Catholic Newman took it upon himself to refute his former Anglican self. In addition, there is a preface in which he sought to answer the charge, that, as an Anglican, he had levelled at the Roman Church, of her being corrupt because of differences between popular piety and official Catholic teaching (e.g. with regard to the honours paid to the Blessed Virgin Mary). He felt that he had already dealt with the

---

[80] *Ibid.*, p. 121.
[81] This is in contrast to Acton. Cf. Coulson, *Common Tradition*, pp. 121–2, and J. Coulson and A.M. Allchin (eds), *The Rediscovery of Newman: An Oxford Symposium* (London, 1967), p. 135.
[82] Newman would, of course, have realized that in practice theology itself can be distorted by political concerns. He himself was labelled a 'Garibaldian' because of his refusal to give enthusiastic support to the Pope's temporal power. Yet there is a sense in which he regarded theology as 'non-political', the regulator of the whole Church system. This is very much the way he describes it in the preface to the *Via Media*: J.H. Newman, *The Via Media of the Anglican Church*, 2 vols (London, 1891), vol. i, pp. xv–xciv. See Coulson, *Common Tradition*, p. 130.
[83] Originally published London, 1837.

charge of innovation in the *Essay on Development*.[84] The second volume contains various of his Anglican writings on the Church, for example, *Tracts LXXI* and *XC*, as well as his *Retraction of Anti-Catholic Statements*. Primarily, though, the *Via Media*, particularly the preface, is a work of apologetics directed at 'those, not a few, who would become Catholics if their conscience would let them'.[85]

As a work of apologetics, it is remarkable of the period in that it frankly admits to conflicts and abuses in the Church, and in this it has relevance for our own time.[86] It is a vindication of Newman's honesty that he dealt with these abuses so openly, and an indication that his aim in the preface was to understand the Church as he encountered her in practice, rather than to elaborate a mere theory.[87] Newman's starting point for his theology of the Church, although he did not formulate his ideas in quite the same terms as contemporary theologians, is that of the Church as sacrament;[88] a notion he learnt, as an Anglican, from his fellow Oxford conspirator,[89] John Keble:

> When Our Lord went upon high, he left His representative behind Him. This was Holy Church, his mystical Body and Bride, a Divine Institution, and the shrine and organ of the Paraclete, who speaks through her till the end comes.[90]

In other words, it is the Church where Christ makes His presence felt, and where He is active today. Given this Christological perspective, Newman is then able to apply the three offices of Christ, Prophet, Priest and King, to the Church herself:[91]

---

[84] Newman, *Via Media*, vol. i, p. xxxvii, and also, *Letters & Diaries*, vol. xxv, pp. 4–5: 'My essay is to answer the Objection "The Roman Church has added to the faith." '

[85] Newman, *Via Media*, vol. i, p. xxxvi. Cf. Gilley's view that the 'whole of Newman's religious pilgrimage can be regarded as an attempt to find a proper balance among' the competing claims of each office of Christ exercised in the Church, as described in the Preface, each of which may be identified with one of the three cities that 'have haunted the European imagination: Rome, Athens and Jerusalem'; Rome the city of government, Athens the city of learning, and Jerusalem the city of faith. S.W. Gilley, 'What has Athens to do with Jerusalem? Newman, Wisdom and the *Idea of a University*' in S.C. Barton (ed.), *Where Shall Wisdom Be Found? Wisdom in the Bible, the Church and the Contemporary World* (Edinburgh, 1999), pp. 155–68.

[86] A. Dulles, 'The Threefold Office in Newman's Ecclesiology' in Ker & Hill, p. 377.

[87] It is to be expected, therefore, that Newman's limited objective in the preface will result in the professional theologian detecting various deficiencies in the work, when examining it from an ecclesiological perspective.

[88] 'Newman's own deeply sacramental theology was formed to a considerable extent by the writings of the Alexandrian Fathers, where he learned of "the mystical sacramental principle", according to which "Holy Church in her sacraments . . . will remain, even to the end of the world, after all but a symbol of those heavenly facts which fill eternity." ' I.T. Ker, *Newman and the Fullness of Christianity* (Edinburgh, 1993), p. 96.

[89] M.R. O'Connell, *The Oxford Conspirators: A History of the Oxford Movement 1833–1845* (London, 1969).

[90] Newman, *Via Media*, vol. i, p. xxxix.

[91] This theme was also prominent in Newman's Anglican theology, cf. 'The Three Offices of

> These offices, which specially belong to Him as Mediator, are commonly considered to be three; He is Prophet, Priest and King; and after His pattern, and in human measure, Holy Church has a triple office too; not the prophetical alone and in isolation . . . but three offices, which are indivisible, though diverse, viz. teaching, rule, and sacred ministry.[92]

He then goes on to connect these three offices (rather tenuously perhaps)[93] with the four notes of the Church laid down in the Nicene Creed, and specifies by whom he sees each office exercised:

> Christianity, then, is at once a philosophy, a political power, and a religious rite: as a religion, it is Holy; as a philosophy it is Apostolic; as a political power, it is imperial, that is One and Catholic. As a religion, its special centre of action is pastor and flock; as a philosophy, the Schools; as a rule, the Papacy and its Curia.[94]

Newman's allocation of these offices has its ambiguities. First, the teaching office he gives to the schools, rather than to the pope and the bishops. As the argument of the preface continues he acknowledges that the bishops do have a teaching function, given their responsibility to preserve unity, but as Dulles has pointed out, this function 'can hardly be called directly doctrinal'.[95] Second, the priestly function is not reserved exclusively to the ordained. In his argument Newman concentrates almost exclusively on popular religion and the beliefs of simple people, and third, when discussing the Regal Office, he reserves this almost exclusively to the pope, making very little mention of bishops, or of their relationship to him. In addition, he states that the pope inherits all three offices himself. This is certainly true. He exercises the Regal Office in his rule, the Prophetical Office in teaching, and the Priestly Office in devotion and in celebrating the sacraments. But to mention this without the corresponding emphasis, that Newman had as an Anglican,[96] on all members of the Church individually inheriting the three offices of Christ to some degree, places too great an emphasis on the pope. When discussing the papacy, Newman also only speaks of it in relation to the Regal Office, forgetting that the pope inherits all three offices, not just the one.

Newman then goes on to set out the guiding principles of each of the offices

---

Christ' in J.H. Newman, *Sermons Bearing on Subjects of the Day* (London, 1871), pp. 52–62. See also M.T. Yakaitis, 'The Office of Priest, Prophet, and King in the Thought of John Henry Newman', Pontificiae Universitatis Gregorianae PhD thesis, 1990.

[92] Newman, *Via Media*, vol. i, p. xi.
[93] Dulles, p. 379.
[94] Newman, *Via Media*, vol. i, p. xi.
[95] Dulles, p. 380.
[96] 'Not the few and the conspicuous alone, but all her children, high and low, who walk worthy of her and her Divine Lord, will be shadows of Him . . . For he is our Prophet . . . our Priest . . . our King.' Newman, *Sermons of the Day*, p. 62.

he has described. For theology, truth is the guiding principle, for worship, devotion and for government, expediency. There are, however, dangers involved:

> Further, in a man as he is, reasoning tends to rationalism; devotion to superstition and enthusiasm; and power to ambition and tyranny.[97]

But abuses in one office can be held in check by the correct operation of the other two. A modern analogy to the working of these offices might be the American political system, which is said to operate as a system of 'checks and balances'. Alternatively, it may be likened to the classical political economy, guided by Adam Smith's[98] 'invisible hand'. Both of these analogies imply an element of competition and creative tension among the offices. Certainly, the gift of infallibility in formal teaching is an aid in preventing disastrous abuses, but it does not amount to impeccability, which is what would be needed to prevent any abuses happening at all.[99]

In the early part of his discussion, Newman argues that the regulating principle of the system he is describing is theology:

> Theology is the fundamental and regulating principle of the whole Church system. It is commensurate with Revelation, and Revelation is the initial and essential idea of Christianity. It is the subject-matter, the formal cause, the expression, of the Prophetical Office, and, as being such, has created both the Regal Office and the Sacerdotal.[100]

As such, the Prophetical Office has a certain jurisdiction over the Regal and Priestly Offices, which Newman considers more liable to excesses, and of these he gives some examples.[101]

Despite this clear statement of the centrality of theology, some scholars have called into question the traditional understanding of this passage. Nicholas Lash has argued that the 'greatness of the preface consists in Newman's refusal to allocate to any one of the three offices a position of privilege or centrality in respect of the others'.[102] Against this it has been maintained by Richard Bergeron,[103] John Coulson,[104] and more recently by H.D. Weidner, that 'the centrality of theology as a "regulating principle" is not only

---

[97] Newman, *Via Media*, vol. i, p. xli.
[98] Author of *Wealth of Nations* (1776), and founding father of Political Economy.
[99] Newman, *Via Media*, vol. i, pp. xlii–xliii.
[100] *Ibid.*, p. xlviii.
[101] *Ibid.*
[102] N. Lash, 'Life, Language and Organization: Aspects of Theological Ministry' in N. Lash, *Theology on Dover Beach* (London, 1979), p. 91.
[103] R. Bergeron, *Les Abus de l'Église d'après Newman: Étude de la Préface à la troisième édition de* La Via Media (Tournai, 1971), pp. 108–21; esp. 113.
[104] Coulson, *Common Tradition*, p. 167.

Newman's own position, and does not upset the balance of the offices, but that it maintains that balance'.[105] It is argued that theology can be the regulating principle without being the dominant principle, since it can regulate by co-ordination, thus maintaining a position of centrality.

In the *University Sermons* and the *Grammar of Assent* Newman was concerned with the practical and the concrete, and he appears to give theology a secondary role to faith. Faith is a real apprehension, whereas theology is notional. As Weidner[106] notes, however, Newman also realised in the *Grammar* that propositions have two functions:

> The notion and the reality assented-to are represented by the one and the same proposition, but serve as distinct interpretations of it. When the proposition is apprehended for the purposes of proof, analysis, comparison, and the like intellectual exercises, it is used as the expression of a notion; when for the purpose of devotion, it is the image of a reality. Theology, properly and directly deals with notional apprehension; religion with the imaginative.[107]

So, viewed from one direction, the proposition can represent the concrete, but viewed from another, the notional. Weidner comments: 'Theology regulates by providing the shape of the field within which authority and devotion view the propositions in their own way ... The "practical, the experiential, the concrete" would tend to shapelessness and over-extension if the field were not defined and co-ordinated with other fields. Likewise, devotion and authority could tend to excess as well as not extending themselves properly to the whole truth unless theology and its propositions were there for co-ordinating purposes.'[108]

When the above passage from the *Grammar* is considered, along with the image of the circle, which Newman developed in his lectures on university education, it would appear that he did intend theology to be the co-ordinating, regulating principle of the Church. The relationship among the three offices is one of interdependence, with theology (the instrument of the Prophetical Office) assuming the position of *primus inter pares* as the regulating principle, maintaining both the balance, and the creativity of the tension among them. Again, theology can only perform this function if the whole Church acts together. If it were not to perform this function, then the offices would encroach into areas where they have no jurisdiction, destroying the balance of the system. This balance could, of course, also be destroyed by the removal of one of the offices from the system completely. This is a reflection of what would happen if the balance of the circle of sciences were to be upset. This

---

[105] H.D. Weidner (ed.), *The Via Media of the Anglican Church By John Henry Newman* (Oxford, 1990), p. lxi.
[106] *Ibid.*, pp. lxi–lxii.
[107] Newman, *Grammar*, p. 108.
[108] Weidner, p. lxii.

could be done by the removal of one of the sciences, the greatest damage being caused by the removal of theology, the science that gives the ultimate form to the circle and the boundaries of the others. Theology, then, is the regulating, co-ordinating principle that gives overall shape, form and stability to the Church.

It must be questioned, however, whether Newman claims too much for the schools themselves. Dulles[109] has argued that Newman's stress on the schools results from his desire to answer the criticisms he made in the *Lectures on the Prophetical Office*. But it must be remembered, that in the past, the various schools engaged in bitter rivalries with one another, and attempted to have their theories given dogmatic status in preference to the others.[110] That being said, Newman is surely right in arguing that the (quest for the) truth must always be borne in mind, and that practical expediency or emotion must not be allowed to ride rough-shod over it.[111]

Although Theology is the regulating principle, the Prophetical Office is not exempt from correction by the other two. This Newman goes on to illustrate:

> Yet theology cannot always have its own way; it is too hard, too intellectual, too exact, to be always equitable, or to be always compassionate; and it sometimes has a conflict or overthrow, or has to consent to a truce or compromise, in consequence of the rival force of religious sentiment or ecclesiastical interests; and sometimes in great matters, sometimes in unimportant.[112]

The rest of the preface is then used to off-set the importance attached to theology at the beginning.

In the section on the Priestly Office Newman contrasts theology and popular devotion. He admits to the fact that differences between the two do occur, but he says that this is inevitable. Here he echoes the *Letter to Pusey*, in which, addressing the same issue, he argued that in matters of devotion, private judgement has a legitimate role.[113] Certainly, the Church is precise in her doctrinal statements, but in matters of devotion, a certain freedom must be accorded to the individual, and unless his devotions clearly imply heretical doctrine, they will be tolerated. In matters of devotion, the Church:

> neither prescribes measure, nor forbids choice, nor, except so far as they imply doctrine, is she infallible in her adoption or use of them.[114]

---

[109] Dulles, p. 383.
[110] J.D. Holmes & B.W. Bickers, *A Short History of the Catholic Church* (London, 1992), pp. 91–2, 96, describe some of the debate over the Franciscans and poverty, and an element of the rivalry between the Franciscans and the Dominicans, including the proscription by the former of the reading of Aquinas by their members.
[111] Dulles, p. 383.
[112] Newman, *Via Media*, vol. i, pp. xlviii–xlix.
[113] J.H. Newman, *Certain Difficulties felt by Anglicans in Catholic Teaching*, 2 vols (London, 1901), vol. ii, p. 28.
[114] Newman, *Via Media*, vol. i, p. lxxv.

It should also be noted, however, that:

> Worship, indeed, being the act of our devotional nature, strives hard to emancipate itself from theological restraints. Theology did not create it, but found it in our hearts and used it.[115]

Thus, Newman saw the religious instinct as antecedent to positive Revelation, perhaps even the primary pre-rational organ of Revelation, and part of the human condition.[116] This instinct is to be respected and is clearly expressed in Catholic devotion to the saints and angels. Polytheism is a corruption of this instinct. What is intended is that man should give glory to God in all of His creation, especially in the holiest part of it. Idolatry is not a reason to limit this instinct.[117]

That said, Newman frankly admits that in some cases devotion and correct theology do seem to be implacably opposed. To substantiate his argument, he cites the case of the woman with the haemorrhage, who touched Jesus' garment in the hope that she would be cured. She was, and Jesus merely said that her faith had cured her. He did not chastise her for what may well have been a superstitious or even idolatrous act.[118] Similarly:

> a poor Neapolitan crone, who chatters to the crucifix, refers that crucifix in her deep mental consciousness to an original who once hung upon a cross in flesh and blood; but if, nevertheless she is puzzleheaded enough to assign virtue to it in itself, she does no more than the woman in the Gospel, who preferred to rely for a cure on a bit of cloth, which was our Lord's, to directly and honestly addressing him.[119]

So, the individual must have a certain liberty in his own devotions and it must also be remembered by those who exercise the Prophetical Office that if such devotions, technically incorrect as they may be, were to be trampled upon, so might be the faith that underlies them. In this connexion, Newman reminds his readers of the exhortations in the Gospels not to throw out the wheat along with the tares, and of St Paul's admonitions to the more sophisticated Christians not to scandalise the weak (cf. 1 Cor. 10 and Rom. 14).

---

[115] *Ibid.*, p. lxix.
[116] Cf. *University Sermon XV* on 'The Theory of Developments in Religious Doctrine' in *Fifteen Sermons Preached before the University of Oxford between A.D. 1826 and 1843*: edited and with an Introduction by M.K. Tillman (Notre Dame, 1997), pp. 312–51, esp. pp. 331 and 336.
[117] *Ibid.*, pp. lxxiv–lxxv; Dulles, p. 384.
[118] Newman, *Via Media*, vol. i, pp. lxvi–lxvii.
[119] *Ibid.*, p. xviii. A modern example might be the veneration accorded the Turin Shroud. Scientific tests have suggested that the Shroud was not Jesus' burial shroud, but it is still venerated by many as such. Although this veneration seems to rest on an unfounded belief, it does, nevertheless, appear to promote true devotion to Christ. Newman's argument, then, would seem to be that although such practices are technically incorrect, if they inspire true devotion to that which they represent (in the case of the shroud, Jesus Christ), they should be tolerated.

Newman also deals with the fact that non-theologians often fear novelty and innovation. This is in contrast to theologians, many of whom are prepared to adopt new theories readily, in the hope that they will provide new and exciting possibilities. As an example, he gives the popular rejection of St Jerome's re-translation of his own version of the psalms.[120] In such cases Newman argues that the Church authorities must, like St Paul, side with the weak so as to avoid scandal and weakening of faith; and on such grounds he explains the Church's treatment of Galileo.[121]

Again on the theme of toleration and compromise, Newman touches on the problem of missionary accommodation. Here he argues that the Church must adapt itself in order to win converts, and cites St Paul who became to the Jews a Jew, that he might gain the Jews, and to them that were without the law, as if he were without the law, and became all things to all men that he might save all.[122]

This ties in with Newman's argument, based on 'the great principle of Economy, as advocated'[123] by many of the Greek Fathers, that it is at times better to leave certain points of faith undefined for the moment, out of charity towards the weaker in faith; a principle he applied to the proposed definition of papal infallibility by the First Vatican Council.[124]

It may therefore appear that Newman is sanctioning deliberate falsehood in matters of religion. This, however, is not so. He is merely pointing out, as he did in the *Grammar*, that debate in matters of religion closely parallels debate in other aspects of life. So:

> Veracity, like other virtues, lies in a mean. Truth indeed, but not necessarily the whole truth, is the rule of Society. Every class and profession has its secrets; the family lawyer, the medical adviser, the politician, as well as the priest. The physician often dares not tell the whole truth to his patient about his case, knowing that to do so would destroy his chance of recovery. Statesmen in Parliament, I suppose, fight each other with second-best arguments, the real reasons for the policy which they are respectively advocating being, as each is conscious to each, not these but reasons of state, secrets whether of Her Majesty's Privy Council or of diplomacy. As to the polite world, which, to be sure, is in itself not much of an authority, I think an authoress of the last century illustrates in a tale how it would not hold together, if every one told the whole truth to every one, as to what he thought of him. From the time the Creator clothed Adam, concealment is in some sense the necessity of our fall.[125]

---

[120] Newman, *Via Media*, vol. i, pp. lii–liii.
[121] *Ibid.*, pp. lv–lvi.
[122] *Ibid.*, p. lxxvi.
[123] *Ibid.*, p. lxi.
[124] 'As to myself personally, please God, I do not expect any trial at all; but I cannot help suffering with the various souls which are suffering.' *Letters & Diaries*, vol. xxv, p. 18.
[125] Newman, *Via Media*, vol. i, p. lix. D. Newsome has pointed out that, despite the obvious Platonism of the *Essay on Development*, Newman's thought as a Catholic was still highly

Newman's treatment of the Priestly Office is impressive. It deals frankly with the charges he brought, as an Anglican, in the *Lectures on the Prophetical Office*, and which are still levelled against Catholicism today. The desire to answer such charges exclusively, however, has led to the preface lacking a full treatment of the Priestly Office. For example, greater mention of the holiness of the Church, the ministry, the sacraments and the liturgy is required.[126]

In his discussion of the Priestly Office, Newman concentrates almost entirely on private devotions, in large part excluding the sacraments and the liturgy. This must be considered a weakness, since it is precisely in those areas that the Priestly Office of Christ is exercised to its greatest degree in the Church. Yet in the *Letter to Pusey*,[127] Newman criticises Pusey for not paying enough attention to the official liturgy of the Church, and for merely bringing to light abuses in popular devotion. As Dulles remarks: 'If Newman had dwelt more on this aspect of worship, he could have established a more positive relationship between devotion and theology. He would have had occasion to discuss the principle *lex orandi, lex credendi*, showing how the sense of the faithful, shaped by participation in liturgical worship, is equipped to detect and repel heresy, as occurred in the Arian crisis.'[128]

It is, however, perhaps not so remarkable that Newman did not do this. After all, when he did it before in 'On Consulting the Faithful', it resulted in a formal accusation of heresy being preferred against him. In addition, his *Letter to the Duke of Norfolk*, published only two years before the *Via Media*, had aroused disquiet in episcopal and curial circles. Given that this followed on from his opposition to the definition of papal infallibility by the First Vatican Council, which became public knowledge with the publication of his letter to Bishop Ullathorne,[129] and his now well-known deference to authority,[130] whatever his private reservations, it is perhaps not surprising that he should

---

influenced by Aristotelianism. Here in the preface he is employing the 'Aristotelian mean' in a description of truth, even though he had rejected the 'via media', that most Aristotelian of concepts. *Two Classes of Men: Platonism and English Romantic Thought* (London, 1974), pp. 62–70.

[126] Dulles, p. 386.

[127] Newman's argument is that Catholics are kept from falling into idolatry because of their devotion to Christ in the Blessed Sacrament: 'a Presence within the sacred walls, infinitely more awful, which claims and obtains from us a worship transcendently different from any devotion we may pay to' our Lady. *Difficulties*, vol. ii, p. 94.

[128] Dulles, pp. 386–7. For the principle *lex orandi lex credendi* in Newman's Anglican Sermons, see P. Murray (ed.), *John Henry Newman Sermons 1824–1843* (Oxford, 1991), vol. i, pp. 67–113.

[129] In a private letter to his bishop, which somehow became public, Newman had described those agitating for the definition of the pope's infallibility as 'an aggressive insolent faction'. *Letters & Diaries*, vol. xxv, pp. 18–19.

[130] For a discussion of Newman's deference to authority see Ker, *Newman and the Fullness of Christianity*, pp. 58–9. But see also, *Letters & Diaries*, vol. xxv, p. 231: 'We have come to a climax of tyranny. It is not good for a Pope to live 20 years. It is anomaly and bears no good

wish to refrain from anything likely to cause controversy. It is true, that had he written as Dulles would have liked, he would have provided a far better treatment of the Priestly Office. It is also likely, however, that he would have once again embroiled himself in bitter and fierce controversy with his own ecclesiastical superiors (many of whom shared the opinion of Monsignor Talbot), and he may well have felt discretion to have been the better part of valour.

Having dealt with the Priestly Office, Newman then goes on to discuss 'the regal office of the Church and her duties to it.'[131] As previously mentioned he saw the Regal Office as the domain of 'the Papacy and its Curia'. This is a vital part of his ecclesiology in the preface:

> If the Church is to be regal, a witness for Heaven, unchangeable amid secular changes, if in every age she is to hold her own, and proclaim as well as profess the truth, if she is to thrive without or against the civil power, if she is to be resourceful and self-recuperative under all fortunes, she must be more than Holy and Apostolic; she must be Catholic. Hence it is that, first, she has ever from her beginning onwards had a hierarchy and a head, with a strict unity of polity, the claim of an exclusive divine authority and blessing, the trusteeship of the gospel gifts, and the exercise over her members of an absolute and almost despotic rule.[132]

Newman makes no mention of the *ecclesia docens* in the preface, and has no notion of collegiality, nor, in this section, of any other factors that might limit the pope's rule.[133]

The instrument of the Regal Office is expediency, the meaning of which in Newman's thought is explained well by Dulles: 'By this he does not mean the self-interest of individual rulers but what rather is dictated by the finality of the Church, which is divinely commissioned to extend its domination and to consolidate itself. Whatever is truly necessary for the survival and mission of the Church, Newman contends, cannot be contrary to God's will. Conversely, whatever is harmful to the unity, sanctity, and expansion of the Church must also be theologically wrong.'[134]

Newman starts by speaking of the missionary activities of St Gregory Thaumaturgus who adopted certain pagan festivals, but invested them with a Christian meaning:

> Having observed that many of the common people were attached to the religion of their fathers from a love of the ancient sports connected with paganism, he determined to provide the new converts with a substitute for those. He instituted

---

fruit; he becomes a god, has no one to contradict him, does not know facts, and does cruel things without meaning it.'

[131] Newman, *Via Media*, vol. i, p. lxxvii.
[132] *Ibid.*, p. lxxx.
[133] Dulles, p. 388.
[134] *Ibid.*

a general festival in honour of the Martyrs, and permitted the rude multitudes to celebrate it with banquets similar to those which accompanied the pagan funerals (*parentalia*) and other heathen festivals.[135]

Since St Gregory was a bishop, as well as a missionary, this is an example of the Regal Office acting, in conjunction with the Priestly Office, in opposition to the Theological. The self-regulating system of checks and balances does not always operate in such a manner, however, and so Newman goes on

> to give instances in which the imperial and political expedience of religion stands out prominent, and both its theological and devotional duties are in the background.[136]

As an example of the Regal Office prevailing over the Theological on the grounds of expediency, Newman cites Pope Stephen I's recognition of heretical baptism as valid,[137] despite the theological arguments to the contrary. He also argues that Pope Leo IX was forced, out of expediency,[138] to reverse his decree which ruled simoniacal ordinations to be invalid. These are instances

> of the Schools giving way to ecclesiastical expedience, and of the interests of peace and unity being a surer way of arriving at a doctrinal conclusion than methods more directly theological.[139]

Elsewhere in the preface, however, Newman attempts to demonstrate that the argument from expediency can be supported directly by theology. Thus, he argues that the infallibility of the pope must extend to the canonisation of saints, on the grounds that if he did not, the Church would be compromised in its prayer and worship if, as according to St Thomas Aquinas 'one who was really a sinner, were venerated as a saint'.[140] This, however, is a strange example. Firstly, he seems to be extending the scope of papal infallibility beyond that which his minimising interpretation allowed. Secondly, in a private note of 1866, he inclined to the view that the pope is not infallible in each canonisation, but merely in recommending the cult of saints.[141] In a letter of 1868, however, he makes the statement, 'to him who thinks it infallible it is such',[142] perhaps implying that it is a matter of theological opinion, and not an article of faith.

---

[135] Newman, *Via Media*, vol. i, p. lxxviii.
[136] *Ibid.*, p. lxxix.
[137] *Ibid.*, pp. lxxxvii–xci.
[138] *Ibid.*, pp. lxxxv–lxxxvi.
[139] *Ibid.*, p. lxxxvii.
[140] *Ibid.*, p. lxxxiv.
[141] *The Theological Papers of John Henry Newman on Biblical Inspiration and Infallibility*, edited by J.D. Holmes (Oxford, 1979), p. 128.
[142] *Ibid.*, p. 112.

The use of this example, like others in this section, rests on the statement that

> no act could be theologically an error, which was absolutely and undeniably necessary for the unity, sanctity, and peace of the Church; for falsehood never could be necessary for these blessings, and truth alone can be.[143]

In principle, Newman is right. It must surely be accepted that there cannot be conflict between the spiritual goals of the Church and her fidelity to the Gospel. He is also to be commended for his admission that the Church is not impeccable, thus realising that any implementation of the principle of expediency by the Regal Office is fraught with difficulties. But it does appear that he has given a poor example in trying to show that expediency can be supported by theology, and it might perhaps have been better, merely to have observed that the pope is infallible in recommending the cult of saints.[144]

It may be that the exaggerated view of papal authority in the preface is the result of trying to placate the more Ultramontane of his contemporaries, as John Coulson has argued,[145] and given the trouble in which he found himself in the past this would seem plausible. But it must be remembered that Newman was trying to understand the Church as he found her, and that in the nineteenth century, particularly following the definition of papal infallibility by the First Vatican Council, the papacy was seen as being at the apex of a strictly hierarchical institution. This view of the Church is reflected in certain passages in the 1878 edition of the *Essay on Development* in which Newman discusses the 'Papal Supremacy'[146] and also in a private letter to Pusey of 23 March 1867, in which he argued that the pope's jurisdiction was universal, on the grounds that

> the Church is a Church Militant, and, as the commander of an army is despotic, so must the visible hand of the Church be; and therefore in its idea the Pope's jurisdiction can hardly be limited.[147]

When writing to Pusey, it might be imagined that Newman would express Catholic claims for the papacy in the manner least likely to give offence to an Anglican theologian. Yet this does not seem to be the case, and the authoritarian element of his ecclesiology, which held the imperial structure of the Church to be the fulfilment of Old Testament prophecies, is strongly to the fore.[148]

---

[143] *Ibid.*
[144] Dulles, pp. 389–90.
[145] Coulson, *Common Tradition*, p. 174.
[146] J.H. Newman, *An Essay on the Development of Christian Doctrine* (London, 1914; 1878 edition), pp. 148–65.
[147] Cited in Ward, vol. II, p. 223.
[148] As Newman asked of the Church, 'does it not . . . closely and literally correspond to the

Once again, the likely reason for this is that Newman was trying to understand the Church as he encountered her. This letter to Pusey was written in the run up to Vatican I, which it seemed likely would define the pope's infallibility. Newman was in the situation of having to defend this doctrine, although it was not at that stage on the council's official agenda.

Furthermore, although Newman makes no specific mention of collegiality, he does suggest that the Regal Office is to be held in check by 'the operation of the other two'. In other words, he does envisage some sort of structural or institutional restraint upon the government of the Church. This reflects a sermon of 1842, 'The Church an Imperial Power', in which he argued that imperial power in the Church could not have been invested in only Peter or the Apostles:

> We must conclude that the power was invested in others also from the size of the empire, for a few persons, though inspired, cannot be supposed to have been equal to the care of all the Church. As Moses found his charge too great for him, and was permitted to have associates in his office, so doubtless would it be with the Apostles.[149]

The problem in the preface seems to be that in his discussion of the Regal Office, Newman has not taken into account the results of his earlier work on the laity and on the relationship between the *ecclesia docens* and the *ecclesia discens*. If, as argued above, theology can only act as the regulating principle if the laity is consulted, this lends a certain authority to their views, and as such the laity, along with the bishops, also shares in the exercise of the Regal Office. This is in contrast to Newman's description of the Regal Office, which takes almost no account of the bishops, and makes no specific mention of the relationship between the *ecclesia docens* and the *ecclesia discens*.[150]

After much discussion, then, of the relationship of the Regal Office to the Prophetical, Newman ends with an example of conflict between the Regal Office and the Devotional:

---

promises of Isaiah about the glory of Jerusalem?' *Essays Critical and Historical*, 2 vols (London, 1891), vol. II, p. 182.

[149] Newman, *Sermons of the Day*, p. 225.

[150] 'In . . . the famous article . . . about consulting the faithful, it seems to us that Newman presented very shrewdly this communion of the *sensus fidelium* and of the exercise of the magisterium.' J.-M.R. Tillard, *Church of Churches: The Ecclesiology of Communion* (Collegeville, Minnesota, 1992), pp. 110–11. It is S.D. Femiano's opinion, however, that Newman's view did not become explicit in the documents of Vatican II, and he would welcome greater authority invested in the laity: 'the process of the development of doctrine sometimes begins in the people; their *consensus* activates the infallible teaching authority of the magisterium. In such cases the faithful's infallibility is not merely a passive reflection of the magisterium's teaching but it is an active exercise of the laity's prerogatives.' *The Infallibility of the Laity* (New York, 1967), p. 136.

That I may not end without an instance of the political in contrast with the Sacerdotal, I will refer to the Labarum of Constantine. The sacred symbol of unresisted suffering, of self-sacrificing love, of life-giving grace, of celestial peace, became in the hands of the first Christian Emperor, with the sanction of his Church, his banner in fierce battle and the pledge of victory for his sword.[151]

In summary, then, Newman has provided an impressive and original account of the three offices of Christ, as they are exercised in the Church. Each is considered in some detail, and the relationship, which is one of creative tension among the three, is discussed. He does not try to cover up abuses and failings in the Church, but admits to them frankly, in order to explain why they occur. The centrality of the Prophetical Office is demonstrated, although the key word regarding the relationship of the three offices to one another is interdependence, and the threefold nature of the Church, which he learnt from the Fathers,[152] has been further developed in Catholic theology.[153] This is despite, first, the fact that the 'argument does not attract the modern mind which considers the ruthless pursuit of truth for its own sake the highest of virtues, and has hardly questioned whether the human appetite for truth, in such matters as nuclear research or genetic engineering, needs the restraint of either authority or popular opinion';[154] and second, the fact that the idea that tension and conflict in the Church could be beneficial, was not a popular one in the pre-conciliar Catholic Church, in which the view of Ullathorne prevailed: 'The Church was peace. They had a deep faith, they did not like to hear that anyone doubted.'[155]

It must be borne in mind, however, that the preface is distinctly limited in places. Newman's incomplete treatment of the Priestly Office may well be explained by his desire to avoid controversy, as well as his desire to understand the Church as he encountered her, but his discussion of the Regal Office requires fuller comment.

With regard to the Regal Office, Newman appears to separate it from the other two. He discusses it as if it is 'the Papacy and its Curia' alone that exercised it, and when speaking of the papacy, gives the impression that it is only the Regal Office that it exercises, forgetting that at the beginning of the preface he noted that the pope has inherited all three offices. This gives the

---

[151] Newman, *Via Media*, vol. i, pp. xciii–xciv.
[152] Such as Eusebius of Caesarea. The history of the triple office is traced in L. Schick, *Das dreifache Amt Christi und der Kirche: Zur Entstehung und Entwicklung der Trilogien* (Frankfurt and Berne, 1982), cited in Dulles, p. 376.
[153] The triple office was given heavier statement in the second chapter of Friedrich von Hügel's *Mystical Element of Religion as studied in St. Catherine of Genoa and her Friends*, 2 vols (London, 1923), vol. i, pp. 50–82, esp. note on p. 53. A brief survey of how the theme was taken up in Catholic theology is provided by Dulles, pp. 393–9.
[154] Gilley, *Newman*, p. 389.
[155] Coulson, *Common Tradition*, p. 112.

appearance that he is in favour of a type of papal absolutism. Furthermore, he fails to make the connexion between the role of the laity in the Priestly Office and their role in the Regal. More important, perhaps, he has no developed concept of collegiality, and makes no mention of the *ecclesia docens*. To use the image of the circle, Newman has failed to find the balance of the *ecclesia docens* with the *ecclesia discens* and with theology. He has excluded the laity, not discussed the role of the bishops in any detail, and has thereby diminished the ability of theology to act as the regulating principle. But this is hardly a fair reflection of his thought on the matter, and appears to be the result of his desire to understand the Church exactly as he encountered her in the last quarter of the nineteenth century.

There is, therefore, a certain amount of inconsistency in Newman's ecclesiology, but it is suggested here that this should not be looked upon as a major failing. Indeed the concept of collegiality was only just beginning to surface towards the end of the nineteenth century,[156] and Newman did envisage some sort of institutional restraint upon the papacy. Rather, this inconsistency should be seen as an example of the creative tension he described as existing among the three offices of Christ, as exercised by His Church.

In other words, the tension that exists in Newman's ecclesiology, over the relationship of 'the Papacy and its Curia' to the bishops, and to the laity, acts as a spur to the contemporary theologian. It serves as a valuable reminder of the claims that have been made in the past for the successor of St Peter, and challenges the theologian to find a way of reconciling the legitimate claims of both hierarchical authority and the freedom of an educated laity in the Church. The results of such research can be regarded as the fruits of the tension in Newman's thought, which parallels the creative tension he described as existing among the three offices of Christ. His understanding of this relationship is a major achievement of the preface.[157]

---

[156] Dulles, p. 392.

[157] At this point, it can be noted with Ker that 'the two principal objections that Newman had made as an Anglican against the Roman Catholic Church, far from being removed, became paradoxically the two major arguments in favour of the Church. Instead of doctrinal developments being seen as accretions, they are now viewed as the essential growth of a living body. Similarly, corruptions in the life of the Church are no longer interpreted in a negative but a positive light: for they are now perceived as the inevitable abuses of a Church which possesses the vitality of Christianity in its fullness and in all the complexity of life itself. In short, both original arguments against Roman Catholicism, doctrinal development and practical corruption, become in effect authentic notes of the true Church – that is to say, of the real not the ideal Church.' Ker, *Newman and the Fullness of Christianity*, p. 122. For as Ker notes elsewhere, 'a Church, which is first and last a communion of vastly different persons, albeit baptized in the same Spirit, is hardly likely to exhibit that kind of orderliness and tidiness that is often vainly desiderated in place of the apparently unresolvable ambiguities and tensions that characterize Catholicism.' I.T. Ker, *Healing the Wound of Humanity: The Spirituality of John Henry Newman* (London, 1993), p. 86.

Conclusion

The key word, then, for understanding Newman's ecclesiology is 'interdependence', for this word characterises the relationship which he envisaged as ideally existing among all those, who, in their different but complementary ways, belong to the Church.

At the Catholic University in Dublin, Newman wanted to integrate clergy and laity, hierarchy and university, in the Church's mission of education. In his discourses on university education, using the image of the 'Circle of the Sciences', he described the interdependence of the various sciences, arguing that the proper form of the circle could be maintained only by a non-political regulator, namely theology; and that theology itself could only perform this role if the legitimate rights of scholarship, the teaching function of the bishops, and the proper boundaries of the academic disciplines within the university were acknowledged and respected. The blurring of such boundaries, the result of a clash between the sceptical liberal temperament of Simpson and Acton, which Newman distrusted, and the autocratic, anti-intellectual stance of the English hierarchy over the *Rambler*, resulted in precisely those problems which Newman envisaged would result from a lack of integration and interdependence among the Church's members. In the preface to the Via Media he addressed this same issue, claiming that the Church is at her best when the competing claims of scholarship, piety and authority, as found in the Church's exercise of Christ's Prophetical, Priestly and Regal Offices, are kept by theology in a dynamic, interdependent relationship.

12

THOMAS ARNOLD: A BICENTENARY APPRAISAL, BEING THE THOMAS ARNOLD MEMORIAL LECTURE, 7 NOVEMBER 1995 ORIEL COLLEGE, OXFORD

DAVID NEWSOME

THE FINAL entry in Thomas Arnold's diary, dated 11 June 1842, two days before his forty-seventh birthday, contains the following reflection: 'How large a portion of my life on earth is already passed . . . Still there are works which, with God's permission, I could do before the night cometh.'[1] Less than twelve hours later he was dead. Like his father before him – a Customs Officer on the Isle of Wight – who died when Thomas was only six; like, too, both his brothers who died before middle age, his life was cut short in its prime. This is worthy of record because we are apt to look upon Arnold as one of the most eminent of 'Eminent Victorians' (notoriously designated as such, indeed, for the purpose of calculated ridicule by Lytton Strachey), when actually barely five years of his life were passed during Victoria's reign. There are, however, good grounds for allowing the label to stand: not only because so many of the attitudes and tensions which we tend to regard as quintessentially 'Victorian' long antedated the accession of the Queen in 1837, and were abundantly evident in the person of Arnold himself, but also because Arnold's influence was arguably greater after his death than before it. As A.O.J. Cockshut has put it: 'He was not a Victorian, but he trained Victorians . . . In an odd way he seems more typical of the decade that followed his death than of any period in his own lifetime.'[2]

Many reasons can be advanced to explain the emergence and expanding

---

[1] A.P. Stanley, *The Life and Correspondence of Thomas Arnold*, 2 vols (London, 8th edition, 1858), vol. II, p. 282.

[2] A.O.J. Cockshut, *Truth to Life. The Art of Biography in the Nineteenth Century* (London, 1974), p. 88.

influence of the moral idealism which lay at the root of what came to to be known as 'Arnoldianism'. Echoes of their Master's voice could be plainly heard from the lips of 'the Doctor's Disciples' – those who had sat at Arnold's feet in his highly-privileged Sixth Form and had acted as his Praeposters. More so at Oxford than at Cambridge, because the more ancient University had always been Arnold's preferred destination for his most favoured pupils. Their veneration for their old Headmaster and the self-conscious high moral stance they adopted was certainly noticed and commented upon, if not always commended, there being uneasy suspicions of moral priggishness. Rather more significant, however, was the studied application of Arnoldian methods followed by former members of his staff, like George Cotton at Marlborough and James Prince Lee at King Edward's, Birmingham, or by an ex-pupil like C.J. Vaughan at Harrow, all of whom served to pass on the Arnoldian legacy to those who were to become the headmasters of the many new public school foundations of the 1850s and 1860s.

Only two years after Arnold's death, Dr George Moberly, Headmaster of Winchester, acknowledged the nature of this legacy in the following words:

> A most singular and striking change has come upon our public schools – a change too great for any person to appreciate adequately, who has not known them in both these times . . . I am sure that to Dr Arnold's personal earnest simplicity of purpose, strength of character, power of influence and piety, which none who ever came near him could mistake or question, the carrying of this improvement into our schools is mainly attributable. He was the first.[3]

It is no unusual phenomenon that a man has to wait until his death before he gains popular acclaim. During his Rugby years Arnold was known – and often attacked – as an outspoken polemicist; and there was a period in the mid 1830s when the decline of numbers in the school reflected public concern over both his religious views and his handling of certain disciplinary issues. Unexpected public recognition came in 1841 when Lord Melbourne, in a rare moment of inspiration, offered Arnold the Regius Professorship of Modern History at Oxford. At the same time, his published sermons were beginning to make a deep impression upon the reading public, whose appetite for such fare – in contrast to our own day – might almost be described as voracious. The Queen read them with approval, we are told.[4] Gladstone, rather surprisingly – in view of his admiration for Newman's Anglican sermons[5] – declared that Arnold's were his special favourite.[6]

As is well known, however, two books, published in 1844 and 1857

---

[3] A.P. Stanley, vol. I, p. 153.
[4] Lytton Strachey, *Eminent Victorians* (London, 1948), p. 205.
[5] C.S. Dessain, *John Henry Newman* (Nelson: London, 1966), p. 44; D.C. Lathbury, *Correspondence on Church and Religion of W.E. Gladstone*, 2 vols (London, 1910), vol. I, p. 485.
[6] Amy Cruse, *The Victorians and their Books* (London, 1935), p. 117.

respectively, ensured that Arnold's name would become a household word. Arthur Stanley, later Dean of Westminster and Arnold's most devoted disciple, received the commission to write the official 'Memoir'. When he saw the papers that had been made available to him, he wrote in his journal: 'If I am not able to make out of them one of the most remarkable biographies that has appeared for a long time, it will be my fault, not theirs.'[7] He need not have worried. By Christmas 1844 the book had gone through four editions in almost as many months. The hero-worship was barely disguised, but that seemed hardly to matter to the many who found the celebrated account of Arnold's work and ideals at Rugby, in the long third chapter, totally absorbing by its revelation of the trials and challenges of one man's mission to create a Christian community out of such unpromising material as a potentially wayward and indifferent society of boys. But there was more to Arnold than this. When Charles Dickens was sent extracts from Arnold's letters, deploring the cruelty of the new Poor Law, he became a convert on the instant. 'I must have that book', he wrote. 'Every sentence that you quote from it is the text-book of my faith.'[8] (One wonders if he noticed another letter of Arnold's, in which he blamed the influence of books 'like Pickwick, Nickleby, Bentley's Magazine etc. etc.' for encouraging 'childishness' in boys.)[9]

Thirteen years after Stanley's *Life*, Thomas Hughes published his *Tom Brown's Schooldays*, scoring an even greater success than Stanley, for this was a book which sold in its thousands both in England and in America. The hero of the story is a boy just like Hughes himself (or as Hughes recalled of himself at Rugby) – an ordinary, decent, not particularly clever, quite unpriggish, outdoor sort of boy. But Arnold is a hero, too, seen from the more distant vantage point of a boy who was never – like Stanley – one of the Doctor's elite, and therefore what he absorbed from Arnold's teaching and his Sunday sermons on moral courage and Christian virtues was a simplified (and – in Stanley's opinion – distorted) distillation of Arnold's ideals. It is easy to see how exhortations to Christian manliness, which to Arnold and Stanley were understood in a Pauline sense, could be translated into something that spoke directly to a boy's admiration for the robust and the physical; in a phrase – 'Muscular Christianity'. E.C. Mack puts it thus:

> Hughes's Arnold has neither the fanatic idealism, the other-worldliness, nor the over-developed sense of sin that the real Arnold possessed. He has become a glorified boy scoutmaster whose strenuous spirituality has been made palatable to Englishmen by presenting it under the guise of the honest manliness of a Kingsley hero.[10]

---

[7] R.E. Prothero, *The Life and Correspondence of Arthur Penrhyn Stanley*, 2 vols (London, 1893), vol. I, p. 319.
[8] Humphry House, *The Dickens World* (Oxford, 1942), p. 93.
[9] A.P. Stanley, vol. II, p. 137.
[10] E.C. Mack, *Public Schools and British Opinion, 1780–1860* (London, 1938), p. 331.

So – less than twenty years after his death – it was becoming increasingly difficult to disentangle the Arnold of history from the legendary figure that his greatest admirers were tending to make of him.

Nevertheless this is what we must now attempt to do. What was he actually like? Of his absolute integrity, no one can seriously doubt. As a young Fellow of Oriel (he was elected at the age of twenty), he went through a period of agonizing doubts over proceeding to Orders because he felt that he could not subscribe whole-heartedly to certain of the Articles of Religion (especially on the nature of the Trinity). It is probably true to say that in the end he stifled these doubts rather than resolved them; but at least he displayed his honesty by careful avoidance of dogmatic preaching thereafter. One early critic (in 1827, when Arnold was still engaged in private tutoring at Laleham) said of him that he suffered from the 'fault of an unsubmissive understanding'.[11] To the accusation of arrogance, levelled at him in 1829 when he had been defending Catholic Emancipation on historical grounds, he gave a lofty reply which hardly exonerates him of the charge: 'I do not consider it to be arrogant', he wrote, 'to assume that I know more of a particular subject, which I have studied eagerly from a child, than those do who notoriously do not study it at all.'[12] He frankly admitted to being ambitious. 'I believe that, naturally, I am one of the most ambitious men alive', he confessed to a Rugby pupil who was seeking advice on a profession, while adding that the only ambitions worthy of the name were to become prime minister, or a governor of a great empire, 'or the writer of works which should live in every age and every country'.[13] A letter of July 1836 to his friend Sir John Franklin, recently appointed Governor of Van Dieman's Land, is altogether more revealing, however. He would be strongly tempted to accompany him to that unhappy convict settlement – as the Bishop, perhaps, or the Principal of a College – because in such a capacity he could assist 'in forming the moral and intellectual character of a new society'.[14] Although the letter continues with sentiments that reveal a painful lack of sympathy for the convict population, at least Arnold had accurately stated what his true aspirations were. If the day came that his work at Rugby had been accomplished, he would seek other realms to conquer, not for the glory of high rank but for the satisfaction of doing a good and lasting Christian work; to repeat the Rugby experiment elsewhere, in fact.

There was one quality above all that enabled him to exercise such an influence over others: earnestness. It was Bonamy Price, commenting on Arnold's relationship with his little coterie of pupils at Laleham, who first discerned it. 'Dr Arnold's great power as a private tutor resided in this, that he gave such an intense earnestness to life. Every pupil was made to feel that there was a work for him to do – that his happiness as well as his duty lay in doing that work

---

[11] A.P. Stanley, vol. I, p. 67.
[12] *Ibid.*, vol. I, p. 209.
[13] *Ibid.*, vol. I, p. 27.
[14] *Ibid.*, vol II, p. 40.

well.'[15] And there, in those two sentences, we have it all. The three words – earnestness, work, duty. They are the words that come, perhaps, first to our minds when we try to describe the dominant ethic of the mid-Victorian period, the prosperous noontide of nineteenth-century England, which Arnold never lived to see. Longfellow, in his 'Psalm of Life', translated Arnoldianism into verse:

> Life is real! Life is earnest!
> And the grave is not its goal:
> Dust thou art, to dust returnest,
> Was not spoken of the soul.

Life was certainly for action. Arnold wanted his pupils to be 'up and doing'. But again we return to the ambiguity of interpretation. As Norman Vance points out, Arnold's ideal was really 'a self-reliant moral maturity which recalls the Coleridgean ideal of self-superintendant virtue'.[17] We may doubt that Thomas Hughes the Rugbeian would have understood language like this. To him, and probably many like him, Arnold's message suggested something more actively heroic – a call to the standard under which 'Christian soldiers' would be called to serve 'for the benefit of the whole nation'.[18]

We are back in the world of Tom Brown again. When Fitzjames Stephen reviewed the book, he made the shrewd observation that what Arnold 'and his admirers' had achieved was 'the substitution of the word "earnest" for its predecessor "serious" '.[19] 'Seriousness' was one of the key words of nineteenth-century Evangelicalism, and to its adherents it bore a technical meaning. The possession of the quality of 'seriousness' meant that you were a 'real' Christian as opposed to a 'nominal' Christian; and one of the hallmarks of a 'serious' Christian was that you exhibited a sort of joyousness in the Lord on every possible occasion, thereby proclaiming your favoured status to the world at large. Arnold was not an Evangelical and would not have used this language. But he was not by nature a solemn man. Bonamy Price has supplied the following slightly improbable picture of him, relaxing with his pupils at Laleham: 'Who that ever had the happiness of being at Laleham, does not remember the lightness and joyousness of heart, with which he would romp and play in the garden, or plunge with a boy's delight into the Thames: or the merry fun with which he would battle with spears with his pupils.'[20] This is

---

[15] *Ibid.*, vol. I, p. 33.
[16] Quoted in Walter E. Houghton, *The Victorian Frame of Mind 1830–1870* (New Haven and London, 1957), p. 221.
[17] Norman Vance, *The Sinews of the Spirit: The Ideal of Christian Manliness in Victorian Literature and Thought* (Cambridge, 1985), p. 71.
[18] *Ibid.*, p. 24.
[19] G.M. Young, *Portrait of an Age: Victorian England*, annotated by G. Kitson Clark (Oxford, 1977), p. 213.
[20] A.P. Stanley, vol. I, pp. 34–5.

one of those vignettes which remind us from time to time that the distance between our own day and the nineteenth century seems measured in light years. I would suggest that another instance occurred earlier. I cannot conceive any headmaster of the present day doing other than rejoice at the prospect of boys reading Dickens for pleasure. Similarly the image of adults 'romping' or 'frolicking' in the way that Bonamy Price describes seems to us more than faintly risible; or if not that, then perhaps 'childish'. One has to remember, however, that of the outdoor games Victorian (and pre-Victorian) adults were wont to play in their lighter moments, a favourite appears to have been – *leap-frog*. After all, Mr Pickwick was tempted to discard his great coat on one sunny afternoon and to persuade Mr Tupman to show his back for just such a game.[21] Thomas Hughes and J.M. Ludlow occasionally invited students of the London Working Men's College to join them for Sunday lunch at their house in Wimbledon, concluding with games of leap-frog in the garden.[22] Two future Archbishops of Canterbury – E.W. Benson, then Master of Wellington, and Frederick Temple, Headmaster of Rugby – together with Charles Kingsley tried collectively to raise the spirits of the first group of Foundationers at Wellington in 1859 by setting an example of sportive play. Temple punted a football about 'wildly', we are told; and Kingsley – quite in character – set in motion a game of leap-frog.[23] One suspects that when everybody else had tired, Kingsley was still leaping higher and more vigorously than the rest. Of all the pictures of Victorian worthies relaxing out-of-doors, however, my favourite is Arthur Benson's description of the solemn Bishop of Durham, Brooke Foss Westcott, on holiday with the Bensons at the seaside. 'On a hot summer afternoon we sat by the sea, and a cock-shy was set up. Westcott threw stones at it, with a deadly intentness, far harder and quicker than any one else.'[24] This was near the nineteenth century's end; but it is a faithful picture of earnestness in play.

All this, however, is to digress. A man of passionate beliefs, whose conception of his appointment to the Headmastership of Rugby in December 1827 was that of a personal mission to turn a potential nursery of vice into a model of a Christian community, was not likely to brook any opposition. He was determined to fulfil what Edward Hawkins predicted of him in his testimonial to the Trustees – 'to change the face of education all through the public schools of England'.[25] As Michael McCrum has pointed out, this was a pretty meaningless phrase at the time. There were only seven such schools in 1827 and most of these studiously avoided deference to Arnold's work, Eton more

[21] C. Dickens, *Pickwick Papers*, chapter xxviii.
[22] J.F.C. Harrison, *A History of the Working Men's College 1854–1954* (London, 1954), p. 38.
[23] David Newsome, *A History of Wellington College, 1859–1959* (London, 1959), p. 101.
[24] A.C. Benson, *The Leaves of the Tree. Studies in Biography* (New York and London, 1911), p. 61.
[25] A.P. Stanley, vol. I, p. 44.

so than any other.[26] In the long run, however – while admitting an element of hyperbole – his prediction was not far off the mark. It will seem strange to us that the Trustees appointed Arnold as Dr Wooll's successor without even an interview; strange, too – although it was to have great significance in elevating the status of headmasters generally – that the Trustees acceded to Arnold's condition that he be given an entirely free hand, without any interference. They might dismiss him, if dissatisfied; otherwise they were to hold their peace. When the Earl Howe presumed, as an individual Trustee, to demand an open admission from the Headmaster that he was the author of his notorious unsigned denunciation of the Tractarians in the *Edinburgh Review*, Arnold's response was one of the frostiest rebuffs ever penned.[27]

Indeed Arnold could display an element of ruthlessness at times. His educational principles were, on the whole, admirable. Anyone who has had experience of schools will testify to the corrupting influence of a single vicious boy. Arnold's answer was to root out all such threats by expulsion. To encourage co-operation from his staff, which he did by regular three-weekly meetings with them and by confirming his respect for them by substantially improving the salary scale, was surely right. One of his major changes for the better was the abolition of 'dames' ' houses and the appointment of housemasters to exercise direct pastoral supervision of their boys. Underlying all his policy at Rugby was his firm conviction that a Christian school should operate on the principle of mutual trust, and this he sought to achieve through his relations with his Sixth Form, who were to be his exemplars in setting the whole moral tone of the school. On the whole that trust was repaid, although doubtless Arnold would have bridled at the cynicism implicit in the well-known maxim that if you fail to trust boys they will do you down, and if you trust them they will – being only boys – sometimes let you down. One particular responsibility, however, he safeguarded in his own person. From 1831, he took over the chaplaincy of the school, so that only his voice should be heard from the pulpit each Sunday. This was to be his most cherished vehicle for the transmission of his ideal of moral purification, and we know from the testimony of his youthful auditors over the years that these twenty-minute addresses – never longer – made a deep and enduring impression.

I think that it would be generally conceded that reliance upon Press reports for an accurate picture of the occasional dramas that spice the life of a public school would constitute a somewhat rash declaration of faith. This, nevertheless, has been the misguided temptation of certain historians, and most notably Professor T.W. Bamford, in efforts to confirm a suspicion that A.P. Stanley's idol must have had feet of clay.[28] Even more misguided, however, has been the

---

[26] M. McCrum, *Thomas Arnold, Headmaster. A Reassessment* (Oxford, 1989), p. 116.
[27] A.P. Stanley, vol. II, pp. 36–7.
[28] T.W. Bamford, *Thomas Arnold* (1960), *passim*.

failure to realize that Arnold, because of his outspoken political writings, had made an inveterate enemy of the Tory press, who seized eagerly upon every opportunity to vilify his reputation. This is the conclusion of a PhD thesis for the University of Hull by Dr Anthony Reeve, who has conducted an exhaustive search for unpublished Arnold letters and papers, and has succeeded in making the most significant contribution to studies of Arnold as an educationalist since Stanley's *magnum opus*.

Dr Reeve does not maintain that Arnold never made a mistake. It was unfortunate that he flogged a boy called Marsh for lying, when in fact he had been telling the truth, but he had no reason to suppose that the master who had reported the boy had himself made a mistake, a fact that did not come to light until forty-eight hours later. Arnold responded in the only honourable way: he made a public apology, wrote to the parents and received in return an expression of entire confidence in his conduct as headmaster, so that there was no question of their son being withdrawn. The Tory press pounced upon another instance of alleged injustice – the expulsion of Nicholas Marshall, claiming, on the unsupported evidence of the aggrieved father, that the boy had been denied any opportunity to state his own case over an incident which could be represented as a gross abuse of power by the Praeposters. Correspondence which Dr Reeve has unearthed reveals that this was simply untrue. Marshall was certainly seen by Arnold after the offence had been reported to him. The boy, furthermore, admitted to taunting the Praeposters, who had intervened to quell a disturbance in which he had been a central figure, and – instead of exercising his right to appeal – he had refused to accept punishment and had come to blows with three of the Praeposters.[29] It is difficult to see what else Arnold could have done other than remove him from the school.

The Wratislaw case of 1839 (so named after the local solicitor who initiated proceedings against the school) has also been re-examined by Dr Reeve in the light of new evidence. This at the time received wide publicity injurious to Arnold's reputation, when the Trustees were taken to court for alleged breach of the original charitable foundation of Lawrence Sheriff, intended to supply local boys with free education, it being further maintained that Arnold had deliberately put every possible obstacle in the way of these Foundationers proceeding from the Lower to the Upper School. Although the Trustees were exonerated on two counts, this last charge went undefended and judgement was found against them. It is now clear, however, that Counsel for the Trustees, either through dilatoriness or through lack of awareness of the seriousness of the issue, failed to send Arnold the relevant affidavits, so that he was given no opportunity to state his own case, which he was confident would have adequately answered all the allegations against him.[30]

---

[29] A.J.H. Reeve, 'Aspects of the Life of Dr Thomas Arnold (1795–1842) in the light of the unpublished correspondence', University of Hull PhD thesis, 1988, pp. 262–4.
[30] *Ibid.*, pp. 356–9.

What was the long-term influence of Arnold's work at Rugby? In the first place he took what at the time were considered to be radical steps in the reform of the Rugby curriculum. These were not, however, in the direction of introducing a serious study of the sciences – for which neglect Corelli Barnett has (not entirely fairly) blamed him and the short-sightedness on the part of the headmasters who slavishly followed his methods, for the lamentable failure to perceive the country's needs for scientific and technical education, thereby contributing to the loss of England's industrial supremacy in the later decades of the century. Arnold's reforms were within the traditional field of the study of the Classics, which had hitherto been largely Latin-based, involving the sentencing of generations of boys to the stultifying exercise of composing imitative Latin verse.

Arnold's aim as a teacher was to imbue his pupils with his own passion for the historians and philosophers of ancient Greece, notably Thucydides, Plato and Aristotle. 'The results of the reorientation, which was so clearly in keeping with the tendencies of the age,' Robert Ogilvie has written, 'were to prove of incalculable benefit . . . To Arnold is due much of the credit for originating the change.'[31] This aspect of Arnoldianism, rightly so described because what Arnold began at Rugby was followed by almost all his disciples in other schools, had its effect in the shaping of the Literae Humaniores School at Oxford. 'By 1866,' Ogilvie continues, 'every Oxford Greats man would be reading Plato and Thucydides, and nearly everyone at Oxford was reading Greats.'[32] This may not seem, especially to non-classicists, to be of earth-shattering importance, one must admit. What Ogilvie would seem to be claiming, however, is that Oxford at least was not unmoved by the change of direction in classical studies at school level, inaugurated by Arnold – a rare instance, perhaps, of the tail wagging the dog. And the text of Thucydides that was studied was Arnold's own scholarly edition. In his preface to the third edition of that work, he concluded with a passage that succinctly summed up his whole approach to the study of history, of which we must say more later. The work on which he had been engaged, he said, was not 'an idle inquiry about remote ages and forgotten institutions, but a living picture of things present, fitted not so much for the curiosity of the scholar as for the instruction of the statesman and the citizen.'[33]

G.M. Young has claimed that 'Arnold reconciled the serious classes to the public schools.'[34] What this really means is that it was Arnold's good fortune to articulate – whether consciously or not – a corpus of ideals and an ethical code which precisely matched what so many of his contemporaries believed

---

[31] R.M. Ogilvie, *Latin and Greek. A History of the Influence of the Classics on English Life from 1600 to 1918* (London, 1964), p. 98.

[32] *Ibid.*, p. 102.

[33] *Miscellaneous Works of Thomas Arnold*, edited by A.P. Stanley (London, 1858), p. 399.

[34] G.M. Young, p. 105.

were the particular needs of their times. Harold Perkin, for instance, has suggested that this was essentially an appeal to the changing society of the early nineteenth century and especially to what he describes as the 'entrepreneurial' classes, who liked what they saw, or what they read about, of Arnold's work at Rugby, not least the encouragement of the competitive spirit. To express it thus – I feel – is somewhat misleading. Arnold rejoiced in the successes of his pupils, but consistently placed the formation of character above the goal of academic success. He would never have approved of 'league tables' of schools. Perkin does, however, concede that Arnold's moral teaching and his ideal of gentlemanly conduct lay at the root of his appeal to this same class. 'His concept of the Christian gentleman was not that of the old chevalier, jealous of his paramilitary honour, but otherwise indifferent to morality,' he writes, 'but that of the new "gentle" gentleman, competing not in duels but in consideration for others.'[35]

What we are seeing is the gradual coming into being of a common ethic, as the different classes of society come more and more to speak as one. This is a process that antedates Arnold's work at Rugby and probably owes more to the Evangelical Revival than to any other cause. It is interesting, for instance, to note Alexis de Tocqueville's account of a conversation with Edward Bulwer (the future Lord Lytton) in 1833 – too early a date for Arnold's influence to have been felt. Bulwer observes that 'there has been an immense revolution in the minds of Englishmen during the last half-century'. He predicts the decline of the aristocracy, noting that common dangers are bringing classes together to seek a common solution.[36] Gertrude Himmelfarb, writing in our own times, comments on the same phenomenon as follows: 'For the first time, a substantial part of the aristocracy and of the working-classes (and in each case the most influential part) shared the ideals and values of the middle classes.'[37] Some thirty-five years ago, when I first ventured into print on the subject of Arnoldianism, I described these ideals in the time-honoured phrase of John Colet as 'Godliness and Good learning'. I am happy to let that stand.

By no means all Arnold's public utterances were received at the time with acclaim.[38] He was a compulsive writer. 'I must write or die', he used frequently to say. Furthermore, he was a man of restless energy, living – it seems – under a 'permanent sense of crisis',[39] which accounts for the tendency to overstatement and the recurring note of urgency in so many of his polemical writings. Here again, he was a man of his times, sharing with many of his contemporaries dark forebodings of imminent cataclysm. Opinions differed

---

[35] Harold Perkin, *The Origins of Modern English Society, 1780–1880* (London, 1969), p. 298.
[36] Alexis de Tocqueville, *Journeys in England and Ireland*, edited by J.P. Mayer (1958), pp. 55–6.
[37] Gertrude Himmelfarb, *Victorian Minds* (London, 1966), p. 277.
[38] A.P. Stanley, vol. I, p. 158.
[39] The phrase is Norman Vance's in Vance, p. 70.

over the form that the blow might take: mob-violence leading to revolution, the consequence of failing to learn the lessons of what befell France in 1789; financial collapse like the disaster of December 1825, which demonstrated so painfully that fortunes easily made could be as easily lost. Such happenings fostered the spread of Millenarianism and expectations of Divine retribution for the sins of national wickedness.[40] Arnold was never a Millenarian, but some of his language gives the hint of an approaching Armageddon. 'The Church as it now stands, no human power can save'[41] (in 1832); 'I cannot, I am sure, be mistaken as to this, that the state of society in England at this moment was never yet paralleled in history' (in a letter to Thomas Carlyle in 1840).[42] So, in his Inaugural Lecture at Oxford in the following year, he warned his audience: 'If there be any signs, however uncertain, that we are living in the latest period of the world's history . . . the importance of not wasting the time still left to us may well be called incalculable.'[43]

Arnold's first most controversial pamphlet on an ecclesiastical theme was his *Principles of Church Reform*, published in 1833, in which he declared his sincere conviction that the State and the National Church are really one and the same body, working for identical ends – the moral improvement of mankind. The major threat to the realization of this ideal was sectarianism, and the worst manifestation of it in his own day was the concept of the Church as a clerical hierarchy, striving for uniformity of opinion and of worship, paying scant regard to the important role of the laity. Of course he had events in Oxford in mind. His proposed measures of radical reform filled almost all churchmen (and Dissenters) with horror – the sharing of church buildings by Christians of all denominations, who would hold their own services under their own chosen forms of worship at different times; all doctrinal tests should be abolished; the order of deacons should be revived, tithes commuted, dioceses and parishes redistributed, and the episcopal order thoroughly remodelled. Only by such sweeping reforms could unity be achieved. 'All societies of men, whether we call them states or churches,' he wrote, 'should make their bond to consist in a common object and a common practice, rather than in a common belief: in other words, their end should be good rather than truth.'[44]

He seems to have known that he was pursuing a dream; but – he observed – quoting a paradox of Hesiod, 'He is a fool who does not know how much the half is better than the whole.'[45] He hotly repudiated, however, imputations of

[40] Boyd Hilton, *The Age of Atonement. The Influence of Evangelicalism on Social and Economic Thought, 1795–1865* (Oxford, 1988), p. 131.
[41] A.P. Stanley, vol. I, p. 264.
[42] *Ibid.*, vol. II, p. 160.
[43] T. Arnold, *Introductory Lectures on Modern History* (1874), pp. 30–1.
[44] T. Arnold, *Principles of Church Reform*, edited by M.J. Jackson and J. Rogan (London, 1962), p. 66.
[45] A.P. Stanley, vol. I, p. 187.

unorthodoxy, claiming to be following in the line of Hooker, Burke and Coleridge. Certainly Coleridge had profoundly influenced Arnold's thought. 'I think with all his faults old Sam was more of a great man than any one who has lived within the four seas in my memory',[46] he wrote in 1836. Arnold's affinity with what has come to be called the Broad Church tradition is even more clearly shown in his work on the 'Interpretation of Scripture'. He never doubted the inspiration of the biblical texts; what worried him was the way in which biblical literalists fought their corner. His professed aim was to place the Bible on 'an imperishable historical base that would be proof against any attack which the most refined modern learning could direct against it'.[47] This required, however, making concessions and admitting techniques of exegesis unpalatable to both Evangelicals and High Churchmen. The Old Testament, for instance, had to be read with an informed understanding of both the context of the events described and the moral code of the times in which they were written. All the Scriptures should be scientifically studied on exactly the same methods and principles as one would employ in a study of the text of Thucydides. Language, being a human instrument, must therefore be subjected to philological analysis.

If one aspired to rise to the rank of a 'Sage' in early nineteenth-century England, there was one sure path to set you on your way: acquire a knowledge of German. This was how the Sage of Highgate (Coleridge) came to exercise the influence that he did; and this is what invested the Sage of Cheyne Row (Carlyle) with an aura of wisdom that his actual writings sometimes failed to confirm. Julius Hare – another Sage – directed Arnold along that same path in 1825, primarily to equip him with the resources to read Niebuhr. Arnold, therefore, was familiar with contemporary German critical scholarship, and it distressed him not a little to see how so many churchmen, for want of that knowledge, took 'alarm at the prevailing spirit' and were therefore afraid 'to yield even points they could not maintain, instead of wisely giving them up, and holding on where they could'.[48]

This was well and wisely said. Not so temperately expressed, nor so wise, however, was Arnold's attack on Newman and the Tractarians in his *Edinburgh Review* article of April 1836, to which the editor added the title 'The Oxford Malignants'. It was understandable, if barely excusable. Perhaps Arnold had never quite forgiven Newman for his off-the-cuff remark 'But is Arnold a Christian?' on learning second-hand of the contents of the *Principles of Church Reform*. The chief reasons for Arnold's violent language, however, were twofold. He had been disgusted at the application by the Tractarians, in an improbable and short-lived alliance with the Evangelicals, of a sort of 'lynch law' aimed to embarrass and humiliate the allegedly heterodox Renn Dickson Hampden on his appointment to the Oxford Regius Professorship of

[46] *Ibid.*, vol. II, pp. 49–50.
[47] *Ibid.*, vol. I, p. 178.
[48] *Ibid.*, vol. I, p. 38.

Divinity. Second, he firmly believed that Newman and his followers stood for everything most damaging to the health of the Church of England: on the one hand by their insistence on the centrality of dogma (to Arnold, Christianity was 'a life rather than a creed'), on the other by their sectarian spirit and their tendency to speak of the Church as if it were an exclusive clerical caste. As he expressed it to Edward Hawkins four years later: 'They have put a false Church in the place of the true, and through their counterfeit have destroyed the reality, as paper money drives away gold. And this false Church is the Priesthood, to which are ascribed all the powers really belonging to the true Church.'[49] He respected Roman Catholics as 'members of Christ's Church just as much as I am'.[50] Insofar as they stood as the enemies of Protestantism, they were 'a fair enemy'. The Newmanites, however, were 'a treacherous one'.[51]

Historians should be wary at predicting the future; and Arnold's forebodings were proved wrong. But his inclination, as we have seen, was towards the cataclysmic; and he belonged to a school of historians – indeed, Duncan Forbes has cast him as the founder of them in this country[52] – who regarded the future with pessimism. These were the Liberal Anglican historians, who derived their inspiration from Niebuhr directly and also from their later study of Vico's *Scienza Nuova*: men such as Julius Hare, Dean Milman, Connop Thirlwall and, faithful disciple of Arnold to the last, A.P. Stanley himself. As a school, they rejected practically every production of recent and contemporary English historical study. Gibbon was anti-religious; Lingard was a romantic antiquarian; Macaulay believed too passionately in Progress, even to the extent of ultimate perfectability. Carlyle, however, shared their belief in the workings of Divine Providence throughout history, and Coleridge had instilled into them the importance of distinguishing 'cultivation' from 'civilisation'. Their pessimism, arising from a cyclical concept of history – civilizations rise only in time to fall – was strengthened by their contemplation of the potentially explosive social conditions of their own times, together with the perilously increased tempo of life within a society preoccupied with material conceits and industrialization.

All these characteristics are found in Arnold's approach to history. There were lessons to be learnt in abundance; not – curiously (for this was his blind spot) – from the 'noisome cavern' of the Middle Ages,[53] but most especially from the history of the ancient world, which demonstrated so many parallels with modern times that he completely rejected the traditional divisions of

---

[49] *Ibid.*, vol. II, p. 204.
[50] *Ibid.*, vol. I, p. 310.
[51] *Ibid.*, vol. II, pp. 245–6.
[52] Duncan Forbes, *The Liberal Anglican Idea of History* (Cambridge, 1952), to which all the summary given in this paragraph is indebted.
[53] A.P. Stanley, vol. II, p. 242.

'ancient' and 'modern'. Time and again, in his teaching of history at Rugby, he would ask his pupils 'What does this remind you of?'[54]

Arnold believed that all nations go through similar stages of development and that history is governed by law just as in the world of nature. On the other hand, there are no timeless lessons to be learnt, and the historian must always proceed with caution and apply his critical judgement to safeguard against 'tearing examples out of context'.[55] The ability to draw analogies in order to read the signs and dangers of one's own times, however, was one of the historian's primary duties. This is why Arnold was so emphatic about the dangers of forcing the pace. One should not do so in the education of the young; similarly a nation must guard against forcing social or political changes too soon. Too much liberty all at once leads – he would say – to too much 'oxygen'.[56] Democracy will come, if it is to come, in its own good time.

Arnold's actual historical legacy was, through his early death, comparatively small. His *magnum opus* on the History of Rome reached no further than the end of the Second Punic War (three substantial volumes none the less). He was full of plans for future projects on his appointment to the Oxford Chair, and his later letters suggest that he had every intention of resigning the Headmastership of Rugby once he had satisfied himself that he had enough funds to enable him to supplement the very meagre salary of a Regius Professor.

And so we must leave him, hoping that we have paid sufficient tribute to a complex character. He was an idealist, who had occasional flashes of discerning realism. 'It would give the vainest man alive a very fair notion of his own insufficiency,' he once reflected, 'to see how little he can do, and how his most earnest addresses are as a cannon ball on a bolster.'[57] He was an autocrat who tended to distrust all authority except his own. He pined for the leisure to enable him fully to relax in his Lakeland retreat, 'Fox Howe', in Ambleside, but restlessness of disposition and his sense of mission would never really have allowed him to, much as he enjoyed the company of his family. He could at one moment cross playful spears with his pupils (not – I suspect – at Rugby), and at another cross angry swords with the leader of the Oxford Movement in a sad conflict of mutual misunderstanding. He loved the study of the past, while always looking, usually with apprehension, at the present and the future. He composed pamphlets galore, many of them ephemeral, but also occasionally revealing that he was a man before his times. The word 'Man', he was wont to define in the following way: 'a being of large discourse, looking before and after'.[58] He might have been describing himself.

What might have been, had he been granted the normal span of years? This was the recurring question in the minds of his admirers. Charles Kingsley

---

[54] R.E. Prothero, vol. I, p. 362.
[55] D. Forbes, p. 16.
[56] *Ibid.*, p. 93.
[57] A.P. Stanley, vol. I, p. 223.
[58] *Ibid.*, vol. I, p. 164.

posed it, after reading Arnold's *Lectures on Modern History*. 'Oh why did that noblest of men die?' he mused in sorrow. 'God have mercy upon England! He takes the shining lights from us, for our National sin!'[59] Stanley reflected that 'What he actually achieved in his work falls so far short of what he intended to achieve, that it seems almost like an injustice to judge of his aims and views by them.'[60]

It is an interesting thought that had Arnold lived a little longer, Stanley would probably never have written his *Life*. The obvious author, according to the fashions of the time, would have been the most literary of Arnold's sons, Matthew, who – in 1842 – was just an undergraduate at Balliol, and a bit of a dandy as well; 'unmotivated' is the word we would use today; but, as his father put it, 'not apt to fix'.[61] What sort of book, I wonder, would have come from Matthew's pen? It would certainly have been a tribute. In 1868 Matthew wrote to his mother as follows:

> The nearer I get to accomplishing the term of years which was papa's, the more I am struck with admiration at what he did in them. It is impossible to conceive him exactly as living now, amidst our present ideas, because these ideas he himself would have so much influenced had he been living the last twenty-five years, and, perhaps, have given in many respects a different course to.[62]

We shall allow Benjamin Jowett the final word. In 1878 he re-read Stanley's *Life* (apparently for the umpteenth time), and as was his oracular wont he sent his judgement to the author: 'There were weak points in Arnold and his friends intellectually, but in that one respect of inspiring others with ideals, there has been no one like him in modern times.'[63]

---

[59] F. Kingsley (ed.), *Charles Kingsley. His Letters and Memories of his Life* (London, 1877), vol. I, p. 88.
[60] A.P. Stanley, vol. I, p. 166.
[61] D.G. James, *Matthew Arnold and the Decline of English Romanticism* (Oxford, 1961), p. 2.
[62] *Letters of Matthew Arnold, 1848–1888*, edited by G.W.E. Russell (1895), vol. I, p. 391.
[63] E. Abbott and L. Campbell, *The Life and Letters of Benjamin Jowett*, 2 vols (London, 1897), vol. II, p. 161.

13

TRACTARIANS AND NATIONAL EDUCATION, 1838–1843

JAMES PEREIRO

THE historiography of the Oxford Movement has long been dominated by the assumption that first generation Tractarians were absorbed by purely theological concerns and had little time or interest for social questions, leaving it for later Anglo-Catholic clergy working in the slums, and for the Christian socialists, to articulate the social gospel latent in Tractarian doctrine. It is only in recent years that attention has been drawn to the study of the abundant materials illustrating early Tractarian concerns in social questions,[1] concerns shown in their writings and direct action which aimed at influencing social life at all levels.

Some of Newman's former pupils, and others who had been under his influence while at Oxford, moved to London to begin their professional careers in Parliament, business or the law. They had been formed or influenced by the *ethos* of the Oxford Movement, and in the mid-1830s they were actively campaigning to spread the new ideas in the metropolis. They were conscious of the fact that the Church's fundamental mission was the salvation of individual souls but, as the Tractarians saw it, the Church was also called to consecrate the nation's soul and social life. The climate of social and political reform of the 1830s presented them with numerous challenges but also with opportunities to guide present and future reforms along more 'Catholic' channels. What was being decided at the time, as they saw it, was whether the new social order then emerging would be configured according to Christian or secular notions of man and society.

---

[1] See for example S.A. Skinner, *Tractarians and the 'Condition of England': The Social and Political Thought of the Oxford Movement* (Oxford, 2004); also his 'Liberalism and Mammon: Tractarian Reaction in the Age of Reform', *Journal of Victorian Culture*, vol. 4.2 (Autumn 1999), pp. 197–227.

The present paper studies the motivations and schemes of those Tractarians who after 1838 tried to influence the debate on national education and shape the policies of the National Society for the Education of the Poor. Their impact on the educational scene has already been noted in previous studies,[2] but little has been done so far to reveal the inner workings of this group.

Tractarians and the National Society for the Education of the Poor

The middle and late 1830s were a time of great ferment in the debate about national education. By that time a number of European countries had already set up, or were in the process of setting up, their own State-funded and regulated educational systems. Ireland had seen the establishment of its system of National Education, and it was felt that the time was ripe for the introduction of similar measures in England. The education of the poor had to date been promoted by the National Society for the Education of the Poor, founded in 1811, and by the British and Foreign Schools Society, founded in 1814. The first was identified with the Anglican Church, and demanded of the schools associated with it that they teach the Catechism and attendance to Church of England public worship. The British and Foreign appeared more comprehensive in its religious policy: religious formation was confined to reading the Bible, and it avoided teaching the tenets of any particular denomination. In fact, because of its refusal to teach the Anglican catechism, the British and Foreign conformed to a purely Protestant pattern of religious education based on the Bible and the Bible only (not without a Protestant gloss from the teacher). Besides, Catholic children were excluded in practice from these schools because the British and Foreign used the Authorised Version.

Since 1833 both societies had shared in the Government grants for education distributed by the Treasury. In the mid 1830s, however, the State attempted to move beyond being a mere provider of funds to educational societies and aimed at taking a more active part in the promotion and supervision of national education, on the plea that the efforts of the educational societies, while praiseworthy, had been unable to provide an adequate extension – in numbers and quality – of the educational system. The Parliamentary Committees of Enquiry of 1834 and 1835, chaired by Lord John Russell and the Earl of Kerry, had shown the magnitude of the problem and started to prepare public opinion for more decided measures on the part of the State. Lord Brougham, whose name had been associated with education for two decades, had

---

[2] See for example H.J. Burgess, *Enterprise in Education. The Story of the Work of the Established Church in the Education of the People prior to 1870* (London, 1958); D. Paz, *The Politics of Working-Class Education in Britain, 1830–1850* (Manchester, 1980); J.L. Alexander, 'Collegiate Teacher Training in England and Wales' (PhD thesis, King's College, London, 1977).

introduced his private member's Bill on national education in successive parliamentary sessions. His proposals, framed in concert with Lord John Russell, included the setting up of an Education Department with the responsibility for the application of funds voted by Parliament and the improvement of education by means of inspection and the creation of training schools for teachers. The Bill also empowered town councils to levy a school-rate in order to establish new schools where needed.[3] Although Brougham's Bills had never been fully debated on the floor of the House of Commons, they gave a clear indication of the views on the subject of education of a large majority of those associated with the Whig government. Around the same time, the recently-founded (1836) Central Society for Education – which included among its members Brougham, Lansdowne, Russell, Spring Rice and Wyse – was putting forward similar ideas in abundant speeches and publications. These men shared a common perception: that the neglect of education which had been demonstrated by recent studies could only be properly remedied by the State taking up the reins of education, as had been done in Prussia, Holland, and, more recently, France. Legislation was needed; *laissez-faire* was a good principle in matters of trade, but not to be extended to education.

A common feature of the different proposals was the establishment of a State Board of Education which, among other responsibilities, would undertake the inspection of the schools already existing and provide for the training of schoolmasters. Prussia and Holland had their Departments of Public Instruction or Ministries of Education, and they were held by many to be the best models for England: they were Protestant countries, and their peoples were examples of morality, religious feeling and respect for authority. The books of Victor Cousin on the educational systems of Prussia and Holland were eagerly read and discussed. His *On the State of Education in Holland* was published in France in 1837, and in England early in 1838.[4] The English edition included some preliminary observations by Leonard Horner, Inspector of Factories and member of the Central Society, which tried to answer those who objected to the import of a foreign system of education. People had contended that the Prussian system of education was well adapted to a country accustomed to an arbitrary form of government and military rule, but that it was not appropriate for a free people and freedom-loving nation. Horner was ready to grant that much but he argued that a state system of education was not equivalent to authoritarianism: Holland had a representative form of govern-

---

[3] The substance of the Brougham's Education Bill can be found in [W.Allen (ed.)], *Education. Speeches and Observations of Lord Brougham, the Marquess of Lansdowne and Lord Lyndhurst in the House of Lords, Tuesday, June 29, 1837* (London, 1837), pp. 18–21.

[4] C.H.V. Cousin, *On the State of Education in Holland as regards Schools for the Working Classes and for the Poor*, Preliminary Observations by Leonard Horner, Esq., FRS (London, 1838). There is also an English edition of his earlier report on Prussia: V. Cousin, *Report on the State of Public Instruction in Prussia* (London, 1834).

ment, and its inhabitants were as jealous of their freedom as were their English counterparts. He felt, moreover, that in the case of England educational reforms could not be rushed in or be mere imitation of those in another country. Reform should be preceded by proper study, by setting up a Parliamentary Commission of Inquiry which would in due course report on the state of education in the country, and recommend the most appropriate measures for its improvement.[5] As a matter of fact, such a Commission had already been set up by Parliament in November 1837. It started its deliberations in February 1838, and under the chairmanship of Robert A. Slaney, who had moved the motion for the Select Committee, was to present its report in July of the same year.

The association of the Whig government with Dissenters and with the Central Society, and their sympathy with their educational ideas was obvious to all: Brougham, Lansdowne and Russell had, at one time or another, occupied the Vice-presidency of the British and Foreign Schools Society, and they were all members of the Central Society. The defenders of the place of the Church in education could read the writing on the wall, and they were not slow to mobilise their effectives to meet the pressure of those who wanted to make education a responsibility of the State. Gilbert Farquhar Graeme Mathison played an important role in re-awakening the flagging energies of the National Society for the Education of the Poor as the educational arm of the Church of England.[6] Having left Oxford without a degree, Mathison had worked for a short period in the opium trade, which he abandoned because of moral scruples. In 1828, after a time in the Colonial Office and as private secretary to the Chancellor of the Exchequer, he had been appointed Secretary to the Mint, where he ran the melting and refining of precious metals as a private and public concern, and was extremely successful in the business. His educational interests were already to the fore, and he had set up a school for one hundred children at the Mint.[7] Mathison, a High Churchman, had shown an interest in

---

[5] Cf. L. Horner, 'Preliminary Observations', in Cousin, *Education in Holland*, pp. lxv–lxvi.

[6] Years later T.D. Acland would regret the lack of credit which Mathison had received in the history of education for his efforts to galvanise and channel the energies of the National Society (cf. A.H.D. Acland, *Memoir and Letters of the Right Honourable Sir Thomas Dyke Acland* (Printed for Private Circulation: London, 1902), p. 88). The *Dictionary of British Educationists*, R. Aldrich and P. Gordon (eds) (London, 1989), does not make any reference to Mathison. It has been remarked that the fact that Gladstone's papers are one of the main sources for the activities of this group should make one cautious of ascribing to him the central role, although that is the impression that the record gives (cf. J.L. Alexander, 'Lord John Russell and the origins of the Committee of Council on Education', *Historical Journal*, vol. 20, 22 (1977), p. 404). The different perception of his contemporaries is illustrated by a letter of Wood to Newman, where he referred to the group moving things in London as the *Mathisonians* (letter dated 10 April 1838, *Halifax Papers Borth.*, Borthwick Library, York, A.2, 42.2, fo. 80r).

[7] Wood to R. Wilberforce, 8 November 1836, *Wilberforce Adds.*, Bodleian Library, Oxford, c. 66, fo. 26. For other biographical details see Mathison's obituary in the *Guardian,* No. 456, 30

the Tracts and corresponded with Newman early in 1836. Through Newman he entered in contact with Samuel Francis Wood – they became close friends – and started to attend William Dodsworth's Margaret Street Chapel.

In the autumn of 1835, Mathison had visited Ireland, and his observations, printed for private circulation in 1836, contained abundant references to the operation of the recently-established Irish system of national education. The National Schools, which were supposed to be non-sectarian and teach a selection of Scriptural texts, had, according to Mathison, become *de facto* Catholic Church schools, were attended only by Catholics and, as far as he could ascertain, used only Catholic books.[8] In the autumn of 1836 it was Wood's turn to visit Ireland. He confirmed Mathison's account: the National Schools had come quietly into the hands of the Catholic clergy, and had become a bonus to Roman Catholic education. Wood had been much impressed by the piety of the Catholic people and their devotion to their priests, in stark contrast with the dismal condition of the Church of Ireland.[9] He felt deeply the need for a crusade at home to renew the attachment of the lower classes to the Church of England. Wood, in a later analysis, identified the cause of the detachment of the middle and lower classes from the Church in the breaking up of the pre-Reformation system of Church education: grammar and chantry schools, and their links with the colleges. The consequent neglect of the education of the lower and middle classes was responsible for the loss of influence of the Church among them.[10]

In Wood's eyes, many causes had prevented the Church of England from exercising 'that complete influence on society, which her divine commission contemplates. Sometimes state jealousy, at other times internal division and weakness, or her own forgetfulness of her high privileges, had interfered with that task.'[11] The tendency in recent years had been to exclude the Church from as many fields as possible, including that of education. Wood contended for the restoration of the Church's privileges: without the recognition of their divine origin the efforts of the Church for the good of society would not produce the blessings which could otherwise be expected. He was not blind, however, to the likelihood of a resistance on the part of the State to grant those privileges or a rebellious disposition on the part of large sections of society to their exercise by the Church.

August 1854, p. 673, and J. Craig, *The Mint. A History of the London Mint from A.D. 287 to 1948* (Cambridge, 1953), pp. 301, 304–5 and 317.

[8] [G.F. Mathison], *Journal of a Tour in Ireland during the Months of October and November 1835* (Printed for Private Circulation only, London, 1836), pp. 5, 47–8, 90 et al.

[9] Cf. Wood to Manning, 3 November 1836, *Manning MSS Bod.* (Bodleian Library, Oxford), Eng. Lett., c. 654, fos 450–1.

[10] S.F. Wood, 'On attaching the Middle and Lower Orders to the Church', *The English Journal of Education*, vol. 1, nn. 2 and 4 (February and April, 1843), pp. 43–9 and 125–30.

[11] [S.F. Wood], 'Griffith's *Christian Church*', *British Critic*, vol. xxii (October, 1837), p. 396.

Mathison went to Holland in the summer of 1837 to study the Dutch system of education. On his return, and while the Parliamentary Commission was starting its work, Mathison and Wood spoke on how to direct the plans on education into a Church channel. There are also records of approaches by Mathison to Thomas Dyke Acland, and others such as Gladstone, Manning, and Samuel and Robert Wilberforce.[12] It may be safely assumed that the small group formed in London in early 1838 to promote Church education was made up of those – Gladstone, Coleridge, Acland, etc. – with whom Mathison had discussed the subject in previous months.

These men felt that a response should be made to Brougham's Bill and other moves, inside and outside Parliament, pointing in the same direction. They considered that the systems of Prussia, Holland, France or Ireland could not be adopted in England because of their lack either of freedom or of proper religious teaching. They felt that, in England, a voluntary system led by the Church was preferable to a Government one, and that it was the energy of the members of the Church, rather than the legislature, that should guarantee her influence.[13] The National Society, in their opinion, was not in a fit state to meet the challenge of the State: school expansion had lost its initial momentum, the running of the Society's business had fallen into a complacent routine, and those who ran it had been drawn into a false sense of security by the granting of State subsidies since 1833.[14] However, in spite of the parlous condition of the National Society, Mathison and his friends thought that the way forward was to re-energise and develop it rather than creating a new society.[15]

Wood clearly described their aim in a letter to Newman: 'to forestall any Government or Abstract-Principle plan by an immediate, silent, and large extension of the funds and energy of the National Society.' They wanted to steal a march on the Government as far as the setting up of a system of National Education was concerned. Wood added that all this was to be achieved by revitalising the committee of the National Society with young men, who would act as the moving force to expand the aims and action of the Society. The training of schoolmasters was Mathison's immediate priority: to imbue them with a love for the Church which they could afterwards pass on to their pupils. After this, came the plans for setting up middle and upper schools, and schools for the middle class, neglected so far by the National Society. The

---

[12] Cf. Acland (ed.), *Memoir of T.D. Acland*, p. 88; in February 1838 Mathison had held conversations on education with Samuel and Robert Wilberforce (cf. A.B. Ashwell, *Life of the Right Rev. Samuel Wilberforce* (London, 1880), p. 11). See also Wood to Manning, 23 March 1838, *Manning MSS Bod*, c. 654, fo. 464.
[13] Cf. G.F.G. Mathison, *How can the Church educate the People?* (London, 1844), pp. 5 ff.
[14] Cf. Burgess, *Enterprise in Education*, pp. 64 ff; see also Alexander, 'Origins of the Committee of Council on Education', pp. 395–415.
[15] Cf. Acland to Pusey, 2 April 1838, *Liddon Bound Volumes (LBV)*, Pusey House, n. 38, lett. 2.

new plans, Wood felt, would remedy one of the shortcomings of the present system: the pupils were leaving the Church's schools 'just when they might begin to be made Churchmen'.[16] Their intention was to make State intervention unnecessary by creating a system of public instruction – from Infant Schools to University – essentially and intimately connected with the principles and ministers of the Established Church.

Mathison and his friends considered that it would be necessary for them not only to mobilise the energies of the National Society; they would also need to keep the reins of future developments in their hands if there was to be any chance of success for their hopes to promote the educational activity of the Church. This was not easy, given the composition of the General Committee of the National Society, to which belonged by right all the bishops of the Church of England. Still, they thought that the prospect of additional support and funds would be a strong inducement for the National Society to take some of them into the Committee and give weight to their proposals. In February of 1838 Mathison approached Joshua Watson, the Treasurer of the National Society, who had enough sympathy for his ideas to arrange for the Archbishop to receive him.[17] On 2 March, Mathison was closeted with Archbishop Howley for two hours, discussing their plans, particularly those connected with the setting up of Training Colleges in order to improve the qualifications of teachers. The Archbishop gave his initial blessing for the plans, which, to start with, they were to set in motion on their own responsibility.[18] As a first step, they prepared a circular on education putting forward their ideas on the subject. At this very moment, however, overwork and anxiety caused Mathison's mental collapse.[19] His friends met on 23 March to consider the course of action to follow in this crisis, and they decided to go ahead with the distribution of the prepared circular.[20] It contained some of the ideas described in Wood's letter to Newman, adding their intention of creating a system of education built around the machinery that the Church offered: parochial, collegiate and diocesan.[21] The aim of the circular was to gather the names of

[16] Wood to Newman, no date (before March, 1838), *Halifax Papers Borth.*, A.2, 42.2, fos 62–5.
[17] Cf. T.D. Acland's note in E. Churton, *Memoir of Joshua Watson* (2nd edn, Oxford and London, 1863), pp. 300–1.
[18] Cf. Wood to Newman, 2 March 1838, *Halifax Papers Borth.*, A.2, 42.2, fo. 71.
[19] Cf. Acland (ed.), *Memoir of T.D. Acland*, pp. 88–9; see also F. Rogers to Newman, 20 March 1838: 'He got wrought up to such a pitch of excitement and anxiety by the National Education scheme that his mind has become actually deranged, and he is at present under medical care' (Birmingham Oratory Archives, *Blachford Letters*).
[20] See Acland to Pusey, 2 April 1838, Pusey House, *LBV*, n. 38, lett. 2. Wood, writing to Manning on 23 March, mentioned the following people as attending the meeting: Gladstone, Acland, Farquhar, Coleridge, Lutwidge, W.M. Praed, and Wood himself (*Manning MSS Bod*, c. 654, fo. 464). Acland's biographer, years later, gave a different list: Lord Sandon, Lord Ashley, Gladstone, S.F. Wood, H. Nelson Coleridge, M. Praed, Lutwidge and Acland (see Acland (ed.), *Memoir of T.D. Acland*, p. 88).
[21] A copy of the *Proposals* can be found at the beginning of the Book of Minutes of the

lay people of substance who were in favour of their plans, avoiding at all costs any hint that this was a High Church initiative. The collecting of signatures should be done, with the greatest possible discretion, by the end of the first week of April. Then the circular, with the names attached to it, was to be sent to the Archbishop.

The circular was sent to people who shared their church views,[22] and, although the response was not all that they would have wished, it was encouraging enough to go ahead with the plans. By 10 April, Wood and Acland were hard at work preparing the plan on national education, which the Archbishop had requested after receiving the circular. This was no easy task. With Mathison's mental collapse had vanished, at least for the time being, his thoughts on education and the contributions made by people like Manning and others: Wood and Acland only had the headings – not developed in detail – of his plan. They asked their friends for help,[23] and used ideas from other sources. At this stage, diocesan seminaries attached to the cathedrals were added to the original proposals, together with an institution in London connected with King's College.[24] Once it was ready, Gladstone had a look through it with Acland and Wood on 11 April, before sending it to Lambeth. Three days later, the Archbishop had a long interview with Sir W.R. Farquhar, Wood, Acland and Gladstone at Lambeth Palace. He gave the plan his entire approval and allowed them to tell people privately that he thought the plan to be for the good of the Church.[25] The Archbishop intimated that, if the list of subscribers to their plans were such as to create confidence in the success of their enterprise, he would agree to be President of an appeal to the public on behalf of Church education.[26]

John H. Spry, Rector of Marylebone, and Joshua Watson, seem to have served as go-betweens with the General Committee of the National Society. This appointed a subcommittee to deal with the group, and a meeting between the two was fixed for 28 April. Wood was at first somewhat apprehensive

Committee of Enquiry and Correspondence 1838 (1839), Church of England Record Centre, London.

[22] Manning received copies of the circular from Wood and Gladstone, and Wood also sent copies to Newman (see Wood to Manning, 23 March 1838, *Manning MSS Bod.*, c. 654, fo. 464; also Wood to Newman, 24 March 1838, *Halifax Papers Borth.*, fo. 75v); Gladstone recorded that he sent a number of circulars without identifying the recipients (cf. M.R.D. Foot (ed.), *The Gladstone Diaries (GD)* (Oxford, 1968), vol. ii, p. 356). Acland wrote to Pusey, etc.

[23] Wood asked Manning to tell him what he had said in his letter to Mathison: 'Anything you said in your letter to poor Mathison is lost' (letter dated 23 March 1838, *Manning MSS Bod.*, 654, fo. 464).

[24] Wood to Newman, 10 April 1838, *Halifax Papers Borth.*, A.2, 42.2, fo. 80v; see also Wood to Manning, Feria Quinta Post Pasch (19 April 1838), *Manning MSS Bod.*, c. 654, fo. 467.

[25] Cf. Wood to Manning, Feria Quinta Post Pasch (19 April 1838), *Manning MSS Bod.*, c. 654, fo. 467; Gladstone recorded the names of those who attended the meeting in his diary's entry for the day (*GD*, vol. ii, p. 363); see also Acland (ed.), *Memoir of T.D. Acland*, p. 89–90.

[26] Cf. Mathison, *How can the Church educate the People?*, p. 8.

about the success of their approach to the National Society. He thought the subcommittee 'a miserable set' of liberal bishops and old laymen, and he suspected that they would try to use the support and funds generated by the circular 'to tinker up their old kettle and nothing more'. Wood and his friends were determined to fight off that attempt, and intended to persuade the National Society to take up their plan; alternatively, they would go their own way.[27] In the event, their meeting with the subcommittee of the National Society on 28 April was successful, and the Society's General Committee decided to set up a Committee of Enquiry and Correspondence to explore the different areas mentioned in the circular.[28] The original 'Mathisonians' – Acland, Wood, Gladstone, and others – formed part of the new Committee, together with some other members of the National Society.[29] The 'young gentlemen', as they were sometimes referred to, counted all along on the invaluable support of Joshua Watson, who considered that he had rendered his best service to the National Society in introducing them to the Council. At times, he would admit that he was not always able to keep pace with their zeal, but he always gave them the benefit of the doubt and the possibility of putting their ideas to the test.[30]

Wood viewed the alacrity with which their plans had been embraced by all – from the Archbishop down – as a sign of the providential character of the enterprise. He felt that it 'ought not to be maimed for want of heads and hands'. This was partly their problem. Pusey, Newman, and the men at Oxford, while giving their hearty approval to the moves in London, were too busy with other matters to be able to do much.[31] By late April the working of their plans had practically fallen on Wood and Acland: 'I am weary of my life', Wood wrote to Manning.[32] The following months were marked by constant Committee meetings.[33] On 16 June 1838 the Committee of Enquiry

---

[27] Wood to Manning, Feria Quinta Post Pasch (19 April 1838), *Manning MSS Bod.*, c. 654, fos 467–8.
[28] Cf. Minutes Book, *General Committee of the National Society*, vol. 4 (January 1838–July 1847), 12 May 1838, pp. 33–9, Church of England Record Centre. See also Wood to Manning, 28/29 April 1838, *Manning MSS Bod.*, c. 654, fo. 471.
[29] The spellings Enquiry and Inquiry appear alternatively in the references to the Committee. The members of this Committee were T.D. Acland, Lord Ashley, the Dean of Chichester (Chandler), H.N. Coleridge, W. Cotton, the Rev Dealtry, Sir W.R. Farquhar, Gladstone, the Rev J. Jennings, R.W.J. Lutwidge, the Rev H.H. Milman, W.M. Praed, Lord Sandon, the Rev J.H. Spry, the Rev J.C. Wigram and S.F. Wood. To these were added, at a later date J.R. Hope, R. Cavendish, the Rev R.W. Brown and T. Tancred; Mathison, who had made a speedy recovery from his nervous breakdown, was co-opted as a member in 1839 (cf. Minutes Book, *Committee of Enquiry and Correspondence, 1838* (1839), pp. 1, 7–8).
[30] Cf. Churton, *Memoir of Joshua Watson*, pp. 299–300.
[31] Wood to Manning, Feria 5 Post Pasch (19 April 1938), *Manning MSS Bod.*, c. 654, fo. 468.
[32] Cf. Wood to Manning, 25 April 1838, *Manning MSS Bod.*, c. 654, fo. 467.
[33] Cf. Minutes Book, *Committee of Enquiry and Correspondence 1838* (1839); see also *GD*, vol. ii, pp. 356 ff.

and Correspondence approved its first report for the General Committee.[34] This was perhaps the most significant of its contributions to the work of the National Society, and – as far as fundamental policies and priorities were concerned – it would have little to add to it in the future.

Its plans were far-reaching. Its Tractarian members envisaged not only the formation of a true national system of education, united and organised in connexion with the Church's ecclesiastical structure, but also a fundamental reshaping of education along Catholic lines, as the Tractarians understood it. First, the Committee touched on the question of middle schools. The Report stated that the support recently promised had been offered 'in the hoped expectation that the National Society will at the present crisis be disposed to extend in all directions the beneficial range of it operations, as far as in law and prudence it may be warranted in so doing',[35] implying that support would not materialise if the Society did not go on to promote middle schools. It seems that some objections were raised against enlarging the Society's field of action. It was argued that the Charter of the Society, by defining its aim as the education of the 'poor', excluded the possibility of extending its operations to middle schools and the middle classes. The argument seems to have been set up as a defensive line by some of the older members of the Committee. The majority in the Committee, however, thought that the word 'poor' was used in a wider context than just those who were considered as paupers, and that the Society was entitled to reach upwards in its educational ventures without transgressing the legal limits of its Charter. It was suggested, however, to seek legal opinion on this respect, and a draft was prepared on the subject to be presented to Counsel. To the relief of the 'young gentlemen', Counsel declared that the Charter's wording could also cover middle and commercial schools. These were a capital element of their plans for teacher training and for raising standards: the middle schools offered the possibility of promotion from the primary to the middle school for those who were better qualified, and it would provide an incentive for teachers to raise standards in the schools. They were also an essential part of that integral system of national education run by the Church at which the Tractarians aimed.

At an organisational level, the hopes of the Committee rested on the revitalisation of the diocesan and district boards, which had been and were still in existence in some dioceses. These had become less and less active as time went by, to the point at which, at that time, only one diocesan committee and four county committees were able to make any grants, while the number of schools had increased considerably.[36] There were in theory about sixty to seventy boards still in existence, and these offered a ready-made structure with

---

[34] Cf. Minutes Book, *Committee of Enquiry and Correspondence 1838* (1839), pp. 12–21.
[35] *Ibid.*, p. 13.
[36] Cf. *Twenty-Seventh Annual Report of the National Society* (London, 1838), pp. 9–11, 25–6.

a diocesan basis, which well suited the ideas of the Committee as to the organisation they wished for the national system of education. Their aim, once more, was to infuse new life into the already existing structure, rather than to create new ones. At a national level, they suggested the creation of several subcommittees – the School Committee, the Finance Committee, and the Committee of Correspondence – to deal with specific areas under the supervision of the General Committee.

The improvement and provision of schoolmasters was close to the hearts of Mathison and his friends, as they realised that this was all-important to promoting and sustaining the programme of expansion of Church education. The present Central School of the National Society was not able to provide the numbers of trained schoolmasters required, and its training methods were the object of increasing criticism. The Committee of Enquiry's report called for the foundation of diocesan training seminaries connected with their respective Cathedrals to prepare teachers at a local level.[37] They also proposed to set up a collegiate hall in London, associated with King's College, to provide more advanced education for schoolmasters.[38] The report also included other recommendations which were dealt with by the General Committee at a later date.

An expectant wait followed. The 'young gentlemen' did not know whether the response of the General Committee would be positive or not, and they were anxious to have their approval, before the summer recess interrupted their meetings, in order to put their plans into operation as soon as possible. The General Committee, listening to the urgent requests of the Committee of Enquiry, approved the report, except for what referred to the collegiate hall in London, on 18 July 1838.[39] Its members seem to have felt that they were being swept off their feet by the flurry of activity and new ideas generated by their young friends, and that by withholding their approval of the hall they would be making a stand somewhere to show that they were still in control of the proceedings. The plans for the London hall, however, were approved after the summer,[40] and premises were acquired in Chelsea in 1841 for what was to become St Mark's College.

The members of the Committee of Enquiry and Correspondence, Acland and Wood in particular, started in earnest to put their plans into action by

---

[37] This point was further developed in their second report (cf. Minutes Book, *Committee of Enquiry and Correspondence*, 30 June 1838, pp. 33–6).

[38] Cf. *ibid.*, pp. 19–21.

[39] Cf. Minutes Book, *General Committee of the National Society*, vol. 4, pp. 51–4.

[40] Cf. *ibid.*, 12 November 1838, pp. 80–3. The General Meeting of the National Society (28 May 1839) included among its resolutions one in favour of promoting the Training School in London, and another requesting the Committee of Enquiry to act as a Committee to collect subscriptions (cf. Appendix, no. VI, in *Twenty-eighth Annual Report of the National Society*, pp. 84–7).

promoting the formation and revitalisation of diocesan boards. They made journeys around the country to carry out these plans, and even used part of their summer holidays in this pursuit. Their efforts found ready welcome in dioceses and districts, and the results were soon clearly perceptible. On 26 December 1838, the Committee claimed that seven diocesan boards had been formed and that eight more were in the process of formation, while other boards had been set up in districts subordinated to the dioceses; diocesan training schools for the education of young men who wanted to become schoolteachers were being set up in connection with several Cathedral establishments, as originally intended, and so on.[41]

All sides in the educational debate recognised the need for an adequate supply of properly formed teachers. In the minds of Mathison and his friends, the setting up of training schools and seminaries was also intended as a means of forming future teachers on Catholic principles. It followed that the nomination of the rectors or directors of those institutions was of paramount importance, if those new training schools were to form educators imbued with a Catholic *ethos*. As a result, the Tractarians and their friends tried to have some Oxford Movement sympathisers appointed as principals of the training colleges. In this they encountered sometimes the reticence, and on other occasions the downright resistance, of the bishops. Blomfield refused to consider Wilson as director of the London training school because of his Tractarian leanings, and Jeffreys found similar opposition to his appointment to the mastership of the Gloucester training school.[42] In view of these difficulties, Newman complained that, after all the work of men like Acland and Wood to set up the Education system of the Church of England, the clergy – mainly the bishops – were rendering their efforts fruitless: 'None are found selfdenying enough to become schoolmasters except those the rest call Puseyites, and therefore reject.'[43] In this climate, the appointment in 1841 of the Rev Derwent Coleridge, sympathetic to the Tractarians, as Principal of St Mark's College was something of a success for the 'young gentlemen'.

In any event, the Committee of Inquiry and Correspondence had succeeded in goading the National Society into action. Successive reports gave an indication of the pace of the Society's progress: some twenty-four boards, in sixteen dioceses and eight subordinate districts, had been set up by June 1839. The London collegiate hall was on its way to become a reality, and training colleges for teachers were being established in dioceses like Chichester, Oxford, Lichfield, London and Gloucester.

---

[41] Cf. *Circular* of the Committee of Enquiry and Correspondence asking support for the Central Establishment in London (dated 26 December 1838). Copy attached to Minutes Book, p. 85.

[42] Cf. Newman to Bowden, 4 November 1839, *The Letters and Diaries of John Henry Newman*, G. Tracey (ed.), (*LD*), vol. vii (Oxford, 1995), p. 177. See also Newman to Bowden, 20 October, *ibid.*, p. 167.

[43] Newman to T. Mozley, 12 December 1839, *LD*, vol. vii, p. 192.

The Debate on National Education

The plan to influence the National Society was not the only front in the 'Mathisonians' campaign to direct national education into a Church of England channel. At this time, there was also a concerted effort in Parliament to gain time for the Church to develop its school system, together with an offensive to win the support of public opinion through articles, sermons, pamphlets, novels, and other writings. The Tractarians were, however, anxious to avoid giving the impression of a co-ordinated campaign: they preferred it to appear as a widespread spirit coming to the surface here, there, and everywhere.[44]

The Parliamentary Commission on Education had continued its sessions during the first half of 1838. Although it had at the outset been weighted with Whigs, the changes introduced in its composition re-established the party balance; a theoretical balance, in fact, as the attendance record of the Tories helped them dominate the proceedings. Robert Slaney, who acted as the Commission's Chairman for most of its duration, seems to have been the author of the first draft of its final report, recommending the creation of a Board of Education. When the draft was put to the vote, Lord Ashley, Lord Sandon, T.D. Acland and W.E. Gladstone vetoed the inclusion of any mention to a Board of Education in the final report. They went even further and added a new clause to the resolutions, saying that the members of the Committee were not prepared to propose any means for meeting the educational deficiency beyond the continuation and extension of the Treasury grants through the National Society and the British and Foreign.[45] These were deliberate delaying tactics, aimed at giving the National Society a head start over the Government as far as setting up a system of national education was concerned. As Gladstone had written in a letter to Hook earlier in the year, their aim was to win 'a safe and precious interval' for the Church.[46] They fully achieved their objectives, frustrating the hopes that the educational radicals had set on the Commission.

The battle for control of national education was also being fought on the theoretical level outside Parliament. The Tractarians and their allies strove to win the minds of the people of England with a flurry of sermons, pamphlets, and the like. The campaign had a double focus: to dispute the grounds for the State's claims to greater control of education, and to disqualify the proposals for a non-denominational system of National Education. One of the first to descend to the arena to defend the rights of the Church in the field of education

---

[44] Cf. Wood to Manning, 23 September 1838, *Manning MSS Bod.*, c. 654, fo. 474.
[45] Cf. 'Report from the Select Committee on Education of the Poorer Classes in England and Wales', PP, *Report Committees*, vol. viii, 1837–9, pp. xii–xv.
[46] Letter dated 12 March 1838, *Gladstone Papers*, British Library, Add. Ms. 44213, fo. 3.

was Henry Edward Manning. He had been asked to preach a sermon at Chichester Cathedral in support of the National Schools on 31 May 1838, and he was in correspondence with Wood about what could be most helpful in the circumstances. Manning's sermon, published towards the end of 1838, focused its attention on what could be called the philosophy of education, and his immediate aim was to refute the idea that it fell to the State, the supreme authority in determining the kind and mode of National Education. He set himself two questions: what kind of education, and under whose control? As he saw it, for Christian men education meant more than mere intellectual or civic formation: its main aim is the remoulding of nature, a shaping of the inward character after a heavenly example. Christ is the author and exemplar of this transformation, and therefore only the Church, as the depositary of his truth and of his grace, can properly educate. There is no education without religion and, he concluded, there is no religion without a creed. All other knowledge was secondary to this one. Even more, religion should imbue every aspect of secular knowledge. The role of the Church in education was defined by the above premises. In this field, she must always be the supreme court, above parents and princes.[47] Samuel Wilberforce, Manning's brother-in-law, would develop similar ideas in his sermon at Portsea in October 1838: only God was able to break the hardness of men's hearts, and rebuild them on the deepest and safest foundation. He added that the Church of England schools were then in need of greater assistance than ever: infidelity was trying, silently and decently, to supersede religion, and nowhere was this shown more plainly than in the new schemes being proposed for education.[48]

The British and Foreign also joined the debate by means of a pamphlet by its Secretary, Henry Dunn. He was in favour of encouraging rather than repressing the work of the existing societies, and attacked the Central Society's insistence on the Government taking up the reins of education. Dunn then went on to suggest the system of the British and Foreign schools as the ideal way forward: to limit religious instruction in the schools to the reading and teaching of the Bible, which would not favour one sect or prejudice another. This system offered another advantage, he added, quoting Cousin: it

---

[47] H.E. Manning, *A Sermon Preached in the Cathedral Church of Chichester in behalf of the Chichester Central Schools. Thursday, 31st May 1838* (London, 1838). Wood thought that the pamphlet could be sent accompanying one of the circulars to the Local Boards; it proved too abstract for the purpose (cf. Wood to Manning, 9 November 1838, *Manning MSS Bod.*, c. 654, fo. 477).

[48] S. Wilberforce, *The Power of God's Word needful for National Education. A Sermon preached at St John's Chapel, Portsea, October 28, 1838* (Portsea and London, 1838). Newman, in his letters to *The Times* in early 1841, would dwell on similar topics and use alike arguments to those in Manning's and Wilberforce's sermons (cf. J.H. Newman, 'The Tamworth Reading Room,' in *Discussions and Arguments on Various Subjects* (7th edn, London, 1891), pp. 254–305).

would make the schools less ecclesiastical and consequently more Christian; priestcraft led to infidelity.[49]

The Whig ministry was not inclined to let the plans of the rejuvenated National Society go unhindered: if Gladstone and his friends were able to use delaying tactics, so was the government. This was not a new tactic; grants for the normal school voted by Parliament in 1835 had been the object of a long and desultory correspondence between the Society and the Treasury, with the latter bent on deferring any grant of money to the National Society on that account.[50] Now, after the failure of the Parliamentary Committee to include the creation of a Board of Education among its recommendations, Lord John Russell presented to Parliament on 12 February 1839 his proposals for a system of national education.[51] They were soon withdrawn, and the Government gave up the attempt to have its educational plans approved by Parliament. They did not abandon them, though, and the long sought after Board of Education was set up, under the title of Committee of Council for Education, by an Order in Council in April 1839, thus avoiding the hazardous piloting of legislation on the subject through Parliament. One of the first measures of the newly-formed Committee of Council for Education was its Minute of 11–13 April, approving the setting up of a state-run normal school, and its annexed model school, in which religious instruction would be confined to the reading of the Bible. The Minute also established that the distribution of school grants was from then onwards to be the responsibility of the Committee of Council, and affirmed the Committee's right of inspection over those schools which received grants of public money. In addition, the Minute opened the way for other educational societies than the National Society and the British and Foreign to apply for grants.

James Philip Kay (later Kay-Shuttleworth), the then Secretary of the Committee of Council, in a much-quoted letter to Lord Russell in 1843, described the animus behind the government's creation of the Committee of Council:

> When your lordship and Lord Lansdowne in 1839 appointed me Secretary of the Committee of Council on Education I understood the design of your Government to prevent the successful assertion on the part of the Church of the claim then put forth for a purely ecclesiastical system of education . . . I, however, understood your lordship's Government to determine in 1839 to assert the claims of the civil power to the control of the education of the country . . . to

---

[49] Cf. H. Dunn, *National Education, the Question of Questions* (London, 1838), pp. 20 ff.
[50] Cf. J. Sinclair (ed.), *Correspondence of the National Society with the Lords of the Treasury and with the Committee of Council for Education* (London, 1839); see also Paz, *Working-Class Education in Britain*, pp. 19–25.
[51] Cf. *Hansard*, 3rd series, xiv, cols 273 ff. See also Mathison, *How can the Church educate the People?*, p. 4; and Alexander, 'Lord John Russell and the Origins of the Committee of Council on Education', pp. 407–13.

secure that the education of the country should be in harmony with all its other institutions – to vindicate the rights of conscience – and to lay the foundations of a system of combined education.[52]

It has been claimed that it was the very success of the rejuvenated National Society that precipitated the Whig government's decision to set up the Committee of Council to prevent the Church strengthening its position in the realm of education. It might be probably truer to say that the Government's plans to gain greater control of education preceded the formation of the group around Mathison, and spurred them to action.[53] The intention behind the Government's initiative was easily perceived by the friends of Church education, and this perception was subsequently reinforced by the knowledge of the part that the British and Foreign had played in Russell's decision to set up the Committee of Council for Education. The Tractarians saw it as a combined move of the Whig Government, the British and Foreign Schools Society and the radicals of the Central Society to undermine Church education.[54] The National Society made use of its annual meeting at Willis's Rooms on 28 May 1839 to respond to the government's moves. The address by the Bishop of London, seconding a resolution proposed by the Earl of Chichester, asserted that education should be Christian, and that religious instruction should be under the superintendence of the clergy and in conformity with the doctrines of the Church in this realm, as the recognised teacher of the nation. The bishop stressed that it was the obligation of the Church to provide that formation – although, the bishop added, the Church's offer was to be taken up only by those who chose to avail themselves of the privilege.[55] The response of the country, in the bishop's view, was almost unanimous in support of the National Society's stance.

Keble, as part of that mobilisation, used his position as Professor of Poetry to promote their educational plans before the University of Oxford, many politicians and other dignitaries. In his Creweian Oration of 12 June 1839, on the occasion of William Wordsworth being granted an honorary degree in Law, Keble had much to say about education, and in particular, the education of the poor (of whom Wordsworth, he said, was the poet). Keble eloquently asked that the doors of the universities be opened to them, as they had been in times

---

[52] Kay-Shuttleworth to Russell, 30 April 1843, quoted in F. Smith, *The Life and Work of Kay-Shuttleworth* (London, 1923), pp. 147–8.

[53] On 12 February 1839 Lord John Russell would mockingly suggest that the Government moves had led to the increase of zeal recently exhibited by the National Society (cf. *Hansard*, 3rd series, xlv, cols 280 and 311).

[54] *The Times* had published the April British and Foreign Schools Society [BFSS] memorandum to Russell, and denounced repeatedly what it saw as the confabulation of Whigs, BFSS and secularists (cf. Alexander, 'Origins of the Committee of Council on Education', p. 407).

[55] Cf. *Speech of the Lord Bishop of London on National Education at the Public Meeting held at Willis's Rooms, on Tuesday, May 28, 1839* (London, 1839).

past, when many of the colleges had been founded for the sake of the poor. That was an ideal to be restored. And, he added, at that very moment men 'had gone forth from the bosom of this Academy' who, 'by divine inspiration', had formed and were promoting a plan of education for the poor in the ethos and principles of the Established Church, a plan which in its higher instances was also intended to re-establish the link between the poor and the universities. And, at this point, a marginal note in the manuscript named the architects of that policy: Acland, Mathison, Wood and others. Keble's oration was not printed, but we may presume that their names were read before all assembled in the Sheldonian Theatre.[56]

The government, in order to strengthen its position, retired the minute of the Committee, but only to reinforce some of its ordinances by an Order in Council of 3 June 1839. The Parliamentary battle which followed had, as a result, a double focus: one political, in so far as the legislature had been excluded from fundamental decisions on the question of national education; the other constitutional religious. Acland and Gladstone took part in the 1839 Parliamentary debate on education, and it appears that Wood provided materials for the speeches of both his friends. The Government when speaking of the National Society and of the Foreign and British had put them on the same level, referring to them as *voluntary* societies. This was a ground that the Tractarians and their friends hotly disputed: they had tried from the very beginning to work always with the tacit or explicit approval of ecclesiastical authority, and had stressed from the first the notion that these initiatives of the National Society were actions of the Church of England *qua* Church, carrying out the role of educator of the English people assigned to her by the constitution of the country. Although the campaign had been a lay initiative in conception and realisation, this was not wholly the result of clerical negligence: it was intended as a means to disabuse the idea that those moves were an attempt by the clergy to impose clerical control on education.[57]

Acland, speaking on 19 June, insisted on the idea that the constitution of the country had established the Church of England as the educator of the people, and this constitutional role of the Church had not been altered by the relief acts allowing Dissenters to keep schools: they were forbidden to teach outside schools endowed by them. There was no excuse to take that educational charge from the Church. She was not failing in the fulfilment of her task, as witnessed by the success of her recent efforts, which Acland went on to describe.[58] Gladstone's speech the following day developed a different line of argument, one reminiscent of his just-published book on Church and State and of Manning's sermon on education. Education's aim is to give children a

[56] Cf. S. Prickett, 'The Social Conscience of the Oxford Movement: A Reappraisal', in Paul Vaiss (ed.), *Newman: From Oxford to the People* (Leominster, 1986), pp. 86 ff.
[57] Cf. Acland to Pusey, 2 April 1838, Pusey House, *LBV*, n. 38, lett. 2.
[58] *Hansard,* 3rd series, vol. xlviii (6 June to 6 July 1839), cols 563–70.

moral system, not just a technical ability. This presupposes religion. Not just any form of it: this would be unconstitutional. To the laughter of some of the Honourable Members, Gladstone affirmed that the State had a conscience, and the means to discover truth: the British Parliament had seen the truth of the Church of England, and, consequently, established it as the religion of the country.[59] The speech of the Bishop of London in the House of Lords on 5 July 1839 bore a different stamp and may not have satisfied the Tractarian members of the Committee of Enquiry because of his insistence on the role of the State in education: as the State had delegated to the Established Church the religious education of the people, this could not be changed without a deliberate and solemn act of the legislature, in all its three estates, following accurate inquiry and mature study and debate.[60] This was more than the Tractarians and their friends were ready to grant the State. The Lords went on to approve a petition asking the queen to dissolve the Committee of Council. It was rejected by Her Majesty.

It may be asked to what an extent the speeches of Gladstone and Acland fully represented the mind of the Tractarians. Were their absolute claims on behalf of the Church of England a non-negotiable principle or were they merely an opening gambit? Was there a more or less clear fall-back position for future negotiations with the government? Their public utterances were clear enough.[61] A letter of Acland to Newman in June 1835, however, opens new perspectives on this question. Acland wanted to have clear the principles in order to decide what political options were open to him and other like-minded public men. The ideal was clear in his mind: education's aim is the promotion of a right moral training, and this can only be guaranteed by entrusting the established Church with the running of the educational system. Acland saw two objections to this absolute claim. The first, at a theoretical level, could be formulated as follows: would it be right to exclude from education those who would not accept Church of England education? He did not think so, and was inclined to look for a system, short perhaps of the ideal, but having a tendency towards it, which would not deny some people access to education. Second, facing the political reality, Acland admitted that there was

---

[59] *Hansard*, 3rd series, vol. xlviii, cols 622–34; see also W.E. Gladstone, *The State in its Relations with the Church* (London, 1838). On Sunday, 21 April, Gladstone had 'read Manning's powerful Sermon on Nat[ional] Education' (*GD*, vol. ii, p. 595).

[60] Cf. *Speech of the Lord Bishop of London in the House of Lords, July 5, 1839 on the Government Plan for Promoting National Education* (London, 1839), pp. 15–20.

[61] The *British Critic* was also a good exponent of those ideas. It is significant that the Tractarian takeover of the High Church quarterly in January 1838 marked a clear shift in the educational line of the magazine: from a quasi utilitarian justification for education, a readiness to grant the State a greater role in it and to accept a diversity of educational agents, it moved towards claiming a more exclusive place for the Church of England in National Education (cf. Skinner, 'Tractarians and the Condition of England', pp. 184 ff). Those differences of approach now found themselves in confrontation within the National Society.

no likelihood of the government or Parliament accepting their absolute claims. In this situation he could see three possibilities. The first two involved the disappearance of the Establishment: the Government would either fund the schools run by the different religious denominations (religion being recognised as the basis of education) or the Government would provide 'knowledge' (as distinct from education) in its own board schools, leaving to the Churches to add the religious element outside school hours. He dismissed these two options, as either involving indifferentism or not being real education. Acland inclined himself for the third possibility: the State acknowledging that education ought to be based on religion, and religion on the Church. National Education would be entrusted to the Established Church but the State would be willing to give some assistance to a secondary system, in the hope of eventually achieving their integration into the proper scheme of national education. Would Newman reject outright entertaining the notion of this secondary system as involving an abdication of principle? He felt, among other things, that not admitting any other educator than the Church could bring about a backlash against it.[62] Unfortunately, Newman's answer is not extant but we have a reference to Acland's plan in the letter Newman wrote to Froude between 11 and 22 June 1835. Newman had actually considered Acland's proposal favourably, in principle, but on second thoughts he gave up that plan as a mare's-nest, adding in his letter that he had written to Acland accordingly.[63]

The agitation surrounding the creation of the Committee of Council was not totally unsuccessful. In face of the opposition the government, by the Order in Council of 3 June 1839, reluctantly sacrificed the normal school. The Committee of Council was, however, preserved to administer the distribution of the sums approved by Parliament for education; beside, from then onwards, grants were conditional on the acceptance by the school of the Committee's right of inspection.

---

[62] Acland to Newman, 10 June [1835], Birmingham Oratory Archives, *1838 Letters*. The letter does not give the year in which it was written. It may have been included among the 1838 correspondence because of the parliamentary educational debates of that year, in which Acland was involved. The editor of *LD*, vol. vi (p. 258, note 1), quoted the opening sentences of the letter, and considered it written in 1838. The internal evidence, and the fact that Newman quoted whole sentences of Acland's letter in his own letter to Froude of 11 June 1835, leave no room for doubt about its actual date.

[63] *LD*, vol. v, p. 79. In June 1838 Newman warned Acland against attempting a compromise: the Liberals would claim that they had accepted their principles. The way forward was to bring together all those opposed to Liberalism (cf. Newman to Acland, 17 June 1838, *LD*, vol. vi, p. 257). Could this be Newman's 1835 answer wrongly dated by the editors of *LD*?

The Right of Inspection

The Tractarians and their friends saw inspection as a thinly-veiled attempt to impose State control over Church schools. The National Society also objected to the inspection as being against Church principles, not proceeding under the sanction of Church authority. One result of the presence of the 'young gentlemen' in the Committee of the National Society was to stiffen its resolution not to accept Government money for its schools for as long as the grants were conditional on conceding the right of inspection to the Committee of Council. Wood and his friends seem to have succeeded, in the face of some wavering on the part of certain other members of the Committee, in imposing their views on the Church's independence from the State in the management of her affairs.

As a result, the National Society became engaged in a long and inconclusive correspondence with the Committee of Council for Education on the subject of inspection. The National Society insisted that inspection should be left to the Church, and its counter-proposal suggested that the inspection could be conducted by the agency of the diocesan boards, then being set up.[64] The Committee of Council, while affirming that 'no terms would be imposed inconsistent with what the Committee understands to be the fundamental principles of the Society',[65] proposed, as a compromise, that the inspectors could be nominated by the Bishop of Chichester, and afterwards appointed by the Committee.[66] This might look like a generous concession but the new men in the National Society felt that one bishop was easy to control by appointment or pressure, and, more to the point, they distrusted Bishop Otter of Chichester, who had voted for the government in the recent debate on education. The National Society reiterated its offer of inspection by diocesan boards. The answer of the Committee of Council was as uncompromising: 'My Lords', Kay wrote on 31 October 1839, 'cannot abandon the condition of inspection.'[67] After further correspondence, the National Society also entrenched itself in principle: they did 'not consider themselves at liberty to accept the grant so long as the above condition is attached to it'.[68]

Wood had hailed the decision not to submit to State inspection as 'the strongest bit of anti-Erastianism which has been afloat for many a day', and he felt at first that this could be a swallow dragging the spring after it.[69] His initial optimism, however, soon gave way to a certain degree of despondency. In a letter to Manning, he complained that the step seemed to have been taken more

---

[64] Cf. letter dated 19 July 1839, in Sinclair (ed.), *Correspondence*, pp. 16–17.
[65] Cf. letter dated 24 July 1839, *ibid.*, pp. 17–18.
[66] Cf. letter dated 17 August 1839, *ibid.*, p. 21.
[67] *Ibid.*, p. 33.
[68] Letter dated 28 November 1839, *ibid.*, p. 34.
[69] Wood to Newman, 29 October 1839, *LD*, vol. vii, p. 179.

on political and polemical feeling than on Church principles.[70] He probably felt that some had seen the educational question as a convenient battering-ram to attack the government, while others had been guided by no higher principle than to keep as much as they could of the previous order, and were ready to sacrifice high principle and long-term considerations to the material and immediate. For the time being, however, the National Society offered a united front in its dealings with the Government, and its position found the support of the generality of the clergy.

The General Committee put into effect on 12 June 1839 the recommendations of the first report of the Committee of Enquiry to set up three subcommittees: the School Committee, the Finance Committee and the Committee of Correspondence.[71] The Committee of Inquiry then ceased to operate. Its most active members – Acland, Wood, and Mathison – were elected members of the General Committee, and the Committee of Inquiry's work was taken over by the subcommittees to which the new members had been appointed.[72] The decision not to apply for grants left many schools in serious financial difficulties, and through the newly-created Finance Committee the National Society bound itself to help financially those schools which were struggling as a result of the new policy of non-cooperation with the State.[73] The financial resources of the National Society were inadequate to supply enough money for all the schools that needed it, and this required an increase in its income to make up for the shortfall. This was the task of the Subscription Committee, under the chairmanship of Lord Ashley. By 1840 it had obtained a considerable degree of support,[74] but the question in many minds was: for how long will the Church be able to keep up that level of voluntary contributions?

---

[70] Wood to Manning, 3 December 1839, *Manning MSS Bod.*, c. 654, fo. 487. Selleck is of the opinion that, although the promotion of the educational question and debate were not subservient to the Tory party, it was used by it to unsettle the government (cf. R.J. Selleck, *James Kay-Shuttleworth. Journey of an outsider* (Ilford, 1994), p. 154).

[71] Cf. Minutes Book, *General Committee National Society*, vol. 4, pp. 162–4.

[72] The General Committee had decided to ask the Committee of Enquiry [CEC] to act as the Committee to organise the General Meeting of 28 May 1839. It was also to prepare the resolutions to be moved, and to find the persons to move them (cf. Minutes Book, *General Committee National Society*, vol. 4, 20 April 1839, p. 144; and Minutes Book, *Committee of Enquiry and Correspondence, 1838* (1839), p. 109). The CEC appointed Acland, Wood, Hope and Lutwidge as a subcommittee to organise the event. The last recorded minutes of the Committee of Enquiry are dated 14 May 1839, and they dealt with the preparation of the meeting at Willis's Rooms.

[73] Cf. Minutes Book, *General Committee National Society*, vol. 4, 4 December 1839, p. 239.

[74] The number of promises of help reached 15,310 – lay and clerical. Mathison, according to Sinclair, was the principal mover of the campaign (cf. J. Sinclair, *Sketches of Old Times and Distant Places* (London, 1875), pp. 205–7).

The Terms of Union

The Committee of Enquiry's brief had also included inquiring into the rules regulating the books used in the schools. Up to that point those schools applying for union to the National Society had to give an assurance that the 'children will be instructed in the Liturgy and Catechism of the Established Church, and constantly attend Divine Service at their parish church, or other place of worship under the Establishment, as far as the same is possible, on the Lord's Day, unless such reasons be assigned for their non-attendance as are satisfactory to the persons having the direction of the School. No religious Tracts will be used in the School but such as are contained in the catalogue of the Society for Promoting Christian Knowledge [SPCK].'[75]

The last limitation was widely resented, and one which the Tractarians felt to be a barrier for the diffusion of Catholic principles and the improvement of education in general. The Committee had not been able to make much progress on this point, and its first report could only agree that: '1st That the Society shall take into its own hands the construction of an authorized list of books for the use of Schools in Union. 2nd That all discretion beyond such list shall be subject to Episcopal Control.'[76] The Committee also suggested studying the possibility of preparing a list of books on every subject of the curriculum.

The question of the terms of union went beyond the confines of the National Society. It had frequently appeared in the questioning of the witnesses called by the Parliamentary Committees on Education since 1834, and the members of the National Society had undergone some hostile questioning about their treatment of Dissenters in National Schools. During the enquiries of the 1837 Committee on Education Gladstone had tried to turn the tables on previous commissioners by questioning Kay, then a poor-law commissioner, in an attempt to extract from him an admission that the Dissenters did not mind Anglican instruction.

Gladstone, in June 1838, had presented to the Committee of Enquiry a paper of suggestions to allow the managers of the schools a certain discretion in exempting Dissenters from Catechism classes – other than Scripture ones – and from attendance to the public worship of the Church; he felt that Scripture teaching would draw them to both, the Catechism and Anglican worship. The proposal did not achieve the level of support necessary for incorporation into the report of the Committee of Enquiry.[77]

The 'young gentlemen' would have liked to see a tightening in the

---

[75] *Twenty-seventh Annual Report of the National Society*, p. 48.
[76] Minutes Book, *Committee of Enquiry and Correspondence 1838* (1839), p. 15; see also p. 3.
[77] Cf. *Gladstone Papers*, British Library, Add. Ms. 44728, fo. 83; see also Minutes Book, *Committee of Enquiry and Correspondence*, 16 June 1838, p. 11.

application of the conditions about the use of the Catechism and the requirement of attendance to public worship, in particular the first. However, there was not full agreement in the Committee of Enquiry about any changes beyond those over the link with the SPCK. In February 1839 the 'young gentlemen' set afoot moves to make more binding the study of the Catechism, but there was a good deal of difference of opinion on the subject. The General Committee was inclined to keep matters in their previous ambiguity.[78] On 19 February it approved the Committee of Enquiry's proposal to break the exclusive link of the National Society with the SPCK. The other conditions of union were not changed, except in so far as the new terms left the instruction in the Holy Scriptures, liturgy and Catechism of the Church of England under the superintendence of the local clergy.[79] The new men were disappointed by the decision. They felt that the conditions, as they stood, were not so clear as to place any definite limit upon the discretion of the clergy in enforcing the terms of union. Even so, Gladstone did not find a seconder in the Committee of Enquiry when he later moved a resolution proposing to entrust to this Committee – in its dealings with the boards, clergy and individual schools – the task of defining more precisely the full implications of the terms of union.[80]

The terms of union as newly redesigned were soon put to the test. The General Committee, meeting on 30 October 1839, read a letter from the Rev J. Gratix, Rector of Halifax, written at the instigation of Horner. Gratix enquired whether instruction in the Church Catechism could be dispensed with in the case of factory children attending school under compulsion, whose parents or guardians objected to it. The rule had until then been applied with a certain degree of flexibility. Now the discussion about the answer to be given to Gratrix's letter seems to have been rather agitated, and the Bishop of London appears to have led the opposition to a strict interpretation of the terms. The Committee stood divided, and the decision was postponed until the next meeting.[81] Newman, in a letter to Bowden, reported – on Mathison's intelligence – that the Bishop of London was trying to prevent the Church Catechism from being an essential condition for union with the National Society, and suggested that he might have the support of other fellow bishops in this matter.[82] The 'young gentlemen' felt that a fundamental principle of the National Society was at stake: to renounce the Catechism would jeopardise the success of their efforts to regain the attachment of the people to the Church of England.

---

[78] Cf. Gladstone on 15 and 20 February 1839, *GD*, vol. ii, pp. 581 ff; see also Gladstone to Manning, 23 February 1839, *Gladstone Papers*, British Library, Add. Ms. 44247, fos 61–2.
[79] Cf. Minutes Book, *General Committee National Society*, vol. 4, pp. 120–3.
[80] Cf. Minutes Book, *Committee of Enquiry and Correspondence*, 2 March 1839, pp. 98–100.
[81] Cf. Minutes Book, *General Committee National Society*, vol. 4, 30 October 1839, p. 211.
[82] Letter dated 4 November 1839, *LD*, vii, p. 177; see also Churton, *Memoir of Joshua Watson*, pp. 300–1.

The question was to be referred several times for further discussion, and the issue was not resolved until the Special Meeting of the General Committee on 29 April 1840. The meeting, attended by an unusually large number of bishops, amounted to a show of episcopal force. Wood knew what was in store for them, and decided to absent himself from the proceedings rather than put his name under a resolution he could not in conscience accept. After some discussion, the General Committee resolved 'that in the case of children employed in Mills and Factories, whose attendance to School is compelled by the statute 3rd and 4th of Willm 4th, chap. 103, the Managers of National Schools, be not considered as breaking the terms of Union if they do not enforce the rule requiring children to be instructed in the Church Catechism, in the case of any child whose parents or guardians, shall declare their wish, that such instruction be not given.'[83] This was not the last word on the matter. The following meeting of the General Committee (6 May) did not approve the minutes of 29 April, the Committee of Correspondence was asked to obtain further information, and the final decision on the matter was adjourned until the next meeting of the Committee on 23 May. At this meeting it was finally decided that there was no sufficient reason for departing from the terms of union agreed on 19 February; the managers of the factory schools, however, were allowed a certain – undefined – amplitude in the interpretation of the terms of union.[84]

The tensions within the Committee seem to have created fracture lines between the younger elements and the bishops, with Joshua Watson inclining himself towards the former in their attempts at raising the *ethos* of the National Society to a more Catholic standard.

A Compromise on Inspection

The pamphlet war had meanwhile moved its focus of attention to the government's right of inspection. James Philips Kay published in 1839 a pamphlet about the recent government measures for the promotion of education, including abundant statistical information on the numbers of those in education against the total of children, and so forth. The pamphlet criticised the

---

[83] Minutes Book, *General Committee National Society*, vol. 4, 29 April 1840, p. 253. Around that time the Committee of Council was proposing a similar clause for those schools of the Church of England not in union with the National Society (Volume of Minutes, etc. presented for 1839–40 by the Committee of the Privy Council on Education to Parliament; quoted in J. Oakley, *'The Conscience Clause'. Its History, Terms, Effect, and Principle. A Reply to Archdeacon Denison* (London, 1866), pp. 3–4). The Poor Law already established that children should not be subject to denominational religious instruction if their parents or guardians objected to it.

[84] Minutes Book, *General Committee National Society*, vol. 4, pp. 254 and 257.

inadequate provision of education, and also the poor quality of much of the education being imparted in the existing schools. Kay dwelt at length on the evil social consequences of the situation, and illustrated this point by means of some statistics about the level of instruction of the prison population at the time, showing that lack of education and criminality went hand in hand. There was also another underlying message of the pamphlet. The social disturbances associated with Chartism and the embryonic trades unions were also attributed to ignorance: men were asking for the unattainable object of wage rates 'above the level resulting for the natural laws of trade'. A good secular education would 'enable them to understand the causes which determine their physical condition, and regulate the distribution of wealth among the several classes of society'.[85] Kay's pamphlet was an instant success, and went through numerous editions.

The critics of the government preyed upon the ideas put forward to defend its plans. From the pages of the *Educational Magazine,* which he edited, and in his lectures on education, Frederic Denison Maurice, who was at the time in close association with Acland and Wood, was one of the first to come out in defence of Church education. Education, as distinct from mere instruction, was one and indivisible; it was the preserve of the Church, as the great educational agent, and she could not prejudice its independence in carrying out this trust by submitting to State inspection.[86] Robert Wilberforce, on his part, questioned the inference – inherited from the Enlightment – that knowledge rather than continuous moral and religious training was the safeguard against moral evil. He accepted that prisoners were the most ignorant amongst the population but added that this did not warrant the establishing of a relationship of cause and effect between the two facts; it was rather the case that those people were also the most destitute. When it came to inspection, Robert was concerned that a method of inspection which had a systematic bearing in any particular direction, by concentrating on a part of the curriculum, would proved irresistible and consequently deform the educational process.[87] Samuel Wilberforce, in a pamphlet which appeared about the same time as that of his brother, claimed that the Government was attempting to take control of schools by stealth: he who managed inspection managed the school. He also disputed Kay's claim that the education provided by the Church schools was insufficient, in quantity and in quality. Samuel turned the tables on the government: the shortfall in educational provision was found fundamentally in the

---

[85] [J.P. Kay], *Recent Measures for the promotion of Education in England* (16th edn, London, 1839), p. 44.

[86] Cf. F.D. Maurice, *Has the Church or the State the Power to Educate the Nation?* (London, 1839).

[87] Cf. R. Wilberforce, *A Second Letter to the Most Noble Marquis of Lansdowne, on the System of Inspection best adapted for National Education* (2nd edn, London, 1840), pp. 16 and 20 ff. It was dated 14 January 1840.

great towns and manufacturing centres, where the Church was weak and Dissent was strong and economically powerful; there it was that men were used and treated as machines. Why were there not more schools promoted by the Dissenters in the towns?[88] When it came to moral education, Samuel did not draw back from an appeal to English pride and insularity: what did the English have to learn from 'the purer French!!! Flemish, Belgic, or central European character . . .?'[89] The Church system was already *in situ*, he concluded: was it not reasonable to reinforce rather than set aside this working and already fast-expanding machinery?[90]

It was now in the interests of the government and its allies to isolate the main agents of the revival of the National Society by making the general public aware of the influences at work within it. A pamphlet by an anonymous clergyman attacked the concept of the relationships between Church and State that inspired the members of the Committee of the National Society, and complained of the small party within the National Society that was behind the objections to State inspection: it was inspired by a papalist theory of Church–State relations.[91] Others followed. The Government's offensive started soon to pay dividends: the general mood of the country was changing, and as the months went by even *The Times* was to abandon its support of the National Society's position, for criticism of its intransigence on the question of inspection.

The Whig administration, on the other hand, clearly realised the unsatisfactory character of the state of affairs. Parliament would not countenance for long that the grants voted for education were spent by the Committee of Council almost entirely on the Dissenting schools. On the other hand, the unity shown by the National Society in 1839 proved, as Wood had intimated, rather superficial. There was soon a cleft between those who were ready for a compromise in the matter of inspection, and the section which wanted to preserve the independence of the Church at the cost of monetary sacrifices. This party seems to have considered the move as a partial disestablishment which would have unleashed the dormant energies of the Church, drugged into complacency and neglect by the financial help of the State. Joshua Watson tended to side with the younger members of the General Committee on this point, and his later resignation from the Treasurership of the National Society in 1842 would be intended as a protest against the acceptance of grants – and the consequent right of inspection by the State – for St Mark's College.[92]

---

[88] Cf. S. Wilberforce, *A Letter to the Right Hon. Henry, Lord Brougham, on the Government Plan of Education* (3rd edn, London, 1840), pp. 25 ff. The statistical material presented by Kay relied fundamentally on the findings of the Manchester Statistical Society, and concentrated mostly on Liverpool and Manchester.

[89] *Ibid.*, p. 32.

[90] Cf. *ibid.*, pp. 36 ff.

[91] Cf. *The Churchman's Protest against the National Society* (London, 1840), pp. 32–3.

[92] Cf. Churton, *Memoir of Joshua Watson*, pp. 298–9; see also Sinclair, *Sketches*, p. 213.

Bishop Blomfield, who had agreed at first in refusing the grants on the condition of inspection by the Government, soon moved towards a more conciliatory position, and was eager to find a compromise.[93] He was not alone: Bishop Phillpotts had earlier clashed with Lord Ashley because of the peer's opposition to a deal.[94] Lord Lansdowne was to take the first steps on behalf of the government in the direction of a compromise. After initial conversations with Bishop Blomfield, Lansdowne wrote a letter to Archbishop Howley containing proposals to serve as basis for an agreement on the subject of inspection.[95] The long drawn out stalemate was broken in July 1840, after negotiations between the Archbishop of Canterbury and the Bishop of London with the Committee in Council, and the agreement was settled by an Order in Council dated 10 August 1840. It provided that the Archbishops of Canterbury and York should be consulted before inspectors were appointed. The Archbishops could suggest to the Committee of Council the names of persons suitable for that office, and no appointment should be made without their concurrence; moreover, if one of the Archbishops were subsequently to object in regard to the work of some of the inspectors, his appointment should be revoked. Finally, the inspectors' reports would be forwarded to the Archbishop and to the local bishops, as well as to the Committee of Council.[96]

Some welcomed this settlement as a victory for the Church, while others felt that the principle of State interference had been granted by the compromise. Acland and Wood published respective letters giving the agreement a guarded approval. The compromise was the best which the circumstances admitted, and they considered that the Whig administration had recognised in it the constitutional functions of the Church of England in education. In return, the Church had conceded the State a limited power of inspection. They, however, were still suspicious of the Government's intentions: the Church should be vigilant and jealous of undue interference. They claimed that what the remonstrances of the House of Lords could not achieve had been won – after much obloquy and hardship – by the resistance of the National Society.[97]

As far as the Finance Committee was concerned, the concordat between the

---

[93] Cf. A. Blomfield, *A Memoir of Charles James Blomfield*, 2 vols (London, 1863), vol. I, p. 270.

[94] Cf. Minutes Book, *General Committee National Society*, vol. 4, 12 July 1839, p. 175. Bishop Otter wrote to Manning on 14 July 1840 to complain of the lack of a spirit of compromise which had animated the members of the Committee of Correspondence (cf. *Manning MSS Bod.*, c. 653, fos 451–2).

[95] Cf. Lord Lansdowne to Archbishop of Canterbury, 6 June 1840, copy in Minutes Book, *General Committee National Society*, vol. 4, pp. 264–6.

[96] A copy of the Order in Council can be found in [Anon] *History and Present State of the Education Question. Being a Collection of Documents Explanatory of the Proceedings of the Committee of Privy Council on Education, from its First Appointment, in 1839, to the Present Time, and of the Steps taken for the Defence of Church Education against the Encroachments of the said Committee* (London, 1850), pp. 21–2.

[97] Cf. *The Educational Magazine*, New Series, vol. ii (August 1840), pp. 65–79.

Church and the Government involved a considerable amount of work in order to process the backlog of applications and to substitute the loans made or promised by the National Society for the grants. The concordat settled the pattern of the relations between Church and Government in the area of education till the late 1840s, and the activity of the National Society settled again into a routine which incorporated the innovations promoted by its younger members, now co-opted into the organs of decision within the society. This was a time of progressive and largely untroubled growth. Of the original plans of the Committee of Enquiry the only major project still outstanding in 1840 was the creation of the London Training College. The year 1841 saw the establishment of St Mark's Training College in Chelsea, which was to absorb a great deal of energy and most of the annual income of the National Society. Its history, not free from controversy, has been told by J.L. Alexander in his thesis on collegiate teacher training.[98]

The work of Mathison and his friends has received little recognition. Their influence, however, has been immense, and the English educational landscape is still deeply marked by the result of their exertions. They were not waging a merely negative campaign; theirs was not an effort to preserve the *status quo*, but an elaborate plan devised by people as expert as those arraigned on the other side of the argument. Some, like Wood, may have been at first unfamiliar with the subject of popular education, but others had long been interested in the educational question. They were, or became, familiar with the most recent bibliography on the matter, and their drafts and discussions showed familiarity with the educational systems of Prussia, Holland, Ireland, the activities of the Kildare Place Society, and so forth.[99]

One of their most important contributions was the creation of a network of training colleges for teachers. St Mark's and the other training colleges connected with the National Society held the initiative in the reform of teacher training in England.[100] Although the expansion of training colleges immediately after 1838 produced a few which were doomed to early failure, enough remained to provide a substantial network, and supply a considerable number of teachers. Even those which failed made their contribution to the general scheme, playing the part of a token occupation force and suggesting that there was no vacuum for the State to fill.

By 1843 the 'young gentlemen' were drawing the balance-sheet of their achievements. A great deal had been done but they were very far still from

---

[98] See footnote 2 above.

[99] See for example Gladstone's suggestions for Subcommittee B of the Committee of Inquiry, *Gladstone Papers,* British Library, Add. Ms. 44728, fos 85–94; it was dated 28 May 1838, probably the day when it was presented to the subcommittee.

[100] J.L. Alexander showed conclusively that the role of Kay-Shuttleworth in the renewal of teacher training in England had been considerably exaggerated, among others by Kay-Shuttleworth himself (cf. Alexander, 'Collegiate Teacher Training', pp. 17, 107 et al.).

their avowed aim of reattaching the English lower and middle classes to the established Church. By that time they seemed to have accepted that it was impossible to recreate a fully developed system of Church education as it had existed before the Reformation. Wood felt that the way forward was through raising in estimation and attainment the parochial school, and that could only be done by the promotion of teachers and masters through the agency of diocesan training colleges. Recruitment, however, had been disappointing. Wood thought that the diocesan clergy should make more of an effort to fill the colleges, whilst also promoting new schools.[101] Mathison, on his part, felt that they had worked hard to build up a system which would contribute to making good Anglicans of the people; now the system was failing because those who had to work it, the clergy, had been rather lukewarm in their support for the training colleges.[102] These had also failed to attract middle-class fee-paying students: the lack of prospects for advancement had acted as a deterrent for possible pupils from the commercial and middle classes.

The Tractarians have been charged with weakening the National Society by introducing into it an element of division between High Churchmen and Evangelicals who had originally worked together, so that the resulting squabbles within the Society sapped its energies, upset its expansion and opened the door to the 1870 Act.[103] That might be the case in the late 1840s, but it hardly represents the developments of the late 1830s and early 1840s, a time of expansion unparalleled in the history of the Society,[104] when Tractarians like S.F. Wood or T.D. Acland could work in close cooperation with Evangelicals like Lord Ashley or High Churchmen like Watson. Besides, it could be argued that without the revitalisation of the National Society by means of new Tractarian blood and energies, together with their successful opposition to state control of schools, the provisions of the 1870 Education Act could have arrived thirty years earlier. The 'Mathisonians' created the space for the voluntary system to grow, and made possible the birth of denominational education in England.[105]

---

[101] Cf. Wood, 'On Attaching the Middle and Lower Orders to the Church', pp. 43–9, 125–30. Mathison would make a similar point: 480 teachers were needed a year for the existing schools; 1600 if there were to be any expansion (cf. Mathison, *How can the Church educate the People?*, pp. 46 ff).

[102] Cf. Mathison, *How can the Church educate the People?*, p. 71.

[103] Cf. Alexander, 'Collegiate Teacher Training', pp. 89–91; see also H.J. Burgess, 'The Work of the Established Church in the Education of the People, 1833–1870' (PhD thesis, London University, 1954), pp. 523–5. Burgess blames in particular the later Denison controversies.

[104] In the period 1837 to 1847 the number of day-schools associated with the Church of England rose from 10,856 to 17,015; the number of Sunday schools followed a declining trend from 6,068 to 5,230 in the same period (*Monthly Paper of the National Society*, vol. xxvii (March, 1848), p. 32).

[105] Mathison mentioned in 1844 that the Wesleyan Methodists were contemplating raising 700 new schools (cf. Mathison, *How can the Church educate the People?*, p. 102). Those plans did not achieve their aim until around 1870, but there had been a rapid growth in the number

By the time the 1870 Education Act came into force, the Church of England schools had been joined by those of Methodists, Catholics and others, creating an educational structure which the State was unable to dismantle or supplant. The fact that even in the 1870s many Church schools did not survive the competition of the newly-established board schools may suggest what would have happened in 1838. The National Society and the British and Foreign would probably have given way to the State in educational matters, and the existing schools would have been absorbed in good measure by a state system established along non-denominational lines. As a result, the Churches would not have been in a position to enter into the partnership with the State that was to mark British education for a long time to come. In the event, even with the loss of some of its number after 1870, the partnership between the religious denominations and the State in education, although considerably modified as years went by, has grown and is still in operation. Mathison, Acland, Wood, Gladstone and those associated with them can be largely credited with having made it possible.

---

of Methodist schools when Mathison was writing: from 22 in 1837 to 332 in 1844 (cf. J.T. Smith, *Methodism and Education, 1849–1902* (Oxford, 1998), p. 236). The Catholic Church counted, with 236 day and 60 Sunday schools in 1843, a considerable increase in numbers since the early 1830s (cf. A.C.F. Beales, 'The Struggle for the Schools', in G.A. Beck (ed.), *The English Catholics, 1850–1950* (London, 1950), p. 367).

14

THE REVEREND CANON HENRY KINGSMILL MOORE, DD, BALL. COLL. OXON., FLS, AND CHURCH OF IRELAND EDUCATION, 1880–1927

SUSAN M. PARKES

HENRY KINGSMILL MOORE was principal of the Church of Ireland Training College, Kildare Place, Dublin for over forty years from 1884–1927. As such he became the leading spokesman on Church of Ireland Anglican education for a generation. Educated at Oxford, Kingsmill Moore was a forceful and dominating personality whose opinions were widely respected and whose expertise on educational matters was widely sought. He was one of the key influences in persuading the Church of Ireland to accept the state-aided National School system of primary education, thus ensuring the survival of the Church of Ireland parish schools. As principal of the Church of Ireland Training College for National School-teachers, the only Anglican training college in the country, he was responsible for its development from its opening in 1884 through to the 1920s. In his final decade Kingsmill Moore was faced with the crisis of the Irish political partition and the loss to the college of most of its students from the northern counties. Throughout his career he successfully championed the cause of small rural schools in Ireland and led the campaign to obtain sufficient government funding for the voluntary denominational training colleges. He was called as an expert witness to give evidence both to the Belmore Commission on Manual and Practical Instruction in Primary Schools (1898) and to the Palles Commission on Intermediate Education (1898),[1] and in 1927 at the end of his career he was appointed as the Protestant representative on the McKenna Committee on

---

[1] *Royal Commission on Manual and Practical Instruction in Primary schools under the Board of National Education in Ireland*, HC 1897 XIII.1. 1898 XLIV.1. *Commission on Intermediate Education (Ireland)*, HC 1899 XXII.175, XXIII.1., XXIV.1.

Inspection.[2] His influence on Protestant education in Ireland, both primary and secondary, was enormous and his legacy to the Church of Ireland College of Education, now so called, was to be long lasting. His portrait, by Sydney Rowley, which hangs in the boardroom of the College today, shows a confident leader, dressed in his academicals, seated in his principal's chair with the centenary book of the College on the table beside him.

Kingsmill Moore wrote an autobiography, *Reminiscences and Reflections from some Sixty Years of Life in Ireland* (London, 1930), in which he recorded his life and work in education. He also became very interested in the history of Irish education and gained a reputation as a historian. In particular, he undertook a study of the work of the Kildare Place Society, the full title of which was the Society for Promoting the Education of the Poor of Ireland. Founded in 1811, this Society had opened a training institution and model school at Kildare Place, Dublin, where it pioneered the Lancasterian monitorial system of teaching. Kingsmill Moore discovered the records of the Society stored in the basements of Kildare Place College, and he used these to write a history of the Society and its work in teacher training, which was published under the title *An Unwritten Chapter in the History of Education; the history of the Society for Promoting the Education of the Poor of Ireland, generally known as the Kildare Place Society* (London, 1904). The book is still regarded as an authoritative study, although somewhat biased, and an apologia for the Kildare Place Society. He also wrote a number of other short books on history and on the teaching of religion, which were widely read within the Church of Ireland community.[3] His contribution therefore to Irish education was both academic and practical, along with a sharp political acumen in public affairs and a determination to uphold and maintain what he considered best for Irish education.

Kingsmill Moore was born in Liverpool in 1853, one of seven children of an Anglican clergyman. His father, Reverend Thomas Moore, a graduate of Trinity College, Dublin, was incumbent of the parish of St Stephen the Martyr, a busy city parish. In 1863 Dr Moore was appointed headmaster of Midleton College, Cork, a school founded in 1696 by Elizabeth Villiers, Countess of Orkney.[4] The school had been in a state of decline in the eighteenth century, but in the nineteenth century a new headmaster, John Turpin, had revived it.

---

[2] *Commission on Inspection of Primary Schools* (Dublin, 1927).

[3] H. Kingsmill Moore, *£200,000 a year for Irish Education: how may it best be spent?* (Dublin, 1891), *The Training of Infants, with especial reference to the Sunday School* (London, 1910), The *Way to Teach the Bible* (London, 1906), *Irish History for Young Readers* (Macmillan: London, 1914), *Ireland and her Church, a short history* (Dundalk, 1937), *The Work of the Incorporated Society for Promoting Protestant schools in Ireland* (Dundalk, 1938), *The Teaching of Our Lord with reference to Finance* (Dundalk, 1942), *Reminiscences and Reflections from some Sixty Years of Life in Ireland* (London, 1930).

[4] Trevor West, *Midleton College, 1696–1996 – a Centenary History* (Cork, 1996), pp. 20–5.

Moore entered the office of headmaster after an unusual arrangement agreed by the governors whereby he exchanged places with the then headmaster, the Rev E.P. Hodgins, who went to take charge of Moore's Liverpool parish. The school had only four pupils in 1863, but by the following year Dr Moore had increased the number to sixty-two. Moore was a very successful headmaster and the school gained a reputation for thorough academic work. Mrs Moore, who died after only three years at Midleton, was an expert gardener and laid out a sunken garden that is still a memorial to her. Her son, Henry, inherited her love of gardening, which was to be one of his favourite occupations later in life.

Kingsmill Moore was educated first at Midleton and then at King Edward VI Grammar School, Bromsgrove where a number of Irish boys attended. His father wished him to go up to Oxford, and in 1873 Kingsmill Moore gained entrance to Balliol College. His experience at Oxford made a lasting impression on him, and in later life he always used the title 'Ball. Coll. Oxon.' which earned him the nickname 'Ball' throughout his career as principal of the Church of Ireland Training College. At the university he came under the influence of Dr Jowett, Master of Balliol, and Professor T.H. Green, the philosopher. He enjoyed sculling and canoeing on the river, organ and piano music, and debating at the Union. He attempted to gain a first class in 'Greats' but overworked, became ill, and had to be content with a 'pass' degree. In 1879 he was ordained for the diocese of Cork, Cloyne and Ross and began his career as a curate, first in Queenstown and later in Fermoy. He married a childhood friend, Constance, daughter of John Turpin, who had been headmaster of Midleton, and entered into forty-four years of 'happy wedlock' with a woman whom he called 'the joy and crown of my life'.[5]

Bishop Robert Gregg of Cork, who appointed him diocesan inspector of schools in 1881, first recognized Kingsmill Moore's ability. His duties were to visit the primary schools in the diocese where Church of Ireland pupils attended, including National Schools. The struggle between the Church and National Schools was still very strong in the diocese, with many clergy still refusing to accept state aid. Since the foundation of the non-denominational National School system in 1831, the Church of Ireland had refused to accept the system, which required religious instruction to be given separately from secular instruction. The Anglican Church Education Society had been founded in 1839 to support parish schools and by 1850 it had raised an annual income of nearly £7000. However, following the disestablishment of the Church in 1869–70, the income of the society had sharply declined and parish schools were faced with a financial crisis. In the1870s and 1880s many Church of Ireland parish schools chose to enter the National School system, accepting non-vested status, which gave them greater control over religious

---

[5] Moore, *Reminiscences and Reflections*, p. 39.

instruction[6] but which provided government salaries for the teachers, and equipment grants. However, many members of the Church considered this decision a betrayal of those who had fought to maintain the right to a 'scriptural education', in which religious education was integrated into all secular subjects, and a bitter rivalry continued between the two parties within the Church. In Cork, Bishop Gregg was determined that the Church of Ireland should recognize its responsibility for pupils who were attending National Schools, and therefore Kingsmill Moore was required to visit both parish and National Schools. In the former he examined all subjects, but in National Schools religion only. He travelled the length and breadth of the diocese, visiting schools in the remote areas of west Cork, where he gained invaluable experience of the education system 'on the ground'. He often had to travel by a horse-drawn side-cart, and in all weathers, but he enjoyed the hospitality of his fellow clergy, and the kindness and interest of the teachers and pupils. As a result of this work Kingsmill Moore published a short pamphlet, *What We are Doing for Our Children*, which was circulated among the clergy and brought him to the notice of senior churchmen. In 1884 he was encouraged by Bishop Gregg to apply for the post of principal of the newly-established Church of Ireland Training College for National School teachers in Dublin. He was interviewed along with four other candidates and was appointed in July 1884 to the post.

The decision of the Church of Ireland to operate a training college for National School teachers had been a difficult one, which had been discussed over a number of years. The College in Kildare Place, Dublin that had been founded by the Society for Promoting the Education of the Poor in Ireland in 1814 consisted of residential accommodation and model schools for infants, girls and boys. By 1855 the Kildare Place Society no longer had sufficient funds to run the College, so the Church Education Society [CES] had taken over the premises to use them for the training of Anglican primary teachers for parish schools. The CES College had operated successfully for twenty years under the leadership of Canon Alexander Leeper, DD, a graduate of Trinity College, Dublin and rector of St Audeon's in Dublin. It trained teachers for church schools that still operated outside of the state-aided National School system. However, in 1878, Leeper had informed the Church of Ireland that the Church Education Society no longer had sufficient funds to run the College and he requested that the Church of Ireland itself should take over the running of the College.[7] Therefore the General Synod of the Church of Ireland was faced with the difficult decision as to whether it should attempt to continue to

---

[6] A non-vested National School was one where the building had not been funded by the state. The denominational manager had stricter control over the teaching of religion and he did not have to allow clergy of another denomination to enter the school to give religious instruction.

[7] S.M. Parkes, *Kildare Place, The History of the Church of Ireland Training College, 1811–1969* (Dublin, 1984), pp. 37–56.

run a voluntary church college without state support, or whether the Church as a whole should accept that the future of Anglican primary education lay within the state-aided system. Many members of the Church still considered that the National School rules, which required the separation of religious education from secular, were unacceptable, and that the long struggle of the Church to maintain its own system of parish schools would be betrayed.

The matter of the training of teachers for National Schools had long been a controversial issue between Church and State in Ireland and the Church of Ireland was to find a strong ally in the increasingly powerful Catholic Church. The Commissioners of National Education in Ireland had founded a non-denominational training college in Marlborough Street in Dublin in 1838 which offered a six month residential training course for National School teachers. However, the Catholic Church had been critical of the non-denominational nature of the college, and in 1863 Archbishop Cullen of Dublin had condemned the college on the grounds of danger to faith and morals, and Catholic students had been forbidden to attend.[8] In 1870 the Powis Royal Commission on Primary Education in Ireland had recommended that denominational boarding houses should be attached to the state college to satisfy the church authorities.[9] However, the Catholic Church was seeking state support for its own denominational colleges, as in England, and the teacher training crisis continued to heighten as the number of untrained teachers, particularly Catholics, continued to rise. In 1874, in order to try to find a solution, the National Board had considered two schemes, one proposed by Professor J.H. Jellett of Trinity College, one of the Protestant commissioners on the National Board, to establish denominational boarding houses for trainee teachers attending the Marlborough Street college; the other, proposed by Sir Patrick Keenan, Resident Commissioner of the National Board and its senior official, to provide state aid for voluntary colleges which undertook to train teachers for the National School system. The Board accepted neither scheme in 1874, but the draft plans were available and 'were on the table'.[10]

Therefore the Church of Ireland General Synod in 1878, when faced with the decision of what to do about the Kildare Place College, decided to wait and see what options were available for the future. It was agreed that the Church should take over the premises in Kildare Place and continue to run a church college until such time as a decision could be made. A management committee

---

[8] P.F. Moran (ed.), *Pastoral Letters and other Writings of Cardinal Cullen, Archbishop of Dublin*, 2 vols (Dublin, 1882), vol. II, p. 141.

[9] *Royal Commission on Primary Education (Ireland)*, HC 1870 (C.6) XXVIII. vol. I, part I, Report of the Commissioners.

[10] *Memorials from the Council of the National Education League for Ireland and from the Elementary Education Committee of the General Assembly of the Presbyterian Church in Ireland on the subject of non-vested training colleges*. HC (210) LIX. 509.

was set up consisting of both lay and clerical members, and in 1879 they wrote to the Commissioners of National Education to ask for details of the Jellett 'Boarding House' scheme of 1874. At the General Synod of 1879 two options were considered, the first that the Church should continue to maintain an independent training college, the second that the Church should apply for state aid for a boarding house attached to Marlborough Street College. The first resolution was accepted by a still conservative Synod and the boarding house scheme was dropped. However, in 1883, under the influence of Keenan, the Resident Commissioner, the government finally agreed to offer state funding to voluntary training colleges. After much protracted debate in the Synod in 1884, the Church of Ireland agreed to apply for state aid under the new scheme to train teachers for church-managed National Schools. The Catholic Church also established two large training colleges for Catholic National School teachers, one for women and one for men, and the 1883 scheme became the foundation-stone of denominational teacher training in Ireland.[11]

In his new role as principal of the Church of Ireland Training College, Kingsmill Moore was to have the strong support and wise advice of William Conyngham, Lord Plunket, Bishop of Meath, who, more than any other figure, ensured the success of the college. Plunket was a member of a distinguished legal family and was grandson of the first Baron Plunket, Lord Chancellor of Ireland, 1830–41. He had served in his youth in missionary work in the west of Ireland and he was appointed Bishop of Meath in 1876 and was to become Archbishop of Dublin in 1884.[12] Plunket was convinced that the Church of Ireland should accept the National School system and thus obtain the necessary financial aid for its schools and teachers, and he was the key influence in persuading the General Synod in 1884 to agree to apply for aid for a denominational training college. He became manager of the Church of Ireland College, and through his leadership reassured churchmen that the future of Anglican primary education lay within the state National School system. One prudent decision was to continue a 'non-government department' within the college that continued to offer teacher training for parish schools. The students attended the same classes as the national teachers in training, but the department received no state aid. The number of 'non-government' students was never large but their presence enabled the college to maintain viability in its early years. The department was phased out in 1903, by which time the majority of clergy had accepted the National School system.

In his first ten years at the college, Kingsmill Moore established himself as a leading authority on Irish education. His main achievements were, first, as a key negotiator for the denominational training colleges in their campaign to obtain additional funding from the government; second, as an advocate for

---

[11] St Patrick's Training College, Drumcondra, run by the Vincentian Order, and Our Lady of Mercy Training College, Baggot Street, Dublin, run by the Sisters of Mercy.

[12] F.D. How, *William Conyngham Plunket, a Memoir* (London, 1900).

small rural schools and their right to particular treatment with regard to state grants; and, third as a spokesman for Church of Ireland education and its important role in the community. In his final years he successfully negotiated a formal link between the Church of Ireland Training College and the University of Dublin, Trinity College, whereby the training college students could proceed to a BA degree on satisfactory completion of their two-year training course. His contribution was widely recognized and his opinion respected, but his sometimes arrogant and dominating manner made others fear and dislike him. As an Oxford-educated Englishman, Kingsmill Moore retained a somewhat superior attitude to his fellow Church of Ireland clergymen, the majority of whom had been educated at Trinity College, Dublin. He liked to be in charge and to organize his colleagues. Though the nickname 'Ball' became one of affection, it did indicate that others 'mocked' the way in which he flaunted his Balliol College education. On the other hand Kingsmill Moore was well able to meet government officials on equal terms, both in Dublin and in London, and he was not intimidated by those in high office. He was at his best when faced with a crisis and in the midst of tough negotiations, and he worked tirelessly alongside his Catholic colleagues in education, particularly the presidents of the Catholic training colleges, in presenting a united front to the government when required. Overall he proved a formidable campaigner for Irish primary education.

Under the terms of the 1883 agreement, the voluntary training colleges received a state grant of only seventy-five per cent of their expenditure. This grant was paid retrospectively on a capitation basis as students successfully completed their training. The colleges received no capital grants to develop facilities or buildings. However in 1890 the colleges gained a major concession from the government known as the Balfour 'Free Home' Scheme whereby they were given capital loans based on the valuation of their existing buildings. Kingsmill Moore and the presidents of the two Catholic colleges, St Patrick's, Drumcondra, and Our Lady of Mercy, Baggot Street, argued that they had been promised parity with the state college in Marlborough Street which was in receipt of full grants. Kingsmill Moore was at the centre of the discussions, travelling to London to lobby their case with the Irish Chief Secretary, A.J. Balfour. This scheme enabled the training colleges, while retaining their voluntary status, to put up new buildings and to improve greatly their facilities. Kingsmill Moore also took the lead in the campaign to defend the position of the small rural schools. Many of the Church of Ireland National Schools were one- or two-teacher schools, and the lowest number of pupils for recognition for a state capitation grant was fifteen. In 1890 this figure was lowered to ten pupils in response to pressure from the Church of Ireland. However, when the Irish Education Bill of 1891 was introduced, to make primary education compulsory and free, it was proposed to pay an average capitation grant to schools in lieu of fees.[13] The Church objected to this policy,

---

[13] *Bill to improve National Education in Ireland*, HC 1892 (420) IV. 645.

pointing out that small schools would suffer, and Kingsmill Moore wrote an influential pamphlet entitled *£200,000 a year for Irish Education: how may it best be spent?* Again, the Church was successful in persuading the government to change its mind, and the terms of the 1892 Education Act included increased teacher salaries and improved financial support for small schools.

In the same year Kingsmill Moore, as president of the Dublin and Central Branch of the Teachers' Guild, was invited to London to give evidence to the Select Committee on the Teachers' Registration and Organization Bill which was chaired by Sir Richard Temple.[14] As a teacher and educator, Kingsmill Moore favoured the registration of all teachers, both primary and secondary, and the establishment of minimum professional qualifications. He informed the committee that the Teachers' Guild had approached the Royal University of Ireland with a view to introducing a diploma in education for teachers that would include theory and practice. (Later Kingsmill Moore was to serve as an examiner for the Royal University when the diploma was introduced in 1898.) He also had the opportunity to make his views public when he was asked to be a witness to the Belmore Commission on Manual and Practical Instruction in the Primary Schools (1898) and also to the Palles Commission on Intermediate Education (1899).[15] To the former he emphasized the need for increased resources for primary teacher training in order to prepare for the new broader curriculum which the government was proposing to introduce in 1900; and to the latter he again stressed the need for professional qualifications and registration for secondary teachers. In 1900 he entered into another battle to defend small schools when the government, in an effort to reduce the number of small schools, decided that the lowest number for recognition of a school was an average attendance of twenty-five pupils. The Church of Ireland rose to the defence of its schools and a major public campaign was launched with Kingsmill Moore to the fore.

Eventually sufficient pressure was brought to bear to defeat the proposal. But the future of Church of Ireland National Schools was bleak as the new structure of grade salaries for teachers, which was introduced in 1900, militated against small schools. In 1908, another attempt was made to raise the average attendance figure to thirty pupils, which would have meant the loss of half the Church of Ireland National Schools, and once again Kingsmill Moore was called to London to lobby the Irish Chief Secretary, Augustine Birrell. The Church of Ireland was again successful, and Kingsmill Moore regarded his work for the small school as one of the most important achievements of his

---

[14] *Select Committee on the Teachers' Registration and Organization Bill*, HC 1890–91 XVII, pp. 287–99.

[15] *Commission on Manual and Practical Instruction in Primary Schools, Minutes of Evidence*, pp. 397–408, HC 1897 (C.8383) XLIII; *Commission on Intermediate Education, Minutes of Evidence*, pp. 439–701, HC 1899 (C.9512) XXIII.

career – and undoubtedly the survival of these schools into the mid twentieth century was due largely to his actions. Also the denominational divide within the National School system was strengthened by the continued existence of Church of Ireland schools.

By 1900 Kingsmill Moore was a widely known and respected figure in Irish education. The College was flourishing and well established, and he turned his energy to other interests. He was elected a canon of St Patrick's Cathedral, Dublin, where he attended regularly. In 1891 he had founded the Church of Ireland Educational Association to develop the teaching of religion in schools. The association was very active and published a programme of religious education for Church schools. He also was appointed secretary to the educational committee of the Standing Committee of the Church of Ireland General Synod and secretary of the Sunday School Society of Ireland. In both positions he was able to influence the course of Protestant education. In the area of secondary education he was a long serving governor of the Erasmus Smith Trust, which ran boys' grammar schools in Dublin, Galway and Tipperary. He was also a governor of The King's Hospital School, Dublin and of the Celbridge Collegiate School for girls, which was run by the Incorporated Society for Promoting Protestant Schools in Ireland. In an area close to his heart, he was chairman of the Island and Coast Society that assisted small island schools. He published a number of education booklets – *Class Teaching* (1888) and *The Fundamental Principles of Education* (1889) – both of which drew on his practical experience of teaching training. His ideas on the 'leading thought' method of religious teaching were published in 1915 in a popular book, *The Way to Teach the Bible* (1906), which was based on his work with the training college students. His principal research interest, however, became the history of the Kildare Place Society. In 1904 he published a history of the society entitled *An Unwritten chapter in the History of Education, being the history of the Society for Promoting the Education of the Poor of Ireland, 1811–1831*.[16] The book, though a partisan defence of the work of the society and its principles of non-denominational education, still remains a standard work on the subject.

Kingsmill Moore's interest in the history of the Kildare Place site led him to organize a centenary celebration in 1911. This event marked the height of his career – he was honoured and praised for his work in establishing the training college and for his leadership in Church of Ireland education. The celebrations were held over a weekend in June 1911 and included a service of thanksgiving in St Patrick's Cathedral, Dublin, with a sermon by the Rev Bernard Reynolds, Prebendary of St Paul's Cathedral and inspector of the church training

---

[16] The Kildare Place Society had pioneered the monitorial system in Ireland and had built a training institution and model schools in Kildare Place. The archives of the Society are held in the Church Ireland College of Education, Rathmines, Dublin.

colleges to the Archbishops of Canterbury and York. Kingsmill Moore addressed a packed lecture hall on the history of the Kildare Place Society, and a garden party was held in the grounds of Iveagh House, the home of the wealthy Guinness family. Lord Aberdeen, the Lord Lieutenant, who gave away the prizes, visited the college and a special centenary ode was composed to mark the occasion. Past students flocked back to the College for the celebrations and *The Centenary Book of the Church of Ireland Training College, 1811–1911* was published with all their names listed. The portrait of Kingsmill Moore by the artist Sydney Rowley was presented to him by his former students, and it portrays the man in his prime, confident and assured, proud of the college and its achievements.

However, the years ahead were to be filled with difficulties, sadness and decline. On the political front the advent of Irish nationalism and the approach of Home Rule for Ireland were very difficult for a man like Kingsmill Moore, who had been a loyal unionist and supporter of the Crown. He was proud of his Oxford degree and of the English connection. Earl Cadogan, the Lord Lieutenant, had been invited to open the new College extension in 1903, and on the occasion of the Royal visit to Ireland in 1911 Kingsmill Moore had much enjoyed attending a garden party at the Viceregal Lodge. The First World War brought a further decline in the number of young men entering the College, and restricted financial resources and other shortages made life at the College difficult. He soldiered on with reduced student numbers and an aging staff, but in 1916 he fell ill and had to take six months' rest. The end of the war brought little respite as the political partition of Ireland loomed ahead. The College had always drawn the majority of its students from the Ulster counties, where the Church of Ireland was strongest, and now it faced the possibility of losing them. In 1922, following the setting up of the Irish Free State and the province of Northern Ireland, the College tried hard to retain the right to train teachers for both jurisdictions, but despite lengthy negotiations with the new Northern Ireland Ministry of Education, the College failed to obtain this privilege. It was now reduced to serving the needs of the Protestant minority in the Free State. The Church of Ireland as a whole did not accept the political division and continued to operate as an all-Ireland institution, but this did not prove possible in the area of teacher education. The crux of the problem for the northern education officials was the compulsory Irish language policy adopted by the Free State Department of Education. The teaching of Irish became compulsory in all National Schools and in the teacher training colleges. 'Partition' created a major division between the two educational systems, which was to widen as the years went by, and the opportunity of retaining the education of northern and southern teachers together was lost.

For Kingsmill Moore the situation was very difficult, and he was now in his late sixties. Nonetheless he showed great courage in striving to adapt the College to the new regime and to ensure its survival. The Irish language had never been taught in the College, and the Irish Literary Revival had made little impact, though Kingsmill Moore himself had written *Irish History for Young Readers* (1912), which was designed for use by Church of Ireland pupils in National Schools. Under the new regulations for training colleges, the Irish language became a compulsory part of the training programme. Kingsmill Moore developed cordial relations with the new officials of the Department of Education, who were sympathetic to the problems of the College and were willing to allow some time for it to adjust. He also had the strong support of Archbishop J.A.F. Gregg of Dublin, who was a manager of the College and determined that the Church of Ireland children would have as good an education as any in the new state. In fact, the acceptance by the College of the need to encourage the teaching of Irish in Protestant schools proved influential among the whole Church of Ireland community, and assisted the integration of that community into the Irish Free State. The standard of Irish among entrants to the College was greatly helped by the setting up of a distinct Church of Ireland preparatory teacher training college funded by the government, in which all subjects were taught in the Irish language. This college, Coláiste Mobhí, was one of seven preparatory colleges set up by the government in 1926 to provide secondary level education in Irish for prospective primary teachers.[17] The respect in which Kingsmill Moore was held in the new state was shown by the invitation to sit on the government committee set up in 1925 to review the new National School curriculum. As the Protestant representative and 'elder statesman', he was able to stress the difficulty which many schools were experiencing with the Irish language course. The final report of the committee recommended a reduction in the amount of Irish to be taught in schools which could now choose to offer either a 'higher ' or 'lower' course depending upon the aptitude of the teachers and pupils.[18] The following year Kingsmill Moore was invited again to sit on the McKenna Committee on the primary school inspectorate and his experience and knowledge of the primary education system proved useful to its deliberations.[19]

The last major achievement of Kingsmill Moore was the establishment of a formal link between the College and the University of Dublin, Trinity College. With the political changes afoot it was considered wise for Protestant institutions in the south to stand together and support each other. In 1922, after extended negotiations, an agreement was drawn up between the two institutions whereby students who had successfully completed their two-year training could proceed to a BA degree at Trinity College. In addition, the students in training were to attend the university on a regular basis for lectures in arts and in theory of education provided by the university's School of Education. A chair of education had been created in the university in 1905, but

---

[17] Parkes, p. 150.
[18] *National Programme Conference Report and Programme* (Dublin, 1926).
[19] *Committee on Inspection of Primary Schools* (Dublin, 1927).

the new arrangement with the training college resulted in the creation of a School of Education and the appointment of a new full-time professor of education whose salary was to be shared between the two institutions. Regrettably, the partnership did not work as well as had been hoped, owing to a personality clash between the new professor of education, R.J. Fynne, and the principal of the Training College. From the start there were arguments over lecture times, examinations and teaching practice. Fynne, who had studied in London, was an expert on Montessori methods and had a much more liberal approach to teacher education. He considered Kingsmill Moore's views to be autocratic and 'out of date'. In particular the two clashed over the practice of 'Crit. Lessons' which were still held in the Training College as an important part of practical training. The principal himself had presided for many years over these sessions, where one student taught a short lesson to pupils from the model school before an audience of students and staff, who 'criticized' afterwards. The ordeal was frightening for many students and Fynne recommended that the practice should end as being 'not in keeping with an institution affiliated to a university'. The conflict between the two men was not just personal but reflected the difference between the more liberal approach of the university and the more didactic and applied methodology of a traditional training college. Sadly, the relationship between the university School of Education and the College remained distant, and neither benefited as much as they might from the link. However, many of the students made use of the privilege offered to proceed to a degree, and some appreciated the lively stimulus of Professor Fynne's university lectures.[20]

By 1927 Kingsmill Moore was a tired and elderly man. He found it very hard to retire and to leave the College that had been his life's work for forty-three years. He did not like the changes and reforms which his successor, the Rev E.C. Hodgins, had to make to modernize the College, and 'the old principal', as he liked to be called, continued to try to interfere in the running of the College. Unwisely, he remained a governor and this did not make things easy for his successor. However, outside of the College, he continued to take an active part in educational matters and to write. His autobiography, *Reminiscences and Reflections*, was published in 1937 and recalled his achievements in a lively, personal style. He continued to take a keen interest in the affairs of the Celbridge Collegiate School and in 1938 published a short history of the Incorporated Society for Promoting Protestant Schools in Ireland, which was a defence of the Society and of its work for Protestant education.[21] He also published a short history of the Church of Ireland in 1937, which emphasized the Irish Celtic roots of the Church, the reforms of the sixteenth century and

---

[20] Parkes, pp. 135–40.
[21] *The work of the Incorporated Society for Promoting Protestant Schools in Ireland* (Dundalk, 1937).

the importance of disestablishment in 1870.[22] In his latter years gardening was his main interest at his house, Cedar Mount, in Dundrum, Co. Dublin, where he had created a beautiful display of flowers and shrubs. This interest resulted in his delightful book, *Joys of the Garden Month by Month* (1936).[23] He was a fellow of Linnean Society and often used this title after his name. He died in 1943 at the age of 89.

Kingsmill Moore's legacy to Church of Ireland education was one of a strong defender of the Church's rights and obligations to provide schooling for its own children, and of the need to speak out on important educational issues of public policy. The College which he led for forty years survived the vicissitudes of the twentieth century and still educates Protestant teachers for National Schools; small rural schools are still valued and protected; and the historical work which he undertook has preserved the records of the Kildare Place Society for posterity. Although he was known and at times disliked for his forceful personality and powerful leadership, his staff at the college served him loyally, and other churchmen recognized his powers of persuasion and untiring energy. His political acumen and determination served the Church of Ireland community well during the critical years of the new Irish Free State and ensured that the Protestant voice, however small, was acknowledged and listened to in the development of public education policy.

In the foreword to Kingsmill Moore's book in 1937 on the history of the Church of Ireland, Archbishop John Gregg of Dublin, wrote of the author:

> There are few men living who have been so closely connected in official ways with the Church of Ireland from soon after its disestablishment in 1870 as the former Principal of the Church of Ireland Training College (1884–1928): his first hand knowledge of the principal events of that period and of the principal actors in them, as well as his membership for nearly forty years of the Standing Committee of the General Synod, enable him to write of the reconstruction of the Church's affairs from the standpoint of one who watched its daily progress.

---

[22] *Ireland and her Church, a short history* (Dundalk, 1938).
[23] *Joys of the Garden, Month by Month* (Dublin and Cork, 1936).

15

'SCOTT'S FOLLY': JOHN SCOTT AND THE DEVELOPMENT OF THE WESLEYAN EDUCATIONAL SYSTEM

JOHN T. SMITH

IN HIS first term as President of the Wesleyan Conference in 1843, John Scott called for the Connexion to create 700 elementary schools within seven years. The Wesleyan Methodists by this time had a mere 234 schools, many of these the result of Scott's personal encouragement. He was to be the instrument through which this target was achieved and through which the Church would become a formidable educational force in the Victorian period, surpassed only by the Church of England and the British and Foreign School Society. As Principal of the Westminster Training College, he became an educationalist of high repute and every year he proclaimed the Wesleyan views on education in his inaugural lecture. He also put the denomination's views to the Newcastle Commission in 1859. Matthew Arnold counted him among his closest friends. Whenever the latter was puzzled by some educational problem, he would say, 'I must consult Scott about it.' Yet he has been largely ignored by historians. He is not mentioned in the *Dictionary of National Biography*, no biography has ever been written about him, and even articles on his contribution to Wesleyan Methodism are limited to those few written shortly after his death in 1868. Yet he was a significant figure in educational circles.

He was born in Copmanthorpe, near York, on 16 November 1792. His father was a farmer and in his early life John often came into contact with the itinerant Wesleyan preachers who visited the village. He was converted at the age of ten at a meeting held in his father's barn. He diligently used to walk to York on Sunday afternoons to attend children's meetings.[1] He joined the Methodist society and became a local preacher when only eighteen. The

---

[1] *Watchman* (22 January 1868), p. 29.

superintendent of the circuit saw him as a promising preacher and recommended him to the ministry, which he entered in 1811, still only nineteen and with few educational advantages. His first circuit, Winterton in Lincolnshire, was an agricultural one and ideally suited to the son of a farmer. In the following years he moved to Patrington in Yorkshire, Hull, Brentford and then in 1817 to Windsor to be Superintendent of the small circuit. In 1833 he was elected to the Legal Hundred and he became Treasurer of the Missionary Society three years later, giving him the opportunity to display his innate financial acumen. However, his greatest contribution to his church was the development of its education policy.

In 1838 a Wesleyan Education Committee (WEC) was established at a time when Wesleyan Methodism could boast only 22 schools. Scott was its chairman from 1844 until his death. In 1841 it presented a draft plan for Wesleyan education that was later modified personally by Scott. All Wesleyan schools had to be 'avowedly and practically connected as to their government and denomination with Wesleyan Methodism as a branch of the visible church of Christ'. All teachers had to be connected with the Wesleyan Church. Every school had to begin and end with prayers and had to use the Authorised Version of the Bible and the Wesleyan hymn book and catechism. However, Scott believed in freedom of conscience and schools were instructed to avoid a 'sectarian exclusiveness, by admitting children whose parents, of whatever denomination, shall voluntarily place them under care'.[2] The deed of settlement upon which all Wesleyan schools were to be founded emphasised that 'no child shall be required to learn any catechism or other religious formulary, or to attend any Sunday school or place of worship to which his or her parent shall on religious grounds object'.[3] Such a stance was applauded later by the Prime Minister, Lord John Russell, who went on to proclaim that 'the principle on which the Wesleyans conduct their schools is the least open to objection'.[4] The aim of Wesleyan education was not proselytism. Scott emphasised to his Westminster students in 1857 that, 'we do not want the State's money to enable us to make Methodists'.[5] In 1855 he commented that if a child's parents attended another church where 'evangelical truth' was taught they (the Methodists) were happy to leave religious guidance to them. However, when the parents did not attend a place of worship, the teacher would endeavour to introduce the child to Methodism. Scott added, 'and if, through the child, he can reach the parents, who may be living ungodly lives, and can bring them under Christian instruction, he widens his range of usefulness.'[6]

[2] *Wesleyan Education Report* [*W.E.R.*] (1849), p. 6.
[3] *Schools and the Education of the Poor. A proposal for a new Methodist school at Great Grimsby* (pamphlet, 1856), p. 2.
[4] *Ibid.*, p. 2.
[5] *W.E.R.* (1857), p. 45.
[6] *Ibid.* (1855), Appendix II, p. 116.

Scott had to contend with a general apathy towards the subject of education within Methodism. J.H. Rigg later pointed out that 'neither the need nor the power of education was appreciated, and many were sceptical as to the tendency and scope of the whole movement.'[7] Scott's first year of Presidency of Conference, 1843, saw much dispute over the subject. Sir James Graham's Bill of that year sought as part of a factory act to establish three hours of compulsory education for children in cotton, flax and silk factories.[8] The new factory schools were to be built and inspected by the government, but Anglicans were placed in a position of great influence. Schoolmasters had to be approved by the bishop as competent to give Anglican instruction. The chairman of each board was to be the local Anglican clergyman and in certain periods of the day there would be instruction in the Anglican catechism and liturgy (although dissenting parents could remove their children). The Bill particularly affected the Wesleyans as they were strong in the factory towns of the North. Moreover, they were suspicious of increasing Tractarian influence within the Established Church. Many Wesleyans were afraid their mother church was being Romanised and feared the possible return of Papal influence within the Established Church. They also maintained religious objections to the development of ritualism and the corresponding decline in the acceptance of absolute Scriptural authority. On 13 May 1843 Scott wrote to Jabez Bunting on the Wesleyan resolutions passed by a special committee on education, which Bunting had missed. Scott described that at the commencement the feeling had been 'very strong and by some of the speakers expressed in no very measured terms'. The Leeds Wesleyans in particular saw no good intentions in the Government proposals and wanted to oppose any system of 'combined' education. They saw grants to educational societies as 'the only practical means of instructing the people'. Other Wesleyans, from the country, were more inclined to support a united system.[9]

The Minutes of Conference of 1843 denounced the Graham Bill as 'the most objectionable and alarming . . . and likely to inflict the greatest injury to the numerous Sunday and weekday schools already supported by the voluntary zeal and liberality of the Wesleyan body.' The Church declared, 'We are friendly to the Establishment but not those grievous errors that are now tolerated within her pale.' In June 1843, Scott, as President, and Bunting saw the Prime Minister, Robert Peel, and Graham to represent the Wesleyan desire for the educational clauses of the Factory Bill to be withdrawn. This did indeed

---

[7] *Ibid.* (1888), p. 50.

[8] Details of the Bill are given in J.T. Ward and J.H. Treble, 'Religion and Education in 1843: Reaction to the Factory Education Bill', *Journal of Ecclesiastical History*, vol. 20 (April 1969), pp. 79–110. The reactions of the Roman Catholic, Congregational and Baptist churches are covered in detail, but coverage of those of the Wesleyan Church is limited.

[9] W.R. Ward, *Early Victorian Methodism: the Correspondence of Jabez Bunting, 1830–1858* (London, 1976), pp. 286–7.

happen. The United Committees of the Church showed their delight at the decision on 28 June with resolutions under the signature of Scott, their chairman, rejoicing that 'those evils have been averted which such clauses were, in their opinion, calculated to inflict upon numerous Sunday and weekday schools now supported by the voluntary zeal and liberality of the Wesleyan and other religious communities and upon their efforts to extend the inestimable benefits of Scriptural Education.'[10] The Committee, however, recognised the urgent duty of 'extending more generally to the children of the labouring classes the advantages of a religious and useful education' and this demanded an active educational policy from the church.

In November, the Special Committee met again to discuss the education question and resolved, under Scott's chairmanship, that it was of paramount importance to give 'a Scriptural and decidedly religious education' to young persons generally and to the poor in particular. Supported by Jabez Bunting, Scott carried a motion committing the Church to the provision of 700 schools in seven years, and a General Education Fund was to be established from a collection taken up throughout the Connexion. Wesleyan Ministers were urged to co-operate with congregations in the establishment and supervision of schools as being 'an integral and indispensable part of their ministerial and pastoral duty'.[11] Meetings were subsequently held throughout the country to raise funds for Wesleyan education. Scott spoke at many of these and raised remarkable sums of money for the period. On 15 February 1844 he went to Waltham St, Hull and to York, where he raised £100 and £400 respectively for

---

[10] *Watchman* (28 June 1843), p. 209. There was already great mistrust of the Anglican High Church before this date, with Jabez Bunting claiming at the Manchester Conference of 1841 that no one on earth or in heaven could reconcile Methodism and High Churchism. O. Chadwick, *The Victorian Church*, 2 Parts (London, 1966), Part I, p. 342, does not analyse the Wesleyan response to the Graham Bill in detail, but he does comment that the Wesleyan body, which had steadily refrained from joining dissenting attacks upon the established church 'joined battle upon these clauses, because of the spirit hostile to the Reformation which filled so many of the clergy'. Graham was disappointed in his hope that Wesleyan Methodism would at least preserve what was its 'middle role between Anglicanism and the Free Churches'. However, John Kent in the *History of the Methodist Church in Great Britain*, vol. 2 (London, 1978), p. 243, claims that 'the rise of Anglo-Catholicism had frightened the Wesleyans into opposition . . . and Graham was unfairly accused of joining in a Puseyite plot for getting the education of the people into the hands of a "priestly monopoly".' He also points out that it was the laity, rather than the ministerial group led by Scott, which really disliked the idea of the State entering the field of education, and that this led to a breakdown in unanimity on the subject in 1846 over government grants to Wesleyan schools, and ultimately to defections from Wesleyan Methodism. David Hempton has argued in *Methodism and Politics in British Society, 1750–1850* (London, 1984), that the bill marked the parting of the ways between Methodism and the Church of England, over Tractarianism. Discussion of this may be found in J.M. Turner, *Conflict and Reconciliation: Studies in Methodism and Ecumenism in England, 1740–1982* (London, 1985), p. 163 and in John T. Smith, *Methodism and Education, 1849–1902* (Oxford, 1998), pp. 9–10.

[11] *Ibid.* (8 November 1843), p. 361.

the fund, this at a time when the average annual salary for Wesleyan schoolmasters was £70. By 1844 over £12,000 had been raised, but regret was expressed that the target of £20,000 had not been achieved.[12] By the following year the total had reached £19,000. The education question was regarded as so important that Scott persuaded Conference to combine the Chapel (building) fund with the General Education Fund and make an appeal to congregations in support of this united fund.[13] Collections and subscriptions continued to be made to the Education Fund. In a letter of 1856 Scott personally praised Islington Circuit for its efforts, though he reflected that other circuits were not as forthcoming.[14] At the 1847 Conference he strongly urged the expediency 'if not absolute necessity' of connecting a school with every principal chapel.[15]

In spite of his success in encouraging the expansion of the Wesleyan school network, Scott recognised the necessity for more funds and he called a meeting of leading Wesleyans in 1847 to consider the Church's application for State grants for their schools. Scott invited J.H. Rigg, who worked under him at Spitalfields, and William Arthur to attend as observers. There were about a dozen of the principal members of the WEC – with such notable figures as Jabez Bunting, Samuel Jackson, William Bunting, Thomas Vasey and George Osborn. Samuel Jackson and William Bunting were totally opposed to allowing the government any share in organising national education. Jackson pleaded for individual liberty in the interest of teachers and for parental right of choice in the education of their children. William Bunting insisted on the danger (he claimed certainty) that if the evangelical churches accepted government grants, the Roman Catholics could not be excluded. Rigg later noted the 'utterly discouraging contrast' between the idealistic view which warned the State not to be involved in national education 'in the faith that the Churches both could and would do the work' and the 'hard reality which had to be faced in the unpreparedness and indisposition of the Churches generally to accept that ideal . . .'[16] After some deadlock, Lord Ashley, later Earl of Shaftesbury, came to speak to Scott in private, after which Scott, using his favourite phrase that they had to 'show cause', persuaded the group to accept the possibility of grants. Rigg recalled his 'slow, unambitious, but sagacious' speech, which analysed the facts of the educational needs of the nation and the conviction on the part of leading statesmen that moral and Christian instruction was a necessity, but also pronounced that the ideas of Jackson and Bunting were great ideals but could not be carried out in practice. Ashley had assured him that no school where the Holy Scriptures in the Authorised Version were not read would be awarded grants, and this was expected to

[12] *W.E.R.* (1844), p. 10.
[13] Methodist Church Archives, letter from J. Scott to Peter Kruse, 23 September 1844.
[14] John Wesley's Chapel, Bristol, letter from John Scott to J. Keeling, 12 July 1856.
[15] *Watchman* (28 July 1847), p. 356.
[16] J.H. Rigg, *Wesleyan Reminiscences: Sixty Years Ago* (London, 1904), p. 108.

dissuade Roman Catholics. He thus secured a guarded and conditional consent to co-operate with the Government and he drew up the resolution to be brought before the Conference, calling on congregations in somewhat negative terms 'not to offer any further connexional opposition to the scheme'.[17] Scott introduced this to the Conference in July 1847 and it was reported in the *Watchman* newspaper:

> He wished the question had not been brought forward . . . owing to the state of feelings of religious parties in this country. On account of the immense difficulty, he wished the government had left all parties to themselves . . . if the Connexion had been left to go on in its former way, they could have built schools and maintained them, as they had built chapels; and they would have succeeded in the course of time, in getting a school connected with each chapel . . . but . . . the government called upon the country to furnish, in a short time, a large number of schools, so that a school should be provided for every destitute population; and that these must not be dame schools, nor schools conducted by uneducated and untrained men, and at a trivial cost – for unless they had first rate masters, they might as well do nothing at all.[18]

He told Conference members that he had to think very carefully before he declined all state aid and had come to the conclusion that 'if the terms are safe' and if they could receive the money on principles that accorded with their own they ought to apply for grants. Again he denied that it would open the door to 'Papists', as they would have to use the Authorised Bible. The Conference was convinced by Scott, and the time of any application was left to Scott's Education Committee 'whose ability, integrity and good intentions' had Conference's confidence. The special committee met in September and Scott met Kay-Shuttleworth, the Secretary of the Committee of the Privy Council on Education, in December 1847. In the following year the Church accepted grants and inspection for the first time, with the proviso that any inspector would be first approved by the Education Committee itself. This was largely Scott's achievement, and the additional finance encouraged the expansion of the Wesleyan educational system.

Scott similarly addressed the problem of teacher training. By the 1840s the Wesleyans were sending forty-two students a year for training at John Stow's academy in Glasgow. In 1843 suggestions had been made for the establishment of a Wesleyan teacher training college. Scott was convinced of the value of the scheme. In 1845, with Thomas Vasey, he visited St John's Training College in Battersea and he encouraged that a similar institution be erected for prospective Wesleyan teachers. He was influential in the choice in 1847 of Westminster as the site of the proposed Wesleyan training college, in spite of the fact that a more salubrious site was offered. Scott wanted an area where

---

[17] *Ibid.*, p. 110.
[18] *Watchman* (28 July 1847), p. 356.

there was an abundance of illiterate children for the 'model' school and he did not wish the potential teachers to be spoiled in training by a long absence away from the dwellings of the poor and among the attractions of 'superior life', so that they might become disinclined and unfit to undertake the arduous and self-denying duties of school teachers.[19] It took ten years to raise the funds for the erection of Westminster College and even when it was completed many Wesleyans predicted it would never be filled. Scott pushed through the measure and Rigg describes this as a marvellous work of faith by a man who 'never either hasted or rested'.[20] The project was even nicknamed 'Scott's Folly' at the time. He badgered the Government to help with the financing of the college, and Kay-Shuttleworth granted him £7,000 in 1849.[21] He requested a further grant two years later and was given an additional £500 for the Model school attached to the college. In November 1850, he dispatched letters from WEC to hold meetings in all district towns to try to raise £10,000 for the Westminster College buildings. The college was finally completed in 1852 and, after his second term as President, Scott was appointed its first Principal.

He decided at the beginning of his principalship of Westminster College to deliver an annual inaugural lecture, although, as he was ill when the College opened, his first was not delivered until 1854. These long analyses of the state of education, both Wesleyan and national, were important in that they achieved a substantial audience through the general and Wesleyan press and the annual Wesleyan Education Report. Matthew Arnold attended some of these inaugurals, as did notable educational figures of the day. Hundreds of teachers were trained during his sixteen-year principalship and were influenced in their practices by his ideas. Scott was concerned with revitalising education. An analysis of his speeches reveals the Wesleyan ethos of education in the mid-Victorian period. He was utterly convinced of its value *per se* and his words were influential in determining Wesleyan attitudes to the subject. In 1854 he pronounced:

> The human intellect gains expansion, and vigour and acuteness by activity. *It must work* or dwindle and starve. It must THINK, think habitually, earnestly, consecutively – or it will lose its power of thinking. The mind must do something, must invent something fresh, must work and wrestle with new problems and deep propositions in order to give hardness and vigour to its own sinews.[22]

He went on to emphasise his belief in the joy of learning:

> Your schools will lack attention, and, in great measure, usefulness if you do not enliven the dryness of school instruction, from time to time, with such

---

[19] F.C. Pritchard, *The Story of Westminster College, 1851–1951* (London, 1951), p. 15.
[20] *W.E.R.* (1888), p. 51.
[21] *W.E.R.* (1849), pp. 61–6.
[22] *Ibid.* (1853), Appendix II, p. 102.

explanations of common things as only a competent knowledge of the principles of physical science will enable you to give.

The emphasis on science in elementary education was in the vanguard of educational thought, with the place of the subject even in the more advanced schools only just being recognised. He did not disparage secular education, and in his 1860 inaugural he pronounced:

> We have no controversy with those who contend that all children should be educated and that education in schools such as ours should give the knowledge which is wanted for this world – should instruct and train them for human society and for the business and pursuits of the present life.[23]

In 1855 he expressed very liberal conceptions of discipline and school atmosphere. He deplored schools where 'sentiments of fear are habitual', and he praised Wesleyan schools which HMIs had found 'present a happier appearance'. He advised future Wesleyan teachers:

> If a teacher is sullen and ill-natured; if, instead of the open countenance and straightforward look, his features are darkened with a scowl, and there is a sinister cast of face seldom thrown off; if he is often out of temper with the children, imputing to their dullness or perverseness what is more justly attributable to his own ill humour and want of skill in commanding and directing them; if he has recourse to the discipline of violence, and reliance is placed on corporeal punishment, rather than upon the influence which mind may exert over mind, – firm and authoritative reason over even untamed passion, you do not wonder at the type the school exhibits: the affections of the children are not won; and the morning face of the master is watched with perhaps as much anxiety, and construed with as much foreboding, as in days when the cane and the ferule were the principal instruments relied on to ensure order and stimulate application.[24]

He does go on to add that 'an over-easy temper' might be as fatal to good order and improvement as harshness and severity and that 'in consequence of kindness, personal attention and leniency, children may, in some rare cases, feel attachment to the teacher, while they care nothing for his authority'. The Wesleyan inspector Armstrong reiterated such feelings when he described some infant schools that he had visited:

> where gladness dances in the eye, and intelligence lights up the countenance of the children; but these are not always among the number where the classification is of the highest order, nor yet where the reading and the writing are well advanced, and the discipline the death-like stillness of inanimate things. An infant school should give play to the emotions, exercise to the limbs, and use to the senses: moral training, and not intellectual forcing, is the highest result. The

[23] *Ibid.* (1860), Appendix II, p. 37.
[24] *Ibid.* (1855), Appendix II, p. 103.

teacher loses power who does not hold the affections of her school, whose rule of action is not the law of love.[25]

Scott was optimistic in seeing education bringing a great improvement in the material comfort of the poor:

> You would like to see the wretched hovel, or still more wretched cellar, with its dingy walls, dirty floor, mean furniture . . . and its depressing gloom, in which the whole family are night and day crowded, exchanged for a cheerful, healthy dwelling, suitably furnished, all things clean and in neat arrangement . . . You would like to see every person in the family washed and clean; and dirty, tattered garments, affording scarcely any protection from the cold, in which multitudes appear, superseded by decent and warm clothing; and the negligent, slatternly appearance of many better clothed men, women and children, changed to cleanliness, neatness and good taste. You would like to see the unwholesome, miserable food on which numerous families live, or rather pine and half starve, exchanged for good, nutritious food, prepared with skill and enjoyed in plenty. You would like no longer to see any one, in the streets or elsewhere, a personification of wretchedness . . . education may extensively affect these changes.[26]

He concluded that the 'foundation of all improvement' was to 'make children generally intelligent' and that, as a precursor, it was necessary 'from the first [to] teach them to think'. His students were encouraged to 'give them thoughts and their thinking right direction, and so train their intellectual powers that they will readily apprehend and appreciate the importance of your lessons, on whatever subject.' As was universal at the time, he also encouraged lessons in cleanliness:

> good clothing and food, with temperate and regular habits, shall be felt essential to comfort, will be a most important step towards the desired change. . . Teach children of both sexes to hate dirt, and disorder and slovenliness, in person, at home, in the school – everywhere. Teach them . . . that a person's comfort and respectability depend mainly on himself . . . expose the evils of intemperance and improvidence.[27]

He recommended that girls learn needlework so that they might make clothes for the family and be taught basic nutrition. Showing much enlightenment, he called for girls to be trained in 'general intelligence and activity'.[28] In 1858, he expressed his condemnation of the long-held conception that it was wrong to educate girls of the lower classes who were destined to 'do the drudgery of life', supposing that it would make them 'dissatisfied and unfit for their proper station'. He believed that the schooling of girls was not, as had

---

[25] *Ibid.* (1861), Appendix I, p. 19.
[26] *Ibid.* (1859), Appendix II, p. 34.
[27] *Ibid.*
[28] *Ibid.*, p. 39.

been claimed, interfering with providential arrangements.[29] His philosophy permeated Wesleyan thinking and their inspector Armstrong even predicted:

> The time will come – but it is not *yet* when all that belongs to womanly education will be valued and sought. Meanwhile, those who have to maintain principle . . . must adhere to the purpose of rearing a higher standard of female worth, so that girls, whether among the humble or the well-conditioned, if found in Wesleyan schools, may come forth qualified the better to discharge the duties of every relation they may have to sustain . . . According to opportunity and ability, each should be taught the principles and habits, as well as the arts, by which she may be qualified to become useful in the station it pleases God to assign her.[30]

Indeed the specimen timetable for Girls' Schools that the Wesleyan Education Committee outlined in its 1865 Report was identical to that of Boys' Schools, with only the addition of needlework. Girls were expected to study reading and arithmetic for five hours each per week and one hour a week was to be spent on history, geography and singing. Similarly with the boys he recommended that they be given education that made them intelligent and trained them for the vigorous use of their understanding. Even though they might not be destined to be clerks, they should be taught good penmanship and drawing, as it prepared them 'to learn with facility any trade or business'.[31] Scott's belief in education in general was shown in his words to the Newcastle Commission in 1860. He told members:

> men whose lives are to be spent in labour, even in the drudgery of labour – ploughmen and hard working labourers – are not at all unfitted for their work by the education which is now given them; but while they will be made more intelligent, they will be much happier in after-life when they can read instructive books, enjoy information and feel pleasure in seeking it.[32]

A love of parents and siblings, he felt, might be fostered by teaching, and both parents and children might be encouraged to regard the home as the most loved spot on earth, 'next to the House of God!'[33] Scott was concerned as chairman of the WEC to ensure the high standards of all Wesleyan schools and he told the Newcastle Commission:

> Our aim is to make every school that we undertake to supply with a teacher, a first-rate elementary school; and if the parents will allow their children to remain long enough under instruction competent, to carry them to any point of learning which they may desire; and this we apply to the merest village school in the

---

[29] *Ibid.* (1858), Appendix I, p. 7.
[30] *Ibid.*, p. 8.
[31] *Ibid.* (1859), Appendix II, p. 38.
[32] *Parliamentary Papers* (*Newcastle Commission*), vol. 21, pt 6 (1861), p. 260.
[33] *W.E.R.* (1859), p. 36.

country as well as to the first school that may be established in any of the large towns.[34]

He believed that it was of no use to set up a school unless the teacher was 'thoroughly qualified to carry it on'[35] and he expected Wesleyan schools to employ first rate teachers. Scott maintained before the Commissioners that if wages were reduced and the good teachers left schools, it would affect the general intelligence and moral habits of the country.[36] He had written to J.B. Dunn on 28 March 1856, after a request for a teacher for the new school at Scarborough, that it was better to wait until after Christmas than to start a school with inadequate and not very competent teachers. 'Whatever inconvenience may come from delay, it is better to defer the opening of the schools than to commence sooner and fail.'[37]

Scott, as most of his Wesleyan contemporaries, saw the religious element in education to be supreme. He told students in 1854:

> This ability to give to children and the young in general a good education in secular learning . . . is not the first in importance. There are higher views of man than those which regard him only in human relations, performing earthly duties . . . he has a nature superior to the merely intellectual.[38]

In similar vein, he addressed a letter to Lord John Russell in 1855, after the publication of the Milner Gibson education bill which would have proscribed all religious instruction in schools receiving State grants.[39] He asked Russell to continue 'to firmly oppose the separation of religion from education in our schools'. He later reiterated the point in an Inaugural:

> Why limit education at any of its stages to the lower views of man, and not adapt it to the higher? Why confine it to what is ephemeral, and exclude from it what is enduring? . . . No one denies that in elementary schools you ought to teach morals . . . by what authority, for what reason, should you be made there to stop, and not teach them to live 'godly'? . . . If what you exclude is left to be taught by parents, and they are disinclined or unable to teach it, then neither at home nor at school are the children taught . . .[40]

Nevertheless, Scott was convinced, as he wrote to the Newcastle Commission in 1860, that: 'the children must be educated religiously; and that all the reasons which require a minister of religion to be a religious man, apply to a school teacher'.[41] He told his students:

---

[34] *Newcastle Commission*, p. 250.
[35] *Ibid.*, p. 254.
[36] *Ibid.*, p. 261.
[37] M.C.A., letter from John Scott to J.B. Dunn, 28 March 1856.
[38] *W.E.R.* (1854), Appendix II, p. 104.
[39] *Ibid.* (1855), p. 10.
[40] *Ibid.* (1860), Appendix II, p. 38.
[41] *Newcastle Commission*, p. 269.

He is a valuable servant of the church. It will be a shame if the church does not recognise and appreciate his labours; if it leaves him alone to struggle with the difficulty and discouragement which he is sure to meet in his arduous work . . . There is One who will certainly observe him . . . That One will notice with the highest approval his care of souls; will watch him with kindest interest when he leads the young into the way of life; when he puts the itinerary into their hands . . .[42]

The daily reading of Scripture was indispensable and in 1857 Scott forwarded to the Government a Wesleyan petition which condemned Sir John Pakington's bill, which would have banned this, no teaching of religion or morals being required:

The [Wesleyans'] experience shows that besides the scripture lesson with which their schools daily open and in which it is sought to make divine truth intelligible to children of all capacities, an able Christian teacher will find throughout the day, when teaching geography, history, physical and moral science, and the knowledge of common things, frequent occasion to illustrate and enforce the truths of religion, and that religious teaching may be made to impart life and spirit to the whole process of education.[43]

Scott did show grievances at the undue influence of the Anglican Church in some areas and he was determined to protect the children of his own denomination. When questioned by the Newcastle Commission in 1860, he expressed his objections to the Anglicans' demands that children in their schools attend Anglican services. Many Wesleyan children attended such schools and he told members that protecting Wesleyan children from such demands had been the only reason for a number of Wesleyan schools to be established in several small places.[44] They had not objected to the learning of the Anglican catechism in school but they were particularly offended that Wesleyan children were required to attend Church and even Anglican Sunday schools:

I have always thought that the church is not wise, as far as its own interests are concerned, in the exclusiveness with which its schools are conducted in a great number of places, for at present, if we could set up schools in many of those places we should do so, because of the exclusiveness of the administration . . . sometimes a clergyman who has been very exclusive, when he finds out that our people are preparing to commence a school, has offered to compromise matters and liberalise the school administration.[45]

He was subject to the same suspicions of Catholicism that were prominent in his church at that period, and in his speech to Westminster College in 1860

---

[42] *W.E.R.* (1855), Appendix II, p. 117.
[43] *Newcastle Commission,* p. 271.
[44] *Ibid.*, p. 254.
[45] *Ibid.*, p. 255.

he advised future teachers to watch out for measures that would 'tamper with the supreme authority of the Holy Scriptures as the Word of God' and that the children should not be taught to 'rest their hopes of future life on ritual observance'.[46] In his last Inaugural, in 1866, he expressed his concern at the rise of the Tractarian movement in the Church of England and, showing how important this issue was in the question of education, he warned future teachers:

> a body now shown to be considerable, of the clergy of our national church, until lately regarded as the great bulwark against Popery, have introduced Popish rites and ceremonies into Divine worship in their churches and are boldly teaching from the pulpit and by the Press the Popish doctrines on which their practices in worship are based . . . Our country therefore is at present in this position: either its people must succumb to Popery, set up, taught, and practised in our national Protestant Churches, or it must do the work of the Reformation afresh, and resist the aggressions of men apparently determined again to establish Popery as the religion of England . . . Even now the trumpet gives no uncertain sound: prepare yourselves for battle. Protest against the idolatry of the Mass, whether in so-called Protestant or Romish Churches . . . teach and train the children to be soundly Protestant.[47]

He concluded:

> Whatever comes to pass, our schools are, and must be, schools for religion. We can dispense with the teaching of the Catechism, if a parent requires it, but we cannot dispense with the Bible. The Bible must be read daily in our schools, and its Divine truths taught, as long as they are Wesleyan schools. We leave others, who like it, to try the experiment, but we have no faith in education without religion . . . Our teachers and our schools are denominational, but our religion is not denominational. It is catholic; anyone may read it in the orthodox theologians of the Protestant Church. But State authority must not throw religion out of our schools, nor settle for us what religion we shall teach the children. We respect the rights of conscience, and maintain that they ought to be respected.[48]

Scott displayed a similar energy against the Government's Revised Code of 1862. He was not opposed to government grants *per se* and told the Newcastle Commission that they helped in reducing ignorance and crime.[49] He also approved of Government inspection and told members that 'teachers that might have performed their work perfunctorily, unconcerned whether their schools made progress or not, have been stimulated to labour with a view to productible results'.[50] Before the introduction of the New Code, in his 1860 Inaugural, Scott warned of attempts at increased government interference in

---

[46] *W.E.R.* (1860), Appendix II, p. 40.
[47] *Ibid.* (1866), Appendix I, pp. 27–8.
[48] *Ibid.* (1866), p. 36.
[49] *Newcastle Commission*, p. 261.
[50] *Ibid.*, p. 268.

schools and emphasised that the Wesleyan stance was that education had to be 'decidedly and thoroughly religious'. Again he stressed that, in spite of new theories on education, even the youngest children should be taught the 'restorative process (of Christianity) for lapsed human nature':

> these are subjects which all men ought to know; and . . . they ought to be taught to children, with a wise adaptation to their opening reason, as early as their understanding can receive them. In this matter, *we* cannot temporise. As a religious people, we have received a precious deposit of Divine truth, 'the truth as it is in Jesus' and we hold it for the benefit of the world; and if we meddle with education at all, we believe we are bound to teach this truth to the children we undertake to instruct.[51]

After the introduction of the New Code, Wesleyan criticism was vociferous. The Code allowed payment of grants in the three R's only, after an HMI examination. Scott organised the lobbying of MPs and pamphlets were composed. In spite of his seventy years, Scott himself toured the country, encouraging teachers and school managers to disregard the limiting aspects of the Code and to continue the existing high standards. He addressed a letter to Earl Granville in 1861, making it clear that Methodism was not content with the Payment by Results system. He told Granville that Wesleyans were convinced that the New Code would 'seriously interfere with the sound processes of education' and he concluded 'surely the intellectual – the moral and religious feeling of the country – will not permit this system to be rashly destroyed and schools compelled virtually to return to the old exploded system'.[52] Armstrong typified Wesleyan reactions in his report:

> Reading, writing and arithmetic cannot be accepted as the complete curriculum of education even for the most neglected and ignorant of our population; indispensable as these are, and carefully as they should be taught, they constitute only a power valuable because of the extent and utility of application. But the presence of this power gives no assurance of its exercise . . . Education must be something more than the creation of a power, if it is to answer any good end . . .[53]

Scott encouraged prospective teachers to see their pupils not as 'machines', but as 'the children of men . . . with human feelings, human interests'.[54] They should not therefore be taught in mechanical ways in the three R's to qualify for grants. Scott castigated the new Code again in his 1863 Inaugural, telling students that it could not be too often repeated, or too strongly impressed upon young people preparing to be educators of youth, that 'by a good education . . . we understand a thorough instruction and a thorough training of the whole

---

[51] *W.E.R.* (1860), Appendix II, p. 36.
[52] *Ibid.* (1861), Appendix II, p. 69.
[53] *Ibid.*, Appendix I, p. 18.
[54] *Ibid.*, Appendix II, pp. 51–2.

man'.⁵⁵ He went on to assert that 'what may satisfy a Government examiner under the New Code will not satisfy us. We have had from the first our own standard of education, we have been working to that standard, and by that standard the managers judge of our schools and their teachers.' He claimed that the new standard 'comprising only reading, writing and arithmetic, must not cause us to reduce our school-instruction within what those limits would seem to indicate.'⁵⁶ He also approved of Matthew Arnold's call for education to 'soften and humanise' people's hearts and he continued to assert the importance of the religious element, 'notwithstanding the sneers with which we are ever and anon met when we declare this conviction'. He maintained that nothing else had an equal power 'to soften the heart, warm its affections . . . excite the imagination to lofty conceptions of truth.' The original intention for creating Wesleyan schools had been to educate the poor in Christian principles and he persisted in calling on teachers, school managers, ministers and Wesleyan people to resist the temptation to reduce the standards of teachers or raise the weekly payment so high as to place education 'above the reach of the humbler classes'.

Scott's last sermon was preached at Greenwich on 5 January 1868, when he led the Covenant Service. He died five days later at the age of 76. J.H. Rigg, his successor at Westminster, wrote in tribute to him:

> The evils of the Revised Code continued to press with almost unabated force on all our schools until the end of his life. But during the whole of that anxious period, Mr. Scott's influence and authority were invaluable for the defence and shelter which they contributed . . . The despondent were cheered, and the disaffected were silenced by the calm confidence which he maintained in the work and in its principles. The strength of an army was in the firmness of that wise and sagacious man.⁵⁷

At his funeral George Osborn remembered 'his noble forehead and his benignant smile . . . his intelligence, his sprightliness and interest in public affairs, together with his habitual placidity, considerate kindness and innocent humour.'⁵⁸ He had the opposite of 'noisy self-assertion'. He was reported to be a gentle and kindly superintendent, who developed acute administrative and financial skills. In his 'Reminiscences', Rigg, who worked under him, called him 'an eminently reasonable man' as superintendent, who did not rule by dictation 'but whose authority was respected'.⁵⁹ After his death, an appraisal of his work in the Minutes of the Methodist Conference commented that 'had his voice been equal to his powers of thought and expression, he would

---

⁵⁵ John Scott, *Varying & Permanent in Popular Education* (pamphlet, 1863), pp. 6–7.
⁵⁶ *Ibid.*, p. 7.
⁵⁷ Pritchard, p. 43.
⁵⁸ *Watchman* (22 January 1868), p. 29.
⁵⁹ Rigg, p. 117.

probably have ranked amongst the first preachers of the day'. These sentiments were reiterated at his funeral by Dr G. Osborn.[60] The Wesleyan Education Committee commented after his death that, as chairman, he represented Methodism to the Government 'with a clearness, a cogency, a gentlemanly firmness and a Christian courtesy, which won from all the recognition of his ability and worth'. To everyone he seemed to be always 'accessible, affable and kind', with a 'fatherly sympathy and advice', with a 'quiet, undemonstrative and consistent piety'.[61] Significantly, Scott's target of 700 Wesleyan schools was finally reached in the year following his death, by which time Wesleyanism could boast over 120,000 scholars. The numbers gave them a voice and a bargaining power second only to that of the Anglican school system. He had not seen this fulfilment, but it was his monument.

Appendix: Scott's Placements

1811	Winterton
1812	Patrington
1814	Hull
1815	Brentford
1817	Windsor (Superintendent)
1819	Colchester
1821	London West
1824	Rochester
1827	Liverpool North
1830	Manchester 3
1833	Bristol Nth, King's Street
1836	London 2nd
1839	London 6th, Hinde Street
1842	City Road
1843	London 1st
1843	President of Conference
1845	London 3rd, Spitalfield
1848	London 8th, Islington
1852	President of Conference
1852–68	Principal of Westminster Training College

---

[60] *Watchman* (22 January 1868), p. 29.
[61] *W.E.R.* (1867), p. 17.

16

ANGLICANISM 'REPRESENTED' OR 'MISREPRESENTED'? THE OXFORD MOVEMENT, EVANGELICALISM, AND HISTORY: THE CONTROVERSIAL USE OF THE CAROLINE DIVINES IN THE VICTORIAN CHURCH OF ENGLAND

PETER B. NOCKLES

THE Oxford Movement, that movement of High Church religious revival led by John Henry Newman, John Keble, Hurrell Froude, and E.B. Pusey, which between 1833 and 1845 centred on the University of Oxford, before spreading out into the parishes, was to remould the Victorian Church of England. It pre-eminently involved an appeal to history; first to that of the Early Church, and in its later phase to that of the Middle Ages. The Movement's appeal to history could be notoriously hagiographic as in the case of the *Lives of the Saints* (1842–4) launched by Newman and James Anthony Froude, but it also served a serious theological purpose. Initially, the Movement's point of reference was Christian Antiquity or the Fathers as well as Councils of the early Church according to the rule of Catholic Consent enunciated by St Vincent of Lerins in the fourth century – *quod semper, quod ubique, et quod ab omnibus*, i.e. Catholic truth was established not by the letter of the Bible alone but by what in the early and undivided Church had been taught 'always, everywhere, and by all'. The series of *Tracts for the Times*, inaugurated in 1833 and from which its authors and followers were accorded the nickname 'Tractarians', repeatedly recalled the example of the doctrine and practice of the primitive Church as a source of imitation and example to a Church threatened by State interference in matters spiritual, as evidenced in the Whig government's suppression of Irish bishoprics.[1] In order to strengthen

---

[1] The literature on the Oxford Movement is immense. See especially, D. Newsome, *The Parting of Friends: a study of the Wilberforces and Henry Manning* (London, 1966); M.R.

an Anglicanism that was losing its political ascendancy as a result of the repeal of the Test and Corporation Acts (1828) and Catholic Emancipation (1829), the Tractarians revived the spiritual basis of the Established Church's authority. The appeal to Antiquity was most fully employed to uphold the constitution of the Christian Church, its episcopal order and apostolical succession against its contemporary detractors or the merely lukewarm. St Ignatius of Antioch and St Clement of Rome especially were cited in support of the apostolic authority of bishops and of the necessity of visible church unity in the face of heresy and schism. More broadly, the Tractarian appeal to the ancient Church was used to underscore the classical Anglican claim to represent a *via media* between the Churches of Rome and Geneva, or as Newman put it, Romanism and ultra-Protestantism.[2]

This essay will focus on a related component of the Oxford Movement's campaign of the 1830s and 1840s – a selective use of earlier Anglican history which entailed an appeal for legitimation to the seventeenth-century Anglican divines (the so-called 'Caroline Divines', though they encompassed Jacobean authors[3]); divines who themselves had been exponents and mediators of an appeal to Antiquity and of patristic orthodoxy. The Caroline epoch was almost as central to Tractarian concerns as the patristic era. The whole Tractarian project rested on the claim to be merely renewing the historic Anglicanism of the seventeenth century to a supposedly 'forgetful generation'. This article will seek to examine that claim, raising the issue of the historical foundations, identity and integrity of Anglicanism. The tension and ultimate divergence between the Tractarian and both traditional High Church and Anglican Evangelical readings of the theology and politics of the seventeenth-century Church of England will form the basis of this study. The Tractarian claim to represent historic Anglicanism was questioned at the time, more recently disputed by W.R. Fryer in a seminal article, 'The High Churchmen of the earlier seventeenth-century' in *Renaissance and Modern*

O'Connell, *The Oxford Conspirators: a History of the Oxford Movement, 1833–1845* (New York, 1969); R. Chapman, *Faith and Revolt: Studies in the Literary Influence of the Oxford Movement* (London, 1970); D.G. Rowell, *The Vision Glorious: Themes and Personalities of the Catholic Revival in Anglicanism* (Oxford, 1983); P. Butler (ed.), *Pusey Rediscovered* (London, 1983); J.R. Griffin, *The Oxford Movement: a Revision* (Edinburgh, 1984); D.G. Rowell (ed.), *Tradition Renewed: the Oxford Movement Conference papers* (Oxford, 1986); R. Imberg, *In Quest of Authority: the "Tracts for the Times" and the development of the Tractarian Leaders, 1833–1841* (Lund, 1987); P.B. Nockles, *The Oxford Movement in Context: Anglican High Churchmanship 1760–1857* (Cambridge, 1994); P. Vaiss (ed.), *From Oxford to the People: Reconsidering Newman & the Oxford Movement* (Leominster, 1996); V.A. McClelland (ed.), *By Whose Authority? Newman, Manning, and the Magisterium* (Bath, 1996).

[2] J.H. Newman, *Lectures on the Prophetical Office of the Church viewed relatively to Romanism and Popular Protestantism* (London, 1837).

[3] F.L. Cross (ed.) (3rd edn, edited by E.A. Livingstone), *The Oxford Dictionary of the Christian Church.* (Oxford, 1997), p. 290.

Studies (1961),[4] and is currently receiving renewed assault from Diarmaid MacCulloch.[5] What is clear is that what was at stake in the nineteenth no less than in the seventeenth century was the issue of what sort of Church the Church of England was.

For Newman and the Tractarians, it was important to convince contemporary churchmen that they had Anglican as well as patristic history on their side, and to harmonise the two sources of historical testimony. 'We have a vast inheritance, but no inventory of our treasures. All is given in profusion; it remains for us to catalogue, sort, distribute, harmonize, and complete.'[6] These often cited words of John Henry Newman from the introduction to his *Lectures on the Prophetical Office of the Church* (1837) show that the Oxford Movement's religious agenda lay in an appeal not only to the model of the primitive church but to the Church of England's mediation of that model via the theological and devotional writings and lives of the Caroline Divines. Newman was able to claim Caroline and even Elizabethan Anglican precedent for the view that the first six centuries of Christianity were normative for doctrine. As Lancelot Andrewes famously put it: 'one canon, two testaments, three creeds, four general councils, five centuries, and the series of Fathers in that period ... determine the boundary of our faith.'[7] Much was also made in Tractarian rhetoric of a canon of 1571 directing preachers to conform to the doctrine of the primitive church as well as of Holy Scripture.[8]

The core doctrines which the Tractarians propagated – the Apostolical Succession, divine-right episcopacy, the authority of the Church as keeper of Holy Writ, the Priesthood and ministerial commission, Apostolical Tradition and a Catholic Consent of the Fathers as interpretative of Scripture according to the rule of St Vincent of Lerins, the Real Presence in the Eucharist, the Eucharistic Sacrifice, Baptismal Regeneration, the Power of the Keys – along with points of discipline and practice such as the necessity of fasting and mortification, frequent communion, observance of Saints' Days and Festivals, almsgiving and celibacy, were set forth in the *Tracts for the Times* by direct reference to the teaching of not only the *Book of Common Prayer* but also of the seventeenth-century divines. Tracts 25 and 26 contained extracts from Bishop Beveridge's sermons, Tracts 27 and 28 were reprints of writings by Bishop Cosin against Transubstantiation, Tract 64 was a reprint of extracts from Bishop Bull on the ancient liturgies and Tract 72 was based on Archbishop Ussher's writings concerning prayers for the dead. Tracts 74, 76, 78,

---

[4] W.R. Fryer, 'The "High Churchmen" of the earlier seventeenth century', *Renaissance and Modern Studies*, vol. 5 (1961), especially p. 112.

[5] See D. MacCulloch, *Thomas Cranmer: a life* (London, 1996), p. 629; D. MacCulloch, *Tudor Church Militant: Edward VI and the Protestant Reformation* (London, 1999), pp. 157–8.

[6] Newman, *Lectures on the Prophetical Office of the Church*, p. 30.

[7] L. Andrewes, *Opuscula quedam Posthuma* (*Library of Anglo-Catholic Theology*) (Oxford, 1852), p. 91.

[8] Nockles, *Oxford Movement in Context*, pp. 118–19.

and Pusey's Tract 81 (on Apostolical Succession, Baptismal Regeneration, Tradition, and the Eucharistic Sacrifice respectively) were all largely *catenae* from writers in the Caroline tradition.

The testimony of the seventeenth-century divines had been repeatedly cited in eighteenth- and early nineteenth-century Anglican apologetic against both the Church of Rome and Protestant Dissent, while their devotional writings, as witnessed by John Wesley's selection in his *Christian Library*, and George Stanhope's posthumous publication of Lancelot Andrewes's *Greek Devotions* in 1730, continued to nourish later generations of High Churchmen.[9] The first twenty years of George III's reign witnessed a revival of the tradition, in its devotional and sacramental as well as political aspects, owing to the exertions of the so-called Hutchinsonian divines, George Horne and William Jones of Nayland, and others in less conspicuous ways.[10] According to F.C. Mather, the Caroline inheritance, of which Bishop Samuel Horsley was a notable exponent at the end of the century, had three interrelated facets. These included the exaltation of state power by the recovery of certain attributes of divine-right monarchy, the defence of the Church of England against dissenters by the assertion of claims to Apostolical Succession, and the defence of the mysterious element in religion in opposition to the plainness of latitudinarianism and the rationalistic creed of Arianism and Socianism.[11] It was, however, as masters of the art of 'holy living' and of catechetics, and as exponents or interpreters of the liturgy, that divines such as Lancelot Andrewes, Jeremy Taylor, and Thomas Ken, and the layman Robert Nelson (1656–1715), retained their widest attraction within Anglican circles.[12] Moreover, the Caroline tradition can be said to have been transmitted at the pastoral and parochial level through such church organisations as the societies for the reformation of manners, the

---

[9] *Private Prayers for every day in the week, and for the several parts of each day: Translated from the Greek Devotions of Bishop Andrewes, with additions, by George Stanhope, D.D. late Dean of Canterbury* (London, 1730).

[10] Nockles, *Oxford Movement in Context*, pp. 13–14; N. Aston, 'Horne and Heterodoxy: The Defence of Anglican Beliefs in the late Enlightenment', *English Historical Review (EHR)*, vol. 108, no. 429 (October, 1993), pp. 895–920. The High Churchmanship of the young Jones and Horne had been forged by their discovery of and subsequent immersion in seventeenth-century Anglican divinity which they found in the library of their patron, Sir Francis Dolben. See W. Jones, *The Memoirs of the Life, Studies, and Writings of the Rt. Rev. George Horne, D.D. late Lord Bishop of Norwich. To which is added his Lordship's own collection of his own thoughts on a variety of great and interesting subjects* (London, 1795), pp. 66–7.

[11] F.C. Mather, *High Church Prophet: Bishop Samuel Horsley (1733–1806) and the Caroline tradition in the later Georgian Church* (Oxford, 1992), p. 305.

[12] G.W.O. Addleshaw, *The High Church Tradition: A Study in the Liturgical Thought of the Seventeenth Century* (London, 1944); C.J. Stranks, *Anglican Devotion: Studies in the Spiritual Life of the Church of England between the Reformation and the Oxford Movement* (London, 1961), especially chapters iii & vi. Thirty-two editions of Nelson's devotional classic, *A Companion for the Feasts and Fasts of the Church of England* (1705) had been published by 1815.

Society for Promoting Christian Knowledge, and the Society for the Propagation of the Gospel.

The appeal to the Laudian era by Anglican writers in the pre-Tractarian period, however, was not entirely uncontentious and attracted the strictures of eighteenth-century Protestant Nonconformists such as Daniel Neal and Samuel Chandler, as well as Anglican latitudinarians such as Samuel Clarke, Benjamin Hoadly and Francis Blackburne.[13] Laud was a particular *bête noire* of the extreme latitudinarian critics of the Whig High Churchmen, Bishop Gibson in the 1730s, and Archbishop Secker in the 1760s. Both Gibson and Secker were condemned as 'spiritual descendants' of Laud, and Blackburne's celebrated polemic *The Confessional* (1766) abounded in anti-Laudian invective.[14] The appeal to Caroline authorities in defence of Anglican credal orthodoxy against Socinians as well as the High Church defence of Anglican apostolicity against both the claims of Protestant dissent and the Church of Rome generated controversy. The contentiousness of Laud and Laudianism, as well as the memory of Charles I, was heightened by the revival of High Church Tory polemic in 30 January sermons during the 1770s in the context of the American War.[15] From the 1790s onwards, High Churchmen such as Archdeacon Daubeny made copious appeals to the Caroline Divines in polemics against Protestant Dissent as well as Roman Catholicism;[16] Daubeny even compiled an edition of seventeen sermons of Bishop Andrewes in 1821 as a polemic against political radicalism.[17] Not only the French Revolution but

---

[13] For examples of the genre, see [M. Tindal], *The Merciful Judgments of High-Church Triumphant on offending clergymen, and others in the reign of Charles I, together with Lord Falkland's speech in Parliament in 1640 relating to that subject* (London, 1710).

[14] See for example, [F. Blackburne], *Memoirs of Thomas Hollis*, 2 vols (London, 1780), vol. 1, p. 227.

[15] J.C.D. Clark, *English Society, 1688–1832: ideology, social structure and political practice during the ancien regime* (Cambridge, 1985), p. 160; J.A.W. Gunn, *Beyond Liberty and Property* (Kingston, 1983), pp. 136, 150; R. Hole, *Pulpits, Politics and Public Order in England, 1760–1832* (Cambridge, 1989), pp. 52–3. Cf. J. Sack, *From Jacobite to Conservative: Reaction and orthodoxy in Britain, c. 1760–1832* (Cambridge, 1993), pp. 126–30. For the origins and earlier history of 30th January sermons commemorating the 'Royal Martyr', see A. Lacey, 'The Office of King Charles the Martyr in the Book of Common Prayer, 1662–1685', *Journal of Ecclesiastical History (JEH)*, vol. 53, no. 3 (July, 2002), pp. 510–26. See note 44.

[16] For examples, see *A Word in Season from the learned Bishop Andrewes, to the governors of this country in Church and State* (London, 1823); C. Daubeny, *On the Nature, Progress, and Consequences of Schism; with immediate reference to the present state of religious affairs in this country* (London, 1818), p. 190.

[17] *Seventeen Sermons of the eminently pious and deeply learned Bishop Andrewes; modernised, for the use of general readers by the Rev. Charles Daubeny* (London, 1821). Another contemporary High Churchman even used Andrewes in an attack on the granting of Catholic Emancipation in 1829. See *The Life and Death of Lancelot Andrewes, D.D. late Lord Bishop of Winchester; by his friend and amanuensis, Henry Isaacson [1650]. Edited and arranged, with a brief Memoir . . . and Preliminary Remarks by the Reverend Stephen Isaacson* (London, 1829), pp. 1–20.

the British constitutional crisis of 1828–32 stirred memories of the Great Rebellion of the 1640s among High Churchmen, with Anglican Evangelicals and British and Foreign Bible Society activists as well as Protestant Dissenters and political radicals being unflatteringly likened to the Puritan fanatics of the mid seventeenth century. Laud became an increasing focus of eulogy, with one biographer, S.H. Cassan, lamenting in 1830 that if Laud had been promoted to Canterbury earlier and Abbot had never been appointed as Primate, 'England in all probability had not seen her Church and State overthrown'.[18]

It was not only eighteenth-century High Churchmen, however, who laid claim to the mantle of the seventeenth-century divines. Richard Hooker and Bishop Joseph Hall, and even Lancelot Andrewes, were favourites of eighteenth-century Evangelical revivalists in their reaction against contemporary latitudinarianism and rationalism. In 1740, Jonathan Warne, a lay Anglican Evangelical defender of George Whitefield, censured the Whig High Churchman Bishop Gibson's teaching on Justification for departing from what Warne called the 'orthodox doctrine of the Church of England' on the subject, taking as his standard a treatise by Bishop Lancelot Andrewes.[19] Likewise, Newman's Evangelical mentor, Thomas Scott of Aston Sandford, explained in his seminal spiritual autobiography *The Force of Truth* (1779), that he owed his progress from a cold rationalism to evangelical conversion to his study of Hooker's writings on the doctrine of Justification.[20] The skilful controversial use made of the writings of the Caroline Divines, notably those of Bishop Richard Montagu, Herbert Thorndike and Bishop William Forbes, in a quite opposite direction, in apparent support of Catholic doctrines and practices by English Roman Catholic apologists such as John Milner and John Fletcher in the half-century from the granting of the first Catholic Relief Act (1778) until Catholic Emancipation (1829), sharpened divisions within the Established Church.[21] High Churchmen such as Bishop Horsley had recourse

---

[18] S.H. Cassan, *Lives of the Bishops of Bath and Wells from the Reformation to the present time* (London, 1830), pp. 42–3. For examples of the High Church Anglican equation of the Calvinist Evangelicalism, Protestant Dissent and radicalism of the Reform era with seventeenth-century Calvinism and Puritanism, see also H.H. Norris, *A Practical Exposition of the Tendency and Proceedings of the British and Foreign Bible Society* (London, 1814), p. 359; A.H. Kenney, *The Principles and Practices of Pretended Reformers* (Dublin, 1819); Daubeny, *Nature, Progress, and Consequences of Schism*, p. 91.

[19] [J. Warne], *The Bishop of London's doctrine of Justification, in his late Pastoral Letter, proved by Bishop Andrewes's sermon on that point, so contrary to the Church of England, that it rather agrees with the Church of Rome. With a postscript in vindication of the Rev. Mr Whitefield's assertions, relating to the errors contained in the book called "The Whole Duty of Man", and Archbishop Tillotson's "Works"* (London, 1740).

[20] T. Scott, *The Force of Truth; an authentic narrative* (London, 1779), pp. 80–1; A.C. Downer, *Thomas Scott the commentator. A memoir of his life. With some account of his principal writings and an estimate of his position and influence in the Church* (London, 1909), p. 40.

[21] P.B. Nockles, 'The difficulties of Protestantism: Bishop Milner, John Fletcher and Catholic

to the Caroline Divines, but the suspicion of Low Churchmen towards them was exacerbated by Catholic apologetical exploitation of them. In his controversial writings of the 1790s and early 1800s, Milner seemed bent on promoting a High Church Anglican–Roman Catholic alliance against Low Church latitudinarianism for tactical reasons. His attack on what he called 'Hoadlyism' for abandoning the high episcopalian and sacramental teaching of Andrewes, Cosin and Taylor,[22] was well suited to this purpose. Milner's Anglican latitudinarian opponent, Archdeacon Sturges of Winchester, who looked upon Bishop Hoadly as a mentor, responded in his *Reflections on the Principles of Popery* (1799) by complaining that the only Bishops of Winchester who had escaped Milner's censure were those proto-Laudians or Laudians, Andrewes, Curle and Mews, who had 'approached nearer to Popery, by which his judgement of them is regulated'.[23] Milner's rhetorical strategy had, as a contemporary complained, directed the debate to a 'question between Protestants high and low church, rather than between them and Papists'.[24] Such internal divisions in interpretation of the Church of England's Caroline inheritance prefigured the divisions which the Oxford Movement was to provoke.

The Oxford Movement capitalised on a pre-existing climate of conservative theological reaction in which knowledge of the teaching of the Caroline Divines was already being recovered. The Caroline Divines achieved a limited vogue among Anglican churchmen in the 1820s, before the dawn of the Movement. In 1824 the works of William Beveridge had been republished in nine volumes, followed in 1827 by the republication of George Bull's works. In 1828, Bishop Reginald Heber's edition of *The Whole Works of Jeremy Taylor* appeared; 1829 saw John Parker Lawson's two-volume *Life and Times of William Laud*, and 1832 an edition of the writings of the Nonjuror Charles Leslie (1650–1722) in seven volumes; the republication of Leslie's *Case of the Regale and Pontificat* (1700) was especially anticipatory of the anti-Erastianism of the Tractarians. When the authors of the *Tracts for the Times* called for a 'rediscovery' of the theology of the seventeenth century, there was already fertile ground at their disposal and a favourable climate in which the call could be heard.

It is clear from his introduction to the *Lectures on the Prophetical Office of*

---

apologetic against the Church of England in the era from the first Relief Act to Emancipation, 1778–1830', *Recusant History*, vol. 24, no. 2 (October, 1998), pp. 193–236.

[22] J. Milner, *The History and Survey of the Antiquities of Winchester* [1798] 2 vols (3rd edn, Winchester, 1839), vol. 1, p. xxxi; vol. 2, p. 46; J. Milner, *Letters to a Prebendary: being an Answer to 'Reflections on Popery' by the Rev. J. Sturges . . . with Remarks on the opposition of Hoadlyism to the doctrines of the Church of England* (2nd edn, Cork, 1802), Letters iv, p. vi.

[23] J. Sturges, *Reflections on the principles and institutions of Popery, with reference to civil society and government, especially that of this kingdom, occasioned by the Rev. John Milner's 'History of Winchester'* (Winchester, 1799), pp. 103–4.

[24] Milner, *Letters to a Prebendary*, p. 465.

the Church that Newman did not regard the Oxford Movement as a passive legatee of the whole Anglican inheritance. The Tractarians looked for what they regarded as the real soul of Anglicanism, smothered, they assumed, under the ultra-Protestantism of the eighteenth century. Moreover, they looked beyond and behind the English Reformation and its formularies. The ultimate point of reference was the early and undivided Church and the attraction of the Caroline Divines lay in their embodiment of primitive Christianity and hence the true Anglican spirit. While the English Reformers, notably Bishop Jewel, had also claimed to be returning to primitive Christian purity, they had been contaminated by the foreign Protestantism of Zurich and Geneva. In Tracts 38 and 41, entitled the 'Via Media', Newman's call for a 'second Reformation',[25] while not designed to undo, was intended to complete, if not correct, the work of the first. This presupposed an agenda whereby the seventeenth-century divines would be called in service not so much to support but to reinterpret the sense or amend the deficiencies of their sixteenth-century predecessors. Such an approach might be characterised as a 'misuse' of the testimony of the Caroline Divines for a purpose for which their writings were not intended. The case, however, can be made out that this was a legitimate use of their testimony because it was precisely to do what the Laudians did in their own day – to reinterpret or refine the Reformation settlement, forge a new consensus and reshape the Church of England in their own image. If later Anglican and Tractarian historiography imposed a polarity between Anglicanism and Puritanism that obscured an Elizabethan and early-Jacobean theological consensus, this was only following the lead of seventeenth-century Laudian apologists, notably Peter Heylin, who wished to marginalise Puritanism from the mainstream of the Church of England.

The Tractarians found the religious history of the Church of England to be something of a Noah's Ark, full of beasts clean and unclean. Although Pusey for a long while remained loyal to them, the Reformers soon came to hold no place of honour in the Tractarian theological canon, largely thanks to Hurrell Froude and his published *Remains* (1838). Froude privately labelled Bishop Jewel as 'what you would call in these days an irreverent Dissenter',[26] and claimed that Jewel's *'Defence of the Apology* disgusted me more than any work I have read'.[27] Froude denounced the Reformation as 'a limb badly set – it must be broken again in order to be righted'.[28] Froude's role was paramount in disconnecting the Oxford Movement from the doctrinal spirit of even the English Reformation. In an influential article full of polemical brio in the *British Critic* in 1841, Frederick Oakeley extended the attack on Jewel and the

---

[25] *Tracts for the Times*, vol. 1, no. 38, 'Via Media. No. I', p. 2.
[26] *The Remains of the Late Reverend Richard Hurrell Froude*, [eds. J. Keble & J.H. Newman], 4 vols (vols 1–2, London, 1838–9; vols 3–4, Derby, 1839), vol. 1, p. 379.
[27] *Ibid.*, p. 380.
[28] *Ibid.*, p. 251.

Reformers, and claimed inspiration from Froude's *Remains*.[29] Under Froude's influence, Newman privately distanced himself from the Reformers, especially Cranmer. He had, it is true, publicly praised the Reformers as late as the mid 1830s, though for largely tactical purposes,[30] but by 1838, in the wake of Froude's *Remains*, privately he was expressing relief that he no longer needed 'all sorts of fictions and artifices to make out Cranmer or others Catholic'.[31] By 1841, in expressing sympathy for Oakeley's line, he could confide to Pusey: 'I fear I must express a persuasion that it requires no deep reading to dislike the Reformation. "A good tree cannot bring forth evil fruit"... Whence all this schism and heresy, humanly speaking, but for it?'[32] He only faulted Ward and Oakeley for being too impatient, but defended their 'running down the Reformers' on the ground 'that our Church cannot be right till they are exposed, till their leaven is cast out, and till the Church repents of them'.[33] In his pre-Tractarian days, Keble had identified himself with Cranmer and Ridley. In 1830, after reading the High Churchman A.P. Perceval's eirenical *Christian Peace-Offering* (1829), he even urged Perceval to 'consider what the Reformers as well as what the Fathers have written, before you send it out again'. Keble was concerned lest 'any good person should lay himself open to the slightest appearances of explaining away the formularies to which he is pledged'.[34] However, by 1835, under Froude's influence, he maintained that 'Hooker wrote many things in order to counteract in a quiet way the Ultra Protestantism of... Cranmer and his school'.[35] In various places in the preface to his 1836 edition of Hooker's *Works*, Keble cautiously and guardedly pointed up examples of this subtle counteraction, especially in relation to Hooker's apparent insistence, in contrast to Jewel, on the reality and exclusive virtue of sacramental grace.[36] In private, Keble was less guarded. By 1836, he could bracket the Reformers as of 'the same class with the puritans and radicals', confiding to his brother Thomas Keble:

---

[29] F. Oakeley, *The subject of Tract XC examined, in connection with the Thirty-Nine Articles, and the statements of certain English divines, to which is added the case of Bishop Montague, in the reign of King James I* (London, 1841), p. x.

[30] J.H. Newman to J.W. Bowden, July 1835, *Letters and Diaries of John Henry Newman* [hereafter, *LD*], vol. 5, T. Gornall (ed.) (Oxford, 1981), p. 94.

[31] J.H. Newman to T. Henderson, 9 December 1838, HEN 2/4/3, Pusey House Library, Oxford [hereafter, PHL)].

[32] J.H. Newman to E.B. Pusey, 13 August 1841, *LD*, vol. 8, G. Tracey (ed.) (Oxford, 1999), pp. 242–3.

[33] *Ibid.*, p. 243.

[34] J. Keble to A.P. Perceval, 16 February 1830, Liddon Bound Volumes [hereafter, *LBV*] (transcript), PHL.

[35] J. Keble to J.H. Newman, 21 January 1835, *LBV* 9/38 (transcript), PHL.

[36] *The Works of that Learned and Judicious Divine, Mr Richard Hooker: with an Account of his Life and Death by Isaac Walton. Arranged by the Rev. John Keble, M.A. late Fellow of Oriel College, Oxford,* 3 vols in 4 [Oxford, 1836] (3rd edn, Oxford, 1845), vol. 1, especially pp. lxxxvii–xci.

I have very little doubt that if we had lived in those times, neither my father, nor you, nor [George] Prevost nor [Benjamin] Harrison would have had anything to do with them. And I think we shall never be able to take our ground against the Romanists or Puritans till we have separated ourselves and our liturgy from them.[37]

In the preface to the third volume of Froude's *Remains,* he agreed with Froude that the Reformers 'were not a party, to be trusted on ecclesiastical and theological questions.'[38] Keble even found Hooker himself to be somewhat deficient in his apostolical principles and in need of supplementation from the subsequent schools of Laud and the Nonjuror Charles Leslie.[39] As John Gascoigne has shown, Keble's preface to his edition of Hooker's *Laws of Ecclesiastical Polity* sought not only to rescue Hooker from the taint of liberal principles attributed to him by Locke and the Low Churchman Benjamin Hoadly, but also to insist that the later Hooker, while shrinking 'from the legitimate result of his own premises,' was moving towards the Laudian doctrine of *jure divino* episcopacy and higher sacramental doctrine than that of his Calvinist contemporaries.[40] For Keble, Hooker was a 'middle term between Laud and Cranmer, but nearer the former' and 'in a transition state when he was taken from us; and there is no saying how much nearer he might have got to Laud, if he had lived twenty years longer'.[41] Moreover, Hooker had 'his full share in training up for the next generation, Laud, Hammond, Sanderson, and a multitude more such divines: to which succession and series, humanly speaking, we owe it, that the Anglican church continues at such a distance from that of Geneva, and so near to primitive truth and apostolical order'.[42] MacCulloch, while conceding the deep insights of Keble's preface, regards his ecclesiological and sacramentalist gloss on Hooker as an exercise in special pleading.[43] For the Tractarians, reverence for Hooker and his apparent successors made it easier and safer for them to ditch the Reformers. When the

---

[37] J. Keble to T. Keble, 14 November 1836, Keble papers, Keble College Library [hereafter KCL], Oxford.
[38] *Remains of the late Rev. Richard Hurrell Froude,* vol. 3 (Derby, 1839), p. xix.
[39] Keble, 'Preface', *Works of . . . Hooker,* vol. 1, p. lxxvii.
[40] J. Gascoigne, 'The unity of Church and State challenged: responses to Hooker from the Restoration to the nineteenth-century Age of Reform', *Journal of Religious History,* vol. 21, no. 1 (February, 1997), pp. 73–4. For earlier readings or 'misreadings' of Hooker, which Keble sought to counteract, see D. MacCulloch, 'Richard Hooker's Reputation', *EHR,* vol. 117, no. 473 (September, 2002), pp. 773–812. For a recent reappraisal of Hooker which places him closer to the 'Reformed' camp and argues against identifying him as an early exponent of the *via media,* see B.D. Spinks, *Two faces of Elizabethan Anglican Theology. Sacraments and Salvation in the Thought of William Perkins and Richard Hooker* (London, 1999).
[41] J. Keble to R.H. Froude, August 1835, J.T. Coleridge, *A Memoir of the Rev. John Keble, M.A. Late Vicar of Hursley* (3rd edn, London, 1870), p. 201.
[42] Keble, 'Preface', *Works of . . . Hooker,* vol. 1, p. cvii. However, see also n. 157 for Keble's disagreement with Hooker on eucharistic doctrine.
[43] MacCulloch, 'Hooker's Reputation', p. 809.

Tractarians were in danger of becoming embarrassed by a widely supported scheme to erect a Martyrs Memorial at Oxford in 1838, perceived as being directed against them, the facetious counter-suggestion was made privately by the Tractarian Henry Woodgate that any countenance to the scheme should involve the inclusion of Laud among the list of martyrs.[44] After some hesitation, Keble refused to countenance the idea of a memorial, maintaining that 'anything which separates the present church from the Reformers, I should hail as a great good'.[45]

For the Tractarians, the Caroline Church, along with its individual Nonjuring successors, represented the apogee of Anglicanism. Oakeley's attack on Jewel may have represented an extreme position, and Ridley was more favourably portrayed by some Tractarians. Manning, in his sermon *The Rule of Faith* (1838), even included Cranmer as well as Ridley in his *catenae* of predominantly Caroline divines in favour of the doctrine of 'Scripture and the Creed attested by Universal Tradition'.[46] James Mozley, however, expressed a characteristic Tractarian view when he conceded: 'I should not rank the Reformers among these standard divines, who seem indeed to have been a decided reaction upon them, i.e. very much more High Church. Compare Laud and Jewel'.[47] The Tractarians focused primarily on a narrow range of divines covering the period from the 1600s to the 1680s, with Hurrell Froude dating the rise and fall of what he called the Church of England's 'genus of Apostolical divines' from the beginning of the reign of King James I until the Revolution of 1688–9 and the separation of the first Nonjurors (i.e. the period from Saravia to Bishop Ken).[48] An exception, however, was sometimes made for the early-Elizabethan Bishop of Gloucester, Richard Cheyney, and other Elizabethan divines such as Bishops Alley of Exeter and Guest of Rochester,

---

[44] H.A. Woodgate to J.H. Newman, 2 March 1839, *LD*, vol. 7, G. Tracey (ed.) (Oxford, 1995), p. 45. Newman, however, recognised the mixed intentions of the proposers, noting that the 'Memorial to the Reformers' could be either 'an Ultra Protestant or an Anglican testimony'. J.H. Newman to H. Mozley, 2 November 1838, *LD*, vol. 6, G. Tracey (ed.) (Oxford, 1994), p. 335. The idea of Laud as an Anglican 'martyr' was popularised by the Tractarians, and linked by association with Charles I who had been declared a Martyr in the state service for 30 January in the Book of Common Prayer. [F.W. Faber], *The Autobiography of Dr. William Laud, Archbishop of Canterbury, and Martyr. Collected from his Remains* (Oxford, 1839), p. xvi. For an earlier identification of Laud as an Anglican martyr, who 'like St Cyprian of old ... died nobly for the Church', see J.P. Lawson, *The Life and Times of William Laud, D.D. Lord Archbishop of Canterbury*, 2 vols (London, 1829), vol. 2, p. 545. See Lacey, 'The Office for King Charles the Martyr'.

[45] J. Keble to E.B. Pusey, 18 January 1839, PHL, *LBV*50/16. Pusey, however, was prepared to support a tablet commemorating 'the blessings of the Reformation' in a Martyrs' Church. E.B. Pusey to J. Keble, 13 January 1839, Keble Papers, KCL.

[46] H.E. Manning, *The Rule of Faith: Appendix to a Sermon* (London, 1838), p. 6.

[47] J.B. Mozley to A. Mozley, 9 July 1842, *The Letters of the Rev. J.B. Mozley, D.D. Edited by his sister* (London, 1885), p. 133.

[48] *Remains of the late Rev. Richard Hurrell Froude*, vol. 2, p. 381.

all of whom the Tractarian Alexander Forbes, Bishop of Brechin, regarded as 'the germ in fact of the afterwards distinguished school of Andrewes and the Caroline divines'.[49] Others placed the key shift of theological gear in a Catholic direction to Richard Bancroft's St Paul's Cross sermon in 1589 preaching *jure divino* episcopacy, the anti-Puritan treatises of Hadrian Saravia (1590)[50] and Matthew Sutcliffe (1591) or Thomas Bilson's *Perpetual Government of Christ's Church* (1593),[51] and cited Archbishop Whitgift's chaplain, Benjamin Carier (a later convert to Rome) as an early exponent of the *via media*,[52] Nonetheless, the Tractarians tended to exalt seventeenth-century Anglican divinity at the expense of that of the later sixteenth century. Froude's anti-Erastianism fuelled an extreme historical *renversement d'alliance*: he sympathised with the Elizabethan Puritans in their controversy with Whitgift because he argued that the former, unlike the latter, upheld 'a *jus divinum,* though not the true one'. Froude admired the 'mar-prelate' polemicist, John Penry, and even considered writing 'An Apology for the early Puritans'.[53]

Tractarian exaltation of the seventeenth-century divines was also at the expense of the eighteenth century, with as few exceptions. For most Tractarians, especially Froude and Newman, eighteenth-century Anglicanism

---

[49] *An Explanation of the Thirty-Nine Articles: with an Epistle Dedicatory to the Rev. E.B. Pusey. By Alexander Penrose Forbes, D.C.L. Bishop of Brechin,* 2 vols (Oxford, 1867), vol. 1, pp. xi–xii. For a later 'High Church' reading of the eucharistic doctrine of Bishops Guest and Cheney, see F.O. White, *Lives of the Elizabethan Bishops of the Anglican Church* (London, 1898), p. 130, pp. 173–6. For an early claim that Bishop Cheney was a precursor of nineteenth-century 'Anglo-Catholicism', see *Puseyism; or the New Apostolicals* (London, 1838), pp. 4–5, 142–4.

[50] For the significance, if not novelty, of the doctrine of Bancroft's sermon, see T. Lathbury, *A History of the English Episcopacy; from the period of the Long Parliament to the Act of Uniformity; with notices of the religious parties of the time, and a review of ecclesiastical affairs in England, from the Reformation* (London, 1836), p. 63. See also, W.D.J. Cargill Thompson, 'Sir Francis Knollys's campaign against the *jure divino* theory of episcopacy', C.W. Dugmore (ed.), *Studies in the Reformation: Luther to Hooker* (London, 1980), pp. 118–19. Hurrell Froude commented (*Remains*, vol. 1, p. 327): 'It seems to me that Saravia and Bancroft are the revivers of orthodoxy in England.'

[51] Newman's curate at the University church of St Mary the Virgin, the Tractarian Robert Eden, edited a new edition of Bishop Bilson's work. For the significance for the Tractarians of Bilson's teaching on *jure divino* episcopacy, see *The Perpetual Government of Christ's Church. By Thomas Bilson, D.D. Bishop of Winchester. A new edition with a biographical notice by the Rev. Robert Eden, M.A. late Fellow of Corpus Christi College, Oxford* (Oxford, 1842), pp. ii–iv.

[52] According to a nineteenth-century writer, when Carier first fled abroad, he declared in a letter to Archbishop Abbot that he was no papist, but 'merely anxious to heal the breach between the Anglican, and the ancient European, Church, by the establishment of the religion which he called Catholic. He distinguished between the Protestants and Puritans of the English Church, disliked Calvin and Calvinism, and disowned all communion with the Reformed churches of France and the Netherlands . . .' J. Tayler, *A Retrospect of the Religious Life of England: or the Church, Puritanism, and Free Inquiry* (London, 1845), p. 97.

[53] *Remains of the late Rev. Richard Hurrell Froude*, vol. 1, p. 327.

represented the Church in the desert. In Tractarian polemic, the Hanoverian Church was condemned not only for latitudinarianism and Erastianism, but for an apparent neglect of, and departure from, the 'sounder divinity' of the seventeenth century. Hugh James Rose had set the tone for disparagement of the divines of the eighteenth century in his Durham *Lectures on Church History* in 1834,[54] which won praise from Hurrell Froude.[55] When the *Works* of Lancelot Andrewes were published in 1842, a Tractarian reviewer, J.B. Mozley, took the opportunity to point out their neglect in the previous century, complaining that:

> Such men ought to have been looked upon by us at this day not as ancients, but as moderns, as if they lived amongst us, and were our own bishops and professors. But as it is they extend their hand to us over a century of puritanism, and another century of indifferentism; and we must lay hold of that hand, and pull them over to us as we can.[56]

The eighteenth century was condemned for publishing 'hardly any theological works but those of its own divines', such as Jortin and Leland; Mozley lamenting that 'the Warburtonian school carried their dicta with a high hand, in a period of intellectual and religious poverty, amongst minds that had not data by which to measure or resist them'. The consequence was that 'people fell into that narrow-mindedness which naturally follows, when they feed upon their own shadows and reflections, and spin a religious system out of their own heads'.[57] The Nonjurors, however, were honoured for their apparent defence of church liberties in 1689 and thereafter. William Copeland even compared the line then taken by Archbishop Sancroft and Bishop Ken against the Williamite 'new order' with the 'protest of Athanasius and a handful of Catholics against the Arianising Emperor Constantine in the fourth century',[58] choosing, though, not to dwell on the central political dimension or what John

---

[54] H.J. Rose, *The Study of Church History recommended: being the Triennial Divinity Lecture delivered in Bishop Cosin's Library, April 15, 1834, before the Right Rev. the Dean, the Chapter, and the University of Durham* (London, 1834), especially pp. 44–63.

[55] Froude welcomed attacks on 'the divines of the last century, on whom Rose has laid the lash pretty sharply I see in his Durham lecture'. *Remains of the late Reverend Richard Hurrell Froude*, vol. 1, p. 379.

[56] *British Critic*, vol. 31, no. cxi [J.B. Mozley], 'Bishop Andrewes's Sermons' (January, 1842), p. 169.

[57] *Ibid*. Rose (*Study of Church History*, p. 56) had argued that the eighteenth-century latitudinarian divines 'could not write a history of the Christian Church, for her proud, and happy, and holy days are her primitive days, and they had no reverence, and no love for primitive antiquity'.

[58] *British Critic*, vol. 22, no. xci [W.J. Copeland], 'Account of the Non-Jurors' (January, 1837), p. 51. On links between the Tractarians and the Nonjurors, see H. Broxap, *The Later Nonjurors* (Cambridge, 1924); J.H. Overton, *The Nonjurors: their Lives, Principles, and Writings* (London, 1902); Nockles, *Oxford Movement in Context*, chs. i–ii.

Findon calls the 'state point' as distinct from 'church point' behind the original Nonjuring separation.[59]

If the Reformation was a weak point in the Tractarians' armoury, they would seem to have been on much firmer ground in appropriating seventeenth-century Anglican divinity. Newman, however, was interested in the Fathers before he became familiar with the Caroline Divines. His reading of the Caroline Divines before 1833 was sketchy and unsystematic.[60] This helped subordinate the Caroline Divines to the Fathers in his theological thought and method. Moreover, while Keble's knowledge of and reverence for the seventeenth-century divines is undisputed, David Forrester has revealed that until Newman introduced him to them in 1829, Pusey, who was then already Regius Professor of Hebrew at Oxford, had little acquaintance with the Caroline Divines. When Pusey came across William Beveridge (1637–1708), he even commented to Newman that he thought he had been 'higher Church than I am'.[61] Old High Churchmen argued that it was precisely a relative ignorance and misunderstanding of seventeenth-century Anglican teaching on the part of the Tractarian leaders which ultimately blew the Movement off course. Edward Churton criticised the writings of Tractarian extremists such as John Mason Neale in the 1840s partly because they 'are perfectly ignorant of what our best Divines of the seventeenth century have said, who were able to break the heads of a hundred such writers as they'.[62] Charles Wordsworth, later Bishop of St Andrews, maintained in his autobiography that the Tractarians 'threw themselves into the study of the Fathers without the steadying guidance which that study pre-eminently requires'. Apart from Keble in the case of Hooker, and Newman in the case of Bishop Bull, Wordsworth maintained that the Tractarians made no deep study of the leading seventeenth-century divines. He found it significant that the *Library of Anglo-Catholic Theology*, designed to propagate the teaching of those divines, was set up only in 1841, in belated response to the anti-Tractarian Parker Society, and five years after the commencement of the *Library of the Fathers*.[63] The modest initiative 'for a projected society for reprinting some of our standard writers in divinity' came

---

[59] J. Findon, 'The Nonjurors and the Church of England, 1689–1716' (D.Phil. thesis, Oxford, 1977), p. 156.
[60] T.M. Parker, 'The rediscovery of the Fathers in the seventeenth-century Anglican tradition', J. Coulson & A.M. Allchin (eds), *The Rediscovery of Newman* (London, 1967), pp. 41–5. Cf. H.D. Weidner (ed.), *The Via Media of the Anglican Church by John Henry Newman* (Oxford, 1990), pp. xxi–xxv. Newman himself conceded that when he came to study the Caroline Divines, 'the doctrine of 1833 was strengthened in me, not changed'. J.H. Newman, *Apologia pro vita sua* (London, 1864), p. 121.
[61] D. Forrester, *Young Doctor Pusey: A Study in Development* (London, 1989), p. 85. See also note 109.
[62] E. Churton to W. Gresley, n.d. [1846], PHL, Gresley Papers, GRES 3/7/59, PHL.
[63] Chas. Wordsworth, *Annals of my early Life: 1806–1846* (London, 1891), p. 343.

in late 1839 from Herbert Evans, a minor correspondent of Newman, who had only a distant connection with the Tractarian leaders.[64]

The *Library of Anglo-Catholic Theology* attracted the suspicion of anti-Tractarian propagandists because the majority of the committee were deemed to be either authors of the *Tracts for the Times* or closely allied to them.[65] However, the committee encompassed old High Churchmen such as H.H. Norris, R.S. Barter, G. Moberly, Hook, Churton, and Gresley, as well as the Tractarians, Newman, Keble, Pusey, and Robert Wilberforce.[66] Many of the editors in the series, such as John Sherron Brewer (on Herbert Thorndike), J.H. Parker (on Laud), William Scott of Hoxton and James Bliss (also on Laud), and Arthur West Haddan, Newman's curate at St Mary's in 1842, were not within the Movement's inner circle. John Keble edited Bishop Thomas Wilson's *Works* for the series, but expressed disappointment to Newman in 1838 when George Moberly decided 'to edit an English divine, Bishop Cosin, instead of translating St Ambrose'.[67] Other contributors who can be regarded as Tractarian disciples, such as the first editor William Copeland and the treasurer and secretary Charles Crawley, became dissatisfied with the content and tone of some authors whose works they edited. Haddan's edition of Bramhall's *Works* was published in the series in five volumes between 1842 and 1845. As Crawley explained to Newman in 1841, Copeland's 'deeper study of the works in which his editorial office engaged him made him acquainted with some objectionable features in them which he had overlooked before and which were too much for his sensitive mind to tolerate'. Crawley himself sympathised, stating: 'I could not but respect his scruples and agree with him in his opinion as to the character of some passages which he pointed out to me in Bramhall for instance'.[68] The Library was soon 'in a tottering condition', while according to Newman, 'Copeland has given up the editorship because our divines do not go far enough for him', though the fact was that many of the best writings of the Caroline Divines had been or were being published elsewhere.[69] Copeland's scruples were assuaged and he retained the

---

[64] *LD*, vol. 7, pp. 190–1. For details of the Library's officers and publications, see *LD*, vol. 8, 'Appendix 2', pp. 521–3.

[65] *Remarks on a late Advertisement from Oxford (with some notice of an extensive and valuable article in the 'Quarterly Review', published in March last). By an aged layman* (London, 1842), p. 4.

[66] *LD*, vol. 7, p. 190.

[67] J. Keble to J.H. Newman, 7 August 1838, Keble Papers, KCL. John Cosin (1594–1672), a personal friend of Laud and Richard Montagu, was Bishop of Durham from 1660 until his death. Thomas Wilson (1663–1755), was a high church disciplinarian. He was closely asociated with the Nonjurors, but was Bishop of Sodor and Man from 1698 until his death.

[68] C. Crawley to J.H. Newman, 16 January 1841, *LD*, vol. 8, p. 18.

[69] J.H. Newman to F. Rogers, 10 January 1841, *LD*, vol. 8, p. 10. Newman explained that the books which Copeland 'took pleasure in were for the most part gone – and he was forced upon such as he did not merely not like, but could not tolerate'. J.H. Newman to C. Crawley, 14 January 1841, *ibid.*, p. 16.

office of superintending editor until 1843, though his disagreement over the process of selection led him temporarily to withdraw from the project at this time. Moreover, the primary source of his disquiet appears to have related to the republication of the writings of 'controversial church writers'; he would have preferred a more exclusive emphasis on the devotional and sacramental literature of the Caroline tradition. Copeland's friend the old High Churchman Edward Churton could sympathise thus far, conceding that 'we want to show to the Christian world the life and substance, not the form and outline, of catholic truth'. He admitted that Bramhall's writings might be 'hard and sinewy' rather 'than winning and comely', but insisted that it was a duty to the Church of England to republish his controversial writings against papists and Presbyterians, and on schism and rebellion.[70] Such Tractarian misgivings were matched by anti-Tractarian perceptions that, far from supporting the Tractarian cause, many of the proposed publications were likely to 'subvert their own, new system'.[71] On the other hand, the same critic seemed to concede that the republications of at least some of the works of the seventeenth-century divines could serve Tractarian purposes and disarm the unsuspecting reader: 'It may be urged that many, or most, of the AUTHORS whose works are mentioned in the list from Oxford, are generally to be considered sound divines. This is granted. But it must also be considered, that error is seldom more dangerous than when it is blended with truth.'[72]

Newman's objections to the project appear to have been more deep-seated than a question of publishing priorities. He emphasised that the project was 'no plan of mine', and that 'neither Pusey nor I was warm about it',[73] or had even been 'for it'.[74] His unease partly stemmed from a reluctance to tie the Movement too much to the teaching of earlier Anglican divines *per se*, even to those of the seventeenth as well as of the sixteenth century. As he confided revealingly to Charles Crawley in January 1841:

> For myself, I have never had any desire, or made any effort to manage our divines – I do not want to make them better than they are – I do not wish to bring the early Church to their judgment seat – Really I think one can bear to differ from them. The idea of our wishing to stand or fall by Jewell, Hicks, or Waterland! Nay or by Jeremy Taylor, or Jackson or Laud themselves.[75]

Both Newman and Pusey conceded 'the absurdity of calling it Anglo-Catholic Library' and felt it would 'look very meagre' when 'many of our first

---

[70] E. Churton to W.J. Copeland, 30 May 1840, Churton Papers, Sutton Coldfield [hereafter, SC] (private possession).
[71] *Remarks on a late Advertisement from Oxford*, p. 5.
[72] *Ibid.*, p. 7.
[73] J.H. Newman to F. Rogers, 10 January 1841, *LD*, vol. 8, p. 10.
[74] J.H. Newman to E.B. Pusey, 12 January 1841, *ibid.*, p. 14.
[75] J.H. Newman to C. Crawley, 14 January 1841, *ibid.*, p. 17.

writers' were left out because they had been already reprinted.[76] Newman only went along with the project as a way of countering 'the Protestants of London' and their 'Opposition Society' dedicated to bringing out 'cheaply Reformation works'[77] – 'because the Parker Society will else inundate us with Protestantism pure and undiluted'.[78] Certainly, the absence of Jewel's *Apology* and the works of even Hooker and Ussher attracted adverse notice from an anti-Tractarian critic.[79] In fact, Newman only reluctantly agreed to promote the Library on condition that less Catholic authors were excluded. The old High Churchman Edward Churton wrote to Crawley:

> If you wish to propitiate, and avoid suspicion, why do you insert such names as Montagu and Heylin? You have left out my friend Dr Edward Hyde. Take my word for him, he is worth more than either of the two last . . . Johnson's *Unbloody Sacrifice* is a book, for which only persons of very extreme opinions will thank you.[80]

Newman reacted sharply to the implication that moderation must be the keynote of religious discourse. As he told Crawley:

> I never meant to give in to Churton's supposition that conciliation was the order of the day. If I am interested in the Library, it is in order to get certain books reprinted, and whether this raises a clamour or not I really do not care . . . if their [Montagu's and Johnson's] works are not published, and Johnson's with no great delay, I shall lose great part of the interest I have in the plan – nay I do not think I should care to promote it.[81]

In the event, none of Hyde's *Works* was included in the Library.

Pusey shared Newman's misgivings about the Anglo-Catholic Library. In a letter to Newman in January 1841, he conceded that he 'should hardly be sorry, if the whole thing came to nothing. I never had any great affection for it, except as far as it would give the opportunity of bringing out two or three sets of works, as Laud, Bramhall'. He also warned of the need for careful editing: 'one might have catholic and uncatholic works from the same writer, as Hall, Ussher, Beveridge', which would render their influence 'nugatory'. He concluded: 'I thought it would be unjust to our divines, not to reserve to the editor, the right of explaining ambiguous phrases in a catholic sense, with a benign interpretation'.[82] In short, the writings of the Caroline Divines had to

---

[76] E.B. Pusey to J.H. Newman, 8 January 1841, *ibid.*, p. 13; J.H. Newman to Miss Holmes, 12 February, 1841, *ibid.*, p. 33.

[77] J.H. Newman to F. Rogers, 10 January 1841, *ibid.*, p. 10; J.H. Newman to E.B. Pusey, 12 January 1841, *ibid.*, p. 14; J.H. Newman to Miss Holmes, 12 February 1841, *ibid.*, p. 33.

[78] J.H. Newman to C. Crawley, 14 January 1841, *ibid.*, p. 17.

[79] *Remarks on a late Advertisement from Oxford,* p. 5.

[80] E. Churton to C. Crawley, [30 January] 1841, *ibid.*, p. 53.

[81] J.H. Newman to C. Crawley, 3 March 1841, *ibid.*, p. 54.

[82] E.B. Pusey to J.H. Newman, 8 January 1841, *ibid.*, pp. 13–14.

be packaged. In the end, Newman did not entirely get his way. The ultra-high church John Johnson's *Theological Works,* including his *Unbloody Sacrifice and Altar* (1714–18),[83] edited by R. Owen, appeared in the Library in two volumes in 1847–8, but Montagu's *Works* were not reprinted in the Library. In the wake of the Tractarian conversions to Rome of 1845–6, some of its members resigned or threatened resignation in order 'to take decided steps to distinguish ourselves from the Romanisers', but the committee of the Library as a whole determined to pull together,[84] distancing the project from the taint of Tractarianism and making it into a vehicle for a self-conscious Anglican loyalism.

After his conversion to Rome in 1845, Newman reacted strongly against James Mozley's criticism that he had only paid lip-service to the teaching of the Caroline Divines and had never really believed in the Anglican Church or received it as divine. Paul Elmer More in his *The Spirit of Anglicanism* (1935) conceded Newman's expressions of loyalty to the seventeenth-century divines but questioned its basis – affection rather than intellectual conviction.[85] Yet such was Newman's confidence in Anglicanism in the mid 1830s, that in his controversy with the Abbé Jager in 1834–5, he was anxious lest his arguments in favour of the 'branch theory' and doctrinal 'fundamentals' might unsettle his opponent. 'Those arguments', he later emphasised, 'were not mine, but the evolution of Laud's theory, Stillingfleet's etc. which seemed to me clear, complete and unanswerable'.[86] Viewed in retrospect, Newman's *via media* might seem to have been only a temporary staging-post in a long religious odyssey, with the Caroline Divines tied into a schema of his own devising. At the time, however, the Caroline Anglican standpoint was held and propagated with what Newman himself later called a 'fierceness' that few could exceed.

---

[83] The eucharistic theology of John Johnson (1662–1725), Vicar of Cranbrook, Kent, 1710–25, had close affinities with that of the Nonjurors. Johnson's influential treatise *The Unbloody Sacrifice and Altar, Unveiled and Supported* (1714–18), affirmed a doctrine of eucharistic sacrifice that was 'proper', 'expiatory', and 'propitiatory', and described the elements after Consecration as the 'Sacramental' or 'Eucharistical body and blood' of the Lord.

[84] E. Churton to W. Gresley, 6 February 1846, GRES 3/7/63, PHL. Richard Montagu (1577–1641), was appointed Bishop of Chichester by King Charles I in 1628, Bishop of Norwich in 1638.

[85] *Anglicanism: The Thought and Practice of the Church of England, illustrated from the religious literature of the seventeenth century. Compiled and edited by Paul Elmer More and Frank Leslie Cross* (London, 1935), pp. xxx–xxxi. For a recent hostile reading of Newman's Tractarian career as self-seeking and 'sectarian' in spirit, see F.M. Turner, *John Henry Newman: the Challenge to Evangelical Religion* (Yale, 2002).

[86] J.H. Newman to H. Wilberforce, [27 January] 1846, *LD,* vol. 11, p. 100. In his letter to Martin Routh, President of Magdalen College, Oxford, in January 1837, asking him permission to dedicate his *Lectures on the Prophetical of the Church* to him, Newman explained that he had 'tried, as far as may be, to follow the line of doctrine marked out by our great divines, of whom perhaps I have followed, Bramhall, then Laud, Hammond, Field, Stillingfleet, Beveridge, and others of the same school'.

According to the Anglican theologian, Henry McAdoo, Anglicanism might provide a theological method and *ethos* but was never a theological system.[87] A possible key to Newman's ultimate loss of faith in Anglicanism was his attempt – contrary to his insistence that he made no effort 'to manage our divines'[88] – to erect a coherent doctrinal edifice on a structure not designed to support it. For as Roman Catholic apologists pointed out, not only did the Caroline Divines differ from one another, but a single author such as Jeremy Taylor could contradict himself in different works.[89] The Caroline Divines exhibited a common theological temper and method – a tripartite appeal to scripture, reason, and tradition – but no doctrinal unanimity. The Caroline Divines might have represented 'a school' but it was a school 'which never has spoken as a school'.[90]

Stephen Sykes has argued that Newman chose to overlook what he and Paul Avis, following P.E. Moore, Henry McAdoo, and H.L. Weatherby, assumed to have been the underlying 'liberal spirit' and religious diversity within the Caroline theological tradition; a diversity which later pre-Tractarian Anglican apologists such as Waterland and Van Mildert had conceded. In consequence, Newman created 'the myth of a unique Anglicanism'.[91] It is true that in his Tractarian apologetic Newman sought to complete, not merely reproduce, the 'inheritance' of the seventeenth century. It was not long before his old High Church friend Hugh James Rose was warning him against over-shooting the bounds of Anglican orthodoxy in an anti-Protestant direction.[92] By appealing directly to antiquity, Newman in theory aimed to supplement incoherencies in the Anglican system with points of primitive faith and practice, such as monasticism, which were lacking.[93] It is debatable just how far this was a departure from the Laudian approach; it was certainly in line with the later Nonjuring method. Caroline and later High Church apologists could be more rigid about their positions in their day than Sykes and Avis allow. It has been argued that divines such as Andrewes, Overall and Montagu

---

[87] H.R. McAdoo, *The Spirit of Anglicanism: A Survey of Anglican Theological Method in the Seventeenth Century* (London, 1965), pp. v–vi.

[88] 'For myself, I have never had any desire, or made any effort to *manage* our divines – I do not want to make them better than they are – I do not wish to bring the early Church to their judgment seat'. J.H. Newman to C. Crawley, 14 January 1841, *LD*, vol. 8, p. 17.

[89] [John Milner], *A Vindication of the End of Religious Controversy* (London, 1822), pp. 40–7.

[90] A.W. Haddan, 'The English Divines of the 16th and 17th centuries', A. Weir & W.D. Maclagan (eds), *The Church and the Age: Essays in the Principles and Present Position of the English Church* (London, 1870), p. 230.

[91] S.W. Sykes, 'Newman, Anglicanism and the Fundamentals', I. Ker & A.G. Hill (eds), *Newman after a Hundred Years* (Oxford, 1990), pp. 365–6; H.L. Weatherby, 'The encircling gloom: Newman's departure from the Caroline tradition', *Victorian Studies,* vol. 12, no. 1 (September, 1968), pp. 57–8.

[92] See J.W. Burgon, 'Hugh James Rose: the Restorer of the Old Paths', *Lives of Twelve Good Men,* 2 vols (4th edn, London, 1889), vol. 1, especially pp. 209–26.

[93] Nockles, *Oxford Movement in Context*, pp. 119–20.

promoted a strict imitation of patristic doctrine and practice as normative for the Church of England of the 1620s and 1630s.[94] There may have been a blurring of lines of demarcation between some Laudians and early and moderate Latitudinarians, Laud being more sympathetic to the proto-Latitudinarians Chillingworth and Hales than his spiritual successors could countenance. Anthony Milton, however, has demonstrated that there was a clear breakdown in the early Caroline period of an earlier Reformed consensus rooted in episcopalian Calvinism, with Laudianism in the 1630s triggering the kind of party conflict which the Oxford Movement was to trigger from the 1830s onwards. There was a Laudian hard core within the umbrella of the Caroline Divines. As Milton observes, for Laudians, the *via media* symbolised a determined exclusivity, rather than moderation, while the Tractarians poured scorn on the notion of the 'middle way' being synonymous with 'moderation'.[95] One should beware of accepting at face value assertions of 'Anglican moderation' by Montagu and other contemporary Arminian divines, some of whom doubted even Laud's steadfastness. As Milton concludes, it should 'come as no surprise' that early Laudian divines 'often found their strongest early lay patrons among recusants or church papists'.[96]

The Tractarians valued Laud and Laudianism not for that Arminianism which has preoccupied current historians of the early Stuart Church, and not for being a mere arm or appendage of what has been called 'Carolinism'.[97] Initially, Tractarian commentators identified with the authoritarian political dimension of Laudianism,[98] but then played down the establishmentarianism which appealed to old High Churchmen, arguing that regal power was exalted primarily because royalty was then on the side of the Church and used to raise her sacerdotal claims and 'not to secularise her'.[99] For the Tractarians, Laud

---

[94] Anthony Milton, *Catholic and Reformed* (Cambridge, 1995), pp. 274–5.

[95] *Ibid.*, especially pp. 531, 538–40. The Tractarian F.W. Faber, echoing the Tractarian Newman, ridiculed the idea that the *via media*, in relation to Laud, might stand for 'moderation': 'he [Laud] might remember, that the moderate party in Arian times was popular, and yet not safe, neither did it prevail. And had he lived forty-four years from his Martyrdom, he would have seen some of that church history carried out at home. Moderate men are not tall enough to throw a shadow over posterity, nor of sufficient integrity of heart and purpose to project their influence on after-generations.' [Faber], *Autobiography of Dr. William Laud,* p. xvi. See also notes 112, 167.

[96] Milton, *Catholic and Reformed*, p. 541.

[97] For use of the term, see J. Davies, *The Caroline Captivity of the Church: Charles I and the Remoulding of Anglicanism* (Oxford, 1992), ch. 1.

[98] See P.B. Nockles, 'Newman and early Tractarian Politics', V.A. McClelland (ed.), *By Whose Authority?,* pp. 79–111.

[99] *Christian Remembrancer*, vol. 9, no. 47 [J.B. Mozley], 'Archbishop Laud' (January 1845), p. 266. James Mozley argued (p. 217) that: 'Nothing can show more clearly that Laud's school was not exalting the *Regale* as such, than the marked anti-*Regale* line in which it issued at last. The Nonjuring school, who wrote vehemently against the regale, were legitimate successors of the Laudian one.'

and his school were exemplars, primarily because they were convinced that it was he and his associates who rescued the sacramental doctrine and restored it to the English Church, and to whom they owed thanks for the survival of all her Catholic aspects as regards liturgy, rubrics, ceremonies, altars, and even episcopacy.

According to James Mozley in a lengthy article in the *Christian Remembrancer* in 1845, commemorating the bicentenary of his martyrdom, Laud stopped the Church of England 'just in time, as she was rapidly going down hill, and he saved all the Catholicism which the reign of Genevan influence had left her'.[100] Mozley and others certainly welcomed Laud's breach of the Genevan or Calvinist sense of the Articles. However, unlike the 'high and dry' school of Bishops Marsh and Pretyman-Tomline, who a generation earlier had been obsessed by the need to repudiate the Calvinist interpretation of Article 17 in support of predestination made by their Anglican Evangelical opponents,[101] the Tractarians were mainly concerned with the sacramental and ecclesiological implications of what they disparagingly called 'Genevan' influence. Newman especially felt that Arminianism, as mediated through the Dutch theologian and jurist Hugo Grotius (1583–1645), had an underlying tendency towards rationalism and depreciation of the sacraments. In a revealing review article on Le Bas's *Life of Archbishop Laud* in the April 1836 number of the *British Critic*, Newman blamed 'our reunion with foreign Protestantism' at the Synod of Dort, for the introduction of what he called the 'plague' of 'latitudinarian indifference', seeking all the time to exempt Laud from responsibility for the trend. As Newman explained:

> Hales, who accompanied Sir Dudley Carleton to the Synod of Dort, made acquaintance there with Episcopius, the disciple of Arminius, brought back his doctrines to England, and communicated them to Chillingworth. We have evidence in history of the great disquiet which this importation gave to Laud, who prevailed on one of these two divines to abandon or conceal his opinions. However, the contagion ran its course; in the next reign it gave rise to a school in Cambridge, under Tillotson and others, diffused itself through the nation in the writings of the celebrated Mr Locke, which drew upon him the condemnation of Laud's own university, and evinced its inbred hatred to the Church, by co-operating in the separation of the Nonjurors, in the erection of the Presbyterian Kirk, and in the ascendancy of Hoadly and his party.[102]

In adopting this historiography, Newman was reverting to a characteristically Protestant genre of tracing the history of doctrinal error and corruption while turning it on its head at the expense of Protestantism. He also appears to

---

[100] *Ibid.*, pp. 299–300.
[101] See Nockles, *Oxford Movement in Context*, pp. 191–3.
[102] *British Critic*, vol. 19, no. lxxxviii [J.H. Newman], 'Le Bas's Life of Archbishop Laud' (April, 1836), p. 369.

have been influenced by his reading of his favourite late Caroline divine, George Bull, author of a *Defence of the Nicene Faith* (1685). Bull did not share the admiration of the Laudians Hammond and Bramhall for Episcopius and Grotius, whom he regarded as undermining the authority and function of the Fathers.[103] Newman's historical view of Arminianism also matched that of an old High Churchman, Edward Churton. In a sermon in 1836, Churton had maintained that the influence on Hanoverian Anglicanism of Dutch Arminian theologians such as Episcopius and Limborch had been pernicious in undermining sacramental doctrines, and 'actually operated against those views of the hierarchy that Laud who is said to have imbibed it, held'.[104]

Newman was uneasy about Dutch Arminianism because it represented an Erastian lay movement which rose and fell in alliance with a republican party, though it was the theological character of Dutch Arminianism that most concerned him. He maintained that the apparently rationalising virus introduced by Dutch Arminianism had infected even the High Churchmanship characteristic of the eve of the Oxford Movement. Along with Froude, Newman regarded doctrinal Calvinism as holding on to a higher sense of supernatural order and sense of the transcendent than that of much of 'orthodox' pre-Tractarian High Churchmanship. In a striking passage in his *Autobiographical Memoir*, when referring to the Oxford of the 1820s, Newman observed: 'a cold Arminian doctrine, the first stage of liberalism, was the characteristic . . . both of the high and dry Anglicans of that day and of the Oriel divines'.[105] Newman's Tractarian friend Samuel Wood made a similar point. On Newman's prompting, Wood in May 1837 proposed an article for the *British Critic* in which, as Wood explained, he would:

> point out that the Arminianism . . . which succeeded the Calvinism of the Reformation and was its reaction, and which assumes to itself . . . the name of Orthodoxy, is just as non-catholic and more Rationalistic, and as far removed from the Mysterious and True System as Calvinism.[106]

---

[103] R. Nelson, *The Life of Dr George Bull, late Lord Bishop of St David's. With the History of those Controversies in which he was engaged* (2nd edn, London, 1714), pp. 370–7.

[104] E. Churton, *The Church of England a Witness and Keeper of the Catholic Tradition*, p. 13. Churton argued (p. 39), in similar vein to Newman, that John Tillotson, the late seventeenth-century latitudinarian Archbishop of Canterbury, borrowed from continental Arminian theologians, 'with too little regard to the points in which their expositions [e.g. on baptism] differ from the authorised statements of the Church of England . . .'.

[105] H. Tristram (ed.), *John Henry Newman: Autobiographical writings* (London, 1956), p. 83. Stephen Thomas comments on the significance of this passage: 'the potential slide into liberalism was here not presented as so often, via Evangelical Protestantism, popular or otherwise, but via the upholders of the creed, liturgy, establishment, Arminianism and orthodoxy – the Zs, who are lumped together with *Noetics* such as Whately and Hawkins.' S. Thomas, *Newman and Heresy: the Anglican Years* (Cambridge, 1991), pp. 14–15.

[106] S.F. Wood to J.H. Newman, 29 May 1837, *LD*, vol. 6, p. 77.

This viewpoint received later corroboration in a survey of Anglican eucharistic teaching by H.C. Grove in 1857. Grove argued that in the seventeenth century, the highest doctrine of the eucharist emanated from Calvinist as much as from classical Laudian divines. He traced the Zwinglian notions in the following century to the influence of 'Arminian' rather than Calvinist divines.[107]

Newman's selectivity in citing the Caroline Divines in order to suit his then current rhetorical purposes represented a ubiquitous practice in controversial writing, shared by all sides, and one which had been perfected by Roman Catholic controversialists such as Bishop John Milner.[108] A marked gap, however, between Newman's public veneration and private criticism of certain of the Caroline Divines was evident at the time of his exposition of his theory of the *via media*. If, in his reading of the seventeenth-century divines, Newman found a discordant note, he privately expressed dismay. Newman's judgements on individual Caroline Divines could be as critical as any of Hurrell Froude's on the Reformers. Froude himself as early as 1834 had chided Newman for printing Cosin's *History of Popish Transubstantiation* as Tract 27 because of what Froude regarded as its unacceptable Protestantism.[109] Newman came to regard William Chillingworth as the patron of later latitudinarianism and an 'ultra-Protestant', on account of his celebrated maxim, 'the Bible only, the religion of protestants',[110] a view which mirrored the way in which Chillingworth had been presented and claimed by the school of Hoadly and Blackburne and its heterodox tail. Chillingworth's standpoint, however, was more subtle than Newman allowed. Edward Churton, who was better conversant with the nuances of Chillingworth's theology than was Newman, even planned in 1836 a new edition of Chillingworth's works in order to demonstrate that Chillingworth was 'a good churchman and a good loyalist', whose views had been misinterpreted by, and were far removed from, later ultra-latitudinarians. Churton may have overstated his case, but he had a point when he impressed upon Newman that 'the doctrine of

---

[107] H.C. Grove, *The Teaching of the Anglican Divines of the Time of King James I and King Charles I, on the Doctrine of the Holy Eucharist, Extracted from their Writings, with an Introduction, containing Remarks on the late works on that subject by Dr Pusey and Mr Keble* (London, 1858), pp. 6–7, 15–16.

[108] See Nockles, 'The Difficulties of Protestantism', especially pp. 206–9.

[109] R.H. Froude to J.H. Newman, January 1835, *LD*, vol. 5, p. 18. Even the conservative patron of the Tractarians, Hugh James Rose, normally a restraining Protestant voice, could complain that the Calvinist Bishop Beveridge had been used in the *Tracts for the Times:* 'my respect for him has been much diminished by the close study of some of his works. It is not only that he puts forth hot Calvinism (sometimes I am inclined to think without knowing it) but that there is a looseness and occasionally a weakness in his reasoning and an extravagance which make him anything but a useful or safe guide'. H.J. Rose to A.P. Perceval, 28 January 1834, *LBV* (transcript), PHL. Newman, on the other hand, held Beveridge in high regard and seemed untroubled by his Calvinism.

[110] [Newman], 'Le Bas's Life of Archbishop Laud', p. 368.

Chillingworth ... is good Oxford divinity', and that Laud had 'something to do with this'.[111] Indeed, Laud had prompted his godson Chillingworth's abandonment of Roman Catholicism in 1632, and influenced Chillingworth in his writing *The Religion of Protestants, a Safe Way to Salvation* (1637), commonly regarded as the first classic of Anglican latitudinarianism. In this often misunderstood work, while Chillingworth argued for liberty against the supposed exclusiveness of Rome, he took a high view of the nature of the Church and priesthood. Moreover, the preface contained a spirited defence of Laudian innovations in ritual. Anthony Milton's suggestion that Laud's, albeit corrective, hand in Chillingworth's and Hales's writings may have pointed to Laud's own moderation on issues of pure doctrine, bears out a favourite argument of Churton which only confirmed Newman's unease and which found no echo in standard Tractarian panegyrics on Laud.[112] Newman also found fault with statements in the writings of Henry Hammond and Jeremy Taylor, asking Churton rhetorically in 1837: 'how come Taylor to be so liberal in his *Liberty of Prophesying*? And how far is Hammond tinctured as regards the Sacraments with Grotianism?'[113] Newman's only objection to the posthumous publication of Froude's 'paper on the Latitudinarians' (the 'Essay on Rationalism' published in his *Remains*), was that it did not take sufficient account of Grotius's 'influence on our Church for good and bad'.[114] While he recommended Taylor's spiritual writings to his younger sister in a letter of June 1837, he proceeded to describe him as 'a writer essentially untrustworthy – i.e. if some external attraction meets him, he cannot resist it ... The necessity, for example, of seeming an anti-Papist will draw all his nails out'.[115]

---

[111] E. Churton to W.J. Copeland, 12 April 1836; E. Churton to W.J. Copeland, 21 May 1836, Churton Papers, SC. Churton proposed a new study of Chillingworth, aiming 'to show that the principles of Chillingworth were not what Coleridge (S.T.) and Alexander Knox have expressed as their general view of them; and consequently that the claim of fraternisation [with the heterodox] made by Hallam (*Constitutional History*) and the Dissenters of the Socinian cast is not well founded. H.J. Rose thinks it will be difficult to make out C[hillingworth]'s orthodoxy. I hope not.' E. Churton to W.J. Copeland, 21 March 1836, Churton Papers, SC.

[112] Milton, *Catholic and Reformed*, pp. 165–7. At the time of the Denison eucharistic controversy of the mid-1850s, Churton returned to the theme of Laud's relative doctrinal liberality: 'Laud was in truth a much more Broad Churchman, than the world seems yet willing to suppose. But at any rate it cannot be denied that he was the discerning patron of both Chillingworth and Taylor; and where will the English Churchman find the just principles of Religious Liberty laid down, if not in the *Religion of Protestants*, and the *Liberty of Prophesying*?'. E. Churton, *A Legal Argument in the Case of Ditcher versus Denison* (London, 1856), p. 22. Cf. notes 95, 167 for Tractarian repudiation of the notion of Laud's doctrinal 'moderation'.

[113] J.H. Newman to E. Churton, 14 March 1837, *LD*, vol. 6, p. 41. Henry Hammond (1605–60) was a Laudian who was also part of the Great Tew circle. A Chaplain in Ordinary to King Charles I, he was most renowned for his popular *Practical Catechism* (1645). See note 122.

[114] J.H. Newman to J. Keble, 26 February 1839, *LD*, vol. 7, p. 42.

[115] J.H. Newman to Mrs J. Mozley, 4 June 1837, *LD*, vol. 6, p. 81.

In late 1839 when Newman's first doubts about Anglicanism were sown by Wiseman's celebrated article in the *Dublin Review*,[116] Newman entered a first stage in a process of disillusionment with the Caroline Divines. Conscious of incipient doubts as to the English Church's catholicity, he initially turned again to them, especially Henry Hammond, complaining in a letter to Pusey on 1 January 1840 of the difficulty of obtaining a copy of Hammond's *Of Schisme. A Defence of the Church of England, against the Romanists* (1654).[117] Thereafter, Newman soon lost interest in employing the Caroline Divines as weapons in the armoury of Anglican apologetic against Rome. In his article, 'The Catholicity of the English Church' in the *British Critic* in 1840, he cited Stillingfleet, Barrow, Dodwell, and Hickes, as proponents of the Anglican branch theory of independent episcopal churches, but distanced himself somewhat from it, hinting at the persuasiveness of St Augustine's apparently contrary view – that the judgment of the whole Church was to be preferred over particular Churches.[118] Manning's suggestion to Newman in 1839, that the anti-Romanist writings of 'our James the Second divines', be reprinted,[119] fell on deaf ears. By this date, the old High Churchman Joshua Watson complained of the Tractarians, 'no Jeremy Taylor or Bishop Bull is to be found amongst their prophets, no dissuasives from Popery, no statements of the corruptions of Rome to alarm and restrain them'.[120] By January 1841 Newman was suggesting privately to Frederic Rogers that Wiseman was no more unscrupulous a controversialist on the Roman side than Jeremy Taylor, Laud, or Stillingleet were on the Anglican side. With singular even-handedness he pronounced that it was 'as rare a thing, candour in controversy, as to be a Saint'.[121]

The only purpose in which the Caroline Divines remained useful to Newman was that of showing how ideas put forward by the Tractarians had in the past been accepted as legitimate within the Church of England. As his *via media* construct collapsed, Newman would find the testimony of Caroline divinity, and especially spirituality, valuable and consoling. As the arguments from apostolicity became more problematic for Newman, the Anglican devotional tradition became even more important as a mark of the Church of England's Catholicity. In March 1840 he delighted in the 'most splendid present' from William Anderdon of a four-volume edition of Henry

---

[116] See J.H. Newman, *Apologia pro vita sua* (London, 1864), pp. 211–12.

[117] J.H. Newman to E.B. Pusey, 1 January 1840, *LD*, vol. 7, p. 195. Pusey wrote to say that Manning had lent him a copy of the book. Manning was responsible for a reprint of the work which was published in 1841.

[118] *British Critic*, vol. 27, no. cv [J.H. Newman], 'The Catholicity of the English Church' (June 1840), pp. 55–63.

[119] H.E. Manning to J.H. Newman, 23 October 1839, Manning Papers, Ms Eng Lett c. 654, fol. 43, Bodleian Library, Oxford.

[120] E. Churton, *Memoir of Joshua Watson*, 2 vols (London, 1861), vol. 2, p. 275.

[121] J.H. Newman to F. Rogers, 10 January 1841, *LD*, vol. 8, p. 10.

Hammond's *Works* (1674–84).[122] Sensitive by this date to suggestions that he was raising sympathies for Rome, he protested in a letter to Keble that if this was true, it was only true in the same sense that Hooker, Taylor, and Bull had, inadvertently, done so:

> Their argument may be against Rome, but the sympathies they raise must be towards Rome so far as Rome maintains truths which our Church does not teach or enforce. Thus it is a question of degree between our Divines and me. I may, if so be, go further; I may raise sympathies more; but I am but urging minds in the same direction as they. In short, would not Hooker, if Vicar of St Mary's, be in my difficulty?[123]

Faced with cases of individuals poised to join the Church of Rome at this time, Newman urged waverers to immerse themselves in what he still regarded as the spiritual treasures of the Caroline tradition, notably the devotional writings of Lancelot Andrewes, Jeremy Taylor, John Cosin, and Thomas Ken. Newman's interest in propagating this devotional tradition had been illustrated in 1836 by Tract 75 in which he virtually canonised Bishop Ken in an anniversary service which he composed on the lines of the Roman Breviary,[124] and was continued in 1840 by his translation and arrangement of the *Greek Devotions* of Bishop Andrewes in Tract 88.[125] Even Laud was honoured primarily for his religious and priestly, and not political character. In the preface to his edition of Laud's *Sermons* in 1842 for the first volume of the seven-volume collection of Laud's Works in the *Library of Anglo-Catholic Theology*, William Scott, Vicar of Hoxton, adopted an apologetic tone, lamenting that they revealed Laud 'more as a statesman rather than as a theologian'. Scott insisted, however, that other sermons that had not survived, and the evidence of his *Diary* and *Conference with Fisher the Jesuit*, as well as his sufferings under persecution, testified 'that his religion was deep and earnest'.[126] Other Tractarian reprints of Laud's writings aimed to demonstrate

---

[122] J.H. Newman to H.E. Manning, 11 March 1840, *LD*, vol. 7, p. 254.

[123] J.H. Newman to J. Keble, 6 November 1840, *ibid.*, p. 433.

[124] *Tracts for the Times. By members of the University of Oxford. Vol. III for 1835–6* [J.H. Newman], *No. 75: On the Roman Breviary as embodying the substance of the Devotional Services of the Church Catholic*, 6. 'Matin Service for March 21. Bishop Ken's Day' (new edn, Oxford, 1840), pp. 135–45. Newman defended the publication of selections from the Roman Breviary in 1839–40 by Tractarian editors from the Caroline precedent of John Cosin's *Hours of Prayer* in 1627. J.H. Newman, *A Letter to the Right Reverend Father in God, Richard, Lord Bishop of Oxford, on occasion of No. 90 in the series called the 'Tracts for the Times'* (Oxford, 1841), p. 10.

[125] *Tracts for the Times . . . vol. V for 1838–40*, [J.H. Newman], *The Greek Devotions of Bishop Andrews, Translated and Arranged* (3rd edn, London, 1843), pp. 1–96.

[126] *Works of the Most Reverend Father in God, William Laud D.D. sometime Archbishop of Canterbury*, 7 vols, vol. 1: *Sermons*. Edited by W. Scott (Oxford, 1847), p. vii; [Faber], *Autobiography of Dr. William Laud*, pp. xvi–xvii.

the point. Frederick Faber's 1838 edition of Laud's *Private Devotions*, first published in 1667, and his 1839 edition of Laud's *Autobiography*, both had the hagiographic purpose of promoting Laud for his spirituality. Tractarian appropriation of the Laudian devotional heritage, also served a contemporary anti-Evangelical controversial and polemical purpose. Faber's preface highlighted the opposition of Laud's 'sound and healthy principles of practical religion' to 'the views and feelings of the Puritanical party'.[127] Faber made explicit the link between Laud's opposition to the Puritan devotional temper of his day and the current Tractarian opposition to popular Evangelical religiosity:

> A reprint of this manual seemed the more necessary when so many devotional books are being published, which put forward a system of practical religion, a little refined in its details, but to all intents and purposes the same with that, in opposition to which Archbishop Laud wrote, and acted, and in the end shed his blood.[128]

Although Pusey and Keble were never close to abandoning their Anglican allegiance, they also came to view and employ the testimony of the Caroline Divines in a new way; not only deferring to the early church as a storehouse of polemical weapons against the Church of Rome, but 'as the ultimate expounder of the meaning' of the Church of England.[129] It was clear that the Caroline Divines would now be valued by the Tractarian leaders exclusively as expositors of primitive faith and practice rather than in their anti-Roman controversial capacity. The Caroline Divines increasingly were called into service by Pusey and others, to support contentious Tractarian interpretations of ecclesiology, and sacramental doctrine on baptism, the eucharist, the

---

[127] *The Private Devotions of Dr William Laud, Archbishop of Canterbury, and Martyr. Edited by the Rev. Frederic W. Faber, B.A. Fellow of University College, Oxford* (Oxford, 1838), p. viii. James Mozley likewise explained away perceptions of Laud's dry spiritual tone, by the neglect of this aspect even by friendly or hagiographic authors. Thus, while Mozley regarded Heylin as admirable in his treatment of Laud the statesman and ecclesiastic, he commented: 'we are not led into the inner and deeper part of his character: the *homo interius* was not in Heylin's line. We go to another document for this. The Diary reveals a different man from what the exterior man presented.' [Mozley], 'Archbishop Laud', p. 203. Faber's Tractarian enthusiasm for publishing the Diary contrasted with the earlier attitude of Laud's old High Church biographer, Charles Le Bas, for whom it consisted 'chiefly of dry memoranda of passing events, made obviously for his own private convenience'. Le Bas maintained that 'we cannot appeal to the Diary of Laud in support of his literary and theological reputation'. *British Critic*, vol. 6, no. 11 [C. Le Bas], 'Life and Times of Archbishop Laud' (July, 1829), pp. 419–20. It also contrasted with the contemptuous attitude to Laud's spirituality by some Victorian Evangelicals. See J.C. Ryle, 'Archbishop Laud and his times', *Church Association Lectures, 1869, delivered at St James's Hall, London. Revised by the authors, with an introduction by the Chairman*, J.C. Colquhoun (London, 1869), p. 160.

[128] *Private Devotions of Dr William Laud*, p. ix.

[129] H.P. Liddon, *Life of Edward Bouverie Pusey*, 4 vols (London, 1893–4), vol. 2, p. 140.

religious life, confession and absolution, that were deemed part of primitive faith and practice.

Of course, some individual Caroline Divines were more amenable for this purpose than others. Significantly, Pusey, like Henry Manning, came to have a special regard for Herbert Thorndike, because, as Pusey put it, Thorndike had 'seen further than others'.[130] Significantly, in explaining a shift in his own position, Pusey commented to Manning in 1845: 'It was Thorndike who first broke in upon the acquiescence which I had ever yielded to our hereditary maxim that a particular church had a right to reform itself. A misgiving, expressed by him, raised the question in my mind'.[131] In his *Just Weights and Measures* (1662), while adhering to the standard Anglican apologetical gambit of blaming Rome for the breach in church unity at the Reformation, Thorndike argued that should the Church of England move in a more Protestant direction in order to conciliate or comprehend Puritans and presbyterians, then the incidence of guilt for the schism might shift.[132] However, if he urged a greater distance from Geneva, he also encouraged the possibility of reunion with Rome. Thorndike was more critical than most Caroline Divines of faults in the English Reformation, even referring to 'that horrible act of abolishing the monasteries under Henry VIII', and admitting that 'the tares of Puritanism were sown together with the grain of the Reformation in the Church of England'.[133] In his *Epilogue of the Tragedy of the Church of England* (1659), Thorndike in effect asserted a right of revision for the Anglican, in the light of a better understood Catholicism than had been displayed at the time of the Reformation itself. Tractarians could also identify with his advocacy of a restoration of penitential discipline and primitive practices such as prayers for the dead. In an archidiaconal charge of 1841, Manning appealed to Thorndike's *Just Weights and Measures*, to support his call for a practical restoration of the Church's powers of the keys through auricular confession, approvingly citing Thorndike's assertion: 'the Church is founded upon the power of the Keys. And therefore when that power is not in force ... there it is a Church in hope rather than in deed and being'.[134] In a letter to Priscilla Maurice in 1850, Manning explained how between 1832 and 1836 his 'mind was opening to Hooker and through Hooker to Thorndike', whom he described as 'the most Roman of our divines'.[135]

---

[130] E.B. Pusey to H.E. Manning, 9 July 1844, *LBV* (transcript), PHL. Herbert Thorndike (1598–1672) was a Fellow of Trinity College, Oxford, and after the Restoration was made a Prebendary of Westminster Abbey.
[131] E.B. Pusey to H.E. Manning, 12 August 1845, *LBV* (transcript), PHL.
[132] T.A. Lacey, *Herbert Thorndike, 1598–1672* (London, 1929), p. 114.
[133] Quoted in *ibid.*, p. 107.
[134] H.E. Manning, *A Charge delivered at the ordinary Visitation of the Archdeaconry of Chichester in July 1841* (London, 1841), p. 27.
[135] H.E. Manning to Miss P. Maurice, 30 August 1850, Manning Papers, Ms. Eng. Lett. c. 659,

It was partly because he felt that Roman Catholic controversialists had garbled statements of Thorndike so as to turn them against the integrity of the Church of England that a Tractarian editor in 1841 justified republication of some of his writings.[136] Nonetheless, Thorndike's theological reputation was rendered suspect by Tractarian patronage. A leading old High Church divine, Christopher Wordsworth junior, warned that he was a less safe guide than Bramhall,[137] while a Tractarian tutor at Christ Church, Thomas Morris, was assured by a correspondent: 'Montagu and Thorndike . . . may very possibly approach nearer to your views than their contemporaries in general'.[138] Le Bas, in his review of Lawson's biography of Laud in the *British Critic* in 1829, reproduced in his own *Life of Archbishop Laud* (1836), probably had Bishops Montagu and William Forbes in mind when he explained away 'some hazardous and indiscreet passages' in various Laudian writers, 'such as the honour due to the Virgin, to Saints, Images, Reliques, etc'. For Le Bas, writing on the eve of the Oxford Movement, it was a matter for complaint that the Laudian divines had 'ventured to put forth some divinity, in which certain Romish practices and opinions were treated with more of tenderness and indulgence, than would now be thought defensible'.[139] Within a few years, Tractarian writers found scope for their own more ambitious brand of High Churchmanship in such divinity.

In the preface to the second edition of his published sermon *The Revival of Popery* (1838), assailing the Tractarians from the university pulpit, the 'High and Dry' churchman, Godfrey Faussett, Oxford's Margaret Professor of Divinity, played into Tractarian hands by attacking them for advocating a eucharistic doctrine 'closely bordering on consusbstantiation' which, according to Faussett on the basis of Newman's citations, had also been taught by Cosin, Andrewes, and Bilson.[140] Newman was grateful for what he claimed to

---

fol. 160, Bodleian Library. On Manning's debt to Thorndike and other Caroline Divines, see J. Pereiro, *Cardinal Manning. An Intellectual Biography* (Oxford, 1998), pp. 16, 57.

[136] *Tracts of the Anglican Fathers*, 4 vols, vol. 2. Pt. 6: *Thorndike on the Rights of the Church in a Christian State, and the Authority of the Church in Controversies of Faith* (London, 1841), pp. vii–viii.

[137] C. Wordsworth (Jun.) to J. Watson, 14 February 1843, Wordsworth Papers, Ms 2147, fol. 162, Lambeth Palace Library.

[138] J.D. Robertson to J.E. Morris, 14 August 1843, Morris Papers, 1/13/2, PHL.

[139] C.W. Le Bas, *The Life of Archbishop Laud* (London, 1836), p. 374. William Forbes (1585–1634) was appointed first Bishop of Edinburgh shortly before his death.

[140] G. Faussett, *The Revival of Popery: A Sermon Preached before the University of Oxford at St. Mary's, on Sunday, May 20, 1838* (2nd edn, Oxford, 1838), p. ix. On the other hand, Faussett (p. 22) appealed to Jeremy Taylor, and (notes, pp. 43–4) Hooker and Waterland in favour of a purely spiritual or heavenly presence of Christ in those who received the eucharist worthily. See also note 145. Godfrey Faussett (1771–1853), a 'High and Dry' Churchman, was a Canon of Christ Church, Oxford, and Margaret Professor of Divinity in the University of Oxford, from 1811 until his death.

be an unguarded admission of the Caroline lineage of Tractarian sacramental teaching. Yet elsewhere in his response, he complained:

> You speak as if the opinions held in the works you censure were novel in our Church, and you connect them with the 'revival of popery'. Does any one doubt that in all those points of doctrine on which a question can occur, there is a large school in our Church, consisting of her most learned men, mainly agreeing in them. Does any one doubt that they are borne out in the main by Hooker, Andrewes, Montagu, Hammond, Bramhall, Taylor, Thorndike, Bull, Beveridge, Ken, and Wilson, not to mention others?[141]

In general, however, the Tractarian utilisation of Caroline divinity in favour of controversial doctrines was rejected by old High Churchmen as selective and unfair. Even the High Church Bishop Phillpotts, in an episcopal Charge in 1842, rejected the Tractarian claim made by the anonymous author [Newman] of Tract 38 in the guise of 'Clericus', that 'in the seventeenth century the theology of the body of the English Church was substantially the same as theirs'. As proof, the author of the Tract had professed, in stating the errors of Rome, to 'follow closely the order observed by Bishop Hall in his *Treatise on the Old Religion*'.[142] Rejecting this claim, Phillpotts pointedly commented that the writer may have followed the order of Bishop Hall's anti-papal treatise of 1628, but had departed widely 'from his truly Protestant sentiments on more than one article'.[143] Phillpotts proceeded to enumerate the Tract writer's palliation of the invocation of saints, honour paid to images, prayers for the dead, and reluctance to engage in controversy with Rome over Transubstantiation.

Old High Churchmen disputed Pusey's claim of sanction for the condemned eucharistic teaching of his Oxford sermon of 1843, *The Holy Eucharist, a Comfort to the Penitent*, from seventeenth-century Anglican divines such as Andrewes, Overall, and Bramhall.[144] When Bishop Sumner of Winchester in 1842 refused to ordain Keble's curate, Peter Young, to the priesthood for failing to deny the Real Presence 'excepting in the faithful

---

[141] J.H. Newman, *A Letter to the Rev. Godfrey Faussett, D.D., Margaret Professor of Divinity, on Certain Points of Faith and Practice* (2nd edn, Oxford, 1838), pp. 19–20.

[142] *Tracts for the Times*, vol. 1, no. 38, p. 11.

[143] *A Charge delivered to the Clergy of the Diocese of Exeter, by the Rt. Rev. Henry Phillpotts, Lord Bishop of Exeter at his Triennial Visitation in the months of August, September, and October 1839* (London, 1839), p. 78. For discussion of the context and content of Hall's *Old Religion*, see Milton, *Catholic and Reformed*, pp. 141–6.

[144] A. Härdelin, *The Tractarian Understanding of the Eucharist* (Uppsala, 1965), p. 213. Pusey's sermon had been condemned by six Oxford doctors of divinity. Keble complained to Pusey: 'I am really quite at a loss to imagine how they can justify this sentence without condemning almost all the writers in your Catena, and certainly all the Fathers.' J. Keble to E.B. Pusey, 1 July 1843, *LBV*, PHL. On the other hand, a later commentator has maintained that Pusey misrepresented the eucharistic teaching of Bishop Andrewes. W.H. Mackean, *The Eucharistic Doctrine of the Oxford Movement: A Critical Survey* (London, 1933), pp. 85–6.

receiver' (the standard Cranmerian doctrine, which also was widely regarded as Hooker's position), Keble likewise appealed to Andrewes, Taylor, Ken, and Wilson, in support of what he claimed was the Church's leaving the nature of the Presence an open question. In article 18 of his formal letter of protest to Bishop Sumner in March 1842, Keble was explicit in his appeal to a narrowly particular period in the doctrinal history of Anglicanism, stating that the bishop's ground of refusal was wrong:

> Because if any one generation of Divines were to be specified whose views of the meaning of our Formularies might well be considered binding on their successors it would be that of the Revisers of the Prayer Book after its restoration in 1660: and three of those at least, Bishop Cosin, Bishop Sparrow, and Mr Thorndike, have recorded their judgement to be substantial.[145]

At a later date, in the 1850s, the citation of Caroline authorities in favour of a eucharistic doctrine of an objective real presence, by Archdeacon George Anthony Denison of Taunton and Bishop Alexander Penrose Forbes of Brechin, also proved contentious; the High Church opponents of Denison and Forbes being insistent that such teaching contradicted that of the Caroline Divines.[146] Typical of the Tractarian utilisation of seventeenth-century theological authorities in order to serve a contemporary polemical agenda was a pamphlet by the Recorder of New Sarum, J.D. Chambers, *The Doctrine of the Holy Eucharist, as expounded by Herbert Thorndike . . . with notes, forming a digested series of authorities in Archdeacon Denison's Case* (1855). Even the later Anglo-Catholic scholar T.A. Lacey, in his biography of Thorndike published in 1929, concluded that it

> was a collection of isolated sentences and paragraphs, chosen for an obvious polemical purpose, and therefore necessarily giving a one-sided account of what it purported to contain. It was effective for its immediate object, making it impossible to condemn the archdeacon's specific teaching as unwarranted innovation, but it did some disservice to Thorndike.[147]

---

[145] *LD*, vol. 8, Appendix 6, p. 595. For details of the Young case, see Liddon, *Life of Edward Bouverie Pusey*, vol. 2, pp. 30–4. The extent to which seventeenth-century Anglican divines were used as a definitive court of appeal in the eucharistic controversies provoked by Tractarian teaching was evident in Oakeley's private account to Pusey of the Bishop of London's rejection of two ordination candidates on account of their eucharistic views, and what followed: 'The questions were "Is there a Real Presence in the Eucharist? Is there any Sacrifice?" They answered affirmatively, but were rejected the first day. They presented themselves however a second time with authorities from later English Divines, and the Bishop retracted his decision.' F. Oakeley to E.B. Pusey, n.d. [1842], *LBV* 58/9, PHL.

[146] R. Strong, *Alexander Forbes of Brechin. The First Tractarian Bishop* (Oxford, 1995), p. 157. Strong (p. 142) shows that in 1860 it was proposed that Bishop Forbes not be prosecuted for his eucharistic teaching, 'if Forbes could agree to abide by the words of Bishops Taylor, Ken and Wilson'. It was a matter of interpretation, and Forbes rejected the gloss on the Caroline Divines placed by his accusers. See also note 219.

[147] Lacey, *Herbert Thorndike*, p. 138.

Pusey applied the same technique as late as 1878 in the preface to his edition of the seventeenth-century French Catholic Abbé Gaume's *Manual for Confessors*, in which he ransacked Caroline Anglican authorities in defence of the doctrine and practice of auricular confession and sacramental absolution, which second generation Tractarians were bent on reviving; not only selecting over eighty pages of testimonies from such authorities in its favour, but citing copiously from the Visitation Articles of Bishops Andrewes, Overall, Montagu, Wren, Juxon, Duppa, and others, from 1619 to 1679. According to Pusey, 'these Bishops wished to revive or secure or guard the use of confession in every parish of their dioceses',[148] an inference which old High Churchmen rejected. Similarly, in 1881 in a critique of Judgements of the Judicial Committee of the Privy Council, Pusey even claimed the Caroline Divines as forerunners of Ritualism: 'they saw what it was good to do, and what could not be done then, and laid up a provision for the future, when minds should be suited to it'.[149]

Newman's avowal to Charles Crawley in January 1841 that he never 'made any effort to manage our divines' was belied by the evidence of his celebrated Tract 90.[150] Nowhere did Newman employ the testimony of the Caroline Divines to such controversial effect than in that Tract when he sought to give a 'catholic' interpretation to the Thirty-Nine Articles. He exploited the 'catholic latitude' which Laud, in reaction against prevailing Calvinist rigidity, had won for later interpreters of the Articles, claiming that Bramhall, Laud, Taylor, Bull, and Stillingfleet, had allowed of much greater freedom in the private opinions of individuals subscribing them, than he had contended for.[151] Even Dean Church admitted that Newman's citations of the Caroline Divines in Tract 90 were one-sided.[152] For example, Newman's appeal to the testimony

---

[148] E.B. Pusey, *Advice for those who Exercise the Ministry of Reconciliation through Confession and Absolution . . . Being the Abbe Gaume's Manual for Confessors. Abridged, Condensed and Adapted to the Use of the English Church* (Oxford, 1878), pp. xli–xliii; W. Maskell, *An Enquiry into the Doctrine of the Church of England upon Absolution* (London, 1849), p. 137. Pusey's claim is only partially borne out by Dr Fincham's recent elucidation of the evidence of Laudian era Visitation Returns. Bishops Montagu of Chichester (1628) and Wren of Norwich (1636), however, appear to have included searching questions on confession before communion. See Kenneth Fincham (ed.), *Church of England Record Society. Volume 5. Visitation Articles and Injunctions of the Early Stuart Church*, vol. II (Woodbridge, 1998), pp. xxiii–xxv.

[149] E.B. Pusey, *Unlaw in Judgments of the Judicial Committee . . . A Letter to the Rev. H.P. Liddon* (London, 1881), pp. 26–7. For an example of Victorian Anglo-Catholic appeals to the Caroline Divines even in support of Ritualism and the use of eucharistic vestments, see T.T. Carter, *The Royal Commission on the Eucharistic Vestments. A Letter to the Rt. Hon. W.E. Gladstone, M.P.* (2nd edn, London, 1867), p. 33.

[150] See P.B. Nockles, 'Oxford, Tract 90, and the Bishops', D. Nicolls & F. Kerr (eds), *John Henry Newman: Reason, Rhetoric, and Romanticism* (Bristol, 1991), pp. 28–87.

[151] J.H. Newman to R.W. Jelf, 15 March 1841, *LD*, vol. 8, pp. 85–7.

[152] R.W. Church, *The Oxford Movement. Twelve Years, 1833–1845* (London, 1891), pp. 286–7.

of Henry Hammond in favour of his interpretation of Article 20 seemed strained and misleading. While Hammond was cited in support of the infallibility of General Councils, no authority was given, while statements from Hammond suggesting that General Councils were fallible, were ignored. Similarly, Bramhall was quoted apparently out of context in favour of a doctrine of a 'comprecation of the saints', while Bramhall's strong anti-Romanism and semi-Erastian theory of church and state was overlooked. Edwin Abbott observed in the 1890s that Newman 'seemed to assume that every opinion, however extreme in the direction of Rome, that had been once expressed by any one high church bishop or divine, and had not been authoritatively censured, at once became part of justifiable Anglican doctrine.'[153] Abbott can be regarded as unfairly biased against anything which Newman was likely to write, but the testimony of Newman's sister-in-law Anne Mozley cannot be dismissed in this way. According to her, in the heyday of Newman's *via media* phase, he selected 'here a teacher, there an authority', but accepted 'them no further than they fell in with his views'. She felt that he snatched at 'every chance saying of any of our Divines', even though 'the whole tenor of the work has no weight with him'.[154] A classic instance of Newman's selective use of Anglican divines was his readiness to abandon Hooker when formulating his own doctrine of Justification. In his *Lectures on Justification* (1838) Newman concluded, 'since we are not allowed to call any man our master on earth, Hooker, venerable as is his name, has no weight with any Christian, except what is agreeable to catholic doctrine'.[155]

This, of course, begged the question of what was 'agreeable to catholic doctrine'. While anxious to enlist Hooker as a patron of catholic views and 'in the great point of the sacraments' as 'almost or entirely with us',[156] Keble treated him in similarly selective fashion. He admitted that Hooker's 'notion of Regal, or rather State, power' and 'dislike to anything approaching to Justification by inherent grace' separated him from the Tractarians, and conceded that Hooker was not his master, and that he had dared to differ widely from him in his own Preface to Hooker's *Works*.[157] The problem in this case was

---

[153] E.A. Abbott, *The Anglican Career of Cardinal Newman*, 2 vols (London, 1892), vol. 1, p. 250.

[154] [A. Mozley], 'Dr Newman's Apology', *Christian Remembrancer*, vol. 48 (July, 1864), p. 178.

[155] J.H. Newman, *Lectures on Justification* (London, 1838), p. 442.

[156] J. Keble to H.H. Norris, 13 November 1837, Ms. Eng. Lett. c. 469, fol. 92, Bodleian Library.

[157] Keble was also forced to concede that his own later doctrine of an Objective Real Presence was a departure from Hooker's position: 'I am forced to feel that Hooker, making the best of it for Calvin and his school, has been led on this subject, as on the Apostolical Succession, to use language inconsistent with what I believe to be "a vital doctrine of the Gospel" . . .' 'Remarks upon Hooker's View concerning the Real Presence', *Letters of Spiritual Counsel and guidance, by the late Rev. J. Keble, M.A. Vicar of Hursley*. Edited by R.F. Wilson, M.A. (5th edn, Oxford, 1885), p. 215; J. Keble, *On Eucharistical Adoration* (Oxford, 1857), pp. 124–5.

that Newman's presentation of a *via media* doctrine of Justification rested upon the teaching of only post-Restoration Caroline Divines over a mere thirty-year period from which such notable Anglican apologists as Hooker, Andrewes, and Hall, were necessarily absent.[158] On the question of Justification, Newman was forced to be even more selective than on other doctrinal issues with seventeenth-century Anglican testimonies. Yet even on the eucharist selectivity was practised. When in the 1850s Keble came to alter his own eucharistic views in favour of an 'objective' real presence, he was shamelessly selective in citing earlier Anglican authorities, claiming: 'I see no disingenuousness in adopting words, from Ridley (e.g.) or any other, to express one's own view, without stopping to inquire whether, on other occasions, the same author might not have employed different or even contradictory language.'[159]

James Mozley and Frederick Oakeley perfected this process of selective citation in the cause of 'unprotestantising' the Church of England. Mozley engaged in controversy with William Sewell, an old High Churchman who had hitherto allied himself with the Tractarians. In his article on the Church of England 'Divines of the Seventeenth Century' in the *Quarterly Review* in 1842, Sewell aimed to settle the then raging party conflict provoked by Tractarianism, by looking back 'to the old standard Theology of the English Church, and to ascertain the sentiments of our acknowledged great Divines on some of the debated questions of the present day'.[160] In short, the seventeenth century was called in to adjudicate on the theological conflicts of the nineteenth. While Sewell's article represented a panegyric on a wide selection of Caroline Divines, highlighting their devotional attributes, his selections were also designed to embarrass extreme Tractarians. Sewell emphasised the anti-Romanism of the Caroline Divines, their glorification of the English Reformation and work of the Reformers, their throwing back the charge of schism upon 'the Church and Court of Rome, their qualification of the right of the spiritual independence of the Church by a respect for the claims of the civil power to partake in ecclesiastical affairs, and their cautions against the dangers of private interpretation in studying the Fathers'.[161] In laboured detail, Sewell turned their testimony on a wide range of doctrine and points of discipline against what he regarded as Tractarian deviations from Anglican faith and practice.

In response, James Mozley in an eloquent article in the *British Critic* in 1842 conceded that many of the earlier Caroline Divines had been too anti-Roman in the heat of controversy and not assertive enough of the

---

[158] A. McGrath, 'John Henry Newman's Lectures on Justification: the High Church Misrepresentation of Luther', *Churchman*, vol. 97, no. 2 (1983), p. 112.
[159] Cited in Mackean, *Eucharistic Doctrine of the Oxford Movement*, p. 126.
[160] [W. Sewell], 'The Divines of the Seventeenth Century', *Quarterly Review*, vol. 69 (March, 1842), p. 472.
[161] *Ibid.*, especially pp. 478–549.

independence of the Church from the State, but warned against the 'illogical inference' being drawn that they were therefore mere Protestants in the 'modern sense'.[162] Mozley maintained that the Caroline Divines went as far as the Tractarians, if one but separated, as he told his sister, 'their real spirit from their controversial phraseology'. Mozley was sensitive to criticism that his article might seem 'hard upon our old divines', insisting that he had 'meant to be quite otherwise', considering them 'the great defenders of our Church, to whom we owe everything'.[163] Mozley countered the claim of old High Church contemporaries that they, rather than the Tractarians, were the true heirs of the Laudian mantle, highlighting the affinity between the dynamic character of both the Laudian and Tractarian movements. Just as the Tractarians were reviled as innovators in the 1830s, so had the Laudians been in the 1630s. Against Sewell, Mozley justified the apparent Tractarian breach of earlier parameters of High Churchmanship by appealing to the precedent of the Caroline Divines, insisting that 'our church divinity has been . . . a progressive, not a stationary one. The Laudian school was as clearly a new development of the church, in its day, as history can show it'.[164] Sewell had been misleading in not distinguishing between the Jacobean and the later Caroline Divines. Mozley complained that half of Sewell's *catenae* had been 'taken from the Calvinistic era of the Church, which ought not to have been done, or at any rate without mentioning the fact (if he was aware of it), or drawing some distinction between that and the sounder divinity which succeeded it'.[165]

In his 1845 *Christian Remembrancer* article, Mozley was even more contemptuous of the old High Churchman's latter-day patronage of Laud. For

---

[162] [J.B. Mozley], 'The Development of the Church in the Seventeenth Century', *British Critic*, vol. 33, no. cxiv (October, 1842), pp. 302–4.

[163] J.B. Mozley to A. Mozley, 9 July 1842, *Letters of the Rev. J.B. Mozley, D.D. Edited by his Sister* (London, 1885), p. 133. Mozley, however, conceded: 'I certainly think they, in common with their R.C. opponents, were much harsher in their language than they needed to be. It was an age of controversy, and everybody used strong terms.'

[164] [J.B. Mozley], 'Development of the Church in the Seventeenth Century', p. 344. Mozley (p. 345) used the example of Bishop Tomline's selective use of seventeenth-century Anglican divinity in order to make his case against Calvinism in controversy with the Evangelical Scott in the 1810s: 'See how Bishop Tomline, in his controversy with Scott, is obliged to apologise for the divines before that time.' For the contrary Anglican Evangelical use of divines before that time, see note 211. The issue of how far Laudianism represented a High Church development or advance which was cut short in 1640 was debated privately between the Tractarian T.E. Morris and the High Churchman J.D. Robertson. See Robertson's claim: 'You tell me that I have not proved that Laud etc. considered their "development" as final. The burden of proof lies with you . . . The character of their minds appears sufficient to preclude any idea of their having looked further.' J.D. Robertson to T.E. Morris, 14 August 1843, Morris Papers, 1/13/2, PHL.

[165] Mozley (p. 335) complained that Sewell had relied too much on pre-Laudian divines such as Bilson, Davenant, Ussher, Richard Field, and Thomas Jackson, whom he regarded as not 'exactly fair samples of Church of England theology, though very good representatives of her before she got out of the Calvinistic atmosphere'.

old High Churchmen, Laud and his party were not partisans or innovators: their theology and concept of the Church were clearly implied in the formularies of the Elizabethan Church. Their ceremonialism was about matters indifferent and had limited sacramental significance. They had discouraged theological controversy and merely wished to redress the balance against Puritan disturbers of the Church's peace. Mozley wielded his pen against this ameliorating or minimalist interpretation of Laudianism:

> He [Laud] appears before us, in short, in the first instance, as an innovator upon the dominant and authorised theology of the day. A High-Churchman of the 'old school' can now appeal to his sanction and name; but Laud was not one of an 'old school' himself; there was no 'old school' of High-Churchmanship for him to belong to; the 'established school' of the Church was then Calvinistic; Calvinism was the theology of the Church dignitary, the Bishop, the Dean, the College Head. The maintainer of another system had to assume the character which thinks for itself, and will not follow the lead; a free, independent, and original one. Laud's High-Churchmanship was no more made to his hand than his archiepiscopate.[166]

As it had been for Laud, so, Mozley implied, was it for the Tractarians. They too, far from being passive legatees and conservers of a received establishment orthodoxy, had been prepared to challenge the ecclesiastical consensus of their day and had not been stifled in the comforting embrace of the 'High and Dry' Churchmanship characteristic of the cathedral close. Mozley clearly had a contemporary ecclesiastical target in view, and the Tractarian experience of being at the receiving end of episcopal and Oxford Heads of House strictures, when he concluded:

> There is a reproach, however, in the shape of praise from which we are anxious to rescue him [Laud] – the praise of a class who know next to nothing about him, and simply regard him as the patron of Church opulence and comfort, of easy posts of dignity and the Establishment system . . . The dead cannot help themselves here, and persons who have not one single sympathy with Laud's self-devotion, deep priestly feeling, love of Church doctrine or discipline, and who, if they had lived in that day, would not have stirred a finger to save the Church from sinking into a Presbyterian establishment, can now safely eulogise him, and smoothly thank him for the official powers which they enjoy from him, and which they employ against that very Catholic spirit in the Church which they were originally instituted to defend.[167]

Frederick Oakeley, who by the early 1840s had earned the reputation of

---

[166] [J.B. Mozley], 'Archbishop Laud', pp. 208–9. The old High Churchman Charles Le Bas, however, made a similar point: 'When Laud commenced his academic residence, Oxford bore a greater resemblance, in many respects, to a colony from Geneva, than to a seminary of Anglo-Catholic divinity.' C.W. Le Bas, *The Life of Archbishop Laud* (London, 1836), p. 5.

[167] *Ibid.*, p. 300.

being in the 'Romanising' vanguard of the Movement, also explained away what he regarded as the harsh anti-Romanism which 'disfigured the pages of English divinity' as 'a sort of traditionary mode of speaking, adopted by these writers, because their immediate predecessors had adopted it, or because it was expected of them'.[168] In his defence of Tract 90, Oakeley took a more historical approach than his friend and mentor, W.G. Ward, interpreting the Thirty-Nine articles in the light of seventeenth-century precedents. Like Newman, Oakeley appealed to the precedent of the English Franciscan friar and chaplain to Queen Henrietta Maria, Dr Christopher Davenport, *alias* Franciscus a Sancta Clara [1598–1680], for an earlier attempt to bridge the gap between the Thirty-Nine Articles and Roman Catholic teaching.[169] Davenport had argued his case by frequent reference, as when explaining Article 28 on the eucharist, to the high sacramental teaching of the then contemporary Anglican divines Andrewes and Montagu, in a way which prefigured Newman's and Oakeley's line of argument on the Articles.[170] Drawing on the apparent evidence of the seventeenth-century Anglican historians Peter Heylin and Thomas Fuller, Oakeley went even further than Newman by arguing that the Articles were drawn up with the deliberate intention of comprehending Roman Catholics as well as Protestants, rather than being merely 'patient' of a catholic interpretation.[171] Oakeley also made use of extracts from the seventeenth-century bishops Forbes and Montagu, and Thorndike, in favour of eucharistical adoration, the invocation of saints, reverence for images, and the doctrine of purgatory, as support for a Catholic interpretation of the Articles.[172]

In correspondence with Oakeley over the second edition of his *The Subject of Tract XC. Historically Examined* (1845), Manning undermined the historical basis of Oakeley's argument, arguing that any subscription to the Thirty-Nine Articles by English Catholics early in Elizabeth's reign entailed mere concession or surrender by a large 'compliant body' to the governing powers

---

[168] Oakeley, *Subject of Tract XC*, p. 11.
[169] *Ibid.*, pp. 35–6.
[170] *Paraphrastica exposito articulorum confessionis Anglicanae: The Articles of the Anglican Church paraphrastically considered and explained, by Franciscus a Sancta Clara (Dr Christopher Davenport), to which are prefixed an introduction and sketch of the life of the author. Edited by the Rev. Frederick George Lee* (London, 1865), p. 58. For discussion of Sancta Clara's work and other precedents for Tract 90, see G. Tavard, *The Quest for Catholicity: a Study in Anglicanism* (London, 1963), pp. 149–60.
[171] F. Oakeley to H.E. Manning, 27 January 1845, Manning Papers, Ms. Eng. Lett. c. 654, fol. 88, Bodleian Library; Oakeley, *Subject of Tract XC*, p. 29. Oakeley argued that such comprehension was intended by the fact of Roman Catholics frequenting the established church services in the early part of Elizabeth I's reign. F. Oakeley, *The Claim to "Hold, as distinct from Teaching", explained in a Letter to a Friend* (London, 1845), pp. 12–13.
[172] Oakeley, *Subject of Tract XC*, pp. 53–71; [J.B. Mozley], 'Development of the Church in the Seventeenth Century', especially pp. 360–1.

of the Reformation state.[173] In a letter to Gladstone about Oakeley's pamphlet, Manning argued that no other Roman Catholic had ever taken Sancta Clara's line, and that 'Forbes, and Montague, not to mention Thorndike, the closest approximators to the Roman doctrine, never dreamed of a mere verbal controversy'.[174] Nonetheless, while Oakeley's logic may have been flawed, he had a better grasp of seventeenth-century Anglican sources than his biographer P. Galloway gives him credit.[175] In his historical defence of Tract 90 he had reproduced the details of the case of Bishop Montagu who, in 1625, had been assailed by Puritan parliamentary opponents for apparently contravening the Protestant interpretation of the Thirty-Nine Articles in his writings. Oakeley found parallels with the outcry against Tract 90 and drew a pointed analogy between contemporaries who sought to exclude Tractarian teaching and 'the Puritans of former times'.[176] Moreover, some credence for Oakeley's argument is provided in a manuscript by Montagu entitled 'Concerning Recusancie of communion with the Church of England' [c. 1635]. Montagu's 'little writing for the recusants' appeared to be designed to entice English Catholics to conform by minimising the differences between Rome and Canterbury. It included an acknowledgement of the power of the keys, the sanctity of holy places, altars, the eucharistic real presence and sacrifice, extreme unction, and penance in absolution, and an avowal that between the two Churches, 'the differences are not great, nor should make a separation'.[177] The anonymous annotation made at the end of the tract – 'It is the same way from Rome to London, which is from London to Rome; Why then may not a Protestant go to the Popish Mass',[178] is an indication of the perceived pacific

---

[173] H.E. Manning to F. Oakeley, 25 January 1845, Manning Papers, Ms. Eng. Lett. c. 654, fol. 75, Bodleian Library.

[174] H.E. Manning to W.E. Gladstone, 28 December 1844, Manning Papers, Pitts Theological Library, Emory University, Georgia [I wish to thank Professor Peter Erb for use of his transcript of the original letter]; H.E. Manning to F. Oakeley, 25 January 1845, Manning Papers, Ms Eng lett. c. 654, fol. 79, Bodleian Library.

[175] See P. Galloway, *A Passionate Humility: Frederick Oakeley and the Oxford Movement* (Leominster, 1999), especially ch. 6: 'An unbalanced logic'.

[176] Oakeley, *The Subject of Tract XC historically examined* (2nd edn, London, 1845), p. x.

[177] Richard Montagu: 'Concerning Recusancie of Communion with the Church of England' [c. 1635], Anthony Milton and Alexandra Walsham (eds), *From Cranmer to Davidson: A Church of England Miscellany. Edited by Stephen Taylor* (Woodbridge, 1999), p. 93.

[178] *Ibid.*, p. 101. The editors comment (p. 80) that 'the points that Montagu dealt with – the identification of the pope as antichrist, predestination, the location of the church before Luther, divisions over the eucharist – were all issues where English protestants were themselves potentially divided, and where Montagu was essentially choosing to place the Church of England closer to Rome than to the "puritans" who upheld the views with which he disagreed.' Dr Milton, however, has kindly drawn my attention to the fact that the anonymous annotation at the end of the Montagu manuscript only survives on the copies that seem to have been made by hostile sources. Therefore, caution needs to be observed in interpreting Montagu's intentions.

and ecumenical intention of the document. Walsham, one of the editors of 'Concerning Recusancie', argues elsewhere that Laud, Cosin and others may have thought that the introduction of semi-Catholic gestures and trappings might check potential Protestant converts to Rome. Furthermore, she suggests that the Laudian programme of the 1630s, by making the boundaries between Rome and Canterbury appear more fluid, may have induced some of those who were 'conservative' in religion and denied Catholic ministry to be more ready to conform.[179] Thus current scholarship bears out that Oakeley had a case for his eirenical reading of Laudian divinity of the 1630s.

Oakeley himself was candid in conceding that citations from the seventeenth-century divines could be used to support a 'one-sided view' and might just as readily be employed against aspects of Tractarian teaching. He explained that 'all that *catenae* necessarily show, and all that, as a matter of fact, they are genuinely intended to show, is that certain doctrines are not *new*'. He argued that the object of such citations was: 'not to justify the Caroline Divines, any more than to ground particular doctrines upon their authority, but merely to show what they have felt themselves at liberty to say without protest. And this fact has its own weight, whatever these divines may chance to have said elsewhere.' The fact that contradictions might exist between Caroline and Tractarian teaching could safely be ignored, because there was no need to press the Caroline Divines 'into our service beyond the point for which they are here claimed'.[180] Oakeley was himself critical of the Caroline Divines for what he claimed was their deficiency in relating the connection 'between the forms and spirit of true religion' and defective understanding of 'the sacramental theory of the church'.[181] Moreover, even Pusey privately conceded a discrepancy between his own developed eucharistic doctrine and that of the Caroline Divines. In a letter to Manning in 1843 at the time of his condemned sermon in which he publicly claimed to be but following Andrewes and Overall, he lamented, in relation to the eucharistic oblation and real presence as taught by the seventeenth-century divines, that there was much 'indistinctness' in Caroline teaching as to both doctrines.[182]

Latitudinarian critics of the Oxford Movement, notably Thomas Arnold, were quick to point up an affinity between contemporary Tractarianism and

---

[179] See A. Walsham, 'The Parochial roots of Laudianism revisited: Catholics, Anti-Calvinists and "Parish Anglicans" in early Stuart England', *JEH*, vol. 49, no. 4 (October, 1998), pp. 620–51.

[180] Oakeley, *Subject of Tract XC*, pp. 3–4. James Mozley made a similar point: 'There is an illogical tendency in ordinary minds, when the sanction of any school has been claimed and proved for *certain* points, to imagine that sanction undone, because the same cannot be proved for certain *other* points; to suppose that agreement clear and manifest on certain subjects, is null and void, because it does not apply to all.' [J.B. Mozley], 'Development of the Church in the Seventeenth Century', p. 302.

[181] *Ibid.*, p. 31.

[182] E.B. Pusey to H.E. Manning, n.d. [Sept. 1843], PHL, *LBV*.

the Laudianism and Nonjuring principles of an earlier age. One such critic in 1838 reminded his readers that in the 1630s, 'Laud, Pocklington, and others of that school published sentiments, both on doctrinal and ecclesiastical points, very similar to, if not worse than, those which are now emanating from an English university, and well known by the designation of "Oxford Popery".'[183]

Partisan Tractarian identification with the Caroline Divines, however, initially did not lead to an unmeasured reaction against them by the Movement's Evangelical opponents on the lines expressed by eighteenth-century latitudinarians and Socinians. One Tractarian defender of Pusey's 1843 sermon complained of his critics:

> What authorities Dr. Pusey may have collected, either from the Fathers or from the Divines of our Church, to bear out his statements, is of course nothing to them. They only see in the Church of England their own modern preaching Church, they have no other idea in their heads of her than this: abstracted from the system of the day, she is a chimera, and all her Divines put together seem to have no more to do with settling a question of this kind, than so many disciples of Zoroaster, and worshippers of the Grand Lama. We are the Divines of the Church of England, say they, we are the loudest talkers, we are her trumpets and mouthpieces now, whoever may have been before.[184]

The evidence of anti-Tractarian publications does not bear out this claim. On the contrary, opponents of Tractarianism chose the historical ground. While some Anglican Evangelical critics of the Oxford Movement equated Tractarianism and Laudianism as related manifestations of Antichrist, carrying the 'mark of the Beast',[185] many of them laid claim to a Jacobean or early Caroline theological inheritance, identifying with the episcopalian Calvinist school of Ussher, Davenant, Carleton, and Hall. Pusey's Anglican Evangelical correspondent, Anne Tyndale, pointed out in a note attached to a letter to Pusey in the mid-1830s that the eighteenth-century Evangelical Revival had represented a revival of the theology not only of the Reformers but of 'Hooker, Ussher, Hall, and other great divines of the early-17th century', in reaction against the latitudinarian and Arminian theology of the

---

[183] 'Report of the Edinburgh Commemoration Meeting, 20 December 1838', cited in W.E. Gladstone, *Church Principles considered in their Results* (London, 1840), p. 559. For Arnold's attack, see [T. Arnold], 'The Oxford Malignants and Dr Hampden', *Edinburgh Review*, vol. 63, no. 127 (April, 1836), pp. 225–39. Arnold contended (p. 235) that the 'Oxford conspirators' were 'the very Nonjurors and High Church clergy of King William's, and Anne's, and George the First's reign, reproduced, with scarcely a shade of difference'.

[184] *British Critic*, vol. 35, no. cxviii, 'Dr. Pusey's Sermon' (October, 1843), p. 471.

[185] R. Rabett, *Archbishop Laud more than half a Papist: or Laudism (after the lapse of two centuries) Revived, under the appelation of Puseyism* (London, 1842), pp. i–ii, 15–17; P. Maurice, *Postcript to the Popery of Oxford: The Number of the Beast* (London, 1851), p. 2.

eighteenth century.[186] Like the Tractarian Newman, Anglican Evangelicals espoused an historiography of doctrinal corruption but gave it a different twist. Whereas the Tractarians blamed the compromises of the post-1688 Church, as John Walsh has shown, the Anglican Calvinist Evangelical revivalists of the eighteenth century had tracked the decay of Reformation doctrine in England back beyond the Restoration to Laud and the Laudians, arguing that 'Arminianism' or the 'free-will heresy' had 'set off a causal chain which led on to Latitudinarianism and outright infidelity'.[187] Early Victorian Anglican Evangelicals and Tractarians could agree in repudiating the doctrinal latitude and aridity which they both ascribed to the eighteenth century and jointly decry the theological school of Tillotson and Hoadly, but for different reasons and from different theological standpoints. They also differed over the favoured historical period from which they drew inspiration in opposition to the heterodoxy of the eighteenth century. Thus Rose's Durham *Lectures on Church History* won support from an Evangelical commentator for an attack on such eighteenth-century rationalist divines as the Lutheran Mosheim and latitudinarian Anglican Jortin, as 'cold and heartless historians'. The writer parted company from Rose, however, for having dared to criticise Joseph Milner as a church historian.[188]

Moderate Anglican Evangelicals such as William Goode, and Protestant Churchmen such as James Garbett and George Stanley Faber, by appealing to the same seventeenth-century historical sources, sought to confute the Tractarians on their own ground in order to prove that the controversy was not one between the 'Catholic' and 'Genevan' schools of doctrine but between orthodox Protestantism and semi-Romanism. Goode's *Divine Rule of Faith and Practice* (1842), according to one reviewer, exposed the Tractarians as guilty of 'a convenient process of misquotation, and accumulating catenas of later Divines, simply by detaching passages from the context and applying them in a manner diametrically opposite to that which their authors designed'.[189] Goode contended that:

> so far from having the support they claim in the writings of our great divines, they are refuted and opposed in the most decisive way by all the best even of their own chosen witnesses; and that their appeal to these writings as in their

---

[186] A. Tyndale, 'Extract on the term "Evangelical" ', n.d. [c. 1835], Tyndale/Pusey Papers, CUP 5/104, PHL.

[187] J. Walsh, 'Origins of the Evangelical Revival', J. Walsh & G.V. Bennett (eds), *Essays in Modern Church History in Memory of Norman Sykes* (London, 1966), p. 149.

[188] J. Scott, *A Vindication of the Rev. Joseph Milner, M.A. and his "History of the Church of Christ", against the judgment pronounced upon it by the Rev. Hugh James Rose, B.D.* (London, 1834), pp. 6–11.

[189] H. Fish, *Jesuitism traced in the movements of the Oxford Tractarians* (London, 1842), pp. 61–2.

favour is one of the most unaccountable, and painful, and culpable however unintentional misrepresentations with which history supplies us.[190]

The fanatical anti-Tractarian controversialist Charles Pourtales Golightly (1807–85) took a similar view. Golightly was outraged by Archdeacon Clerke of Oxford's assumption that the sentiments of the Tractarians 'were in the main in accordance with those of the leading divines of our church'. Golightly contended that this was 'a mischieviously erroneous statement', and was confident that Clerke would be contradicted, especially by the High Church Bishop of Exeter, later himself accused of pro-Tractarian bias.[191] Even Laud and Heylyn, normally *bêtes-noires* of Low Churchmen, were defended by Garbett and Goode, because they 'still venerated the scriptural founders of the Reformed Church'.[192]

Garbett and others cited Laud, Andrewes, Bramhall, and a litany of Caroline authors, to refute Pusey's interpretation of the eucharistic doctrine of the Church of England based on their testimony.[193] Goode even defended not only

---

[190] W. Goode, *The Divine Rule of Faith and Practice, or, a Defence of the Catholic Doctrine of Holy Scripture*, 2 vols (London, 1842), vol. 1, p. xxiii. Goode (p. xxix) claimed the Tractarian *catenae*, revealed 'a great want of acquaintance even with the works of our own great divines'. See also the more moderate Garbett's nuanced critique of Tractarian appeals to seventeenth-century Anglican authorities: 'the same one-sidedness, which is observable in their views of the Reformers and of the Fathers, is quite as strongly marked in the adduction of authorities from the Church of England, of dates subsequent to the Reformation . . .'. J. Garbett, *Christ, as Prophet, Priest, and King: Being a Vindication of the Church of England from Theological Novelties, in Eight Lectures Preached before the University of Oxford, at Canon Bampton's Lecture, in the Year MDCCCXLII.* 2 vols (Oxford, 1842), vol. 2, pp. 484–5.

[191] Golightly also quoted extensively from divines such as Andrewes, Jackson, Hammond, Pearson, Bramhall, and Bingham, as well as Hooker, Ussher, Hall, and Beveridge, to argue that Tractarian teaching on Justification, Sin after Baptism, and Reserve, was not the teaching of the Church of England. [C.P. Golightly], *A Letter to the Right Reverend Father in God, Richard, Lord Bishop of Oxford, Containing Strictures upon Certain Parts of Dr. Pusey's Letter to his Lordship. By a Clergyman of the Diocese, and a Resident Member of the University* (Oxford, 1840), pp. 10–14. According to Thomas Mozley, Golightly's religion 'was that of Scott, and Newton, and Cecil, and Baxter, and certain select Puritans, not without a little High Church seasoning'. T. Mozley, *Reminiscences Chiefly of Oriel College and the Oxford Movement*, 2 vols (London, 1882), vol. 2, p. 110. However, Edward Goulburn who had known Golightly well disputed this, maintaining: 'I should be disposed to say that, at the time I knew him, Hooker and Bishop Hall would more exactly represent Golightly's views than the divines who are named by him [Mozley]'. E.M. Goulburn, *Reminiscences of Charles Portales Golightly. A Letter Reprinted with Additions, and a Preface, from 'The Guardian' Newspaper on January 13, 1886* (Oxford, 1886), pp. 14–15.

[192] J. Garbett, *The University, the Church, and the New Test. A Letter to the Lord Bishop of Chichester* (London, 1845), p. 73. Garbett reminded Tractarian critics of the term 'Protestant': 'No great English divines even of those [Laudian and Nonjuring] schools popularly considered the most Romanizing have ever held the name of protestant as other than a title of honour.' J. Garbett, *Christ as Prophet, Priest, and King*, 2 vols (Oxford, 1842), vol. 1, p. 433.

[193] J. Garbett, *A review of Dr Pusey's Sermon, and the Doctrine of the Eucharist according to the*

Andrewes but the ultra-Laudians Bishops Forbes and Montagu, and Thorndike, from Oakeley's attempt to enlist them in support of his historical defence of the principles of Tract 90, denying also that Laud countenanced Sancta Clara's interpretation of the Thirty-Nine Articles. While Goode denied that the later Church of England could be officially committed to every position advanced by those divines, he was anxious to deny Oakeley's inference that they provided a legitimate precedence for Tract 90 and advanced Tractarian teaching.[194] Goode also argued that the Tractarian exaltation of oral tradition departed from Caroline teaching. He maintained that even Laud in his controversy with Fisher the Jesuit had confined the divinity of Tradition to the apostolic age alone. The only precursors of the Tractarian position of making an 'imaginary "Catholic Consent" ' into 'a divine informant and part of the Rule of Faith' were not even Laud or the Laudians but merely 'a few individuals, such as Brett, Hickes, Johnson, and others, forming a small and extreme section of a small and extreme party in our Church, namely the Nonjurors; and even among these it would be difficult to find one who agreed with their system as now developed'.[195] Likewise, Anglican Evangelical critics accused the Tractarians of deception in their *catenae patrum* on the theological questions of Justification and Sanctification, though they conceded that Newman's favourite Anglican divine, Bishop Bull, whom Garbett criticised for what he regarded as a defective view on Justification by Faith, supported the Tractarian theory of an infused, as distinct from an imputed, righteousness.[196] The Anglican Evangelical Henry Fish, in his *The Jesuitism of the Oxford Tractarians* (1842), was particularly critical of Pusey for citing Hooker and Andrewes 'in confirmation of Mr Newman's views of Justification: whereas the views of both those men were the very reverse of Mr Newman's'.[197] Moreover, the strength of the Evangelical argument was

    Church of England (London, 1843), p. ci. Garbett argued that 'Doctor Pusey goes beyond the non-juring divines, who are more Protestant than he!'

[194] W. Goode, *Tract XC historically refuted; or A Reply to a work by the Rev. F. Oakeley, entitled "The Subject of Tract XC historically examined"* (London, 1845), pp. 120–1, 131–51; Goode, *Divine Rule of Faith and Practice*, vol. 1, pp. xxi–xxii.

[195] Goode, *Divine Rule of Faith and Practice*, vol. 1, pp. xxiii–xxiv.

[196] Garbett, *Christ as Prophet, Priest, and King*, vol. 1, pp. 437–8.

[197] Fish, *Jesuitism . . . of the Oxford Tractarians*, pp. 61–2; [C.P. Golightly], *New and Strange Doctrines extracted from the Writings of Mr Newman and his Friends, in a Letter to the Rev. W.F. Hook, by one of the original subscribers to the 'Tracts for the Times'* (Oxford, 1841), pp. 12–13. Garbett likwise contrasted the 'evangelical' teaching on Justification of Andrewes, Hall, and Jackson, with that of Bull. Garbett, *Christ as Prophet, Priest, and King*, vol. 1, pp. 438–9; C.P. McIlvaine, *Oxford Divinity compared with that of the Romish and Anglican Churches; with a special View of the Doctrine of Justification by Faith* (London, 1841), pp. iii–iv. A modern Evangelical theologian, Alistair McGrath, supports this view. McGrath argues that Newman's teaching on Justification rested on the support of only the post-Restoration Caroline Divines over a mere thirty year period, from which such earlier 'High Church' worthies as Hooker and Andrewes were necessarily absent. A. McGrath, 'The Anglican tradition on Justification', *Churchman* (1984), p. 40.

conceded by Newman's Tractarian friend, Samuel Wood. Wood warned Newman of the danger of resting his teaching on Justification on earlier Anglican precedent: 'Is not the "peculiar" [i.e. Evangelical] view of justification in some sense their stronghold, inasmuch as it is only false as being partial and distorted, and has there not been a great school on that side ever since the Reformation?'[198]

For old High Churchmen, the Anglican Evangelical appeal to history as a controversial strategy was no less disingenuous in one direction than was Tractarian appeal in another. Goode claimed support for a repudiation of Apostolic Tradition as even a subordinate rule of faith in the writings of anti-Evangelical 'High and Dry' divines such as Bishops Herbert Marsh and Pretyman-Tomline,[199] but he was on shaky ground in claiming sanction from even Laud and his school. Goode's attempt to prove that divines in the Caroline tradition ranging from Ussher through Jackson to Stillingfleet and Patrick, and at a later date, Waterland and Van Mildert, also were opposed to the authority of tradition in any sense, not merely an exaggerated one, was far-fetched in the view of even many moderate High Churchmen.[200]

Goode sought to undercut the Tractarian doctrine of the visible church by reference to the Caroline Divines. In 1843 he republished short treatises by Thomas Jackson (1579–1640) and Robert Sanderson (1587–1663), both moderate Laudian authors whom the Tractarians esteemed. Goode contended that while Jackson held a high view of visible Churches ruled by bishops, he also taught that it was possible to a member of the mystical Body of Christ without being a member of an episcopal communion.[201] Goode inferred too much from the evidence. Goode's sense of priority for an invisible church of

---

[198] S.F. Wood to J.H. Newman, 8 April 1837, *LD*, vol. 6, p. 53.

[199] Goode stood by 'the Protestant view well laid down by Bishop Marsh', himself a High Churchman of sorts, in his *Comparative View of the Churches of England and Rome* (1814). W. Goode, *The Case As It Is: or, A Reply to the Letter of Dr. Pusey to His Grace the Archbishop of Canterbury* (London, 1842), p. 73.

[200] *Christian Remembrancer*, vol. 23 (June, 1840), pp. 394–411; *British Magazine*, vol. 18 (July, 1840), pp. 34–9; *Church of England Quarterly Review*, vol. 7 (April, 1840), pp. 307–8.

[201] W. Goode (ed.), *Two Treatises on the Church. The First by Thomas Jackson D.D. commended by Dr. Pusey as "one of the best and greatest minds our Church has nurtured"; the Second by Robert Sanderson, D.D. formerly Bishop of Lincoln; to which is added a Letter of Bishop Cosin on the Validity of the Foreign Reformed Churches* (London, 1843), especially pp. v–xii; Goode, *Divine Rule of Faith and Practice*, vol. 1, pp. 685–707. Goode contended (*Two Treatises*, pp. iii–iv): 'If we go back to the works of the great divines of our Church, not of the school of Calvin, we shall find that the very views now advocated by the Tractarians are stigmatised as of the essence of Popery.' Another anti-Tractarian writer concluded: 'Their catenas parade, with the most unblushing effrontery, the names of divines who have directly and clearly opposed their views, as of advocates in their favour.' *Non-Episcopal Ordination: an Abridgment of an Article in the 'Christian Observer' for November 1851. Setting forth the Opinions of the Fathers of the Church of England from Archbishop Cranmer to Archbishop Howley* (London, 1856), p. 3.

true believers, the doctrine of the first generation of Elizabethan divines such as Whitaker and Perkins, was not shared by Laudian exponents of *jure divino* episcopacy, with their emphasis on church visibility and succession. Moreover, Goode's compilation of a *catenae patrum* of Anglican divines opposed to the absolute necessity of episcopal orders for valid ordination could be regarded as misleading because of a disregard for context and changing circumstances.[202]

It could be argued that in questioning the validity of the non-episcopal orders of continental Protestant churches, the Tractarians, by insisting on the maxim 'no bishop, no church', departed from a more moderate Elizabethan and Jacobean consensus, as adhered to by Hooker and even Andrewes, and at a later date, even Cosin, for each of whom episcopacy appeared to be the *bene esse* rather than *esse* of the church. Norman Sykes made much of this argument at the expense of the Tractarians, whom he portrayed as innovators in this matter, but he overstated his case.[203] The Caroline Divines had separated the case of the foreign reformed churches, for whom the argument of necessity could excuse their abandonment of episcopacy, from that of the English dissenting bodies and Scottish Presbyterian Kirk, who could make no such plea. Goode showed that Andrewes and others refused to 'unchurch' the foreign Reformed churches, and that Bishop Cosin when in exile in Paris had communicated 'rather with Geneva than Rome,'[204] but he inferred more from this than was warranted. As Anthony Milton observes, Andrewes defended episcopacy on *jure divino* grounds and did not explicitly recognise presbyters' rights to ordain in cases of necessity.[205] The Elizabethan instances of

---

[202] *Church of England Quarterly Review*, vol. 11 (April, 1842), p. 363.

[203] N. Sykes, *Old Priest and New Presbyter* (Cambridge, 1956), especially pp. 30–84. John Kent makes the unsubstantiated claim that Sykes 'won' the historical argument against the Tractarians on the status of the foreign Protestant churches and episcopacy as normative. See J. Kent, *The Unacceptable Face: The Modern Church in the eyes of the Historian* (London, 1987), pp. 102–3. For a critique of Sykes's argument, see A.L. Peck, *Anglicanism and Episcopacy: a Re-examination of the Evidence with Special Reference to Professor Norman Sykes's 'Old Priest and New Presbyter'* (London, 1958), pp. 40–1; J. Pinnington, 'Anglican openness to Foreign Protestant Churches in the Eighteenth Century: a Gloss on the Old Priest and New Presbyter Thesis of Norman Sykes', *Anglican Theological Review*, vol. 51 (1969), pp. 133–40. See also A.J. Mason, *The Church of England and Episcopacy* (Cambridge, 1914), pp. 449–50.

[204] Goode, *The Case as it is*, p. 17. To counter the Tractarians, Goode drew up his own *catenae patrum* of high church divines apparently opposed to the absolute necessity of episcopal orders for valid ordination. See W. Goode, *A Reply to Archdeacon Churton and Chancellor Harrington on the term, 'Church of Scotland' in the Fifty-Fifth Canon, and on Non-Episcopal Ordinations* (London, 1852), pp. 31–2; W. Goode, *A Vindication of the Doctrine of the Church of England on the Validity of the Orders of the Scotch and Foreign Non-Episcopal Churches* (London, 1852), pp. 11, 26–7; W. Goode, *Brotherly Communion with the Foreign Protestant Churches desired and cultivated by the highest and best Divines of the Church of England* (Cambridge, 1859), pp. 17–34.

[205] Milton, *Catholic and Reformed*, pp. 486–7.

presbyterial ordination such as of William Whittingham, Dean of Durham, and Walter Travers, Master of the Temple, could be presented as unfortunate anomalies. Laud wished to break the Church of England's sense of unity with the Reformed churches of the continent.[206] He made life difficult for foreign Protestant or stranger churches in England because they set an example of alienation from the national Church and might, given the Laudian association of extreme Calvinism with rebellion, prove to be seed-beds of political disorder. Furthermore, the reluctant pre-Tractarian acceptance of the orders of continental non-episcopal Churches had become increasingly grudging before the Oxford Movement, as circumstances detracted from the plea of necessity: a plea that had always amounted to a polemical rather than strictly historical statement. In 1893 the Anglo-Catholic Charles Gore edited a new edition of the Nonjuror William Law's famous 'Bangorian letters' of 1717 directed against Benjamin Hoadly, in order to refute the view that 'the real insistence upon the "necessity" of episcopal succession, and what goes with that in ecclesiastical principles, is a modern growth in the Anglican church'.[207] The growth of heterodoxy in continental Protestant churches at a later date further contributed towards a hardening of attitudes; Hugh James Rose by the 1820s was linking the rising heterodoxy among foreign reformed Churches to a failure to re-establish apostolic discipline.[208]

Even old High Churchmen, however, were troubled by the apparent plausibility of Goode's arguments and evidence. After anxious consultation with Howley in 1842, Archdeacon William Rowe Lyall, an old High Churchman, conveyed to Bishop Bagot of Oxford the Archbishop's concern that 'if Dr Pusey and Mr Newman believe their opinions to be founded on the authority of the Ancient and Anglican Fathers . . . it is for them to make good their opinions by showing that Mr Goode is guilty of the fault with which he charges others.'[209] Tractarian polemicists stepped forward, notably Pusey in his monumental *Letter to the Archbishop of Canterbury on the Present Crisis in the Church* (1842), but the waters had been muddied, and the controversy was not resolved conclusively. One Tractarian sympathiser, Roundell Palmer, first

---

[206] Laud opposed 'escape clauses for the foreign churches' on the question of episcopacy. Milton, *Catholic and Reformed*, p. 489. However, it is a measure of later Tractarian 'extremism' on this question that J.M. Neale could even fault Laud for too great 'moderation' towards foreign Protestants, criticising his supposed concurrence in the Isle of Rhe expedition on behalf of the French Huguenots, 'an expedition undertaken to support rebels, and to defend heresy'. J.M. Neale, 'The Laudian Reformation compared with that of the Nineteenth Century', *Lectures Principally on the Church Difficulties of the Present Time* (London, 1852), p. 185.

[207] *William Law's Defence of Church Principles. Three Letters to the Bishop of Bangor, 1717–1719. Edited by J.O. Nash and Charles Gore* (London, 1893), pp. 9–10.

[208] H.J. Rose, *A Letter to the Lord Bishop of London, in Reply to Mr Pusey's Work on the Causes of Rationalism in Germany* (London, 1829), p. 144.

[209] W.R. Lyall to Bishop Bagot, 14 January 1842, Bagot Papers, PHL.

Earl of Selborne, later observed that Goode's *Divine of Faith and Practice* was widely read 'and told, in the intellectual circles with which I came into contact in London'. Palmer was convinced that it acted as 'a considerable check to the influence (until then progressive) of the "Tract" literature', and lamented that no real attempt was made to respond. Palmer recalled that 'some of those who placed confidence in the Oxford divines, but were ignorant of the Fathers, waited anxiously for answers which never came'.[210]

Significantly, some of those High Churchmen and Tractarians who seceded to Rome after the Gorham Judgment in 1850 came to concede that Evangelicals such as Goode had had the better of the purely historical argument. The Gorham controversy in 1849–50 over baptismal regeneration, provoked by Bishop Phillpotts's refusal to institute George Cornelius Gorham as rector of Bampford Speke, Devon, found High and Low Churchmen battling over rival interpretations of the Anglican formularies and appealing to the views of the Reformers and Elizabethan divines. In the ensuing pamphlet warfare, High Churchmen exploited the testimony of various Caroline Divines to attempt to settle the disputed theological issues at stake. Goode, on the other hand, teased Bishop Phillpotts, by appealing to a long line of testimonies from Anglican divines in support of Gorham's understanding of a regeneration as a 'charitable hypothesis' in the baptismal service:

> For a long period after the Reformation you have not a single witness that you can lean upon in our Church. And even when the current tone of theology among us began to change, in Laud's time, so entirely different were even Laud's views from those of your Lordship, as to the character of such doctrine as that of Mr Gorham, that he not only made no opposition to the promotion in the Church of men holding it, but actually recommended them for the Episcopal office.

Goode repeatedly made use of Laud's name as a rhetorical device to embarrass Phillpotts, exclaiming: 'Have we really got so far on the way to Rome, that Laud himself has been left in the distance, as the patroniser of heretics, as a friend to those who denied an Article in the Creed, because he supported men holding these views [on baptism]?'[211]

High Churchmen disputed Goode's assumption that the moderate Calvinist episcopalian divines of Laud's early days, such as Bishops Carleton and Prideaux, coincided with Gorham in their understanding of baptism, or the

---

[210] Roundell Palmer's ms. marginalia comment on volume 2, pp. 406–7 of his copy [in the Bodleian Library] of T. Mozley, *Reminiscences Chiefly of Oriel and the Oxford Movement*, 2 vols (2nd edn, London, 1882). I owe this reference to Dr Simon Skinner, Fellow of Balliol College, Oxford. Golightly also reported that he had heard 'that some of the Newmanites acknowledge that Mr Goode has done harm to their cause'. C.P. Golightly to W.S. Bricknell, 16 May 1842, Bricknell Papers, BRIC 1/2, *PHL*.

[211] W. Goode, *A Letter to the Bishop of Exeter; containing an Examination of his Letter to the Archbishop of Canterbury* (London, 1850), p. 45. Cf. note 164.

bold assertion that even Laud acquiesced in it by apparently supporting the promotion of all moderate Calvinists. Goode was again criticised for inferring too much from limited evidence. In an earlier dispute with Anglican Evangelical opponents of baptismal regeneration in 1842–3, itself a partial re-run of an earlier controversy of 1812–15, High Churchmen had derided Evangelical claims to appropriate the Reformers on their side, accusing them of selectivity, one-sidedness and special pleading. Similarly, in the Gorham dispute, High Church protagonists cited the opinions of Cranmer, Ridley, and even Bucer, apparently in favour of baptismal regeneration, in order to counter Goode's appeal to Reformed divines in support of Gorham.[212] Much was made of the unfairness implied in the Judgment itself that Jewel, Ussher, and even Hooker, Taylor, and Pearson, could be claimed 'as countenancing the hypothesis of Mr Gorham'.[213] Nonetheless, after further study of Caroline authorities, James Mozley, perhaps the most accomplished Tractarian theologian, came to accept the fairness of an historic latitude recognised by the Gorham Judgment, in a striking personal *volte face*. As he put it in his influential *The Primitive Doctrine of Baptismal Regeneration* (1856): 'I look in vain into the writings of Hooker, Laud, Jeremy Taylor, Pearson, and others of that school for any sign that they considered the hypothetical interpretation of the statements regarding the baptised in our formularies as a bar to a clergyman officiating in the Church'.[214]

Moreover, the conversion of several Tractarians to Rome was aided by their perception that Goode and other Low Churchmen had exploded the High Church notion that the doctrine of unconditional baptismal regeneration was the only doctrine allowed by the Church of England. Goode and others effectively undermined the High Church case in favour of baptismal regeneration based on Reformation principles, by exploiting the well known Tractarian antipathy to the Reformers.[215] Some Tractarians were prepared to believe the worst of the Reformers and came to accept the anti-sacramental Evangelical presentation of the Reformers' views. To the embarrassment of High Churchmen but the delight of Goode, Phillpotts's chaplain, William Maskell,

---

[212] F.C. Massingberd, *A Letter to the Rev. William Goode, M.A. Showing that the Opinions of Cranmer, Ridley, and Bucer, concerning Holy Baptism were Opposed to those Contained in a Letter of Peter Martyr, lately Published by him. With Comments on his Inferences from that Letter* (London, 1850), p. 6.

[213] *A Brief Vindication of Jewel, Hooker, Ussher, Taylor, and Pearson, from Misrepresentations in the recent Baptismal Judgment. By a Fellow of a College* (Cambridge, 1850), p. 3.

[214] J.B. Mozley, *The Primitive Doctrine of Baptismal Regeneration* (London, 1856), p. lii; J.B. Mozley, *A Review of the Baptismal Controversy* (London, 1862); W. Maskell, *A Second Letter on the Present Position of the High Church Party in the Church of England* (London, 1850), pp. 11–33.

[215] Gorham's original advertisement for a curate 'free from Tractarian error' had served as a spark for the controversy, and Goode sought to discredit the high church case by drawing attention to the link. W. Goode, *The Doctrine of the Church of England as to the Effects of Baptism in the Case of Infants* (London, 1850), pp. 2–3.

while seceding to Rome in part reaction against the Gorham Judgment, came down in favour of the Evangelical representation of Anglican teaching on baptism based on the Thirty-Nine Articles and known opinions of the English Reformers and Elizabethan divines. To the dismay of High Churchmen in 1850, the High Church Maskell conceded that the Caroline Divines ultimately had failed in the controversial uses to which not only Tractarians but a preceding generation of High Churchmen had put them. As Maskell candidly admitted:

> catenae are useful enough, within their proper and reasonable limits; they create difficulties sometimes whilst they seldom suffice to establish a conclusion: employed, however, as they have been, of late years by own [high church] party, they are not merely a packed jury, but a jury permitted only to speak half of their mind.[216]

Newman himself had reached a similar conclusion by the eve of his conversion to Rome in 1845, his earlier confidence in the seventeenth-century divines evaporating as 'he read the Fathers more carefully, and used his own eyes in determining the faith and worship of their times'.[217] Maskell in 1850 and Newman in 1845 reached Rome by very different routes. However, in both cases their path to Rome had been eased by a common sense of betrayal and of having been, in Newman's words, 'taken in' by the Caroline Divines, whose language he had adopted to the sacrifice of his own words.[218] Alexander Forbes, the Tractarian Bishop of Brechin, did not take the step of conversion, but in the wake of the outcry against his eucharistic teaching from within the Scottish Episcopal Church in the late 1850s, he also came close to throwing the Caroline Divines overboard and abandoning his Anglican allegiance. Forbes's brother Scottish bishops condemned his eucharistic teaching from the apparent vantage-point of the seventeenth-century Anglican divines. Keble and Pusey became alarmed in 1859 precisely because their Scottish friend seemed to blame those divines for being able to be claimed by both sides in the eucharistic controversy, and thus as not being explicit enough in favour of his own, supposedly Catholic, teaching.[219]

Attitudes towards the Caroline Divines underwent a further shift among second and third generation Tractarians or Anglo-Catholics (as they came to be called) and their opponents. The early Tractarians closely identified with

---

[216] Maskell, *Second Letter on the Present Position of the High Church Party*, p. 16.
[217] J.H. Newman to E.B. Pusey, 19 February 1844, *LBV* (transcript), PHL.
[218] In his retractions of anti-Roman language in 1843, Newman explained that he had said to himself: ' "I am not speaking my own words, I am but following almost a consensus of the divines of my Church. They have ever used the strongest language against Rome, even the most able and learned of them. I wish to throw myself into their system. While I say what they say, I am safe." ' *Conservative Journal*, 28 January 1843, p. 5.
[219] Strong, *Alexander Forbes*, pp. 156–7.

the political principles of the Caroline Divines, anathematising rebellion and upholding passive obedience and non-resistance. They invested monarchy with a sacral quality and reverenced Charles I as the 'Royal Martyr' who had died for episcopacy.[220] However, while the image of the suffering Church of England under the Great Rebellion and deprivation of the Nonjurors for conscience sake appealed to the Tractarians, from the start they were never entirely at ease with the Court associations of classical Laudianism, inseparable as these were to Laud's campaign. There was no equivalent in the Oxford Movement to the close relationship between monarch and religious leader that characterised the Laudian movement. The Tractarians may have regarded this as a sign of the spiritual superiority and more popular basis of their own Catholic revival,[221] but there were others who regarded this lack of any connection with a great institution of the realm and the Tractarian failure to secure, as did the Laudians, the commanding levers of power in church and state as a weakness. In an article entitled 'Church and King' in the *British Critic* in 1839, Thomas Mozley spoke for the Tractarian generation when he conceded to 'our being unable to estimate the feeling which made a Herbert, or a Laud, such zealous competitors for royal favour'.[222] John Mason Neale was one of the first among the apologists of the nineteenth-century Catholic Revival to distance it from that of the seventeenth century. In a series of lectures delivered and published in 1852 under the title *The Laudian Reformation compared with that of the Nineteenth Century*, Neale contrasted the former highly unfavourably with the latter, complaining that even the Laudian Church in its glory was compromised by what he termed 'a fearful Erastianism', which tainted, he claimed, even Andrewes and which 'blazes forth in Overall, and Montague, and Cosin'.[223] The Tractarian sensitivity to the isolation of the Church of England was also evident in Neale's charge against the Caroline Divines of being guilty of a practical 'Donatism'.[224]

---

[220] Nockles, *Oxford Movement in Context*, pp. 67–79.
[221] Neale, 'Laudian Reformation compared with that of the Nineteenth Century', pp. 171–3. See Neale's comment (p. 180): 'What way could the Church make among Chartists, if she came among them, clothed in the aristocratical garb of Caroline times.'
[222] [T. Mozley], 'Church and King', *British Critic*, vol. 25, no. c. (April, 1839), 325–6. However, see James Mozley's comment ('Archbishop Laud', p. 217): 'He [Laud] was obliged to make his way at Court, to get any of the practical acting power of the nation into his hands... a courtier he must be; he must gain access to the great political lever, if he was to put a finger on the ecclesiastical.'
[223] Neale, 'Laudian Reformation compared with that of the Nineteenth Century', p. 179. Even as early as 1839, the Tractarian Faber had questioned 'whether the view taken by Laud and others of the King's Supremacy, and the limits by which he would have bounded it in Church matters, was precisely accurate'. [Faber, ed.], *Autobiography of Dr William Laud,* p. viii. Cf. note 99. James Mozley was more sympathetic to Laud's political preoccupations, arguing that he was not Erastian, but clung to the old medieval notion of the Church as a political estate of the realm. [J.B. Mozley], 'Archbishop Laud', pp. 215–16.
[224] Neale, 'Laudian Reformation compared with that of the Nineteenth Century', p. 181.

Pusey and others continued to use Caroline precedents to support the Anglo-Catholic cause, even Ritualism; the Anglo-Catholic view of the Laudian tradition, became increasingly condescending and detached. The Caroline Divines were simply not Catholic enough, and most Anglo-Catholics preferred either Sarum or Roman over Caroline models of worship. In a revealing article in the *Church Quarterly Review* in July 1883, the Laudian movement of the seventeenth century was dismissed as only 'to a small extent sacerdotalist or ritualistic', aiming merely 'at securing a moderate conformity to the Prayer Book, nothing nearly so close as is found in even the lowest Evangelical parishes nowadays'. The Laudians, the writer complained, made a point of only one piece of ritualism, 'the placing and fencing the altar in a way which is practically universal now'.[225] Above all, unlike the Tractarian revival, the Laudian reforms were imposed from above and did not originate from below. The very fact of their unpopularity and opposition to the established order, which had impressed the early Tractarians, was now adduced as a sign of weakness. Laudianism was portrayed as the creed of a small cluster of academic dignitaries, opposed by the 'prevalent tone of opinion'. A 'high church school was doubtless rising' after 1590, it was conceded, 'but the tradition of sixty years was against it'.[226] The trend in Anglo-Catholicism towards detachment from the Caroline inheritance was evident in T.A. Lacey's biography of Thorndike (1929) which, with its patronising tone of both praise and criticism of Thorndike,[227] expresses the enormous condescension of posterity.

A shift in attitude to Caroline Anglicanism is also discernible on the anti-Tractarian side. Some Anglican Evangelicals never followed the attempt by divines such as Goode and Garbett to utilise the Caroline Divines, Laud included, against the Tractarians but rather, in branding Tractarianism as a true successor to Laudianism, castigated both as equally un-Protestant, if not anti-Protestant. The very success of the Tractarian appropriation of the Laudian tradition in their favour encouraged this tendency among their Anglican Evangelical opponents. In contrast to Goode, J.C. Ryle, later Bishop of Liverpool, both in a lecture on Richard Baxter in 1853 and then in a lecture to the ultra-Protestant Church Association published in 1869 as 'Archbishop Laud and his Times', attacked Laud head-on. Praising the Puritan party, Ryle almost identified himself with the charges raised by Laud's fanatical contemporary enemy, the Puritan William Prynne. For Ryle, 'Laud did more harm to the Church of England than any churchman that ever lived. He inflicted a wound that will never be healed; he worked mischief that will never be repaired'.[228] Ryle accepted the Tractarian claim that Laud deliberately 'set

---

[225] *Church Quarterly Review*, vol. 16, no. 32, 'The Catholic Side of Anglicanism' (July, 1883), p. 427; Neale, 'Laudian Reformation compared with that of the Nineteenth Century', p. 186.
[226] *Ibid.*
[227] See Lacey, *Herbert Thorndike*, pp. 53–4, 67.
[228] J.C. Ryle, 'Archbishop Laud and his times', p. 142. Ryle (p. 163) even maintained that Laud

himself to oppose the current theology of his day', and blamed him for rallying 'around him in an Arminian Cave of Adullam every churchman who was discontented with the doctrines of the Reformation'.[229] Moreover, Ryle made explicit the link between a Laudian and a Tractarian plot, albeit separated by two centuries, to 'High-Churchmanise and un-Protestantise' the Church of England – Laud was 'the father of Tractarianism'.[230] In both cases, the engine of un-Protestantising was shown to be 'a great and suspicious stir about the sacrament of the Lord's Supper, and attaching an ominous importance to the precise position of the Lord's Table'.[231] The Laudian notion, propagated by Newman, of the Church of England holding a *via media* position between Geneva and Rome, was anathema to Ryle, who regarded it 'as about as absurd as to say the Isle of Wight occupies a middle position between England and France!'[232] Yet even Ryle fell back on the standard Anglican Evangelical expedient of offsetting denigration of Laud with praise for other contemporary bishops, notably Hall, Prideaux, Bedell, and Ussher, as 'good men' and 'bright exceptions among the bishops, both as to doctrine and practice'. It was left to a High Church critic of Ryle's anti-Laudian 1853 lecture to remind Ryle that,

> Hall was so impressed with the schismatical violence of the Puritan party, that, at the request of Laud, he wrote his immortal work, 'Episcopacy by Divine Right Asserted'. You will pardon me for referring you also to the dedication of his 'Apology against the Brownists', in which you will see, that his view of the Church in his days strangely contrasts with the opinion which you have given to the world. Prideaux and Ussher were 'good men', and were made bishops, as was also Bedell . . . These are considered 'good men', as opposed to Laud, whose very name is cast out as evil. But who procured their promotion? Why Archbishop Laud himself![233]

In reaction against the Oxford Movement and early Ritualism, other more moderate Evangelicals and Low Churchmen came to take up a more critical posture towards the Laudian experiment. Even Goode shifted tack in his later

---

'did more harm to the reformed Church of England than any man that ever lived – more than Gardiner, Cranmer, Cardinal Pole, and Bloody Mary, all put together'.

[229] *Ibid.*, p. 145.

[230] *Ibid.*, pp. 161–2. Ryle argued that far from being 'a new invention of these latter days', Tractarianism was 'two hundred years old'. *Baxter and his Times. A Lecture by the Rev. J.C. Ryle, A.B. Rector of Helmingham, Suffolk. Delivered before the 'Young Men's Christian Association', in Exeter Hall, February 1, 1853* (London, n.d.), p. 5; Rabett, *Archbishop Laud more than half a Papist*, especially pp. iii–vii.

[231] Ryle, 'Archbishop Laud and his times', p. 151.

[232] *Ibid.*, p. 162.

[233] *A Letter to the Reverend J.C. Ryle, A.B. in Reply to his Lecture on 'Baxter and his Times', 'Delivered before the Young Men's Christian Association. By a Clergyman of the Diocese of Exeter* (Exeter, 1853), p. 32. Ryle (*Baxter and his Times*, p. 4) claimed that 'good bishops' such as Davenant and Hall were 'snubbed', while 'bad bishops, like Montague and Wren, were patted on the back and encouraged'.

writings and assailed Laud as a precursor of the Ritualists of the 1860s. Fearful that the Anglican Bishops of the 1860s might sanction an unacceptable degree of ritualism that mirrored what was allowed by their episcopal successors of the 1630s, Goode argued that in both cases episcopal authority might be exercised in defiance of the law of the Church. The historical analogy was invoked as a direct warning. Laud's campaign to place the Lord's Table altarwise was portrayed as an example of 'how the most gross violation of the ecclesiastical law in an important point of ritual may be introduced and enforced by episcopal authority for the promotion of party purposes'.[234] The implication was that the Bishops of 1867 should not fall into the same trap. C.P. Golightly, an inveterate anti-Tractarian, in the same year and in the same context of early Ritualist controversies, wrote *A Brief Account of the Romeward Movement in the Church of England in the days of Archbishop Laud*, with a similarly contemporary agenda in mind. According to Golightly, in the 1630s, 'serious and systematic efforts were made, like those which we witness in our own day, to undo the work of the Reformation'.[235] Golightly, however, cleared Laud himself from dishonest Romanising intentions, while blaming others such as Montagu of harbouring them.[236] The fall-back Evangelical position of employing the Jacobean and early Caroline divines of the episcopalian Calvinist school of Ussher, Davenant, and Hall, against the Tractarians remained an option.[237] Moreover, the editor of the 1869 *Church Association Lectures*, J.C. Colquhoun, fell back on Garbett's earlier challenge to Pusey, 'that not one Anglican churchman of any school for three hundred years ever held the dogmas of Dr Pusey and his allies'.[238] In short, such critics wanted to use Laudianism both as bugbear and warning against Tractarianism, while at other times denying that the latter historically was supported by the former. The Anglican Evangelical urge to reappropriate the Caroline inheritance resurfaced in 1927 at a time of Low Church opposition to a High Church-inspired revised Prayer Book. Hall and Ussher were prominent in citations of Caroline testimonies to alliance with foreign Reformed Churches, hostility to the 'idolatry' of Rome, and opposition to eucharistic adoration and

---

[234] W. Goode, *Remarks on the Episcopal Resolution passed in the Upper House of the Southern Convocation on the Subject of Ritualism* (London, 1867), pp. 12–13.

[235] C.P. Golightly, *A Brief Account of the Romeward Movement in the Church of England in the days of Archbishop Laud* (London, 1878), p. 1. This work had been first published by Golightly as a preface to his *The Present Position of the Right Rev. Samuel Wilberforce in Reference to Ritualism* (London, 1867), bearing the motto: 'there is no new thing under the sun'. As early as 1841, Golightly had called the Tractarians, 'the Laudian school of divinity'. [C.P. Golightly], *Strictures on No. 90 of the 'Tracts for the Times'. By a Member of the University of Oxford*, 2 parts (Oxford, 1841), part 2, p. 86.

[236] Golightly, *Brief Account of the Romeward Movement in the Church of England in the days of Archbishop Laud*, pp. 10–13.

[237] Ryle, 'Archbishop Laud and his times', p. 160.

[238] J.C. Colquhoun, 'Introduction', *Church Association Lectures, 1869*, p. xi.

reservation (key issues in the 1927 Prayer Book revision). According to C.S. Carter, the *via media* between Rome and Protestant sectaries adopted by the Caroline Divines extended only to points of discipline, not doctrine. The Caroline Divines were defended as at one with the Reformers, the only difference being that the former held a somewhat higher doctrine of ministry.[239] The message was clear – modern Anglo-Catholicism stood condemned by both.

In conclusion, the Tractarians could take some credit in forcing even their opponents to take seriously the testimony of the seventeenth-century divines. Looking back from the start of the Oxford Movement, from the vantage-point of 1842, James Mozley could maintain:

> If our memory fails us not, the appeal to those divines was received at the time [1833] in a way any thing but complimentary or respectful to their authority. The language was . . . why evoke from their quiet and obscurity a set of musty and moth-eaten folios, to sit in judgment upon us – why sound a retreat from the nineteenth to the seventeenth century . . . but such is not the language which any moderate, any decent churchman can hold now . . .[240]

However, at the same time, any residual Anglican consensus in appealing to the Caroline Divines broke down in the era of the Oxford Movement. The Victorian Church of England was a prey to party division forged by the legacy of history. There was a sense in which the Tractarians and even some of their more conservative High Church supporters sheltered behind the authority of the Caroline Divines in order that they might be better able to rebut charges of being a mere 'party' in the Church. As William Sewell put it in 1842: 'If we are afraid of party in the Church – that at least cannot be called a party which collects itself round those whom the Church has so long regarded as her own special teachers'.[241] However, this was to presume precisely that which their opponents challenged – the claim or presumption to be exclusively the nineteenth-century mouthpiece of seventeenth-century Anglicanism. In fact, the Tractarians appealed to the Caroline Divines in a subtly different way from that of their High Church predecessors: eventually more as polemical support in defence of their own position within the Church of England and for long disused or disputed points of faith and practice such as prayers for the dead and private confession, rather than primarily as polemical support in defence of the Church of England as an institution against her denominational adversaries. They tended to play off the Caroline Divines against the Reformers, regarding the former as a corrective of the latter. One advanced Tractarian writer summed up this attitude in 1879 with a bold claim:

---

[239] C.S. Carter, *The Anglican Via Media: being Studies in the Elizabethan Religious Settlement and the Teaching of the Caroline Divines* (London, 1927), especially chs vi–ix; C.S. Carter, *The Caroline Church* (London, n.d. [1913]), especially chs vii–viii.
[240] [Mozley], 'Development of the Church in the Seventeenth Century', pp. 300–1.
[241] [Sewell], 'Divines of the Seventeenth Century', p. 472.

It is then to the Caroline prelates and divines that the Anglican Church owes its theology, almost its existence as a Church. They had inherited a position they would never have voluntarily chosen, and did their best, under terrible disadvantages, to improve it. From the nature of the case, their work was reactionary and reconstructive: 'to gather up the fragments that remained'.[242]

The Tractarian attempt to appropriate exclusively the theology of the seventeenth-century divines as well as the early Fathers in their favour was ambitious and even provoked some mockery. Edwin Abbott, in his critical study of Newman published in 1892, pointed out the irony of the task of 'extracting the "Divine Wisdom" of eighteen centuries of Christian divinity being entrusted to a little group of Oriel men in 1837'.[243] The Tractarians, however, never claimed originality, but merely to be following 'the old paths'. One can make out a case that the Tractarian presentation of the Caroline Divines as proto-Anglo-Catholics in the nineteenth-century mould was an example of latter-day High Church Anglican myth-making, but there was some substance behind the myth.

There was a genuine immediacy to the analogy commonly drawn between what the Tractarians were attempting in the 1830s and what the Laudians attempted in the 1630s. Yet though history appeared to be repeating itself and affinities were drawn between the Laudianism of the 1630s and Tractarianism of the 1830s, the Oxford Movement was not a mere replication of the teaching of the Caroline Divines, even of the Laudian hard core. Firstly, the Tractarians were not interested in Arminianism as such. In private, they found fault with various Caroline authors, with Newman lamenting the longer-term impact of what he called 'Grotianism', mediated via Chillingworth, Hales, and even Hammond, in lowering the tone of Anglican theology. Moreover, while Hurrell Froude and others referred to 'the holy and blessed Martyr St. Charles, and 'St. William of Canterbury',[244] the Movement grew increasingly out of sympathy with the uniquely Laudian theocratic synthesis of statecraft and religion. By the time of James Mozley's bicentennial panegyrical article on Laud in 1845, the political dimension of the Laudian heritage had been almost jettisoned.

It suited Tractarian propagandist purposes to claim an earlier Anglican lineage and testimony when rallying support for their own contested doctrines, but selectivity was necessary and openly avowed. By the compilation of *catenae*, the Tractarians did not claim the theology of the extracts as in itself normative or authoritative but merely intended to show that Tractarian opinions on the respective doctrines involved had the testimony or warrant of 'a

---

[242] Henry Nutcombe Oxenham M.A. (ed.), *An Eirenicon of the Eighteenth Century. Proposal for Catholic Communion by a Minister of the Church of England New edition, with introduction, notes, and appendices* (London, 1879), pp. 8–9.

[243] Abbott, *Anglican Career of Cardinal Newman*, vol. 2, p. 82.

[244] *Remains of the late Rev. Richard Hurrell Froude,* vol. 1, p. 177.

chain of witnesses' and could be a useful springboard for the propagation of more advanced sacramental teaching. Newman defended the reprint of Cosin's *History of Popish Transubstantiation* as Tract 27, on the ground that it was a useful weapon against 'Hoadlyism' on the eucharist, 'not as if Bishop Cosin was a defence of us, but as containing a true view'.[245] Tractarian polemicists, when presented with the teaching of individual Reformers or later divines who contradicted them, were always ready to use the argument that catholic truth did not depend on 'the personal opinions, or private judgement, of any man, or men, of station or influence, however high'. On the other hand, they were no less ready to ransack the tomes of Anglican divinity and pile on *catenae patrum* of seventeenth-century divines for the support of their own positions. Tractarian propaganda on behalf of the Catholicism of the Caroline Divines was also well served by citations of shocked Puritan, Nonconformist, and Whig testimonies, as by the historians Daniel Neal (author of a four-volume *History of the Puritans*, 1732–7) and Henry Hallam (author of a Whiggish *Constitutional History of England* in the 1820s), to their supposedly 'popish' inclinations.

The testimony of the Caroline Divines was used by both old High Churchmen and later Tractarians to support their own opposed positions on the subject of Roman Catholicism. Sewell was no less selective in his citations than Mozley or Oakeley, and Protestant High Churchmen such as Le Bas in 1829, facing the prospect of Catholic Emancipation, needed to explain away 'incautious' eirenical language and ecumenical overtures towards Rome on the part of some Laudians.[246] It is possible to overstate Laudian hopes of reconciliation with Rome. Montagu's manuscript on recusancy might be viewed as a tactical device to reconcile Roman Catholics to the Church of England, while Laud distanced himself from Montagu's dealings with the papal emissary Panzani in the 1630s. Laudian anti-Romanism, however, was formulated on a very different basis to that of Elizabethan Calvinist divines – J.C. Ryle rightly recognised that the Laudians took up 'a new view of the Church of Rome', based on 'the perpetual visibility of the Church of Christ, derived from the Apostles to the Church of Rome', and as conceding that Rome was a true, if corrupt, branch of the Church of Christ.[247] Anthony Milton stresses the significance of the new emphasis placed by the Laudian divines on the Church of England's continuity with the pre-Reformation Latin Church and its hierarchy[248] – a legacy which Tractarians and later Anglo-Catholics eagerly embraced and from which only those who seceded to Rome departed.

---

[245] Härdelin, *Tractarian Understanding of the Eucharist*, pp. 14, 45.
[246] [Le Bas], 'Life and Times of Archbishop Laud', p. 440. The Tractarian Neale, however, complained that the Laudians did not seriously contemplate reunion. Neale, 'Laudian Reformation compared with that of the Nineteenth Century', pp. 181–2.
[247] Ryle, 'Archbishop Laud and his times', p. 161.
[248] Milton, *Catholic and Reformed*, pp. 158–60, 298–300.

Newman sought a doctrinally rigid synthesis which ran counter to the underlying diversity of Caroline divinity, but some current Anglican commentators in their search for a common 'Anglican identity' and 'integrity' might be open to the charge of imposing their own 'liberal catholic' and ecumenical gloss on a tradition which eludes neat categorisation. For Sykes, Avis, and others, the Caroline Divines become subsumed within a liberal Anglican tradition denoting comprehension, toleration, consensus, and latitude, and become historical tools in the construction of a new 'paradigm' for contemporary Anglicanism.[249] Yet for all its Great Tew circle links, Laudianism had a hard edge and one susceptible of Tractarian resuscitation two centuries later. Tractarian contemporaries felt that Newman had broadened and popularised a tradition that in Laud's hands had been narrow, elitist, and Court-centred.

Neither Tractarians nor Laudians rested content with an inherited Protestant orthodoxy, but sought to redefine and remould the Church of England of their day in order to carry forward their own agenda. For all the secessions of some of their number to Rome, the former, quite as much as the latter, were engaged in a 'struggle for Anglicanism'. Before they were forced to settle for a mere right to observe certain catholic doctrines and practices within the widening comprehensive fold of Anglican teaching, the Tractarians had sought the removal of Evangelical or classic Protestant doctrines from the Church of England's formal polemic, just as Laudians such as Montagu had sought the removal of Calvinist doctrines from the Church's formal polemic two centuries earlier. If the Tractarians were selective in their *catenae patrum* of Caroline extracts, they were no more so than what Peter McCullough has revealed of the strategy of the Laudian editors of Bishop Andrewes's *Ninety-Six Sermons* (1629).[250] The Tractarians were well aware that, as Diarmaid MacCulloch convincingly demonstrates, the Reformation might have gone much further but for the death of Edward VI in 1553,[251] but this was no source of embarrassment for them. Like some Laudian commentators, the Tractarians gloried in the 'superintending Providence' that had intervened.[252] Unlike old High Churchmen, the Tractarians increasingly were not concerned to fashion the 'myth' of a conservative Reformation on even the Laudian model of Heylin. Hurrell Froude had cured them of that tendency in High Church apologetic. Yet Laudianism provided no real precedent for later

---

[249] Avis, *Anglicanism and the Christian Church*, ch. 18.
[250] P.E. McCullough, 'Making Dead Men Speak: Laudianism, Print, and the Works of Lancelot Andrewes, 1625–1642', *Historical Journal*, vol. 41, no. 3 (October, 1998), pp. 401–24. McCullough points out that the *Library of Anglo-Catholic Theology* edition of Andrewes's works (1841–56) scrupulously preserved the order of the *XCVI Sermons*.
[251] MacCulloch, *Thomas Cranmer* pp. 618–20.
[252] *Tracts for the Times . . . Vol. V for 1838–40*, No. 86 [I. Williams]: 'Indications of a Superintending Providence in the Preservation of the Prayer Book and in the Changes which it has undergone' (3rd edn, Oxford, 1843), 4 parts, pp. 1–144.

Tractarian attempts to cut the Church of England off from her sixteenth-century Reformation moorings. Nicholas Tyacke recently has argued, in the case of Andrewes, that there was a wholesale Laudian abandonment of mainstream Elizabethan Protestantism.[253] This was the view of Hurrell Froude, who claimed that Laud's preface to the Thirty-Nine Articles in 1628 'certainly intended to disconnect us from the Reformers'.[254] It was the assumption which underlay James Mozley's periodical polemic of the 1840s. However, it was Puritanism and not Elizabethan Protestantism that was the bugbear for Laudians, though Bishop Montagu, with his private talk of 'Puritan Bishops', was as scatter-gun in his employment of the 'Puritan' label against opponents as the Tractarians would be in bandying the term 'ultra-Protestant' or 'Genevan' against their own Evangelical critics. Moreover, recent research by Kenneth Fincham lends some credence to Tractarian propaganda, by revealing the extent to which the Laudian campaign of the 1630s amounted to a 'new conformity' and standards of 'orthodoxy' in terms of the *Book of Common Prayer*, canonical and ritual observance which amounted to a substantial modification of the terms of the 'old conformity' characteristic of the Elizabethan and Jacobean Church.[255] Yet while the Laudians refurnished or even altered a house already built, it is more questionable to regard them as pioneers or founders of an entirely 'new Anglicanism' on the lines of Tractarian rhetoric. Laudianism constituted just one fall-out from an apparently (though not in reality) unified Elizabethan protestant tradition that was fragmenting of its own accord.[256] Tractarianism represented a further stage in the process of doctrinal polarisation within Anglicanism and of the disintegration of the English Protestant tradition.

Tractarian converts to Rome lost faith in the integrity of the Laudians as expositors of Catholicism, partly because they came to realise that they could no longer be regarded as proof of what the Church of England believed, since 'they were clearly in a minority, even in their day'.[257] From this Catholic standpoint, Tractarianism, like Laudianism, was viewed as a sort of 'Patristico-Protestantism', an eclectic amalgam of primitive doctrines and

---

[253] N. Tyacke, 'Lancelot Andrewes and the Myth of Anglicanism', P. Lake & M. Questier (eds), *Conformity and Orthodoxy in the English Church, c. 1560–1660* (Woodbridge, 2000), pp. 5–33, especially pp. 32–3.

[254] *Remains of the late Rev. Richard Hurrell Froude*, vol. 1, p. 380.

[255] K. Fincham, 'Clerical Conformity from Whitgift to Laud', *Conformity and Orthodoxy*, Lake & Questier (eds), pp. 125–58.

[256] Milton, *Catholic and Reformed*, especially pp. 531–46.

[257] [P. Le Page Renouf], *The Character of the Rev. William Palmer, MA, of Worcester College, as a Controversialist... Considered in a Letter to a Friend at Oxford* (London, 1843), pp. 9, 5–6; [G.D. Ryder], 'Notes Preparatory to a History of the Church of England's Claim to the Apostolical Succession', *Thoughts on Some Questions of the Day* (London, 1869), p. 33. See P.B. Nockles, 'Sources of English Conversions to Roman Catholicism in the Era of the Oxford Movement', McClelland (ed.), *By Whose Authority?*, pp. 1–40.

practices, only tolerated by the laxity of a liberal establishment rather than owned as the authoritative teaching of a living Church speaking with one voice as the Movement of 1833 had envisaged.[258] The convert Manning, himself a one-time devotee and propagator of Laudian divinity, came to regard the Laudian school as no more 'the legitimate voice or exponent of the Anglican Church' than any of the other schools within the pale of the Established Church.[259] Some Victorian Catholic writers retained an affection for Laud, but faulted him for failing to follow out the logic of his principles, leading his Church down a blind alley, and sowing a degree of confusion which ultimately prevented the Church of England from knowing 'either what it was or what it wanted'.[260] Tractarian converts to Rome, such as Thomas Allies, came to conclude that at best, the Laudian divines and the Tractarians alike had found out or recovered for themselves mere fragments of Catholicism which had been either 'violently cast out' by the Reformers or, as in a few cases, somehow suffered to remain in the Anglican formularies. Such 'Catholicism' as they espoused, however, was in spite of and not because or the result of the system in which they found themselves.[261] It represented the mere shadow, rather than substance, of an old devotional and sacramental world that had been lost.

Old High Churchmen and moderate Tractarians, however, continued to value the Caroline Divines as articulators of the *via media* between Rome and Protestant Dissent. The presentation of Laud as loyal exponent of the Anglican *via media* was a prominent feature of the 250th anniversary of his death in 1895 – Laud's lasting legacy was represented as saving episcopacy and establishing the correct position of the altar.[262] However, by the twentieth century even these apparent achievements could be viewed as uncontentious and

---

[258] W. Maskell, *Protestant Ritualists* (London, 1872), pp. 12–13; F. Oakeley, *Historical Notes on the Tractarian Movement (A.D. 1833–1845)* (London, 1865), pp. 100–3; J. Gordon, *Reasons of my Conversion to the Catholic Church. Letters to a Friend* (London, 1849), p. 19; F.A. Paley, *A Brief Review of the Arguments alleged in Defence of the Protestant Position. Addressed to those who call themselves 'Anglo-Catholics' in the Church of England* (London, 1848), p. 25.

[259] Cited in Pereiro, *Cardinal Manning*, p. 163.

[260] [T. Longueville], *A Life of Archbishop Laud. By 'A Romish Recusant'* (London, 1894), pp. 474, 478.

[261] T.W. Allies to H.E. Manning, 3 November 1848, Manning Papers, Ms Eng. Lett. c. 657, fol. 110, Bodleian Library.

[262] W.E. Collins, *Lectures on Archbishop Laud* (London, 1895), p. 124. For earlier non-Tractarian High Church eulogies of Laud as saviour of the Church of England, see J. Baines, *The Life of William Laud, Archbishop of Canterbury, and Martyr* (London, 1855), pp. 267–9; S.H. Cassan, 'William Laud: Martyred by the "Saints" ', *Lives of the Bishops of Bath and Wells*, pp. 33–4. Not all High Churchmen took this line. For the view that the survival of 'catholic' aspects of the Church was not due to Laud, but that on the contrary these survived in spite of the discredit he cast upon them, see A.C. Benson, *William Laud, sometime Archbishop of Canterbury, a Study* (London, 1887), pp. 219–20.

acceptable to both High and Low Church parties, apart from a few extremists on either side.[263] Moderate High Churchmen repudiated Anglo-Catholic attempts to claim the seventeenth-century divines as precedents for the Ritualism and medievalism being espoused later in the nineteenth century. Francis Meyrick translated some of the lesser known polemical treatises of Bishop Andrewes such as *Tortura Torti*, written against the Roman Catholic Cardinal Robert Bellarmine and in defence of King James I, precisely in order to highlight the Protestant and anti-papal side of seventeenth-century divinity. According to Meyrick in his *Old Anglicanism and modern Ritualism* (1901), the then 'new medievalist party' looked 'with as much contempt on the Anglicanism of the seventeenth century as on the Protestantism of the eighteenth century'. Nonetheless, it was important to disabuse loyal but misguided High Churchmen who defended 'the medievalists' on the false 'belief that ritualism, as it exists at present, is historically justified by being a legitimate successor to the Caroline school of divinity'.[265]

Anglican Evangelicals remained ambivalent, claiming lineage from the school of Jacobean episcopalian Calvinist divines, but repudiating the Laudian inheritance. The Reformation historiography of Heylyn and Collier was anathema to Anglican Evangelical polemicists long before the rise of the Oxford Movement.[266] Their recurrent attempts to drive a wedge between acceptable Jacobean Calvinist and unacceptable Laudian divines harked back to the distinction which Richard Baxter in the 1650s had drawn between those whom he labelled 'the old episcopal divines', such as Jewel, Pilkington, Hooper, Latimer, Cranmer, Hall, Davenant, and Morton, and the 'new episcopal divines' of his own day, such as Taylor, Hammond, Bramhall, and Sheldon: a distinction which the Laudian Bramhall indignantly repudiated as a 'chimera of his own brain, without any ground'.[267] Significantly, in the light of Peter McCullough's research on the precedent of the Laudian-glossed publication of Andrewes's writings after his death and then Puritan recreations of Andrewes after 1641, Victorian Anglican Evangelicals also appealed to the works of an earlier crypto-Puritan Andrewes as well as from Hooker, Hall, Ussher, Downham, Davenant, and Jackson against the Arminian school of Laud, Hammond, Taylor, Sheldon, and Bull, in order to support their own doctrines of Justification and Election.[268] In contrast, there was a long tradition

---

[263] E.C.E. Bourne, *The Anglicanism of William Laud* (London, 1947), pp. 22–3. Laud was also presented as more in harmony with the theology of the English Reformers than many later High Church divines assumed. A.S. Duncan-Jones, *Archbishop Laud* (London, 1927), p. 73.
[264] F. Meyrick, *Old Anglicanism and Modern Ritualism* (London, 1901), p. 1.
[265] *Ibid.*, p. 231.
[266] P.B. Nockles, 'A Disputed Legacy: Anglican Historiographies of the Reformation from the era of the Caroline Divines to that of the Oxford Movement', *Bulletin of the John Rylands University Library of Manchester*, vol. 83, no. 1 (Spring 2001), pp. 121–67.
[267] M. Sylvester (ed.), *Reliquiae Baxterianae*, 2 vols (London, 1696), vol. 2, p. 387.
[268] Fish, *Jesuitism . . . of the Oxford Tractarians*, pp. 61–2; Garbett, *Christ as Prophet, Priest,*

of English and Catholic utilisation of High Church Anglican writers from Hooker onwards for propagandist purposes.[269] This tradition lived on and was revitalised by Victorian Catholic writers in response to the Oxford Movement. Mid nineteenth-century Catholic controversialists such as the Jesuit Fr William Waterworth in his *Origin and Development of Anglicanism* (1854) followed Bishop Milner's line in exploiting Caroline Anglican admissions in favour of Catholic doctrines and practices such as the veneration of saints and prayers for the dead, thereby embarrassing or undermining their Protestant contemporaries.[270]

As we have been recently reminded by historians of the early modern Church, the content and criteria of orthodoxy and conformity in the Church of England was from the beginning in a state of constant flux, modification, and reconstruction, even the Church's foundation documents being capable of endless gloss and reinterpretation.[271] This survey reveals that the same applies to the competing nineteenth-century Anglican readings of seventeenth-century English church history. The Tractarian Newman privately conceded the partisan nature of the Oxford Movement's reading of earlier Anglican history, confiding in 1839: 'I fear . . . as regards the "Theocratic Philosophy of History". . . Our Church is not, alas, sufficiently at unity in itself, to enable us to take more than what in matter of fact is a *party* view of history'.[272] The Tractarians have been blamed for a 'defensive narrowing of historical vision' by abandoning the Reformation and disowning the Lutheran tradition.[273] Tractarian reinterpretations of Anglicanism, however, had a long pedigree and anti-Tractarians employed the same technique of a selective reading of the past. Meanwhile, contemporary liberal Anglican theologians pursuing their own current agenda are no more immune from the perennial

---

    and King, vol. 1, p. 439n. See McCullough, 'Making Dead Men Speak', pp. 417–24; Milton, *Catholic and Reformed*, p. 533.

[269] Nockles, 'The Difficulties of Protestantism', pp. 193–236. This tradition of English Catholic apologetic can be dated at least as far back as John Brereley's *The Protestant Apology for the Roman Church* (1608).

[270] J. Waterworth, *The Substance of Six Historical Lectures on the Origin and Progress in this Country, of the Change of religion called the Reformation, Delivered in the Catholic Church of the Holy Trinity, Newark* (Newark, 1839), p. 5.

[271] P. Lake & M. Questier, 'Introduction', *Conformity and Orthodoxy*, pp. ix–xx.

[272] J.H. Newman to S. Fox, 23 October 1839, *LD*, vol. 7, p. 170. Newman's attention was being drawn by his correspondent to the work of John Duff Schomberg, later published as *The Theocratic Philosophy of English History; being an Attempt to impress upon History its true Genius and Character, and to present it, not as a disjointed Series of Facts, but as one grand whole* (1842).

[273] For Tractarian antipathy to Luther and Lutheranism, see J.C. Hare, *Vindication of Luther* (London, 1855); W.P. Haugaard, 'A myopic curiosity: Martin Luther and the English Tractarians', *Anglican Theological Review*, vol. 66, no. 4 (October, 1984), pp. 391–401; A.E. McGrath, 'Newman on Justification: an Evangelical Anglican evaluation', *Newman and the Word*, T. Merrigan & I. Ker (eds) (Louvain, 2000), pp. 91–107, especially p. 107.

tendency to use or reinterpret history for their own 'present-centred' purposes for which Victorian churchmen can be accused.[274] In the nineteenth-century debates, both sides had their historical heroes and villains. The seventeenth-century divines served very different, often contradictory rhetorical and controversial purposes for competing parties within the Victorian Church of England, as well as between the Church and other denominations. The *protean* quality of the texts of seventeenth-century Anglican divinity ultimately eluded Tractarian efforts to appropriate them definitively in support of all the Movement's doctrines and practices and to pass them off as the Church of England's 'official' teaching, as the Movement's converts to Rome recognised. Newman's undoubted attempts to 'manage' the Caroline Divines, which he denied, were doomed to fail. The authentic voice of an earlier apparently stable and uniform Anglicanism, as claimed both by Evangelical patronage of the Parker Society and Tractarian promotion of the *Library of Anglo-Catholic Theology*, was incapable of conclusive resolution. Historically, one can speak only of 'Anglicanisms' rather than 'Anglicanism'. The Church of England was a denomination constantly being remade by its leaders, with the Laudian heritage, merely one of its manifestations, remodelled in the Williamite and Hanoverian eras, and then only partially recovered in the nineteenth century. The Caroline Divines left an ambiguous, disputed legacy to the Victorian Church of England, which has echoed down the ages and which flickers into life even today,[275] but which reflected a more deep-seated ambiguity inherent within the Anglican Reformation formularies themselves.

---

[274] See Avis, *Anglicanism*, pp. xiii–xviii. Cf. B.W. Young, 'Knock-Kneed Giants: Victorian Representations of Eighteenth-Century Thought', J. Garnett & C. Matthew (eds), *Revival and Religion Since 1700* (London, 1993).

[275] Anglican church party readings of Anglican history are not quite dead and the spirit of the later Goode or even Ryle has recently found renewed expression. Thus, it is interesting to note an example of a contemporary throwback to a Victorian Evangelical mindset of intolerant criticism of Newman for daring 'to regard the Caroline Divines as somehow defining the essence of Anglicanism'. The author sits in aggrieved judgement on 'Newman's arbitrary historical positivism', which is modestly described as 'quite unacceptable'. See A.E. McGrath, 'Newman on Justification', p. 106; McGrath, 'Emergence of the Anglican tradition on Justification', p. 41.

SELECTED PUBLICATIONS OF VINCENT ALAN McCLELLAND

Books

Cardinal Manning: His Public Life and Influence 1865–92 (Oxford University Press, 1962, pp. xii, 256).

English Roman Catholics and Higher Education 1830–1903 (The Clarendon Press, Oxford University Press, 1973, pp. x, 453).

The Liberal Education of England's Youth: Idea and Reality (University of Hull, 1979, pp. 23).

The Churches and Education (editor and contributor), (History of Education Society, 1984, pp. vi, 107).

Private and Independent Education (editor and contributor), (University of Hull Institute of Education, 1986, pp. 107).

Christian Education in a Pluralist Society (editor and contributor), (Routledge, 1988, pp. ii, 239).

Advances in Teacher Education (editor and contributor), (Routledge, 1989, pp. vii, 218).

The Needs of Teachers (editor and contributor), (Cassell, 1996, pp. 131).

By Whose Authority? Newman, Manning and the Magisterium (editor and contributor), (Downside Abbey, 1996, pp. x, 290).

From Without the Flaminian Gate: 150 years of Roman Catholicism in England and Wales 1850–2000 (editor and contributor), (Darton, Longman and Todd, 1999, pp. xviii, 406).

Contributions to Books and Symposia

'Thomas William Allies'; 'Peter Augustine Baines'; 'Kenelm Digby'; 'Ambrose Lisle March Phillipps de Lisle'; 'James Warren Doyle'; 'William Ewart Gladstone'; 'Henry Edward Manning'; 'William Bernard Ullathorne'. Contributions to *The New Catholic Encyclopedia* (Catholic University of America, Washington DC, USA. 1967).

'A Catholic Eton: By Hook or By Crook? John Henry Newman and the Establishment of the Oratory School', in C. Brock and R. Ryba (eds), *A Volume of Essays for Elizabeth Halsall* (*Aspects of Education,* University of Hull, 1980), pp. 3–17.

'The Church and Religious Education', in John Cumming and Paul Burns (eds), *The Church Now* (Gill and Macmillan, 1980, pp. 109–20).

'John Dewey', contribution to *The Fontana Biographical Companion of Modern Thought* (1983), pp. 179–80.

'Gladstone and Manning: A Question of Authority', in P.J. Jagger (ed.), *Gladstone, Politics and Religion* (Macmillan, 1984), pp. 148–70.

'Some Educational Implications of the Oxford Movement', in V.A. McClelland (ed.), *The Churches and Education* (History of Education Society, 1984), pp. 52–69.

'History of the Church's Involvement in Higher Education (University) in England and Wales', in D.J. Mullins (ed.), *Towards a Policy for Higher Education* (*Report of the Committee for Higher Education of the Department of Christian Doctrine and Formation of the RC Bishops Conference*, 1985), pp. 18–25.

'Towards the Year 2000: Accountability and the British University', in H.M. Chang (ed.), *University Education in the Next Century* (Chinese University of Hong Kong, 1985), pp. 56–62.

'The Liberal Education of England's Youth: Idea and Reality', in P. Gordon (ed.), *The Study of Education,* vol. III (Woburn, 1988), pp. 40–57.

'*Sensus Fidelium*: The Developing Concept of Voluntary Effort in Education in England and Wales', in W. Tulasiewicz and C. Brock (eds), *Christianity and Educational Provision in International Perspective* (Routledge, 1988), pp. 61–88.

'Tractarian Intellectualism and the Silent Heritage 1840–50', in J.F. Champ (ed.), *Oscott College 1838–1988* (Oscott, 1988), pp. 83–92.

'The Effect of the Council on Catholicism: Great Britain and Ireland', in A. Hastings (ed.), *Modern Catholicism: Vatican II and After* (Oxford University Press & SPCK, 1990), pp. 365–76.

'Henry Edward Manning and the Rights and Dignity of Labour', Chapter in P. Furlong and D. Curtis (eds), *The Church Faces the Modern World: 'Rerum Novarum' and its Impact* (Earlsgate, 1994), pp. 191–203.

'Authority and Freedom: John Henry Newman and the Formation of Youth', in R. Aldrich (ed.), *In History and In Education* (Woburn, 1996), pp. 58–73.

'Parents, Church and School: Meeting the Educational Needs of the Christian Family', in J.M. Feheney (ed.), *Education and The Family* (Veritas, 1995), pp. 18–29.

'Wholeness, Faith and the Distinctiveness of the Catholic School', in T.H. McLaughlin, J. O'Keefe and B. O'Keeffe (eds), *The Contemporary Catholic School: Context, Identity and Diversity* (Falmer, 1996), pp. 155–61.

'*Phylacteries of Misery* or *Mystic-eyed Hierophants*? Some Ecclesiastical and Educational Challenges in England of the Irish Diaspora 1850–1902', in Susan M. Parkes (ed.), *Education and National Identity: The Irish Diaspora* (History of Education Society Publication, 1997), pp. 15–32.

'School or Cloister? An English Educational Dilemma, 1794–1880', contribution to the published papers of the History Symposium, English Benedictine Congregation, vol. 15, 1997, pp. 1–30.

'Religious Instruction in Schools: A Theology of Catholic Education', in J. Redford (ed.), *Hear O Islands: Theology and Catechesis* (Veritas, 2002), pp. 132–9.

'School and Studies', in A. Cramer (ed.), *Lamspringe: An English Abbey in Germany, 1643–1803* (Ampleforth Abbey, 2003), pp. 103–19.

'Vaughan, Herbert Alfred Henry Joseph Thomas (1839–1903)'; 'Jackson, Joseph Devonsher (1783–1857)'; Scurr, John (1876–1932)', entries in the new *Oxford Dictionary of National Biography* (Oxford University Press, 2004).

Articles

'Documents Relating to the Appointment of a Delegate-Apostolic for Scotland 1868', *The Innes Review*, vol. viii, no. 11, 1957, pp. 93–8.

'Ruskin's Apologia', *The Downside Review*, vol. 79, no. 255, 1961, pp. 128–34.

'Manning's Idea of a University', *The Tablet*, vol. 216, no. 6381, 1962, pp. 828–30.

'Manning and the Universities: A Reappraisal of the Background to the Kensington Venture', *The Tablet*, vol. 217, no. 6410, 1963, pp. 335–7.

'Archbishop Ullathorne and Religious Education', *Pax*, vol. 54, no. 310, 1964, pp. 124–30.

'The Athens of the North: Ushaw and Catholic Education in the 19th Century', *The Tablet*, vol. 218, no. 6474, 1964, pp. 798–9.

'The Protestant Alliance and Roman Catholic Schools, 1872–1874', *Victorian Studies*, vol. 8, no. 2, 1964, pp. 173–82.

'The 1880 Central School Scheme: Part 1: How Great Was The Need?', *The Tablet*, vol. 219, no. 6532, 1965, pp. 852–4.

'The 1880 Central School Scheme: Part 2: The Need Examined', *The Tablet*, vol. 219, no. 6533, 1965, pp. 877–9.

'The 1880 Central School Scheme: Part 3: The Final Outcome', *The Tablet*, vol. 219, no. 6534, 1965, pp. 901–3.

'The Kensington Scheme', *The Month*, new series, vol. 33, no. 3, 1965, pp. 173–82.

'The 1890s and After in France', *The Aylesford Review*, vol. viii, no. 1, 1966, pp. 97–103.

'Lady Macbeth', *The Aylesford Review*, vol. viii, no. 1, 1966, p. 54.

'Robbins in Retrospect', *Pax*, vol. 54, no. 316, 1966, pp. 36–41.

'Scots Jesuits and Episcopal Authority 1603–1773', *The Dublin Review*, vol. 240, no. 508, 1966, pp. 111–32.

'Discipline in Schools', *The Month*, new series, vol. 1, no. 37, 1967, pp. 166–71.

'Ethics and Historiography', *The Aylesford Review,* vol. ix, no. 1, 1967, pp. 15–20.

'Going to University', *The Harvest*, new series, vol. 1, no. 5, 1967, pp. 4–5.

'The Irish Clergy and Archbishop Manning's Apostolic Visitation of the Western District of Scotland, 1867; Part 1: The Coming of the Irish', *The Catholic Historical Review*, vol. 53, no. 1, 1967, pp. 1–27.

'The Irish Clergy and Archbishop Manning's Apostolic Visitation of the Western District of Scotland, 1867; Part 2: A Final Solution', *The Catholic Historical Review*, vol. 53, no. 2, 1967, pp. 229–50.

'From Douai to Dublin: Four Hundred Years of Educational Endeavour', *Studies*, vol. 59, no. 233, 1970, pp. 40–52.

'A Hierarchy for Scotland 1868–1878', *The Catholic Historical Review*, vol. 56, no. 3, 1970, pp. 474–500.

'The History of Education: Aid to National and International Understanding', *The European Teacher*, vol. 7, no. 2, 1970, pp. 19–22.

'Modernism: An Essay in Religious Education', *Pax*, vol. 60, no. 325, 1970, pp. 29–35.

'Milestones in the History of Special Education in Britain', *The Irish Journal of Psychology*, vol. 1, no. 1, 1971, pp. 36–42.

Contribution to 'Symposium: Report on Teacher Training', *Oideas*, Earrach 1971, pp. 18–19.

'Wiseman, Manning and The "Accademia": An Experiment in English Adult Education', *Paedagogica Historica*, vol. 9, no. 2, 1971, pp. 414–25.

'The Liberal Training of England's Catholic Youth: William Joseph Petre (1847–93) and Educational Reform', *Victorian Studies*, vol. 15, no. 3, 1972, pp. 257–77.

'The Universities' Education Board and the Chaplains, 1895–1939: The History of a Troubled Relationship', *The Ampleforth Journal*, vol. LXXVII, 1973, pp. 69–84.

'Herbert Vaughan, The Cambridge Teachers' Training Syndicate and Public Schools 1894–1899', *Paedagogica Historica*, vol. 15, no. 1, 1975, pp. 16–38.

'The "Free Schools" Issue and the General Election of 1885: A Denominational Response', *History of Education*, vol. 5, no. 2, 1976, pp. 141–54.

'Change and Continuity', *Pax*, no. 345, 1980, pp. 65–9.

'Educating for Life: A Challenge for the Nineties', *The Month*, second new series, vol. 14, no. 10, 1981, pp. 333–8.

'School or Cloister? An English Educational Dilemma, 1794–1889', *Paedagogica Historica*, vol. 20, no. 1, 1980, pp. 108–28.

'Corporate Reunion: A 19th Century Dilemma', *Theological Studies*, vol. 43, no. 1, 1982, pp. 3–29.

'Teacher Education: The Making of Persons', *Durham and Newcastle Research Review*, vol. x, no. 56, 1986, pp. 307–8.

'An Education for our Time', *The Clergy Review*, vol. 1, no. 7, 1987, pp. 275–9.

'Recent Trends in Teacher Education in England', *Irish Educational Studies*, vol. 7, no. 1, 1988, pp. 1–15.

'The Making of Young Imperialists: Rev. Thomas Seddon, Lord Archibald Douglas and the Resettling of British Catholic Orphans in Canada', *Recusant History*, vol. 19, no. 4, 1989, pp. 509–29.

'Manning's Work for Social Justice', *The Chesterton Review*, Cardinal Manning Special Issue, 1992, pp. 525–37.

'*O Felix Roma!* Henry Manning, Cutts Robinson and Sacerdotal Formation, 1862–1872', *Recusant History*, vol. 21, no. 2, 1992, pp. 180–217.

'Spiritual Nemesis: Henry Edward Manning and the Road to Rome', *The Allen Review*, no. 6, 1992, pp. 4–8.

'Der Grundbegriff der Katholischen Erziehung', Engagement, *Zeitschrift für erziehung und schule*, 2–3 (Aschendorff Verlag, 1994), pp. 249–60.

'Religion, Community and Coherence', in Elizabeth Ashton and Brenda K. Watson (eds), *Aspects of Education*, vol. 51, 1994, pp. 28–34.

'Partnership and Quality in Teacher Education', *Studies in Education,* vol. ii, no. 2, 1995, pp. 30–4.

'Unity, Partnership and Quality in Teacher Education: A United Kingdom Perspective', *European Journal of Teacher Education*, 18 (1), 1995, pp. 59–67.

'Bourne, Norfolk and the Irish Parliamentarians: Roman Catholics and the Education Bill of 1906', *Recusant History*, vol. 23, no. 2, 1996, pp. 228–56.

'St Edmund's College, Ware and St Edmund's College, Cambridge: Historical Connections and Early Tribulations', *Recusant History*, vol. 23, no. 3, 1997, pp. 470–82.

'Self-Integration and Denominational Schooling in England and Wales', *Parents and Teachers*, vol. 5, no. 9, 1998, 3000 words.

'The Manning Archive', *Catholic Archives*, no. 19, 1999, pp. 79–82.

'Changing Concepts of the Pastoral Office: Wiseman, Manning and the Oblates of St Charles', *Recusant History*, vol. 25, no. 2, 2000, pp. 218–36.

'The Restoration of the Hierarchy, 1850: A Question of Authority', *The Month*, second new series, vol. 33, no. 8, 2000, pp. 297–308.

INDEX

Acland, Thomas Dyke 255–6, 265–7
Almond, Dom Cuthbert 104
America, Benedictines 96–7
Ampleforth Abbey 103–4, 105
Anglican Church *see* Church of England
Anglican Evangelicals 347–51, 360–1, 367
Anglicanism *see* Church of England
Anglo-Catholics *see* Tractarians
anti-Catholicism 139–40, 144, 146, 150–2
   attacks on convents 152–3, 155, 161
   conspiracy theory 153–4
   Poor Law Guardians 7
   in Victorian England 162
anti-Communism 124–5, 135
anti-Tractarians 322–3, 347, 358
Apologia pro Vita Sua 186
Arian controversy 213
Arminianism 328–9
Arnold, Dr Thomas
   admired by Kingsley 247–8
   ambition 237
   attack on Tractarians 245–6
   Broad Church 245
   complexity of character 247
   Fellow of Oriel 237
   ideal 238
   influence on University of Oxford 242
   influence on Victorians 234–5
   Laleham 237, 238
   Liberal Anglican historian 246–7
   Principles of Church Reform 244
   religious doubts 237
   research by Dr Anthony Reeve 241
   at Rugby 235, 239–43
   Stanley's memoir 236
   Tom Brown's Schooldays 236
   Wratislaw case 241
Arnold, Matthew 248
Australia, Benedictines 100–1
Baudelaire, Charles 190–1
Beaumont Lodge 92
Beck, Bishop George Andrew 12–13

Belloc, Hilaire 194
Benedictines
   in America 96–7
   army chaplains 106–7
   Australia 100–2
   and British imperialism 95–6, 108–9
   education 103–5
   French Revolution 97
   lay schools 103
   Liverpool 96
   missionary work 97–8, 100–3
   patriotism 95, 106
   return to England 95–6
   universities 105
   in Wales 100
Benson, R. H. 194
Bewick, Bishop John William 60
Bilsburrow, Bishop Romanus, OSB 100
Birdsall, Dom John Augustine 101
Blessings in Disguise 199
Blue Army of Fatima 133–4
Blundell, Dom Odo 107
Board of Education *see* Committee of Council for Education
Board Schools 8, 9 *see also* school boards
Bradley, Meta, on Virginia Crawford's marriage 32
British and Foreign Schools Society 250, 252, 262, 278
Brogan, Colm 111–12, 116–19, 127–32, 137
Brogan, Sir Denis 110, 111, 119–22
Brougham, Henry, Lord, Education Bill 250–1, 254
Brown, Bishop Thomas Joseph 100
Brown, Bishop William F., OSB 55
Buckley, W. F. Jr 129–31
Burton, Bishop George Ambrose 107
Burton, Canon Edwin 163, 174, 178, 179–80
Butler, Fr Robert 35
Butt, Dorothy 55
Byles, Marianne Caroline 14

Callista 186
Calumnies against Convents 153, 155–6, 160
Cambridge University 105
Camm, Dom Bede 94–5, 107–8
Cannadine, David 98
Capes, John Moore 208–9
Caroline Divines 309, 341
  anti-Tractarians 358
  appeal to Catholics 314
  appeal to Tractarians 310–11
  Library of Anglo-Catholic Theology 321–5
  loss of favour 356–7
  moderate Tractarians 366
  Newman's attitude to 325–6
  political principles 357
  as proto-Anglo-Catholics 362
  use made of writings 313
  works republished 314
Carroll, Bishop John 97
Catéchisme du Patron 50
Catholic Church
  adaptability 225
  attack from liberal ideas 144
  three offices of Christ (Newman) 219–20
  undermining Protestantism 150
Catholic education 1–2, 4–5, 6, 7, 85
Catholic Emancipation 172, 309
The Catholic Encyclopedia 173–4
Catholic literary revival 189–90
Catholic London a Century Ago 173
Catholic Poor School Committee 5
Catholic Social Action, 1891–1931 49
Catholic Social Guild 54
Catholic Socialist Society 116
The Catholic Student Magazine 118
Catholic Women's Suffrage Society 55
Central School of the National Society 259
Central Society for Education 251, 252
Chadwick, Bishop James 58–9
Chamberlain, Joseph 7, 9, 34
Chandler, Dom Richard Paul 96–7
Chesterton, G. K. 183–4, 199
  Catholic literary revival 193
  on Gothic architecture 194
  on tradition 194
Chillingworth, William 330–1
Christian Democratic Union 55
The Church and the Worker 54
Church Education Society 281, 282–3

Church History of England 85–6
Church of England 2, 4, 5, 10
  Caroline Divines 361–2
  contaminated by foreign Protestantism 314
  divisions 361
  doctrinal polarisation 365
  plurality 369
  role in education 253, 254–6, 261, 273, 277, 294
Church of Ireland
  disestablishment 281
  National School system 281–2
Church of Ireland College of Education 280, 282
  links with Trinity College Dublin 289–90
Church of Ireland Educational Association 287
Church of Ireland Training College for National School-teachers *see* Church of Ireland College of Education
Churton, Edward 323, 330–1
Clarke, Fr Thomas Tracy 91–2
Coleridge, Samuel Taylor 184–5, 245, 246
Collegio Romano 79
Collier, Dom William Bernard 99
Committee of Council for Education 263, 267
  school inspection 268
conservatism 114–15, 122–7
  and Marianism 133
Consitt, Edward 59–61, 65
conspiracy theory, anti-Catholicism 153–4
convents
  abuse of nuns 158
  stereotypical view 140
conversion to Catholicism, relation to tradition 183–4
Copeland, William J. 322–3
Coulston, Gabriel 60–1
Cowper-Temple clause 9
Crawford, Donald 32 *see also* Crawford, Virginia
Crawford, Virginia
  biography of Frederic Ozanam 56
  and Captain Henry Forster 32–3
  Catholic Social Guild 54
  Catholic Women's Suffrage Society 55
  Christian Democratic Union 55
  conversion to Catholicism 35
  divorce 33–4

education 31
enters convent 52
friendship with Cardinal Manning 29, 35–6
gossip concerning 32–3
journal extracts (re Cardinal Manning) 36–49
journalism 28, 35, 51
later life 56–7
marriage 31–2
parents 31
People and Freedom Group 56
political activity 52–3, 54
relationship with Sir Charles Dilke 29
sisters 31–2
social work 32, 52–3
Spanish Civil War 55–6
St Joseph's home 55
visit to Canada 53
visit to Dublin 54
visit to Lavington 50
visits to Europe 51–2, 53
writing as Clarence Ford 51
Cullen, Paul, Cardinal 5, 283

Dalrymple, Martha Mary *see* Smith, Eustacia
Daubeny, Archdeacon Charles 312–13
Davenport, Dr Christopher 344
Davis, Dom Charles Henry 102
Davis, H. Francis 12, 13
The Dawn of the Catholic Revival 176
de-Christianization 3–4
de Grey, Thomas, Lord 6
Decadents 190–2
  conversion to Catholicism 192–3
denominational education 1–4, 5, 6, 9
  Ireland 283
desacralization *see* secularization
Dilke, Ashton Wentworth 31
Dilke, Maye (née Smith) 30, 34–5
Dilke, Sir Charles 28–9, 32–3
  friendship with Cardinal Manning 29–30
  marries Emilia Francis 34
  response to Crawfords' divorce 33–4
directions on spiritual care (Manning) 13–14
Discourses on the Scope and Nature of University Education see The Idea of a University
Dissenters, education 270
'Divines of the Seventeenth Century' 341

Douai 103
Douglass, Bishop John 173
Downside Abbey 103–4, 105, 106, 107
Dream of Gerontius 187
dual system of education 2, 3, 8–9
Dutch system of education 251

ecclesia discens 212, 213, 215, 230
ecclesia docens 212, 213, 215, 230
The Edmundian 171
Edmundian Association 182
education
  administration 7
  Benedictines 103–5
  C of E diocesan and district boards 258, 260
  Cardinal Manning's philosophy 262
  Catholic 1–2, 4–5, 6, 7, 85
  Church-State partnership 278
  denominational 1–4, 5, 6, 7, 9
  Dissenters 270
  dual system 2, 3, 8–9
  Dutch system 251
  duty of parents 4, 10–11
  elementary 1–11
  of girls 300–1
  Jesuit 118
  New Code 305–6
  Parliamentary Commission of Enquiry 251–2
  payment by results 305
  Prussian system 251
  role of religion 302, 304–5
  role of State 4–6, 10–11, 250–1
  school inspection 268, 272
  secularization 2, 8, 9, 263–5
  terms of Union 270–2
  Tractarians 258, 260, 261, 270, 277
  Wesleyan Methodist 293
Education Act (1870) 1–3, 6–7, 9, 11, 277, 278
  conscience clause 7
elementary education 1–11
Elgar, Sir Edward 106
Eliot, T. S. 194–6
English Martyrs 64
Established Church *see* Church of England
The Eternal Priesthood 26–7
Eurocentricism 99
The Eve of Catholic Emancipation 176
Evelyn Innes 52
Eyre, Monsignor Charles 59

Faber, Rev Frederick William 334
Factory Education Bill (1843) 294
fall of Rome (1870) 64
Faussett, Professor Godfrey 336
Faust legend 192
feminism 137–8
fides implicita 214–15
Fincham, Kenneth 365
'Finis Coronat Opus' 192
Fitzpatrick, Sir Percy 107
The Force of Truth 313
Forgotten Shrines 108
Forster, Captain Henry 32, 33
Forster's Bill *see* Education Act (1870)
Fraser, Hamish 110, 132–7
French Revolution 3, 10
  Benedictines 97
Froude, James Anthony, *Lives of the Saints* 308
Froude, Rev Richard Hurrell 330
  anti-Erastianism 319
  attack on Bishop Jewel 315
  influence on Newman 316
Fynne R. J. 290

Galecki, Bishop Antonio 142
Gallagher, Tom 110
Gasquet, Francis Aidan, Cardinal 108
Gillow, John 210–12, 214–15
Gladstone, William Ewart 1–2, 7, 265–6
Goode, William 349–55, 359–60
Gorham decision 17–18n, 354–5
Gothic revival 185
Graham, Sir James 294
Grammar of Assent 222
Gray, John Bede *see* Tatham, John Bede
Gregg, Archbishop John 291
Gregg, Bishop Robert 281, 282
Gregory XVI 98
Guinness, Sir Alec 199
Gwydir, Dom Basil 107

Haggard, H. Rider 153
Haig, Field Marshall Alexander 107
Hall, Dom Placid 105
Handley, James E. 110
Hankinson, Dom Michael Adrian 99
Hanoverian Church 319–20
Hanson, Rev Eric, SJ 113
Hare, Archdeacon Julius 17
Harrison, Helen (née Smith) 31
Harrison, Robert Richens 31
Hedley, Bishop Cuthbert, OSB 104–5

Heloise and Abelard 52
Help and Comfort for the Sick Poor By the Author of 'Sickness, its Trials and Blessings' 25–6
Herbert, Lady Elizabeth 14–15
Herbert, Sidney, 1st Baron Herbert of Lea 14n
Heylin, Rev Peter 315
hierarchical authority in Catholicism 207–8
High Churchmen, writings used for propaganda 368
Hints on the Service for the Visitation of the Sick 20–1
historians, Liberal Anglican 246
History of St Edmund's College Chapel 172
history, tendency to reinterpret 368–9
'Hoadlyism' 314
Hogarth, Bishop William 58
Holland, Rev W. Lancelot 153
  attack on Fr Sydney Smith 155–6
Hooker, Richard 316–17, 340–1
Hopkins, Rev Gerard Manley, SJ 189–90
Horner, Leonard, Dutch system of education 251–2
The Horrors of Roman Catholic Convents and the Suffering of Sister Barbara 150–3
Howard, Christopher 1
Howard, Edward, Cardinal 66
Howley, Archbishop William, role of C. of E. in education 256
Hume, Basil, Cardinal 109
Huysmans, J. K. 190–2

The Idea of a University 202–8
Ideals of Charity 53–4
identity, religious 111
Ile de France *see* Mauritius
Imperialism, Benedictines 95–6, 108–9
industrial society, immorality 125
Irish language teaching 288–9
Irish national schools 6
The Irish Sketch Book 139
Italy Today 55

Jerusalem 94
Jesuits, friction with Vicars Apostolic 79–80
Jubilee 82–3
Justification 340–1

INDEX

Kay, James Philips 272–3, 297, 298
Kay-Shuttleworth, James Philips *see* Kay, James Philips
Keble, John 264–5, 316–17, 334, 337–8
  eucharist 341
  preface to *Laws of Ecclesiastical Polity* 317
A Key to Labour Problems 50
Kildare Place Society *see* Society for Promoting the Education of the Poor in Ireland
Kingsley, Rev Charles 239
  on Thomas Arnold 247–8
Kingsmill Moore, Rev Dr Henry
  at Balliol College 281
  canon of St Patrick's Cathedral, Dublin 287
  Church of Ireland Educational Association 287
  clash with R. J. Fynne 290
  defence of rural schools 285–7
  diocesan inspector of schools 281–2
  historian 287–8, 290
  Irish language teaching 288–9
  later life 290–1
  legacy to Church of Ireland education 291
  parents 280–1
  Principal of Church of Ireland College of Education 279, 284–90
  Reminiscences and Reflections from some Sixty years of Life in Ireland 280, 290
  Society for Promoting the Education of the Poor in Ireland 280, 287
  teachers' training, Ireland 286
Knowles, Dom David 108
Kuehnelt-Leddihn, Erik von 110

laity, role in Catholic church 210–18, 230, 232
Larkin, Dr William P 112
Latin Mass, Appeal to preserve 198
Latitudinarianism 346–7, 348
Laud, Archbishop William
  accusations of Romanising 360
  attitude to reformed Churches 353
  contentiousness 312
  controversy with Fisher 350
  eulogised 313
  legacy to Church of England 366
  loss of favour 366
  moderation 331
  Tractarians' view 333–4
  'via media' 327
Laudians
  abandonment of mainstream Protestantism 365
  anti-Catholicism 363
  attitude of Tractarians 327–31
  Caroline Divines 315
  Church and State 357
  criticised for 'Romish' practices 336
  loss of favour 358, 362
  Mozley attacks old High Church 341–3
  remoulding the Church of England 364
Lavington 50
lay schools, Benedictines 103
League for European Freedom 123
leap-frog 239
Lectures and Essays on University Subjects see The Idea of a University
Lectures on Justification 340
Lectures on the Present Position of Catholics in England 212
Lectures on the Prophetical Office of the Church 226, 310, 314
Leeper, Canon Alexander 282
Leslie, Shane 52
Liberal Anglican historians 246
liberal state
  nature (Manning) 5
  relationship with churches 4, 10
Library of Anglo-Catholic Theology 321–5
Liddon, Canon Henry Parry 35
Life of St Edmund of Canterbury 172
Liverpool, Benedictines 96
Lives of the Saints 308
Lockhart, Elizabeth 23n
Loss and Gain 186
Lucas, Frederick 85
Luck, Bishop Edmund, OSB 103
Lyrical Ballads 184
Lythgoe, Fr Randal, SJ
  at 22nd General Congregation 91
  achievements 92–3
  background 76–7
  building programme 87–8
  at Collegio Romano 79–82
  death 92
  at Dole 83–4
  education 77
  educational work 85
  Jesuit novice 79
  in Malta 90

Lythgoe, Fr Randal, SJ (*cont.*)
  Manning's opinion 75
  missionary work 84
  in North Wales 89–90
  ordination 83
  in Paris 82
  Provincial Superior 86–8
  return to London 90
  visits to Europe 79
  in Yarmouth 90–1

MacGavigan, Jack 125
MacMillan, Frank 129, 135
Manning, Henry Edward, Cardinal
  apocalyptic view of society 3–4
  attitude to Society of Jesus 75
  and Bernard Ward 165–6
  Caroline Divines 318
  directions on spiritual care 13–14
  and education 1–11
  episcopal appointments 62
  The Eternal Priesthood 26–7
  friendship with Virginia Crawford 29, 35–49
  and Henry O'Callaghan 61–2, 64–5
  illness 21–2, 26
  and Mgr George Talbot 59
  nature of liberal state 5
  pastoral care 12, 18–19, 26
  The Pastoral Office 26
  philosophy of education 262
  political alliances 10
  rejection of Laudianism 366
  relationship with Priscilla Maurice 19–21, 23–6
  Vatican Council 1–2
Marianism, and conservatism 133
Marlborough St training college 283
marriage, ideal state for women 147
Marylebone Park House 85
masculine Catholicism 137
Masonic threat to Catholicism 153–4
Massingberd, Rev Francis Charles 20, 20n, 23
Mathison, Gilbert Farquhar Graeme 252–5, 259, 260, 276
Maurice, Rev John Frederic Denison 273
Maurice, Priscilla 15–17
  correspondence with Cardinal Manning 23, 26
  Help and Comfort for the Sick Poor By the Author of 'Sickness, its Trials and Blessings' 25–6

Hints on the Service for the Visitation of the Sick 20–1
  illness 18–19
  on pastoral care of the sick 18–26
  Prayers for the Sick and Dying by the Author of 'Sickness, its Trials and Blessings' 26
  relationship with Cardinal Manning 17, 19–21, 23–6
  Sacred Poems for Mourners 21
  Sickness, its Trials and Blessings 18, 22–3, 25
Mauritius 97–100
McCarthyism 131
McClelland, V.A. 1, 3, 9
McGahey, Mick 111
Menology of St Edmund's College 172
metaphysical poets 184–5
Methodist Conference 1843, reaction to Factory Education Bill 294–5
Methodist education 293
  boys 301
  debate on state funding 296–7
  General Education Fund 295–6
  girls 300–1
  role of religion 302, 304–5
  school building programme 292, 295
  standards 306
  state inspection 297
  teachers' training 297–8
Methodists 10
Middleton, Rev Reginald, SJ
  Glasgow Catholic Institute 117
  social Catholicism 116
Milner Gibson education bill 302
Milner, J. 314
Moberly, Dr George 235
Modernists 194, 198–9
Molesworth Commission 101
monasticism 103
The Monk 140
Montagu, Bishop Richard 345
Moore, George 52
Moore, Maurice 54
Morris, Bishop William Placid, OSB 98
Mozley, Anne 340
Mozley, James 328, 341–3, 355, 361
Mussolini, Benito 55

National Education League 7, 8–9
National Education Union 5
National Schools England, Dissenters 270

INDEX

National Schools Ireland 281–3
  teachers' training 283–4
National Society for the Education of the
  Poor 250, 254–5, 257–8, 261, 278
  Committee of Enquiry 257, 259, 269,
    270, 276
  General Committee 257–9
  Mathison, Gilbert Farquhar Graeme
    252–5
  school inspection 268, 274
  schools' finance 269
  Wood, Samuel Francis 257
Neale, Rev John Mason 357
Neve, Rev Frederick 63
Newcastle Commission 301–2, 303, 304
Newdegate, Charles Newdigate, MP 141
Newman Association 127
Newman, John Henry, Cardinal *see also*
  three offices of Christ
  adaptability of Catholic Church 225
  as Anglican 201
  Apologia pro Vita Sua 186
  Arian controversy 213
  Arminianism 328–9
  attitude to Reformers 316
  avoiding controversy 226–7, 231
  Callista 186
  Caroline Divines 325–6, 330–2, 339–40
  centrality of theology 221–3, 233
  Church unity 201
  conversion to Catholicism 186, 200–1
  creative tension in Church 232
  criticism from Arnold 245–6
  criticism of discourses on education
    205–6
  discourses on education 203–8
  doctrinal rigidity 364
  Dream of Gerontius 187
  editor of *The Rambler* 209–11
  Grammar of Assent 222
  hierarchical authority in Catholicism
    207–8
  The Idea of a University 202–8
  influenced by Froude 316
  instructive poetry 187
  interdependence in ecclesiology 233
  Lectures on Justification 340
  *Lectures on the Present Position of
    Catholics in England* 212
  *Lectures on the Prophetical Office of the
    Church* 226, 310, 314
  on *Library of Anglo-Catholic Theology*
    324
  Lives of the Saints 308
  Loss and Gain 186
  'On Consulting the Faithful in Matters
    of Doctrine' 212–13
  popular devotion 223–4
  principal of expediency 227–31
  purpose of university education 202,
    204–5, 206
  Rector of Dublin University 201–2
  refutation of Anglicanism 218
  relationship between theology and
    faith 222
  religious instinct 224
  role in Catholic literary revival 189–90
  role of Catholic laity 210–8
  *Sermons addressed to Mixed
    Congregations* 186–7
  suspicion of heresy 215
  'The Pilgrim Queen' 187–9
  theology of the Church 219
  Tracts for the Times 201
  Via Media of the Anglican Church 217,
    218–35, 314, 325
Nightingale, Florence 14
Nonconformist Churches 4, 5, 10
Nonjurors 318, 320–1

Oakeley, Rev Frederick 315, 341, 343–4,
  346
Oblates of St Charles Borromeo 61–2n
O'Callaghan, Bishop Henry
  arrival in Tynemouth 68–9
  biography 62–7
  breakdown in relationship with
    Wilkinson 70–1
  and Cardinal Manning 61–2
  consecration 66–8
  later life and death 74
  nomination for episcopacy 64–5
  reluctance to become bishop 58, 65–7,
    72–3
  resignation 70, 72
  return to Rome 69
Old High Church
  Anglican Evangelicals 351
  reaction to Goode 353–5
'On the Nature of the Gothic' 185
O'Neill, Dom Peter Augustine 100
Orientalism 100
Ornamentalism 98
Oscott College 165–6
Oxford Movement 185, 249 *see also*
  Tractarians; *Tracts for the Times*

Oxford University 105
Ozanam, Frederic 56

Pakington education bill 303
Pall Mall Gazette 28, 35
Parker Society 321, 324
Parliamentary Commission on
    Education 261
pastoral care 15–16n
    Manning, Henry Edward, Cardinal 12, 18–19, 26
Pastoral Letter (1869) 4–5, 11
The Pastoral Office 26
Patmore, Mrs Coventry *see* Byles, Marianne Caroline
patriotism
    Benedictines 95, 106
    Catholic conservative 122
    of Catholics 106, 113
Pattison, Mark, on Virginia Crawford's marriage 32
People and Freedom Group 56
Perkin, Harold, on Thomas Arnold 243
Petre, Monsignor Lord 105, 164
Phillpotts, Bishop Henry, rejection of Tractarian view of Caroline Divines 337
The Picture of Dorian Gray 192
Pilgrim Paths in Latin Lands 94–5
Pius VII 98
Plater, Rev Dominic, SJ, 114–15
Plunket, Lord William 284
Polding, Archbishop John Bede, OSB 101–2, 106
Poor Law Guardians, anti-Catholicism 7
Pope-Hennessy, Sir John 99–100
popular devotion 223–4
Prayers for the Sick and Dying by the Author of 'Sickness, its Trials and Blessings' 25
Pre-Raphaelites 185–6
presbyterial ordination 353
Priestly Office of Church 223–7, 231
Principles of Church Reform 244
Propaganda 215
Prophetical Office of Church 221–3
Prussian system of education 251
Pugin, Augustus 185
Purcell, Edmund Sheridan 1
Pusey, E. B. 324, 334–5, 339, 346, 358

Quinn, Dermot 2, 3

The Rambler 208–19
    dispute over role of Catholic laity 210–18
    Newman editor 209–11
    'On Consulting the Faithful in Matters of Doctrine' 212–13
    Simpson editor 209
Ramsay, Dom Leander 105
Rawlinson, Dom Stephen 106–7
Raynal, Dom Paul Wilfrid 100
A Rebours 190–2
Reeve, Dr Anthony 241
Reflections on the Principles of Popery 314
Regal Office of Church 227–31
religious instinct 224
Remains of the Late Reverend Richard Hurrell Froude 315
Reminiscences and Reflections from some Sixty years of Life in Ireland 280, 290
Rerum Novarum 49, 53
The Revival of Popery 336
The Rock, attack on convents 146–7
Rogerson, Mrs 33–4
Romanos Pontifices 64
Roothaan, Fr Jan Philip 89–91
Rosebery, 5th Earl of 34
Rosetti, Dante Gabriel 186
Royal Commission (1885) 3
Rule of St Benedict 107
Ruskin, John 185–6
Russell, Lord John, proposals on education 263
Ryle, Bishop J. C. 358–9

Sacred Poems for Mourners 21
Said, Edward 100
Salvado, Rudesindo 102
Sassoon, Siegfried 197
Scarisbrick, Dom William Benedict 99–100
School Boards 2–3, 7–8, 9
schools
    Irish national 6
    local rates assistance 1, 2, 7–8
    secular 7–8
    state inspection 6, 268, 272, 297
Scott, John
    appraisal by colleagues 306–7
    biography 292–3
    chair of Wesleyan Educational Committee 293–4

education of girls 300–1
inaugural lectures 298–304
placements 307
principal of Westminster College 298–9
protection of Methodist education 303–4
role of religion in education 302, 304–5
standards in education 306
Scottish Catholic Renewal Movement 127
Scottish-Polish Society 124
secular education 2, 8, 9
secularization 3–4, 10
Selby, D.E. 2, 3–4, 9–10
Select Committee on the Teachers' Registration and Organization Bill 286
The Sequel to Catholic Emancipation 177
Sermons addressed to Mixed Congregations 186–7
Sewall, Fr Nicholas 78
Sewell, Rev William 341, 361
Sickness, its Trials and Blessings 18, 22–3, 25
Simpson, Richard, role of Catholic laity 216–17
sisterhood, as alternative to marriage 25
Sitwell, Edith 196–7
Slater, Dom Edward Bede 98
Smith, Eustacia 31
  liaisons with Sir Charles Dilke 33
Smith, Rev Sydney, SJ 153–4
  response to Holland 158–61
Smith, Thomas Eustace 31, 34
social differentiation, decline of 243
Society for Promoting Christian Knowledge (SPCK) 270, 271
Society for Promoting the Education of the Poor in Ireland 280, 282
Spanish Civil War 55–6
Speaight, Robert 198–9
St Aloysius' College 112–14, 118
St Bernard's seminary, Olton 165–6
St Beuno's theologate 89–90
St Edmund's College
  affiliation to Cambridge University 169
  centenary celebrations 171–2
  home of Bernard Ward 163–4
St Joseph's home 55
St Mark's College 259, 260
St Mark's Training College, Chelsea 276
Stanley, Arthur, *Life of Arnold* 236
Stanley, Mary 14

State
  moral character 5
  role in education 4–6, 10–11, 250–1
  secular nature 11
Stead, W. T. 28, 30–1, 35
Stone, Rev Marmaduke, SJ 77–8
Stonyhurst College 77–9
Studies in Foreign Literature 52
Subiacan congregation 102–3
Sweetman, Dom Francis 108

The Tablet 85
  fear of suppression of Catholics 148
  on Sr Barbara Ubryk 147–9
Talbot, Monsignor George 59
Tatham, Dom John Bede 96
teachers' training, Ireland 283–4
teachers' training, Methodist education 297–8
Temporal Power 3
Terry, Richard 106
Test and Corporation Acts 309
'The Pilgrim Queen' 187–9
'The Westminster Library' 173
Thompson, Francis 192–3
Thorndike, Rev Herbert 335–6
three offices of Christ
  applied to Catholic Church 219–20
  centrality of theology 221–3
  guiding principles 221
Tierney, Mark 85–6
The Times, Sr Barbara Ubryk 141–6
Tom Brown's Schooldays 236
Tractarians *see also* individual names; Oxford Movement; *Tracts for the Times*
  attitude to Hooker 317
  attitude to Reformation 315–16
  Caroline Divines 311, 318–19, 321–2, 334–5, 362
  conversions to Catholicism 325, 355
  core doctrines 310
  criticism from Arnold 245–6
  episcopacy 352
  Hanoverian Church 319–20
  remoulding the Church of England 364
  school inspection 268
  social concerns 249
  as threat to Methodism 304
  view of Anglicanism 314
  views on education 258, 260, 261, 270, 277

INDEX

Tracts for the Times 201, 308, 310 *see also* Oxford Movement; Tractarians
  subject matter 310–11
tradition, relation to conversion 183–4
Trench, Archbishop Richard Chenevix 21n

Ubryk, Sr Barbara
  American pamphlet on case 158–9
  anti-Catholic response 150–2
  Austrian Commission 156
  case reported in *The Tablet* 147–9
  Cracow riots 143
  death of convent confessor 143, 146, 151, 156, 157, 160
  as Gothic horror 144
  Holland's account 155–6
  incarceration 141–2, 144
  inconsistencies in accounts of case 161–2
  mental illness 144, 147–8, 149, 156, 159
  mythology 146
  outcome of legal proceedings 154–5
  proceedings against convent 148
  recovery 146
  reported testimony 157
  role of Sr Mary 156
  Smith's response to Holland 158–61
  The Times 141–6
  treatment in asylum 149
Ullathorne, Bishop William Bernard OSB 8, 101, 165–6
  role of Catholic laity 216
Universities, Benedictines 105
Ushaw College 58–9

Vance, Monsignor John, description of Bernard Ward 166
Vatican I 1–2, 64
Vatican II 131, 135
Vaughan, Archbishop Herbert 105, 166–7
Vaughan, Archbishop Roger Bede, OSB 102, 105
Via Media of the Anglican Church 217, 218–35, 314, 325

Wales, Benedictines 100
Walled Up Nuns and Nuns Walled In 155–7
Walmesley, Bishop Charles, OSB 97
Ward, Maisie 174–5
Ward, Monsignor Bernard 163
  attitude to Irish Catholics 177
  Bishop of Brentwood 181
  campaign to replace at St Edmund's 180
  The Catholic Encyclopedia 173–4
  Catholic London a Century ago 173
  considered for See of Northampton 179
  correspondence with Edwin Burton 178, 181
  The Dawn of the Catholic Revival 176
  depression 179
  devotion to Bishop Douglass 173
  devotion to St Edmund 167–8
  early career 164–5
  editor of 'The Westminster Library' 173
  education 164
  The Eve of Catholic Emancipation 176
  Fellow of the Royal Historical Society 174
  help received in research 176–8
  historian of English Catholicism 170
  history of St Edmund's College 171
  History of St Edmund's College Chapel 172
  influence in education 169
  interest in sport 168–9
  on Isle of Wight 164
  Life of St Edmund of Canterbury 172
  Menology of St Edmund's College 172
  nickname 167
  obituary 167
  objectivity in writing 175–6
  Oscott College 165–6
  parents 163
  pilgrimage to Shrine of St Edmund 164
  relationship with Cardinal Bourne 180–1
  Secretary of Edmundian Association 165
  The Sequel to Catholic Emancipation 177
  at St Edmund's College 163–4, 166–8
  steam trains 169
  study of Catholic Emancipation 172
  travels 164, 165, 172–3, 178
  Vatican Archives 178
  wit 175
Ward, William George 163
The Waste Land 194–6
Watson, Joshua 274
  Tractarians 332

INDEX

Waugh, Evelyn 196–8
Wesleyan Educational Committee
 (WEC) 293
Westminster College 298
Whigs
 education 263–5
 National Society for the Education of
  the Poor 263
Wilberforce, Mary Sargent 14
Wilberforce, Rev Robert Isaac 14, 273
Wilberforce, Bishop Samuel 262, 273–4
Wilde, Oscar 31, 190–2

Wilkinson, Bishop Thomas William 60–1,
 65, 69–73
Wood, Samuel Francis 277, 329
 National Society for the Education of
  the Poor 257
 role of C of E in education 253–6
 terms of Union 272
Wordsworth, William 184
World War I, Benedictine chaplains
 106–7
Wratislaw case 241